Burials in Charles County Maryland

by the
Charles County Maryland
Genealogical Society

Volume I: A to K

HERITAGE BOOKS
2018

HERITAGE BOOKS
AN IMPRINT OF HERITAGE BOOKS, INC.

Books, CDs, and more—Worldwide

For our listing of thousands of titles see our website
at
www.HeritageBooks.com

Published 2018 by
HERITAGE BOOKS, INC.
Publishing Division
5810 Ruatan Street
Berwyn Heights, Md. 20740

Originally published:
2012

All rights reserved. No part of this book may be reproduced or transmitted in any form or by any means, electronic or mechanical, including photocopying, recording or by any information storage and retrieval system without written permission from the author, except for the inclusion of brief quotations in a review.

International Standard Book Number
Paperbound: 978-0-7884-5760-9

PREFACE

Our goal in publishing this reference book was to create and update the list of burials in Charles County, Maryland. This effort adds to the list published by the Historical Society of Charles County, Inc. in 1987. We have located and recorded information from 168 cemeteries throughout Charles County. As a result of our work, we have 19,309 entries in this publication. This reference includes church, public and private Charles County Maryland cemeteries and burial sites. It includes names, dates and other inscriptions found on the headstones, markers and other resources. While errors are inevitable, all efforts were made to make this reference as accurate as possible. This book was compiled during the years 2004 through 2011. The Trinity Memorial Gardens in Waldorf, Maryland was not transcribed due to its large number of burials.

Each name listed has a three-letter code followed by a number: example ABC001. The three letters designate the cemetery and the number represents the photograph that was taken of the marker or headstone. Depending on the size of the headstone or marker, more than one photograph was sometimes taken. There may have also been a military or footstone marker. If there was no headstone or marker but the burial place was known, then the three-letter code is followed by NoStone, which also indicates that no photograph was taken. The code list for the cemeteries and burial plots can be found following this preface.

In many cases, dates were missing from the headstones and markers. The comment "No Date" was used in place of the missing birth or death dates. Numerous plots were marked by a rock, artificial flowers or ornament and contained no names or other identifying information. Because of the lack of identifying information, these plots have not been included.

Members of the Charles County Maryland Genealogical Society, their friends, spouses and other volunteers generously donated their time and effort to this project. A special "Thank You" goes to the Charles County Maryland Historical Society for graciously contributing funding towards the initial printing of this reference book. Without the help of all those involved, this book would not be possible.

Cemetery Codes

Code	Cemetery Name	Location
ALX	Alexander Methodist Church Cemetery	Chicamuxen
AME	Amery Family Cemetery at "Watsons Choice"	Ryceville
ARA	Maddox Gravesite at "Araby"	Mason Springs
BAS	Bastain at "Ashbank" Family Cemetery	Nanjemoy
BDK	Bean, Dent, Keech at "Dent's Palace"	Dentsville
BET	Ridgate Grave at "Betty's Delight"	Port Tobacco
BFM	Burgess Farm Cemetery	Nanjemoy
BGN	Bragunier & Compton Family Cemetery	Pisgah
BLK	Blake Gravesite	Wayside
BOE	Bowie, John Bernard Grave	Hilltop
BOW	Bowling Family Cemetery	Faulkner
BPG	Brawner & Penn Graves at "Harwood"	Port Tobacco
BRC	Brice Chapel Cemetery	Waldorf
BRD	Brawner & Dean Gravesite	Ironsides
BRO	Contee & Clerklee Graves at "Bromont"	Newburg
BRT	Brandt Gravesite	Bryans Road
BRW	Brawner Catherine Grave at "Federal Oak"	Pomonkey
BUD	Budd and Mason Graves at "Frogs Nest"	Doncaster
BUP	Burgess Gravesite in Pisgah	Pisgah
BUR	Burgess Gravesite at "Burgess Farm"	Riverside
CAR	Carpinter, Dyson, Tolson Graves	Riverside
CHG	Chiles, Rev. Family Cemetery	Nanjemoy
CHH	Chandler, Job Grave at "Chandler's Hope"	LaPlata
CHM	Chambers Grave	LaPlata
CHP	Chapman Family Cemetery	Bryans Road
CHR	Christ Episcopal Church Wayside Cemetery	Wayside
CLV	Calvary United Methodist Church (Oakland Cemetery)	Waldorf
CMX	Chicamuxen United Methodist Church Cemetery	Chicamuxen
COM	Compton, Dr. Wilson Gravesite	Wicomico

Cemetery Codes

Code	Cemetery Name	Location
COO	Cooksey, Dent, Sanders Graves	Dentsville
COX	Cox Graves at "Salem"	LaPlata
CRA	Crain Family Cemetery at "Mt Victoria Farm"	Newburg
CRB	Crabb Graves	Patuxent City
CRP	Cropley and McPherson Graves	Nanjemoy
DAF	Davis and Freeman Family Cemetery	Charlotte Hall
DEN	Dent Graves at "Good Will" near Gilbert Run	Charlotte Hall
DIN	Dent and Lawson Graves at "Dent's Inheritence"	Dentsville
DLV	Dent and Truman at Graves at "Dent's Level"	Pomonkey
DOW	Downs Grave	Nanjemoy
DSP	Dent Graves at "Smith Point"	Nanjemoy
DUD	Dudley Cemetery (Church of the Lord Jesus Christ)	Port Tobacco
DWH	Dent Graves at "Walnut Hill"	Charlotte Hall
EIL	Eilbeck Graves	Bryans Road
ELL	Edelen and Stone Graves at "Ellenborough"	Popes Creek
EMO	Emory Methodist Chapel Church Baptist (Now King James Baptist)	Nanjemoy
FEN	Fenwick Family Cemetery	Bryans Road
FER	Fergusson, Amelia Grave	Port Tobacco
FKE	Franklin Grave at "Exchange"	LaPlata
FRA	Franklin Family Cemetery in Pisgah	Pisgah
GHB	Good Hope Baptist Church Cemetery	Newburg
GIB	Gibbons Graves (Now in Turtle Creek Subdivision)	Malcolm
GIL	Gilroy Cemetery	Doncaster
GLR	Gilroy, Dr. & Wife Gravesite	Doncaster
GMC	Graves at "Mount Carmel Monastery"	LaPlata
GOL	Golden, Sidney Family Graves	Doncaster
GOS	Good and Simpson Graves	Ryceville
GRA	Gray Family Cemetery at "Mansion Hall"	Ironsides
GRE	Lingan at "Green Hill" Grave	White Plains
GRY	Gray Family Cemetery	Port Tobacco

Cemetery Codes

Code	Cemetery Name	Location
GUN	Gunston - Fowke Graves	Welcome
GUS	Gustavus Brown at "Rose Hill"	Port Tobacco
HAI	Haislip Graves	Rison
HAM	Hammack Cemetery	Doncaster
HAN	Hancock Cemetery	Nanjemoy
HAR	Harris Family Cemetery at "Mt. Tirza"	Newburg
HAW	Hawkins Family Cemetery at "Fair Fountain"	LaPlata
HDV	Stone Cemetery at "Habre de Venture"	Port Tobacco
HER	Heritage Memorial Park Cemetery	Waldorf
HGH	Holy Ghost Catholic Church Cemetery	Issue
HML	Carrington, Jane Grave at "Hanson - Moores Lodge"	LaPlata
HNT	Huntt Cemetery	Waldorf
HOY	Hoytt and Lothrop Graves	Nanjemoy
HRD	Harris and Clagett Graves at "Hard Bargain"	Mt Victoria
HSM	Hargraves and Smoot Graves	White Plains
HSN	Hanson Grave	Pisgah
HWK	Hawkins Family Cemetery	LaPlata
LAG	Stonestreet Graves at "La Grange"	LaPlata
LEE	Lee Family Cemetery	Newburg
LOC	Locust Grove Family Cemetery	Bryans Road
LUM	LaPlata United Methodist Church Cemetery	Dentsville
MAC	Macedonia Baptist Church Cemetery	Bryans Road
MAD	Maddox Grave in Nanjemoy	Nanjemoy
MAS	Mason, Dr. Gravesite	Chicamuxen
MCD	McDaniel Graves	LaPlata
MHB	Mt. Hope Baptist Church Cemetery	Nanjemoy
MIL	Millar Cemetery at "Walnut Landing"	Riverside
MKT	Tubman, Dement Graves at "Markett Overton"	Bryans Road
MOR	Moran, Sus.[h] Grave	Patuxent City
MRB	Marbury Baptist Church Cemetery	Marbury

Cemetery Codes

Code	Cemetery Name	Location
MRH	McDaniel Graves in "Waldorf"	Waldorf
MRN	Moran, William Gravesite at "Dubois"	Charlotte Hall
MRS	Marshall Family Cemetery at "Marshall Hall"	Bryans Road
MTR	Mount Rest Cemetery (Christ Church Port Tobacco Parish)	LaPlata
MTZ	Mount Zion Cemetery	Malcolm
MUL	Mulberry Grove Family Cemetery	Port Tobacco
NJB	Nanjemoy Baptist Church Cemetery	Nanjemoy
NME	Newtown Methodist Church	LaPlata
NOR	Norman Graves	Nanjemoy
NPH	Naylor Graves at "Poplar Hill"	Malcolm
NSP	New St. Peter's Catholic Church Cemetery	Waldorf
NYR	Naylor Graves in "Brandywine"	Brandywine
NZN	Nazarene Church Cemetery	Pisgah
OAK	Oak Grove Baptist Church Cemetery	Nanjemoy
ODE	Old Durham Episcopal Church Cemetery	Ironsides
OFE	OldFields Episcopal Church Cemetery	Hughesville
ONZ	Old Nazarene Church Cemetery	Stump Neck
OSB	Osborn Family Cemetery	Waldorf
OSM	Old Shiloh Methodist Church Cemetery	Bryans Road
OSP	Old St. Peter's Catholic Church Cemetery	Waldorf
OTC	Old Trinity Episcopal Church Cemetery at "The Glebe"	Charlotte Hall
PAR	Parnham Family Cemetery	Newport
PAT	Patuxent Friends Cemetery (Quaker)	Patuxent City
PER	Perry, Edmund Grave	Welcome
PGN	Pleasant Grove Baptist Church Cemetery (New)	Marbury
PGO	Pleasant Grove Baptist Church Cemetery (Old)	Marbury
PIS	Pisgah United Methodist Church Cemetery	Pisgah
PKH	Park Hill Cemetery	Marbury
POM	Pomonkey Metropolitan United Methodist Church Cemetery	Pomonkey
POS	Posey Family Cemetery	Chicamuxen

Cemetery Codes

Code	Cemetery Name	Location
PRC	Price, Martha H. Grave	Nanjemoy
PRI	Price Graves at "Melwood"	Ironsides
PTC	Twiford Graves at "Port Tobacco Courthouse"	Port Tobacco
PUM	Pumphrey Graves	Grayton
REN	Rennoe Graves	Doncaster
RIS	Rison Family Cemetery	Nanjemoy
RML	Mitchell, Barnes and Compton Graves at "Rosemary Lawn"	Welcome
RND	Estep, Martin and Wall Graves at "Round Hill"	Hughesville
ROB	Robertson & Stone Graves at "Equality"	Bel Alton
SAC	Sacred Heart Catholic Church Cemetery	LaPlata
SAU	Saunders Graves at "Cherry Hill"	Doncaster
SCA	St. Catherine's Catholic Church Cemetery	McConchie
SCL	St. Charles Catholic Church Cemetery	Glymont
SHI	Shiloh Community United Methodist Cemetery	Shiloh
SIC	St. Ignatius Catholic Church Cemetery at "Chapel Point"	Port Tobacco
SIG	St. Ignatius Catholic Church Cemetery at "Hilltop"	Hilltop
SJB	St. John's Baptist Church Cemetery	Benedict
SJE	St. John's Episcopal Church Cemetery	Pomonkey
SJO	St. Joseph's Catholic Church Cemetery	Pomfret
SKI	Skinner Graves	Port Tobacco
SMC	St. Mary's Catholic Church Cemetery	Bryantown
SMI	Smith Chapel United Methodist Church Cemetery	Pisgah
SML	Smallwood Grave at "Smallwood State Park"	Marbury
SMO	Smoot Graves	LaPlata
SMT	St. Mathews Methodist Church Cemetery	LaPlata
SMY	St. Mary's Catholic Church Cemetery in Newport	Newport
SPK	Speake Grave	Pisgah
SPL	St. Paul's Episcopal Church Cemetery (Piney Parish)	Waldorf
STE	Stewart Grave at "Ellerslie"	Port Tobacco
STO	Stoddert Graves	Bryans Road

Cemetery Codes

Code	Cemetery Name	Location
STM	St Marks Cemetery (New, no burials yet)	LaPlata
STR	Stromatt and Skinner Graves	Nanjemoy
STW	Brown, Clagett, and Wheeler Graves at "Strawberry Hill"	Bryans Road
SWN	Swann Family Cemetery	Ryceville
THO	Thompson, Clarinda Grave	Ironsides
TOW	Townshend Grave	Malcolm
TRI	Trinity Episcopal Church Cemetery	Newport
TRM	Trinity Memorial Gardens Cemetery (Not Transcribed)	Waldorf
TUB	Tubman Family Cemetery	Pomfret
TUR	Turner Family Graves at "Watsons Choice"	Ryceville
WAT	Waters Grave	Gallant Green
WAV	Harris and Hungerford Graves at "Waverly"	Morgantown
WHS	Stoddert Family Cemetery at "West Hatton"	Mount Victoria
WIL	Wills Cemetery at "Preference"	LaPlata
WMT	William Mitchell Grave at "Smith Point"	Nanjemoy
WOD	Wood Grave	Faulkner
WTS	Watson, Jane Grave at "Greenwood Farm"	Pisgah
ZBC	Zion Baptist Church Cemetery	Welcome
ZWU	Zion Wesley United Methodist Church Cemetery	Waldorf

Last Name	First Name	Middle Name	Date of Birth	Date of Death	Transcription / Notes	Cemetery Code
A	S.		No Date	1808	This might be Samuel Amery; father of Thomas Amery	AME011
Aaron	Doris	L.	1917	1999	In Loving Memory	HER017
Aaron	Joseph	M.	1915	1982	In Loving Memory	HER017
Aaron	Mary	E.	1942	1990		HGH4218
Aaron	Thomas	B.	1940	No Date		HGH4218
Abell	Alex	L.	1882	1931		SCL2124
Abell, III	Benjamin	C.	Jan. 21, 1950	Sep. 16, 1979		SMC2071
Abell, Jr., Col.	Benjamin	C.	Dec. 25, 1917	Dec. 18, 1971	Col.	SMC2071
Abell	Carlisle	Frank	Sep. 30, 1912	Jun. 21, 1996	Sep 12, 1940	PKH140
Abell	Charles	C.	Jun. 5, 1872	Mar. 18, 1908		PIS123
Abell	Charles	L.	1927	No Date	Father / In Loving Memory / Mother	SIG061
Abell	Charles	R.	Jan. 13, 1908	May 29, 1998	Dunrovin: It's true, I will never tell	PIS067
Abell	Clyde	Mitchell	Nov. 28, 1914	Mar. 14, 2007	Together Forever / March 22, 1937	PKH012A
Abell	Crystal	E.	1916	1980		PKH005
Abell	Doris		No Date	No Date	Stone: 58 / Numbered Stonemarkers have been placed on unmarked graves by church (info is from church records)	CMX2004
Abell	Ella	V.	May 11, 1907	Dec. 11, 1992		PKH050
Abell	Elsworth	H.	Apr. 22, 1903	Apr., 1903	In Memory Of Ellsworth H. Abell / our baby / Infant s/o George & Neta Abell / Aged 1 day / Footstone: Elsworth	CMX1002
Abell	Eva	A.	1885	1970		SCL2124
Abell	Evelyn	A. Willett	Feb. 27, 1916	May 16, 2007	Together Forever / March 22, 1937	PKH012A
Abell	Fannie	I.	Sep. 5, 1906	Jul. 12, 1907	d/o C. C. & R. B. Abell	PIS122
Abell	Frank	A.	Feb. 17, 1935	Oct. 13, 1979	We Love you	SIG108
Abell	Frank	M.	Apr. 28, 1873	Apr. 21, 1945	Tho lost to sight to memory dear	CMX1010
Abell	George	I.	1869	1926		PKH006
Abell	Gilbert	L.	1907	2001		SCL2125
Abell	Hazel	B.	1906	1962		PKH058
Abell	Irwin		1906	1980		PKH005
Abell	Janice	M.	No Date	1950	Baby	PKH051
Abell	Jean	G.	1928	1988	Father / In Loving Memory / Mother	SIG061

Last Name	First Name	Middle Name	Date of Birth	Date of Death	Transcription / Notes	Cemetery Code
Abell	Lee	S.	May 14, 1886	Aug. 3, 1886	In Memory of our dear brothers / Footstone: Lee	CMX1002
Abell	Mary	E.	Jun. 17, 1927	No Date	"Nancy" / Married Aug 21, 1948	SJO4018
Abell	Mattie	I.	Jul. 24, 1936	Oct. 3, 1996	We Love You	SIG108
Abell	Media	B.	Aug. 3, 1841	May 11, 1894	In memory of our dear Father & Mother / Footstone: Mother	CMX1001
Abell	Nettie	Mae	Dec. 16, 1920	No Date	Sep 12, 1940	PKH140
Abell	Park	C.	Apr. 20, 1877	Aug. 21, 1918	In memory of my Beloved husband / All the plans of life is broken. All the hopes of life are fled. Counsel, comfort and adviser Alas! Alas! For thou art dead	PKH047
Abell	Parran	Cecil	Dec. 29, 1926	Mar. 28, 2003	Married Aug 21, 1948 / FM US Merchant Marine WW II / back of stone: Parents of Patti F. Joni L. Parran D.	SJO4018 / SJO4018A
Abell	Robert	Meredith	Nov. 20, 1914	Jul. 19, 2002	Beloved husband, Daddy, Relative and friend. A strong hard working farmer who enjoyed nature and took great pride in growing huge sweet cantaloupes. Devoted to God and his family. "Blessed are the peacemakers".	PKH084
Abell	Ronald	Gene	Jan. 7, 1957	Dec. 4, 2007	Age 50 / s/o the late Carlisle Abell and the late Nettie Mae Shannon Abell. h/o Brenda Abell / He is buried close to the road and to the right of Park Abell / info is from Maryland Independent Newspaper Dec 12, 2007)	PKHNoStone
Abell	Ronald	Stephen	Dec. 26, 1954	Nov. 4, 2003		SIG062
Abell	Ruth		Aug. 9, 1923	No Date	"Louise" / Loving wife, mother and friend "Weeze" devoted her life to being a great homemaker, canner, cook, quilter and volunteer. "God is love and he that dwelleth in love dwelleth in God and God in him. John 4:16	PKH084
Abell	Sarah	J.	Jul. 13, 1880	Jul. 8, 1965	Tho lost to sight to memory dear	CMX1010
Abell	Thelma	V.	1915	1982		SCL2125
Abell	W.	Raymond	Mar. 18, 1866	Feb. 17, 1896	In Memory of our dear brothers Footstone: Raymond	CMX1002
Abell	Waughneta		1875	1958		PKH006
Abell	William	C.	1904	1959		PKH057
Abell	William	I.	Aug. 9, 1838	Aug. 5, 1905	In memory of our dear Father & Mother Footstone: Father	CMX1001
Abernethy	Charles	W.	No Date	No Date		SIC7065

Last Name	First Name	Middle Name	Date of Birth	Date of Death	Transcription / Notes	Cemetery Code
Abernethy	Marie		No Date	No Date		SIC7065
Able	Clifford	C.	Apr. 4, 1971	Oct. 14, 2006		SMC3025
Able	Gary	G.	1976	1996		SMC3031
Able	Jerry	G.	1936	No Date	Together Forever	SMC3028
Able	Judy	L.	1950	2001	Together Forever	SMC3028
Abramowicz	Nicholas	J.	Aug. 22, 1977	Apr. 8, 1979		NSP603
Ackerman	Raymond	C.	1893	1963		CMX1126
Ackson	Alease		1894	1984	The "J" may be missing from the funeral home marker, so it is listed twice under the last name of Ackson and as Jackson	DUD036
Acton	Ann	Maria	Aug. 13, 1822	Mar. 7, 1897	In loving remembrance of / "Weep not; she is not dead but sleepth". / Footmarker: A.M.A.	SPL1053
Acton	Annie	L.	Dec. 28, 1869	May 10, 1910		OFE2012
Acton	Ava	Theresa	No Date	Jan. 8, 2008		SMC4226
Acton	Elizabeth		No Date	May 7, 1874	Info is from church records	OFENoStone
Acton	Elizah	G.	Nov. 2, 1881	Jul. 22, 1882	Stone is lying on ground	SPL5035
Acton	Emma	R.	1879	1947	Thy Memory Shall Ever Be A Guiding Star To Heaven	CLV229
Acton	Frances	Olevia	Jan. 23, 1855	Feb. 24, 1890	In memory of Frances Olevia Action Beloved w/o Richard A. Acton / Asleep in Jesus oh how sweet to be for such a slumber meet. With Holy confidence to sing, that death has lost it's painful sting.	OFE1041
Acton	James	C.	May 9, 1864	Jun. 1, 1965	Stone is lying on ground	SPL5036
Acton	John	H.	May 31, 1834	Mar. 21, 1911	Father	OFE4087
Acton	John	Lester	No Date	Mar. 12, 1942	Age 38 / info is from church records	OFENoStone
Acton	John	T.	Nov. 8, 1868	Nov. 23, 1923		OFE2012
Acton	Martha	A. E., Sasscer	1833	1928	w/o John Acton Sasscer "Rest sweet Rest"	SPL6130
Acton	Martha	E.	Dec. 12, 1839	May 9, 1874	Mother	OFE4087
Acton	Mary	Ellen	Jan. 13, 1883	Feb. 4, 1886	Safe in the arms of Jesus / d/o R.A. & F.O. Acton	OFE1043
Acton	Mary	M.	1916	1987		MTR4289
Acton	Ruth	P.	Jun. 6, 1884	Aug. 14, 1884	Stone is lying on ground	SPL5034
Acton	Sadie	Beatrice	No Date	Jan. 8, 2008		SMC4226
Acton	Sara	E.	Jul. 30, 1842	Aug. 1, 1921	Asleep in Jesus	SPL5038

Last Name	First Name	Middle Name	Date of Birth	Date of Death	Transcription / Notes	Cemetery Code
Acton	Sonthorn	William	No Date	Aug. 4, 1919	Age 27 / info is from church records	OFENoStone
Acton	Walter		Sep. 1, 1896	Mar. 14, 1897	Info obtained from the Historical Society research located at the College of Southern MD, LaPlata, MD.	PATNoStone
Acton	William	E.	Oct. 19, 1860	Aug. 15, 1869	Stone is lying on ground	SPL5037
Acton	William	H.	1872	1923	Thy Memory Shall Ever Be A Guiding Star To Heaven	CLV229
Acton	William	I.	No Date	Jan. 11, 1915	I know that my redeemer liveth / Age 68 years	SPL5038
Acton	William	R.	Sep. 29, 1810	Oct. 16, 1898	In Memory of / Footmarker: W.R.A.	SPL1052
Acton	Wilmer	Thaddus	No Date	Feb. 4, 1967	Age 66 / info is from church records	OFENoStone
Adams	Albert	Francis	Nov. 21, 1906	Dec. 13, 1991	Dates are from ancestry.com	CHR233
Adams	Alexander		1892	1975		SCL3042
Adams	Alice	O., McDaniel	Sep. 3, 1854	May 25, 1889	Return onto thy rest	OSM091
Adams	Amelia		No Date	Oct. 17, 1821	In memory of Amelia Adams consort of Posey Adams who departed this life / in the 53d. year of her age	REN008
Adams	Ann	Elizabeth	1838	Jun. 12, 1864	Ann Elizabeth Adams w/o Warren W. Adams / In her 26th year. Jesus can make a dying bed feel soft as downy pillows are, While on his breast I lean my head, and breathe my life out sweetly down there. Stonemaker: A Gadness Balt. / Birth date is from church records	SPL1050
Adams	Ann	Hope	Sep. 16, 1936	Feb. 16, 1998	Our Mother / God wanted us to learn some things what joy a gentle touch can bring, What kindness and compassion do and how a firm hand helps us too. What strength there is in gentleness. What power lies in a caress. How one can show love for another and so he gave us you. Our Mother	SCL3393
Adams	Anna	H.	1904	1932	Loving wife & mother	NJB102
Adams	Anne		1874	1931	Anne	MTR2169,
Adams	Annie	Viola	Mar. 3, 1895	Dec. 27, 1989		SJO3179
Adams	Arlo	Wendell	Sep. 23, 1916	Oct. 16, 1995	Pop	SJO2020
Adams, Jr.	B.	Rudolph	Aug. 29, 1957	Nov. 13, 1957		SMC3213
Adams, Sr.	B.	Rudolph	Feb. 14, 1928	Nov. 5, 1996		SMC3213
Adams	Bennie	S.	No Date	No Date		SPL4154
Adams	Catherine	L.	Mar. 18, 1927	Mar. 26, 2001	Mother / "Lynn"	SJO2028

Last Name	First Name	Middle Name	Date of Birth	Date of Death	Transcription / Notes	Cemetery Code
Adams	Catherine		1873	1949		SPL5028
Adams	Cecil	Eugene	Nov. 19, 1951	Dec. 6, 1992	US Navy	CHR448
Adams	Charles	A.	Jul. 27, 1909	Jan. 6, 1965	Maryland Pvt Co D 28 Inf TNG BN	SMC3318
Adams	Charles	E.	1939	1983		SMC3321
Adams	Clara	Margaret	May 29, 1910	Sep. 28, 1995		SMC3317
Adams	Clyde	S.	Jun. 30, 1903	Jan. 4, 1964		SJO4057
Adams	Crushaw		Dec. 22, 1916	May 19, 1935		OSP059
Adams	D.	LeLand	Oct. 23, 1909	Jan. 28, 1937		CLV206
Adams	Dennis	R.	Aug. 4, 1875	Dec. 10, 1960		CLV208
Adams	Derrick	Joseph	Nov. 25, 1969	Jan. 1, 1999	"Susie" Beloved Mother & Devoted son / ancestry.com website shows his last name as Adams	SJO2246
Adams	Donna	Theresa, Taylor	Jul. 18, 1968	Mar. 22, 2006		SJO2244
Adams	Doris		No Date	May 22, 1949	Info is from church Records	CLVNoStone
Adams	Dorothy	Taylor	Feb. 17, 1940	No Date	"Susie" Beloved Mother & Devoted son	SJO2246
Adams	Dorothy		No Date	Jun. 26, 1848	In memory of / w/o Samuel Adams who departed this life / in the 91st year of her age.	SPL4046
Adams	E.	V.	Jul. 25	No Date		SPL3037
Adams	Earl		1908	1945		NSP203
Adams	Edna	A.	Mar. 19, 1909	Feb. 2, 2005		SAC1147
Adams	Edward	J.	1870	1941		SPL5028
Adams	Edward	S.	Apr. 9, 1942	Feb. 19, 2002		NSP400
Adams	Edward		Feb. 10, 1886	Aug. 24, 1912	May he rest in peace	SJO2267
Adams	Edwin		Jul. 9, 1831	Dec. 9, 1875	Info is from DAR book Pg 148 located at the College of Southern MD, LaPlata, MD.	ODENoStone
Adams	Effie	A.	Sep. 7, 1876	Dec. 3, 1954		NSP470
Adams	Emily	S.	1838	Oct. 10, 1875	Sacred in the memory of Emily S. Adams Beloved w/o Samuel F. Adams, who departed this life / Aged 37 years. / She was a fond, devoted wife and affectionate mother, she bore all her sufferings with great christian fortitude and died as she had lived, with a steadfast faith in her Redeemer. / Stone has been repaired. / Birth date is from church records	SPL1043

Last Name	First Name	Middle Name	Date of Birth	Date of Death	Transcription / Notes	Cemetery Code
Adams	Emma	C.	Dec. 2, 1895	Jun. 3, 1987	Dates are from church records	SPL6119
Adams	Emma	Conner	1898	1967	Eastern Star Emblem	OFE4031
Adams	Eula	M.	1908	1989		NSP467
Adams	Eunice		Nov. 16, 1908	Feb. 6, 1981	Info is from church Records	CLVNoStone
Adams	Evelyn	Pearl	1873	1943		SPL6119
Adams	Frances	L.	Apr. 8, 1910	May 13, 1994		SJO4057
Adams	Francis	B.	Jan. 30, 1911	Jun. 9, 1993	Death date is from website Ancestry.com	SJO2019
Adams	Francis	Lee	1906	1992		ODE289
Adams	Francis	R.	1896	1956	Gone but not forgotten	NJB075
Adams	Francis	R.	1920	1922	Sons of F.R. & E.M. Adams	NJB074
Adams	Franklin		No Date	Oct. 30, 1862	In Memory of / s/o the late Samuel S. and Mary Adams / aged 25 years	OFE4035
Adams	George	Edwin	Nov. 17, 1913	Nov. 15, 1976	Staff Sargent US Army WWII / Masonic emblem etched into stone	SPL3145
Adams	George	R. W.	1869	1945		NSP202
Adams	George	W.	1881	1945		SPL3142
Adams	George	W.	Feb. 7, 1902	Mar. 1, 1907	Suffer little children and forbid them not to come unto me for of such is the Kingdom of Heaven	SCL1263
Adams	Georgiana		1861	1947		NSP250
Adams	Guy		May 15, 1889	Jun. 12, 1889	Infant son / Return into thy rest	OSM091
Adams	H.	Mac	Sep. 11, 1899	Nov. 25, 1981		CLV209
Adams	Harry	Leo	Dec. 15, 1924	Feb. 12, 1982	PFC US Army WWII	NSP913
Adams	Helen	S., Combs	Apr. 30, 1900	Nov. 6, 1992		SJO3172
Adams	Helene	Agnes	Dec. 4, 1911	May 9, 2000	American Legion symbol is on stone	SPL3145
Adams	Herbert	D.	1902	1966		MTR2192
Adams	Herbert	E.	Aug. 28, 1929	Oct. 9, 1971	Maryland PFC 12 Station Hosp. Korea	MTR2197
Adams	Herman	F.	1898	1966		NSP916
Adams	J.	Chapman	1899	1970		NSP920
Adams	J.	Henry	No Date	Jun. 25, 1920	Info is from Christ Church microfilm Reel 3 Pg 230-231 located at the College of Southern MD, LaPlata, MD	MTRNoStone
Adams	J.	Holland	May 17, 1876	Jan. 19, 1944		NSP399
Adams	Jack	W.	Feb. 26, 1893	Aug. 7, 1970	From wife and children	SPL5029

Last Name	First Name	Middle Name	Date of Birth	Date of Death	Transcription / Notes	Cemetery Code
Adams	James	A.	No Date	No Date	Aged 78 years / Father	SPL5027
Adams	James	D.	May 30, 1891	Mar. 25, 1944		SJO3178
Adams	James	Ernest	Mar. 29, 1921	Sep. 3, 1972	"Hardinig" / Info was obtained from the Historical Society Research located at the College of Southern MD, LaPlata, MD.	OAKNoStone
Adams	James	Ernest	Mar. 29, 1921	Sep. 3, 1972	"Harding"	SCA106
Adams	James	L.	1900	1942	Loving husband & father	NJB101
Adams	Jane	E.	No Date	Jul. 18, 1857	Eldest d/o W.W. & Ann E Adams / aged 4 months (info is from the 1940 DAR book page 21)	SPLNoStone
Adams	Janell	K.	No Date	Oct. 7, 2005	No Marker / info is from church records	CLVNoStone
Adams	Janet	Marie	1958	1986		SMC3326
Adams	Jason	Michael	Jan. 14, 1977	May 26, 2006	In Loving Memory	SCL1052
Adams	JoAnn	Sheila	Sep. 15, 1947	Sep. 29, 2009	Age 62 / daughter of the late James E. Harding Adams and the late Catherine Lillian Adams / info is from the Maryland Independent Newspaper Oct 2, 2009, Pg A-14 Col 1	SJONoStone
Adams	Joe		No Date	No Date	Number 29 is inscribed on the lower left of the stone / Infant / info is from church records	CLV459
Adams, Sr.	John	F.	Jan. 24, 1923	May 27, 2001		NSP960
Adams	John	Francis	Dec. 25, 1906	Nov. 25, 1970		NSP266
Adams	John	William	1858	1938		SPL6119
Adams	Joseph	S.	1919	1979	Metal plate attached to marker flush to the ground	SCL3014
Adams	Josephine	U.	May 19, 1863	Jun. 14, 1864	Youngest d/o W.W. and A.E. Adams. / aged 1year, 8mo's, 19days / "Suffer little children to come onto me, for of such is the kingdom of Heaven."	SPL1051
Adams	Kendrick	Tirrell	Apr. 26, 1969	May 2, 2005	"Terry"	SJO2024
Adams	Lakeesha	Dawn	Sep. 16, 1975	Jun. 25, 1996	Beloved Daughter of Henry Adams & Linda Yates Jones	SAC1117
Adams	Lemuel	P.	Jul. 28, 1867	Jan. 9, 1909		SPL4143
Adams	Lemuel	Paul	Mar. 4, 1895	Oct. 12, 1942	Beloved, How we miss you	SJO2010
Adams	Leonard		No Date	Mar. 29, 1802	Oldest identified marker. In memory of Leonard Adams and Mary his wife the former departed this life / aged 79 years and the latter / aged 70 years	SPL6076

Last Name	First Name	Middle Name	Date of Birth	Date of Death	Transcription / Notes	Cemetery Code
Adams	Lillian	Gertrude	Jun. 14, 1904	Apr. 16, 1975		NSP468
Adams	Linda	Joann	1946	1995		SMC3056
Adams	Lola	V.	Oct. 3, 1875	Jan. 6, 1943		CLV207
Adams	Lucy	Gray	1915	1997		ODE289
Adams	M.	E.	No Date	Dec. 25, 1959	Old upright stone	SJO1175
Adams	Margaret	C.	Apr. 30, 1909	Apr. 24, 1994		NSP472
Adams	Margaretta	Hinton	Oct. 7, 1874	Nov. 21, 1957	Name in Religion Sister Maria Trinita b / d / "And in thy name I will lift up my arms" Plot N20	ODE298
Adams	Maria	Georgina	Jan. 23, 1921	Apr. 6, 2001		GMC015
Adams	Marian	Beatrice	1905	1996		NSP225
Adams	Marion		Nov. 13, 1826	Aug. 19, 1879	Sacred to the memory of	OFE4036
Adams	Mary	Alice	1873	1933		SJO2011
Adams	Mary	C.	No Date	Aug. 12, 1859	Mary C. Adams / Departed this life in the 21st year of her age	OFE4033
Adams	Mary	Constance	1889	1927		SPL3118
Adams	Mary	E.	No Date	No Date	Mary E / Adams / aged 68 years / Mother / wife of James Adams	SPL5027
Adams	Mary	E.	1885	1964		SPL3142
Adams	Mary	E.	Aug. 11, 1877	Dec. 28, 1954		SMCE006
Adams	Mary	F.	1899	1988		NSP920
Adams	Mary	Inez	Jul. 8, 1914	Aug. 10, 1953		NSP270
Adams	Mary	Jane	Jan. 11, 1812	Aug. 30, 1899	Beloved w/o the late Dr. Thomas A. Adams / info is from the 1940 DAR book page 82, located at The College of Southern MD, LaPlata, MD.	SJONoStone
Adams	Mary	L.	May 3, 1932	No Date		SMC3213
Adams	Mary	Renshaw	Jun. 18, 1915	Jul. 3, 2000	In loving memory of mother / Jesus saves	NJB340
Adams	Mary	V.	Jan. 24, 1908	May 21, 1985		SJO2019
Adams	Mary		No Date	Apr. 1, 1802	Oldest identified marker. In memory of Leonard Adams and / his wife Mary the former departed this life / aged 79 years and the latter / aged 70 years	SPL6076
Adams	Mary		1918	2006	Thornton Funeral Home Marker	SCL4017A
Adams	Marya	Magdalene	Feb. 17, 1919	Dec. 22, 1996	Nana	SJO2020

Last Name	First Name	Middle Name	Date of Birth	Date of Death	Transcription / Notes	Cemetery Code
Adams	Melissa	Francine, Swann	Sep. 30, 1966	Feb. 4, 2010	Thornton Funeral Home Marker / age 43 d/o Sterling Roscoe Swann Sr. and Carolyn Francine Swann. s/o Rev. Sterling Roscoe Swann Jr. w/o Kirby Adams Jr. / obit appeared in the Maryland Independent Newspaper dated Feb 10, 2010	PGN088
Adams	Norman		No Date	Feb. 23, 1884	(infant) beloved s/o Simon S & Orella C Adams aged 18 mo. / Little Norman was our darling. Pride of all our hearts at home. But an angel came and whispered. Norman darling come home.	OSM095
Adams	Olivita	Thomas	Dec. 4, 1911	Feb. 24, 2002		ODE411
Adams	Orella	C.	Sep. 3, 1857	Feb. 17, 1924	God is our refuge & strength	OSM094
Adams	Phyllis	Missouri	Jun. 18, 1883	Mar. 12, 1971		NSP142
Adams	Posey		No Date	Feb. 26, 1823	In memory of / who departed this life / in the 54th year of his age	REN010
Adams	Robert	J.	1928	2002	Loving son	NJB073
Adams	Rosalie		Aug. 6, 1905	Jan. 30, 1985	I Love You	CLV205
Adams	Ruth		No Date	Mar. 19, 1949	Age 22 hours / info is from church records	CLVNoStone
Adams	S.	Lawrence	No Date	Dec. 20, 1936	Aged 65 years	SMCE007
Adams	Sadie	I.	1905	1998		NSP916
Adams	Samuel	A.	Aug. 20, 1902	Jul. 30, 1992		SAC1147
Adams	Samuel	F.	Mar. 10, 1832	Feb. 17, 1911		SPL1042
Adams	Samuel	Robert	Jul. 25, 1870	Feb. 26, 1935		ODE290
Adams	Samuel	S.	No Date	Oct. 25, 1859	Departed this life in the 67th year of his age Father "Blessed are the pure in heart for they shall see God"	OFE4034
Adams	Samuel	W.	Mar. 26, 1824	May 23, 1900		ODE292
Adams	Samuel	Webster	1885	1983	Masonic Emblem	OFE4031
Adams	Samuel		No Date	Jun. 1, 1841	In Memory of / who departed this life / in the 78th year of his age / Prepare to meet thy God	SPL4047
Adams	Sarah	A.	No Date	Mar. 9, 1879	Asleep in Jesus, w/o Samuel W. Adams d/o Dr. Bennett Dyson / aged 49 years / "As for me, I will behold thy face in righteousness: I shall be satisfied when I awake with thy likeness."	ODE291
Adams	Sarah	J.	No Date	Feb. 9, 1915	w/o W.D. Adams. / aged 65 years. Footstone: Mother	SPL3116

Last Name	First Name	Middle Name	Date of Birth	Date of Death	Transcription / Notes	Cemetery Code
Adams	Sebright		Nov. 16, 1902	Aug. 23, 1925		OSP073
Adams	Simon	S.	Sep. 16, 1841	Jun. 3, 1917	God is our refuge & strength	OSM094
Adams	Susan		No Date	Mar. 12, 1858	In Memory of / d/o Samuel S. and Mary Adams / in the 26th year of her age	OFE4032
Adams, Dr.	Thomas	A.	May 18, 1808	Aug. 14, 1850	A kind husband, a tender parent, a warm friend and an exemplary christian. / Info is from the 1940 DAR book page 82, located at The College of Southern MD, LaPlata, MD	SJONoStone
Adams	Thomas	Norman	No Date	Feb. 23, 1884	Beloved s/o Simon S & Orella Adams / aged 18 mos. Side of stone: Little Norman was our darling pride of all our hearts at home, but an angel came and whispered, Norman darling, due come home.	OSM093A
Adams	Unknown		No Date	No Date		NJB103
Adams	Unknown		No Date	No Date	Info is from church records	SPLNoStone
Adams	Unknown		No Date	Nov. 21, 1932	d/o Clyde and Lucile Adams	SJO2002
Adams	Unknown		No Date	Apr.il 7, 1931	d/o Clyde and Lucile Adams	SJO2001
Adams	Unknown		No Date	No Date	Nothing on stone except the name Adams	PKH100
Adams	V.	Eugene	Jun. 22, 1906	Aug. 1, 1908		OSP038
Adams	Verbal	C.	Oct. 9, 1878	Apr. 19, 1940		NSP469
Adams	Vernon	G.	1919	No Date	Sons of F.R. & E.M. Adams	NJB074
Adams	Virginia	Harrison	1906	1996		CHR233
Adams	Virginia	Lee	1865	1906		SPL6119
Adams	Vivian	W.	Jun. 17, 1910	Jun. 9, 1996	Vivian W. Adams / Member of Sons of the American Revolution	NSP471
Adams	W.	A.	No Date	Apr. 18, 1915	s/o W.D. & E.A. Adams / age 31 (info is from the 1940 DAR book page 31)	SPLNoStone
Adams	W.	D.	1884	Apr. 13, 1915	Info is from church records	SPLNoStone
Adams	W.	D.	No Date	Oct. 4, 1907	Footstone: Father / Age 68 years	SPL3116
Adams	Warren	W.	No Date	Jun. 19, 1864	Youngest son of W.W. & A.E. Adams. / Aged 1m, 9d. / Suffer little children who come unto me: for of such is the kingdom of heaven.	SPL1045
Adams	Wiley	M.	1948	No Date		SMC3056
Adams, Sr.	William	R.	Nov. 2, 1895	Dec. 26, 1981	Info is from church records	CLVNoStone

Last Name	First Name	Middle Name	Date of Birth	Date of Death	Transcription / Notes	Cemetery Code
Addison	French	Bowie	Apr. 18, 1889	Mar. 26, 1972	Onward Christian soldier	CHR603
Addison	Josephine	Roberts	Mar. 28, 1885	Jul. 10, 1963	w/o French Bowie Addison "May the Angels lead her to Paradise" / Obit in Washington Post Newspaper dated Jul 12, 1963 shows her last name as Addison	CHR602
Adell	Norine	E.	Jul. 26, 1913	Nov. 8, 2004		SPL3022
Adell	William	C.	Jun. 7, 1907	Jul. 19, 1989		SPL3022
Adkins	Mary	Lou	Nov. 27, 1943	No Date	Thy Kingdom Come Thy Will Be Done	SCL1109
Adkins	Rodney	A.	Dec. 30, 1938	Oct. 1, 1988	Thy Kingdom Come Thy Will Be Done / Footstone: PFC US Army	SCL1109
Ager	Elmer	R.	Nov. 7, 1935	No Date		NSP894
Ager, Sr.	Elmer	R.	Mar. 14, 1909	Jun. 16, 1953		NSP883
Ager	Patricia	C.	Jul. 12, 1943	May 21, 1996		NSP894
Agostinho	Joaquim		1911	1983	Arehart Funeral Home Marker / Cement Cross	SIG131
Aguayo	Jorge		Dec. 4, 1903	Mar. 11, 1994	Ashes are buried in front of Statue / Per Sister Miriam John at Mt Carmel. Maria died before Jorge. They could not speak English. Maria and Jorge are buried in Plot A	GMC012
Aguayo	Maria		Nov. 26, 1900	Mar. 15, 1990	Ashes are buried in front of Statue / Per Sister Miriam John at Mt Carmel. Maria died before Jorge. They could not speak English. Maria and Jorge are buried in Plot A	GMC012
Aguilera	Joseph	A.	Jun. 2, 1912	Jul. 5, 1962		SCL3406
Ahlstrom	Albin	A.	Feb. 28, 1916	Aug. 22, 2001		SAC3039
Ahlstrom	Mabel	T.	Feb. 15, 1931	Mar. 22, 1991		SAC3039
Akin	Jonathan		No Date	Apr. 11, 1838	11th of 4 mo 1838	PAT017
Akin	Lydia		May 27, 1811	Oct. 10, 1876	27th of 5 mo 1811 / 10th of 10 mo 1876	PAT018
Albarado	Jerry	P.	Sep. 22, 1940	Jul. 24, 2006	Together Forever	SMC3073
Albarado	Shirley	L.	Jul. 14, 1946	No Date	Together Forever	SMC3073
Albers	Edith	M.	Aug. 27, 1891	Nov. 26, 1992		SCL4029
Albers	James	Stanley	Mar. 16, 1906	Jun. 19, 1973	MD TEC4 US Army WW II	SCL4031
Albrittain	Alberta	M.	Jan. 2, 1877	Sep. 5, 1948	Nee Carpenter w/o Warren M. Albrittain	MTR2179

Last Name	First Name	Middle Name	Date of Birth	Date of Death	Transcription / Notes	Cemetery Code
Albrittain	Ann	D.	No Date	Apr. 29, 1887	In Loving remembrance of Ann D. Albrittain Beloved wife of John W. Albrittain / aged 36 years 10 mos. And 25 days. By Faith she lived on earth, in hope she died; By love she lives in heaven (stone has been repaired and a portion where the verse is written is missing)	MTR3050
Albrittain	Barbara	Anne	Jun. 23, 1842	Jun. 2, 1917		SPL3071
Albrittain	C.	A.	May 9, 1813	Jan. 14, 1873	The beloved w/o J. W. Albrittain / "Forever with the Lord! Amen, so let it be: Life from the dead is in that word, tis immortality."	SPL3059
Albrittain	Catherine	Eleanor	Apr. 10, 1926	Oct. 12, 2010	Dates are from Maryland Independent Newspaper dated Oct 15, 2010	SIC8027
Albrittain	Donald	Anthony	Jul. 13, 1957	Jul. 31, 1985	MMFN US Navy	SAC2131
Albrittain	Edith	Eliza	1952	1952		MTR2010
Albrittain	Edmonia	Etheldra	No Date	May 2, 1894	Info is from Christ Church microfilm Reel 2 Pg 171-172 located at the College of Southern MD, LaPlata, MD	MTRNoStone
Albrittain	Eliza	P.	Nov. 19, 1915	Mar. 13, 1962		MTR2011
Albrittain	Emily	Sue	1930	1931		SIC3097
Albrittain	Ernest	George	Dec. 12, 1875	Mar. 17, 1928		MTR3199
Albrittain	Etheldra	Thelma, Ross	Mar. 26, 1894	Feb. 23, 1924	Jesus calls us oer the tumul	MTR2015
Albrittain	Evelyn		1883	1972		SPL3057
Albrittain	George	Edward	Jun. 28, 1922	Jun. 30, 1973		SIC8027
Albrittain	George	H.	1839	1892		SPL3057
Albrittain	George		No Date	Mar. 15, 1929	Info is from Christ Church microfilm Reel 3 Pg 234-235 located at the College of Southern MD, LaPlata, MD	MTRNoStone
Albrittain, Sr.	Henry	B.	Jan. 13, 1904	Sep. 6, 1992	Married Apr 10, 1928	SAC3113
Albrittain	Henry	E.	1872	1946		MTR3171
Albrittain	Jacquelyn	Cavalier	Jun. 11, 1962	Jul. 31, 1985		SAC2131
Albrittain	James	W.	1891	1966		SIC7050
Albrittain, Jr.	James	W.	Apr. 2, 1919	Oct. 19, 1919	Our loved one	SCL3095
Albrittain	Jane		1872	1945		MTR3172
Albrittain	Jerome		No Date	May 29, 1908	Info is from Christ Church microfilm Reel 3 Pg 220-221 located at the College of Southern MD, LaPlata, MD	MTRNoStone

Last Name	First Name	Middle Name	Date of Birth	Date of Death	Transcription / Notes	Cemetery Code
Albrittain	John	L.	1924	1981		SIC7041
Albrittain	John	W.	Mar. 21, 1810	Jun. 20, 1882		SPL3058
Albrittain	John	W.	Aug. 20, 1926	Oct. 21, 1929		SCL3096
Albrittain	John	Warren	Oct. 15, 1844	Oct. 4, 1919	Father	MTR3049
Albrittain	Lemuel		1885	1958		SIC7040
Albrittain	Leona	C.	Feb. 5, 1905	Feb. 1, 1985	Married Apr 10, 1928	SAC3113
Albrittain	M.	Louise	1896	1986		MTR3169
Albrittain	Maggie S.	Cooksey	Feb. 24, 1883	Dec. 18, 1922		MTR3199
Albrittain	Mary	A.	Dec. 12, 1863	Oct. 25, 1946	Mother / w/o John W Albrittain	MTR3048
Albrittain	Mary	E.	Apr. 30, 1847	Jan. 2, 1874	d/o John W. & Cecelia A.	SPL3060
Albrittain	Mary	E. Miles	1891	1961		SIC7050
Albrittain	Mary	Ephelia	No Date	May 19, 1903	Info is from Christ Church microfilm Reel 1 Pg 90-91 located at the College of Southern MD, LaPlata, MD	MTRNoStone
Albrittain	Mary	Katherine, Wills	Jun. 2, 1929	No Date	Together	SIC7042
Albrittain	Mary	Louise	1894	1961		SIC7040
Albrittain	Mary	R.	1840	1902		SPL3057
Albrittain	Mary	Katharine	Sep. 4, 1905	Dec. 8, 1928	d/o Warren M-Alberta M Albrittain	MTR2179
Albrittain	Pearl	M.	1899	1982		MTR3170
Albrittain	Thomas	Warren	Sep. 4, 1930	May 20, 2009	"Buck"	SIC7046
Albrittain	Warren	M.	Sep. 18, 1872	Jul. 1, 1956		MTR2179
Albrittain	William	J.	Oct. 19, 1870	Aug. 17, 1887	Our beloved boy / s/o John W. & Ann D. Albrittain / Loved in life, in death remembered	MTR3051
Albrittain, Sr.	William	Miles	Jul. 8, 1928	No Date	"Willie" / Together	SIC7042
Alderman	Anna	Harrison	No Date	May 2, 1963	Name is shown on church records but burial location is unknown	CHRNoStone
Alexander	James	R.	1936	1959		OSM029
Alexander	Patricia	V., Estep	1943	1977		PGN010
Alexander	Rebecca	Ellen	1915	1999		DUD018
Alexander	Unknown		1925	May 24, 1925	3 days old. Not sure if Alexander is first or last name. / info is from church records	SHINoStone
Alford	James	A.	Apr. 1, 1858	Apr. 11, 1922	James A Alford and his wife Marion L. Adams	MTR2165
Alford	Marion	L.	Aug. 16, 1866	Feb. 24, 1942	James A Alford and his wife Marion L. Adams	MTR2165

Last Name	First Name	Middle Name	Date of Birth	Date of Death	Transcription / Notes	Cemetery Code
Alger	Helen	Elizabeth	Feb. 10, 1908	Jan. 24, 1991	Peace and Love be with you forever	MTR4095
Alger, Jr.	Howard	Franklin	Apr. 1, 1960	Jul. 22, 1985	Beloved Frank / God shall wipe away all tears	MTR4096
Alger	Judy	Ellen	Sep. 17, 1933	Jul. 23, 1995	Courage, strength, compassion and Love, a beautiful person	MTR4076
Allard	Betty	Hall	Jun. 26, 1937	No Date		CLV374
Allard	Emily	Jane	May 01, 1998	May 24, 2004	Forever In Our Hearts	CLV388
Allard	Robert	Owen	Sep. 23, 1937	Aug. 19, 2004		CLV374
Allard	Unknown		No Date	Jul. 13, 1992	Marker / Baby Boy Allard / Forever in our Hearts	CLV388
Allcorn	Anna	E.	May 16, 1904	Oct. 9, 1978		SPL6197
Allen	Clyde		No Date	1991	Info from church records	OSMNoStone
Allen	Delores	E.	Feb. 1, 1937	Feb. 21, 1994	In God's care / Mother	SJO1159
Allen	Dorothy		No Date	Dec. 1, 1976	Info is from church records	SHINoStone
Allen	Floyd	W.	1931	1980	CPL US Army Korea	OSM111
Allen	George	T.	May 18, 1902	Aug. 7, 1982	Gift of daughter	NSP056
Allen	Gertrude		1907	1984		DUD037
Allen	John	Francis	Jul. 23, 1860	Feb. 4, 1909	An honest man is the noblest work of God	PIS144
Allen	Lawrence	W.	No Date	Nov. 16, 1936	Father	SJE102
Allen	Mary	E.	Dec. 1, 1900	Dec. 26, 1984	Gift of daughter	NSP056
Allen	Sarah	C.	Jun. 6, 1929	Oct. 8, 1987	Mother	SJE102
Allen	Viola	H.	1905	1980		OSM110
Allison	H.	Bryan	Jan. 9, 1920	Oct. 15, 1993	Son	LUM033
Allison	Lenzy	Dodson	Feb. 28, 1917	Aug. 4, 2004	Wife	LUM033
Almo	Adele	H.	Sep. 29, 1921	Oct. 8, 1987		NSP1030
Almo	Jerry	J.	Feb. 25, 1912	Feb. 4, 1989		NSP1030
Almo	Margaret	M.	1891	1963	A good mother / A religious woman	NSP1031
Alston	Renee	Savoy	Jul. 29, 1973	Apr. 22, 2006	Beloved wife, mother, daughter	SMC3081
Altemus	Catherine	J.	Jan. 15, 1911	Dec. 5, 1995		HGH4213
Alva	Cesar	A.	Oct. 21, 1927	No Date		NSP834
Alva	Fernanda	M.	Jul. 1, 1927	Mar. 8, 1986		NSP834
Alvey	Catherine	L.	Apr. 14, 1944	Aug. 23, 2003	Married Aug 20, 1960	LUM168
Alvey	Clair	Cecelia	Jul. 24, 2003	Aug. 17, 2007	Our little angel	SIC9095

Last Name	First Name	Middle Name	Date of Birth	Date of Death	Transcription / Notes	Cemetery Code
Alvey	Cora		No Date	May 22, 1951	Age 63 / info is from church records	OFENoStone
Alvey	Druscilla	Wood, Goldsmith	No Date	Dec. 10, 1930	Age 77 / info is from church Records	OFENoStone
Alvey	Elmer	N.	Sep. 14, 1945	Apr. 12, 1987	Father is on a separate stone near this one	OFE4041
Alvey	Els pett ?	Jeannette	No Date	Mar. 11, 1943	Age 78 / info is from church records	OFENoStone
Alvey	George	H.	1905	1970	Have Mercy	LUM200
Alvey	George	Henry	1933	2002	Husband and wife	LUM208
Alvey	Hope	M., Cameron	Apr. 7, 1964	No Date	Always in our hearts, together Mar 28, 1986 / Back of stone: Cameron, Alvey	ODE330
Alvey	Irene		Feb. 1, 1927	May 8, 1927		OFE4040
Alvey	John	M.	Dec. 24, 1951	Dec. 8, 2003	Always in our hearts, together Mar 28, 1986 / Back of stone: Cameron, Alvey	ODE330
Alvey, Sr.	John	Melvin	Dec. 16, 1974	Jul. 12, 1982	In loving memory / grandson	SIC8013
Alvey, Jr.	Lewis	McArthur	Aug. 16, 1942	Mar. 27, 1978		LUM156
Alvey	Margaret	H.	Aug. 11, 1910	Jul. 1, 1994		OFE4042
Alvey	Margaret	Ruth	1923	2002	Husband and wife	LUM208
Alvey	Martha	E.	1916	1995	Have Mercy	LUM199
Alvey	Mary	L.	No Date	Apr. 14, 1931	Age 1 1/2 months / info is from church records	OFENoStone
Alvey	Rickey	A.	Nov. 7, 1961	Dec. 7, 1961		LUM155
Amery	Anna		No Date	Sep. 6, 1815	Sacred in the memory of / consort of Thomas Amery / who departed this life / Aged 35 years, 3 mo's. and 13 days Footstone	AME008
					In memory of Samuel J. E. Amery who departed this life / aged 28 years 3 mo's and 4 days / For ye are dead and your life is hid with Christ in God. When Christ who is our life shall appear then shall ye also appear with Him in Glory / 3rd Chapter 3 & 4th verses of Colossians / Footstone (This footstone was recently made to match the other two already here)	
Amery	Samuel	J. E.	No Date	Aug. 26, 1840		AME002
Amery	Thomas		No Date	Dec. 4, 1840	Sacred to the memory of / who departed this life / Aged 60 yr's 9 mo's and 1 day / Footstone	AME005
Amidon	Charles	K.	1902	1960	Middle name is Kieran per church records	MTR2017
Amidon	R.	Louise	1903	2002	First name is Rebecca, per church records	MTR2017
An??	Harriett		Feb. 9, 1926	Mar. 18, 2000		ALX028

Last Name	First Name	Middle Name	Date of Birth	Date of Death	Transcription / Notes	Cemetery Code
Anastasi	Anthony	J.	Apr. 29, 1960	Aug. 12, 2004	"Absent From the Body and Present With the Lord" / Beloved Husband and Father	SAC5107
Anderson	Bessie	B.	1886	1970	Headstone says Anderson on one side and Adams on the other side, church records show last name as Anderson	SPL3149
Anderson	Charles	L.	1892	1975	Pvt. US Army WW I	MTR3202
Anderson	Dorothy	M.	1913	1982		MTR3201
Anderson	Ellen	Grabis	Aug. 4, 1928	No Date	Rest in peace	SMC1017
Anderson	Elmer	Lee	Jun. 9, 1926	Jul. 12, 2001	Rest in peace	SMC1016
Anderson	James	Edward	1965	1971	Info is from the Historical Society Research located at The College of Southern MD, LaPlata, MD	SCLNoStone
Anderson	Jerome	Vernell	Feb. 25, 1973	Dec. 16, 1999	Beloved son, brother, father and friend. Yea, I have loved thee with an everlasting love. Jer 31:3	SCL4195
Anderson	John	S.	Mar. 16, 1846	Aug. 11, 1911		SJE071
Anderson	Lloyd	H.	Oct. 24, 1886	Apr. 6, 1972	Together Forever	SMC4115
Anderson	Margaret	Dyer	Dec. 9, 1894	Dec. 18, 1991		SIC4064
Anderson	Mary	O.	Jun. 6, 1909	Apr. 3, 1983	Together Forever	SMC4115
Anderson	Nannie	Bell	1881	1945		SPL3098
Anderson	Oscar	P.	1877	1967	Headstone says Anderson on one side and Adams on the other side, church records show last name as Anderson	SPL3149
Anderson	Robert	L.	1891	1959		SPL3098
Anderson	Robert	Lee	1949	1950	Baby	SMCE030
Anderson	Ruth	E.	Sep. 28, 1903	Jul. 30, 1978		SJO2023
Anderson	William		No Date	Jan. 1961	Info is from church records	SHINoStone
Andrews, Sr.	Arthur	James	Aug. 24, 1900	Jun. 10, 1975	GY SGT US Marine Corps World War I	SMC4031
Andrews	Elizabeth	Marie	Jul. 5, 1927	Mar. 20, 1981		SMC4040
Andrews	Mary	Margaret	Jan. 1929	Feb. 1995	Aunt / Resting Peaceful	SMI124
Andrews	William	A.	Aug. 19, 1949	Mar. 11, 1968	Maryland, PFC 189 Assault Heli CO Vietnam	SMC4030
Andrews			No Date	Sep. 2, 1967	Baby	MTR3148
Angel	Stephanie	Diane	1972	2007	Brinsfield-Echols Funeral Home	SMY4005
Angelini	Elizabeth	Marie	No Date	Nov. 2, 1984	Our little angel	NSP344

Last Name	First Name	Middle Name	Date of Birth	Date of Death	Transcription / Notes	Cemetery Code
Annie, Aunt	Unknown		No Date	May 26, 1878	2 people are buried in this plot but only Aunt Annie is listed on the records / info is from church records	OFENoStone
Anselmo	Peter	J.	1914	1982		NSP533
Antonelli	Anthony	P.	1914	1996	Together Forever / "Tony" / "Joan"	SJO5025
Antonelli	Jennie	J.	1916	1995	Together Forever / "Tony" / "Joan"	SJO5025
Appell	George	Alvin	No Date	Nov. 25, 1956	Info is from Christ Church microfilm Reel 4 Pg 278-279 located at the College of Southern MD, LaPlata, MD	MTRNoStone
Appell	George	Washington	No Date	Dec. 7, 1931	Info is from Christ Church microfilm Reel 3, Pg 236-237 located at the College of Southern MD, LaPlata, MD	MTRNoStone
Appell	Mary	Ellen	No Date	No Date	Info is from Christ Church microfilm Reel 4 Pg 276-277 located at the College of Southern MD, LaPlata, MD	MTRNoStone
April	L.	Jun	1920	2001		NSP844
April	N.	Raymond	1927	2000		NSP844
Arbogast	Connie	Ann	Apr. 1, 1969	Apr. 1, 1969	Budded on earth to bloom in heaven	NJB210
Arch	Anthony	E.	Dec. 28, 1924	Apr. 1, 1992	US Army WW II	SMC4263
Arch	Anton		1884	1980		SMCD258
Arch	Hedwick		1889	1944		SMCD258
Arch	Lucia		1865	1942		SMCD258
Archbold	Annie	M.	1875	1923		OFE2090
Archbold	Eloise	Dyson	1895	1995		OFE2088
Archbold	Olive	J.	1871	1939		OFE2081
Archbold, Rev.	Walter	D.D.	1873	1941		OFE2089
Arehart	C.	Louise, Mudd	Jun. 9, 1917	Mar. 11, 2002		NSP500
Arehart	Roy	C.	Aug. 27, 1905	Jan. 8, 1986		NSP500
Aris	Anthony	Leo	Oct. 13, 1969	Jan. 19, 1994		SJO4048
Armiger	Charlotte		1900	1975	(Lottie)	SPL5018
Armiger	Virgil		1904	1973		SPL5018
Armstrong	Mary		1952	1998	Use to have a Thornton Funeral Home Marker / Info is from Irma Simpson research at The College of Southern MD, LaPlata, MD	SMYNoStone
Armstrong	Robert	P.	Jun. 1, 1923	Sep. 8, 1963	Maryland PFC US Army World War II	HGH3013
Armstrong	Zacharey	Edward	No Date	Sep. 10, 1993	Infant / Too Little, Too Soon, Too Sweet	SAC1062

Last Name	First Name	Middle Name	Date of Birth	Date of Death	Transcription / Notes	Cemetery Code
Armsworthy	Audrey	C.	1925	2005		SIC9092
Armsworthy	Emma	E.	1898	1989		SIC2112
Armsworthy	James	C.	1884	1959		SIC2112
Armsworthy	Joseph	H.	1926	No Date		SIC9092
Arnold	Helen	L.	Jun. 8, 1842	Aug. 15, 1896	Sister	ODE179
Arnold	Thomas	J.	No Date	No Date	Buried Jun 27, 1909, age 69 / information is from Old Durham Church microfilm pg 158-159 located at the College of Southern MD, LaPlata, MD.	ODENoStone
Arnold, Mrs.	Unknown		No Date	Jan. 29, 1917	Residence is listed as Malabar, Fl. / info is from Christ Church microfilm Reel 3 Pg 226-227 located at the College of Southern MD, LaPlata, MD	MTRNoStone
Artes	Unknown		No Date	No Date	Arehart Funeral Home Inc. Marker	SJE020
Arwood	Glenn	A.	1926	No Date		NSP783
Arwood	Jean	M.	1930	No Date		NSP783
Ashburn	Leland	E.	Jan. 29, 1941	No Date	m. Oct 13, 1962	NSP891
Ashburn	Rose	A.	Aug. 2, 1942	No Date	m. Oct 13, 1962	NSP891
Ashton	Caroline	Grace	Sep. 6, 2000	Sep.t 11, 2000	Our Little angel	HGH4082
Ashton	Eliza	Armistead	Apr. 26, 1852	Oct. 9, 1902		CHR524
Ashton	Helen	D.	1881	1958	Mother	SCL3344
Ashton	Patricia	Muschette	Mar. 15, 1939	Jun. 22, 1989		SIC6063
Ashton	Wm.	Henry	Nov. 7, 1885	Jun. 7, 1964	Father	SMI123
Atchison	Annie		No Date	No Date	Number 21 inscribed on lower left of stone / info is from church records	CLV041
Atchison	Carlton		No Date	Dec. 26, 1946	Info is from church records	CLVNoStone
Atchison	Catherine	J.	Jan. 31, 1917	Oct. 21, 1997		CLV431
Atchison	E.		No Date	1941	Old upright stone	SJO1176
Atchison	E.		No Date	No Date	Number 255 inscribed on the lower left of the stone	CLV371B
Atchison	Elizabeth	J.	No Date	Jul. 1, 1982	Number 241-A inscribed on the lower left of the stone info is from church records	CLV403
Atchison	Elmer	M.	Mar. 3, 1942	Jan. 11, 1971		CLV044
Atchison	Evelyn		Jun. 1, 1952	Jun. 1, 1952	Info is from church records	CLVNoStone

Last Name	First Name	Middle Name	Date of Birth	Date of Death	Transcription / Notes	Cemetery Code
Atchison	Everett		No Date	No Date	Number 20 inscribed on lower left of stone info is from church records	CLV042
Atchison	James	E.	Dec. 20, 1908	Mar. 25, 1973		CLV431
Atchison	Joseph		No Date	Oct. 19, 1939	Aged 26 - No Marker / info is from church records	CLVNoStone
Atchison, Mrs.	M.	E.	No Date	Apr. 16, 1941	Old upright stone	SJO1177
Atchison	Marjorie		Sep. 10, 1925	Jul. 16, 2006	Age 80 / Green funeral home Marker	NJB001
Atchison	Ronald	L.	1958	1971	Father and Son	CLV370
Atchison	Rose	W.	No Date	No Date	Number 12-D is inscribed on lower left of stone / First name is from church records	CLV023
Atchison	Unknown		No Date	No Date	Number 19 inscribed on lower left of stone	CLV043
Atchison	Unknown		No Date	No Date	Number 9 inscribed on lower left of stone	CLV021
Atchison	Unknown		No Date	No Date	Number 11 inscribed on lower left of stone	CLV020
Atchison	Unknown		No Date	No Date	Number 8 is inscribed on lower left of stone	CLV011
Atchison	William	E.	1907	1969	Father & Son	CLV370
Atchison	William	H.	No Date	No Date	Number 241 inscribed on the lower left of the stone info is from church records	CLV404
Atherton	Ellen	R.	1872	Jan. 4, 1947	Wife	ODE130
Atherton	Philo	D.	1867	1939	Wife	ODE130
Atlee, Sr.	Charles	W.	1856	1933	Father	POM129
Atlee	Ethel	E.	1883	1960	Mother	POM130
Atlee, Sr.	Godfrey	A.	Jan. 18, 1911	Sep. 5, 1938	Follow Me, Date of birth was changed on stone from 1918 to 1917	POM185
Atlee	Lavinia	E.	1917	1987		POM128
Atlee	Louise	I.	Feb. 21, 1907	Mar. 4, 1976	Follow Me	POM185
Atlee	Mabel	I.	1920	1981	Mother	POM129
Aud	Ann		1889	1972	In memory of / in the 65th year of her age	OFE4065
Aud	James		No Date	Sep.t 2, 1855	Departed this life / aged about 62 years (death year may be 1851 or 1854)	SMCB003
Auglis	Janis		No Date	Oct. 11, 1851	In Latvia Beloved father	CHR342
Austin	(C)arrie	R.	May 28, 1877	Jul. 21, 1951	Arehart Funeral Home Marker	OSB009
Austin	Everett	L.	1898	1986	Aarehart Funeral Home Marker	OSB008
Austin	Josephine	E.	1898	1974	At rest	ODE417
			1897	1960		

25

Last Name	First Name	Middle Name	Date of Birth	Date of Death	Transcription / Notes	Cemetery Code
Austin	Paul	Daniel	1897	1929	Beloved h/o J. Elizabeth - C. Austin / At rest (stone has fallen) middle name is from church records	ODE416
Austin	Ruth	H.	Oct. 8, 1884	May 18, 1958		TRI292
Austin	Sadie	C.	Feb. 15, 1898	Aug. 16, 1983	At rest	ODE431
Austin	William	C.	Mar. 28, 1896	Jan. 31, 1970	At rest	ODE431
Auth	Bernard	F.	Jan. 8, 1912	Mar. 7, 1981		SIC6043
Auth	Edith	Robey	Aug. 24, 1906	Jan. 22, 1990		SMCA250
Auth	Eleanor	N.	Oct. 6, 1915	Oct. 6, 2003		SIC6043
Auth	Hubert	Peter	Sep. 23, 1908	Dec. 19, 1979	CSP US Navy WW II	SMCA251
Auth	Joseph		1982	1982	Arehart Funeral Home marker	SAC1012
Aydelotte	Robert	L.	1900	1983	Thornton's Funeral Home Marker	MAC006
Aydelotte	Sarah	C.	Jul. 5, 1913	Jul. 29, 2004		SMY2070
Ayer	Philip	Howard	Dec. 5, 1928	Jun. 18, 2008	Age 79, s/o Philip Melvin Ayer and Katherine Viola Melin Ayer Born in Cincinnati Ohio / info is from the MD Independent Newspaper, Jul 1, 2008	CLVNoStone
Ayers	George	William	Sep. 30, 1927	Apr. 21, 1933	"To know, to esteem, to love, and then to part with our little son who left us with a broken heart." / white stone laying on the ground	HGH1153
Ayers	Martha		No Date	No Date	Small pointed stone with name etched on it by hand	HGH1154
Ayres	Constance	G.	Oct. 16, 1953	Mar. 24, 2007	Info was obtained from the Catholic Cemetery Assoc.	SIG075
Ayres	Pearl	E., Deakins	Dec. 17, 1898	Aug. 30, 1987		MRB059
B.	F.	D.	No Date	No Date	Footstone with the initials F.D.B.	SMCW049
B.	H.	T.	No Date	No Date	Footstone with the initials H.T.B.	SMCW048
B.	J.	T.	1865	1946	Initials on stone J.T.B. (This may be the h/o Cora I. Burgess, James T. Burgess)	PIS248
B.	T.	R.	No Date	No Date	Footstone with the initials T.R.B.	SMCW050
Bachmeier	Cecilia	B., Arch	1902	1991	Mother	NSP437
Bachmeier	Dorothy		1936	1947		NSP436
Bachmeier	Karl	B.	1898	1966	Father	NSP437
Badamo	Rama		Nov. 16, 1966	Jul. 25, 2005	"Kira" / wife and Mother	SIC9057
Baden, Sr.	Ambrose	A.	May 22, 1899	Dec., 29, 1972	In loving memory	NSP583
Baden	Andrew	D.	1904	1960		NSP462

Last Name	First Name	Middle Name	Date of Birth	Date of Death	Transcription / Notes	Cemetery Code
Baden	Annie	May	Aug. 14, 1896	Dec. 12, 1976		NSP866
Baden	Bridget	Agnes	Aug. 31, 1913	Jun. 1, 1977	Mother	NSP868
Baden	C.	Norwood	1923	1990		SIG063
Baden	Charles	Edward	1894	1905	Married Jun 14, 1947	OSP156
Baden	Charles	P.	1860	1904		OSP154
Baden	Cora	K.	1903	1993		NSP464
Baden	Evelyn	Duley	Dec. 13, 1902	No Date	In loving memory	NSP583
Baden	Frances	Marie	1934	1935		NSP459
Baden, Sr.	G.	Ralph	1906	1968		NSP463
Baden	Genevieve	D.	1924	No Date	Married Jun 14, 1947	SIG063
Baden	Halbert	D.	1877	1933		NSP460
Baden	Joseph	Halbert	Jul. 31, 1914	Aug. 20, 1993	PFC US Army WW II	NSP869
Baden	Kerby	A.	1891	1934		NSP512
Baden	Louise	Burnham	Aug. 29, 1891	Feb. 14, 1972		OFE3029
Baden	Lucy	V.	1879	1947		NSP461
Baden	Margaret	T.	1937	1999		NSP465
Baden	Mary	A.	1824	1904		OSP155
Baden	Mary	C.	1861	1933		NSP508
Baden	Mary	Teresa	1868	1921		OSP157
Baden	Maureen	Philomena	Jul. 15, 1949	Jun. 9, 1954	Beloved d/o Joseph H and Bridget M. Baden	NSP867
Baden	Thomas	B.	1857	1927		NSP507
Baden	William	Thomas	Mar. 11, 1896	May 16, 1972		NSP866
Bagley	Barbara	M.	1896	1961		LUM054
Bagley	Jesse		1882	1959		LUM054
Bagnato	Jonathan		No Date	Jul. 1985	Gone but not forgotten - "Til we meet again / Wife, Mother, Nanny / Grandson / 7 days	SJO4015
Bagnato	Mary	Jean	Dec. 29, 1930	Jan. 19, 1985	Gone but not forgotten - "Til we meet again / Wife, Mother, Nanny / Grandson 7 days	SJO4015
Bagnato	Nazzareno	G.	Oct. 8, 1928	No Date	Gone but not forgotten - "Til we meet again" / Wife, Mother, Nanny / Grandson	SJO4015
Bailey	Alice	Jean	Mar. 28, 1930	Mar. 8, 1938		MTR3024

Last Name	First Name	Middle Name	Date of Birth	Date of Death	Transcription / Notes	Cemetery Code
Bailey	Allen	M.	1881	1956		NJB479
Bailey	Barry	Warwick	Feb. 18, 1934	Apr. 16, 1982	In Loving Memory / Beloved Husband of Elaine, Beloved father of Erin age 12, Shannon Age 10, Ryan Age 2 (there is a strike over on the middle name by the stone maker)	MTR3040
Bailey	Benjamin	F.	Nov. 11, 1865	Aug. 3, 1929		SMY3177
Bailey	Charles	R.	Jun. 12, 1913	Jun. 23, 1994	Together forever	HGH4061
Bailey	Chloe	Rebecca	1864	1907	footstone	CHR069
Bailey	Constance	B.	1944	1972	Our Father Who Art In Heaven	SMI062
Bailey	Constance	Raye	No Date	Aug. 5, 1932	Infant d/o Leon & Frances Bailey / Aged 3 months	MTR3025
Bailey	Earl	Rodney	Mar. 20, 1926	Dec. 2, 1977	Rest in peace / Beloved husband and father / Footstone: CPL US Marine Corps WW II	SCL3028
Bailey	Edwin	D.	Dec. 15, 1849	Sep. 7, 1927		OSM006
Bailey	Eleanor	G.	Jul. 5, 1850	Feb. 25, 1942		OSM005
Bailey	Elizabeth	Alethia	No Date	Jan. 22, 1911	(Nee Lloyd) In her 87 year	HGH1072
Bailey	Elmer	Domnick	1894	1946		HGH1138
Bailey	Emma	E.	Oct. 14, 1921	No Date	Together forever	HGH4061
Bailey	Emma	S.	Mar. 6, 1878	Jun. 25, 1968		SMY3177
Bailey	Francis	Malcolm	1909	1977	TEC4 US Army WW II	SMY3207
Bailey	George	Robert	Nov. 16, 1925	Jan. 25, 2009	Age 73 s/o late Mary Bailey (info is from the Maryland Independent Newspaper Wed. Jan 28, 2009 page A10 Col 1)	SHINoStone
Baines, Sr.	James	E.	Dec. 7, 1915	Nov. 2, 1971		HGH1060
Bailey	James	Ignatius	1863	1932	Footstone	CHR069
Bailey	James	L	1908	1966		CHR074
Bailey	Josiah	Read	Dec. 23, 1892	Dec. 13, 1946		TRI050
Bailey	Lela	Turner	Apr. 17, 1893	Oct. 11, 1946		TRI050
Bailey	Leon		1895	1935		MTR3027
Bailey	Leonard	Martin	May 28, 1893	Feb. 24, 1945	Beloved husband and father	OSM156
Bailey	Lilly	M.	May 16, 1884	Mar. 31, 1949		PKH010
Bailey, Sr.	Louis	Vernon	Jan. 7, 1920	Jan. 10, 1963	Maryland PVT AGF REPL DEPOT 1 World War II	HGH2051
Bailey	Mary	C.	Dec. 15, 1844	Jan. 12, 1931		HGH3087

Last Name	First Name	Middle Name	Date of Birth	Date of Death	Transcription / Notes	Cemetery Code
Bailey	Nettie	Mae	1880	1952		NJB398
Bailey	Ralph	V.	1951	1985	"Dinky" Beloved husband and father	HGH2049
Bailey	Richard		1886	1958		NJB398
Bailey	Ruth	Jackson	1900	1980		HGH1138
Bailey	S.	Ralph	1915	1975		HGH2050
Bailey	Sterling		1912	1967		HGH2052
Bailey	Unknown		No Date	No Date		CHR068
Bailey	Unknown		No Date	No Date		CHR067
Bailey	Unknown		No Date	No Date		CHR066
Baker	Anthony	James	Apr. 12, 1961	Nov. 8, 1997		SJO5090
Baker	Anthony	James	Apr. 12, 1961	Nov. 8, 1997		SJO5026
Baker	Billy	C.	Mar. 19, 1936	May 31, 1994		SCL3298
Baker	Braxton	Bragg	1923	Oct. 22, 2009	Together forever / Age 85. Born in Alabama and died in Charles County, MD. h/o the late Hilda Baker. He retired from the Navy after 33 yrs of service. (info is from the Maryland Independent Newspaper Wed. Oct 28, 2009 Pg A12 Col 3)	SMC1042
Baker	Clarence	C.	1917	2002	Married May 1, 1938	SJO1065
Baker	DeVonte	A.	Jun. 17, 1993	Mar. 23, 1996	In God's Care	SIC9068
Baker	Hilda	E.	1917	2006	Together forever	SMC1042
Baker	Irene	Annetta	May 9, 1859	Jan. 17, 1923		NJB072
Baker	Joseph	Bradley	Jun. 12, 1925	Apr. 24, 1992	Pvt US Army WW II	SJO5064
Baker	Joseph	Bradley	Jun. 12, 1925	Apr. 24, 1992	Pvt. US Army WW II	SJO5059A
Baker	Mabel		Jul. 12, 1921	Mar. 24, 2003	"Miss Mabel" / Eternal Peace	PGN066
Baker	Mary	Alma	Feb. 23, 1930	Apr. 17, 2004		HGH4007
Baker	Reuben	Eugene	Feb. 11, 1949	Aug. 24, 2002		ALX020
Baker	Rosie	C.	1923	2004	Married May 1, 1938	SJO1065
Baker	Shirley	Ann	Dec. 6, 1944	Feb. 8, 1994		SMC2114
Baker	Shirley	Mae	Nov. 29, 1950	Jul. 15, 1994	In Remembrance / Loving Mother, Daughter and Sister	SMY2122
Baker	Spriggs	A.	Jul. 23, 1943	Jan. 1, 2005		SMC2115
Baker	William	M.	1917	1960		SMY2093

Last Name	First Name	Middle Name	Date of Birth	Date of Death	Transcription / Notes	Cemetery Code
Baker	William	T.	Sep. 12, 1850	Mar. 4, 1933	Masonic emblem engraved on stone	NJB071
Baker	Ollie		1928	2009	Thornton Funeral Home Marker	SJO5066
Bakr	Barbara	Woodland	Jul. 27, 1946	Nov. 27, 1987	Mother / At rest	NSP060
Baldus	Carl	R.	1883	1950		SMY3125
Baldus	Mary	Madeline	1898	1976		SMY3126
Baldus, Rev.	William	Joseph	1880	1947		SMY3097
Baldwin	Alice		1921	1926		SJE040
Baldwin	Kathleen		No Date	1927	Infant	SJE039
Baldwin	Nellie	E.	1888	1928		SJE038
Baldwin	Randolph	M.	1875	1929		SJE037
Baldwin	William	H.	1913	1953		SJE041
Balenger	Gertrude	Stone	1914	2005	Death leaves a heartache no one can heal / Mother / Love leaves a memory no one can steal	SMC4220
Balenger	Theodore	E.	Mar. 28, 1962	Jan. 16, 2004	"Ted" / The soul that suffers is stronger than the soul that rejoices	SMC4221
Bales	Marcus	Joseph	Nov. 30, 1956	Aug. 13, 1999		SIC9004
Ball	Fannie		1905	1979		MHB200
Ball	Florence	C.	1894	1970	La Plata MD / Cheverly MD	SAC5049
Ball	Willie		No Date	Jul. 17, 1976	Info is from Shiloh Church Records	SMTNoStone
Bamberger	Carolyn	Marie	Sep. 11, 1941	Apr. 15, 2006	In Loving Memory / Beloved Wife, Mother, & Nana	SAC1029
Bamberger	Mary	Catherine	No Date	Aug. 29, 1990	Our Daughter / Bye Nana and Pap Pap	SAC1009
Bamberger	Raymond	David	No Date	Jan. 20, 1990	Our Son	SAC1010
Bambrick, S.J.	George	P.	Aug. 26, 1918	Aug. 17, 1989	IHS / Born 26 Aug 1918 / INGR. 1 March 1945 / Died 17 Aug. 1989 (In Priests Plot)	SIC1026
Baner (?)	William	McConchie	No Date	Oct. 2, 1913	Info is from Christ Church microfilm Reel 3 Pg 224-225 located at the College of Southern MD, LaPlata, MD	MTRNoStone
Bankhead	Marie	Smallwood	No Date	Jul. 29, 1926		HGH3094
Bankins	Norman	Leonard	Apr. 25, 1922	Mar. 21, 1987	M SGT US Army	SMC4114
Banks	Charles	H.	1916	1975		PKH154
Banks	Marion		No Date	Mar. 31, 1923	At Rest, Aged 81 years / This day brings back sad memorys of our dear one gone to rest, And those who think of him today Are the ones who loved him best	POM001

Last Name	First Name	Middle Name	Date of Birth	Date of Death	Transcription / Notes	Cemetery Code
Banks	Mary	E.	1918	1997		PKH154
Banks	Vera	Jean, Washington	1949	1979		NSP303
Bannister, Sr.	Alfred		No Date	No Date	His stone is buried in these bushes per church members. He was a Rector of Zion Baptist	ZBC125
Bannister	Edward	John	May 24, 1924	Dec. 8, 1995	PFC U.S. Army World War II	OAK060
Bannister	Gilbert		1924	1987		OAK212
Bannister	Raymond		Aug. 24, 1911	May 19, 1968	Thornton Funeral Home Marker	OAK222
Bannister	Robert	Lee	Jul. 21, 1945	Oct. 15, 1997	Eternally You've Gone But Not Forgotten	MHB117
Banque	Hugh		No Date	Aug. 30, 1866	In memory of / who departed this life Aug. 30, 1866 Aged/ 82 years & 11 months. The deceased was a native of Burgundy, France, But passed the last 60 years of his life in the United States. Footstone: H. B.	CHR560
Barbaza	Apolinar	V.	Jun. 18, 1934	No Date		NSP031
Barbaza	Bienvenida	G.	Oct. 30, 1938	No Date		NSP031
Barber	Eliza	Crain	Apr. 12, 1871	Jul. 29, 1942	d/o Yates & Eliza Crain Barber	CHR056
Barber	Eliza	Crain, Morgan	Feb. 22, 1841	May 27, 1909	his wife / "Not changed but glorified"	CHR058
Barber	Emma		No Date	Jan. 17, 1915	Aged 22 / info is from church records	OFENoStone
Barber	Frank		No Date	Jan. 13, 1927	Age 72 / info is from church records	SHINoStone
Barber	Frederick	S.	Sep. 26, 1880	Sep. 21, 1948	s/o Yates & Eliza Crain Barber	CHR055
Barber	George		No Date	May 15, 1931	Age 100 / info is from church records	OFENoStone
Barber	Gilbert	W.	1899	1987		HGH4036
Barber	Grace	K.	1896	1996		HGH4036
Barber, Dr.	James	Morgan	Oct. 17, 1939	Jul. 11, 1949	Info was provided by a family member	WAV1014
Barber, Sr.	James	S.	Oct. 12, 1906	Sep. 10, 2006		SAC5112
Barber	John	Benjamin	Mar. 22, 1867	Feb. 18, 1989	Beloved Husband & Father	SAC4062
Barber	Juliette	Wood, Hungerford	Jun. 11, 1918	Jan. 11, 1957	Info was provided by a family member	WAV1014
Barber	Laura	Loretta	Jun. 5, 1868	Jan. 17, 1977	Beloved Wife & Mother	SAC4062
Barber	Mary	Eleanor	No Date	Jan. 25, 1962		CHR060
Barber	Mary	Elizabeth	Jun. 19, 1941	Nov. 27, 1933	Age 100 / info is from church records	OFENoStone
Barber	Mary	R.	1904	No Date		SAC5112
Barber	Ruth	W.		1999		HGH4036

Last Name	First Name	Middle Name	Date of Birth	Date of Death	Transcription / Notes	Cemetery Code
Barber	S.		No Date	May 1918	Info is from church records	SHINoStone
Barber, P.S.J.	Samuel		1814	Feb. 22, 1864	IHS / Ob. 22, Feb 1864 / AET. 50 (In Priests Plot) Ancestry.com 1860 census shows birth as 1814 and he was 46 years old.	SIC1027
Barber	Walter	Yates	Jan. 12, 1876	Mar. 16, 1959		CHR059
Barber	Yates		Mar. 11, 1822	May 1, 1884		CHR058
Barberio	Mary	Louise	Nov. 11, 1920	Jan. 30, 2009	Mom	SMC1007
Barbour	Alice	A.	No Date	May 3, 1937	Aged 87 years 29 days / Info is from the 1940 DAR book page 64	TRINoStone
Barbour	Blanche	D.	Aug. 29, 1892	Nov. 17, 1965		SMI074
Barbour	Bradley	Stephen	Aug. 24, 1988	Oct. 4, 1988	Our Beloved Son	SAC4070
Barbour	Charlotte	M.	1888	1967		MTR3106
Barbour	Clara	P.	Oct. 18, 1884	Jan. 28, 1910	Children of J.S. & M.S. They will never be forgotten, Never shall their memories fade sweetest thoughts will ever linger around the graves where they are laid	SIC4042
Barbour	Daisy	M.	1889	1970		NSP674
Barbour	Dorothy	Frances	Feb. 28, 1917	No Date		SIC8084
Barbour	Dorothy	W.	Aug. 22, 1918	May 2, 2004		SCL4109
Barbour	Elizabeth		No Date	No Date	Info is from the 1984 church cemetery transcription list	SICNoStone
Barbour	Francis	Bruce	Apr. 25, 1894	Jun.e 3, 1971		SAC1130
Barbour	George	W.	Nov. 12, 1861	Jan. 19, 1929		TRI147
Barbour	George		Jul. 30, 1871	Jun. 21, 1949		ALX072
Barbour	Gladys	B., Miles	1899	1940		MTR3075
Barbour	Henry	L.	Jun. 9, 1912	Aug. 9, 1999		SCL4109
Barbour	J.	Samuel	Sep. 14, 1858	Jun. 25, 1931	Rest in peace.	TRI151
Barbour	James	A.	Aug. 24, 1876	Aug. 19, 1907	Beloved h/o Mary Barbour / They who knew him best will bless his name and keep his memory dear while shall last; Thy will be done.	TRI150
Barbour	James	Terence	Jan. 22, 1964	Mar. 30, 1989	In Loving Memory	SMY2123
Barbour	James	Walter	May 13, 1916	Jun. 14, 1981	Tec 5 US Army WW II	SIC8084
Barbour	James		No Date	No Date	Info is from the 1984 church cemetery transcription list	SICNoStone
Barbour	Jane	E.	1869	1881		ALX061

Last Name	First Name	Middle Name	Date of Birth	Date of Death	Transcription / Notes	Cemetery Code
Barbour	John	F.	Feb. 8, 1831	Dec. 18, 1900	May he rest in peace.	TRI148
Barbour	Keyonia	M.	1985	1988	Adams Funeral Home Marker	ZBC041
Barbour	Laura	E.	Jul. 24, 1909	Jun. 5, 1993	dates are from ancestry.com / There is a DAR emblem on the stone	CHR242
Barbour	Lee	S.	Sep. 12, 1891	Mar. 23, 1910		SIC4042
Barbour	Lloyd	E.	Jun. 27, 1919	Mar. 17, 1996		SCA038
Barbour	M.	Lillian	Jul. 22, 1890	Jan. 28, 1907		SIC4042
Barbour	Margaret		Sep. 10, 1915	Jul. 11, 1989	In Loving Memory	SMY2147
Barbour	Marion	H.	Nov. 17	No Date		SCA038
Barbour	Mary	A.	Nov. 7, 1839	Aug. 2, 1883	M.A.B.	TRI147
Barbour	Mary	Lucilla	1865	1934	Mary Lucilla, info is from church records	MTR3076
Barbour	Mary	Susie	Aug. 10, 1859	Nov. 9, 1947		SIC4042
Barbour	Nellie	N.	1882	1963		SMY2056
Barbour	Phyllis	Buckley	1918	1981	Trusted advocate-Mariner, States Attorney 1951-1955. Devoted Husband & Father / Devoted wife and mother. She was our constant, strength and inspiration	MTR3122
Barbour	Robert	Guy	1885	1958		MTR3106
Barbour	Robert	Taylor	Nov. 22, 1911	May 27, 1998	Trusted advocate-Mariner, States Attorney 1951-1955. Devoted Husband & Father / Devoted wife and mother. She was our constant, strength and inspiration / WOJG US Army WW II / Has an SAR emblem	MTR3122
Barbour	Robert	Thomas	1856	1935	Robert Thomas Barbour, info is from church records	MTR3077
Barbour	Samuel	D.	Feb. 7, 1882	Aug. 28, 1909	Children of J.S. & M.S. They will never be forgotten, Never shall their memories fade sweetest thoughts will ever linger around the graves where they are laid	SIC4042
Barbour	Sidney	C.	1889	1964		NSP674
Barbour	Susan	Iola	Nov. 25, 1894	Feb. 24, 1993		SAC1130
Barbour	Thomas	A.	1883	1953		MTR3074
Barbour	Thomas	T.	Aug. 2, 1909	Feb. 28, 1996	dates are from ancestry.com / SAR Emblem	CHR242
Barbour	William	E.	Jan. 30, 1887	Mar. 23, 1949	Maryland PFC 78 Field ARTY 6 Div WW I	MTR3078
Barbour	William	F.	Jan. 16, 1911	Jun. 8, 1991	In Loving Memory	SMY2147
Barbour	William	H.	1877	1958		SMY2056

Last Name	First Name	Middle Name	Date of Birth	Date of Death	Transcription / Notes	Cemetery Code
Barbour	William	H.	Feb. 15, 1881	Feb. 19, 1952		SMI075
Barbour	Willie		1914	1996	Father, There is a life above and all that life is Love	SMI073
Barbour	Yolanda	N.	1986	1988		ZBC040
Bardroff	John	E.	1858	1954	Adams Funeral Home Marker	MTR2047
Barger	Alberta	Smith	May 27, 1930	No Date	Beloved wife and Mother	ODE337
Barger	Blair	Barnard	Mar. 23, 1920	Mar. 30, 1983	Lt. US Navy WW II	ODE337
Barker	W.	Cephas	1893	1972		MTR2198
Barker, M.D.	William	R.	Oct. 2, 1859	Jun. 21, 1901		SMY1124
Barkley	G.	E.	Aug. 3, 1892	Oct. 8, 1931		SJE107
Barkley	Mary	E.	1871	1959		SJE108
Barkley	S.	B.	Mar. 1, 1855	Oct. 24, 1912		SJE109
Barkley	T.	H.	Sep. 7, 1889	Nov. 8 1916		SJE110
Barkley	Theresa	Celestia, Edelen	No Date	No Date	w/o Samuel Chase Barkley / info is from the Historical Society Research and the 1940 DAR book pg 199 located at the College of Southern MD, LaPlata, MD,	SMCNoStone
Barletta	Samuel	F.	1930	1994	US Air Force Korea	SMC4285
Barley	Sarah	Ludlow	Dec. 21, 1938	No Date	Abide in love	SPL3081
Barley	Warren	E.	Jun. 20, 1936	Mar. 10, 2002	Abide in love	SPL3081
Barnard	Donald	H.	1948	1985	Don's Gone Fishing	LUM085
Barnard	Henry	A.	Jun. 24, 1910	Oct. 29, 1969		LUM152
Barnard	M.	Virginia	Apr. 1, 1909	Oct. 9, 1977		LUM153
Barnard	Theresa	A.	Dec. 2, 1969	No Date	Maryland Independent 1/9/2004 Pg. A-9 lists Teresa as daughter of John Louie & Teresa M Facchina Burke	SJO4003
Barnard, III	James	M.	Jun. 25, 1968	No Date	Maryland Independent Newspaper Jan 9, 2004 Pg. A9, shows James as son-in-law of John Louie & Teresa M Facchina Burke	SJO4003
Barnes	Alexander	Hanson	Mar. 15, 1890	Apr. 7, 1979		MTR1159
Barnes-Perkins	Ann	Willette	Oct. 16, 1934	Sep. 15, 1997		SAC3097
Barnes	Annie	E.	Oct. 11, 1828	Jan. 18, 1903		SJE051
Barnes	Arthur	Nalley	No Date	Jan. 1896	Buried Jan 25, 1896 age 7 mo's. / Info is from Old Durham Church microfilm pg 83-83 located at the College of Southern MD, LaPlata, MD	ODENoStone

Last Name	First Name	Middle Name	Date of Birth	Date of Death	Transcription / Notes	Cemetery Code
Barnes	Arthur	Nalley	1895	1896		MTR1153
Barnes	Benton	Chiles	1871	1935	son of Benton & Mary Brawner Barnes / his wife / daughter of George E. & Frances Robey Lyon	MTR4033
Barnes	Benton		Jun. 9, 1826	Jan. 16, 1896		ODE143
Barnes	Beverly	Hanson	Apr. 21, 1900	Nov. 24, 1951		MTR1151
Barnes	Carolyn	E.	Jul. 17, 1923	Mar. 6, 1996	Thinking of you	SIG031
Barnes	Charles	E.	Jun. 11, 1924	May 27, 1981	PFC US Army WW II	SCL3231
Barnes, Sr.	Charles		Oct. 1, 1899	May 12, 1973		SMT016
Barnes, Jr.	Clifford	C.	Mar. 22, 1993	Apr. 15, 1999	"C.J." / Beloved Son, Grandson, Nephew, Brother and Friend / His Gentle Soul Has Gone to be an Angel	SAC1083
Barnes	Corinne	E.	Mar. 14, 1905	Jul. 6, 1975		SJO1028
Barnes	Dewayne		1956	1983	Montgomery Brothers funeral Home Marker	ZBC065
Barnes	Edith	Cooksey	Jul. 2, 1906	Apr. 1, 1969		MTR1157
Barnes	Edna		1928	2006	Thornton Funeral Home	ZBC093
Barnes	Edward	J.	Oct. 7, 1881	Mar. 14, 1972		SCA107
Barnes, Sr.	Edward	J.	Feb. 15, 1915	Aug. 24, 2000		SCL4224
Barnes	Ellen	Nalley	Nov. 25, 1862	Aug. 6, 1924		MTR1148
Barnes	Ernest	C.	1905	1980		MTR4034
Barnes	Esther	K.	Mar. 3, 1888	May 17, 1956		MTR1154
Barnes	Ethel	Cochrane	1888	1972		MTR1188
Barnes	Ethel	Lee	May 18, 1884	May 30, 1957		MTR1147
Barnes	Francis	H.	Aug. 25, 1920	Feb. 8, 1945	Maryland, PFC 366 INF WWII	SCA024
Barnes	Frank	Shepherd	1868	1940		ODE136
Barnes, Jr.	George	Edward	Aug. 25, 1958	Sep. 10, 2000	Son / Lo I will be with you always until the end of the world	LUM201
Barnes	Hanson		Oct. 26, 1860	Dec. 11, 1941		ODE141
Barnes	Hattie	E.	1892	1974	Loved in Life by the children	SCA135
Barnes	Henry	Robertson	May 6, 1886	May 15, 1970	Ever mindful of the needs of others	MTR1155
Barnes	Ida	Jane	No Date	May 1935	Buried May 7, 1935 / info is from Old Durham Church microfilm pg 160-161 located at the College of Southern MD, LaPlata, MD	ODENoStone
Barnes	Jane		18	1914		SMT018

Last Name	First Name	Middle Name	Date of Birth	Date of Death	Transcription / Notes	Cemetery Code
Barnes	Janie	E.	Mar. 16, 1906	Feb. 2, 1950	d/o Benton & Mary E. E. Barnes	SMT016
Barnes	Jennie		No Date	May 5, 1935		ODE140
Barnes	John	G. H.	Feb. 6, 1845	Aug. 6, 1849	s/o Richard S and Mary J. Barnes	RML015
Barnes	John		Apr. 25,, 1931	Aug. 11, 1947		HGH2025
Barnes	Joseph	T.	Mar. 13, 1925	Dec. 8, 1989	US Army TEC 5 1943 - 1946	SCL3327
Barnes	Joseph		No Date	No Date	Info is missing from Funeral Home Marker	HGH4212
Barnes	Juanita	M.	1959	1975	Funeral Home Marker / info is from the Historical Society Research located at The College of Southern MD, LaPlata, MD	LUMNoStone
Barnes	Katherine	S.	Dec. 16, 1898	Jan. 13, 1984		MTR1160
Barnes	Louie	A.	Jul. 28, 1900	Apr. 4, 1978		SJO1027
Barnes	Mable	C.	1879	1965	son of Benton & Mary Brawner Barnes / his wife / daughter of George E. & Frances Robey Lyon	MTR4033
Barnes	Marie		No Date	Nov. 23, 1905	Info is from Christ Church microfilm Reel 3, Pg 218-219 located at the College of Southern MD, LaPlata, MD	MTRNoStone
Barnes	Marion	Blanche	Nov. 11, 1873	Mar. 17, 1916	Marion Blanche Barnes / beloved wife of Harry B. Barnes / Rest in peace	SJO2323
Barnes	Mary	E. C., Brawner	No Date	No Date	w/o Benton Barnes / Mother	ODE142
Barnes	Mary	Elizabeth	No Date	Oct. 30, 1882	Info is from Christ Church microfilm Reel 1 Pg 320-321 located at the College of Southern MD, LaPlata, MD	MTRNoStone
Barnes	Mary	J.	Jan. 1806	Jan. 8, 1852	In Memory of Mary J. Barnes d/o Jas & Ann W. Robertson / aged 46 years / erected by Richard Barnes as a memorial of conjugal love and his high admiration of her character which shed ____ A sacred halo o'er her life where every virtue brightly shown in mistress, mother friend and wife while Jesus claimed her for his own. Then let that thought from tears and grief her spirit softly wispers give the dearest sweetest full relief that Jesus died that I might live. / Footstone: with the initials M.J.B.	RML017
Barnes	Mary	Jane	1870	1943		SHI260
Barnes	Mary	Loretta, Sanders	Sep. 10, 1879	Jan. 6, 1961	Beloved w/o Frank Shepherd Barnes	SJO6015
Barnes	Mary	Peggy	1950	1985		SJO3340

Last Name	First Name	Middle Name	Date of Birth	Date of Death	Transcription / Notes	Cemetery Code
Barnes	Mary	R.	Dec. 12, 1840	Jun. 28, 1842	d/o Richard & Mary J. Barnes	RML013
Barnes	Mary	Elizabeth	Jul. 16, 1896	Jul. 4, 1980	Gallant lady so well beloved	MTR1158
Barnes	Miriam	Burr	Oct. 29, 1907	Jun. 26, 1971		MTR1152
Barnes	Noble	E.	Nov. 14, 1833	Oct. 28, 1905		SJE051
Barnes	Olive	C.	Oct. 29, 1917	No Date		SCL4224
Barnes	Otis	Allison	1903	1986		MTR1189
Barnes	Richard		No Date	Sep. 21, 1898	Info is from Christ Church microfilm Reel 1 Pg 84-85 located at the College of Southern MD, LaPlata, MD	MTRNoStone
Barnes	Robert	H.	18	1947		SMT017
Barnes	Roger	Wellington	Jul. 4, 1910	Jul. 9, 1911	In sad but loving memory / Our Darling Baby / Safe in the arms of Jesus	GHB044A
Barnes	Stephen	R.	Jan. 20, 1971	Jun. 24, 2008	In God's Care	SJO5091
Barnes	Stephen	R.	Jan. 20, 1971	Jun. 24, 2008	In God's Care	SJO5027
Barnes	Unknown		No Date	No Date	Only the name Barnes is on the stone	SCA025
Barnes	Unknown		Oct. 1836	Oct. 1836	Infant d/o Richard & Mary J. Barnes	RML011
Barnes, Rev.	W.	H.	No Date	No Date		SHI043
Barnes	Wallace	E.	Dec. 7, 1936	Jan. 1, 2004		SAC5116
Barnes	Wallace	Shepherd	Sep. 7, 1894	Jan. 18, 1984		MTR1156
Barnes	William	Clay	Jul. 12, 1887	May 4, 1912		MTR1150
Barnes	William	I.	Apr. 13, 1894	Mar. 16, 1925	Beloved s/o Wm. H. & Mary J. & Beloved husband & father of Lottie C. & Wm. W. & Robt. O. age 30,	SHI263
Barnes	William	M.	Feb. 4, 1858	Oct. 2, 1912		MTR1149
Barnett	Elnora	L.	1899	1960		SCL1031
Barnett	Isabell	M.	1920	1940		SCL1031
Barnett	Paul	Anthony	Sep. 30, 1958	Jul. 20, 1995		SCL1027
Barnett	Sidney	J.	Sep. 23, 1922	Mar. 6, 1989		SCL1026
Barnett	Thomas	S.	Sep. 12, 1931	Dec. 23, 1993	CPL US Army Korea	SCL1074
Barnett	Zanita	Carolyn	Oct. 30, 1962	No Date		SCL1027
Barnhill	Unknown		No Date	No Date	Old looking stone with no names or dates	ODE352
Barres	Shamus	Welch	Feb. 18, 1916	Jul. 9, 2001		NJB266
Barrow	Betty	E.	1924	No Date		OSM087

Last Name	First Name	Middle Name	Date of Birth	Date of Death	Transcription / Notes	Cemetery Code
Barrow	George	William	Feb. 13, 1916	Mar. 22, 1989	TEC 5 US Army WWII	OSM087
Barrs, Jr.	Edward	W.	1917	1920	Info was obtained from the Historical Society Research located at the College of Southern Md, LaPlata, MD	OAKNoStone
Bartlett	Wm.	Henry	Feb. 12, 1923	Aug. 7, 2005	Footstone: Henry William Bartlett / PFC US Army World War II / Feb 12, 1923 / Aug 7, 2005 (Note:First and middle name are reversed)	CHR598
Barton	Jonathan	Andrew	Jun. 27, 2000	Oct. 24, 2000	J A B / Our Little Angel	SMY2103
Barton	Ralph	Dewey	1898	1966	Per church records, first name is Ralph	MTR1085
Barton	William		Feb. 22, 1934	Dec. 26, 2000	Hungerford plot	CHR143
Bartz, Jr.	Herman	Leo	1943	No Date	Info is from church records	SPL3040
Bartz, Sr.	Herman	Leo	Oct. 3, 1918	Jan. 8, 1990	Info is from church records	SPL3040
Bartz	Lucille	C.	Sep. 9, 1922	Feb. 29, 1996	Info is from church records	SPL3040
Basford	Ida		No Date	Aug. 31, 1879	Child / info is from church records	OFENoStone
Basford	Thomas	Frederick	No Date	Feb. 28, 1940	Age 60 / info is from church records	OFENoStone
Bassaford	Francis	Wilmer	Apr. 13, 1906	Jul. 20, 1906	s/o William F and Martha Bassaford	SMCA203
Bassford	Esther	M.	Apr. 22, 1917	Apr. 4, 2002		SMCD211
Bassford	James	E.	May 25, 1909	Mar. 29, 1989	Beloved wife and mother	SMCD211
Bassford	Leona		Jan. 19, 1929	Mar. 11, 1991		SMC3173
Bassford	Martha	C.	Dec. 9, 1883	Apr. 11, 1926	Mother / May they rest in peace	SMCA202
Bassford	Michael	E.	Jan. 29, 1959	Feb. 15, 1959	Infant son	OFE4103
Bassford, Sr.	Robert	F.	Feb. 27, 1935	Jun. 26, 1997		OFE4102
Bassford	Unknown	James	No Date	Jun. 11, 1882	P. 70 / info is from church records	OFENoStone
Bassford	Unknown		No Date	No Date	Infant of Wm and Leona Bassford	SMCA204
Bassford, Mrs.	Unknown		No Date	Jan. 1891	Info is from church records	OFENoStone
Bassford	William	B.	Feb. 14, 1924	Sep. 27, 1990	MM2 US Navy WW II	SMC3174
Bassford	William	F.	Aug. 9, 1874	Sep. 26, 1960	Father / May they rest in peace	SMCA202
Bastain	Albert		1869	1949	Asleep in Jesus/ gone but not forgotten	NJB514
Bastain	Alice	H.	Jul. 23, 1875	Apr. 13, 1950	In loving memory of / At rest	NJB250
Bastain	Belle		Apr. 14, 1922	Jul. 2, 2003		ODE296
Bastain	Brittania	Dodd	1925	No Date		NJB309
Bastain	Eddie		Nov. 14, 1877	May 21, 1960		NJB249

Last Name	First Name	Middle Name	Date of Birth	Date of Death	Transcription / Notes	Cemetery Code
Bastain	Edward	C.	1920	1985	CPL US Army WWII	NJB315
Bastain	Elizabeth		1873	1946	According to the census records of 1900, 1910 and 1920 she goes by Mary, Elizabeth and Lizzie	ODE295
Bastain	Ethel	Pearl	Feb. 5, 1914	Mar. 20, 1956	She has gone but not forgotten	NJB248
Bastain	Herbert	Harvey	May 16, 1917	Jan. 14, 1979	TEC 5 US Army WW II	ODE296
Bastain	Horace	E.	1899	1978		NJB310
Bastain	Lester	Horace	Nov. 7, 1923	Feb. 16, 1984	PFC US Army WWII	NJB314
Bastain	Mamie	N.	1897	1975		NJB310
Bastain	Mary	K.	1880	1954	Asleep in Jesus / gone but not forgotten	NJB514
Bastain	Norman	M.	1907	1944		ODE305
Bastain	Oscar	Leo	1915	1991		NJB309
Bastain	Samuel		1871	1946		ODE295
Bastain	Thomas	E.	Jul. 23, 1904	Jan. 27, 1999	Mother / Father	NJB232
Bastain	Violet	C.	Oct. 12, 1908	Feb. 19, 1996	Mother / Father	NJB232
Bastain / Bastin	Amos		Oct. 15, 1882	Abt 1933	Info is from a Bastain relative / s/o Lorenzo and Duedema Bastin / last name may be spelled Bastin	BAS002
Bastian	Caroline	M.	No Date	Jul. 1919	Buried Jul 10, 1919 / Census records show she is the d/o Samuel and Mary Elizabeth Bastin/Bastain (other info is from Old Durham Church microfilm pg 158-159 located at the College of Southern MD, LaPlata, MD)	ODENoStone
Bastian	Janice	E.	Dec. 18, 1941	Dec. 20, 1941		NJB231
Bastian	Thomas	E. P.	No Date	Jan. 29, 1904	Buried Feb 1, 1904 / Thomas E.P. Bastian / Census records show he is the son of Samuel and Mary Elizabeth Bastain / Bastin (other info is from Old Durham Church microfilm pg 85-86 located at the College of Southern MD, LaPlata, MD pg. 85)	ODENoStone
Bastin	Frank		No Date	Jul. 1885	11 mo.'s / info is from Old Durham Church microfilm pg 79-80 at the College of Southern MD, LaPlata, MD	BASNoStone
Bastin	Louis		No Date	Jul. 1875	2 yrs. / Info is from Old Durham Church microfilm pg 79-80 located at the College of Southern MD, LaPlata, MD	BASNoStone
Bastin	Josephine		No Date	Apr. 1885	Age 36 / info is from Old Durham Church microfilm pg 79-80 at the College of Southern MD, LaPlata, MD	BASNoStone

Last Name	First Name	Middle Name	Date of Birth	Date of Death	Transcription / Notes	Cemetery Code
Bastin, Jr.	Samuel	N.	No Date	Oct. 1924	Buried Oct 9, 1924 / age 2 yrs, 8 mo's. Name is also spelled Bastian, Bastian (Other Info is from Old Durham Church microfilm located pg 59 at the College of Southern MD, LaPlata, MD)	ODENoStone
Batchelder	Catherine	H.	Jan. 6, 1977	Nov. 20, 2007		SAC1143
Batchelor	Alvin	Earl	May 30, 1938	Oct. 15, 2005	In loving memory / Father	SJO3124
Batchelor	Elaine	Ann	No Date	No Date	In loving memory / Mother	SJO3124
Bateman	Elizabeth	J.	No Date	Jan. 26, 1896	Name is shown on church records but burial location is unknown, date is the burial date, not death date	CHRNoStone
Bateman	George	Ignatius	May 15, 1875	Nov. 11, 1955		MTR1129
Bateman	Henrietta		No Date	Jul. 1, 1949	Info is from church records	CLVNoStone
Bateman	Joseph	Henry	Feb. 13, 1877	May 20, 1935		MTR4117
Bateman	Kathleen	A.	1913	No Date		PKH141
Bateman	Lydia	V., Swann	Apr. 2, 1871	Oct. 19, 1926		MTR4117
Bateman	Mable	Virginia	Apr. 17, 1908	Nov. 27, 1993	Nee Sollars	CLV307
Bateman	Mary	Elizabeth	Feb. 24, 1877	May 5, 1946		MTR1130
Bateman	Perry		No Date	Jan. 25, 1936	Name is shown on church records but burial location is unknown, date is the burial date, not death date	CHRNoStone
Bateman	Philip	C.	1913	1982		PKH141
Bateman, Sr.	Thomas	Roland	Jul. 1, 1905	Nov. 19, 1975		CLV306
Baxter, Mrs.	Ann	M.	No Date	Jul. 14, 1855	Sacred to the memory of / a native of Cha. County Md. And consort of Reuben Baxter who departed this life / on the 21st year of her age / May she rest in peace (info is from the Historical Society Research located at the College of Southern MD, LaPlata, MD)	SICNoStone
Baxter	Belle	E.	1882	1940	R. I. P.	SJO2069
Baxter	J.	Leonard	Sep. 19, 1881	Aug. 26, 1908	In memory of / stone has fallen off it's base and is laying on the ground	SJO2067
Baxter	Mary	Catherine	Feb. 18, 1924	Mar. 10, 2001		SMC3083
Baxter	Reuben		No Date	Nov. 1892	Buried Nov 1892 (info is from Old Durham Church microfilm pg 83-84 located at the College of Southern MD, LaPlata, MD)	ODENoStone
Bayne	Helena	J.	1902	1990		NSP439

Last Name	First Name	Middle Name	Date of Birth	Date of Death	Transcription / Notes	Cemetery Code
Bayne	James	J.	1905	1966		NSP439
Beale	Mary	P., Travers	Dec. 9, 1922	Dec. 29, 2003	In loving memory "Dad" / "Mom"	SJO3111
Beale	Rufus	S.	Jul. 4, 1911	Apr. 21, 1997	In loving memory "Dad" / "Mom" / Thornton funeral home marker shows his first name as Sweeney	SJO3111
Beall	Donald	V.	Nov. 17, 1934	Jun. 4, 1991	In loving memory "Bigga Boss" / US Army	SJO3106
Beall	Shirley	A.	Nov. 6, 1946	No Date		SMC2016
Beall	Stanley	L.	May 11, 1943	No Date		SMC2016
Bealle	Dorothy	M.	Nov. 23, 1919	Nov. 10, 2002	Mother	SJO3114
Bealle	James	L.	May 2, 1910	Aug. 28, 1977	website Ancestry.com shows last name as Bealle	SJO3115
Bean	Agnes	Gardiner	Nov. 10, 1900	Dec. 19, 1983		NSP682
Bean	Alice	Berry	Jan. 24, 1853	Dec. 17, 1913	Beloved w/o John H. Bean / Lord remember me when thoust comest into my Kingdom.	SPL4101
Bean	Alonza		1903	1977	Together Forever	SCA139
Bean	Amelia		No Date	Jan. 16, 1830	w/o Henry H. Bean. / Died in the 70th year of her life	SPL3127
Bean	Amelia		No Date	Sep. 16, 1840	who departed this life / in her 19th year	BDKNoStone
Bean	Ann		Mar. 20, 1792	Dec. 12, 1877	d/o Hezekiah Dent and Martha his wife / in her 86th year "For so he giveth his beloved sleep"	BDKNoStone
Bean	Carlton	E.	Sep. 16, 1894	Feb. 12, 1977		NSP625
Bean	Catherine	Contee, Keith	Apr. 9, 1861	Aug. 27, 1892		SPL3042
Bean	Charles	E.	Nov. 7, 1917	Sep. 14, 1919	s/o C.E. & M.I. Bean	HNT055
Bean	Doris	M.	Dec. 28, 1928	Jun. 10, 1971		SPL4120
Bean	Drucilla		Nov. 30, 1883	Jun. 27, 1972		SPL4100
Bean	Edward	D. R.	Feb. 3, 1915	Nov. 9, 1926	s/o W. I. - Emma F. Bean / Rest in Peace	SAC1057
Bean	Elizabeth		Mar. 13, 1782	Dec. 26, 1867	In memory of / Thy word is a lamp unto my feet and a light unto my path / Rev: 21:23	SPL3125
Bean	Emma	F.	May 30, 1878	Oct. 22, 1956	Wife of Wm. I. Bean	SAC1055
Bean	Ethel	A.	Jan. 13, 1885	Dec. 2, 1973	Maryland Nurse, Army Nurse Corp. WWI	SPL4099
Bean	Francis	J.	Aug. 2, 1921	Apr. 19, 1978		SIC8081
Bean	Francis		1904	1988	Thornton Funeral Home Marker	SMT041
Bean	George	Robert	Oct. 2, 1913	Jan. 14, 1943		SPL4107
Bean	Henry	Arthur	Jul. 25, 1889	May 27, 1968		SPL4102

Last Name	First Name	Middle Name	Date of Birth	Date of Death	Transcription / Notes	Cemetery Code
Bean	Henry	H.	1753	May 22, 1840	Revolutionary soldier plaque / 1753-1840 / placed by Port Tobacco chapter of DAR / Birth date is from church records	SPL3128
Bean	J.	Milton	1881	1935		SPL4105
Bean	James	Hanson	Sep. 8, 1929	Jun. 14, 1987	Pvt. US Army Korea	SPL4108
Bean	James	T.	No Date	Aug. 20, 1850	s/o H. H. and M. A. Bean d / age 14 days	BDKNoStone
Bean	John	H.	1848	1940	Lord Remember me when Thous comest into thy Kingdom	SPL4101
Bean	John	L.	No Date	No Date	Info is from the Historical Society Research located at the College of Southern MD, LaPlata, MD	SICNoStone
Bean	Kathy		No Date	No Date	Info is from Christ Church microfilm Reel 1 Pg 320-321 located at the College of Southern MD, LaPlata, MD	MTRNoStone
Bean	Linda	L.	Jul. 2, 1950	Jan. 4, 1951		SPL4109
Bean	Margaret	E.	May 13, 1876	Jul. 14, 1876	Daughter of E.D.R. & Louisa R. / Of such is the kingdom of heaven	SPL3119
Bean	Margaret	Iola	Aug. 27, 1896	Mar. 28, 1962		NSP625
Bean	Martha		1889	1988	His wife - R. I. P.	SJO2062
Bean	Mary	A. E.	Jan. 3, ?	Mar. ?	w/o Dr. H. H. Bean and d/o James Miltmore, in the 29th year of her life	BDKNoStone
Bean	Mary	R.	Oct. 31, 1927	Jun. 9, 1993		SCL4008
Bean	Pauline		1905	1977	Together Forever	SCA139
Bean	R.		No Date	No Date	Initials only on Footstone (Info is from church record)	SPLNoStone
Bean	Robert	L.	1955	1973		SJO2026
Bean	Ruth	L.	Dec. 27, 1923	No Date		SIC8081
Bean	Sarah	Rebecca	No Date	Jan. 5, 1865	Beloved w/o E.D.R. Bean / In the 24th year of her age. / Memorial of affection to our Loved one, who rests in Heaven. Where they have no need of the sun, neither of the moon, to shine in it: for the glory of God does lighten it, and the Lamb is the light thereof.	SPL3120
Bean	Sarah		Jan. 1, 1784	Jul. 4, 1865	In memory of / footstone: S.B.	SPL3126
Bean	Sidney	A.	Sep. 17, 1887	Jul. 31, 1974	CPL US Army	SPL4103
Bean	Teresa	Estella	Sep. 26, 1917	Nov. 10, 1926	Dau of W. I.-Emma F. Bean / Rest in Peace	SAC1056
Bean	Thomas	Edward	Apr. 4, 1927	Jan. 16, 2002	WW II	SPL4119

Last Name	First Name	Middle Name	Date of Birth	Date of Death	Transcription / Notes	Cemetery Code
Bean	Wilford	D.	No Date	Jun. 24, 1838	who departed this life / in the 13th year of his age	BDKNoStone
Bean	William	A.	1888	1939	R. I. P.	SJO2062
Bean	William	I.	Dec. 28, 1877	Jul. 7, 1931		SPL4098
Bean	Wm	N.	Feb. 2, 1792	Sep.t 16, 1867	To my Beloved grandfather / Father I give my spirit up. I trust it in thy hand; my Dying flesh shall rest in Hope and rise at they command.	OFE2057
Bean, Jr.	Francis	J.	May 19, 1947	Dec. 17, 1976		SIC8077
Bean, Sr.	James	F.	Sep. 17, 1924	Dec. 27, 2000	USN WW II	SCL4008
Beans	Charles	F.	Oct. 17, 1901	Jul. 30,1986		OAK216
Beans	Helen	T.	May 21,1899	Aug. 7, 1986		OAK217
Beason	Marie		1946	2001	Funeral Home Marker / info is from church records	PGN057
Beattie	Bernardine	H.	Mar. 5, 1913	Apr. 20, 1993		SIC1112
Beattie	Mary	Joanne	Apr. 18, 1934	Dec. 7, 2005		MTR2208
Beattie	William	Allison	May 14, 1930	Jun. 25, 2002	CPL US Air Force WWII SGT US Army Korea	MTR2207
Beck	Dora	B.	Jan. 4, 1917	Feb. 25, 2004	Eastern Star	LUM130
Beck	Esther	E.	1862	1919	Located in the Kemp plot	MTR3095
Beck	Ethel	F.	Feb. 23, 1907	Jul. 27, 1989	Together forever with the Lord	NJB274
Beck	George	E.	Sep. 3, 1909	Apr. 8, 1989	Together forever with the Lord	NJB274
Beck	Rose	Apt	1897	1957	Peace	NSP387
Beck, Sr.	Harry	E.	Sep. 22, 1918	May 24, 1987	Masonic Emblem	LUM130
Beck, Capt.	William		1860	1937		CMX2014
Beckwith	Margaret	A.	Apr. 23, 1914	Jan. 9, 2008		SIC8089
Beckwith	Richard	W.	May 21, 1914	Aug. 6, 1991		SIC8089
Bednarik	Anna		No Date	No Date		HGH4164
Bednarik	John	Stephen	Mar. 6, 1919	Nov. 4, 1995		HGH4092
Bednarik	John		No Date	No Date		HGH4164
Bednarik	Rebecca	Milbren	Sept.6, 1923	Feb. 3, 2006		HGH4092
Beecher	William	B.	1884	1934		SJE021
Belfield	Lloyd		1928	1970	Rest in Peace Dad	SJO5061
Belfield	Mary	Helen	1948	1975	Rest in Peace	SJO5060
Bell	Agnes	H.	1923	1999		SCL2095

Last Name	First Name	Middle Name	Date of Birth	Date of Death	Transcription / Notes	Cemetery Code
Bell	Annette		No Date	Mar. 7, 2006	Info is from church records	CLVNoStone
Bell, Sr.	Bernard		Jun. 1, 1908	Oct. 2, 1983		SMC1174
Bell	Brian	Keith	Aug. 13, 1965	Nov. 7, 1988	He will give you peace in the midst of the storm	NSP244
Bell	Dorothy	May, Alvey	May 18, 1919	Jun. 6, 2008	Age 90 / d/o the late James King and late Lillian King. w/o the late Roger Bell and the late Bernard Alvey. Info is from Maryland Independent newspaper Wed. Jul 2, 2008 Pg A-10 Col3	PIS034
Bell	Dorothy		1921	1975	Thornton Funeral Home marker	BRC004
Bell	Edna	Link	Mar. 25, 1906	Feb. 24, 1993	In loving memory	CHR458
Bell	Frank		1908	1968	Masonic Emblem	PIS035
Bell, Miss	Hattie		No Date	Mar. 1929	Info is from church records	SHINoStone
Bell	Hillary		No Date	Jul. 8, 1925	77 yrs. 11 mos. / info is from church records	SHINoStone
Bell	James	Albert	Feb. 22, 1916	Jan. 20, 2004		SMC1131
Bell	John		1877	1937	Headstone and marker	PIS047
Bell, Jr.	Joseph		1923	1985	Thornton Funeral Home marker	BRC003
Bell	Leroy		1904	1986	Father	SMC1206
Bell	Mary	Ann	Mar. 19, 1899	Nov. 5, 1971		NSP179
Bell	Mary	Katie	Aug. 13, 1918	Jun. 10, 1989		SMC1131
Bell	Mary	Marie	1922	1978		SMC1176
Bell	Mary	N.	1912	1992	Eastern Star	PIS035
Bell	Patricia	A.	1948	1983	Daughter	SMC1206
Bell	Roger	A.	1914	1963	Masonic Emblem	PIS034
Bell	Russell		1948	1988	Thornton Funeral Home marker	BRC002
Bell	Susanna		Nov. 7, 1841	Sep. 3, 1924		SCL3358
Bell	Sydney		No Date	May 15, 1927	Age 70 / info is from church records	SHINoStone
Bell	Thomas	Albert	1894	1986		SMC1205
Bell	William	A.	1946	1979	Billy	SMC1175
Bell	William	A.	1918	1992		SCL2095
Bellamy	Jewel	Webb	Apr. 6, 1919	Jul. 10, 2000	Write me as one who loves his fellow men	LUM022
Bender	Barbara	C.	Dec. 17, 1895	Jun. 30, 1983		SMCD168
Bender	Edward	F.	Aug. 21, 1919	Nov. 9, 1922	Baby / At rest	SMCD169

Last Name	First Name	Middle Name	Date of Birth	Date of Death	Transcription / Notes	Cemetery Code
Bender	Fred	J.	Jul. 9, 1921	Jul. 3, 1962	The birth date of 21st was covered up with 9th	SMC3239
Bender	Fred	S.	Aug. 17, 1889	Oct. 2, 1986		SMCD168
Bender, Rev., S.S.	Lawrence	Anthony	Nov. 14, 1924	Feb. 5, 2004	There is a lot of information on the stone in reference to his life.	SMCD164
Bender	Leonard	John	Jul. 8, 1935	Dec. 16, 1957	Maryland PFC Ordnance Corps	SMC3245
Bender	Mary	Arabelle	Sep. 23, 1922	Jul. 3, 1962		SMC3238
Bender	Walter	Leo	Aug. 1, 1931	Oct. 14, 1989	US Army	SMC3252
Benjamin	Unknown		No Date	Jan. 8, 1964	Info is from church records	CLVNoStone
Benner	Dorine	E.	1932	1999		SMC3011
Benner	James	R.	1931	2002		SMC3011
Bennet	Lavonne		No Date	No Date	Artificial flowers, rock with a verse on it. (information provided by trustee at church)	SMI099
Bennett	Allison	Jane	Aug. 8, 1965	Jun. 2, 2005	In God's loving care	CHR090
Bennett	Andre		1963	2008	Thornton Funeral Home marker	SMY2029
Bennett	Elizabeth		Jan. 18, 1930	May 29, 1997	Beloved Mother	SMY2029
Bennett	Ernest	E.	1924	1979	PFC US Army WW II	SJO3145
Bennett	Florence	E.	May 14, 1889	May 14, 1974		SJO3142
Bennett	G.	J.	Feb. 22, 1916	May 9, 1986	SI US Navy WW II	SJO3141
Bennett	Irving	L.	Feb. 18, 1953	Jun. 7, 1977	Trust in the Lord, Believe in the Lord	SJO3144
Bennett, Sr.	James	A.	Aug. 29, 1907	Nov. 2, 1972		LUM126
Bennett	Louis	Elmore	Apr. 16, 1932	Dec. 13, 2006	PFC US Army Korea	SJO3080
Bennett	Mary	E.	Sep. 23, 1908	Jan. 31, 1995	Wife of Francis Bennett	SAC4096
Bennett	Mary	R.	May 10, 1909	Sep. 30, 1967		LUM126
Bennett	Rebecca	Ann	Jul. 29, 1941	Dec. 12, 1941	Our darling / She was too pure for this cold world, too gentle to stay, so God's holy angels came, and bore our darling away	LUM125
Bennett	Sherron	M.	Jun. 20, 1959	Apr. 8, 2002	Loving Daughter	ZBC059
Bennett	Timothy	Joe	Sep. 28, 1955	Mar..5,1991	Tim's Gone Fishing	GIL005
Bennett	William	A.	Apr. 28, 1883	May 28, 1974		SJO3142
Bennett	William	H.	Apr. 17, 1934	Oct. 4, 1972	Maryland CPL US Army Korea	SJO3131
Benton	Daniel	William	1867	1950		TRI082

Last Name	First Name	Middle Name	Date of Birth	Date of Death	Transcription / Notes	Cemetery Code
Benton	Doris	E.	May 20, 1922	Jul. 13, 1923	Our baby / Darling we miss thee	TRI080
Benton	Ethel	Moran	Jul. 22, 1903	Mar. 16, 1937		TRI111
Benton	Herman	Lee	Dec. 20, 1949	Feb. 28, 2004	In loving memory	SMC2033
Benton	Huntt	F.	1907	1948	Rest in peace	TRI086
Benton	Mildred	S.	1903	1986	Together forever	TRI087
Benton	Preston	S.	1904	1981	Together forever	TRI087
Benton	Ruth	M.	1910	1969	Rest in peace	TRI085
Benton	Sue	Ella	1873	1925		TRI082
Berardelli	Helen		Mar. 12, 1922	Jun. 4, 1990		SCL4108
Berbig	Dominic	Guy	1881	Jun. 16, 1942		CLV287
Berbig	Dorothy	M.	Dec. 25, 1897	Jun. 21, 1990	Nee King	CLV284
Berbig	J.	John	Mar. 16, 1890	Sep. 2, 1957	Death date is from church records	CLV285
Berbig	Linnie	May	Apr. 27, 1916	Jun. 25, 1921		CLV288
Berbig	Virgie	Irene	1881	Apr. 29, 1952	Death date is from church records	CLV286
Berger	Lawrence	L.	1943	No Date		SIG069
Berkeley	Jean	Marie	Feb. 23, 1946	Mar. 13, 1993	Together Forever	NSP662
Berkeley	R.	E.	May 21, 1944	No Date	"Mike" / Together forever	NSP662
Berry	A.	Benton	1859	1901		MTR4007
Berry	Ada	Turner	1880	1967		OSM042
Berry	Alice	Lois	Dec. 17, 1930	May 27, 1933	At rest	SPL4008
Berry	Alverta	Blanche	Jul. 11, 1919	May 3, 1999		SPL4071
Berry	Amos	D.	Sep. 2, 1859	Jun. 13, 1860	S/o George W. & June E.V. Berry	MTR1175
Berry	Annie	E.	Apr. 13, 1892	Jun. 3, 1973	At rest	SPL4017
Berry	Arthur	W.	Jun. 16, 1891	Mar. 19, 1965		SPL4017
Berry	Asenith		1876	1956		MTR1181
Berry	Beal	T.	Jun. 22, 1856	Mar. 28, 1857	s/o W.L. and M.E. Berry / aged 11m, 6d / Dates are from church records	SPL6058
Berry	Benjamin	B.	1880	1966		SPL3027
Berry	Benjamin	F.	1915	1950	Erected by E. Day	SPL3030
Berry	Benjamin	F.	Aug. 10, 1865	Nov. 22, 1901		OSM137
Berry	Bernard	M.	Sep. 24, 1880	Dec. 19, 1910	Beloved h/o Mable A. Berry	SPL1047

Last Name	First Name	Middle Name	Date of Birth	Date of Death	Transcription / Notes	Cemetery Code
Berry	Burnard	H.	Apr. 26, 1824	Aug. 2, 1852	IHS / In memory of / who departed this life / in the 28th year of his age / In mansions of the blest freed from the cares of death and sin	OSP164
Berry	Carl	Benjamin	Jun. 13, 1914	Feb. 19, 1992	"Pop" / Absent in body but present in spirit. Forever in our hearts.	SPL4007
Berry	Carlisle		No Date	Jun. 10, 1941	Info is from Christ Church microfilm Reel 4 Pg 268-269 located at the College of Southern MD, LaPlata, MD	MTRNoStone
Berry	Cassie	M.	1876	1941		SPL3027
Berry	Charles		Jan. 7, 1878	Sep. 30, 1889	Our darling / s/o William T & Julia Berry / I loved my darling little Charley, and would have had him stay, but let our Father's will be done, He shines in endless day.	SPL1041
Berry	E.	Alberta	1902	1991		MTR1259
Berry	Edward	Guy	May 16, 1883	Jan. 15, 1920		SPL4016
Berry	Edward	T.	1857	1944		MTR1259
Berry	Edward		Apr. 14, 1851	Jun. 10, 1920		SPL4012
Berry	Effie	E.	1877	1933		MTR1259
Berry	Eleanor	Wells	1908	1981		MTR1122
Berry	Eleor		No Date	May 17, 1889	Info is from Christ Church microfilm Reel 2 Pg 165-166 located at the College of Southern MD, LaPlata, MD	MTRNoStone
Berry	Elizabeth	J.	1820	1855	w/o Geo. W. Berry	MTR1171
Berry	Elizabeth		1874	1955		MTR1180
Berry	Ella	Maude	1869	1914		MTR4008
Berry	Emma	A.	No Date	Mar. 11, 1898	Beloved w/o Edward Berry who departed this life in her 47th year. Blessed are the dead who died in the Lord.	SPL4013
Berry	Ernest		1898	1977	Beloved Father	MHB138
Berry	Ethel	A., Moore	Mar. 9, 1915	Jul. 29, 2000		SPL4006
Berry	Fannie	Morris	1869	1944		MTR1119
Berry	Flora	T.	Dec. 18, 1882	Jan. 13, 1885	Our babe / d/o William T. & Julia Berry / Of such is the kingdom of heaven.	SPL1040
Berry	Frances	E.	Mar. 1, 1852	Jan. 12, 1941		OSM039
Berry	G.	W.	Feb. 8, 1845	Mar. 3, 1930		OSM040
Berry	George	Tarleton	No Date	Sep. 17, 1955	Info is from Christ Church microfilm Reel 4 Pg 276-277 located at the College of Southern MD, LaPlata, MD	MTRNoStone

Last Name	First Name	Middle Name	Date of Birth	Date of Death	Transcription / Notes	Cemetery Code
Berry, Jr.	George	W.	1847	1932		MTR1176
Berry	George	Washington	No Date	Aug. 19, 1932	Info is from Christ Church microfilm Reel 3, Pg 238-239 located at the College of Southern MD, LaPlata, MD	MTRNoStone
Berry	George	Washington	1818	Mar. 1, 1899	Name and dates are from church records	MTR1171
Berry	Harriet	A.	1885	1886		SPL4014
Berry	Helen	C.	Sep. 4, 1891	Sep. 12, 1904	Children of E.T. & Kate E. Berry	MTR1260
Berry	Henry	Bruce	Nov. 3, 1877	Oct. 26, 1956		MTR4035
Berry	Ida	May	1864	1903		MTR4062
Berry	James	Carlisle	1887	1941		MTR1086
Berry	James	Horace	Jun. 28, 1915	Feb. 16, 2002	WW II	SPL4071
Berry	Jane	E.	1833	1924		MTR1171
Berry	Jennifer	Lynn	No Date	Jun. 27, 1978		NSP538
Berry	John	Nally	1780	1842	MD Pvt. 43 Regt. Md. Militia - War of 1812	SPL6054
Berry	John	Walter	Jun. 22, 1862	Sep. 23, 1945		SPL6055
Berry	Juanita	S.	1886	1956		NSP494
Berry	Kate	E.	Jan. 25, 1853	Jul. 3, 1899	Wife of E. T. Berry	MTR1261
Berry	Kate	T.	Jan. 5, 1910	May 3, 1984		MTR1262
Berry	Katherine	V.	Sep. 12, 1879	Dec. 22, 1942	w/o Bruce Berry	OAK182
Berry	Kathryn		Jul. 14, 1874	Oct. 17, 1947		SPL6116
Berry	Lillian	V.	May 14, 1886	Aug. 14, 1967		SPL4012
Berry	Lloyd	M.	1877	1965		SPL4016
Berry	Louis	Wickliffe	1900	1989		OSM042
Berry	Mabel	A.	1892	1925		MTR1121
Berry	Malcolm		1864	1931		SPL1046
Berry	Mamie	H.	Mar. 15, 1882	Feb. 27, 1890	Children of E.T. & Kate E. Berry	MTR1167
Berry	Margaret	E.	No Date	Jul. 23, 1864	w/o William L. Berry / in the 32nd year of her age. / She was a tender mother here, and in her life the Lord did fear; we trust our loss will be her gain, and that with Christ she's gone to reign.	MTR1260
Berry	Margaret	E.	1881	1890		SPL6057
Berry	Maria	C.	No Date	Apr. 29, 1884	Departed this life / Aged 64 years	SPL4015
						SJO4170

Last Name	First Name	Middle Name	Date of Birth	Date of Death	Transcription / Notes	Cemetery Code
Berry	Mary	Edith	No Date	Oct. 23, 1942	Info is from Christ Church microfilm Reel 4 Pg 268-269 located at the College of Southern MD, LaPlata, MD	MTRNoStone
Berry	Mary	J.	Jan. 25, 1853	Aug. 17, 1913	Rest in Peace	SPL1038
Berry	Mary	R.	No Date	May 5, 1861	Sacred to the memory of / who departed this life on the 5th of May 1861 aged 9 years 5 months and 5 days / Dearest daughter thou hast ____ The loss most deep for (stone is laying on the ground, broken and parts are missing)	OSP166
Berry	Mary	Ruth	1878	1918		MTR1176
Berry	Mary	Jane	1853	1890		MTR1176
Berry	Matilda		1895	Apr. 1984	A rock marks the spot / info is from church records / ancestry.com shows birth date as Jan 21, 1892	PGN023
Berry	Paul	A.	Apr. 17, 1899	Jun. 5, 1899	Children of E.T. & Kate E. Berry	MTR1260
Berry	Pearle		1898	1988	Father	MHB096
Berry	Pearlie		1898	1988	Thornton Funeral Home Marker	MHB150
Berry	Robert		1889	1984	Thornton Funeral Home	MHB151
Berry	Roy	T.	Jul. 24, 1887	Mar. 8, 1908	Children of E.T. & Kate E. Berry	MTR1260
Berry	Somerset	Dyson	1851	1935		MTR4062
Berry	Stanley		1924	1993	Thornton Funeral Home Marker	ALX111
Berry	Susan	R.	1830	1889		MTR4004
Berry	Tarleton		1881	1955		MTR1179
Berry	William	Ashton	1867	1962		MTR1120
Berry	William	Edward	Dec. 16, 1912	Feb. 5, 1994		SPL4006
Berry	William	H.	1813	1899		MTR4006
Berry	William	L.	Oct. 6, 1822	Jun. 1, 1878	I know that my redeemer liveth.	SPL6056
Berry	William	T.	Nov. 16, 1850	Dec. 10, 1882	The blood of Christ cleanseth from all sin. A. H. Lyeth, Balt.	SPL1039
Berry	William	W.	1885	1973		MTR1170
Berry	Wm	Herbert	1855	1892		MTR4005
Besche	Anthony	C.	Feb. 12, 1917	Dec. 15, 1972		NSP748
Besche	Mark	S.	Sep. 16, 1953	Sep. 27, 2001		NSP747
Besit	K.		1867	Apr. 24, 1905	K. BESIT B 1867 DIE 1941 SEP 10	SMCW032

Last Name	First Name	Middle Name	Date of Birth	Date of Death	Transcription / Notes	Cemetery Code
Bettis	Mary	L.	Apr. 17, 1926	Jan. 7, 1983		SMC3275
Beverlin	Burtis		Jan. 30, 1916	Apr. 14, 1967	Father	PIS031
Beuchert	Gyongyver	G.	Jul. 12, 1942	No Date	Together forever / Married May 4, 1963	SMC2034
Beuchert, Sr	Jerome	J.	Feb. 16, 1916	May 18, 1985		SMC2043
Beuchert, Jr	Jerome	Joseph	Nov. 26, 1939	Jan. 19, 2004	Together forever / Married May 4, 1963	SMC2034
Beuchert	Jessie	Richards	Jan. 12, 1917	Sep. 17, 1995	A mother is a mother still, the Holiest thing alive	SMC2044
Bettis	Paul	E.	Aug. 31, 1930	Aug. 22, 1991		SMC3275
Beverlin	Donnis	J.	1947	1955	Daughter / I Pray Thee Lord My Soul to Keep	PIS024
Beverlin	Lily	Bell	May 3, 1945	Jun. 8, 1960		PIS030
Beverly	Michael	Lamont	Feb. 22, 1975	Jun. 28, 2008	Age 33 / Born in P.G. County, MD, Died LaPlata, MD / info is from Maryland Independent Newspaper, Friday Jul 4, 2008 Page A12 Col 2	HGH4015
Bibb	Ralph	A.	1901	1964		CLV120
Bibb	Thelma	M.	1903	1979		CLV120
Bibby	Francis	Grafton	Jun. 1, 1895	Jan. 19, 1899	In loving remembrance of our darling boy	ODE121
Bibby	John	G. S.	No Date	Nov. 5, 1905	District of Columbia-Hosp. Steward US. Navy Buried Sep 29, 1892 (info is from Old Durham Church microfilm located at the College of Southern MD, LaPlata, MD)	ODE120
Bibby, Mrs.	Unknown		No Date	Sep. 27, 1892	Plot N6 / Info is from Sister Miriam John at Mt Carmel Monastery	ODENoStone
Biddle	Sharon	A.	Nov. 10, 1936	Apr. 23, 2000		GMC024
Bigger	Grover	C.	1887	1946		POM009
Bigger	Minnie		1894	1989		POM248
Biles	Abram		1858	1930		NJB259
Biles	Amelia		1862	1931		NJB259
Biles	Annie	Viletta	No Date	Apr. 8, 1881	Info is from Christ Church microfilm Reel 1 Pg 318-319 located at the College of Southern MD, LaPlata, MD	MTRNoStone
Biles	Edward	James	No Date	Apr. 13, 1883	Info is from Christ Church microfilm Reel 1 Pg 320-321 located at the College of Southern MD, LaPlata, MD	MTRNoStone
Biles	Frederick		No Date	Sep. 6, 1891	Info is from Christ Church microfilm Reel 2 Pg 167-168 located at the College of Southern MD, LaPlata, MD)	MTRNoStone

Last Name	First Name	Middle Name	Date of Birth	Date of Death	Transcription / Notes	Cemetery Code
Biles	William	H.	1824	Dec. 23, 1883	In memory of / PVT CO A 5 NYHA Civil War / This is a memorial stone, exact burial site is unknown. Info is from Christ Church microfilm Reel 1 page 320-321 located at the College of Southern MD, LaPlata, MD	MTR1272A
Billingsley	Vernon	E.	Apr. 22, 1925	May 17, 1945	District of Columbia / Pvt. Engrs.	MRB027
Birch	Joshua	David	No Date	1979		CLV101
Birchby	Constance	D.	1885	1927		TRI355
Birchby, Rev.	Ernest	Lee	Mar. 26, 1879	Jun. 22, 1922		TRI354
Birchby	John	Pinsent	Jun. 7, 1917	Oct. 20, 1976		TRI357
Birchby	Madeline	W.	Sep. 26, 1916	Jul. 1, 1971	God called her home, it was His will. But in my heart I love her still. Her memory is as dear today as in the hour she passed away.	TRI356
Birckhead	Annie	E.	1881	1928		SPL4026
Birckhead	Thomas	E.	1880	1932		SPL4028
Bishop	Ann	Dawson	1844	1921		HGH1007
Bivins	Agnes	F.	1891	1992		SAC4024
Bivins	Charles	R.	1858	1920	RIP	SAC4082
Bivins	James	L.	Dec. 15, 1914	Jun. 30, 1985		SAC4023
Bivins	John	W.	1953	1972		SAC4058
Bivins	Joseph	F.	1915	1977	Tec 5 US. Army WWII	SAC4060
Bivins	Louis	M.	1888	1962		SAC4024
Bivins	Martha	P.	1860	1934	RIP	SAC4082
Bivins	Sally	Elizabeth	Dec. 10, 1931	Jul. 6, 1955	Your Loving Children	SAC4069
Bivins	Sarah	E.	1911	1963	Raymond Funeral Home marker	SAC4070A
Black	Florence	Carroll, Taylor	May 26, 1908	Mar. 12, 1985	Love, Husband and Children	SJO2249
Black	Olga	Virginia	Oct. 2, 1927	Mar. 27, 1996	Trusting Jesus on earth praising Jesus in heaven / Beloved friend husband Father and Grandfather / Married Dec 24, 1949 Our best christmas gift ever / Cherished friend, wife mother and grandmother	CMX2167
Black, Sr.	Robert	Dean	Nov. 19, 1925	Dec. 9, 1999	Trusting Jesus on earth praising Jesus in heaven / Beloved friend husband Father and Grandfather / Married Dec 24, 1949 Our best christmas gift ever / Cherished friend, wife mother and grandmother	CMX2167

Last Name	First Name	Middle Name	Date of Birth	Date of Death	Transcription / Notes	Cemetery Code
Blackburn	Clemence	Pauline	Oct. 2, 1904	Aug. 1, 1990	In loving memory	ODE083
Blackburn	Helen	Enslow	Aug. 8, 1918	No Date		ODE079
Blackburn	Levi	Carroll	Jun. 3, 1907	Mar. 23, 1969		ODE079
Blacklock	Elizabeth	Sabina, Matthews	May 25, 1875	May 16, 1949	w/o Julian Chandler Blacklock	SIC4132
Blacklock	James	Sydney	Mar. 3, 1912	Jan. 26, 1995		SIC4063
Blacklock	Julian	Chandler	Mar. 25, 1871	Aug. 24, 1957	Husband of Elizabeth Sabina Matthews	SIC4134
Blacklock	Mildred	Shorter	Dec. 2, 1920	No Date		SIC4063
Blackmon	Ben	Marion	Oct. 12, 1923	No Date		SIC6045
Blackmon	Mary	Scott	Sep. 27, 1925	No Date		SIC6045
Blackwelder	Dorothy	W. Ford	Jul. 17, 1911	Jan. 1, 1987	Dorothy was good	LUM175
Blackwelder	Leroy	J.	Aug. 29, 1931	No Date		LUM175
Bladen	Effie	I.	Feb. 23, 1931	Dec. 22, 1933	d/o E.L. & M.E. Bladen	SJO6033
Bladen	Ernest	Lee	Jul. 3, 1900	Oct. 14, 1977		SJO1078
Bladen	Mary	E.	Feb. 21, 1912	Nov. 25, 1992		SJO1078
Blair	Mildred	Bernice	Sep. 24, 1916	No Date		SPL2014
Blair	William	Preston	Jul. 29, 1905	Apr. 18, 1977		SPL2014
Blake	John	Derrick	Dec. 6, 1956	Jan. 21, 2002	(Dee)	NJB281
Blake	John	H.	Aug. 26, 1797	Mar. 1983	Here repose the remains of John H. Blake born in Georgetown, D.C. August 26, 1797 died at Elmwood August 24, 1863	BLKNoStone
Blake	Katherine	H.	Mar. 23, 1931	Apr. 30, 1981		NJB280
Blanchard	Elizabeth	Warren	Mar. 13, 1861	Mar. 4, 1901		SJE046
Blanchard	Robert	Warren	May 21, 1896	May 20, 1969		SJE046
Blanchard	William	W.	No Date	Mar. 12, 1914	Aged 33y, 10m / He is not dead, but sleepeth	OSM002
Bland	Iris	Ophelia	1951	1981	Funeral home marker	MAC021
Bland	James	D.	Apr. 23, 1933	Apr. 11, 1983	Love always wife and children	MAC019
Bland	Mary	Alice	1894	1978	Funeral Home marker	MAC024

Last Name	First Name	Middle Name	Date of Birth	Date of Death	Transcription / Notes	Cemetery Code
Blandford	Benjamin	W.	No Date	Jul. 16, 1872	Sacred in the memory of / an affectionate husband and father, a kind neighbor, a zealous and faithful vestryman, and a consistant Christian, He fell asleep in the communion of the Catholic Church / aged 63 years. "The souls of the righteous are in the hand of God and there shall no torment touch them"	SPL4134
Blandford	Clarence	K.	Oct. 6, 1878	Mar. 10, 1879	s/o Wm.H. & Delia Blanford	SPL4116
Blandford	Jessie	C.	Mar. 19, 1880	Mar. 28, 1880	Infant d/o W.H. & Delia Blanford	SPL4113
Blandford	Mary	Amelia	Sep. 30, 1872	Jun. 23, 1891	d/o William & Delia Blanford.	SPL4131
Blandford	Mary	F.	No Date	Sep. 18, 1916	Age 68 years	SPL4112
Blandford	Mary	O.	Mar. 5, 1819	Nov. 30, 1882	Them also which sleep in Jesus will God bring with him. 1st Thess 4:14 Asleep in Jesus, peaceful rest, Whose waking be supremely blest, No fear, No woe shall dim that hour, That manifests the Saviors power.	SPL4133
Blandford	William	H.	Apr. 3, 1843	Feb. 20, 1882		SPL4132
Blaskey	Elizabeth		Aug. 7, 1893	Oct. 20, 1974		NSP918
Blevins	Erika	Maryanna	Jan. 21, 1920	Jan. 10, 2007	Age 86, born in Dresden Germany, daughter of Willy Paul Robert Petzold and Elizabeth Anna Mudach Petzold / info is from the MD Independent Newspaper dated Jan 11, 2007	CLVNoStone
Blockum	Ruth	Mary	Dec. 25, 1909	May 30, 2000		SAC1053
Bloom	John	H.	Jun. 7, 1890	Feb. 19, 1977	PVT US-Army World War I	SCL2037
Bloom	Laura	F.	Jul. 3, 1904	Nov. 22, 1994	County Leitrim Ireland	SCL2039
Bloom	Robert	H.	1874	1927		PAT013
Bloom	Sarah	Fible	Mar. 27, 1864	Jul. 30, 1947		PAT013
Blume	Judy	Golding	1940	1994	Our loving daughter and sister	PKH142
Blundon	Agnes	M.	Jun. 20, 1868	Jun. 19, 1896	Beloved w/o R.F. Blundon / United on earth remembered in death	OFE2010
Blundon	Joseph	A.	1888	1962		SIC7034
Blundon	Mary	V.	1878	1976		SIC7034
Blunt	Edith	Lloyd	May 26, 1915	Jul. 3, 1985		MTR1133

Last Name	First Name	Middle Name	Date of Birth	Date of Death	Transcription / Notes	Cemetery Code
Blunt	Edith	Matthews	Oct. 31, 1875	Jan. 25, 1946	William Laird & his wife Edith Matthews, children - William Laird, Jr., Harriet Woodward, Harry Woodward, John Matthews	MTR1134
Blunt	Harriet	Woodward	Dec. 2, 1909	Feb. 15, 1910	William Laird & his wife Edith Matthews, children - William Laird, Jr., Harriet Woodward, Harry Woodward, John Matthews	MTR1134
Blunt	Harry	Woodward	Jul. 5, 1906	Jul. 20, 1982	William Laird & his wife Edith Matthews, children - William Laird, Jr., Harriet Woodward, Harry Woodward, John Matthews	MTR1134
Blunt	John	Matthews	May 31, 1908	Sep. 29, 1945	William Laird & his wife Edith Matthews, children - William Laird, Jr., Harriet Woodward, Harry Woodward, John Matthews	MTR1134
Blunt	William	Laird	Jul. 5, 1870	Mar. 28, 1937	William Laird & his wife Edith Matthews, children - William Laird, Jr., Harriet Woodward, Harry Woodward, John Matthews	MTR1134
Blunt, Jr.	William	Laird	Jan. 5, 1902	Jan. 16, 1902	William Laird & his wife Edith Matthews, children - William Laird, Jr., Harriet Woodward, Harry Woodward, John Matthews	MTR1138
Boardly	Frank		No Date	Sep. 6, 1926	Age 65 years / info is from church records	SHINoStone
Boarman	A.	Alberta	1887	1972		HGH1071
Boarman, Dr.	Alan	S.	1884	1957	On the front side of this stone is Edelen	SMCD177
Boarman	Albert	J.	Mar. 14, 1845	Apr. 22, 1897	In memory of	SMCD195
Boarman	Anita		Nov. 29, 1890	Nov. 10, 1897	Our darling / Eldest d/o J.M. and B.S. Boarman	SIC3104
Boarman	Annie	E.	1881	1954		SMCD206
Boarman	Barbara	Ann	1938	1956		HGH1212
Boarman	Belle	Simms	Sep. 12, 1865	Jun. 27, 1947		SIC3103
Boarman	Cecelia		No Date	May 6, 1931	Twin to John Boarman	HGH1209
Boarman	Dorothy	S.	No Date	No Date	My Beloved sister (Info is from Irma Simpson research located at The College of Southern MD, LaPlata, MD)	SMYNoStone
Boarman	Edward	A.	1874	1970		HGH1071
Boarman	Elizabeth	A.	Nov. 26, 1865	Mar. 14, 1933	"My Jesus Mercy"	SMCE010
Boarman	Elizabeth		No Date	Jan. 29, 1857	w/o John W. Boarman and Eldest d/o the late Alexius Lancaster in the 30th year of her age	SMY1047
Boarman	Eugene		Oct. 27, 1877	Nov. 13, 1954		HGH1081

Last Name	First Name	Middle Name	Date of Birth	Date of Death	Transcription / Notes	Cemetery Code
Boarman	Francis	Carroll	Jul. 31, 1921	Mar. 5, 2004	Info is from the Maryland Independent Newspaper Mar 10, 2004 Pg A-11	HGHNoStone
Boarman	George	T.	1856	1942	Mother - Father	SMY1101
Boarman	Henrietta		No Date	Mar. 7, 1863	Aged 56 / Henrietta Boarman / w/o Dr. Walter F. Boarman / info is from the Historical Society Research and the 1940 DAR book pg 190 located at the College of Southern MD, LaPlata, MD.	SMCNoStone
Boarman	Ida	Cecelia	1917	1952		HGH1210
Boarman	Ida	E.	Aug. 25, 1883	Oct. 22, 1934	Loved in life in death remembered	HGH1086
Boarman	Ione		Dec. 1, 1891	Jul. 26, 1892	infant d/o J.M.& B.S. Boarman	SIC3106
Boarman	J.	W.	No Date	Aug. 28, 1897	Aged 73 years May she rest in Peace Note: The church has placed parts of stones and loose stones in a plot by themselves	SMY1003 SMY1004
Boarman, Jr.	James	Wise	Nov. 8, 1917	Sep. 13, 1998		SMY2014
Boarman, Sr.	James	Wise	Aug. 8, 1887	Oct. 23, 1970		SMY3218
Boarman	John	M.	Apr. 2, 1862	Dec. 5, 1929		SIC3103
Boarman	John	R.	Nov. 19, 1822	Feb. 5, 1902	Given by his son Eugene Boarman	HGH1083
Boarman	John	W.	1904	1965		HGH1211
Boarman	John	W.	Mar. 25, 1863	Jun. 20, 1946		HGH1230
Boarman	John	Walter	1896	1944	Son	OFE2007
Boarman	John		No Date	May 6, 1931	Twin to Cecelia Boarman	HGH1209
Boarman	Joseph	R.	1894	1915	Matched records with the Historical Society Research located at the College of Southern MD, LaPlata, MD	HGH1258
Boarman	Joseph	S.	No Date	Aug. 6, 1851	IHS / Sacred to the memory of / Who departed this life / In the 53d year of his age / May he rest in peace, Amen /stone maker: A Gaddess Balto	SMCD199
Boarman	Leonard	A.	Jul. 24, 1921	Jun. 1, 1990	CPL US Army WW II	SMY3219
Boarman	M.	Henrietta	1871	1947		SMCD205
Boarman	Marie	M.	Aug. 9, 1939	Dec. 23, 2005	In Loving Memory / Loving Wife & Mother	SMY2131
Boarman	Mary		No Date	Aug. 15, 1786	IHS / Consort of R Boarman / Aged 21 years (stone is broken off the base and is near stone for James Gardiner)	SMCD230
Boarman	Mary	J.	Aug. 4, 1873	Jun. 17, 1942		HGH1231

Last Name	First Name	Middle Name	Date of Birth	Date of Death	Transcription / Notes	Cemetery Code
Boarman	Mary	B.	Jan. 12, 1929	No Date		SMY3219
Boarman	Mary	Elizabeth, Gardiner	No Date	Jun. 13, 1908	Beloved w/o John W. Boarman / aged 70 years and 3 months / Requiescat in pace	SMY1048
Boarman	Mary	F.	Nov. 28, 1851	Jul. 12, 1915	By her daughter Agnes Hill	HGH1084
Boarman	Mary	L.	1874	1916	Mother - Father	SMY1101
Boarman	Raphael	H.	No Date	No Date	Sacred to the memory of / Erected by his beloved wife. E. M. Boarman...May he rest in peace / Stone is leaning against it's base	SMY1142
Boarman	Raphael		No Date	May 19, 1829	IHS / To the memory of / who died / Aged 80 years / (stone is broken off the base and is near stone for James Gardiner)	SMCD230
Boarman	Rebecca		No Date	Oct. 1, 1856	In memory of / Consort of Benedict L. Boarman who departed this life / in the 57th year of her age. May she rest in peace Stone maker was A Gaddess Maker, Balt	SMY1093
Boarman	Shirley	E.	Apr. 30, 1941	Jul. 25, 1969		SJO3050
Boarman, S.J.	Sylvester		No Date	Jan. 7, 1811	IHS / OB. 7 Jan 1811 / AFT 64 (In Priests Plot)	SIC1009
Boarman	Thomas	Edgar	Apr. 26, 1870	Mar. 12, 1922	"My Jesus Mercy"	SMCE010
Boarman	Walter	W.	Nov. 10, 1871	Jan. 20, 1952		HGH1082
Boarman, Dr.	Walter	F.	Aug. 10, 1797	Oct. 2, 1854	Our Father / Farewell, my wife and children all / From you a father, Christ doth call / Mourn not for me it is in vain / To call me to your sight again	SMCD196
Boarman	Willard	A.	Jun. 12, 1920	Jan. 30, 2008	In Loving Memory/ Served 6 Years / Loving Husband & Father	SMY2131
Boarman	William	I.	1883	1946		SMCD204
Boarman	Mary	Maria	Apr. 9, 1919	May 9, 1990		SMY2014
Bodie	Margaret	M.	1889	1954	Beloved w/o Mulford Bodie buried at sea 1953	HNT063
Boggess	Florence	M.	Oct. 30, 1876	Dec. 30, 1947	Date of death is very light on stone	NJB138
Boggess	Thomas	L.	Jan. 20, 1859	Apr. 1, 1934		NJB138
Boggs	Lettie	C.	Aug. 16, 1872	Feb. 21, 1943	Daughter	SPL1078
Boies	Virginia	O.	Feb. 13, 1921	Aug. 10, 1991		ODE439
Boies	William	Dayton	Jan. 1, 1916	Apr. 1, 1984	TEC 5 US Army WW II	ODE439
Bolden	Oden		No Date	Jul. 15, 1951	Age 60 / Info is from the Historical Society Located at the College of Southern MD, LaPlata, MD	BRCNoStone

Last Name	First Name	Middle Name	Date of Birth	Date of Death	Transcription / Notes	Cemetery Code
Bolger	Catherine		1859	1939	Mother	SCL3313
Bollman	Lottie	M.	1883	1962		OSM041
Bollman	Richard	W.	1885	1962		OSM041
Bolton, Major	Frank	A.	Mar. 6, 1891	Dec. 9, 1985	Frank A Bolton / Maj. US Army WW I & WW II (Dates are from church records)	MTR1081
Bolton	Melissa	Dement	May 24, 1894	Oct. 26, 1961		MTR1082
Bond	Benjamin		May 28, 1911	Jan. 3, 1969	Unmarked stone to right of Irving Milstead Sr	ALX020A
Bond	Bennie	L.	Aug. 15, 1915	No Date		SAC4009
Bond	Catherine	P.	1900	1987	Thornton Funeral Home Marker	SMT043
Bond	John	H.	Mar. 22, 1913	Mar. 6, 1992		SAC3038
Bond	Kevin		1965	1984		SHI029
Bond	Letitia		No Date	Jun. 5, 1895	Name is shown on church records but burial location is unknown, date is the burial date, not death date	CHRNoStone
Bond	Lucille	Johnson	Feb. 3, 1920	No Date		MTR1096
Bond	M.	Genevieve	1909	No Date		SAC2123
Bond	Madeline	Elizabeth	Sep. 21, 1916	Jun. 20, 1988		SAC3055
Bond	Mary		No Date	Jan. 11, 1849	w/o Zachariah Bond; departed this life in communion with the Catholic Church / in her 54th year / "Erected to her sacred memory by surviving relatives"	TRI031
Bond	Mary		1858	Apr. 17, 1943		SHI148
Bond	Thelma	V.	May 3, 1918	Nov. 11, 2007	In God's Care / Mother	ALX017A
Bond	Thomas		1857	Jun. 14, 1949		SHI148
Bond	Wayne	Lewis	Mar. 14, 1908	Mar. 20, 1973	Maryland TEC5 US Army WW II	MTR1096
Bond	Zachariah		Oct. 14, 1780	Sep. 11, 1851	Erected by surviving relatives in grateful memory of / stone lying down	TRI033
Bonds	Beulah	Blythe	May 31, 1913	Dec. 28, 1991		PGN036
Bondurant	Carol	Ann	1948	Sep. 10, 1983		SPL6035
Bonebrake	Eva	H.	1877	1950		HGH1160
Bonebrake	James	H.	1875	1947		HGH1160
Booker	Mary	E.	1837	Apr. 15, 1925	Aunt / Beloved Aunt of Mary J. Barnes & Others & sister of Annie Turner, Amelia Simms, Georgianna Shade / Our Loved one age 88	SHI105

Last Name	First Name	Middle Name	Date of Birth	Date of Death	Transcription / Notes	Cemetery Code
Boone	Alice	V.	Jan. 12, 1857	Jun. 26, 1910	wife of R. A. Boone (Left side of stone)	SMCE031
Boone	Baldwin	Neale	Feb. 3, 1930	Dec. 23, 1983	His Wife / SGT US Army	SAC3035
Boone	Charles	Daniel	Feb. 8, 1938	No Date		SMC2099
Boone	Edward	D.	Jan. 25, 1811	Jan. 27, 1889		SMCE035
Boone	Edward	S.	May 21, 1891	May 31, 1891		SMCE036
Boone	Edward	Valentine	No Date	No Date	s/o Edward D and Mary E Boone / 7 years old / info is from the Historical Society Research and the 1940 DAR book pg 194 located at the College of Southern MD, LaPlata, MD,	SMCNoStone
Boone	Elizabeth		No Date	Aug. 5, 1862	IHS / Erected by Sylvester Boone in memory of his beloved wife who departed this life on the 5th of August 1862 at the residence of her son in law in Alexandria, VA., leaving a daughter and her grandchildren to mourn her loss / longing for heaven May she rest in peace. Amen / in the 59th year of her age / Stonemaker: C. L. Neale, Alex. Va.	OSP109
Boone	Gertrude	Marie	Nov. 24, 1937	May 27, 2001	In loving memory, Forever in our hearts	SMI059
Boone	Maria	Teresa	Jan. 25, 1934	Jul. 22, 1997	His Wife	SAC3035
Boone	Mary	F.	May 12, 1847	May 23, 1924		SMCE037
Boone	Rebekah	Compton	Jul. 22, 1904	Jan. 24, 1992	Daughters of the American Revolution Emblem	SMC2126
Boone	Richard	A.	Jun. 13, 1840	Nov. 19, 1931	(Right side of stone)	SMCE031
Boone	Richard	Grantley	Jun. 24, 1892	No Date		SMCE038
Boone	Richard		1933	No Date		SMC1121
Boone	Theresa		1939	1989		SMC1121
Boone	Vivian	Edelen	Oct. 28, 1942	No Date		SMC2099
Boone	William	McKinley	Apr. 10, 1894	Apr. 14, 1977	US Army Emblem	SMC2126
Boone	William	Patrick	Dec. 25, 1965	Aug. 20, 1985		SMC1126
Booth	Charles		1854	1919	Beloved h/o Julia Ann	SMCB006
Booth	Charles		May 29, 1923	May 2, 2001		SMC3126
Booth	Doris	C.	Nov. 18, 1919	Jan. 22, 2000		SMC3127
Booth	Edward	W.	1912	1972		SMC3314
Booth	George	L.	1873	1949		SMCE062

Last Name	First Name	Middle Name	Date of Birth	Date of Death	Transcription / Notes	Cemetery Code
Booth, Jr.	George	L.	1899	1967		SMC3308
Booth	Henrietta	Gaynor	No Date	Feb. 10, 1924	In Memory Of / Age 79 Years / Erected by her daughter Emma T Booth	MHB251
Booth	Joseph	Louis	Feb. 3, 1926	Nov. 14, 2001	In God's loving care	NSP298
Booth	Julia	Ann, Chapman	1836	No Date	w/o Charles Booth / Her death date isn't on the stone	SMCB006
Booth	Mellie	G.	1880	1965		SMCE062
Booth	Pearl	Edith	Nov. 30, 1928	Jan. 5, 1961		NSP298
Boothe	John		No Date	Feb. 26, 1805	In memory of John Boothe, Merchant of Boyd's Hole. / aged 54 years (info is from DAR book Pg 144 and the Historical Society Research, located at College of Southern MD, LaPlata, MD. (Stone is hard to read)	ODE009
Boothe	Mary	M.	Apr. 8, 1922	Jun. 6, 2003	Rest in peace / A loving wife and mother	SMC3299
Booze	Peter	Edward	1880	1943		NSP181
Borrell	Emily	Louise	Nov. 25, 1977	Feb. 4, 2000	Always A Winner Always Brave In the Attempt "EMS" Remember, I Love You	SCL2015
Borza	Andrew	S.	1914	1994		SMC2021
Borza	Sally	M.	1914	1999		SMC2021
Boschulte	Rubina	Penny	1939	2000	Beloved Mother / Beloved Grandma / The family jewel	SCL4116
Boswell	Bernard	S.	1900	1946		ODE277
Boswell	Bernard	Smith	No Date	Aug. 14, 1890	Age 19 / s/o Bernard and Roberta Ellen Ratcliff Boswell (info is from Old Durham Church microfilm located at the College of Southern MD, LaPlata, MD pg 81 and Old Register, lists of families pg. 2)	ODENoStone
Boswell	Bessie	L.	Jun. 6, 1890	Apr. 8, 1982	Gone but not forgotten	MTR3138
Boswell	Bessie	R.	1892	1958	Mother	NSP444
Boswell	Chloe		No Date	Nov. 23, 1863	In memory of / w/o John Boswell died in the 73rd year of her age / Into thine hand I commit my spirit, thou hast redeemed me O Lord God of truth.	SPL3131
Boswell	Edith	Wilmer	Dec. 15, 1856	Feb. 22, 1874	d/o William & Mary F Boswell. "He shall gather the lambs in his arms, and carry them in his bosom."	MTR2028
Boswell	Elizabeth	C.	No Date	Sep. 24, 1842	In her 26th year / info is from the Historical Society Research and the 1940 DAR book pg 193 located at the College of Southern MD, LaPlata, MD.	SMCNoStone

Last Name	First Name	Middle Name	Date of Birth	Date of Death	Transcription / Notes	Cemetery Code
Boswell	Henry	Heber	1861	1936	s/o William and Mary F. Boswell	MTR2027
Boswell	James	Thomas	Dec. 17, 1873	May 3, 1936	In memory of / who departed this life in the 84th year of his age. / Having a desire to depart and to be with Christ which is for better	SJENoStone
Boswell	John		No Date	Sep. 9, 1869		SPL3132
Boswell	Joseph	H.	Dec. 25, 1875	Mar. 8, 1946		SJE002
Boswell	Lillian	E.	Mar. 5, 1885	Aug. 31, 1965		SPL4004
Boswell	Lizzie	Campbell	Jun. 5, 1849	Dec. 29, 1866	d/o William and Mary F. Boswell / I know that my redeemer liveth	MTR2050
Boswell, Mrs.	Margaret	Brooke	No Date	Jan. 1920	Buried Jan 9, 1920 age 45 (info is from Old Durham Church microfilm lpg 159 ocated at the College of Southern MD, LaPlata, MD)	ODENoStone
Boswell	Maria	Campbell	No Date	Nov. 23, 1905	d/o William and Mary F. Boswell / entered into eternal life / Blessed are the pure in heart	MTR2044
Boswell	Mary	E. C.	Jul. 31, 1844	Feb. 17, 1881	Beloved w/o Charles A. Boswell / Blessed are the dead who died in the Lord.	SPL4138
Boswell	Mary	Fullerton	1852	1936	d/o William and Mary F. Boswell	MTR2054
Boswell	Mary	Fullerton	Nov. 17, 1825	Jan. 25, 1906		MTR2052
Boswell	Maynard	Perry	No Date	Apr. 1928	Buried Apr 26, 1928 (info is from Old Durham Church microfilm pg 160-161 located at the College of Southern MD, LaPlata, MD)	ODENoStone
Boswell	Milton	P.	Jan. 6, 1925	Mar. 29, 1988		ODE276
Boswell	Olive	J.	1902	1930		ODE277
Boswell	Roberta	E.	No Date	Oct. 1929	Buried Oct 12, 1929 / age 82 (info is from Old Durham Church microfilm pg 160-161 located at the College of Southern MD, LaPlata, MD)	ODENoStone
Boswell	William		Aug. 19, 1821	Jul. 18, 1883		MTR2052
Boswell	Willie		Mar. 21, 1865	Jan. 29, 1878	Willie Boswell / s/o William & Mary F. Boswell / Angels of Jesus, angels of light, Singing to welcome the pilgrims of the night	MTR2026
Boswell	John	Samuel	1871	May 13, 1938		SJENoStone
Boswell	Thomas	Edward	No Date	Nov. 27, 1903	In the 71st year of his age	SJENoStone
Boteler	Daniel	Harmon	Feb. 22, 1917	Jan. 11, 2006		HGH4084
Boteler	Naomi	Crigler	Aug. 19, 1919	No Date		HGH4084

Last Name	First Name	Middle Name	Date of Birth	Date of Death	Transcription / Notes	Cemetery Code
Boucher	Edward	J.	1927	No Date		SMC4262
Boucher	Jean		1931	No Date		SMC4262
Boudreaux	Janice	A.	May 17, 1940	Dec. 3, 1999	"Jan"	SCL4211
Boudreaux	John	H.	Jun. 23, 1925	May 16, 2002	"Jake"	SCL4211
Boudreaux	Shauna	Lynn	Mar. 17, 1986	Dec. 8, 1987	Our Little Angel	SCL3050
Bowdish, Jr.	George	F.	Mar. 5, 1926	Jul. 18, 1990		NSP983
Bowdish	Madge	M.	Jan. 24, 1905	Aug. 10, 1979		NSP984
Bowen	Gladys	B.	No Date	Dec. 31, 1968	Name is shown on church records but burial location is unknown	CHRNoStone
Bowen	Katherine	Marie	Aug. 4, 1988	Jan. 24, 1989	"The brightest star that ever shown"	SPL7010
Bowen	Lloyd		No Date	Feb. 4, 1940	Age 57 / info is from church records	CLVNoStone
Bowie	Agnes	Carpenter	Jul. 9, 1917	No Date	Devoted Wife and Mother	SCL2044
Bowie	Albert	W.	Jan. 3, 1882	Jul. 13, 1959		NZN043
Bowie	Alexander	F.	Aug. 18, 1843	Aug. 21, 1910		MTR1035
Bowie	Algie	G.	1877	1950		PIS079
Bowie	Alice	Alberta	Mar. 9, 1903	Sep. 7, 1984		NJB460
Bowie	Alice	V.	Jul. 1855	Apr. 21, 1888	w/o Wesley Bowie / footstone: A. V. B.	PIS141
Bowie	Allard	N.	1885	1946	h/o Eula V. Bowie	NJB077
Bowie	Amber	Lynn	Dec. 12, 1971	Sep. 25, 1994	Beloved daughter and granddaughter / Our angels	NZN052
Bowie, Sr.	Andrew	W.	Mar. 4, 1942	Jun. 5, 2000	"Andy"	SAC1154
Bowie	Angela	Lynn	Dec. 12, 1971	Dec. 16, 1971	Beloved daughter and granddaughter / Our angels	NZN052
Bowie	Anna	M.	1923	1986		NJB245
Bowie	Archie	G.	1907	1970	Located in the Kemp plot	MTR3091
Bowie	Archie	McDonald	May 14, 1941	Sep. 23, 1993		LUM040
Bowie	Aubrey	D.	Jul. 7, 1916	No Date	Only one date on stone, not sure if it's a birth or death date	CMX2012
Bowie	Benjamin	F.	1906	1973		NJB121
Bowie	Blanche	G.	Aug. 17, 1886	Sep. 20, 1943		MTR4077
Bowie, Ed.D.	Blanche	Lucile	Oct. 5, 1910	Aug. 26, 1997	Devoted her life to education, Professor Emerita University of Maryland National & International Lecturer	MTR4079
Bowie	Carrie	F.	Feb. 5, 1892	May 5, 1965		ODE065

Last Name	First Name	Middle Name	Date of Birth	Date of Death	Transcription / Notes	Cemetery Code
Bowie	Charles	I.	1917	1981	"I love you"	NJB060
Bowie, Sr.	Charles	William	Jul. 25, 1917	Sep. 26, 1979	CPL US Army World War II	SCL2044
Bowie	Charlotte		May 1821	Jun. 1905	Rest in Peace / By her only Daughter	PIS090
Bowie	Clara	Alberta	Sep. 1, 1886	Feb. 13, 1949	Mother / God is love	PKH103
Bowie	Clara	E.	No Date	Jun. 15, 1907	Our Baby / aged 3 months	SJE103
Bowie, Jr.	Claude	Edward	Jul. 9, 1958	Dec. 4, 2003	Father	SJO4047
Bowie, Sr.	Claude	Edward	Feb. 27, 1922	Apr. 22, 1982	PFC US Army / Dates are from church records	SPL4139
Bowie	Cora	E.	1919	1988	Beloved how I miss you	LUM042
Bowie	Cora	L.	1921	1924		NJB473
Bowie	D.	W.	Aug. 18, 1895	Apr. 23, 1929	Father / Asleep in Jesus	PIS055
Bowie	Daisy	L.	1915	1980	Gone from home but not from our hearts	ODE070
Bowie	Della	Milstead	1903	1989		CMX2039
Bowie	Dorothy Cecelia	Bateman	May 2, 1907	Aug. 27, 1994		MTR1131
Bowie, Sr.	Douglas	W.	May 8, 1944	Feb. 10, 1992		NJB123
Bowie	Edith	M.	May 22, 1882	Dec. 23, 1968		NJB351
Bowie	Edna	E.	Oct. 7, 1894	Oct. 5, 1985		NZN043
Bowie	Elizabeth	R.	1882	1960		NZN030
Bowie	Elizabeth	Stoddert	No Date	No Date	Here lies Major John Truman Stoddert, his wife Elizabeth Stoddert, his children, Truman Stoddert, Elizabeth Stoddert, Lucy Stoddert Brown, Gustavus Brown, Elizabeth Stoddert Bowie, his grandchildren, John Robert Bowie Stoddert, William Truman Stoddert, James Truman Stoddert, Mary Bowie / Memorial Stone	WHS001
Bowie	Elmer	E.	1917	1979		NZN055
Bowie	Emory	Lee	May 5. 1906	Jul. 13, 1967		NJB119
Bowie	Erika	Raye	No Date	Dec. 18, 1988	"our baby" / She was my everything created on earth to bloom in heaven	NJB082
Bowie	Ethelbert		1847	1897	At rest	NJB470
Bowie	Eula	V.	Jan. 15, 1904	Apr. 23, 1995	w/o Allard N. Bowie	NJB076

Last Name	First Name	Middle Name	Date of Birth	Date of Death	Transcription / Notes	Cemetery Code
Bowie	Everett	Glenn	May 15, 1927	Mar. 26, 2008	Age 80 ho/ Mildred Welch who died March 31, 2006. s/o Allard and Eula Bowie. MD Independent Newspaper Wed. Apr 2, 2008 Page A-10 Column 2	ODENoStone
Bowie	Fannie	I.	1874	1954	Mother	PIS028
Bowie	Fannie	R.	No Date	Nov. 12, 1942		LUM045
Bowie	Florence E.	Rye	Sep. 28, 1911	Oct. 23, 2001	Rest in peace	NJB135
Bowie	Gail	M.	Jul. 21, 1955	Sep. 9, 1981		NJB122
Bowie	George	Curtis	May 14, 1917	Jan. 9, 1990	CPL US Army WW II	ODE052
Bowie	George	Kenneth	1935	1959	The Lord is my shepherd	LUM044
Bowie	George	L.	1889	1893		NJB472
Bowie	George	R.	1913	1979	Beloved how I miss you	LUM042
Bowie	Grace		1886	1981		SPL4140
Bowie	Hamilton	A.	1889	1958		PIS185
Bowie	Hamilton		Mar. 8, 1865	Jan. 15, 1889	s/o H. H. & Mary E. Bowie	PIS181
Bowie	Hannah G.	Willett	Jun. 1, 1872	Jan. 20, 1920		SIG045
Bowie	Harriet	Cecelia	No Date	Feb. 7, 1910	Twin Sister of Annie L. Bowie Hodge	SIG044
Bowie	Harriett	C.	Oct. 31, 1854	Apr. 15, 1928	IHS / The faithful are certain of their reward	SIG019
Bowie	Harry	Benjamin	Nov. 4, 1901	Jan. 5, 1979		NJB460
Bowie	Harry	C.	Jan. 14, 1882	Nov. 7, 1925		MTR4077
Bowie	Helen	D.	1920	1970	Located in the Kemp plot	MTR3091
Bowie	Helen	L.	Aug. 22, 1947	Jul. 25, 1953	Rest in peace	NJB136
Bowie	Helen	V., Lees	1917	2005		NZN054
Bowie	Henry	H.	1845	1925	Father	NZN044
Bowie, Jr.	Henry	J.	May 25, 1927	Feb. 28, 1976	PFC US Army WWII	NJB491
Bowie	Henry	Joseph	Dec. 5, 1903	Dec. 27, 1964		NJB488
Bowie	Henry		No Date	No Date	Identified on church's unmarked grave list as Stone: 53	CMXNoStone
Bowie	Howard	N.	1901	1982	Located in the Kemp plot	MTR3091
Bowie	Irma	Frances	Mar. 23, 1909	Mar. 14, 1926		NJB088
Bowie	Jackie	M.	May 21, 1987	May 8, 1989	Our little Angel	ODE059
Bowie	James	B.	Aug. 19, 1891	Jun. 9, 1950	We will meet again	ODE066

Last Name	First Name	Middle Name	Date of Birth	Date of Death	Transcription / Notes	Cemetery Code
Bowie	James	H.	Aug. 18, 1851	Mar. 20, 1881	s/o Uriah and Charlotte A. Bowie (info is from the Historical Society Research located at The College of Southern MD, LaPlata, MD)	FRANoStone
Bowie	James	R.	Mar. 5, 1969	Mar. 11, 1986	Verse on stone: Oh! I have slipped the surly bonds of earth and danced the skies on laughter-silvered wings and while with silent lifting mind, I've trod the high untrespassed sanctity of space, put out my hand and touched the face of God.	NJB272
Bowie	James A.	Buddis	1844	1918		PIS162
Bowie	Jane	Rosalie	1878	1963	Sister of Clara Cecelia Gibbons	MTR4169
Bowie	Jennie	E.	1894	1980		PIS185
Bowie	Jessie	A.	1879	1947		SPL4140
Bowie	Jim		No Date	No Date	Stone: 52 -/Numbered Stonemarkers have been placed on unmarked graves by church. Metal nameplate is attached to marker	CMX2040
Bowie	John	Bernard	Apr. 28, 1870	Jul. 26, 1939	This stone is by itself on the right side of St Ignatius Church Hilltop near the road, but does not belong to St Ignatius Church. It is on private property.	BOE002
Bowie	John	J.	1920	1975	Our Father / info is from The Historical Society Research at The College of Southern MD, LaPlata, MD	SJONoStone
Bowie	John	T.	No Date	Jan. 13, 1930	At Rest / (Age 67 in 1920 census, death date is from Maryland Independent Newspaper dated Jan 24, 1930)	PIS052
Bowie	John	T.	1920	1975		NZN053
Bowie	John	Thelbert	Dec. 5, 1955	Mar. 27, 1993	We love you and miss you	LUM041
Bowie, Jr.	John	Thomas	Sep. 18, 1949	Dec. 16, 1975	PVT US Marine Corps Vietnam	NZN049
Bowie	Joseph	E.	Oct. 20, 1875	Aug. 29, 1934		NJB351
Bowie	Joseph	W.	1914	1969		NJB245
Bowie	Joseph	William	Jul. 19, 1930	Dec. 11, 1958	A friend to his country and a believer in Christ	NJB120
Bowie	June	K.	Apr. 26, 1943	Feb. 24, 2001	Mother	NZN057
Bowie	Kathleen	A.	Sep. 28, 1926	Aug. 8, 1928	Beloved d/o Harry B. & Alice A. Bowie / our little one is living in our hearts	NJB459
Bowie	Leo	C.	Jun. 15, 1915	Sep. 12, 1976	The Lord is my Shepherd	SIG143
Bowie	Leora	Alice	Feb. 19, 1942	Feb. 13, 1943	Budded on earth to bloom in heaven	NJB137

Last Name	First Name	Middle Name	Date of Birth	Date of Death	Transcription / Notes	Cemetery Code
Bowie	Linda	L.	1946	No Date		SIG064
Bowie	M.	Scelena	Sep. 23, 1841	Jan. 19, 1880	In memory of / d/o Sarah A. & Pliny Bowie / Stonemaker was Flannery Bros.	PIS182
Bowie	Maggie	M.	1878	1933		NZN045
Bowie	Marcellus		1875	1957		PIS116
Bowie	Margaret	Anne	Aug. 7, 1930	Aug. 26, 1932		NJB486
Bowie	Margaret	C.	May 1850	Dec. 22, 1912	w/o Wesley Bowie / footstone: M.C. B.	PIS137
Bowie	Margaret	L.	Jul. 22, 1907	Mar. 23, 1910	Beloved d/o A. W. & V. H. Bowie / Sleep in the arms of Jesus	PIS101
Bowie					Sometimes in our life we have gone astray, but never forgetting the love you showed and gave so dearly in your life. Love always / Back of stone: Loving Mother, Billy, Bobby, Bubbles, Buddy, Jerry, Johnny, Leo, Sparkie, Georgie	
Bowie	Marion	F.	Aug. 28, 1919	Oct. 12, 1987		ODE057
Bowie	Mary	Clara	May 4, 1849	Dec. 31, 1918	Mother	SJE105
Bowie	Mary	E.	1860	1915	At rest	NJB470
Bowie	Mary	E.	1853	1919		NJB375
Bowie	Mary	E.	1912	1994		NJB121
Bowie	Mary	Ellen	Aug. 3, 1919	Nov. 9, 1926	d/o Harry C-Blanche G	MTR4078
Bowie	Mary	Frances	Jun. 24, 1959	Apr. 13, 1988	"Love Always" / Robin, Corleta, family & friends	NJB059
Bowie	Mary	P.	Apr. 30, 1888	Apr. 9, 1906	Beloved d/o W. J. and H. C. Bowie / May she rest in peace and sleep in the arms of Jesus	SIG018
Bowie	Mary	Simmons	1845	1932	Mother	NZN044
Bowie	Mary		No Date	No Date	Here lies Major John Truman Stoddert, his wife Elizabeth Stoddert, his children, Truman Stoddert, Elizabeth Stoddert, Lucy Stoddert Brown, Gustavus Brown, Elizabeth Stoddert Bowie, his grandchildren, John Robert Bowie Stoddert, William Truman Stoddert, James Truman Stoddert, Mary Bowie / Memorial Stone	WHS001
Bowie	Maximillian		1868	1939		NZN045
Bowie	Merle	Robey	1890	1973		PIS103
Bowie	Mildred	Belle	Jul. 7, 1903	Jul. 4, 1954		NJB487
Bowie	Mildred	Welch	Sep. 30, 1928	Mar. 31, 2006	Beloved wife and mother	ODE451

Last Name	First Name	Middle Name	Date of Birth	Date of Death	Transcription / Notes	Cemetery Code
Bowie	Miriam	E.	Mar. 9, 1919	Nov. 21, 1989	The Lord is my Shepherd	SIG143
Bowie	Morris	E.	1912	1961		NZN054
Bowie	Naomi	R.	1923	1978		NZN055
Bowie	Nathaniel	N.	1875	1949		PIS104
Bowie	Nellie	S.	1877	1936		PIS079
Bowie	Nellie		No Date	No Date	Baby	NJB471
Bowie	Nellie		1886	1904	d/o John T. & Susie W. Bowie	PIS165
Bowie	Nora	E.	1893	1930	Mother	NJB425
Bowie	Norris	T.	Feb. 26, 1925	Mar. 6, 1986		CMX1036
Bowie	Ora Tucker	Hancock	Jul. 31, 1888	Oct. 18, 1913		NJB087
Bowie	Pamela	Ann	No Date	Jan. 17, 1958		SIG142
Bowie	Pliny		Mar. 11, 1815	Jan. 1, 1890	In memory of / Father of H. H. & Grandfather of Lee Pinkney & Heister C. Bowie	PIS184
Bowie	R.	Meredith	Jul. 14, 1928	Nov. 29, 1959		NZN048
Bowie	Randolph	P.	Jul. 24, 1944	May 20, 1979	"Lucky" / we love and miss you	LUM212
Bowie	Richard	N.	1885	1967	Father	NJB423
Bowie	Richard	T.	Jul. 10, 1894	Sep. 6, 1974	Son / Mother	NJB307
Bowie	Robert	Henry	Apr. 16, 1884	Feb. 4, 1961	Beloved Father and Grandfather	CMX2075
Bowie	Roger	H.	Dec. 14, 1936	Jun. 13, 1937		CMX2128
Bowie	Ronald	Alvin	Oct. 17, 1933	Mar. 25, 2004		NJB457
Bowie	Ronald	L.	1942	1988		SIG064
Bowie	Rosalie		Nov. 17, 1862	Sep. 22, 1899	He giveth his beloved sleep	SJE104
Bowie	Russell		Nov. 24, 1898	Jan. 3, 1952		NZN047
Bowie	Sadie	M.	Dec. 17, 1890	Apr. 24, 1942	We Commit Thee to God	OFE4043
Bowie	Samuel	Irving	Apr. 19, 1910	Aug. 16, 1993	Rest in peace	NJB135
Bowie	Sarah	A.	Apr. 11, 1823	Feb. 19, 1881	In memory of / Beloved w/o Pliny Bowie	PIS183
Bowie	Sarah	E.	1886	1975		PKH117
Bowie	Sarah	Angeline	Dec. 8, 1872	Dec. 16, 1948	Son / Mother	NJB307
Bowie	Shirley	A.	1929	1970	Our Mother	SIG071

Last Name	First Name	Middle Name	Date of Birth	Date of Death	Transcription / Notes	Cemetery Code
Bowie	Sidney	Allison	Apr. 21, 1917	Nov. 28, 2007	Age 90 / .s/o the late Hamilton A Bowie and the late Jennie E. Bowie. H/o Mae Bowie. Info is from Maryland Independent Newspaper dated Nov 30, 2007	PISNoStone
Bowie	Simeon	Francis	Dec. 7, 1839	Mar. 27, 1904	Father There remainth therefore a rest to the "people of God"	SJE105
Bowie	Stanley	S.	1909	1981	Located in the Kemp plot	MTR3091
Bowie	Susan	Ward, Simmons	1847	1905		PIS162
Bowie	Sussie	W.	Apr. 16, 1855	May 12, 1927	His Wife / (Age 68 in 1920 census)	PIS052
Bowie	Tammy	L.	No Date	1964	Information is from the Historical Society Research located at The College of Southern MD, LaPlata, MD	SIGNo Stone
Bowie	Teri	Lou	Oct. 15, 1949	May 7, 1998	In loving memory	NZN056
Bowie	Thomas	E.	Mar. 17, 1832	Nov. 14, 1895	Our father / I have fought a good fight. I have finished my course. I have kept the faith. / Erected by his son T.M. Bowie	NJB376
Bowie	Unknown		No Date	1946	Infant Son of Charles W. & Agnes Bowie	SCL2044
Bowie	Unknown		No Date	No Date	Infant girl of H.J. & Mildred Bowie	NJB484
Bowie	Unknown		No Date	No Date	Infant boy of H.J. & Mildred Bowie	NJB485
Bowie	Uriah		Jan. 1817	Jan. 1900	"Gone but not forgotten" / By his only daughter	PIS117
Bowie	Viola	H.	Oct. 15, 1887	Dec. 22, 1910	w/o A. W. Bowie / May she rest in peace	PIS102
Bowie	W.	B.	Sep. 29, 1856	Jul. 30, 1922		NJB468
Bowie	W.	J.	Feb. 17, 1838	Nov. 5, 1906	h/o H. C. Bowie / May he rest in peace. Gone but not forgotten	PIS091
Bowie	Walter		1909	1993	Gone from home but not from our hearts	ODE070
Bowie	Wesley	F.	Sep. 20, 1884	May 15, 1935	Resting in hope of a glorious resurrection	PKH102
Bowie	Wesley		Dec. 12, 1846	Nov. 23, 1925	footstone: M.C. B	PIS139
Bowie	William	C.	1878	1946		PKH117
Bowie	William	Howard	Sep. 19, 1932	Jun. 19, 1936		MTR1132
Bowie	William	L.	Apr. 6, 1945	Apr. 15, 1997	A free spirit	ODE071
Bowie	William	Leon	No Date	Jul. 26, 1978		NJB228
Bowie	William	T.	1880	1964		NZN030
Bowie	Wm.	Frances	Jul. 18, 1916	Jul. 5, 1933	Though lost to sight to memory dear / Name is from cemetery records	PKH116
Bowie	Zachary	Tyler	No Date	Jun. 21, 2000	Beloved s/o Ronnie and Crystal	SIG067

Last Name	First Name	Middle Name	Date of Birth	Date of Death	Transcription / Notes	Cemetery Code
Bowles	Billy	J.	Oct. 29, 1923	Nov. 4, 1972	Virginia, SGT Army Air Forces WW II	LUM037
Bowles	Catherine	Marie	No Date	Aug. 1, 2003		SMCI007
Bowles	Lindsay	Ann	No Date	Feb. 2, 1980		LUM038
Bowles	Margaret	V.	Dec. 23, 1926	Jul. 15, 2004		LUM037
Bowling	A.	Olive	Jun. 21, 1915	Aug. 29, 1976	In loving memory	TRI442
Bowling	Agnes	B.	Jul. 20, 1906	Jan. 4, 1983		SMY3047
Bowling	Aloysius	E.	Dec. 30, 1857	Nov. 23, 1905	He is listed on the headstone with Benj. F. & Mary E. Bowling as A E. Bowling. He also has a separate headstone with the name Aloysius E. Bowling	SMCD034 SMCD035
Bowling	Aloysius		No Date	Jan. 1, 1850	IHS / Sacred to the memory of / who departed this life / aged 39 yrs, 11 mo's and 24 days / Eternal rest grant to him O Lord / Stone Maker was A. Gaddess	SMCA121
Bowling	Amelia	E., Brooke	1875	1954		SMCD030
Bowling	Anna	M.	Sep. 10, 1832	May 31, 1898	In memory of / d/o Wm F and Teresa Bowling / Rest in peace	SMCA136
Bowling	Annie	E.	Jan. 27, 1898	Jan. 11, 1981	Susie never truly leaves us	LUM182
Bowling	Annie	Summers	Jul. 8, 1874	May 24, 1932	His wife	OSP089
Bowling	Augustus	W.	1910	1981		LUM171
Bowling	Benj	F.	Mar. 3, 1831	May 27, 1904		SMCD036
Bowling, Rev., C.S.P.	Benjamin	Franklin	Jan. 10, 1897	May 5, 1980	Ordained Sept. 24, 1921	SMCE014
Bowling	Benjamin	Tyler	Jan. 21, 1907	Oct. 26, 1987		TRI368
Bowling	Bernard	Lee	Sep. 4, 1945	May 17, 1946	Our Darling	SMY3061
Bowling	Betty	F.	Jan. 13, 1916	Oct. 26, 1982		SMC1093
Bowling	Brent	Guy	Jul. 5, 1963	Apr. 19, 2007		SMY3117
Bowling	Catherine	M.	1946	1982	(Kitty) This may be Catherine M. Robey that is on the church records	MTR2045
Bowling	Catherine	P.	Mar. 17, 1929	No Date		LUM120
Bowling	Catherine	S.	1904	1968		LUM109
Bowling	Charles	A.	1895	1963		LUM147
Bowling	Charles	Albert	1871	1954		SMCD109
Bowling	Charles	Allen	Aug. 18, 1956	Mar. 4, 2005		SMCD140

Last Name	First Name	Middle Name	Date of Birth	Date of Death	Transcription / Notes	Cemetery Code
Bowling	Charles	D.	Mar. 25, 1926	Jul. 2, 1977	"Rabbit" / m. Sept 20, 1945	LUM178
Bowling	Charles	Elsworth	Oct. 30, 1922	Oct. 31, 1922	Baby / Asleep in Jesus, blessed thought	LUM148
Bowling, Sr.	Charles		1867	1948	Rest in Peace	LUM183
Bowling	Clara	L.	Aug. 28, 1907	Oct. 21, 1978	Together forever	TRI360
Bowling	Corinne	M.	Feb. 23, 1905	May 3, 1905		SMCD061
Bowling	Daisy	M.	1885	1956		LUM163
Bowling	Dorothy	R.	Oct. 14, 1907	Dec. 25, 1987	Rest in Peace	LUM141
Bowling	Earnest	DeDales	May 9, 1920	Sep. 16, 1920	s/o Thos. W. & Mary D. Bowling	LUM166
Bowling	Eleanor	D.	Jul. 1, 1908	Jun. 11, 1998		SMY3042
Bowling	Eleanor	Forbes	1873	1942		SMCD109
Bowling	Elease	Williams	Oct. 19, 1916	No Date	m.Oct 19, 1945 / Devoted parents and grandparents	LUM121
Bowling	Elizabeth	Cooksey	Jun. 16, 1928	Sep. 30, 2002		HGH1201
Bowling	Elizabeth	L.	Jan. 25, 1933	Feb. 18, 1933	Of such is the kingdom of heaven / footstone: E.L.B.	TRI361
Bowling	Elizabeth	S.	Mar. 11, 1838	Sep. 18, 1920		SMCA135
Bowling	Ella	Maureen	Mar. 18, 1918	Nov. 8, 2002		SMCD142
Bowling	Emma	Aline	Mar. 28, 1885	Jan. 25, 1924		SMCD032
Bowling	Estelle	V.	1876	1935	w/o Robert P Bowling Sr / At rest / footstone: mother.	TRI340
Bowling	Ethel	M.	Apr. 8, 1883	Sep. 15, 1945	Age 62 years	LUM160
Bowling	Frances	Eleanor	Mar. 16, 1920	Jun. 3, 2001	In loving memory	SMY3060
Bowling, Jr.	Frank	A.	Oct. 7, 1923	Sep. 11, 1994		LUM120
Bowling, Jr.	Frank	O.	Jul. 12, 1877	Aug. 16, 1953		LUM204
Bowling	Frank	V.	Jan. 11, 1890	May 27, 1965	This is a flat stone that was covered with grass. It can be found in front of and a little to the left of the stone for Sophia Dyer	SMCD295
Bowling	Frank	A..	No Date	May 1960		LUM122A
Bowling	Frederick	Thomas	1874	1949		SMCD030
Bowling, Sr.	Garth	Edward	May 16, 1916	Jul. 15, 2001	m.Oct 19, 1945 / Devoted parents and grandparents / Masonic Emblem / footstone - TEC 5 US Army WWII	LUM121
Bowling	George	Forbes	1905	1957		SMCD143
Bowling, Sr.	George	M.	Oct. 12, 1893	Feb. 26, 1995		SMC4047
Bowling	George	P.	Jan. 9, 1900	May 22, 1999		SMY3047

Last Name	First Name	Middle Name	Date of Birth	Date of Death	Transcription / Notes	Cemetery Code
Bowling	George	W.	1925	2000		SMC1009
Bowling	George	Washington	Nov. 3, 1915	Mar. 8, 2008	s/o the late Thomas Bowling and the late Marie Simpson Bowling. h/o the late Mary Katherine Farrall Bowling. Info is from Maryland Independent Newspaper dated Wednesday Mar 12, 2008 Page A-12 Column 1	BOW004
Bowling	Gertrude	H.	Mar. 29, 1886	Dec. 15, 1955		SMCE008
Bowling	Gertrude	H.	Jul. 4, 1863	Apr. 19, 1951		SMCE012
Bowling	Gladys	Pauline	Jun. 18, 1912	Feb. 10, 2006	Together forever	SMC4106
Bowling	Grace	B.	1911	1996		LUM171
Bowling	Harry	R.	Feb. 7, 1867	Sep. 7, 1947		SMCD103
Bowling, Jr.	Harry	R.	Sep. 25, 1895	Feb. 16, 1976	US Navy World War I	SMCD105
Bowling	Helen	L.	Sep. 20, 1906	Jun. 10, 1957		SMC2194
Bowling	Henry	S.	Feb. 28, 1903	Apr. 22, 1978		SMY3042
Bowling	Irene	Auguste	Jun. 14, 1915	Nov. 27, 2003		SMCD010
Bowling	J.	Hayden	1890	1959		SMC4074
Bowling	J.	Shakespeare	1904	1970		LUM108
Bowling	Jacob	B.	Jul. 12, 1874	Jun. 5, 1951		LUM161
Bowling	Jacob	V.	1914	2003		CLV027
Bowling, Jr.	James	H.	Jun. 24, 1925	No Date		SMC4130
Bowling	James	M.	Apr. 16, 1859	Jun. 22, 1936		SMCE012
Bowling	James	Patterson	Jun. 14, 1927	Mar. 10, 1987		SMY3046
Bowling	James	Thomas	Jan. 29, 1894	May 3, 1957		LUM144
Bowling	James	W.	1946	1963		LUM164
Bowling	James	W.	Jul. 27, 1932	Feb. 11, 1990		LUM105
Bowling	John	Clinton	Oct. 14, 1957	Jun. 1, 1984	Come unto me all ye that labour and are heavey laden and I will give you rest. Matthew 11:28	SMC4123
Bowling	John	R.	Mar. 28, 1905	Nov. 15, 1982	Together forever	TRI360
Bowling	John	S.	Mar. 20, 1897	Aug. 21, 1955		LUM159
Bowling, Sr.	John	W.	Dec. 28, 1902	May 28, 1987		SMC2195
Bowling	Joseph	Glenn	Feb. 27, 1963	Nov. 22, 1981		SMC4105
Bowling, Atty.	Joseph	T.	1901	1970		SMCE016

Last Name	First Name	Middle Name	Date of Birth	Date of Death	Transcription / Notes	Cemetery Code
Bowling	Joseph	W.	Aug. 3, 1895	Dec. 11, 1975		LUM157
Bowling	Josephine	A.	1931	1985		LUM142
Bowling	Joshua	A.	Dec. 10, 1980	Jun. 2, 1999	A Loving Son, Brother & Father; So Much Love, So Little Time	TRI154
Bowling	Leonarda	Rosa	Aug. 13, 1932	No Date		SIC6067
Bowling	Lessie	Swann	Sep. 28, 1903	Nov. 3, 1981		TRI368
Bowling	Lloyd	S.	1930	No Date		LUM142
Bowling	Louise	B.	Oct. 21, 1928	Dec. 12, 1997		SMCD4130
Bowling	Louise	Steuart	1863	1923	She has a headstone and a footstone	SIC4030
Bowling	Lucy	Q.	1848	1939		SMCA146
Bowling	M.	Catherine	Nov. 13, 1887	Jan. 23, 1969		SMC4047
Bowling	Margaret	C.	1924	2000		SMC1009
Bowling	Margaret	Ellen	Feb. 17, 1899	Mar. 30, 1900		SMCD106
Bowling	Margaret	Ellen	Feb. 17, 1899	Mar. 30, 1900		SMCA171
Bowling	Margaret	McP	May 10, 1868	Dec. 26, 1952		SMCD104
Bowling	Margaret		No Date	Jun. 15, 1819	IHS / Sacred to the memory of / who departed this life / in the 56th year of her age	SMCD297
Bowling	Margaret		1911	No Date		LUM108
Bowling	Marie	F.	1919	No Date		CLV027
Bowling	Marie	T.	May 27, 1860	Jan. 13, 1953		SMCD011
Bowling	Marsham		No Date	Aug. 21, 1847	Sacred to the memory of / who departed this life / in the 75th year of his age / May the Lord be merciful to him, Amen	SMCD299
Bowling	Martha	E.	Nov. 3, 1921	May 6, 2001		SMC4050
Bowling	Martha	L.	1911	1984		LUM172
Bowling	Martha	R.	1890	1992		SMC4074
Bowling	Marvetta	Vera	Aug. 10, 1952	Aug. 17, 1952		LUM139
Bowling	Mary	C.	1873	1938	Let our Father's will be done	LUM162
Bowling	Mary	Dozier	Aug. 10, 1909	Apr. 20, 2005	Name is from church records	MTR1022
Bowling	Mary	E.	Aug. 4, 1834	Dec. 13, 1907		SMCD036
Bowling	Mary	Emily	Jan. 13, 1901	Dec. 4, 1989		SMCD132

Last Name	First Name	Middle Name	Date of Birth	Date of Death	Transcription / Notes	Cemetery Code
Bowling	Mary	Emma, Huntt	1861	1929		HNT023
Bowling	Mary	G.	1899	1993		SIC3133
Bowling	Mary	J.	Oct. 19, 1834	Apr. 30, 1882	In memory of / Beloved wife of William I Bowling / R I P Age 84....Her middle name appeared in her husbands obit notice located in the Maryland Independent Newspaper dated Wednesday Mar 12, 2008 Page A-12 Column 1	SMCD222
Bowling	Mary	Katherine	May 11, 1919	Oct. 27, 2002		BOW006
Bowling	Mary	Lelia	Dec. 22, 1891	Aug. 29, 1966		SMCD131
Bowling	Mary	Madeline	1903	2002		LUM147
Bowling	Mary		No Date	1826	w/o Thomas Bowling / died 1826 / aged 24 / info is from the Historical Society Research and the 1940 DAR book pg 193 located at the College of Southern MD, LaPlata, MD.	SMCNoStone
Bowling	Mary	Margaret	No Date	Sep. 28, 1841	Aged 8 yr. 8 mos. / info is from the Historical Society Research and the 1940 DAR book pg 192 located at the College of Southern MD, LaPlata, MD.	SMCNoStone
Bowling	Matthew	Wade	Apr. 19, 1977	May 12, 1977		LUM136
Bowling	Maureen		Jan. 3, 1952	Sep. 19, 1971		SMCD141
Bowling	Mildred	C.	1923	1981		LUM165
Bowling	Mortimer	Brooke	Sep. 17, 1908	Sep. 8, 1973		SMCD009
Bowling	Nannie	S.	1871	1949	Rest in Peace	LUM183
Bowling	Nellie	M.	Apr. 17, 1880	May 14, 1964		LUM204
Bowling	Norma	Lee	1937	2004		LUM106
Bowling	Philip	Semmes	1865	1949		SIC4030
Bowling	Phillip	B.	Nov. 10, 1904	Mar. 9, 1974		MTR1022
Bowling, Sr.	R.	P.	1871	1940	h/o Estelle V Bowling / At rest / footstone: father.	TRI340
Bowling	Rachel		No Date	Jan. 10, 1880	IHS / In memory of / d/o Wm F & Teresa Bowling / age 50 years / May she rest in peace	SMCA124
Bowling	Robert	P.	1902	1972		LUM109
Bowling	Rose	B.	1898	1963		SIC3134
Bowling	Ruey	P.	1894	1973		SIC3134
Bowling	Ruth	D.	Jun. 26, 1904	Jan. 24, 1993		SMCE015

Last Name	First Name	Middle Name	Date of Birth	Date of Death	Transcription / Notes	Cemetery Code
Bowling	Ruth	P.	No Date	Mar. 1960		LUM122B
Bowling	Sharon	Gayle	Jul. 9, 1951	Jul. 10, 1951		LUM138
Bowling	Susie	L.	Feb. 11, 1864	May 28, 1947	May she rest in peace	SMCD013
Bowling, Sr.	T.	Oden	Oct. 4, 1911	Nov. 15, 1976	In loving memory	TRI442
Bowling	T.	Seger	No Date	1956	son	LUM149
Bowling	Teresa		No Date	Jul. 25, 1886	IHS / In memoriam / w/o Wm F Bowling / Aged 84 years / May she rest in peace	SMCA127
Bowling	Thomas	Herbert	Feb. 24, 1946	Feb. 8, 2006	Age 59, s/o Jacob V. Bowling and Marie E. Higgs Bowling / info is from the MD Independent Newspaper	CLVNoStone
Bowling	Thomas	R.	Oct. 14, 1843	Sep. 5, 1919		SMCA122
Bowling	Thomas	W.	1876	1957		LUM163
Bowling	Thomas		No Date	Sep. 18, 1829	Aged 27 years / info is from the Historical Society Research and the 1940 DAR book pg 192 located at the College of Southern MD, LaPlata, MD.	SMCNoStone
Bowling	Unknown		No Date	No Date	Infant d/o P.S. & L. S.	SIC4033
Bowling	Velma	E.	Jan. 5, 1925	Apr. 30, 1997	"Toots" / m. Sept 20, 1945	LUM178
Bowling	Victor		Nov. 30, 1851	Dec. 10, 1865	Died at St. Charles College / R.I.P	SMCA138
Bowling	Viola	Lyon	Jul. 1, 1896	Feb. 21, 1984		LUM144
Bowling	Violet		No Date	Mar. 24, 1883	d/o A M & Violet Bowling / Back side of stone: Little Sister / aged 2 years and 2 months / Not sure if death day is 21 or 24	SMCA133
Bowling	W.	Wilson	1918	2001		LUM165
Bowling	Wallace	E.	1902	1960		LUM172
Bowling	Wallace		1835	1904	Pvt. / 2nd Maryland Infantry Co A Confederate States of America / Duty is the sublimist word in our language. Do your duty in all things, you cannot do more, you should never wish to do to less-Gen. Robert E. Lee; Footstone: Pvt, Co A 2 MD Inf CSA	TRI271
Bowling	Walter	Brent	Aug. 5, 1954	Aug. 7, 1954		LUM140
Bowling	Walter	W.	Sep. 6, 1904	Oct. 28, 1984	Rest in Peace	LUM141
Bowling, Jr.	Walter	W.	Mar. 14, 1927	Nov. 12, 1998	m. Sep 18, 1948	LUM135
Bowling	Washington	P.	1869	1956	Let our Father's will be done	LUM162
Bowling, Sr.	William	Clayton	Jun. 18, 1908	Aug. 6, 1971	Together forever	SMC4106

Last Name	First Name	Middle Name	Date of Birth	Date of Death	Transcription / Notes	Cemetery Code
Bowling	William	F.	1833	1917		SMCA147
Bowling	William	I.	Oct. 19, 1832	Aug. 29, 1867	In memory of / Beloved husband of Mary J Bowling / R I P	SMCD223
Bowling	William	Sinclair	Mar. 28, 1908	May 4, 1984		SIC6067
Bowling	William	T.	Jun. 24, 1910	Sep. 1, 1996		SMC1093
Bowling, Jr.	William	V.	Apr. 2, 1970	Oct. 31, 2006		LUM228
Bowling, Sr.	Willson	C.	1893	1969		SIC3133
Bowling	Winifred	Faye	May 6, 1950	Nov. 19, 1950		LUM137
Bowling	Winifred	Garner	Dec. 15, 1927	Nov. 22, 2005	m. Sep 18, 1948	LUM135
Bowling, Sr.	Wm.	F.	Mar. 9, 1801	Jun. 10, 1866	Sacred to the memory of / Blessed are the dead who die in the Lord / R.I.P.	SMCA128
Bowman	Ada	C.	May 1890	No Date	old cement stone cross	SCA074
Bowman, Mrs.	Ada	C.	May 28, 1920	Sep. 26, 1964	Info was obtained from the Historical Society Research located at the College of Southern Md, LaPlata, Md	OAKNoStone
Bowman	Addell		1920	1979		SMI052
Bowman	Anna	R.	Mar. 23, 1888	Aug. 24, 1989		SJO1172
Bowman	Carl		1953	1971	Info is from the Historical Society Research located at the College of Southern MD, LaPlata, MD	ZBCNoStone
Bowman, Jr.	Charles	H.	Jan. 21, 1914	Apr. 9, 1990		SCL3076
Bowman	Charles	Ulysses	May 21, 1921	May 30, 1984	TEC 5 US Army WW II	SCL3300
Bowman	Christian		2000	2000	Thornton Funeral Home Marker	SMI100
Bowman	Dorothy	Mae	May 25, 1944	Jan. 26, 1974	Our Beloved / Rest in Peace	SMI048
Bowman	Ethel	Mabel	1912	2004	Daughter	SCL3411
Bowman	Eva	S.	Oct. 10, 1899	Dec. 29, 1980	Mother	SCL3299
Bowman	Gloria	V.	Aug. 11, 1927	Dec. 18, 1969	In Loving Memory	SMY2084
Bowman	James	C.	Jan. 31, 1917	Oct. 23, 1954		SCL3332
Bowman, Jr.	James	Louis	Nov. 16, 1970	Sep. 16, 1989		SIG098
Bowman	John	W.	1913	1976	Thornton Funeral Home Marker	SMI115
Bowman	John	B.	Aug. 30, 1924	Dec. 13, 1996	Husband of The Late Gloria V Bowman	SMY2011
Bowman, Sr.	Joseph	E.	Jun. 18, 1937	Oct. 6, 2003	SN US Navy	SMI098
Bowman	Joseph	H.	Feb. 18, 1911	Sep. 7, 1975		SMY2060

Last Name	First Name	Middle Name	Date of Birth	Date of Death	Transcription / Notes	Cemetery Code
Bowman	Joseph	Stephen	Apr. 8, 1947	Nov. 28, 1990	SP 5 US Army Viet Nam	SCL3077
Bowman, Capt.	Joseph		No Date	Apr.il 8, 1717	Here lyes the body of Joseph Bowman Of Whitehaven who died / 1717 aged 32 yrs. (info is from the 1940 DAR book page 142 located at the College of Southern MD, LaPlata, MD) He is not buried at Old Durham Church. The stone was found on Wade's Bay a few yards back from the shore. Rev. Stevenson of Old Durham Church had it moved to his Church yard.	ODENoStone
Bowman	Levi	A.	Oct. 8, 1907	Feb. 13, 1976	Pvt US Army WW II	SMI051
Bowman	Lillie	H.	1924	1977	Info is from Historical Society Research located at The College of Southern MD, LaPlata, MD	SACNostone
Bowman	Lucille	M.	Aug. 22, 1917	Aug. 17, 1962		SMI066
Bowman	Mary	Louise	Jun. 15, 1924	No Date		SCL3075
Bowman	Nellie	A.	1914	1987	Mother	SMI101
Bowman	Ophelia		Aug. 24, 1938	Oct. 7, 1990	Wife / (Barbara) Mother	SMI068
Bowman	Patricia	Elvira	Nov. 26, 1950	Jul. 28, 2003		ZBC085
Bowman	Rebecca		No Date	No Date	Painted on a piece of wood attached to a pole	SMI129
Bowman	Robert	B.	Nov. 28, 1909	Feb. 22, 1986	Deacon	MAC072
Bowman	Shelia		1956	2010	Rock marks the spot	PGN089A
Bowman	Thomas	N.	Oct. 20, 1911	Apr. 3, 1978		SMI102
Bowman	Ulysses	G.	Mar. 29, 1892	Dec. 14, 1968	Father (death date is from familysearch.org)	SCL3301
Bowman	Wesley		No Date	No Date	Painted on a piece of wood attached to a pole	SMI130
Bowman	Wilhemeina		Dec. 17, 1951	Mar. 2, 2004	"Willie" / Always in our hearts	SCL3078
Bowman	William	Clifton	May 29, 1938	Nov. 21, 1973		SMI067
Bowman	William	H.	Apr. 3, 1918	Feb. 23, 1999	(Cabby) Father	SMI069
Bowman	William	H.	Jan. 1, 1912	Mar. 14, 1980		SAC3080
Bowman	William		1941	2005	Thornton Funeral Home Marker	SMI097

Last Name	First Name	Middle Name	Date of Birth	Date of Death	Transcription / Notes	Cemetery Code
Boyd	Andrew	J.	Apr. 8, 1982	Apr. 11, 2002	A J / Verse on stone: With love you were our guide. Gone for now but with the tide, while your days passed way too fast. Our memories remain Till Together at last. Back of stone: Our world is blessed and beautiful but you're where you need to be You have new jobs to work on So we will Pray and let you be. We will miss your hugs and kisses You gave them oh so free but soon we will be together A day that will bring much Glee! From all of us you touched and left behind. Love never ends, Never stops	SCL3117
Boyd	Mary	Ann	Jun. 2, 1937	Apr. 28, 2009		SMC3104
Boyer	Mary	Helen	1889	1940		SJE035
Boykin	Louise	H.	1885	1981		SJE250
Boykin	Margaret	J.	Dec. 19, 1880	Jul. 10, 1904	Beloved Wife Of R. M. Boykin	SCL2148
Boykin	Margaret	J.	Mar. 6, 1904	Sep. 17, 1907	Daughter of R.M. & M.J. Boykin	SCL2146
Boykin	Robert	Eugene	Aug. 23, 1902	Jan. 1903	Son of R.M. & M.J. Boykin	SCL2147
Boykin	Robert	M.	1877	Sep. 23, 1954		SJE250
Boykin	William	H.	No Date	Apr. 1919	Age 6 months	SJE248
Bracken	Gladys	Mallory	Jul. 9, 1900	Oct. 4, 1970		SIC8010
Bracy	Lottie	W.	Jun. 12, 1932	Apr. 6, 1981		CLV009
Bradburn	Eleanore	C.	Feb. 24, 1925	Nov. 10, 1983		SAC2037
Bradburn	Francis	E.	Aug. 31, 1876	Jan. 10, 1959		SAC2020
Bradburn	John	B.	Jul. 28, 1926	Mar. 10, 1971		SAC2017
Bradburn	Joseph	A.	Sep. 25, 1898	Sep. 6, 1956		SAC2018
Bradburn	Joseph	Ford	Feb. 27, 1921	Aug. 10, 1983		SAC2021
Bradburn	Murial	L.	Jul. 12, 1897	Jul. 23, 1952		SAC2019
Bradford	Catherine	Cooper	Oct. 1, 1922	Jan. 2, 1993		SCA062
Bradford	Harry	L.	Aug. 12, 1912	Jul. 15, 1997		SCA063
Bradley	Harold		1901	1996		MTR1084
Bradley	Mary	W.	Aug. 19, 1886	Jul. 19, 1937	There is death, the stars go down to rise upon some fairer shore, and bright in heavens jewelled crown, they shine forever. / nee Darg	SPL3086

Last Name	First Name	Middle Name	Date of Birth	Date of Death	Transcription / Notes	Cemetery Code
Bradley	Movetta	Nadine, Butler	Aug. 17, 1960	Feb. 14, 2011	age 50 / d/o Thomas "Llois" and Patricia Bradley, w/o Gregory Carl Bradley Sr. (obit appeared in the Maryland Independent Newspaper dated Feb 18, 2011)	PGN092
Bradley	Myrtle	Y.	1903	1974		MTR1084
Bradshaw	Elendor	Jane	Mar. 30, 1827	Feb. 7, 1910	Info is from The College of Southern MD, LaPlata, MD	HAN013
Bradshaw	Jane	Barnett	1934	1970	MAMA	SCL1030
Bradshaw	Oventon		1821	May 3, 1898	Info is from The College of Southern MD, LaPlata, MD	HAN013
Bradshaw	Raymond	G.	1963	1979	In loving memory of our son	HGH4185
Brady	Albert		Jan. 12, 1943	Jun. 8, 1996	Nearer my God to thee / "Doc"	SPL5020
Brady, S.J.	John	J.	Mar. 13, 1910	Jan. 30, 1993	IHS / S. J. / Nat. 13 March 1910 INGR 30 July 1932 / Obit 30 Jan 1993 (In Priests Plot)	SIC1006
Brady	Judith	Ann	Oct. 2, 1944	No Date	Nearer my God to thee	SPL5020
Brady	Mary	Plowden	No Date	May 9, 1879	Beloved w/o William Brady / d/o Dr. Thos. A. & Mary J. Davis departed this life / A devoted wife, daughter and Christian. To know her was to love her R.I.P.	SJO3091
Bragunier	Benjamin	H.	Aug. 20, 1888	Nov. 10, 1894	children of D. J. and M. L. Bragunier / on same stone with Benjamin Brangunier	BGN011
Bragunier	Daisy	E.	Nov. 16, 1880	Apr. 28, 1940	Mother / "w/o Wm. P. Bragunier	PIS212
Bragunier	James	Noel	May 19, 1882	May 8, 1883	son of D.J. & M. L. Bragunier	BGN009
Bragunier	Kittie	E.	Jan. 8, 1885	Nov. 3, 1894	children of D. J. and M. L. Bragunier / on same stone with Benjamin Brangunier	BGN011
Bragunier	Mary	L.	Mar. 27, 1847	Nov. 26. 1927	Footstone	BGN003
Bragunier	Wm	P.	Sep. 27, 1878	Sep. 11, 1960	Father	PIS212
Brake	Gustella		1925	1981		POMNoStone
Branan	John	Stouten	Mar. 10, 1920	Oct. 9, 1998	In loving memory	NSP136
Brand	Alfred		1891	1938	Rest in Peace / Buried Feb 29, 1938 / age 48 (info is from Old Durham Church microfilm pg 161 located at the College of Southern MD, LaPlata, MD)	ODE125
Brandt	Richard	H.	No Date	Nov. 25, 1831	Sacred to the memory of / who departed this life / in the 26th year of his age	BRT002
Bransom	Clarence	Isaah	Apr. 26, 1926	Nov. 5, 1971	Maryland S1 USNR WW II	POM078
Bransom	Rosie	Jenkins	Jan. 15, 1879	Feb. 17, 1970		POM227
Bransome	Annie	E.	1887	1938	Mother	POM077

Last Name	First Name	Middle Name	Date of Birth	Date of Death	Transcription / Notes	Cemetery Code
Bransome	George	R.	1907	1973		POM071
Bransome	John	E.	1881	1950	Father	POM077
Bransome	Lawrence	L.	Mar. 29, 1947	Aug. 23, 1991	website Ancestry.com shows last name as Bransome	SJO3115
Branson	Alice	R.	Feb. 7, 1915	Oct. 17, 2000	Mother	POM073
Branson	Bernard	M.	Apr. 30, 1930	Jan. 26, 1976	CPL US Army Korea	POM070
Branson	Brenda		1951	1992	Thornton's Funeral Home Marker	MAC016
Branson	Caroline		Jul. 15, 1906	May 18, 1985	In Memory	POM219
Branson	Frances		No Date	Nov. 5, 1913	Aged 34 years, At Rest	POM036
Branson	Helen	E.	Mar. 14, 1914	Feb. 28, 1984		SCL1043
Branson, Jr.	Joseph	S.	Mar. 24, 1937	Sep. 26, 1992	In Loving Memory	POM079
Braun	Donna	Christine	Aug. 27, 1988	Dec. 12, 1988	Baby	SJO6005
Braun	Jason	F.	Nov. 28, 1973	Jun. 7, 1975		SCA036
Braunstein	Cecilia	E.	Aug. 8, 1916	Oct. 15, 2006	Married 63 years	SIC9017
Braunstein	David	W.	Apr. 11, 1941	No Date		SIC9018
Braunstein	William	L.	Sep. 25, 1914	Mar. 23, 2001	Married 63 years	SIC9017
Brawner	Alexander	M.	Jun. 15, 1887	Nov. 17, 1980		SCL4180
Brawner	Amanda	E. D.	Jul. 18, 1813	Sep. 15, 1874	Amanda E.D. Brawner / w/o James L. Brawner / age 61 years, 2 months, 2 days (Info was obtained from the Historical Society Research located at the College of Southern MD, LaPlata, MD)	BPGNostone
Brawner	Ann		No Date	Dec. 17, 1906	Info is from Christ Church microfilm Reel 3, Pg 220-221 located at the College of Southern MD, LaPlata, MD	MTRNoStone
Brawner	Bertha	L.	Feb. 4, 1894	Apr. 7, 1986		SCL3302

Last Name	First Name	Middle Name	Date of Birth	Date of Death	Transcription / Notes	Cemetery Code
Brawner	Catherine	A.	No Date	Jan. 2, 1816	Sacred to the memory of / who departed this life / in the 68th year of her age, leaving a husband and two sons to deplore her death (Broken) deceased and you would ( ) with her and entombed every virtue that acclaims her sex ( ) be her sleep until her savior bids her rise and with him ascends triumphant to the skies. Info is from the Historical Society Research located at The College of Southern MD, LaPlata, MD. Note: Picture was obtained from the file of J. Richard Rivoire at the College of Southern MD, LaPlata, MD.	BRW001
Brawner	Catherine	E.	Feb. 10, 1834	Feb. 5, 1893	w/o J. Alex. Brawner / Verily, Verily I say unto you, that but believeth in me hath everlasting life	MTR4093
Brawner	Cecelia		1931	1983		ZWU003
Brawner	Charles	P.	May 8, 1885	Aug. 27, 1906		SCL2166
Brawner	David	Leroy	Oct. 3, 1957	Aug. 5, 2000	In loving memory of / without farewell you asleep with only memories for us to keep in life we loved you dearly in death we love you still you hold a place in our hearts no one can ever fill / The Brawner Family	SJO1069
Brawner	Edgar		Nov. 18, 1820	Nov. 9, 1892	In memoriam / to the memory of our beloved father RIP by his children	SJE175
Brawner	Edna	M.	Jul. 7, 1904	Jan. 19, 1989		SCL4180
Brawner	Edward	C.	Mar. 31, 1918	Mar. 9, 1969		SCL4178
Brawner	Emma	L.	No Date	Dec. 23, 1895	Buried Dec 24, 1895 (info is from Old Durham Church microfilm pg 83-84 located at the College of Southern MD, LaPlata, MD)	ODENoStone
Brawner, Mrs.	Emma		No Date	May 2, 1907	Buried May 4, 1907 age 66 (info is from Old Durham Church microfilm pg 85-86 located at the College of Southern MD, LaPlata, MD)	ODENoStone
Brawner	Eugene	H.	Aug. 11, 1851	Aug. 10, 1916	May He rest in peace	SCL2165
Brawner, Jr.	Eugene	H.	Mar. 29, 1883	Jan. 28, 1898		SCL2170
Brawner	Francis	L.	Apr. 7, 1935	May 30, 2006		SJO1080
Brawner	Frederick	T.	1932	1978	SGT US Air Force Korea Vietnam	SCL4179
Brawner	Gerard	Briscoe	1860	Jul. 15, 1887	Blessed are the pure in heart for they shall see God (Stone is broken, unable to see birth info)	MTR4070

Last Name	First Name	Middle Name	Date of Birth	Date of Death	Transcription / Notes	Cemetery Code
Brawner	Gleness	Ann	Nov. 28, 1966	Feb. 20, 2007	In loving memory	SJO1092
Brawner	Henry	M.	Oct. 17, 1807	Oct. 16, 1836	In memory of / who departed this life / aged 29 years of one day, leaving a devoted wife, Catherine Brawner and three helpless children, Henry G., John A. and Henrietta Middleton Brawner / Info is from the Historical Society Research located at the College of Southern MD, LaPlata, MD	BPG006
Brawner	Horace		No Date	Nov. 25, 1851	Sacred to the memory of / infant s/o Wm H. and Mary C. Brawner who departed this life / aged 19 months and 20 days / Footstone	BRD001
Brawner	I.	Thaddeus	Jan. 19, 1829	Oct. 8, 1852	Earths proudest volume ends in how he lies and dust to dust concludes her noblest son / In life displaying the bright qualities of the true man. In death illustratiing the meek sublimit of the true faith. He lived a benefactor. He died a Christian.	SCL2167
Brawner	J.	Alexander	Jun. 9, 1835	Jun. 12, 1886	Asleep in Jesus blessed sleep	MTR4092
Brawner	James	Douglas	1853	1938	According to the Old Durham Church microfilm pg 161 located at the College of Southern MD, his first name is James	ODE282
Brawner	James	Walter	No Date	Jun. 18, 1851	s/o Amanda and James D. Brawner / age 14 years / Info was obtained from the Historical Society Research located at the College of Southern MD, LaPlata, MD	BPGNostone
Brawner	James		Mar. 2, 1927	Aug. 31, 1980	(Buster)	SJO1082
Brawner	James		1953	2008	Thornton Funeral Home Marker	SJO1066
Brawner	James		No Date	Jan. 1899	Info is from Old Durham Church microfilm pg 83-84 located at the College of Southern MD, LaPlata, MD	ODENoStone
Brawner	James			Apr. 28, 1846	Sacred to the memory of / who fell asleep in Jesus / age 58 years, 1 month, 10 days, the righteous is taken away from the evil to come, he shall enter into peace. Erected by his bereaved wife, Mary Brawner and his affectionate son, James L. Brawner (Info was obtained from the Historical Society Research located at the College of Southern Maryland, LaPlata, MD)	BPGNostone
Brawner	John	Dyer	Jan. 24, 1919	Sep. 19, 1971	Maryland Cpl 195 Gen Hosp WW II	SIC7070

Last Name	First Name	Middle Name	Date of Birth	Date of Death	Transcription / Notes	Cemetery Code
Brawner	Joseph	Harrison	Feb. 6, 1942	Aug. 30, 2006		SJO1091
Brawner	Margaret	E.	No Date	Apr. 15, 1855	Sacred to the memory of / infant d/o Wm H. & Mary C. Brawner who departed this life / aged 3 months. Footstone	BRD004
Brawner	Margaret	J.	Nov. 4, 1854	Dec. 22, 1890	Beloved Wife Of E.H. Brawner / At Rest	SCL2149
Brawner	Mary	A.	No Date	Mar. 20, 1821	Sacred to the memory of Mrs Mary A. Brawner w/o James Brawner Esq. who departed this life the 20th March 1821 aged 27y 2m & 20d / Early not sudden was poor Mary's fate Soon not surprising death his visit paid / Footstone: M.B. was leaning up against a tree and isn't near the headstone	RML005
Brawner	Mary	Alice	Oct. 13, 1911	Apr. 15, 1982		HGH4024
Brawner	Mary	Catharine	No Date	Jan. 20, 1891	Buried Jan 22, 1891 age 70 (info is from Old Durham Church microfilm pg 81-82 located at the College of Southern MD, LaPlata, MD)	ODENoStone
Brawner	Mary	E.	No Date	May 9, 1889	Buried Jul 7, 1889 age 21 (info is from Old Durham Church microfilm pg 81-82 located at the College of Southern MD, LaPlata, MD)	ODENoStone
Brawner	Mary	Morris	Jan. 29, 1901	Jul. 1, 1983		ODE287
Brawner	Mary	J.	No Date	Sep. 16, 1851	In memory of / consort of Thaddeus Brawner who departed this life / aged 23 years. Confined in the tomb neath this cold lap of earth. Sleeps the child of religion, and true moral worth. When the sun bids us farewell, and seems to seek rest, tis but to be welcomed another worlds guest. So she has but left us less fortunate here. To shine with fresh glory in heavens bright sphere. And now that the sun of her mortal's life's set, The moon of her memory still beams o'er us yet.	SCL2168
Brawner	Mary	Waring	Oct. 10, 1888	Jan. 6, 1972		SCL2164
Brawner	R.	Franklin	Apr. 12, 1913	May 15, 1958		SCL3305
Brawner	Raymond		May 26, 1876	Jan. 28, 1882	In Memory of / Eldest Son of W.H & M. J Brawner / Stone Mason was: Bradley, Wash D.C.	SCL2169
Brawner	Richard	Francis	Apr. 18, 1893	Feb. 13, 1969		ODE286
Brawner	Robert	C.	May 10, 1885	Jun. 23, 1962		SCL3302

Last Name	First Name	Middle Name	Date of Birth	Date of Death	Transcription / Notes	Cemetery Code
Brawner	Robert	Massie	No Date	Mar. 26, 1916	Aged 56 yrs	ODE285
Brawner	Robert	S.	No Date	Jun. 19, 1858	Sacred to the memory of / s/o Wm H. and Mary C. Brawner who departed this life / aged 2 years and 2 days / Footstone	BRD007
Brawner	Robert		1955	2008	Thornton Funeral Home	SJO1081
Brawner	Rose	Davis	Feb. 14, 1838	Aug. 19, 1890	In memoriam / To the memory of our Beloved Mother / w/o Edgar Brawner / R.I.P. / By her children	SJO3096
Brawner	Ruth	Norman	Mar. 17, 1865	Oct. 4, 1951	Beloved w/o William Francis Brawner	ODE283
Brawner	Ruth	Norman	Jun. 29, 1891	Sep. 23, 1984	Beloved d/o William Francis & Ruth Norman Brawner	ODE281
Brawner	Washington	Briscoe	Jun. 27, 1871	May 14, 1904		MTR4071
Brawner	William	Francis	Nov. 18, 1845	Apr. 12, 1919		ODE284
Brawner	William	L.	No Date	Jan. 1892	Buried Jan 17, 1892 (info is from Old Durham Church microfilm pg 81, located at the College of Southern MD, LaPlata, MD)	ODENoStone
Brawner	Willliam	Francis	No Date	Jan. 11, 1894	Age 22 s/o John James and Emeline Haislip Brawner (info is from Old Durham Church microfilm pg. 83 located at the College of Southern MD, LaPlata, MD)	ODENoStone
Braxton	Delores	Bernadette, Coby	Jan. 16, 1950	May 31, 2009	In God's Care / Mother / Age 59 / w/o William Marvin Braxton, d/o Edward and Madeline Coby / Info is from The Maryland Indedpendent Newspaper dated Jun 5, 2009	PGN086
Bray	James	William	Jun. 15, 1927	Sep. 19, 1981	M SG US Army WWII Korea Vietnam	SMC4057
Brayfield	Elias		1822	Nov. 1880	Info is from church records	TRINoStone
Brayfield	John	Samuel	No Date	No Date	Info is from church records, buried Aug 8, 1880. Note: s/o Elias Brayfield	TRINoStone
Brayshaw	Ilbert	de Lacy	Oct. 26, 1891	Jun. 28, 1934	In a large plot with "H" cornerstones, grouped around a large family stone "Hungerford".	CHR010
Brayshaw	Katherine	H.	Aug. 28, 1889	Mar. 16, 1932	Hungerford plot	CHR011
Breig	John	William	Jul. 27, 1921	Jul. 15, 2000	In loving memory	SCL1179
Breig	Marybelle		Dec. 14, 1920	No Date	In loving memory	SCL1179
Brensinger	Florence	C.	1943	No Date	She touched life with a Loving hand	HER012
Brensinger	Lester	E.	1937	1982	Too well Loved to ever be forgotten	HER012

Last Name	First Name	Middle Name	Date of Birth	Date of Death	Transcription / Notes	Cemetery Code
Brent	Adele		Jan. 10, 1865	Feb. 21, 1939	Located in Brent Merrick Plot	SMY1149
Brent	Alice		Feb. 13, 1861	Oct. 1, 1887	Located in Brent Merrick Plot	SMY1171
Brent	Ann	Nellie	No Date	Mar. 20, 1833	In memory of / d/o George & Matilda Brent who departed this life / aged 6 years and 10 months (located in Brent Merrick Plot)	SMY1166
Brent	Anne		Sep. 17, 1768	Feb. 22, 1807	Sacred to the memory of / the w/o John Brent. She was / Sic transit gloria mundi / Requiescat in pace Stone no longer exists	GMCNo Stone
Brent	Catherine	Ann	No Date	Jan. 9, 1813	In memory of Catherine Ann Brent daughter of George & Matilda Brent who departed this life / aged 11 months (located in Brent Merrick Plot)	SMY1169
Brent	Catherine	Merrick	May 12, 1830	Aug. 31, 1877	In Memoriam / Mother / w/o George Brent / Father / Footstone: D/o William Duhurst Merrick and Catherine Thomas; the d/o of Major William Thomas and Catherine Brooke Boarman Requiescant in Pace (located in Brent Merrick Plot)	SMY1153
Brent	Ella		Jun. 5, 1857	Jul. 10, 1858	Child of Geo. & Catherine Brent / As sweet a bud as ever bloomed in this vale of tears has been ripped by the frost of death (located in Brent Merrick Plot)	SMY1170
Brent	George		No Date	Aug. 22, 1838	My Father / Sacred to the memory of / who departed this life / in the 52nd year of his age (located in Brent Merrick Plot)	SMY1163
Brent	George		Sep. 28, 1817	Jan. 6, 1881	In Memoriam / Mother / w/o George Brent / Father / Footstone: D/o William Duhurst Merrick and Catherine Thomas; the d/o of Major William Thomas and Catherine Brooke Boarman Requiescant in Pace (located in Brent Merrick Plot)	SMY1153
Brent	George		Mar. 4, 1867	Mar. 7, 1932	His wife	SIC2101
Brent	John		No Date	No Date	Death could be after his wife's Feb. 22, 1807. Probably buried here next to his wife, Anne Brent. (Notes from Sister Miriam John at Mt Carmel Monastery)	GMCNo Stone
Brent	John F. X.	Parnham	No Date	Sep. 9, 1825	In memory of / s/o George & Matilda Brent who departed this life / aged 6 years 2 months (located in Brent Merrick Plot)	SMY1168

Last Name	First Name	Middle Name	Date of Birth	Date of Death	Transcription / Notes	Cemetery Code
Brent	Josephine	Burch	1873	1902		SMCC042
Brent	Josephine		Jan. 12, 1856	Mar. 2, 1935	Located in Brent Merrick Plot	SMY1150
Brent	Margaret	L.	Aug. 10, 1872	Oct. 10, 1927	Located in Brent Merrick Plot	SMY1174
Brent	Mary	Leila, Matthews	Aug. 5, 1868	Nov. 25, 1958	His wife	SIC2101
Brent	Mary		Apr. 24, 1859	Nov. 29, 1905	Located in Brent Merrick Plot	SMY1173
Brent	Matilda		No Date	Sep. 18, 1829	In memory of / d/o George & Matilda Brent who departed this life / aged 6 years 2 months (located in Brent Merrick Plot)	SMY1167
Brent	Matilda		No Date	Nov. 6, 1835	My Mother / Sacred to the memory of / w/o George Brent & d/o Maj. Wm Thomas of St. Mary's Co. who departed this life / in the 49th year of her age (located in Brent Merrick Plot)	SMY1160
Brent	Matilda		Dec. 14, 1850	Oct. 9, 1882	Located in Brent Merrick Plot	SMY1152
Brent	Nannie	Merrick	Dec. 26, 1870	Aug. 16, 1904	Located in Brent Merrick Plot	SMY1172
Brent	Unknown		No Date	No Date	Several young children of George & Matilda Brent / Info is from the 1940 DAR book page 153	SMYNoStone
Brent	Unknown		No Date	No Date	Several young children of George & Matilda Brent (info is from the 1940 DAR book page 155)	SMYNoStone

Last Name	First Name	Middle Name	Date of Birth	Date of Death	Transcription / Notes	Cemetery Code
Brent, Jr.	William	Leigh	Sep. 28, 1820	Mar. 17, 1833	To the memory of / who was born at Martinsville in the state of Louisiana upon the 28th of September 1820 and died at Washington City D.C. upon the 17th March 1833 aged twelve years, five months and seventeen days. This stone is erected by his mourning and affectionate father and mother, William L. Brent and his wife, Maria Fenwick. No early care had worn the tender ties that bound him here, no grief his heart had bowed, only too pure for earth, he seemed to rise, to his own heaven as doth some silver cloud before the winds grow loud. He's gone! in silence make his grave but not in tears we would not from its home, recall his happy soul perchance to brave a weary lot__ too gentle far to roam through years of grief to come, oh God! "Thy will be done in this and in all things for thou art mercy itself and tenderly tempers the wind to the shorn lamb" Stone maker was J. Birth Fecit W. City D.C.	FEN002
Brent	William	Merrick	Dec. 12, 1853	Aug. 17, 1923	Located in Brent Merrick Plot	SMY1151
Brent, Dr.	Wm.	Thomas	Jun. 14, 1810	Aug. 7, 1859	To my brother / s/o George & Matilda Brent / aged 49 years 1 mo and 24 days Left side of stone: Christian hope bids us believe we will meet in a better world where sufferings, sorrow and affliction will be no more forever. Right side of stone: Affection drops the tear of sorrow & of bitter grief upon the grave of the noble & good. Back of stone: Behold he taketh away who Can hinder him: or who will say unto him whose doest thou.	SMY1155 SMY1156
Breslin	Joseph	John	Mar. 10, 1873	May 19, 1971	F1 US Navy SP AM War	SCL1121
Brewer	Unknown		No Date	No Date	No other info on stone	SMCE001
Brickman	Patricia	S.	No Date	Mar. 1972	Temporary Headstone that was donated by Cemetery Committee marked PSB 3/72, information is from church records	CHRNoStone
Bridaham	Jessie		1856	1935		SJE114
Bridget	Aleine		Feb. 20, 1904	Mar. 7, 1906	d/o Oden & Hattie Bridget / Sleep on sweet Aleine, and take thy rest, God called thee home, he thought it best; gone but not forgotten / footstone: I.A.B.	TRI257

Last Name	First Name	Middle Name	Date of Birth	Date of Death	Transcription / Notes	Cemetery Code
Bridgett	Annie	H.	1883	1935	Our mother; she was the sunshine of our home / footstone: A.H.B.	TRI234
Bridgett	Benjamin	Lewis	Jul. 6, 1981	Feb. 10, 1988	Orange was Ben's favorite color and a word that has no Rhyme. Thee will not be another like him until the end of time. Love, Daddy	SIC5066
Bridgett	Charles	T.	Oct. 25, 1849	Sep. 21, 1935	At rest / footstone: C.T.B.	TRI297
Bridgett	Dennis	O.	1878	1959		TRI177
Bridgett	Earl	K.	1926	1926		TRI236
Bridgett	Edward	E.	1918	1999		SAC2093
Bridgett	Frances	Olive	1908	1968		SMY2160
Bridgett	Francis	E.	Apr. 5, 1917	May 6, 2001	Sgt US Army Air Forces WWII	TRI173
Bridgett	Hammond	D.	No Date	Apr. 19, 1905	Departed this life / Aged 28y, 2m, 2d / By his wife / footstone: H.D.B.	TRI293
Bridgett	Heidi	Denison	Oct. 26, 1949	Feb. 10, 1988	"There were birds in the trees but I never heard them singing, no I never heard them at all until there was you." Love, Mel	SIC5097
Bridgett	Helen	Elaine	1961	1970	Daughter	CHR409
Bridgett	Henry	G.	1881	1919	Erected by the employees of St Elizabeth Hospital Washington DC.	TRI295
Bridgett	John	T.	1852	1925	Beloved h/o Martha F.	TRI226
Bridgett	Joseph	Carlyle	Mar. 21, 1905	Jan. 7, 1907	s/o D O & A H Bridgett / Another little lamb has gone to dwell with him who gave, another little darling babe is sheltered in the grave; gone but not forgotten / footstone: J.C.B.	TRI259
Bridgett	L.	Lennis	Oct. 31, 1923	No Date	Beloved wife and mother	TRI173
Bridgett	Lewis	N.	Jun. 22, 1926	No Date		SIC5096
Bridgett	Mabel	Elizabeth	Feb. 19, 1917	1918	Thomas Reginald Bridgett	TRI174
Bridgett	Nelson	B.	1907	1918		TRI261
Bridgett	Oden	Lee	1915	1936		TRI252
Bridgett	Oscar	P.	1875	1967		TRI176
Bridgett	Rosalie	M.	1912	2001		SAC2093
Bridgett	Ruby	E.	Jan. 8, 1930	Jun. 2, 1987		SIC5096
Bridgett	Sarah	L.	Dec. 18, 1840	Nov. 14, 1921	Hope / At rest.	TRI296

Last Name	First Name	Middle Name	Date of Birth	Date of Death	Transcription / Notes	Cemetery Code
Bridgett	Thomas	Reginald	May 9, 1914	Nov. 25, 2000	Mabel Elizabeth Bridgett	TRI174
Bridgett	Thornton	K.	1903	1957		LUM196
Bridgett	Wayne	Randall	Nov. 25, 1952	Nov. 23, 2003	Trinity Episcopal Church Parking Lot Improvements / In memory of our loving son / Mom - Evelyn Powell Bridgett / Dad - Leon Brichby Bridgett. Note: This stone is outside the entrance to the church cemetery	TRI452
Bridgett	Woodrow	W.	1912	1915		TRI233
Bright	Bianca		Jul. 14, 2005	Jul. 25, 2005	Number 230-D inscribed on marker info is from church records	CLV426
Briscoe	Adrian	L.	May 11, 1973	Jun. 22, 1991	The beloved s/o Ronnie and Barbara	SCL4095
Briscoe	Agnes	C. Proctor	Aug. 8, 1902	Dec. 25, 1984		HGH4198
Briscoe	Alton	A.	1929	1960		SMCB023
Briscoe	Annette		1948	1963	Thornton Funeral Home Marker	MHB167
Briscoe	Austin	J.	1900	1969		SMC3142
Briscoe	Charles	A.	1906	1985		SJO3290
Briscoe	Delia	E.	Oct. 24, 1936	May 19, 2006	"Annie" / In loving memory	SJO3075
Briscoe	Edith	N.	1904	1984		SMC3143
Briscoe	Elenor	E.	Apr. 18, 1883	Apr. 12, 1916	In memory of / Merciful Jesus grant her eternal rest	SJO2301
Briscoe	Elijah		1903	1955	Cement cross, name is written with wire	POM158
Briscoe	Elizabeth	Ann	1879	1979	Beloved mother (Eliza)	SMC3288
Briscoe	Frank		Dec. 31, 1914	Jan. 6, 1996	TEC 4 US Army World War II / Thornton Funeral Home	MHB031
Briscoe	Genevieve	M.	1920	1981	In bushes	MAC007
Briscoe	George	A.	Mar. 23, 1908	Feb. 17, 1998		SJO3074
Briscoe	George	F.	1932	1980	s/o George A. & Mary E. Briscoe	SJO3077
Briscoe	Gerard		No Date	Apr. 25, 1848	Sacred to the memory of / who died in the 40th year of his age	SJE159
Briscoe	Gerard		No Date	Jun. 22, 1862	Sacred to the memory of my dear son who died a prisoner of war in the Old Capital Washington D.C. on the / in the 21st year of his age. In my hand no price I bring simply to thy cross I cling.	SJE158

Last Name	First Name	Middle Name	Date of Birth	Date of Death	Transcription / Notes	Cemetery Code
Briscoe	Harriett	A.	No Date	Feb. 3, 1899	Mother / Harriett A. Briscoe / aged 52 years / Oh the misery of that dreary day when I've held her dying head till death stole upon her softly and ( ) her soul had fled. / R.I.P. by her children	SJO3293
Briscoe	James	Arthur	Mar. 4, 1928	Jan. 27, 1969	Maryland CPL US Army	SJO3289
Briscoe	John	Thomas	No Date	Feb. 29, 1880	In Memory of / aged 48 years	SMY1148
Briscoe	Josephine	M.	1914	No Date	Forever in our hearts	SCL1215
Briscoe	Laura	King	Nov. 6, 1903	Jul. 10, 1993	Beloved Aunt	POM146
Briscoe	Laura	C.	1904	1963		POM176
Briscoe	Lewis		No Date	May 2, 1889	Father / who departed this life / aged 49 years. Prayer is a fruitful gift of faith for they are the flowers that never decay / R.I.P. By his children	SJO3295
Briscoe	Lewis		No Date	No Date	Info is from church records	SHINoStone
Briscoe	Loretta		1914	2001	Thornton Funeral Home Marker	MHB009
Briscoe	Lucy	F.	1900	1959		SMC3142
Briscoe	Marguerite	Wedding	Feb. 16, 1927	Sep. 26, 1995	Rest in peace	NJB091
Briscoe	Mary	E.	Feb. 21, 1911	No Date		SJO3074
Briscoe	Mary	E.	No Date	May 20, 1866	To the memory of / wife of Gerrard Briscoe / in the 54th year of her age. "I know that my Redeemer liveth" / Info is from the 1940 DAR book page 46. She was moved to St. John's from Catawba	SJE159A
Briscoe	Mary	G.	1912	1961	Sacred to the memory of my dear daughter / Blessed are the pure in heart for they shall see God (stone is laying on the ground)	NSP327
Briscoe	Mary	H.	No Date	Nov. 8, 1862		SJE157
Briscoe	Mary	Jane	1912	1981	Cement stone with funeral home marker	MAC035
Briscoe	Mary	L.	1932	1960		SMCB024
Briscoe	Mary		No Date	Jan. 3, 1843	Age 64 / In memory of / Departed this life /She was the 2nd wife of Richard Sothoron Briscoe and sister of Richard's first wife (Theodosia McPherson. She was born 1778. Mary was living in Wash. D.C. when she died. / Additional information was supplied by J. Richard Rivoire Jul 2009	MAC038

Last Name	First Name	Middle Name	Date of Birth	Date of Death	Transcription / Notes	Cemetery Code
Briscoe	Nathan	R.	1917	No Date		MAC007
Briscoe, Sr.	Raphael		Apr. 22, 1911	Apr. 18, 1985		SJO1134
Briscoe, Doct.	Richard	S.	No Date	Apr. 18, 1849	Aged 43 years / s/o Richard Sothoron Briscoe and his first wife Theodosia MacPherson Briscoe. Dr. Briscoe never married, lived with his parents in Wash. D.C. until 1830's when he went to live at Catawba. He died in Baltimore. / additional information was supplied by J. Richard Rivoire Jul 2009	MAC013
Briscoe	Richard	Sothoron	1768	1843	Husband of Theodosia MacPherson and Mary MacPherson (sisters) He moved to Wash D.C. after Theodosia died. Richard died from pneumonia at his home in Wash D.C He and his wife Mary died 3 days apart and had a shared obit notice. Their remains were removed to the family burying place in Charles County. (Markett Overton - Catawba) Info is from J. Richard Rivoire Jul 2009	MACNoStone
Briscoe	Robert	E.	Jan. 23, 1958	Jun. 1, 1996	"Robbie"	SJO3076
Briscoe	Robert	Francis	Jan. 7, 1940	Jul. 26, 1998		SPL7003
Briscoe	Rufus	N.	Dec. 18, 1966	Jan. 29, 1994		NSP051
Briscoe	Sarah	M.	May 23, 1880	Dec. 18, 1959		SJO3288
Briscoe	Theodosia	L., MacPherson	Jan. 30, 1771	Dec. 6, 1806	1st w/o Richard S. Briscoe / Info is from the 1940 DAR book Page 98 / She was the d/o William and Mary (Stone) MacPherson. Theodosia was the mother of Mary (Dement) Bender, Lucinda (Dement) Briscoe and (Dr.) Richard S. Briscoe. / Additional information was supplied by J. Richard Rivoire Jul 2009	MACNoStone
Briscoe	Thomas	Edward	Jun. 27, 1913	Nov. 28, 1978	US Army WW II	SJO1133
Briscoe	Unknown		1912	1981	Thornton's Funeral Home Marker	MAC034
Bristow	James	Patrick	Mar. 1, 1962	Mar. 8, 1962		SAC1001
Bristow	Ruth	E.	1934	No Date		GMC036
Bristow, Jr.	Wier	M.	1933	2005	OCDS Plot W44	GMC036
Brittle	M.	Rebecca	Feb. 14, 1934	May 16, 2008		HGH1133
Broadneaux	Eloise	Rudd	1914	1994	Beloved wife-Mother-Educator	ZBC036

Last Name	First Name	Middle Name	Date of Birth	Date of Death	Transcription / Notes	Cemetery Code
Bronner	Ann		Jun. 1, 1827	Sep. 9, 1907		SIC4023
Brook	Matthew		No Date	12 ? 196 ?	Age 74 / Info is from the Historical Society Research located at The College of Southern MD, LaPlata, MD	SIGNo Stone
Brookbank	Annie	Turner	1866	1903		TRI017
Brookbank	Daniel		1866	1913		TRI019
Brookbank	Esther	Noland	Oct. 2, 1920	Jul. 18, 1978		LUM031
Brookbank	Etta	E., Ewy	1893	1943		TRI022
Brookbank	J.	Spencer	1889	1967		TRI022
Brookbank	Leonard	D.	Apr. 29, 1899	Dec. 18, 1980		TRI018
Brookbank	Marjorie	R.	1902	1928	Beloved w/o Marion E. Brookbank / at rest	SMY3145
Brookbank	Thomas		1862	1942		TRI017
Brookbank	William	Francis	Aug. 10, 1906	Aug. 18, 1988		LUM031
Brooke	Alexander		1867	1867		SMY1081
Brooke	Amanda	C.	1832	1902		SMY1032
Brooke	Annie		1876	1906		SMY1081
Brooke, M. D.	David	A. M.	1829	1903	And his wife / their children	SMY1081
Brooke	Edwardina	Keech	1844	1905		SMY1081
Brooke	Eleanor	V.	1883	1979		SJE164
Brooke	J.	Compton	1872	1949		SJE164
Brooke	Mary	Rosella	1873	1875		SMY1081
Brooke	Mary		1757	Feb. 26, 1800	Obit 26th Feby. 1800 Aetatis 43 (Wife of Ignatius Baker Brooke, Jr.) Stone no longer exists	GMCNo Stone
Brooke, P.S.J.	Matthew		No Date	1705	Buried Under Sacristy (In Priests Plot)	SIC1001
Brooke	Susan	E.	Apr. 20, 1851	Feb.. 21, 1888	In memory of / Faithful unto death	SJE178
Brooks	Arthur		No Date	No Date		POM045
Brooks	Benedict	Ignatius	No Date	Feb. 10, 1977	Aged 85 yrs. (info is from Historical Society Research located at The College of Southern MD, LaPlata, MD)	SACNostone
Brooks	Carrie		1903	1985	Montgomery Bros. Funeral Home Marker	OAK128
Brooks	Cenia	Duckett	No Date	No Date		POM045
Brooks	Daisy	Avant	No Date	No Date		POM045
Brooks	Eliza	Ann	No Date	No Date		POM045

Last Name	First Name	Middle Name	Date of Birth	Date of Death	Transcription / Notes	Cemetery Code
Brooks	Evelyn	B.	Sep. 27, 1912	Jan. 6, 1933		SJO2099
Brooks	Florian	R.	Jul. 22, 1897	Jun. 18, 1983		SJO1168
Brooks	Gertrude	Hawkins	Nov. 22, 1899	Aug. 16, 1965	Info is from church records	SHI066
Brooks	Gwendolyn	D.	1950	1972		NSP312
Brooks	Harry		No Date	No Date		POM045
Brooks	J.	Carroll	Mar. 26, 1894	Jun. 13, 1983		SJO1168
Brooks	James	W.	1915	1985	Montgomery Bros. Funeral Home Marker	OAK127
Brooks	John	Wesley	No Date	No Date	Rusted metal funeral home marker. Name is illegible. (Grave is located within a bricked plot) h/o Minnie Thomas Brooks / info supplied by a church member	PGO013
Brooks	Joseph	W.	Sep. 22, 1897	Oct. 2, 1967	Info is from church records	SHI066
Brooks	Joseph		1917	1976	Info is from the Historical Society Research located at The College of Southern MD, LaPlata, MD	SCLNoStone
Brooks	Joseph		No Date	No Date		POM045
Brooks	Josephine		No Date	No Date		POM045
Brooks, Jr.	Lawrence	E.	Jan. 16, 1967	Oct. 31, 2000		SMC1082
Brooks	Lucille	M.	1932	1975	Information is from the Historical Society Research located at the College of Southern MD, LaPlata, MD	SMINoStone
Brooks	Mary	Delia	1905	1971	Robinson Funeral Home Marker	SMCE034
Brooks	Mary	E.	1893	1967		POM235
Brooks	Mary	M.	Aug. 1, 1879	Aug. 22, 1917	May she rest in peace. By her husband Wm. N. Brooks / Tall white stone that is near a tree. The stone is leaning and looks like it might fall soon.	SJO2100
Brooks	Minnie	Thomas	Jul. ? 1891	Apr. 12, 1970	Beloved mother and grandmother / Grave is located within a bricked Plot / w/o John Wesley Brooks and m/o Lloyd E. Thomas Sr.	PGO014
Brooks	Naomi	Rogers	No Date	No Date		POM045
Brooks	Odelle	Bond	Oct. 20, 1917	Apr. 21, 1987		SPL5057
Brooks	Raymond		1905	1965		POM220
Brooks	Roy		No Date	No Date		POM045
Brooks	Ruth		1916	No Date		POM220
Brooks	Susie	E. W.	Dec. 12, 1850	Jun. 17, 1946	In Memory of our Mother	ZBC172

Last Name	First Name	Middle Name	Date of Birth	Date of Death	Transcription / Notes	Cemetery Code
Brooks	Walter		Apr. 27, 1892	Feb. 4, 1962	Maryland PVT CO D 401 RES Labor BN QMC WWI	MAC023
Brooks	George	W.	Jun. 5, 1877	Dec. 23, 1916	May he rest in peace	SIC4103
Brosco	Stephen	James	Jan. 2, 1964	Apr. 25, 2007	Beloved Father, Son, Brother	SAC2079
Brown	A.	Demetrius	1961	2008	Thornton Funeral Home Marker	SJO4024
Brown	Ada	C.	1900	1977	At Rest	POM224
Brown	Agnes	Marie	Oct. 31, 1904	Aug. 2, 1992	In Loving Memory	SCL1055
Brown	Agnes		No Date	No Date	Old cement cross	ZWU006
Brown, Rev.	Alexander		No Date	Aug. 5, 1975	Info is from Shiloh Church records	SMT054
Brown	Allen	T.	Apr. 28, 1914	Jan. 7, 1971		SCL1127
Brown	Alton	Emanuel	May 29, 1936	Feb. 7, 2006	BTFN US Navy	SCL3421
Brown	Amelia		Apr. 11, 1903	Dec. 18, 1971		SMI004
Brown	Andrew		No Date	Nov. 24, 1968	Info is from church records	SHINoStone
Brown	Ann Agnes	Barnes	Sep. 10, 1830	Jun. 2, 1902		MTR1275
Brown	Anna		No Date	Feb. 1956	Info is from church records	SHINoStone
Brown	Anne	Schmidt	Oct. 8, 1899	Aug. 27, 1970	Quoniam in aeternum misericordia ejus / at Xenia, Ohio / Married at New York Aug 15, 1927, Died at LaPlata / Age did not wither her nor custom stale her infinite variety. Sie Zeugete vondem Licht, das wahrhaftiae Licht welches alle Menschen erleuchtet die in diese Welt Kommen / Back of stone: Sie Zeugete Von dem Licht. das wahrhaftiae Licht welches alle Menschen erleuchtet die in diese Welt Kommen.	MTR2163A
Brown	Annette	E.	Nov. 6, 1897	Sep. 1, 1973		ZBC187
Brown	Annie		No Date	Dec. 28, 1930	Info is from Christ Church microfilm Reel 3, Pg 236-237 located at the College of Southern MD, LaPlata, MD	MTRNoStone
Brown	Ardie		Aug. 22, 1903	Apr. 19, 1974		NJB063
Brown	Augustus	W.	1929	1985		OSM112
Brown	Austin		1938	2005	Thornton Funeral Home Marker	SMT038
Brown	Benjamin	F.	1887	Feb. 11, 1961	Info is from church records	SHI112
Brown	Bernice		1922	May 8, 1985	Thornton Funeral Home Marker / death date is from church records	SHI032
Brown	Bertha	Theresa	Nov. 1, 1908	Dec. 10, 2002	Our beloved Momma B	SCL3368

Last Name	First Name	Middle Name	Date of Birth	Date of Death	Transcription / Notes	Cemetery Code
Brown	Bessie	E. Lyon	No Date	Aug. 13, 1889	Info is from Christ Church microfilm Reel 2 Pg 165-166 located at the College of Southern MD, LaPlata, MD	MTRNoStone
Brown	Blanche	C.	1917	No Date		SAC3024
Brown	Burley	V.	Mar. 18, 1904	Dec. 22, 1970		POM225
Brown	Carolyn	R.	1910	1982	At Rest	POM223
Brown	Carroll	Robert	Dec. 14, 1925	May 21, 1949		OSM082
Brown	Cecil	Jerome	Jul. 5, 1957	Dec. 28, 1992	In Loving Memory	SCA120
Brown	Celesta	B.	1912	2001		SCL3107
Brown	Charity	A.	1857	1945	Rest in Peace	SJO2102
Brown	Charles	H.	1850	1938	Rest in Peace	SJO2102
Brown	Charles	R.	Nov. 3, 1882	Dec. 8, 1909	Beloved s/o Mr. & Mrs. Charles H. Brown / aged 27 yrs, 1 mo., & 5 dys. / May he rest in peace	SJO2105
Brown	Charles	R.	1911	2003		SCL3107
Brown	Charles	R.	Aug. 5, 1919	Dec. 1, 2001	Father / Love Always	PGN061
Brown	Charles	W.	Apr. 10, 1917	Jun. 26, 1992		MHB050
Brown	Charles		No Date	Nov. 1, 1895	Aged 55 Years	MHB252
Brown	Clarence	William	Mar. 28, 1919	Feb. 2, 1995		NSP120
Brown, Rev.	Clark		No Date	Jan. 12, 1817	"He is interred in the church on the left side as you approach the altar." Info is from the files of J. Richard Rivoire.	CHRNoStone
Brown	Daniel	W.	1914	1985	Thornton Funeral Home Marker	SHI084
Brown	Doris	Tederick	May 5, 1926	Sep. 11, 1992		NJB294
Brown	Dorothy	H.	Aug. 23, 1915	No Date		NSP405
Brown	Dorothy		1911	2000	Thornton Funeral Home Marker	SAC3056
Brown	Earl	L.		1907	1967	Cherrydale, VA / Charles CO. MD / Known as "the man on the hill" KOI 2955 unit 3 / moved to Charles CO as a boy. Retired from Naval Powder Plant. Built first Crystal Radio Receiver in SO. MD.	OSM114
Brown	Earl	Donald	Sep. 12, 1951	Aug. 13, 2001	Beloved son, husband, father, brother, friend. / Offshore fisherman	OSM113
Brown	Eddie		1941	2005	Thornton Funeral Home Marker	SMT039
Brown	Edward	Columbus	Jun. 9, 1921	Mar. 28, 1993	US Army WW II / In memory of my loving Uncle	ZBC094

Last Name	First Name	Middle Name	Date of Birth	Date of Death	Transcription / Notes	Cemetery Code
Brown	Eliza	E.	Jan. 24, 1839	Jun. 1, 1910	Info is from 1940 DAR book pages 54, 99 & 100	STWNoStone
Brown	Elizabeth	E.	Aug. 7, 1854	Aug. 15, 1889	w/o Dr. Gustavus R. Brown & d/o Frederick & Maria L. Stone	MTR1278
Brown	Elizabeth	H.	Dec. 1859	No Date	Date is from 1900 census / she is the w/o James H. Brown and m/o Parron & Emma Brown per 1920 census info is from ancestry.com	SHI109
Brown	Elizabeth	M.	1914	1988	Loving mother and grandmother	POM242
Brown	Ellen		1911	1966	w/o Randolph Brown	SHI079
Brown	Eloise	E.	Apr. 28, 1923	Apr. 23, 2002	Mother / Love Always / Eastern Star Emblem	PGN060
Brown	Elwood	A.	Jul. 22, 1922	Mar. 30, 1983	US Army WW II	MHB153
Brown	Emma	E.	Sep. 1878	No Date	Date is from 1900 census / she is the d/o James & Elizabeth Brown per 1920 census info is from ancestry.com	SHI109
Brown	Emma	L.	Jun. 22, 1923	Apr. 11, 1996		SMC4198
Brown	Ernest	William	May 11, 1922	Apr. 3, 1992	Info is from church records	SHINoStone
Brown	Estelle	N.	1913	1982	Mother	SAC3098
Brown	Estelle	V.	1912	1999		SMC3328
Brown	Evangeline	E.	1921	1987		SMC4043
Brown	F.	Marie	1886	1983		SJO1004
Brown	Fannie	E.	Jul. 26, 1910	Feb. 18, 1980	Eastern Star Emblem	PGN015
Brown	Fillmore	A.	Nov. 1, 1918	Aug. 1, 1972		NJB062
Brown	Frances	L.	1913	1985	Thornton Funeral Home Marker	SMT026
Brown	Frances	O'Neill	1924	1944		SIC6080
Brown	Frederick	J.	May 29, 1925	Apr. 12, 1991		SCL3369
Brown	Frederick	James	1904	Oct. 11, 1984	Death date and middle name is from church records	SHI016
Brown	Genevieve	S.	Sep. 10, 1914	Nov. 21, 1983		SCL1127
Brown	George	E.	1914	1991		SAC3024
Brown	George	F.	1933	1982		SCA055
Brown	George	T.	Apr. 8, 1869	Dec. 2, 1899	Age 30 yrs	POM069
Brown	Gertrude		No Date	Apr. 2, 1965	Info is from church records	SHINoStone
Brown	Gordon	F.	Jun. 19, 1926	No Date		SJO6057
Brown	Grace	M.	Feb. 25, 1894	Feb. 19, 1979		SHI083

Last Name	First Name	Middle Name	Date of Birth	Date of Death	Transcription / Notes	Cemetery Code
Brown	Gracy	Ann	Dec. 1, 1827	Dec. 12, 1882	Sacred to the memory of / w/o William Brown	NJB414
Brown	Gus		1865	1946	Dad / At rest	OSM135
					Sacred to the memory of / This tombstone is erected by his beloved wife Margaret Brown in testimony of her respect and affection and as a monumnet of his skill as a physician and his learning as a scholar of his wisdom as a philosopher his patriotism as a citizen and his generosity as a friend of his elegant_____ and his hospitality as a neighbour his tenderness as a husband and father and of his benevolence as a man. He died / Aged 56 years.	
Brown, Dr.	Gustavus	Richard	No Date	Sep. 30, 1804		GUS003
Brown, Dr.	Gustavus	Richard	Sep. 12, 1851	Jul. 20, 1911		MTR1276
					Here lies Major John Truman Stoddert, his wife Elizabeth Stoddert, his children, Truman Stoddert, Elizabeth Stoddert, Lucy Stoddert Brown, Gustavus Brown, Elizabeth Stoddert Bowie, his grandchildren, John Robert Bowie Stoddert, William Truman Stoddert, James Truman Stoddert, Mary Bowie / Memorial Stone	
Brown	Gustavus		No Date	No Date		WHS001
Brown	Gustavus		Aug. 17, 1783	Jun. 1, 1841	In Memory of / flat stone elevated on cinder blocks	HDV019
Brown	Harold	E.	Feb..11,1920	Jun..16,1944	TEC 5 US Army/Maryland	MHB271
Brown	Hattie	Marie	No Date	Aug. 3, 1960	Info is from church records	SHINoStone
Brown	Helen	Ann	Oct. 27, 1934	Sep. 30, 1987		SMC3330
Brown	Helen	Ann	Oct. 27, 1984	Sep. 30, 1987		SMC3320
Brown	Helen	Dorsey	No Date	1964	Info is from church records	SHINoStone
Brown	Helen		Jun. 4, 1912	Jul. 5, 2002	"Nellie" / Mother	PGN064
Brown	Irene	D.	Sep. 1, 1918	No Date	All creatures great and small. God loves us all	ODE308
Brown	Isaac	C.	No Date	Feb. 9, 1887	Aged 15 yrs. / Right bottom of stone is broken off	SCL3103
Brown	James	C.	Jun. 28, 1933	Nov. 5, 1962	Maryland PVT CO L 14 Infantry Regt Korea	SMC3329
Brown	James	Calvin	1927	1976		SCL3351
Brown	James	F.	1892	1978		SJO1004
Brown	James	F.	Mar. 13, 1902	Jan. 18, 1959	PVT US Army WW II	SCL3333

Last Name	First Name	Middle Name	Date of Birth	Date of Death	Transcription / Notes	Cemetery Code
Brown	James		Jun. 1848	No Date	Date is from 1900 census / He is the h/o Elizabeth Brown and f/o Parron and Emma Brown per 1920 census / info is from ancestry.com	SHI109
Brown	James	H.	Apr. 11, 1917	Jul. 15, 1974	Beloved s/o Mr. & Mrs. James F. Brown	SJO1003
Brown	James	R.	Aug. 10, 1909	Oct. 17, 1986		OAK204
Brown	James	Richard	1901	Jul. 17, 1985	Middle name and death date is from church records	SHI106
Brown	James	W.	1880	1964		NSP307
Brown	James	William	Jun. 19, 1925	May 14, 1995	In Loving Memory	SCA120
Brown	Janie	I.	Jul. 19, 1895	Jul. 12, 1954		PKH040
Brown, Jr.	John	Atkins	Aug. 28, 1930	Jul. 16, 1987	Do unto others as you would have others do unto you	NSP831
Brown	John	Childs	Jun. 26, 1944	Jul. 22, 1973	Maryland PFC US Army	SMC3289
Brown	John	F.	1912	1996	Father	SAC3098
Brown	John	H.	1920	1994	In loving memory	SMC2059
Brown	John	Randolph	Oct. 15, 1908	Oct. 5, 1992	Father	SHI080
Brown	John	Wesley	No Date	Mar. 23, 1893	Info is from Christ Church microfilm Reel 2 Pg 169-170 located at the College of Southern MD, LaPlata, MD	MTRNoStone
Brown	Johnson	M.	1909	1981		SPL3061
Brown	Joseph	H.	Sep. 19, 1879	Dec. 13, 1910		POM069
Brown	Joseph	Harris	1909	1976	Commandery 309 SGT	SCL1106
Brown	Joseph	Melvin	Oct. 29, 1945	Jun. 12, 2002	Father	SMC4160
Brown	Joseph	S.	Mar. 7, 1960	Mar. 6, 1997	"Peter"	SMC4161
Brown	Judith	H.	Jun. 18, 1940	Jul. 23, 1944		NSP412
Brown	Julia		No Date	No Date	In Memory Of / Could be someone else but Stone is Hard to read	SMT046
Brown	Kent		No Date	Jul. 6, 1968	Info is from church records	SHINoStone
Brown	Kent		No Date	Jul. 6, 1968	Death date is from church records	SHI205
Brown	Kevin	F.	Jun. 1954	Sep. 1954		SJO6057
Brown	Lawrence	Alfred	Sep. 15, 1932	Jul. 11, 2000	CPL US Army	SCL3370
Brown	Lawrence		1984	1984	A rock marks the spot / info is from church records	PGN024
Brown	Lena		No Date	Mar. 10, 1965	Info is from church records	SHINoStone
Brown	Leonard	B.	1911	1961		SMC3328

Last Name	First Name	Middle Name	Date of Birth	Date of Death	Transcription / Notes	Cemetery Code
Brown	Leroy	P.	Sep. 11, 1916	Apr. 1, 1990	All creatures great and small. / God loves us all	ODE308
Brown	Lillian		No Date	Feb. 10, 1923	7 mos. 5 days / info is from church records	SHINoStone
Brown, Mrs.	Lizzie		No Date	Jan. 7, 1927	Age 65 / info is from church records	SHINoStone
Brown	Louise	V.	1916	1987	In loving memory	SMC2058
Brown	Louise		1891	1963	Mother at rest	OSM136
Brown	Louise		1895	1979	Thornton Funeral Home Marker	DUD045
Brown	Lucy	Stoddert	No Date	No Date	Here lies Major John Truman Stoddert, his wife Elizabeth Stoddert, his children, Truman Stoddert, Elizabeth Stoddert, Lucy Stoddert Brown, Gustavus Brown, Elizabeth Stoddert Bowie, his grandchildren, John Robert Bowie Stoddert, William Truman Stoddert, James Truman Stoddert, Mary Bowie / Memorial Stone	WHS001
Brown	M.	Bernice, Simms	Aug. 20, 1930	Nov. 16, 1998	Loving Mother and Grandmother	SCA126
Brown	M.	Gertrude	Jul. 11, 1907	Aug. 15, 2002		SMC2051
Brown	Mabel	Willett	Jun. 24, 1908	Dec. 1, 1992		PKH131
Brown	Marcellus		1903	1990	Funeral Home Marker	SMI077
Brown	Margaret	Berry	1894	1973		SIC6078
Brown	Margrie		1922	1998	Thornton Funeral Home Marker	OAK009
Brown	Marion	Hancock	Jun. 23, 1876	Sep. 12, 1898	Family member gave birth and death dates but, has birth year as 1877, and it says 1876 on the stone	HAN004
Brown	Marjorie	Jane	May 10, 1930	Jan. 28, 2001		SJO6057
Brown	Mary	A.	1937	No Date	In Loving Memory	SMY2020
Brown	Mary	Anna, Pryor	Apr. 10, 1910	Nov. 14, 2007	d/o the late Charles Pryor and late Ida Bell Hawkins Pryor. w/o James Brown. m/o William Brown. Mary was buried on Nov. 24, 2007. Info is from Maryland Independent Newspaper Wed. Nov. 21, 2007	SCL1045A
Brown	Mary	Brent	1899	1934		SIC2013
Brown	Mary	G.	1880	Feb. 1968	Info is from church records	SHI111
Brown	Mary	L.	Sep. 24, 1938	Jan. 7, 2007	In loving memory	SAC3012
Brown	Mary	Louise	Jun. 27, 1959	Apr. 26, 1979	Info is from church records	SHI078
Brown	Mary	M.	1890	1975		NSP323
Brown	Mary	Madeline, Wade	Mar. 26, 1884	Jan. 4, 1953	Mother / May she rest in peace O' Lord	SMCB022

Last Name	First Name	Middle Name	Date of Birth	Date of Death	Transcription / Notes	Cemetery Code
Brown	Mary	Mason	Jan. 16, 1907	Jan. 8, 1993		SMT001
Brown	Mary	Viola	1915	1940		NSP229
Brown	Mary	G.	1924	1986		OSM112
Brown	McLain		1865	1930		NJB113
Brown	Melvin		1959	2002	Thornton Funeral Home Marker	SCA042
Brown	Muriel	A.	1902	1938	Information is from the Historical Society Research located at the College of Southern MD, LaPlata, MD	SMINoStone
Brown	Nannie	C.	Dec. 25, 1918	Dec. 31, 1975		SHI156
Brown	Naomi		1915	1982	Montgomery Brothers Funeral Home Marker	MHB129
Brown	Odean	E.	1904	1985		SHI106
Brown	Oma	C.	Feb. 1, 1893	Mar. 9, 1979	d/o Belle S. and John M. Boarman	SIC3089
Brown	P.	D.	No Date	No Date	Information is from the Historical Society Research located at the College of Southern MD, LaPlata, MD, and the 1984 church cemetery transcription list	SICNoStone
Brown	Parron	H.	Feb. 1879	No Date	Date is from 1900 census / He is the s/o James & Elizabeth Brown per 1920 census / info is from ancestry.com	SHI109
Brown	Paul	Dennis	1892	1974		SIC6078
Brown	Rebecca		No Date	Feb. 4, 1970	Info is from church records	SHINoStone
Brown	Rex	A.	Jul. 10, 1910	Sep. 25, 1981		NSP405
Brown	Robert	S.	No Date	Oct. 20, 1975	Aged 18 years / Information is from the Historical Society Research located at the College of Southern MD, LaPlata, MD	SMINoStone
Brown	Robert		No Date	May 16, 1966	Info is from church records	SHINoStone
Brown	Roland	Cecil	May 15, 1942	Dec. 10, 1980		SCL3350
Brown	Rosie	M.	Jan. 11, 1897	Apr. 4, 1963		ZBC145
Brown	Russell		No Date	No Date	Funeral Home Marker	SCA133
Brown	Sally		Apr. 28, 1788	Dec. 28, 1849	In Memory of / w/o Gustavus Brown (flat stone elevated on cinder blocks)	HDV017
Brown	Samuel		No Date	Nov. 16, 1924	Info is from church records	SHINoStone
Brown	Sarah		No Date	Mar. 31, 1937	Mother / Age 92	SCA016
Brown	Thelma	V.	May 30, 1944	Oct. 10, 1949		SCL3352

Last Name	First Name	Middle Name	Date of Birth	Date of Death	Transcription / Notes	Cemetery Code
Brown	Thomas		No Date	Mar. 6, 1908	Right bottom of stone is broken off	SCL3103
Brown	Thomas	E.	Feb. 13, 1920	Aug. 2, 1984	Loving memories / Agnes Davis	ZWU007
Brown, Sr.	Thomas	F.	1936	1993	In Loving Memory	SMY2020
Brown	Virgile		Nov. 25, 1912	Oct. 26, 1994	Info is from church records	SHINoStone
Brown	Walter	A.	Sep. 11, 1937	No Date	In loving memory	SAC3012
Brown, Sr.	William	A.	Nov. 14, 1909	Sep. 21, 1979		SMC2051
Brown	William	E.	May 22, 1922	Apr. 9, 1992		SHI036
Brown	William	H.	No Date	No Date	Age 53 yrs	POM038
Brown	William	Vincent	No Date	Nov. 1927	Age 15 / info is from church records	SHINoStone
Brown	William		Aug. 14, 1823	Jul. 13, 1882	Sacred to the memory of / Born in the Parish of Urgust in the north of Scotland	NJB413
Brown	Willie	Mae	1926	1971		SPL3061
Brown	William		Jul. 3, 1930	No Date	Info is from Christ Church microfilm Reel 3, Pg 236-237 located at the College of Southern MD, LaPlata, MD)	MTRNoStone
Brown-Travers	Dorothy	H.	Dec. 8, 1912	Aug. 29, 1998	Ancestry.com shows her birth year as 1911 and she is listed as Dorothy H. Travers	POM097
Bruce	Arnim	R. C.	May 29, 1923	Aug. 30, 1983	Verse on stone: To those leaning on the sustaining infinite, Today is big with blessing rest in peace / Our precious pearl of great price. An example in loving. Rest in Peace / Back of Stone: "Love is like a resting place. A shelter from the storm. It exceeds to give you comfort. It is fur to keep you warm. And Ev'n though skies are troubled when you are most alone. The memory of love will bring you home."	MTR2214
Bruce	John	Fergusson	No Date	Feb. 14, 1903	s/o William H. and Constance J. Bruce (stone is broken)	MTR2141
Bruce	Miguel	Angel	Sep. 6, 1989	Jul. 30, 1990	To Heaven is a star shining for you	MTR2218

Last Name	First Name	Middle Name	Date of Birth	Date of Death	Transcription / Notes	Cemetery Code
Bruce	Pearl	P. B.	Sep. 15, 1935	Dec. 15, 1981	Verse on stone: To those leaning on the sustaining infinite, Today is big with blessing rest in peace / Our precious pearl of great price. An example in loving. Rest in Peace...Back of Stone: "Love is like a resting place. A shelter from the storm. It exceeds to give you comfort. It is fur to keep you warm. And Ev'n though skies are troubled when you are most alone. The memory of love will bring you home."	MTR2214
Brunk	Edna Mae	Leland	Aug. 29, 1910	Jun. 16, 1984	Do not stand by my grave and cry I am not there - I did not die - I live with the risen Lord / dates are from ancestry.com	CHR269
Brunk	Owen	K.	No Date	Apr. 12, 1991	Cremated, Not buried in cemetery (info is from church records)	CHRNoStone
Brunner	Dean	Jerome	Oct. 8, 1965	Apr. 24, 1981	Only the good die young	SAC2104
Bryan	Alexander	M.	1852	1927		SJE143
Bryan	Alexander	M.	1907	1968		SCL1205
Bryan	Carolyn	Sue	Oct. 29, 1969	Jan. 6, 1970		NSP386
Bryan	Dorothy	H.	Jun. 2, 1909	Sep. 30, 1997	Nee Mary Blair Pryor Walker Zimmer	SCL1207
Bryan	Ella	Clagett	1854	1902		SJE144
Bryan	George	K.	1890	1953		ODE293
Bryan	George	R.	1849	1937		SJE138
Bryan	Hester	B.	1898	1977		ODE293
Bryan	Jimmy		Feb. 27, 1947	Apr. 28, 1957	Our Darling	NSP440
Bryan	John	Richard	Mar. 13, 1874	Mar. 8, 1956		SJE139
Bryan	Nannie	Truman, Chapman	Dec. 12, 1899	Nov. 27, 1993	"True"	MTR1225
Bryan	Oliver	N.	Jul. 4, 1820	Jul. 11, 1891		SJE160
Bryan	Richard	W.	Oct. 30, 1818	Apr. 23, 1889	In memory of	SJE161
Bryan	Robert	Edward	Nov. 27, 1893	Jul. 29, 1965	Maryland SFC 489 Aero Const Sq WW I	MTR1225
Bryan	Sarah	Ann, Dement.	Dec. 3, 1813	Apr. 26, 1894	In memory of / Mary E. Briscoe was her sister / w/o Richard W. Bryan / addt'l info is from J. Richard Rivoire Jul 2009	SJE162
Bryan	Sue	L.	1880	1919		SJE138

Last Name	First Name	Middle Name	Date of Birth	Date of Death	Transcription / Notes	Cemetery Code
Bryan	Wilhelmina		1849	1891	w/o George R. Bryan	SJE138
Bryan	Wm.	Clagett	1875	1954		SJE142
Bryan, Jr.	William	Zachary	Aug. 4, 2003	Aug. 31, 2003	Green Funeral Home Marker	NJB288
Bryant, Jr.	Albert	Franklin	Feb. 7, 1944	Feb. 19, 2002		NSP118
Bryant	Alice	Cooksey	Nov. 23, 1930	No Date		CHR300
Bryant	E.	Camalier	Mar. 10, 1923	Oct. 12, 1994	Co. C 186th Engr, Combat Bn. TEC5 US Army World War II	CHR300
Bryant	Edgar	F.	Jan. 5, 1861	Dec. 1, 1940	In Loving Memory	CHR335
Bryant	Fred	W.	Aug. 11, 1913	May 1979	Funeral home marker is laying on top of another stone. According to Christ Epis. Ch. Records he is buried in NW lot 41 site 4 / info is from church records and web site familysearch.org	MTR3143
Bryant	Gladys		No Date	No Date	A rock marks the spot / info is from church records	PGN035
Bryant	Lorenzo	O.	1869	1937		NJB194
Bryant	Martha	M.	Aug. 10, 1895	Sep. 15, 1930		SJO2107
Bryant	Mary	O.	1870	1948		NJB194
Bryant	Nancy	L.	May 11, 1965	No Date	Beloved d/o Camalier & Alice Bryant	CHR304
Bryant	William	J.	Jun. 29, 1907	Oct. 8, 1964		NJB193
Bryniczka	Harriett	Iris	Jul. 18, 1915	Oct. 2, 1987	2nd Lt US Army WWII	CMX1139
Buchanan	Gilbert	Marvin	Feb. 18, 1935	Nov. 28, 1994	PFC US Army	NZN023
Buchanan	Gladys	L.	Jul. 25, 1908	Jul. 1, 1986		NZN038
Buchanan	Lorraine	Mary	Sep. 1, 1944	Sep. 30, 1997	Beloved wife	NZN022
Buchanan	Michael	Roy	Nov. 23, 1962	Jul. 15, 1991	Forever in our hearts till we meet again	NZN039
Buchanan	Robert	P.	Dec. 19, 1932	Jun. 6, 1933		NZN024
Buchanan	Unknown		No Date	Sep. 21, 1960	s/o W. R. B. & Norma Lee B. (info is from Christ Church microfilm Reel 4 Pg 280-281 located at the College of Southern MD, LaPlata, MD)	MTRNoStone
Buchanan	William	K.	Aug. 21, 1936	Sep. 2, 1936		NZN025
Buchanan	William	R.	Nov. 27, 1910	May 21, 1984		NZN037
Buchholtz	Ann	L.	1886	1961		ODE064
Buck	Florence	M.	1896	1956		MTR3110
Buck	George	E.	1925	1946		MTR3112

Last Name	First Name	Middle Name	Date of Birth	Date of Death	Transcription / Notes	Cemetery Code
Buck	Kenneth	O.	1917	1954		MTR3111
Buck	Oliver	G.	1894	1970		MTR3109
Buckler	Andrew	C.	Apr. 8, 1911	May 10, 1975	Together forever	NSP1023
Buckler	Beatrice	I.	Oct. 28, 1926	No Date		SMC4182
Buckler	Blanche	L.	1907	1967		OFE3003
Buckler	Brenda	K.	Jul. 16, 1955	No Date	Married Feb 25, 1972	SAC4074A
Buckler	Edward	Dominic	Feb. 10, 1924	May 14, 1975		SMC1265
Buckler	F.	Edna	Jan. 11, 1916	Mar. 29, 1997	Together forever	NSP1023
Buckler	Florence	L.	Apr. 3, 1882	Oct. 22, 1965		SMCD210
Buckler	Frances	M.	Jun. 27, 1918	May 20, 1986	May she rest in peace	SMC1239
Buckler	Francis	E.	Nov. 6, 1874	Apr. 21, 1901	s/o Wm. A. and Mary J. Buckler (info is from the Historical Society Research and the 1940 DAR book pg 184 located at the College of Southern MD, LaPlata, MD.	SMCNoStone
Buckler	George	W.	Oct. 6, 1876	Nov. 17, 1953		SMCD209
Buckler, Sr.	Henry	L.	1919	1993	Married Jan 22, 1943	SMC4167
Buckler	James	P.	1904	1970		OFE3003
Buckler	James	R.	Aug. 28, 1947	Oct. 11, 2003		SMC4168
Buckler	John	A.	Oct. 5, 1949	Oct. 27, 1997	Married Feb 25, 1972	SAC4074A
Buckler	Joseph	Carroll	Oct. 5, 1941	May 18, 1948	Son of Mr and Mrs. Edward Buckler	SMCD315
Buckler	Josephine	E.	Feb. 14, 1955	Jan. 29, 1989	Sister / In God's care / Beloved Daughter & Mother	NSP1022
Buckler	Kelly	Jo	1945	No Date		SMC2085
Buckler	Kenneth	O.	1942	1991		SMC2085
Buckler	Margaret	R.	1925	1998	Married Jan 22, 1943	SMC4167
Buckler	Martin	W.	Jun. 4, 1917	Jan. 20, 1998	Lt Col US Air Force WWII Korea Vietnam	SMC1135
Buckler	Mary	J.	Sep. 1, 1837	Dec. 25, 1899	w/o Wm. A. Buckler / info is from the Historical Society Research and the 1940 DAR book pg 184 located at the College of Southern MD, LaPlata, MD.	SMCNoStone
Buckler	Mary	Roseann	Mar. 27, 1951	Dec. 20, 1952		SMCD316
Buckler	Maurice	R.	Jun. 1, 1919	Oct. 1, 1938		SMCD208
Buckler	Norma	L.	1922	1994		SMC1134
Buckler	Perry	A.	Apr. 8, 1922	May 24, 1985	At rest	SMC1238

Last Name	First Name	Middle Name	Date of Birth	Date of Death	Transcription / Notes	Cemetery Code
Buckler	Phillip	X.	Dec. 2, 1926	Nov. 15, 1973	Beloved husband & father	SMC1262
Buckler	Thomas	L.	Jan. 7, 1924	Jun. 1, 1988		SMC4182
Buckler	Vincent	M.	1919	1989		SMC1134
Buckley	Agnes	R.	1893	1988		SIG021
Buckley	Frances		1908	1963		OFE2101
Buckley	James	M.	1880	1963		SIG021
Buckley	L.	Ralph	1903	1970		OFE2101
Buckley	Rosemary	Conay	Mar. 30, 1897	Feb. 4, 1985	In Loving Memory	MTR3046
Budd	Artimacia	T.	No Date	Aug. 19, 1862	In memory of / who departed this life on the 19th day of August 1862 in the 84th year of her age. A faithful good wife and a sincere friend, the like of herself you seldom can find. The poor or afflicted no'er to her door, to go away hungry because they were poor. A mistress most kind to her servants and thine. You could always depend on her as a friend but like the rest of us, she is gone home to that goal where no traveler comes from. God rest her sole. / Footstone: A. T. B.	BUD004
Budd	Clara	M.	May 16, 1868	Aug. 5, 1939	May she rest in peace	SIC2135A
Budd	John	G.	Feb. 28, 1862	Dec. 18, 1936		SAC2038
Budd	Joseph	A.	Sep. 20, 1861	Mar. 25, 1915	Rest in Peace	SIC2135A
Budd	William		No Date	Jun. 8, 1840	In memory of / who departed this life Monday / in the 57th year of his age / Footstone: W. B.	BUD002
Buddecke	Mary	Isabelle, Brawner	Nov. 17, 1862	Mar. 23, 1896	Beloved w/o Geo. Douglas Buddecke	SJO3098
Bugin, Sr.	Edward		Apr. 23, 1923	Jul. 8, 1994		SMC4164
Bugin	Julia	M.	Jan. 24, 1925	Feb. 1, 2007		SMC4163
Bujarski	Severin	E.	Feb. 1, 1920	Jan. 14, 2003	EMI US Navy WWII SKI IWO JIMA	SJO1103
Bullis	Blanche	V.	1901	1983		CMX2032
Bullis	Opal	M.	1928	No Date		CMX2031
Bullis	Shirley	L.	1938	1985		CMX2032
Bullock	Madeline	Rison	Nov. 1, 1924	Mar. 9, 1946	Absent not dead	NJB513
Bullock	Rosie	Bowman	Jan. 28, 1920	Jun. 14, 1962		SMI050
Bundy	Norma	Jones	Nov. 15, 1929	Mar. 21, 1989	One worthy of remembrance	SJO1071

Last Name	First Name	Middle Name	Date of Birth	Date of Death	Transcription / Notes	Cemetery Code
Bunnell	David	R.	Dec. 31, 1933	Nov. 13, 2005	In loving memory	NJB306
Bunnell	Eileen	A.	Sep. 23, 1937	No Date	In loving memory	NJB306
Burch	A.	Louise	1920	1991	Together forever	SMC2186
Burch	Amelia	Josephine, Mudd	Feb. 22, 1832	Jan. 28, 1872	w/o Wm. Mason Burch / info is from the Historical Society Research and the 1940 DAR book pg 200 located at the College of Southern MD, LaPlata, MD. (matched this stone to the date for Amelia Burch	SMCC031
Burch	Augustine		No Date	Aug. 6, 1834	IHS / Sacred to the memory of AUGUSTINE BURCH who departed this life Aug't 6, 1834 In the 56th year of his age. / May the Lord be merciful to him	SMCW014
Burch	Augustine	Oliver	Jan. 30, 1781	Jun. 10, 1861	s/o Justinian & Bethethland Dade Burch / erected 1953 replacing original stones / aged 80y, 4m, 10d / May he rest in peace	TRI114
Burch	Austin	Miles	Aug. 22, 1846	Sep. 9, 1910	"Beloved Farewell"	OSP040
Burch	B.	La-Vega	May 7, 1855	Jun. 23, 1898		SIC4020
Burch	Babe		Feb. 19, 1890	Feb. 26, 1890	Our Babe / s/o J W & Carrie Burch	SMCA087
Burch	Bernard		Oct. 31, 1889	Oct. 22, 1965		SMCC049
Burch	Betty	Lucille	Aug. 17, 1940	Nov. 11, 1977		SJO4058
Burch	C.	Alene	1877	1963		SMCC041
Burch	Caroline	T.	No Date	Jun. 30, 1887	w/o James M Burch / Aged 70 / info is from the Historical Society Research and the 1940 DAR book pg 193, at the College of Southern MD, LaPlata, MD.	SMCNoStone
Burch	Catherine	C.	1912	1993	May they rest in peace	SIC7085
Burch	Charles	E.	1907	1957		NSP871
Burch, Jr.	Christine	H.	Oct. 20, 1933	No Date	Our Father which art in heaven	NSP974
Burch	Clarence	V.	1916	1984	Father	NSP1019
Burch	D.	Ewell	1864	1952	Rock of Ages / "I have fought a good fight. I have finished my course. I have kept the faith."	TRI053
Burch, Jr.	David	Leroy	Jul. 16, 1961	May 9, 1970		NSP981
Burch, Sr.	David	Leroy	Jan. 6, 1937	Dec. 1, 1997		NSP980
Burch	E.	Lucille	1909	1988		SMCA206

Last Name	First Name	Middle Name	Date of Birth	Date of Death	Transcription / Notes	Cemetery Code
Burch	Eberta	May	No Date	Sep. 18, 1917	In memory of / Beloved w/o J.C. Burch / Loved in life, in death remembered.	SPL1027
Burch	Edward	B.	1898	1909		SMCA206
Burch	Edward	Edelen	Jan. 16, 1860	Jan. 15, 1952	Info is from the Maryland Independent Newspaper Fri. Jan 18, 1952) (s/o Franklin Burch; h/o Mary Steward Welch	SICNoStone
Burch	Edward	W.	1916	1999	Together forever	SMC2186
Burch	Elizabeth	Ida	1853	1933		SMCC028
Burch	Elizabeth		No Date	Aug. 18, 1853	w/o Benjamin F. Burch / in the 35th year of her age / info is from the Historical Society Research and the 1940 DAR book pg 200 located at the College of Southern MD, LaPlata, MD.	SMCNoStone
Burch	Elmer	E.	1896	1920		SMCA206
Burch	Emily	T.	Feb. 5, 1841	Feb. 20, 1916	J. Marine Burch / His wife / Rest In Peace	SMCE023
Burch	Emma	B.	Jun. 24, 1888	Sep. 11, 1974	d/o James M. and Caroline Burch / info is from the Historical Society Research and the 1940 DAR book pg 193, at the College of Southern MD, LaPlata, MD.	SPL1017
Burch	Emma	T.	Mar. 11, (?)	Jan. 15, 1870		SMCNoStone
Burch	Ernest	E.	1872	1920		SMCA206
Burch	Estelle	Cross	Apr. 11, 1930	May 1, 1996		SIC6060
Burch, Jr.	Francis	A.	Feb. 18, 1922	Jan. 10, 1999		SIC6060
Burch, Sr.	Francis	A.	1890	1964		SIC6058
Burch	Francis	D.	Feb. 18, 1843	Mar. 6, 1879		SMCA083
Burch	George	E.	1904	1973	May they rest in peace	SIC7085
Burch	George	F.	Jul. 31, 1929	Jun. 15, 1979		SMC3185
Burch	George	H.	1870	1909	At Rest	SMCA150
Burch	George	W.	Feb. 22, 1893	Oct. 5, 1975		SMC3193
Burch	George	W.	Jun. 10, 1896	Aug. 13, 1964		NSP445
Burch	Grace	Cecelia	Sep. 15, 1851	Dec. 6, 1922	"Beloved Farewell"	OSP039
Burch	Henry	T.	Dec. 24, 1838	Apr. 13, 1859	IHS / Sacred to the memory of	SMCA114

Last Name	First Name	Middle Name	Date of Birth	Date of Death	Transcription / Notes	Cemetery Code
Burch	Isabel		No Date	Jun. 23, 188	Age 63 / info is from the Historical Society Research and the 1940 DAR book pg 183 located at the College of Southern MD, LaPlata, MD.	SMCNoStone
Burch	J.	Henretta	1840	1909	At Rest	SMCA132
Burch	J.	Marine	Feb. 17, 1837	Sep. 12, 1925	J. Marine Burch / His wife / Emily T. Burch / Rest In Peace	SMCE023
Burch	J.	Regina	Aug. 7, 1896	Nov. 29, 1977		NSP536
Burch	James	Hayden	Oct. 24, 1924	May 29, 1979	Pfc US Army WW II	SIC6059
Burch	James	M.	Jan. 10, 1811	Oct. 20, 1892	In his 82nd year / info is from the Historical Society Research and the 1940 DAR book pg 193 located at the College of Southern MD, LaPlata, MD.	SMCNoStone
Burch	James		Oct. 21, 1892	Nov. 6, 1892	s/o Jas W and Carrie Burch	SMCA086
Burch	James		1845	1919	At rest	SMCA085
Burch	Jane	B.	Jun. 6, 1806	Jan. 10, 1864	Aged 57y, 7m, 5d / Why lament departed friends or shake at death's alarms, death's but the servant Jesus sends to call us to his arms	TRI117
Burch	Jane	Millar	1877	Dec. 1879	Info is from church records, buried Dec 28, 1879. Note: b. 1877; d. Dec 1879; d/o John Alexander & Mary Wood Burch	TRINoStone
Burch	Jennie	G.	1904	1986		SAC1149
Burch	Jennings	Ewell	May 27, 1905	Jun. 24, 1960	Pennsylvania, PFC, US Army, WWII.	TRI058
Burch	Jeremiah	Walter	No Date	Apr. 20, 1875	To Our Parents / in his 68th year / and his wife Maria Dorothy Burch / in her 57th year / In loving remembrance by their daughter Anna M. Hughes	SMCE039
Burch	Jesse	C.	Aug. 21, 1869	Jul. 18, 1953		SPL1018
Burch	John	Alexander	1824	1908	h/o Mary Wood Cartwright	TRI119
Burch	John	Patrick	Oct. 27, 1931	Feb. 1, 1968	Maryland AA US Navy	SMC3186
Burch	John	Russell	Mar. 13, 1935	Nov. 3, 2005		SIC6061
Burch	John	Kelly	Jul. 9, 1976	Oct. 25, 1994		SMY2080
Burch	Jonnie		No Date	No Date	Aged 3 yrs. (located in Burch Plot)	SIC4022
Burch	Joseph	A.	1919	1984	Father	SMC1105
Burch	Joseph	B.	1914	1979		SMC2184
Burch	Joseph	L.	Jul. 24, 1934	No Date	Our Father which art in heaven	NSP974

Last Name	First Name	Middle Name	Date of Birth	Date of Death	Transcription / Notes	Cemetery Code
Burch	Joseph	S.	1893	1963		SAC1149
Burch	Justinian		1742	1805	In honor of Revolutionary War Patriot / dedicated May 27, 1993 Port Tobacco Chapter DAR / Burch lot-burial site unknown.	TRI1112
Burch	Leo	Franklin	Sep. 9, 1928	Jan. 16, 1976		SMY2079
Burch	Lewis	Norbert	1908	1973	TEC 5 US Army WW II	OFE3039
Burch					d/o Wm Mason and Amelia Josephine Burch / info is from the Historical Society Researchand the 1940 DAR book pg 200 located at the College of Southern MD, LaPlata, MD.	SMCNoStone
Burch	Lizzie		May 3, 1870	May 4, 1883		SMCA143
Burch	Louis	.	1878	1958		SMC2184
Burch	Lucy	Dyer	No Date	No Date		WIL007
Burch	M.	A.	No Date	Sep. 9, 1909	d/o Dr. Francis R and Katherine Wills / age 75 Rest in Peace	TRI053
Burch	M.	Servilla	1869	1927	Rock of Ages / w/o D. Ewell Burch	SMCW003
Burch	Mabel		Sep. 1896	Sep. 1896	Infant d/o J.W. & MARY C. Burch Age 6 Months	HGH4280
Burch	Margaret	Lloyd	Jul. 27, 1916	May 11, 2003		SMC1120
Burch	Margaret	R., Howe	Apr. 6, 1906	Apr. 21, 1984	To Our Parents / Jeremiah Walter Burch in his 68th year / and his wife / in her 57th year / In loving remembrance by their daughter Anna M. Hughes	SMCE039
Burch	Maria	Dorothy	No Date	Apr. 12, 1876		SMCA073
Burch	Martha		No Date	No Date	Mother	SMCC029
Burch	Mary	C.	Feb. 9, 1869	Feb. 15, 1924	Eldest d/o Wm Mason & Josephine Mudd Burch / Requiescat in pace	SMCA078
Burch	Mary	C.	May 27, 1856	Jan. 14, 1898	IHS / Beloved w/o James W. Burch / aged 42 years / May her soul rest in peace	SMCA206
Burch	Mary	E.	1874	1950		SIC6058
Burch	Mary	E.	1900	1977		SMY2079
Burch	Mary	Elsie	Oct. 6, 1934	No Date		SMC3194
Burch	Mary	M.	Dec. 4, 1906	Nov. 7, 1993		
Burch	Mary	S. Welch	No Date	Jan. 26, 1908	Beloved w/o Edward E. Burch / age 41 years / She leaves 6 girls & 2 boys to mourn her death	SIC4045
Burch	Mary	Wood Cartwright	1840	1892	w/o John Alexander Burch	TRI119

Last Name	First Name	Middle Name	Date of Birth	Date of Death	Transcription / Notes	Cemetery Code
Burch	Mattie	C.	1881	1953	Info is from church records	SMCA143
Burch	Mildred		No Date	May 6, 1927		MTRNoStone
Burch	Myra	G.	Dec. 13, 1966	No Date	Bobby / In Loving Memory / Wed May 27, 1989	SIG104
Burch	Nannie	M.	Aug. 24, 1853	May 30, 1925	His wife	SIC4020
Burch	Oliver		1713	1795	In honor of Revolutionary War Patriot / dedicated May 27, 1993 Port Tobacco Chapter DAR / Burch lot--burial site unknown	TRI113
Burch	Paul	C.	Dec. 27, 1894	Jun. 24, 1919	To my beloved husband / Blessed are the dead who die in the Lord, Even so saith the Spirit for they rest from their labor.	SPL1026
Burch	Rebecca	Wood	Apr. 17, 1786	Dec., 1866	d/o Benjamin & Jeane Wood / Erected 1953 replacing original stones / In the 82nd year of her age / "Dearest mother thou hast left us. We'e thy loss most deeply felt. But it's God that hath bereat us. He can all our sorrows heal".	TRI114
Burch	Richard	Hamilton	May 22, 1909	Dec. 27, 1950	In memory of	SMCA268
Burch	Robert	E.	Jul. 2, 1963	Jan. 14, 2005	Bobby / In Loving Memory / Wed May 27, 1989	SIG104
Burch	Rose	P.	1917	1995	Mother	NSP1019
Burch	Rose		1816	1903	At Rest	SMCA116
Burch	Russell	A.	No Date	No Date	Information is from the 1984 church cemetery transcription list	SICNoStone
Burch	Sandra	Clapp	Jun. 19, 1940	No Date		SIC6061
Burch	Sarah	Ann, S.	No Date	Oct. 25, 1852	IHS / Sacred to the memory of / w/o Rob't L. Burch who departed this life / in the 40th year of her age	SMCC044
Burch	Sarah	F.	1853	1890	At rest	SMCA085
Burch	Stanislous	Kostka	Mar. 15, 1886	Sep. 19, 1962		SMCC040
Burch	Stephen		No Date	No Date	Father	SMCA073
Burch	Susanna	D.	No Date	Feb. 25, 1846	IHS / Sacred to the memory of SUSANNA D.Wife of Aug'ste BURCH who departed this life Feb 25, 1846 In the 63d year of her age. / May the lord be merciful to her.	SMCW016
Burch	T.	Damian	Sep. 9, 1968	Apr. 8, 1970	Son	SIC1094
Burch, Sr.	Thomas	Benjamin	Jul. 30, 1910	Mar. 21, 1989		HGH4280

Last Name	First Name	Middle Name	Date of Birth	Date of Death	Transcription / Notes	Cemetery Code
Burch	Theresa	E, Lyon	No Date	Dec. 27, 1917	Beloved w/o Basil Burch / aged 78 years / R.I.P	SMCA205
Burch	Thomas	F.	No Date	Oct. 9, 1860	In memory of / aged 38 years old	OFE4061
Burch	Thomas	R.	Mar. 11, 1837	Nov. 14, 1899		SMCA130
Burch	Unknown			Jul. 16, 1882	Child of Mr. and Mrs. Thomas Burch / info is from church records	OFENoStone
Burch	William	E.	1840	1921	At Rest	SMCA132
Burch	William		1813	1876	At Rest	SMCA116
Burdette	Emma	Jones	1876	1957		MTR2138
Burdette	Eunice	Eveline	1903	1988		MTR2138
Burdette	John	Purdum	1868	1945		MTR2138
Burdick	Dixon	C.	Sep. 17, 1914	Jul. 22, 1969	Captain USNR WW II	SMC4191
Burdick	Mary	King	Dec. 14, 1912	Jul. 1, 1988	Social Worker	SMC4190
Burg	Katharine	Schoenbeck	Sep. 20, 1897	Jan. 9, 1919	w/o Simon Burg	SMCA225
Burgess, Jr.	Alton	Parker	Feb. 14, 1936	Dec. 18, 1953		ODE268
Burgess, Sr.	Alton	Parker	Oct. 5, 1904	Jul. 20, 1970		ODE269
Burgess	Angelica		No Date	No Date	Sacred to the memory of	BUR001
Burgess	Cora	I.	Mar. 14, 1862	Apr. 9, 1925	Beloved w/o James T. Burgess / At rest	PIS240
Burgess	Eleanor	Wilcox	1913	2000		ODE471
Burgess	Elsie	V., Shelton	Jul. 9, 1902	Jun. 15, 1995	Under his name it says: A.E.R. Veteran WW I, France CO B. 20th Engineers Under her name it says: Faithful wife for 73 years and devoted mother	ODE467
Burgess	Emma	J.	Jul. 31, 1874	Jul. 23, 1942		ODE434
Burgess	Francis	B. F.	Mar. 15, 1868	Nov. 16, 1935		ODE434
Burgess	Francis	Earl	1914	2002		ODE471
Burgess	Franklin	C.	Sep. 14, 1893	Jan. 17, 1957		ODE435
Burgess	Irene	Garnett, Jennison	Sep. 26, 1939	Jul. 27, 2003	After Glow Poem by Helen Lowrie Marshall is on back of stone	BFM001
Burgess	Jane	Young	Aug. 19, 1859	Apr. 5, 1944	d/o Hon. Francis B. F. and Elizabeth Young Burgess	ODE258
Burgess	John		No Date	Feb. 27, 1845	In memory of / who departed this life / In the 73rd year of his age	BUP006
Burgess	Jordan	Louis	Jan. 21, 2003	May 16, 2003		NZN040
Burgess	Marian	Hancock	Apr. 30, 1913	Nov. 24, 2004		ODE409

Last Name	First Name	Middle Name	Date of Birth	Date of Death	Transcription / Notes	Cemetery Code
Burgess, Jr.	Richard	Archie	Dec. 5, 1933	Mar. 15, 2000	After Glow Poem by Helen Lowrie Marshall is on back of stone	BFM001
Burgess, Sr.	Richard	Archie	May 13, 1911	Apr. 7, 1992		ODE409
Burgess	Teresa		1777	Sep. 28, 1861	Info is from Port Tobacco Times Vol. XVIII No. 24 dated Oct 10, 1861	SIGNo Stone
Burgess	Thomas	Alexander	Oct. 15, 1795	Oct. 11, 1861	Age 66 /Info is from Port Tobacco Times Vol. XVIII, No. 30 dated Nov. 23, 1861.	SIGNo Stone
Burgess	Viola	Dent	Jun. 23,1913	Nov. 30, 2001		MHB011
Burgess	Wilfred	Clayton	Jan. 20, 1896	Dec. 25, 1999	Under his name it says: A.E.R. Veteran WW I, France CO B. 20th Engineers Under her name it says: Faithful wife for 73 years and devoted mother	ODE467
Burgess	William	F.	No Date	Sep. 30, 1841	In memory of / who departed this life / In the 27th year of his age. How short the race our friend has run. Cut down in all his bloom. His course but yesterday begun, Now finished in the tomb. / Footstone with initials W. F. B.	BUP002
Burke	Anna	Augusta	Aug. 21, 1905	Jul. 14, 2002		HGH4165
Burke	Robert	Emmett	Apr. 13, 1917	Oct. 24, 1982	BMC US Navy	HGH4166
Burke	Robert	W.	Dec. 12, 1988	Jul. 16, 1993	Beloved grandson of Mary Flint Forster	SAC2068
Burke	Theresa	M.	Feb. 28, 1933	Dec. 30, 2002	Facchina	SJO4003
Burke	John	L.	Dec. 23, 1932	Jan. 5, 2004		SJO4003
Burko	Gladys	B.	Oct. 26, 1922	Feb. 3, 1980		HGH4070
Burleson	Altia	L.	Apr. 14, 1913	Nov. 5, 2002		ZBC012
Burleson, Jr.	William	J.	Apr. 8, 1947	May 12, 1987		ZBC012
Burleson, Sr.	William	J.	Apr. 12, 1914	Feb. 9, 1994		ZBC012
Burnett	Anna	E.	Mar. 1, 1928	Jan. 24, 1989		MTR4259
Burnett	Cecil	G.	Sep. 9, 1916	Mar. 23, 1992		MTR4259
Burnett	Gary	Cecil	1946	1964		MTR4258
Burnham	George	Byron	Sep.t 19, 1894	Feb. 6, 1981		OFE3028
Burnham	Harry	W.	Jun. 2, 1909	Aug. 6, 1961		OFE3034
Burnham	Henry	W.	Nov. 1, 1859	May 6, 1940		OFE3031
Burnham	Kathleen	Warburton	May 5, 1903	Mar. 22, 1987		OFE3030
Burnham	Paul	E.	Jan. 6, 1889	Sep. 19, 1961		OFE3035

Last Name	First Name	Middle Name	Date of Birth	Date of Death	Transcription / Notes	Cemetery Code
Burnham	Sarah	L.	Jan. 10, 1864	Jul. 13, 1940		OFE3032
Burns	Beatrice	L.	Mar. 13, 1907	Mar. 2, 1989	"Abe"	MHB160
Burns	Eva	D. Short	Jun. 23, 1969	Aug. 18, 2007	Loving wife, mother & sister / Back of stone: The Lord watch between me and Thee. While we are absent, one from the other. Genesis 31:49	SJO1115
Burns	George		Apr. 5, 1891	Mar. 9, 1979	"Abe"	MHB160
Burns	Lanny	B.	1864	1941	Mother	MHB187
Burns, Sr.	Larry	E.	Apr. 28, 1957	Apr. 28, 1988	In God's Care	ZBC047
Burrough	Richard	J.	No Date	Feb. 22, 1916	Age 76 / info is from church records	OFENoStone
Burrough, Mrs.	Richard		No Date	Aug. 31, 1899	Info is from church records	OFENoStone
Burroughs	Blanche	G.	1902	1983		SMC2143
Burroughs	Catherine	B.	Mar. 19, 1926	Feb. 3, 1993		SMY3178
Burroughs	Clara	P.	1893	1981		SCL2139
Burroughs	Clarence	R.	1877	1962	Ancestry.com shows b. Sep 1, 1877 d. Jul 21, 1962	CHR079
Burroughs	Daniel	R.	1929	1967	Son	CHR082
Burroughs, Jr.	Dewayne	A.	No Date	Nov. 22, 1977	3 mos. (info is from Historical Society Research located at The College of Southern MD, LaPlata, MD)	SACNostone
Burroughs	Donald	R.	1943	1988	F.N & D.B. / Married Apr 19, 1969	SMC2131
Burroughs	Eugene	S.	1902	1982		SMC2143
Burroughs	George	Amory	No Date	Feb. 26, 1928	Son	CHR076
Burroughs	H.	Bruce	1868	1935		HNT004
Burroughs	Henry	D.	1893	1968		SCL2139
Burroughs	Hortense		No Date	1954	Mother	HGH3091
Burroughs	James		No Date	May 2, 1847	Sacred to the memory of / who departed this life May 2nd 1847, aged 44 years Footstone: J. B. (located behind the church)	CHR614
Burroughs	James		No Date	1927	Father	HGH3091
Burroughs, Jr.	James		Mar. 1, 1948	Jul. 6, 1977		HGH3032
Burroughs	Jane		No Date	Nov. 9, 1846	Sacred to the memory of Jane, w/o James Burroughs who departed this life Nov. 9th 1846 aged 35 years Footstone: J. B. (located behind the church)	CHR612

Last Name	First Name	Middle Name	Date of Birth	Date of Death	Transcription / Notes	Cemetery Code
Burroughs	Joseph	Leonard	Oct. 5, 1900	Jul. 4, 1902	s/o H. Bruce & Laura Huntt Burroughs / First name is from Historical Society Research located at College of Southern MD, LaPlata, MD	HNT006
Burroughs	Laura	Huntt	1874	1965		HNT005
Burroughs	Mary	M.	1904	1966		CHR079
Burroughs	Mary	Posey	1874	1940		SCL3271
Burroughs	Mary	V.	1938	1938	Daughter	CHR078
Burroughs	Walter		1922	1986	Son	HGH3091
Burroughs	Wilson	McKenney	Dec. 2, 1925	Jan. 26, 2007	Son	CHR077
Burton	Allendra		1980	2001	Thornton Funeral Home	SJO1155
Burton	Annie	M.	Aug. 28, 1929	Oct. 26, 1997	In Loving Memory	SCA028
Burton	Catherine	S.	Jan. 28, 1916	Nov. 20, 1973	Mother / stone is sunken	SJO1166
Burton	Charles	W.	Apr. 23, 1964	Jun. 26, 2008	SK 3 US Navy Beloved husband and father	SJO1153
Burton	Hazel	Hancock	Apr. 17, 1917	No Date		LUM221
Burton	Hazel	Marie, Shillingburg	Nov. 14, 1920	Oct. 5, 2007		LUM117
Burton, Jr.	Joseph	Leroy	Jan. 4, 1963	Jul. 23, 2005	AM2 US Navy Persian Gulf, Operation Desert Storm	SJO1154
Burton, Sr.	Joseph	Leroy	Nov. 3, 1936	Sep. 12, 2009	Age 72 / s/o the late Walter and Late Catherine Burton / info is from Maryland Independent Newspaper Wed. Sep 16, 2009	SJONoStone
Burton	Robert	Blaine	Aug. 26, 1918	Sep. 7, 2001	"Bob"	LUM117
Burton	Shermica	Latasha	Sep. 16, 1977	Jul. 3, 1986	Daughter / "Our Golden Child"	SJO1157
Burton	William	Stanton	Jul. 28, 1916	Jun. 5, 2006		LUM221
Burttes	James	N.	No Date	Apr. 13, 1879	Info is from church records	OFENoStone
Burttes	Sarah		No Date	Jun. 30, 1905	Info is from church records	OFENoStone
Burttes	Thomas		No Date	May 27, 1895	Info is from church records	OFENoStone
Bury	Benedict	C.	Feb. 27, 1902	Nov. 26, 1962		LUM056
Bush	Agnes	V.	Dec. 7, 1888	Jan. 26, 1960		SCL1173
Bush	Brenda	Ann, Edelen	Mar. 9, 1959	Feb. 9, 1991	In loving memory	SMC1138
Bush, III	Charles	H.	1960	1994		SAC5033
Bush, Jr.	Charles	H.	Aug. 5, 1942	Mar. 18, 1996		SAC5034
Bush	Dorothy	E.	Mar. 3, 1943	No Date		SAC5034

Last Name	First Name	Middle Name	Date of Birth	Date of Death	Transcription / Notes	Cemetery Code
Bush	Elizabeth		No Date	Jul. 4, 1906		SIC5023
Bush	George	C.	Oct. 24, 1884	Sep. 17, 1963		SCL1173
Bush	George	Cecil	Mar. 9, 1918	Oct. 6, 1980	F2 US Navy WW II	SCL1172
Bush	Harriet		No Date	Nov. 29, 1900		SIC5023
Bush	Jane		1828	Jan. 27, 1902	R.I.P.	SIC4097
Bush	Martha		No Date	Jun. 9, 1909		SIC5023
Bush	Mary	G.	No Date	Jul. 11, 1910		SIC5023
Bush	Mary	Veronica	May 21, 1919	Aug. 12, 1993		SCL1171
Bush	Theresa		No Date	Jul. 4, 1906		SIC5023
Bush	Wm		1823	Jan. 5, 1897	R.I.P.	SIC4097
Bushee	William	Robert	Dec. 14, 1936	Apr. 10, 1992	PFC US Army	SCL1258
Busser	Mauri		Aug. 26, 1962	Dec. 24, 1982	Back of Stone: Be Yourself / I was blind but now I see all the foolish things people pretend to be. As I grow older and start to understand, the more I want to be an independent woman. All my life I can truly say I've been myself in every way. I'm not trying to do myself as thee. I'm doing all right just being me. By M. Mauri	SAC2134
Buster, Sr.	Freddie	W.	1939	2000		SCA029
Bute	Anna	M.	Sep. 21, 1884	May 29, 1959	God Giveth his beloved rest	PIS004
Buteaux	Alexander		Jun. 30, 1873	Sep. 1, 1938		SCL3308
Butler	A.		No Date	No Date	(White Cross)	SAC4098
Butler	Agnes	Briscoe	1921	1985	"Minnie" / Too well loved to ever be forgotten	HGH4199
Butler	Agnes	E.	1908	1933	Old round top stone with metal plate screwed onto front. Info is etched onto metal plate	SCL3381
Butler	Alfred	Lee	Sep. 19, 1894	Sep. 13, 1965	In God's Care	SMC4007
Butler	Alice	B.	1905	1986		SMY3174
Butler	Alice	E.	Apr. 7, 1859	Mar. 2, 1891	Beloved wife of Cornelius I. Butler..May she rest in peace / Presented by Cornelius I. Butler in memory of the Butler Family	SCL2194
Butler	Anna	E.	1915	1988	In loving memory of	HGH4151
Butler	Annie	H.	1876	1950		SCL1244
Butler	Annie		No Date	No Date		ZWU019

Last Name	First Name	Middle Name	Date of Birth	Date of Death	Transcription / Notes	Cemetery Code
Butler	Arthur		Oct. 3, 1906	Jan. 22, 1976	Loving Parents	SMC4069
Butler	Benjamin	J.	Aug. 25, 1911	Apr. 22, 1996		SMC2008
Butler	Benjamin		No Date	Sep. 12, 1880	Info is from church records	OFENoStone
Butler	Bernard	R.	1941	1987		HGH4252
Butler	Bessie	C.	Oct. 16, 1899	Aug. 6, 1919		SCL4077
Butler	Calvin	L.	Feb. 7, 1952	May 6, 1974	PVT US Marine Corps	HGH2028
Butler	Catherine	E.	1919	1998	Mother	SCL1240
Butler	Catherine	Ford	1946	2001	Till we shall meet and never part	SMC4142
Butler	Catherine	Teresa	May 21, 1932	Jun. 30, 1990	St. Theresa / A Loving Family Together Forever	SAC4072
Butler	Cecelia		1927	1984		SJO3359
Butler, Jr.	Charles	A.	Apr. 19, 1970	Feb. 6, 1990		SMC3090
Butler, Sr.	Charles	A.	May 30, 1946	No Date		SMC3091
Butler, Sr.	Charles	E.	Jan. 16, 1911	Apr. 18, 1994		SCL1243
Butler	Charles	H.	No Date	Oct. 7, 1907	Homemade cement base with marker on top	HGH3056
Butler, Sr.	Charles	L.	Mar. 2, 1940	Aug. 2, 2005	Beloved Husband (Buck) Forever in our hearts / In loving memories, your family	PGN076
Butler, Jr.	Charles	S.	Jun. 11, 1938	May 19, 2004		HGH4257
Butler, Sr.	Charles	S	1912	2001	In loving memory	HGH4250
Butler	Charles	W.	Apr. 4, 1881		(Stone is sunken into ground)	NSP281
Butler	Charlotte		No Date	Jun. 5, 1894	Aged 51 years (info is from the 1940 DAR book page 21)	SPLNoStone
Butler	Cornelious		Feb. 22, 1845	Dec. 17, 1918	In memory of our dear father / May he rest in peace by his loving children B.P. & C.B.	SCL1264
Butler	Cos		No Date	Jul. 22, 1951	Age 65 / info is from church records	OFENoStone
Butler	Daniel	T.	Nov. 28, 1942	No Date	Together Forever	SJO1034
Butler	Delephine		No Date	Nov. 2, 1900	Homemade cement base with marker on top	HGH3057
Butler	Elizabeth	Eleanor	Aug. 30, 1939	Feb. 14, 2003	In Loving Memory	SHI090
Butler	Ella	R.	Apr. 19, 1907	May 25, 1989	Mother	SMC1211
Butler	Ellen	M.	Aug. 15, 1807	Dec. 28, 1890	Loving Mother of Cornelius Butler	SCL2196
Butler	Elsie	F.	Aug. 15, 1922	Jul. 18, 1990		SJO1073
Butler	Emma	R.	Jun. 18, 1883	Oct. 10, 1888	Loving child of Cornelius Butler	SCL2195

Last Name	First Name	Middle Name	Date of Birth	Date of Death	Transcription / Notes	Cemetery Code
Butler	Eugene	W.	Jul. 30, 1914	May 13, 1984	US Army WW II	DUD035
Butler	Evelyn	R.	Jul. 13, 1909	Jan. 25, 1961		SHI141
Butler	Florine		Jul. 12, 1919	Jun. 12, 1988	Thornton Funeral Home Marker	SHI188
Butler	Florence	Gertrude	Jan. 3, 1925	Jul. 8, 2004	Mother	SMY2076
Butler	Frances	L.	Sep. 12, 1945	Nov. 15, 2004	Together Forever	SJO1034
Butler, Sr.	Francis	Richard, Xavier	Aug. 28, 1924	Dec. 28, 1995		SCA090
Butler, Sr.	Francis	Robert	Nov. 8, 1924	Apr. 20, 2008	Thornton Funeral Home Marker / age 84 s/o the late Marie Janie Butler and the late Robert Butler. He was in the Navy, h/o Rose Butler / Obit appeared in the Maryland Independent April 25, 2008	PGN084
Butler	Frances	V.	Jan. 17, 1850	Apr. 6, 1916	Mother / R.I.P.	SCL2220
Butler	Francis	J.	May 17, 1957	Nov. 17, 1993		SMC3095
Butler	G.	P.	No Date	Dec. 26, 1941		SHI146
Butler	George	B.	1893	1965		SMY3189
Butler	George	E	1872	1955		SCL1245
Butler	George	T.	May 23, 1941	Jul. 8, 1978		SJO3012
Butler	Gladys	M.	No Date	Aug. 5, 1923	Homemade cement base with marker on top	HGH3059
Butler	Grace	Ann	Mar. 1, 1893	Dec. 7, 1967	In loving memory of our mother	SMC3316
Butler	Hattie		No Date	Oct. 28, 1903	Aged 26 years	POM117
Butler	Helen		No Date	Feb. 1961	Info is from church records	SHINoStone
Butler	Ida		1951	1986	Thornton Funeral Home Marker	OAK194
Butler	Ignatius		1873	1949		SJO1150
Butler	Inez	G., Keys	No Date	Sep. 7, 1933	In God's care / Mother / Trust in God	SIC3100
Butler	Irene	M.	Jul. 18, 1904	Aug. 18, 1971		SJO1074
Butler	Irma	J.	Jul. 30, 1921	Apr. 6, 1995	In God's loving care / Forever in our hearts	PGN044
Butler	J.	Kenny	Feb. 2, 1972	Jul. 23, 1990	Our Beloved Son / Brother in Our Hearts Always	SAC4073
Butler	J.	Samuel	Nov. 18, 1875	Feb. 3, 1964		SCL4079
Butler	James	C.	Feb. 2, 1937	Nov. 16, 1994	Dad	SJO3019
Butler, Sr.	James	C.	Sep. 23, 1909	Feb. 25, 1969	Metal plate attached to stone that is painted blue	SJO3334
Butler	James	C.	Oct. 15, 1936	Dec. 10, 2007	St. Jude / A Loving Family Together Forever	SAC4072
Butler	James	F.	Oct. 9, 1938	Jan. 25, 1989	Rest in peace	NSP110

Last Name	First Name	Middle Name	Date of Birth	Date of Death	Transcription / Notes	Cemetery Code
Butler	James	H.	No Date	Jul. 26, 1935	Age 68 yrs 1 mo 10 dys / large cement base with a cement cross on top	HGH3066
Butler	James	Henry	Jul. 1, 1945	Apr. 7, 2004	In Loving Memory	SHI090
Butler	James	J.	1894	1967		SMY3174
Butler	James	J.	1923	1946		NSP161
Butler	James	L.	May 26, 1907	Jun. 29, 1994		SJO4026
Butler, Sr.	James	V.	Oct. 8, 1918	Jan. 10, 1991		SMY2075
Butler	James	W.	Feb. 27, 1900	Apr. 7, 1970		SJO1075
Butler	Jerry	A.	Oct. 17, 1951	Sep. 18, 2000		HGH4201
Butler	John	A.	Aug. 20, 1806	Feb. 6, 1879	Loving Father of Cornelius Butler	SCL2196
Butler	John	A.	1965	No Date		SMC3293
Butler, Jr.	John	Allen	Apr. 21, 1915	Nov. 21, 1982	In loving memory of our father	SMC3292
Butler	John	Garrett	Jan. 15, 1897	Apr. 9, 1960	Maryland Pvt 16 Co 154 Depot Brigade WW I	SHI189
Butler	John	O.	1906	1987	"Connie"	SIC9020
Butler	John	B.	Sep. 7, 1969	Oct. 24, 2001		SMY2095
Butler	Jorden	Lee	2005	2005	Arehart Funeral Home Marker	HGH1259
Butler	Joseph	Calvin	Mar. 11, 1904	Apr. 29, 1969	Maryland CPL Army Air Forces WW II	SJO1076
Butler	Joseph	E.	Nov. 17, 1935	Jul. 19, 1977	Son & brother	SMC1209
Butler	Joseph	Earl	Jan. 7, 1918	Dec. 10, 1992	In loving memory	SIC9011
Butler	Joseph	L.	1951	1954	Info is from the Historical Society Research located at the College of Southern MD, LaPlata, MD	SICNoStone
Butler	Joseph	M.	1953	1995	On earth / In heaven	SMC4159
Butler	Joseph	N.	Feb. 2, 1901	Sep. 29, 1986		SCL3233
Butler	Joseph	S.	Jul. 19, 1890	Aug. 27, 1971	Maryland PFC US Army World War I	HGH3047
Butler	Joseph	W.	1918	2001	Father	SCL1240
Butler	Joseph		1906	1991	Our trust is in God	NSP998
Butler	Josephine	M.	Jan. 9, 1929	Jan. 19, 1974		SJO3358
Butler	Juanita	M.	1942	1991		SMC4214
Butler	Julia	C.	1887	1981		SAC4099
Butler	Karen	Denise	Jul. 25, 1958	May 2, 1999		HGH4322
Butler	Kenneth	T.	Jan. 6, 1956	Mar. 4, 2006		HGH4202

Last Name	First Name	Middle Name	Date of Birth	Date of Death	Transcription / Notes	Cemetery Code
Butler	Kenneth	V.	Jun. 2, 1933	Aug. 20, 1998	Forever In Our Hearts	SAC4007
Butler	Kervick		No Date	Oct. 4, 1903	Homemade cement base with marker on top	HGH3058
Butler	Landonia	Johnson	Dec. 22, 1937	Sep. 20, 2004		SCA088
Butler	Laura	J.	No Date	Mar. 9, 1915	Loving Memory / w/o J. S. Butler / Aged 38 years / Gone but not forgotten	SCL4078
Butler	Lawrence	DeSales	Oct. 9, 1930	Oct. 30, 1972	s/o Thomas & Mary Butler	SJO3112
Butler	Lawrence	E.	Jul. 29, 1951	May 9, 2008	Loving Son, Father and Pop-Pop	SMC4128
Butler	Lena		Oct. 31, 1915	Oct. 16, 2007	Loving Parents	SMC4069
Butler	Leo		No Date	No Date	Funeral Home Marker	OAK193
Butler	Lillian	Mae	1898	1965	In loving memory of our mother	SJO4191
Butler	Lloyd	W.	1945	1989	Brother	SJO1077
Butler	Louis	DeSales	1945	2002	Till we shall meet and never part	SMC4142
Butler	Louis		May 4, 1926	May 27, 1992	US Army World War II	SMC2039
Butler	Lowndes		1893	1966		HGH3063
Butler	M.	Julia	1869	1950		SJO1150
Butler	Magdalen	R.	Aug. 31, 1947	Jan. 30, 1995		SMY2094
Butler	Mamie	R.	Feb. 13, 1944	Jun. 22, 2007		SMC2019
Butler	Marie	J.	Feb. 15, 1903	Nov. 3, 1994	Gone But not forgotten / Children	PGN043
Butler	Martin	W.	Feb. 14, 1907	Apr. 26, 1986		SJO1073
Butler	Mary	Agnes	Mar. 31, 1892	May 8, 1978		SAC4012
Butler	Mary	E.	May 13, 1921	No Date		SJO3113
Butler	Mary	E.	Mar. 12, 1924	Mar. 6, 1979	In loving memory / death date on stone was changed from 1976 to 1979	SIC8075
Butler	Mary	E.	1928	1987	Love you	HGH3008
Butler	Mary	E.	No Date	Sep. 7, 1909	Homemade cement base with marker on top	HGH3055
Butler	Mary	Goldena	Sep. 29, 1951	Apr. 5, 1975		HGH3014
Butler	Mary	Hazel	Jun. 3, 1915	Aug. 2, 2006		SMC4162
Butler	Mary	R.	No Date	Feb. 16, 1967	Mrs. Mary R. Butler / 84 years (Kelson Funeral Home Marker R.F.D. 1 Box 134 Aquasco, MD.	SMCW034
Butler	Mary	V.	Sep. 27, 1912	Feb. 26, 1989		NSP040

Last Name	First Name	Middle Name	Date of Birth	Date of Death	Transcription / Notes	Cemetery Code
Butler	Mary		Jan. 30, 1945	Jun. 28, 2009	Thornton Funeral Home Marker / Age 64 / d/o the late Thomas Desales & Mary Edith Butler / info is from Maryland Independent newspaper Fri. Jul 3, 2009 Page A-11 Col. 2	SJO3014A
Butler	Mary	M.	Aug. 5, 1898	Sep. 15, 1991	In God's Care	SMC4007
Butler	Matilda		No Date	Jan. 17, 1915	Info is from church records	OFENoStone
Butler	Mattie		No Date	1938	Old cement cross with only one date of 1938	SHI136
Butler	Mazie	A.	Apr. 4, 1888	Apr. 4, 1937		SHI267
Butler	Nathan	A.	Jun. 22, 1949	Apr. 29, 2000	Forever loved your Daughter and Grandson	PGN055
Butler	Oscar	DeSales	May 10, 1914	Jan. 25, 1976	Beloved husband and father	SMC4068
Butler	Oscar	Jerome	Dec. 11, 1942	Jun. 20, 2006	Our Dad on earth God's Angel in Heaven	SMC4158
Butler	Paul	Eugene	1928	1985	In loving memory	SMC3315
Butler	Robert	Daniel	Dec. 7, 1904	Dec. 27, 1967		SPL2015
Butler	Robert		Mar. 5, 1896	Mar. 27, 1979		PGN012
Butler, Jr.	Robert	P.	Feb. 9, 1929	Aug. 22, 1998	Beloved son & brother / Bubba	SMC1107
Butler, Sr.	Robert	P.	Sep. 5, 1905	Jun. 30, 1977	Husband & father	SMC1212
Butler	Sarah	E.	1908	1985		NSP998
Butler	Shanita		1990	1993		SAC1021
Butler	Steven	H.	Nov. 20, 1962	May 16, 1983	Son	NSP283
Butler	T.	R.	No Date	Mar. 20, 1955		HGH3064
Butler	Theresa	E.	Oct. 9, 1946	No Date		SMC3091
Butler	Theresa	O.	Dec. 5, 1938	No Date	Mom	SJO3019
Butler	Thomas	D.	Nov. 19, 1914	Nov. 25, 1991		SJO3113
Butler, Sr.	Thomas	Reed	1917	1988	Your wisdom and love linger to help us through	HGH4200
Butler, Mrs.	Unknown		No Date	Aug. 1873	w/o Joseph Butler / info is from church records	OFENoStone
Butler	Unknown		No Date	No Date	Child of Joe / Info is from the 1984 church cemetery transcription list	SICNoStone
Butler	Wayne	Cyril	Feb. 8, 1947	Mar. 25, 2003		SJO5050
Butler	William	B.	1900	1973	Info is from the 1984 church cemetery transcription list	SICNoStone
Butler	William	E.	Jul. 9, 1939	Apr. 5, 2006		SMC2019
Butler	William	H.	Jan. 29, 1904	No Date		SMC4162

Last Name	First Name	Middle Name	Date of Birth	Date of Death	Transcription / Notes	Cemetery Code
Butler	William	Harold	Apr. 29, 1943	Mar. 24, 1997		NSP232
Butler	William	L.	1938	1974		SMC3249
Butler	William	Ralph	Oct. 7, 1911	Feb. 28, 1974	Maryland CPL US Army WWII	NSP282
Butler	William	S.	Oct. 19, 1890	Jul. 17, 1891	Loving child of Cornelius Butler	SCL2195
Butler	Z.	Alfred	No Date	Oct. 25, 1892	In memory of / aged 49 years / Today be mine, tomorrow thine.	SJO3014B
Button	Elizabeth	Katherine	No Date	Jul. 10, 1904	Info is from Christ Church microfilm Reel 3, Pg 218-219 located at the College of Southern MD, LaPlata, MD s/o A.H. and Mary F. Lambert / s/o J.S. and Mary F. Button / "who died for us that whether we wake or sleep we should live together with Him	MTRNoStone
Button	Frederick	S.	May 1, 1877	Oct. 26, 1897		MTR1277
Button	John	Francis	Oct. 6, 1874	Aug. 28, 1908		MTR1282
Button	John	S.	Mar. 29, 1840	Jan. 7, 1880	In memory of / Loved in life, remembered in death (According to church records, he was the first person buried in Mt. Rest Cemetery	MTR1273
Button	Sarah	Jane	Feb. 22, 1846	Feb. 6, 1872	Sacred to the memory of / beloved w/o John S. Button / Fell Asleep in Jesus / Oh faith, lift up my drooping love, Tell of the promised home, The ( ) earth's chill clouds above, Where parting cannot name! In hope I ( ), for strength I pray. And peace is surely won. As from my bleeding heart I say thy will be done. / verse is hard to read	SPL6161
Byles	Katherine	Auguste, E.	No Date	Oct. 26, 1887	Info is from Christ Church microfilm Reel 2 Pg 165-166 located at the College of Southern MD, LaPlata, MD	MTRNoStone
Byrd	Magnolia	Elizabeth, Wilson	Feb. 27, 1937	Mar. 14, 2006	Mother	OAK061
Byrd	Veronica	Smith	Aug. 27, 1921	Aug. 8, 2003		SCL4177
Byrne	Amelia	Helwig	Sep. 20, 1887	Jun. 28, 1922	Tis but the casket lies here. The gem that filled it sparkles yet.	NJB478
Byrne	Barbara		May 26, 18	May 27, 18	d/o LT. Comdr. And Mrs. J. A. Byrne / No year is listed on the stone	SCL3221
Byrnes	Mary	Ellen	Nov. 28, 1905	Oct. 11, 1997	Loving Mother	SJO5021
C.	C.	A.	No Date	No Date	Footstone with initials C.A.C. (Could be footstone for Clara A. Cox)	SJO3340B
C.	C.	M.	No Date	No Date	Footstone with the initials M.C.C.	SMCW046

Last Name	First Name	Middle Name	Date of Birth	Date of Death	Transcription / Notes	Cemetery Code
C.	J.	J.	No Date	No Date	Footstone with initials J.J.C. (to the left of this is a stone missing from the base) (probably footstone for Josephine J. Cox)	SJO2345
C.	T.	E.	No Date	No Date	Footstone with the initials T.E.C. This is probably the footstone for Teresa E. Carrico consort of Geo. W. Carrico (headstone is missing)	SMCA081
Cahill	Diane	Swann	1935	1984	Devoted m/o Troy, Tracy & Darren	OFE1012
Caimi, Rev.	Luke	A.	1918	No Date	Ordained May 31, 1958	HGH4188
Cain	Pauline		1924	1999		HGH4120
Cain	Thomas		1924	No Date		HGH4120
Cairns	Elizabeth	C.	1923	No Date		OFE1085
Cairns, Sr.	Melvin	R.	1919	1994	In loving memory	OFE1085
Calvert	Cornelious		Sep. 15, 1884	Nov. 28, 1952	Maryland PFC 401 Res Labor BN QMC World War I	HGH3012
Cammayo	Ines	T.	Jan. 21, 1927	Oct. 19, 2002		NSP937
Cammayo	Tomas	G.	Feb. 13, 1924	Dec. 9, 1996		NSP937
Campbell, Sr.	Albert	G.	May 1, 1910	Dec. 28, 1989	"AB" / "Ella"	MTR4052
Campbell	Ann		No Date	Nov. 13, 1913	Mother / Aged 75 yrs / May she rest in peace	SCL1072
Campbell	Bartholomew	I.	1884	1975	Flat piece of cement / artificial pink flowers mark the site	SMY2134
Campbell	Calvin	A.	193	198	Note: Found letters laying on ground next to flowers. (located to the Left of Louis Campbell)	SAC3057
Campbell	Denny		1939	1998		PKH092
Campbell	Donald	StClair	1893	1940		MTR4074
Campbell	Elizabeth	A.	1849	1923	May she rest in Peace. / Stone is broken off base and is laying on the ground in a bush	SMY1015A
Campbell	Emma	C.	1920	2003		SIC9072
Campbell	Frances	L.	Sep. 11, 1892	May 16, 1987		SMC1085
Campbell	Francis	Arthur	Dec. 27, 1873	Nov. 9, 1886	R.I.P. Small upright stone that is in a bush.	SMY1015B
Campbell	Francis	J.	Apr. 16, 1923	Jul. 15, 1974	In Memory of	SAC5045
Campbell, Sr.	Haskell	N.	Nov. 14, 1936	May 14, 2001		SMY2096
Campbell	James	C.	1941	1976	Info is from the Historical Society Research located at The College of Southern MD, LaPlata, MD	SCLNoStone

Last Name	First Name	Middle Name	Date of Birth	Date of Death	Transcription / Notes	Cemetery Code
Campbell, Corpl.	Jos.		No Date	No Date	Corpl. Co K 19 U.S.C. inf (his stone is placed close to the woods away from most of the other stones)	SMY1125
Campbell, Jr.	Joseph	A.	Jul. 18, 1949	Jun. 25, 1950		SCL3106
Campbell	Joseph	Harvey	Aug. 24, 1943	Oct. 16, 1989	Married May 22, 1970 / US Navy Vietnam	CHR114
Campbell	Kyle	Daniel	Jul. 16, 1990	Oct. 22, 1990	Our baby boy is in God's care	PKH093
Campbell	Louis	E.	1916	1981		SAC3058
Campbell	Louise	E.	Oct. 23, 1919	Sep. 3, 2006		SMC1084
Campbell	Louise		1888	1953		SMY2133
Campbell	Louise		1921	1992	Sisters / Together Forever (on same marker with Cecelia Massey)	SCL3027
Campbell	Margaret	E.	1924	1988		SMY2108
Campbell	Mary	E.	1846	1929	Mother	SMY3194
Campbell	Mary	Ellen	Apr. 26, 1910	May 1, 1996	"AB" / "Ella"	MTR4052
Campbell, Jr.	Michael	Lovell	Jan. 1, 1993	May 31, 2002	The Lord is my Shepherd	PGN062
Campbell	Natalie	Martin	Jul. 14, 1910	Nov. 10, 2000		SMY3108
Campbell	Raymond	A.	Jul. 29, 1913	Oct. 23, 1982	In Loving Memory	SCL3022
Campbell	Ruth	Ann	Aug. 25, 1948	No Date	Married May 22, 1970	CHR113
Campbell	Viola	L., Hackerson	Mar. 4, 1932	Aug. 11, 1990	Your loving Mom / "Singe" / Love Always	SCL3105
Campbell	Virginia	E.	Oct. 20, 1873	Dec. 6, 1933		SPL3020
Campbell	William	A.	1915	1987		SMY2108
Campbell	William	Dean	Nov. 9, 1908	Sep. 15, 1995		SMY3108
Campbell	William	H.	1842	1919	Father	SMY3072
Camphor	Morris		No Date	Sep. 1981	Info is from church records	SHINoStone
Canady	Valerie		Jun. 29, 1963	Dec. 21, 1988	In loving memory of our daughter Valerie / killed in the bombing of Pan Am 103 over Lockerbie, Scotland / William James, Loulie Dodson	ODE047

Last Name	First Name	Middle Name	Date of Birth	Date of Death	Transcription / Notes	Cemetery Code
Candland	Anna	Lee	Apr. 22, 2002	Sep. 3, 2003	Cherished d/o Benjamin and Kimberley Candland / For behold all little children are alive In Christ. Moroni 8:22 / "The Crown without the conflict" / Back of stone: "The Lord takes many away even in infancy, that they may escape the envy of man, and the sorrows and evils of this present world. They were to pure too lovely to live on earth. Therefore, if rightly considered, instead of mourning, we have reason to rejoice, as they are delivered from evil and we shall soon have them again, notwithstanding all this Glory, we for a moment lose sight of it and mourn the loss, but we do not mourn as those without hope. Joseph Smith Jr.	ODE076
Cangiano	Kevin	M.	Nov. 29, 1979	Jun. 10, 2002	In loving memory / Our Beloved Son	NSP736
Cannon	James	T.	1900	1977		SJO4071
Cannon	Marjorie	A.	1903	1983		SJO4071
Cannon	Vernon	W.	Dec. 7, 1883	Jul. 14, 1927		HNT056
Cant( )	Jennie		No Date	Oct. 17, 1918	Info is from Christ Church microfilm Reel 3, Pg 228-229 located at the College of Southern MD, LaPlata, MD	MTRNoStone
Canter	Alice	E.	Aug. 15, 1834	Apr. 4, 1902	w/o Henry A Canter	OFE2093
Canter	Andrew	Lewis	Mar. 19, 1831	Oct. 18, 1910		OFE1044
Canter	Andrew	Mitchell	Aug. 22, 1891	Dec. 7, 1930		OFE2042
Canter	Andrew	Richard	Aug. 20, 1873	Oct. 2, 1954		OFE1027
Canter	Ann	M.	Feb. 14, 1914	Jun. 3, 1914		OFE1046
Canter	Ashby	H.	May 11, 1810	Jul. 26, 1885	In Memory of	OFE3010
Canter	Barbara	Ann	Jun. 23, 1912	Aug. 29, 2001		OFE1029
Canter	Bessie	Viola	1932	1934	d/o Robt. And Nellie Canter	OFE3015
Canter	Blanche	Lamarr	Dec. 30, 1884	Dec. 18, 1895	IHS	OFE2044
Canter	Caroline	Celeste	1905	1995		OFE1031
Canter	Charles	Richard	1865	1950	Mother / under a tree	OFE2020
Canter	Dorothy		Feb. 14, 1937	Dec. 30, 1996	SP4 US Army	OFE3038
Canter	Dorothy	L.	1928	No Date	"Dottie"	OFE3036
Canter - Welch	Dorothy	Virginia	Apr. 4, 1924	Mar. 25, 1994	Beloved m/o Mary Cordelia and Dianna	OFE3018

Last Name	First Name	Middle Name	Date of Birth	Date of Death	Transcription / Notes	Cemetery Code
Canter	E.	Blanche	Jan. 17, 1878	Aug. 9, 1888	In memory of / d/o Andrew E. & Jane Canter / Weep not, she is not dead but sleepeth.	OFE1042
Canter	Edwin	Henry	Jul. 19, 1929	Mar. 21, 1954	Our son Jimmy / In remembrance "Jimmy"	OFE3016
Canter	Elizabeth		1862	1952		OFE2069
Canter	Francis	Albert	1866	1939		OFE2017
Canter, Sr.	Francis	Wilson	1920	Dec. 15, 1981	"Tommie" / info is from church records	OFE3036
Canter	Frank		No Date	Jul. 12, 1939	Age 73 / info is from church records	OFENoStone
Canter	Frank	W.	1897	1964		OFE3037
Canter	Harry	H.	Aug. 17, 1888	Feb. 8, 1970		OFE2063
Canter	Henry	A.	Mar. 13, 1826	Jun. 9, 1913	May he rest in peace	OFE2021
Canter	Henry	Edgar	Jun. 17, 1869	Jun. 8, 1948		OFE1048
Canter	Henry		Jan. 26, 1795	Dec. 6, 1866	In Memory of / ? ? Thee do ? Of Gods put my ? ? Trust	OFE4028
Canter, Jr.	James	E.	Aug. 19, 1952	Apr. 3, 2008	"Butch"	SMC3071
Canter, Sr.	James	E.	Jun. 29, 1929	No Date		SMC3070
Canter, Mrs.	Jane		No Date	Mar. 17, 1875	Info is from church records	OFENoStone
Canter	Jane	Lamarr	1837	1914	His wife	OFE1045
Canter	John	A.	No Date	Aug. 20, 1871	Aged 62	OFE3007
Canter	L.	H.	Feb. 13, 1825	Sep. 23, 1883		SMCD101
Canter	Leonard	G.	Jun. 8, 1873	Mar. 29, 1955		OFE2034
Canter	Levi		Dec. 12, 1832	Dec. 22, 1900	Son	OFE4030
Canter	Levin		1862	1955		OFE2069
Canter	Lillian	M.	May 8, 1876	Jan. 28, 1956		OFE2034
Canter	Luke		Oct. 27, 1850	Feb. 28, 1928	In remembrance / Beloved Grandfather	OFE4024
Canter	Maggie	Virginia	Mar. 15, 1878	May 17, 1958		OFE1047A
Canter	Marguerite	C.	1901	1978		OFE3037
Canter	Marianne	M.	Jun. 26, 1928	No Date		SMC3070
Canter	Mary	C.	No Date	Jul. 22, 1873	Aged 40 years / Stonemaker Baddeus, Balto	OFE4096
Canter	Nellie	Erma	Sept 24, 1901	Oct. 30, 1978		OFE3016
Canter	Nelson	Emmett	Jun. 10, 1917	Feb. 19, 1985	SP5 US Army, WWII, Korea	OFE1028
Canter	Oscar	Robert	Jun. 20, 1919	Nov. 22, 1999	In Remembrance "Billy"	OFE3019
Canter	Pammelia	Anne	Nov. 3, 1873	Jun. 22, 1899	w/o Luke Canter	OFE4025

Last Name	First Name	Middle Name	Date of Birth	Date of Death	Transcription / Notes	Cemetery Code
Canter	Richard	Henry	1861	1916	Father / under a tree	OFE2019
Canter	Robert	Edward	Feb. 18, 1895	Apr. 27, 1951		OFE3016
Canter	Robert		Aug. 15, 1813	Oct. 22, 1885	In Memory of	OFE3009
Canter	S.	E. D.	Jan. 30, 1830	Jan. 26, 1892		SMCD101
Canter	Sarah	Anne	No Date	No Date	Buried lot - 40 Calverton Manor May 1837 Reinterred 1887 (At Oldfields Episcopal Ch)	OFE4030
Canter	Sarah	Virginia	Jan. 15, 1900	Jun. 24, 1901	IHS	OFE2043
Canter	Sarah	Virginia	Sep. 24, 1863	May 8, 1948		OFE2040
Canter	Stouten	Horatio	Sept. 6, 1857	Nov. 3, 1933	IHS	OFE2041
Canter	Unknown			Aug. 1934	Infant Canter buried at Robert Canter place on Aug 20, 1934 / info is from church records	OFENoStone
Cantrell	Garry	Randall	Apr. 9, 1960	Aug. 8, 1970		MTR3127
Cappers	Miriam	Matthews	Nov. 28, 1913	No Date	May they rest in peace	SIC1067
Cappers, Jr.	William	Frederic	Sep. 9, 1919	Apr. 22, 1978	May they rest in peace	SIC1067
Caraol	Roland	Donald	No Date	Jun. 26, 1966	Aged 6 / Info was obtained from the Historical Society Research located at the College of Southern Md, LaPlata, Md)	OAKNoStone
Card	Alma	Ruth	1902	1983	Sister	HGH2061
Card	Frances		Oct. 16, 1933	No Date	Nee Montgomery / Beloved wife and mother	SMC3196
Card	Mary	E.	1897	1968	May their souls rest in peace	MTR1089
Card	Stephen	G.	1880	1927	May their souls rest in peace	MTR1089
Card	William	G.	Oct. 9, 1925	Aug. 5, 1995	TEC 5 US Army WW II	SMC3195
Carey	Thomas	Edwin	Aug. 13, 1936	Aug. 1, 1977	US Navy Korea	CMX2079
Cargill	Bernadette		Aug. 31, 1918	May 31, 1997		SMY2017
Cargill	George	H.	Jan. 28, 1914	No Date		SMY2017
Cargill	Louis	H.	Feb. 9, 1948	Mar. 25, 1975		NSP931
Carl	Rebecca	Lyon	No Date	Jan. 22, 1921	Info is from Christ Church microfilm Reel 3, Pg 230-231 located at the College of Southern MD, LaPlata, MD	MTRNoStone
Carley	Gulielmus	E.	Jun. 30, 1888	Mar. 5, 1965	IHS / COAD. S. J. / NATUS 30 Jun. 1888 / INGR. 29 Oct. 1909 / OBIIt 4 Mar. 1965 / R.I.P. (In Priests Plot)	SIC1037
Carnahan	Robert	Paul	No Date	1963	Baby	CLV421
Carney	Jonathon	D.	1925	2001	LTC US Army WW II Korea Vietnam	MTR4017

Last Name	First Name	Middle Name	Date of Birth	Date of Death	Transcription / Notes	Cemetery Code
Carney	M.	Elizabeth	1937	No Date	Beloved Wife	MTR4018
Carpenter	Agnes	H.	1907	1990		SIC7001
Carpenter	Annie	Catherine	Apr. 5, 1897	Aug. 28, 1900	d/o T M & M R Carpenter	TRI208
Carpenter	Bertha	Mae	Oct. 4, 1911	Apr. 19, 2004	My presence shall go with thee, and I will give thee rest. Ex 33:14	NJB332
Carpenter	Bettie	Adams	May 8, 1834	Jan. 14, 1893	His wife	ODE090
Carpenter	Betty	G.	Oct. 8, 1930	Jul. 6, 1983	Thy Kingdom come thy will be done	SCL4012
Carpenter	Broadie	M.	1889	1962		NJB443
Carpenter	Catherine	Carol	No Date	Aug. 9, 1956	Age 53 / Info is from the Historical Society Research located at the College of Southern MD, LaPlata, MD	PISNoStone
Carpenter	Cecelia	B.	1903	1996		PIS238
Carpenter	Cecil	A.	Aug. 17, 1915	Sep. 4, 1933		NJB444
Carpenter	Charles	D.	Apr. 30, 1863	Dec. 26, 1930	Father / Asleep in Jesus aged 42 years 12 months 22 days. May he rest in peace / Erected by his devoted wife	PIS205
Carpenter	Charles	L.	Mar. 9, 1836	May 31, 1878		SMY1043
Carpenter	Clara	A.	Jul. 27, 1920	No Date		SCL3269
Carpenter, Jr.	Clarence	D.	Nov. 29, 1924	No Date	Married July 16, 1943	SCL4047
Carpenter	Clarence	Daniel	1891	1971		SJO3239
Carpenter	Clarence	Mitchell	1920	2004		SJO3237
Carpenter	Della	E.	Jun. 24, 1895	Jul. 5, 1895		PIS203
Carpenter	Edith	V.	1890	1970		NJB443
Carpenter	Etta	Adams	1893	1967		SJO3238
Carpenter	Francis	K.	1901	1985		SIC7001
Carpenter	George	M.	Jan. 17, 1849	Nov. 6, 1925		MRB046
Carpenter	George	W.	Sep. 10, 1922	Jan. 11, 2000	Forever in our hearts	PIS237
Carpenter	George	W.	Sep. 5, 1818	Jan. 20, 1904	His wife	ODE090
Carpenter	Harry	A.	Jun. 9, 1885	Jun. 26, 1922	Tall Stone / Soft Southern sun shine brightly here. Warm southern winds blow gently here. Green sod above. Lie light-Lie light. Good night Dear heart, Good night, Good night.	MRB053
Carpenter	Inez		No Date	Apr. 4, 1991	Info is from church records	CHRNoStone
Carpenter	J.	Edward	1891	1927		SCL3264

Last Name	First Name	Middle Name	Date of Birth	Date of Death	Transcription / Notes	Cemetery Code
Carpenter	J.	Wesley	1853	1935		SCL3266
Carpenter	James	G.	1896	1934		SCL3263
Carpenter	John	B.	Apr. 26, 1823	Feb. 28, 1897	In Memory of / "Blessed are the dead who die in the Lord." / His children arise up and call him Blessed / Erected by his four sons.	PIS109
Carpenter	Keith	D.	No Date	Sep. 4, 1975	Infant Son	SCL4090
Carpenter	Kirby		Aug. 13, 1865	May 17, 1894	In Memory of / This modest stone what few vain marbles can, May truly say. Here lies an honest man.	PIS084
Carpenter	Lemuel	P.	Sep. 3, 1926	No Date	Thy Kingdom come thy will be done	SCL4012
Carpenter	Lucille	A.	May 31, 1925	Jun. 28, 1994	Married July 16, 1943	SCL4047
Carpenter	Maria	R.	May 23, 1873	Nov. 6, 1962		TRI246
Carpenter	Mark	Sixtus	Dec. 28, 1960	Dec. 6, 2001	Loving Memories last forever	SCL4013
Carpenter	Mary	Agnes	May 31, 1886	Feb. 4, 1962	Info is from the Historical Society Research located at the College of Southern MD, LaPlata, MD	SMCNoStone
Carpenter	Mary	E.	1867	1940		SCL3267
Carpenter	Mary	E., Delozier	Aug. 10, 1850	Jan. 30, 1924		MRB046
Carpenter	Montgomery	Adams	1871	1931		ODE082
Carpenter	Otis	Douglas	Dec. 6, 1910	Jan. 30, 2000	My presence shall go with thee, and I will give thee rest. Ex 33:14	NJB332
Carpenter	Robert	G.	1889	1958		SCL3268
Carpenter	Ruth	E.	1892	1976		SCL3265
Carpenter	Ruth	V.	Jul. 26, 1891	Jun. 23, 1892	d/o Kirby & Rachel Carpenter	PIS106
Carpenter	Sadie	Mae	1895	1969	w/o James G. Carpenter	SCL3262
Carpenter	Sarah	A.	Oct. 1, 1871	Dec. 23, 1931	Mother / Asleep in Jesus	PIS205
Carpenter	Thomas	D.	1897	1960		PIS238
Carpenter	Thomas	M.	Apr. 11, 1863	Jan. 19, 1945		TRI246
Carpenter	Unknown		Jan. 8, 1900	Feb. 15, 1900	Infant of C. D. & S. A. Carpenter / Born to soon	PIS204
Carpenter	Virginia		1829	May 6, 1891	In Memory of / w/o J. B. Carpenter / Gone but not forgotten / Erected by her five sons	PIS110
Carpinter	Unknown		No Date	No Date	Stone with Surname on it only	CAR006
Carr	Francis		No Date	Jun. 11, 1900	Name is shown on church records but burial location is unknown, date is the burial date, not death date	CHRNoStone

Last Name	First Name	Middle Name	Date of Birth	Date of Death	Transcription / Notes	Cemetery Code
Carrico	Ambrose	E.	No Date	Mar. 23, 1887	In his 23rd year whilst a student for the Oly Priesthood at St. Charles College. / info is from the Historical Society Research and the 1940 DAR book pg 187 located at the College of Southern MD, LaPlata, MD	SMCNoStone
Carrico	Anna	F.	Aug. 20, 1852	May 4, 1934	His wife	SMCD160
Carrico	Anne	E., Dent	1837	1888	on the back of this stone is Jno F & Francis L infants of Thos A & A E Carrico (wife of Thos. A Carrico M.D.)	SMCA075
Carrico	Annie	J.	Mar. 10, 1874	Oct. 19, 1945	On the back of stone is Rudolf and Eleanor Carrico	SMCA027
Carrico	B.	Hamilton	Jul. 19, 1852	Feb. 9, 1908		SMCD160
Carrico	Beulah	Sisson	No Date	No Date		SMC2147
Carrico	Eleanor	Mae, Forbes	Nov. 6, 1920	Jan. 26, 2003	She is on the back of the stone for Louis and Annie Carrico	SMCA028
Carrico	Francis	L.	No Date	No Date	Infant of Thos A & A E Carrico (This is on the back of the stone for Thos & Anne Carrico	SMCA076
Carrico	Francis	Percy	Oct. 30, 1891	Dec. 6, 1891	Infant son of B Hamilton & Anna Frances Carrico / May he rest in peace	SMCD180
Carrico	Geo	Emory	1893	1975	As rest	SMCD162
Carrico	George	W.	Jul. 21, 1821	No Date	In memory of his son / stone sunk unable to read death date / info is from the Historical Society Research and 1940 DAR book pg 181 located at the College of Southern MD, LaPlata, MD.	SMCNoStone
Carrico	Jane	F.	No Date	Mar. 20, 1885	Relict of Thomas Carrico / aged 58 / info is from the Historical Society Research and the 1940 DAR book pg 187, at the College of Southern MD, LaPlata, MD.	SMCNoStone
Carrico	Jno	F.	No Date	No Date	Infant of Thos A & A E Carrico (This is on the back of the stone for Thos & Anne Carrico	SMCA076
Carrico	Leila	Gladys	Oct. 10, 1899	Oct. 7, 1999		SMCD179
Carrico, M.D.	Louis	C.	Nov. 23, 1860	Mar. 12, 1921	On the back of this stone is Rudolf and Eleanor Carrico	SMCA027
Carrico	M.	Frances	Dec. 29, 1877	Jun. 21, 1941	d/o the late Dr. Thomas A. and Anne Dent Carrico / Requiescat in pace	SMCA071
Carrico	Maria	R.	1897	1999	At rest	SMCD162
Carrico	Mary		No Date	Dec. 11, 1848	Erected by Thomas Carrico in memory of his wife Mary in the 53rd year of her age. May the Lord be merciful to her. Amen	SMCW044

Last Name	First Name	Middle Name	Date of Birth	Date of Death	Transcription / Notes	Cemetery Code
Carrico	Mary		No Date	Dec. 11, 1848	Erected by Thomas Carrico in memory of / his wife / aged 53 / info is from the Historical Society Research and the 1940 DAR book pg 187 located at the College of Southern MD, LaPlata, MD.	SMCNoStone
Carrico	Rudolf	A.	Feb. 26, 1908	Jun. 9, 1969	He is on the back of the stone for Louis and Annie Carrico	SMCA028
Carrico	Sarah		No Date	Aug. 13, 1853	Erected by Thomas Carrico in memory of his mother / in the 91st year of her age. / May the Lord be merciful to her.	SMCC050
Carrico	Teresa	E.	No Date	Jul. 23, 1884	Erected by B. Hamilton Carrico / In memory of his mother / consort of Geo. W. Carrico / In the 66th year of her age / info is from the Historical Society Research and the 1940 DAR book pg 181 located at the College of Southern MD, LaPlata, MD.	SMCNoStone
Carrico	Thomas		No Date	Apr. 1881	Aged 88 / info is from the Historical Society Research and the 1940 DAR book pg 187 located at the College of Southern MD, LaPlata, MD.	SMCNoStone
Carrico, M.D.	Thos	A.	1827	1902	on the back of this stone is Jno F & Francis L infants of Thos A & A E Carrico	SMCA075
Carrico	Thomas	Carlyle	Dec. 2, 1916	Jun. 9, 1985		SMC2147
Carrington	Elizabeth	A.	No Date	Oct. 9, 1890	In Memory of / w/o Samuel Carrington / aged 56 years..at rest (laying next to this stone is one that says father, no other information)	MTR3052
Carrington	Jane	S.	Aug. 21,1839	Oct. 28, 1870	In Memory Of	HML005
Carrington	John		No Date	Feb. 1869	Parted Below United Above / Sacred to the Memory of / aged 62 years / Press one kiss upon her forehead gently close those dark black eyes. Do not weep she is only sleeping We will meet her in the skyes / Stonemaker was Barker W.D.C.	SJE084
Carrington	Samuel		No Date	Oct. 15, 1893	In Memory of / Aged 77 years / At Rest	MTR3054
Carrington	Tiffani	C.	Jul. 29, 1977	Dec. 21, 1996	An Angels work is never done /Etched on the stone: Bryans Road Volunteers Charles County / Medical Emergency Technician	SCL4184
Carro	Mary	Katherine Richards	No Date	No Date	Transferred from John & Elaine Richards to Daughter / Information is from the 1984 church Cemetery transcription list	SICNoStone

Last Name	First Name	Middle Name	Date of Birth	Date of Death	Transcription / Notes	Cemetery Code
Carroll	Annie		Jun. 4, 1904	May 25, 1961	Mother	POM183
Carroll	Austin	C.	May 14, 1919	Mar. 16, 1997		DUD076
Carroll	Benjamin		1859	1939	Thornton Funeral Home Marker	MHB266
Carroll	Carlton	U.	Apr. 26, 1880	Aug. 18, 1968	Thornton Funeral Home	MHB146
Carroll	Charles		1935	2004		MHB239
Carroll	Charlie	Danny	Jan. 29, 1957	Apr. 14, 1993	Loving Son Brother	OAK107
Carroll, Mrs.	D.		No Date	No Date	Broken cross with homemade inscription	OAK084
Carroll, Jr.	Dennis	Gene	Sep. 18, 1996	May 24, 1997	"Man-Man"	SJO3322
Carroll	Dorothy	E.	Jan. 16, 1916	Sep. 29, 2000		DUD078
Carroll	Dottie		No Date	Dec. 1956	Info is from church records	SHINoStone
Carroll	Edna	J.	1913	1993	In Loving Memory of our Mother and Grandmother We Trust Our Loss Will Be Her Gain and That With Christ She's Gone To Reign	MHB045
Carroll	Elmer		No Date	1944	Info was obtained from the Historical Society Research located at the College of Southern Md, LaPlata, Md)	OAKNoStone
Carroll	Glenn		1958	1991	Thornton Funeral Home Marker	MHB064
Carroll	Glynielle	L.	Jun. 20, 1988	May 9, 1991		MHB060
Carroll	Gregory		1959	1981	Thornton Funeral Home Marker	DUD031
Carroll	James	D.	Sep. 2, 1982	May 9, 1991	Love Always	MHB065
Carroll	James		1903	1993	Thornton Funeral Home Marker	MHB058
Carroll	John	H.	1881	1957		SHI059
Carroll	John	W.	No Date	Apr. 27, 1961	Info is from church records	SHINoStone
Carroll	Joseph	K.	Dec. 28, 1946	Feb. 26, 1969	Maryland PFC US Army Vietnam BSM-PH	SJO4124
Carroll	Josephine		No Date	Aug. 30, 1945		POM098
Carroll	Julia		1895	1974	Info was obtained from the Historical Society Research located at the College of Southern Md, LaPlata, Md)	OAKNoStone
Carroll	Katie	M.	Feb. 12, 1927	Mar. 11, 1991	In Loving Memories / Loving Wife and Mother	OAK106
Carroll	Lemuel		No Date	No Date	In Memory Of	MHB221
Carroll	Lena		1896	1978	Thornton Funeral Home Marker	DUD048
Carroll	Leslie		Nov. 6, 1966	Dec. 19, 1995	SRA US Air Force	MHB033
Carroll	Margaret	E.	Mar. 7, 1927	Aug. 20, 1995		SJO4123

Last Name	First Name	Middle Name	Date of Birth	Date of Death	Transcription / Notes	Cemetery Code
Carroll	Marian		1959	1989	Thornton Funeral Home Marker	OAK175
Carroll	Marion	T.	Aug. 28, 1930	May 8, 2001		SJO4124
Carroll	Mattie		1916	1991	Thornton Funeral Home Marker	MHB059
Carroll, Sr.	Melvin	L.	Feb. 20, 1923	Jun. 29, 1977	Father	MHB223
Carroll	Michelle		1971	2006		SCL4020
Carroll	Minnie	Price	1884	1935		MHB145
Carroll	Odean	L.	Sep. 3, 1905	Apr. 11, 1986	Devoted w/o Pearlic A. Carroll	SHI009
Carroll	Pearlie	A.	1902	Oct. 5, 1968	Info is from church records	SHI008
Carroll	Romaine	C.	Jul. 24, 1946	May 9, 2001	"Sally" Loving Mother and Grandmother To Live In Hearts We Leave Behind Is Not To Die	MHB008
Carroll	Rosalie		Jan. 21, 1934	Jun. 10, 2001	Beloved mother and Grandmother…"Now I lay me down to sleep, I pray the Lord by soul to keep" your Loving family	DUD014
Carroll	Roy		1929	1986	Thornton Funeral Home Marker	OAK104
Carroll	Sharnelle	T.	Feb. 26, 1984	May 9, 1991		MHB060
Carroll	Susie		1870	1951		SJO2253
Carroll	Unknown		1964	1983	Thornton Funeral Home Marker	OAK105
Carroll	Walter	S.	Jan. 19, 1924	Nov. 10, 1999	Loving Dad	OAK043
Carroll	Wilbert		1948	1983		DUD082
Carry	Maria		No Date	1889	info is from the 1940 DAR book page 158	SMYNoStone
Carry	Maria		No Date	1889	info is from the 1940 DAR book page 153	SMYNoStone
Carter	Alberta	Adell	Aug. 22, 1904	Jan. 25, 1982	Arehart Funeral Home Marker	SMT007
Carter	Barbara	Sue	Jan. 1, 1945	Nov. 17, 2001	United in love Dec 21, 1962	SPL3082
Carter	Emiline		No Date	Jul. 1892	Age 56 years / May she rest in peace	SCL2218
Carter	Florence	E.	May 26, 1929	Jan. 30, 1965	In Memory of	SCA056
Carter	Frederick		1933	2004	Thornton Funeral Home Marker	OAK032
Carter	George	Arthur	Nov. 21, 1910	May 20 1911	Son of Geo. F & Mary E. Carter	SCL2203
Carter	George	F.	1881	1938	Father	SCL1257
Carter	Helen	T.	Oct. 20, 1917	Dec. 30, 2002		SCL4155
Carter	Henrietta	C.	Nov. 27, 1847	Jan. 10, 1906	Beloved w/o Joseph H. Carter / Gone but not forgotten	SCL1256
Carter	J.	Ralph	1914	1974		SCL3059

Last Name	First Name	Middle Name	Date of Birth	Date of Death	Transcription / Notes	Cemetery Code
Carter	Jacqueline	M.	1936	1997	In Loving Memory	SCL3336
Carter	James	Arthur	1906	1978	Info is from the Historical Society Research located at The College of Southern MD, LaPlata, MD	SCLNoStone
Carter	John	Wilson	No Date	1982	infant	OSM023
Carter	John		Nov. 10, 1958	Sep. 9, 2003	info is from church records	CLVNoStone
Carter	Joseph	Canfield	1887	1960	In Loving Memory	SCL3336
Carter	Joseph	Clinton	Nov. 9, 1909	Sep. 7, 1910	Son of Geo. F & Mary E. Carter	SCL2204
Carter, Sr.	Joseph	Edward	Feb. 5, 1920	Jul. 18, 1991	US Army WWII	SCA046
Carter	Joseph	H.	No Date	Feb. 15, 1920	In Memory of our dear father / eldest son of Henry and Emeline Carter / Age 69 years / May he rest in peace	SCL2219
Carter	Joseph	Lorenzo	Jan. 15, 1904	May 5, 1956	Father	SIC5045
Carter	Keith	R.	Sep. 1, 1912	Jul. 13, 1983		SCL4155
Carter	Kenneth	Wayne	Oct. 22, 1941	No Date	United in love Dec 21, 1962	SPL3082
Carter	Margaret	C.	Apr. 8, 1886	Oct. 6, 1963		SJO3351
Carter	Margaret	R., Deshields	Nov. 17, 1916	Jun. 19, 1990	Info is from a Thornton Funeral Home Marker and from church records	SHI281
Carter	Margaret		No Date	Apr. 15, 1953	There is only one date on the stone	SCL1034
Carter	Mary	Campbell	1898	1999	In Loving Memory	SCL3336
Carter	Nellie	G.	1911	2003		SCL3059
Carter	Pearl	Dolores	Jun. 14, 1932	Jul. 18, 1952	Mother	SMT009
Carter	Robert	Q.	1887	1957		SCL3341
Carter	Sarah	Ann	No Date	Oct. 22, 1928	Mother	SCL2201
Carter	Victoria	E.	1886	1956		SCL3341
Carter	William	A.	No Date	Mar. 21, 1923	Rest In Peace	SCL2202
Carter	William	H.	Mar. 12, 1879	Mar. 12, 1904	s/o J.H. & H.C. Carter / May he rest in peace HMI US Navy Viet Nam / "Skip" Love is love forever more	SCL1255
Cartwright	Robert	C.	Oct. 9, 1946	Jul. 30, 1989	Life's work well done. He rests in peace	MTR3163
Cary	Edw.	L.	1863	1927		OSM134
Cary	Egbert		Nov. 11, 1828	Mar. 8, 1870	11th of 11 mo 1828 / 8th of 3 mo. 1870 Unable to read stone (Information is from the 1940 transcriptions of the Latter Day Saints Microfiche 6047,990-1)	PAT012
Cary	F.	Neal	1884	1937		OSM105

Last Name	First Name	Middle Name	Date of Birth	Date of Death	Transcription / Notes	Cemetery Code
Cary	Francis	Raymond	Aug. 12, 1917	Nov. 22, 1992		SCL1203
Cary	Hazel	Jenkins	Jan. 5, 1919	Feb. 20, 2001		SCL1201
Cary	Jessie	M.	1881	1967		OSM106
Cary	Margaret	G.	1894	1964		MTR4297
Cary	Raymond	B.	1889	1962		MTR4297
Casey, D.M.	Roseanne	McIlvane	1930	2005		SIC9062
Casey, Jr.	Francis	Lawton	1927	1993		SIC9062
Cash	William	R.	Jul. 21, 1900	Jun. 23, 1901	In memory of	SIC2085
Cashmore	Herbert	E.	1898	1987		OSM027
Cassell	William	L.	Dec. 9, 1884	May 30, 1953		CLV452
Castillo	Aaron		1993	1994		SHI178
Castle	D.		No Date	No Date	Thornton Funeral Home Marker	CLVNoStone
Castle	Susan	Elizabeth	Feb. 14, 1958	Sep. 10, 1968	Info is from church records	MTR2007
Casto	Lillian	W.	Sep. 25, 1910	Dec. 26, 1970	May she rest in peace	SJO4117
Caswell	Charles	H.	Mar. 27, 1908	Jun. 12, 1949		SPL6108
Cater	Ann	N.	Mar. 14, 1936	Jan. 6, 2000	Beloved Husband and wife / Forever in our hearts	NSP741
Cater	Robert	B.	Jul. 15, 1930	Jan. 20, 2003	Beloved Husband and wife / Forever in our hearts	NSP741
Cather	Melanie	Gaye	1955	1961		SCL3057
Cato	Robert	L.	Nov. 26, 1915	May 15, 1982	US Army	SIC7067
Caton	Alice A.	Cox	1908	1934	Beloved w/o Harry L. Caton	NJB386
Catto	Martha	H.	1923	2000		ODE294
Catto	Robert	J.	1914	1982		ODE294
Cawood	Eleanor	B.	No Date	Mar. 24, 1858	Sacred to the memory of / w/o H.R.V. Cawood, who departed this life / in the 69th year of her age. Thou hast been faithful in a few thing I will make thee ruler over many things. Matth. XXV 21. The sun is just a spark of fire a transient meteor in the sky, the soul immortal as it's fire shall never die. The soul of origin divine God's glorious image, freed from clay in heavens eternal sphere shall shine a star of day. (This stone is in a different area than the other stones)	LOC012

Last Name	First Name	Middle Name	Date of Birth	Date of Death	Transcription / Notes	Cemetery Code
Cecil, Jr.	Linwood	H.	Oct. 5, 1939	Nov. 23, 1996	In Loving Memory / "Daddy" / SN US Navy / Known by All as Fubby	SAC4076
Cecil, Jr.	Richard	Earl	Mar. 4, 1961	Apr. 11, 1999	SM2 US Navy / Ricky / Gone Fishing	SAC4077
Celentano	Louis	J.	1909	1983		SIC7086
Celentano	Nancy	D.	1921	2001		SIC7086
Cerger	Coy		No Date	No Date	Info is from the Historical Society Research located at the College of Southern MD, LaPlata, MD	ZBCNoStone
Chalk	Julia	C., Barbour	No Date	Jul. 24, 1960	Name is shown on church records but burial location is unknown	CHRNoStone
Chamberlain	Marie	G.	Jul. 26, 1888	Aug. 17, 1984		SIC9023
Chambers	Dorothy	Gray	No Date	No Date		SMY3208
Chambers	Robert	Hayes, Wheeler	May 10, 1867	Dec. 23, 1968	A loyal friend to the Sutton Family (Bronze marker flush to the ground-move leaves to find the marker)	CHM005
Chambers	Ruth	Berry	No Date	May 2, 1923	Age 21 / info is from church records	SHINoStone
Chandler	Caroline	W.	Jan. 6, 1841	Nov. 23, 1898	Faithful unto the End / He giveth his beloved sleep	ODE460
Chandler	Charles	A.	May 15, 1904	May 23, 1904	Info is from the Historical Society Research located at the College of Southern MD, LaPlata, MD	ODENoStone
Chandler	Charles	Todd	Sep. 9, 1906	Oct. 16, 1927	s/o Charles T & Mary A Chandler	ODE459
Chandler	Charles	Todd	1872	Apr. 15, 1938	Aged 66 yrs. / info is from DAR book Pg 147 located at the College of Southern MD, LaPlata, MD	ODE458
Chandler	Ella	L.	1862	1956		SJE098
Chandler	Harold	H.	Nov. 16, 1908	Dec. 18, 1983	Lt Co US Army WW II	ODE461
Chandler	Jane	E.	Feb. 24, 1842	Aug. 13, 1889	In memory of	NJB373
Chandler	Job		1630	1659	Job Chandlers Will states "To be buried in the subsidance to the south and west of ye main dwelling house. His head to be directly to the east under the Paper Mulberry Tree brought from England to feed the silk worms, with his feet directly to the west". Information is from the Charles County Historic Sites Box 7, at the College of Southern MD, LaPlata, MD	CHH001
Chandler	Mary	A.	1878	1951		ODE458

Last Name	First Name	Middle Name	Date of Birth	Date of Death	Transcription / Notes	Cemetery Code
Chandler	Saml	T.	Nov. 20, 1838	Feb. 20, 1894	Co. B 9th Va Cavalry C.S.A / They that know thy name will put their trust in Thee for thou Lord hast never failed them that seek thee / Psalm IX:10	ODE462
Chandler	Thomas	A.	1861	1931		SJE098
Chaney	Ruth	Elaine, McPherson	Oct. 7, 1954	Oct. 11, 1980		SMC2160
Chapman	A.	Grant	Sep. 5, 1879	Jan. 29, 1961		MTR4123
Chapman	Agnes	L.	Nov. 15, 1908	Jan. 17, 1970		SMC3331
Chapman	Alton	E.	Jun. 16, 1918	Dec. 7, 1983	h/o Lucille Chapman	NSP059
Chapman	Amelia	Tabb, Smoot	Oct. 14, 1870	Jul. 17, 1962	Beloved w/o John Grant Chapman III	CHR573
Chapman	Andrew	G.	Jan. 17, 1839	Sep. 25, 1892	In Memory of / Our Father / A lover of hospitality, a lover of good men, sober, just, holy, temperate.	MTR4122
Chapman	Anna		Sep. 14, 1901	Jul. 17, 1975		SJO1132
Chapman	Arthur	Y.	Mar. 4, 1910	Feb. 2, 1969		SMC4147
Chapman	Bernard	H.	Jan. 28, 1923	Jun. 7, 1982	Forever in our hearts	NSP106
Chapman	Catherine	Graham	No Date	Mar. 31, 1930	Info is from Christ Church microfilm Reel 3, Pg 236-237 located at the College of Southern MD, LaPlata, MD	MTRNoStone
Chapman	Cecilia	W.	Jul. 22, 1878	Aug. 16, 1899	Asleep in Jesus, blessed sleep / Info is from Historical Society Research located at the College of Southern MD, LaPlata, MD	MTRNoStone
Chapman	Edith	Roberts	Sep. 6, 1881	Sep. 22, 1881	Our Baby / d/o Andrew G and Helen M. Chapman / He shall gather the lambs in his arms and carry them in.	MTR4120
Chapman	Elizabeth	Parker, Grantt	No Date	Apr. 24, 1856	Relict of Col. Samuel Chapman of this County in the 77th year of her age. She was the m/o Etheldra Jane Chapman Harris (Her stone is broken into pieces) / Info is from the Historical Society Research located at The College of Southern MD, LaPlata, MD. / also from a family member	WAV1015
Chapman	Ellen	S.	1863	1946	Beloved d/o Marshall Stockett & Ellen Chapman - I believe in the resurrection of the dead and the life of the world to come. Amen	MTR1056
Chapman	Ellen	Turner	1843	1926	His wife / at rest	OFE4106

Last Name	First Name	Middle Name	Date of Birth	Date of Death	Transcription / Notes	Cemetery Code
Chapman	Ellen	Stockett	Feb. 6, 1838	Nov. 23, 1933	w/o Marshall Chapman, d/o J.N. & Sophia Stockett of Annapolis, MD / The gift of God is eternal life through Jesus Christ our Lord	MTR1061
Chapman	Elsie	F.	Aug. 20, 1891	Nov. 26, 1980		MTR4142
Chapman	Etheldra	Harris	Jul. 21, 1867	Jun. 17, 1952	d/o Marshall Chapman & Ellen Stockett Chapman / In Thee O Lord have I put my trust.	MTR1054
Chapman	Frances	Lucille	Aug. 29, 1923	Feb. 21, 2003	w/o Alton E. Chapman	NSP328
Chapman	Gale	C.	Oct. 5, 1960	Mar. 4, 1967		SMC4177
Chapman	George	Pearson	Dec. 31, 1869	Jun. 22, 1870	s/o Marshall & Ellen Chapman / And they shall be mine saith the Lord of hosts in that day when I make up my jewels. Malachi III : 17th	MTR1058
Chapman	George	Pearson	Mar. 4, 1837	Oct. 12, 1853	To the Memory of George Pearson Chapman s/o John G. & Susan P.A. Chapman, died in Charlottesville, Va. "Them also which sleep in Jesus will God bring with him." I Thes. 4, 14	MTR1041
Chapman	George		Feb. 12, 1854	Mar. 18, 1918	Hope	SMCB019
Chapman	George		Feb. 24, 1820	Dec. 29, 1840	Info obtained from a handout inside the home	CHPNoStone
Chapman	Georgianna		Nov. 8, 1852	Dec. 6, 1908	Hope	SMCB019
Chapman	Gustavus	Alexander	1777	1780	s/o Pearson Chapman	CHPNoStone
Chapman	Helen	Mary	Feb. 2, 1848	Apr. 28, 1913	w/o Andrew G. Chapman / She hath done what she could St Mark 14 Chapt. 8 Vse	MTR4121
Chapman	Henry	H.	May 5, 1883	Dec. 29, 1962		MTR4142
Chapman	Homer	W.	Oct. 3, 1954	Feb. 8, 1958	Sons of Alton and Lucille Chapman	NSP318
Chapman	Inez	E.	Jul. 1, 1914	Dec. 21, 1990		NSP097
Chapman	Irma	A.	Dec. 18, 1889	Aug. 24, 1970		NSP334
Chapman	J.	Alfred	Jun. 6, 1907	Apr. 19, 1982	In God's Loving Care	SMC4148
Chapman	Jacqueline	V.	Jul. 19, 1953	Jun. 18, 1969		SMC4150
Chapman	John	F.	Jan. 26, 1880	Mar. 9, 1971		NSP334

Last Name	First Name	Middle Name	Date of Birth	Date of Death	Transcription / Notes	Cemetery Code
Chapman	John	Grant	Jul. 12, 1833	Mar. 22, 1890	Sacred to the memory of John Grant Chapman / Eldest son of John Grant and Susan P.A. Chapman born at Thoroughfare House, Prince William Co., Va. and Died at Glen Albin, Charles Co., Md. / Verse on Stone: I am the resurrection and the life he that believeth in me Tho' he were dead yet shall he live and whosoever liveth and believeth in me shall never die. John XI 25 and 26 / "I have fought a good fight, I have finished the course, I have kept the faith; henceforth there is laid up for me a crown of righteousness. Blessed are the dead who die in the Lord for they rest from their labors and their works do follow them. REV. XIV 13.	MTR1235, MTR1236
Chapman	John	Grant	Aug. 22, 1897	Dec. 4, 1950	In loving memory	MTR1230
Chapman	John	S.	No Date	Oct. 20, 1841	age 49 years / "The chill of death now coldly lies, Upon they bright and speaking eyes, Index true of polished thought, And heart with kindly feelings fraught, With frank and gay and winning art Such cheerful joy did e'er impart. That cruel seem'd the fatal blow, when from thy friends the spell it tore But she who yet above thee rest, In union sweet with thee was blest Can meekly bow and kiss the rod, Submissive to thy will O God."	CHP001
Chapman	John		No Date	Aug. 1935	Name is shown on church records but burial location is unknown, date is the burial date, not death date	CHRNoStone
Chapman	John	Grant	Jul. 5, 1798	Dec. 10, 1856	To the memory of / of Charles County, Md. S/o Col. Sam'l & Elizabeth Parker Chapman - And I heard a voice from heaven saying unto me write, blessed are the dead which die in the Lord from henceforth; yea saith the Spirit that they may rest from their labours and their works do follow them. Rev. XIV:13	MTR1044
Chapman, Sr.	Joseph	F.	Feb. 4, 1912	Jan. 18, 2001	US Army	SMC4145
Chapman	Katharine	Graham	Dec. 8, 1862	Mar. 31, 1930	d/o John Grant & Mary Stone	MTR1233
Chapman	Louise	E.	Mar. 10, 1932	Apr. 1, 1957		NSP333
Chapman	M.	Harriett	Apr. 11, 1908	Jul. 4, 2004	In God's Loving Care	SMC4148
Chapman	Marshall			Oct. 14, 1901	S/o J.G. & S.P.A. Chapman aged 67 years. The gift of God is eternal life through Jesus Christ our Lord	MTR1063

Last Name	First Name	Middle Name	Date of Birth	Date of Death	Transcription / Notes	Cemetery Code
Chapman	Mary	Agnes	May 12, 1882	Oct. 30, 1912	Hope	SMCB019
Chapman	Mary	Ann	Nov. 22, 1942	Feb. 23, 1966	In God's Loving Care	SMC4176
Chapman	Mary	Carmel, McGovern	Feb. 18, 1928	Mar. 29, 1980	Grave is enclosed with an iron fence and is set apart from the other graves.	WAV2001
Chapman	Mary	Josephine	Mar. 18, 1878	Jan. 3, 1907	Hope	SMCB019
Chapman	Mary	Stone	Aug. 2, 1902	Jul. 25, 1977	Peace	MTR1241
Chapman	Mary	Caroline, Stone	Jul. 9, 1830	Jan. 31, 1899	Sacred to the memory of / d/o William Briscoe Stone & Caroline Brown of Haberdeventure and w/o John Grant Chapman of Glen Albin, Md. Entered into life eternal on - Blessed are the pure in heart for they shall see God.	MTR1234
Chapman	Matilda	L. A.	Nov. 18, 1799	Mar. 25, 1874	w/o Jno. S. Chapman	CHP002
Chapman	Matilda	Louise	1772	1773	d/o Pearson Chapman	CHPNoStone
Chapman	Mildred	C.	Aug. 10, 1938	Apr. 18, 1998	Mother	SMC4149
Chapman	Nannie	Kent	No Date	Jan. 25, 1899	d/o M & E Chapman, aged 24 years, Make her to be numbered with thy saints in glory everlasting, Amen	MTR1059
Chapman	Nannie	Dorset, Matthews	Jan. 16, 1868	Nov. 1, 1941	his wife	MTR1231
Chapman	Nathaniel		1767		s/o Pearson Chapman	CHPNoStone
Chapman, Dr.	Nathaniel		1842	No Date	Info obtained from a handout inside the home	CHPNoStone
Chapman	Nettie	A.	No Date	Jul. 5, 1909	w/o J.C. Chapman / Aged 27y, 5d	ZWU044
Chapman	Nettie		1889	1949		NSP152
Chapman	Paul	D.	Feb. 25, 1951	Oct. 3, 1970	Sons of Alton and Lucille Chapman	NSP318
Chapman, Jr.	Paul		Nov. 30, 1939	Sep. 28, 2008	On earth / In heaven	SMC3036
Chapman, Sr.	Paul		Oct. 30, 1905	Dec. 7, 1974		SMC3332
Chapman	Pearson		Jun. 24, 1745	1784	Info obtained from a handout inside the home	CHPNoStone
Chapman	Pearson		Sep. 7, 1803	May 10, 1877	Info obtained from a handout inside the home	CHP005
Chapman	Rebecca	B.	Apr. 30, 1888	Sep. 17, 1986	In loving memory	MTR1230
Chapman	Robert	Alexander	Apr. 25, 1845	Oct. 21, 1914		SJE121

Last Name	First Name	Middle Name	Date of Birth	Date of Death	Transcription / Notes	Cemetery Code
Chapman, M.D.	Robert	F.	Jul. 25, 1841	Nov. 12, 1912	Of New York City, seventh s/o Gen. John Grant & Susan P. A. Chapman, born Jul 25, 1841 at LaPlata, Md. Passed to the fuller life. We give thanks to God for his life of service among us. We know that for him faith has become light & that his portion is assuredly in heavenly plans through Jesus Christ	MTR1047
Chapman	Robert	Marshall	Jan. 22, 1886	Jan. 29, 1948		MTR4143
Chapman	Rosie	Lee	1900	1987	Blessed are they who die in the Lord	OAK108
Chapman	S.	M.	No Date	Jun. 8, 1870	age 62 years / Consort of Pearson Chapman / Our Mother / stone broken in half	CHP003
Chapman	Samuel		May 23, 1882	May 23, 1882	(Little) Born & Died on same day	MTR4119
Chapman	Sharon	C.	Jan. 7, 1955	No Date	m. Sep 1, 1973	NSP213
Chapman	Sigismunda	M.	Jul. 16, 1875	Jan. 28, 1899	Unable to read verse on stone	MTR4144
Chapman, Sr.	Spencer	J.	Apr. 4, 1953	Apr. 6, 2005	m. Sep 1, 1973	NSP213
Chapman	Susan	P. A.	Sep. 12, 1801	Jan. 17, 1872	Sacred to the memory of Susan P.A. Chapman daughter of George & Susan P.A. Chapman of Pr. Wm. Co., Va. and wife of John G. Chapman. Yea though I walk through the valley of the shadow of death I will fear no evil, for Thou art with me. Thy rod and Thy staff they comfort me. Psalm XXIII V. 14	MTR1042
Chapman	Susan	Pearson	Sep. 9, 1868	Apr. 17, 1949		MTR1232
Chapman	Susanna	Pearson, Alexander	1766	1815	Info obtained from a handout inside the home	CHPNoStone
Chapman	Thelma	K.	Oct. 24, 1922	Dec. 30, 1982		SMC4146
Chapman	Theodore		Sep. 6, 1908	Mar. 31, 1970	Maryland SGT US Army WWII	NSP313
Chapman	Thomas	D.	No Date	Jul. 5, 1905	In memoriam / aged 66 years / His wife at rest	OFE4106
Chapman	Thomas		No Date	Dec. 14, 1937	Info is from Christ Church microfilm Reel 3, Pg 260-261 located at the College of Southern MD, LaPlata, MD	MTRNoStone
Chapman	Unknown		Jul. 1900	Jul. 1900	d/o Helen Pearson Chapman / info obtained from a handout inside the home	CHPNoStone
Chapman	William	Brown	Oct. 3, 1871	Oct. 13, 1871	s/o Virginia Alexander Chapman and Thomas Foster Chapman	CHPNoStone
Chapman	William	Briscoe, Stone	Jul. 3, 1865	May 13, 1945		MTR1231
Chapman	William	Briscoe, Stone	Jun. 19, 1909	Jun. 25, 1987		MTR1243

Last Name	First Name	Middle Name	Date of Birth	Date of Death	Transcription / Notes	Cemetery Code
Chapman	Wilson	A.	Sep. 18, 1913	Mar. 2, 1993	Col. US Air Force WWII (Grave is enclosed with an iron fence and is set apart from the other graves.)	WAV2001
Chapman	Wm.	H.	No Date	Nov. 6, 1887	In Memory of / In his 19th year	ZWU017
Chappelear	Elizabeth	D.	May 30, 1821	Apr. 10, 1890	Our Mother w/o George Chappelear / aged 68 years 10 months and 10 days	OFE4091
Chappelear	Emily	F.	No Date	No Date	Age 75 / info is from church records	OFENoStone
Chappelear	Eva	M.	1878	1962		OFE4055
Chappelear	G.	J.	Feb. 11, 1839	Oct. 21, 1898		OFE4090
Chappelear	George		Nov. 22, 1800	Apr. 11, 1887	Our Father / Aged 86 years 4 months and 19 Days	OFE4092
Chappelear	John	A.	Feb. 1, 1906	Dec. 15, 1985		OFE4053
Chappelear	John	H.	Nov. 16, 1835	Jul. 11, 1923		OFE4054
Chappelear	John	L.	1873	1961		OFE4053
Chappelear	Mary	E.	1849	1937		SMCE067
Chappelear	Susan	J.	1852	1940		OFE4052
Chappelear, Mrs.	Unknown		No Date	Mar. 27, 1899	Info is from church records	OFENoStone
Chapura	John	S.	1910	1994		SCL1204
Chapura	Kathleen	A.	1916	2007		SCL1204
Chaput	Blanche	C.	1923	No Date		HGH4009
Chaput	Mederic	H.	1926	No Date		HGH4009
Charles	Jessamine	G.	1883	1962		GHB012
Charnock	Benjamin	F.	May 23, 1867	Feb. 14, 1960	h/o Clara Charnock Father	OFE3054
Charnock	Clara		Jun.e 12, 1886	May 7, 1934	w/o Ben Charnock Mother	OFE3055
Charnock	Felicia	Sue	Dec. 11, 1946	No Date	Giant Food is written on a truck carved into the stone. Firemans emblem with Chief Co 3 Waldorf VFD on it. / July 17, 1970	OFE3053
Charnock	Ira		1907	1998	married Nov 7, 1938	NSP727
Charnock	J.	Donald	Feb. 26, 1941	Mar. 19, 2001	Giant Food is written on a truck carved into the stone. Firemans emblem with Chief Co 3 Waldorf VFD on it. / July 17, 1970	OFE3053
Charnock	Viola	Theresa	1909	1976	married Nov 7, 1938	NSP727
Chase	Alice	T.	1901	1982		SJO5006

Last Name	First Name	Middle Name	Date of Birth	Date of Death	Transcription / Notes	Cemetery Code
Chase, Sr.	Ambrose	Cecil	Dec. 24, 1939	Dec. 19, 2002		SMY2003
Chase	Annie	W.	1867	1947	Name and dates etched on a cement cross	POM028
Chase	Annie		1887	1972		SMY2112
Chase	Bernetta		1906	1978	Info is from the Historical Society Research located at The College of Southern MD, LaPlata, MD	SCLNoStone
Chase	C.	William	1925	1942		SJO1169
Chase	Carrie		Aug. 1, 1877	Jul. 8, 1909	w/o Jackson Chase	POM012
Chase	Catherine	L.	Jan. 7, 1930	Feb. 20, 1996	Beloved mother & grandmother	SMC2040
Chase	Catherine	O.	Jan. 14, 1911	Mar. 5, 2000	Married Oct 31, 1927	SIC8021
Chase	Christine	D.	1922	1943		SJO1170
Chase	Damien	A.	No Date	May 15, 1979		SAC1008
Chase, Jr.	Dennis	D.	Oct. 26, 1986	Jun. 15, 1991	Little Dennis	SMC2069
Chase	Dorothy	J.	1904	1990		NSP072
Chase	Edward	B.	1902	1988		SJO5006
Chase	Edward		Mar. 12, 1873	Jul. 26, 1951		SJO1165
Chase	Eleanor	R.	Sep. 28, 1936	No Date		SIC9106
Chase	Eugene	C.	Oct. 12, 1908	Dec. 26, 1988	Mother, Father "Earth hath no Sorrow that heaven cannot heal"	SMI015
Chase	Frances		No Date	Feb. 9, 1912	Aged 82 years / May they rest in peace	SCL1018
Chase	George		No Date	Dec. 21, 1909	Aged 82 years / His wife Frances / Aged 80 yrs. May they rest in peace	SCL1018
Chase, Sr.	George	Dennis	1927	1990	Father / In loving memory	SMC2070
Chase	George	R.	Oct. 8, 1927	May 12, 2005		SMC4187
Chase	Grant	A.	Mar. 2, 1903	Jan. 12, 1993		SJO1173
Chase	Herman	Kenneth	No Date	Jan. 29, 1977	Info is from church records	SHINoStone
Chase	J.	Bap	1828	1908	Father / Aged 80 years	SMCC048
Chase	James	A.	1920	1983		SMC1062
Chase	James	A.	Sep. 10, 1906	Nov. 27, 1971	Married Oct 31, 1927	SIC8021
Chase	James	Leroy	Jul. 28, 1927	Mar. 21, 1981	Loving husband & father	SIC8072
Chase	Jeannetta	M.	Dec. 7, 1900	May 26, 1976		SJO1163
Chase	John	Alexander	Jun. 3, 1934	May 8, 2003		SIC9088

Last Name	First Name	Middle Name	Date of Birth	Date of Death	Transcription / Notes	Cemetery Code
Chase	Joseph	D.	1959	1983		SAC4015
Chase	Joseph	O.	Jun. 29, 1937	No Date		SIC9106
Chase	Lloyd	W.	Apr. 30, 1917	Dec. 18, 1966	Beloved Husband	SHI127
Chase	Lucille	E.	Aug. 19, 1909	May 18, 1995	Mother, Father "Earth hath no sorrow that heaven cannot heal"	SMI015
Chase	Margaret	Viola	1896	1985		SMC2090
Chase	Mary	C., Briscoe	Dec. 21, 1869	Jan. 10, 1916	Wife (on top of stone)	SJO2298
Chase	Mary	Estelle	1923	1985		SMY2009
Chase	Mary	Lavenia	Dec. 30, 1899	Dec. 25, 1993		SMC3210
Chase	Mary	M.	May 28, 1923	May 27, 2003	Mother	SJO2098
Chase	Nick		1889	1962		SMY2114
Chase	Robert		Mar. 13, 1877	Feb. 7, 1955		SJO1164
Chase	Samuel		1865	1935		POM027
Chase	Theresa	Ann	Sep. 17, 1954	Dec. 31, 2006	Beloved Mother / Forever in our hearts	SIC9014
Chase	Theresa	E.	Jan. 29, 1902	Sep. 28, 2001		SJO1173
Chase	Thomas	J.	Aug. 15, 1958	Aug. 13, 1988		SMC4188
Chase, Sr.	Thomas	Jerome	Aug. 2, 1926	Aug. 15, 1973	Father / h/o Mary M. Chase	SJO2098
Chase	William	Oliver	Jan. 30, 1952	Oct. 25, 2003	"Bill"	SIC9107
Chesley	Annie	Marie	1924	1978	Info is from The Historical Society Research located at The College of Southern MD, LaPlata, MD	SJONoStone
Chesley	Barbara	Ann	Jul. 7, 1950	Jan. 26, 1987		SJO1048
Chesley	Carroll	Lancaster	Oct. 2, 1941	Nov. 25, 2003	Verse on stone: Eternal light is shining upon me, I am home with the Lord	SJO4040
Chesley	Cecil	A.	Feb. 23, 1946	Sep. 9, 1999		SJO1033
Chesley	Charles	S.	Dec. 13, 1930	Feb. 5, 1968		SJO2256
Chesley	Clifton	Lamont	1965	1989	In loving memory / Kip	SMC2089
Chesley	Doris	A.	1926	No Date		SJO1013
Chesley	Dorothy	C.	Oct. 10, 1917	Sep. 3, 1972		SJO2257
Chesley	Francis		1922	2007	Thornton Funeral Home Marker	SCL3395
Chesley	James	F.	Jan. 8, 1938	Nov. 11, 1962	Maryland A1C 464 CAM SQ AF	SJO4038
Chesley	James	L.	No Date	Jul. 22, 1928	Age 8 / info is from the Historical Society Research located at The College of Southern MD, LaPlata, MD	SCLNoStone

Last Name	First Name	Middle Name	Date of Birth	Date of Death	Transcription / Notes	Cemetery Code
Chesley	Jane		No Date	Sep. 22, 1926	Age 48 / info is from the Historical Society Research located at The College of Southern MD, LaPlata, MD	SCLNoStone
Chesley	John	E.	1920	No Date		SJO1030
Chesley	John	Francis	Apr. 3, 1914	Jul. 15, 1999		SJO4037
Chesley	Louise	E.	1923	1989		SJO1030
Chesley	Mary	A.	1914	2003		SMY2008
Chesley	Matilda		1855	1926		SJO2255
Chesley	Mattie	J.	Aug. 12, 1896	Feb. 22, 1985		SJO2254
Chesley	Moses		1854	1920		SJO2255
Chesley	Russell	Martin	May 18, 1948	Sep. 11, 2001	A1C US Air Force Vietnam	SJO4039
Chesley	Sherman	J.	Mar. 2, 1953	Oct. 22, 1954		SCL3099
Chesley	Sylvester	W.	1914	1991		SJO1013
Chesley	Thomas	O.	1901	1985		SMY2008
Chesley, Jr.	Thomas	O.	Dec. 29, 1934	Dec. 7, 1980	SP2 US Army	SMY2027
Chesley	William	A.	Mar. 6, 1886	Jun. 5, 1939		SJO2254
Chesley	Mabel	C.	1926	1992	All our love Francis & the girls	SJO4192
Cheslock	Clara	P.	Mar. 17, 1915	Sep. 26, 2002		SIC7033
Cheslock	Joseph	J.	Feb. 4, 1908	Mar. 10, 1996		SIC7033
Chesser	Alden	Willard	Feb. 23, 1894	Jan. 20, 1981	PFC US Army World War I	CHR148
Chesser	Macy	Florence	Dec. 31, 1898	May 3, 1982		CHR147
Chialastri	Robert	Paul	Feb. 17, 1952	Aug. 25, 1997	"Bobby"	HER007
Chichester	Robert	William	Nov. 20, 1983	May 25, 1984	Robbie lives in our hearts forever	OFE4099
Chick	Dorothy	A.	Dec. 14, 1935	No Date	Beloved wife and mother	SMC4252
Chick, Sr.	John	Francis	Oct. 15, 1925	Dec. 19, 1997	SM2 US Navy WW II	SMC4252
Chick	Patricia	L.	1959	1986		SMC4251
Children	Unknown		No Date	No Date	Small stone with "Children" etched at the top it is near the stone for Aloysius Elder	SIC4008
Childress	Donna	M.	Jul. 18, 1957	Apr. 23, 1999	Mom	SMC2151
Childress	Paul	G.	Mar. 9, 1959	Oct. 23, 2000	Dad	SMC2151
Chiles	Ida	H. F.	No Date	No Date	Aged 5 years 11 months & 13 days Footstone: Initials I.H.F.C.	CHG017

Last Name	First Name	Middle Name	Date of Birth	Date of Death	Transcription / Notes	Cemetery Code
Chiles	Janes		No Date	Jun. 12, 1873	Sacred to the memory of / who departed this life D / aged 66 years. "Blessed are the dead which die in the Lord". Stone Maker was Jouvenal Wash'n D.C. Footstone: Initials J.C.	CHG009
Chiles, Rev.	Wm.	J.	May 12, 1810	Apr. 13, 1874	Sacred to the memory of / Stone Maker was Jouvenal Wash'n D.C. Footstone: Initials W.J.C. Stone is broken off base and is leaning up against trees	CHG002
Chiles	William	Shepard	Oct. 11, 1841	Apr. 14, 1889	B & W picture taken around 1974 by J. Richard Rivoire, Current picture showing the stone is turned over and is laying on the ground. Footstone: Initials WSC	CHG006
Chilsey	Francis	T.	No Date	Oct. 3, 1968		HGH3041
Chilton	Eula	Grey, Austin	Mar. 19, 1917	Jul. 1, 1999	Loving Mother / The Lord is my Shepherd	LUM012
Chin	Shee	Tong	Aug. 21, 1895	Sep. 1, 1991		HER013
Ching	Alice	R.	No Date	Dec. 31, 1878	Info is from church records	OFENoStone
Ching	Pearl	E.	Jun. 9, 1892	May 3, 1980		TRI129
Ching	Robert	Lee	May 18, 1920	Mar. 31, 1989		TRI127
Ching	Sophia	M.	Jan. 6, 1848	Apr. 23, 1930	May she rest in peace	TRI104
Ching, Capt.	Thomas	H.	Jun. 11, 1847	Nov. 22, 1923	Captain / I have fought a good fight. I have finished my course. I have kept the faith.	TRI104
Ching	Thomas	M.	Nov. 5, 1886	Aug. 15, 1954		TRI129
Chippendale	Nancy	Frances	1937	2008		PKH022A
Chisley	Agnes	Eleanor	1924	2008	Last number on death date is missing from funeral home marker / info is from Catholic Cemeteries	HGH4287
Chisley	Betty	Ann	Sep. 7, 1953	Oct. 1, 2007	"Betty Boop" / Loved By All	SAC1142
Chisley	Cecil	Jerome	Sep. 18, 1949	Dec. 19, 1988	In Loving Memory	SCA052
Chisley	Daniel	Wade	Jun. 30, 1947	Mar. 30, 1987	SP4 US Army Vietnam	HGH4244
Chisley	Della Ann	Elizabeth	Apr. 5, 1898	Nov. 13, 1967	Wife & Mother	HGH3044
Chisley	Eulalia	E.	1903	1993		HGH4227
Chisley	Francis	N.	Nov. 20, 1939	Sep. 15, 2001		HGH4046
Chisley	Irene		Nov. 27, 1919	Jun. 19, 1946		NSP181A
Chisley	James	M.	1916	1983	In Loving Memory	SCA101
Chisley, Jr.	James	R.	May 31, 1959	Feb. 21, 1978	s/o Mr. & Mrs. James Chisley	ZBC025

Last Name	First Name	Middle Name	Date of Birth	Date of Death	Transcription / Notes	Cemetery Code
Chisley, Jr.	John	Francis	Apr. 20, 1922	Nov. 22, 1999		HGH4174
Chisley	John	F.	1896	1976	"Goldie"	HGH4228
Chisley	Mabel	E. Ford	Mar. 19, 1900	Jul. 21, 1995	Gone but not forgotten	SHI176
Chisley	Mary	G.	1921	1969	In Loving Memory	SCA101
Chisley	Mary	Gustella	Oct. 29, 1921	Dec. 19, 1969	We all love you age 48 / Info was obtained from the Historical Society Research located at the College of Southern Md, LaPlata, Md	OAKNoStone
Chisley	Patricia	Ann	Aug. 14, 1948	Apr. 26, 1996	"Patsy" We Love You We Miss You You're Always In Our Thoughts	SAC4067
Chisley, Jr.	Perry		1997	1997	Arehart Echols Funeral Home Marker	OAK141
Chisley	Rufus	M.	Mar. 16, 1892	Jan. 12, 1976	Husband and father	HGH3043
Chisley	Tanina	Lynn	Aug. 14, 1969	Sep. 3, 1972	Angel of God	HGH3042
Chisley	Thomas	D.	Aug. 6, 1941	Sep. 21, 1995		SCA053
Chriscaden	Althea	S.	Sep. 28, 1880	Sep. 3, 1971		SJE012
Christ	Caroline		Jan. 13, 1840	Jun. 11, 1899	I H S his wife	OFE4005
Christ	Henry		Jan. 10, 1840	Sept 9, 1917	I H S	OFE4005
Christian	Myrtle		1921	1975	Funeral home marker embedded in concrete with an angel statue on top, all are painted white	SCL3284
Cieslik	Albert	Peter	Jan. 21, 1926	Nov. 20, 2003	Beloved Schatz, Papa and Opa / Our love goes with you until we meet again	SJO6001
Cieslik	Anneliese	Ottilie	May 2, 1938	No Date	Beloved Schatz, Papa and Opa / Our love goes with you until we meet again	SJO6001

Last Name	First Name	Middle Name	Date of Birth	Date of Death	Transcription / Notes	Cemetery Code
Cinicola	John	Carmine	Jan. 7, 1944	Jun. 19, 1999	Verse on stone: God looked around his garden and saw an empty place, he then looked down upon the earth, and saw your tired face. So he put his arms around you, and gathered you to rest, God's garden must be so beautiful, he only takes the very best. He knew that you were suffering. He knew you were in pain. He knew that you would never get well on earth again. He saw the road was getting rough and the hills were hard to climb, so he closed your weary eyelids and whispered "peace be thine." It broke my heart to lose you, but you didn't go alone. For a part of me went with you. The day God called you home. Until we meet again, Your loving wife, Laura	SIC9008, SIC9008A
Claffy	Anna	M.	1889	1982		SMCD107
Claffy	William	H.	1883	1962		SMCD107
Clagett	Allan	Page	1887	1956	Located in Clagett Plot	MTR3178
Clagett, Jr.	Allan	Page	Mar. 27, 1914	Jan. 25, 2005	Married Oct 5, 1940	MTR4270
Clagett	Cora	Hawkins	1891	1978	Located in Clagett Plot	MTR3177
Clagett	G.	Marshall	1860	1910	Asleep in Jesus	SJE137
Clagett	Hal	Eugene	Mar. 31, 1940	Nov. 9, 2006		SCL4207
Clagett	Henry	Hawkins	1918	1926	Located in Clagett Plot	MTR3179
Clagett	Horatio		No Date	Feb. 12, 1844	Aged 67 years	HRD019
Clagett	Jennie	Louise	May 26, 1899	Aug. 9, 1900	d/o G. Marshall and Kate D. Clagett / He shall gather the lambs with his arm and carry them in his bosom	SJE136
Clagett	Katherine	Mitchell	Nov. 5, 1918	Nov. 21, 1985	Married Oct 5, 1940	MTR4270
Clagett	Mabel	Bernice	Dec. 25, 1938	Aug. 1, 1994		SCL4207
Clagett	William	H.	No Date	May 22, 1888	Died at his residence in Pomonkey. Aged 76 / info is from the 1940 DAR book pages 54, 99 & 100	STWNoStone
Claggett	Mary	Hannah	Feb. 9, 1846	May 15, 1882	The 1880 census shows her last name is Claggett instead of Glaggett	OSP083
Claggett	Sidney	B.	Jun. 4, 1868	Jan. 3, 1885	Info is from The Historical Society Research located at College of Southern MD, LaPlata, MD	OSPNoStone
Clancy	Ela	S.	Apr. 17, 1868	May 11, 1947		SCL1248

Last Name	First Name	Middle Name	Date of Birth	Date of Death	Transcription / Notes	Cemetery Code
Clark	??? Walter		No Date	Mar. 12, 1899	Info is from Christ Church microfilm Reel 1 Pg 86-87 located at the College of Southern MD, LaPlata, MD	MTRNoStone
Clark	A.	Leon	1948	2008		HGH4051
Clark	Agnes	M.	Mar. 2, 1918	Aug. 28, 2002		HGH4179
Clark	Alcena	K.	Mar. 15, 1907	Jun. 18, 1989	In God's Care	POM019
Clark	Andrew	J.	1892	1971		SAC2025
Clark, Jr.	Andrew	J.	Oct. 10, 1915	Nov. 9, 1926	s/o Andrew J. and Louise Farrall Clark	SAC2024
Clark	Barbara	Lee	Jun. 16, 1946	Jun. 29, 1990	Daughter	PKH106
Clark	Don	Bradford	Apr. 2, 1922	Jul. 9, 1995	Pfc US Army WW II	SHI097
Clark	Dorothy	Maxine	Jun. 8, 1924	Dec. 11, 2008		PKH105
Clark	E.	Elnora	1901	1990		POM063
Clark	Elizabeth	A.	Jan. 31, 1808	Jan. 10, 1874	Sacred to the memory of Elizabeth A. Clark Blessed are the dead which die in the Lord from henceforth. You with the Spirit, that they may rest from their labours.	SPL3133
Clark	Elizabeth		No Date	Nov. 11, 1864	Info is from the Historical Society Research and the 1940 DAR book pg 193 located at the College of Southern MD, LaPlata, MD.	SMCNoStone
Clark	Estelle	Waugh	Jan. 19, 1925	Aug. 15, 1985	Our loving Aunt & Sister	SHI208
Clark	George	R.	Sep. 6, 1940	Apr. 6, 1967		NSP985
Clark	Henrietta		No Date	Aug. 1890	Age 70 / info is from the Historical Society Research and the 1940 DAR book pg 193 located at the College of Southern MD, LaPlata, MD.	SMCNoStone
Clark	James	F.	1922	1976		NSP534
Clark	James	Joseph	Jun. 9, 1922	Jul. 30, 1995	Cox US Navy World War II	HGH4161
Clark	James	M.	Jul. 1897	Dec. 1977		ZBC134
Clark	James	W.	1898	1975		POM063
Clark	John	L.	Sep. 16, 1892	May 27, 1957		HGH3048
Clark	John		1927	2003	Thornton Funeral Home Marker	SHI210
Clark	John		Jul. 24, 1877	Oct. 24, 1958		CRA003
Clark	Katherine	D.	Sep. 1912	Aug. 1995		ZBC134
Clark	Kenneth	R.	1896	1948		MTR1017
Clark	Laura	A.	1908	1982		ZBC188

Last Name	First Name	Middle Name	Date of Birth	Date of Death	Transcription / Notes	Cemetery Code
Clark	Lester	E.	1883	1958		NSP679
Clark	Lillian	A.	Dec. 16, 1923	Apr. 24, 2005	In God's Care	NSP979
Clark	Lorna	Johnson	Jul. 2, 1931	Nov. 6, 2001		SAC2007
Clark	Lottie	A.	1893	1978		NSP679
Clark	Mary	E.	May 12, 1896	Aug. 20, 1991	Beloved Mother	ALX046
Clark	Mary	Louise	1889	1965		SAC2025
Clark	Mary	R.	May 10, 1900	Mar. 15, 1953		SHI159
Clark	Mary	Ruth	Apr. 19, 1901	Jul. 5, 1962		MTR1011
Clark	Mildred	E.	Feb. 21, 1926	Jul. 24, 2005	Beloved mother of Barbara, Pat, James, Larry, Betty	HGH4160
Clark	Mildred	I.	Nov. 29, 1919	Nov. 9, 1998	Mom	CLV315
Clark	Myra		Oct. 5, 1961	Dec. 20, 1978	St Mary's Academy / Class of Lord / In Loving Memory	SCL4136
Clark	Nannie	V., Bond	Mar. 1, 1911	Jul. 9, 1984		SAC4010
Clark	Ora	Abell	Mar. 6, 1879	Jan. 14, 1961		PKH049
Clark	Patricia	Lyons	No Date	No Date		CHR378
Clark	R.	Cassoline	1950	No Date		HGH4051
Clark	Ralph	Abell	May 3, 1921	Dec. 30, 1988	Tec 5 US Army WW II	PKH105
Clark	Richard	R.	Nov. 22, 1917	Oct. 31, 1984	In God's Care	NSP979
Clark	Robert	Sheldon	No Date	No Date		CHR378
Clark	Ruby Lillian	Mitchell	Sep. 23, 1891	Nov. 10, 1918	Beloved w/o Wm. R. Clark / and infant son / A light from our home is gone. A voice we loved is stilled. A place is vacant in our hearts that never can be filled	PKH035 PKH036
Clark	Thomas	Jarrett	Mar. 3, 1920	Sep. 10, 1998	STM3 US Navy World War II	HGH4178
Clark	Thomas	Roger	Mar. 17, 1920	Apr. 14, 1988		SAC2006
Clark	Viola	K.	Dec. 3, 1899	Apr. 17, 1975		MTR1010
Clark	Virginia	F.	Jun. 6, 1922	Oct. 21, 1977		SHI098
Clark	Virginia	Walker	Oct. 23, 1860	Jul. 18, 1929		MTR1013
Clark, Rev.	W.	M.	Oct. 30, 1884	May 13, 1942	s/o Rev. Mitchell and Sarah Clark, Pastor of Pleasant Grove Baptist Church	SMI055
Clark	William	R.	Dec. 16, 1888	Jun. 8, 1950	A light from our home is gone. A voice we loved is stilled. A place is vacant in our hearts that never can be filled	PKH035 PKH036
Clark	William		1922	1985	Thornton Funeral Home Marker	SHI160

Last Name	First Name	Middle Name	Date of Birth	Date of Death	Transcription / Notes	Cemetery Code
Clark	William	Randall	Oct. 15, 1856	May 17, 1947	To my Husband / Aged 39 years / Erected by his wife E.C. Clark	MTR1012
Clarke	Basil	E.	No Date	Sep. 3, 1913		POM062
Clarke	Blanche		1873	1980		HGH3051
Clarke	Earl	Harold	Sep. 18, 1912	Feb. 28, 1977		ODE414
Clarke	Eric	Albert	No Date	Apr. 5, 1984	s/o Eric and Linda Clarke (There is a headstone with Clarke on one side and Gagliardi on the other side)	MTR3129
Clarke	Gardnal		No Date	Mar. 18, 1938	There is only one date on the stone	SCL1032
Clarke	Gordon	Dobson	Jan. 13, 1928	Dec. 23, 1968	District of Columbia SP4 Artillery World War II	CHR341
Clarke	Olivia	Davis	Nov. 1, 1906	May 24, 1999		ODE415
Clayton	Charles	C.	Sep. 21, 1903	No Date		SCL1036
Clayton	Edith	Warren	1891	1951	Clayton Sisters	ZBC169
Clayton	Minnie	Robinson	1888	1954	Clayton Sisters	ZBC169
Clayton	Philomena	L.	Nov. 27, 1906	Jun. 18, 1970		SCL1036
Claytop	Ida	Mae	1920	1947		NSP178
Clegg	Richard	Wayne	Dec. 12, 1965	Jan. 15, 1998	In loving memory of Richard Wayne Clegg / Richie / Forever a part of us Back of stone: Ritchie, you were truly a gift from God to this world and a real strength in our own family. The memories of your smile, laughter and hugs are forever etched in our hearts. You had a passion for life, lived each day to the fullest and because of your sincere kindness and honesty, you were blessed with many genuine friendships. We all miss you so very much and only wish you could have stayed with us a little longer.	SJO5045
Clement	Ashby		Jul. 17, 1895	Jan. 23, 1896	Infant s/o Warren and Sadie Clement / Asleep in the arms of Jesus	SJE235
Clements	Agnes	Irene	Apr. 18, 1907	No Date		SMY3127
Clements	Alexander	I.	Nov. 29, 1862	Mar. 18, 1924		HGH1004
Clements, Jr.	Alexander	I.	Aug. 8, 1897	Mar. 11, 1976	"Alec"	HGH1003
Clements	Anne	Mary	May 20, 1922	Feb. 11, 1985		MTR4262
Clements	Augustine		No Date	Jan. 1939	Name is shown on church records but burial location is unknown, date is the burial date, not death date	CHRNoStone

Last Name	First Name	Middle Name	Date of Birth	Date of Death	Transcription / Notes	Cemetery Code
Clements	Charles		Feb. 1, 1908	Sep. 15, 1966		HGH1004
Clements	Christine	Mudd	Dec. 24, 1902	Feb. 29, 2004		SMY3101
Clements	Edna	M.	1908	1969		HGH1112
Clements	Edward		Mar. 8, 1905	Feb. 4, 1968		SIG039
Clements	George	L.	Jun. 5, 1883	May 23, 1909		SJO3052A
Clements	George	R.	May 10, 1853	Aug. 9, 1909		SJO3052A
Clements	George	W.	Aug. 17, 1913	Nov. 3, 1978		SJO6010
Clements	Gretchen	Perrie	May 19, 1919	Jan. 14, 2000	Death Date is from web site Ancestry.com	SMY3157
Clements	Henry		1782	Oct. 4, 1822	IHS In memory of Henry Clements of Thos. / aged 40 years / Info is from the Historical Society Research at the College of Southern MD, LaPlata, MD	GMCNo Stone
Clements	J.	Percy	May 5, 1875	May 26, 1952		SJO3038
Clements	James	E.	1854	1929		ODE033
Clements	Jane	C.	1839	1874		SJO3279
Clements	Jimmie		No Date	No Date	Baby / located in Clements Plot	SMY3105
Clements	John	A.	1848	1911		MTR4222
Clements	John	Carroll	Oct. 9, 1895	Jun. 8, 1957		SMY3107
Clements	John	O.	1901	1965		HGH1112
Clements	John	W.	Dec. 22, 1861	Sep. 14, 1953		ODE032
Clements	L.	Bertrum	1898	1944	Husband	SMY3106
Clements	Leonard	A.	1889	1952		SIC6073
Clements, Jr.	Leonard	Aubrey	Mar. 11, 1933	Jul. 15, 1975		SIC7006
Clements, Jr.	Leonard	J.	May 15, 1963	Aug. 10, 1967		SMC4028
Clements	Martha	Ann	1836	1866		ODE031
Clements	Martha	Bowling	May 18, 1937	Nov. 22, 1978		SIC7006
Clements	Mary	A.	1850	1940		SJO3279
Clements	Mary	E.	Apr. 8, 1868	Jun. 9, 1955		HGH1004
Clements	Mary	Eleanor	Dec. 6, 1873	Jun. 2, 1967	His Wife	SIG007
Clements	Mary	Florence	1868	1929	his wife	SMY3088
Clements	Mary	L.	Nov. 22, 1913	Feb. 12, 1999		SJO6010
Clements	Mary	Long	Mar. 20, 1888	Aug. 22, 1971		SMY3107

Last Name	First Name	Middle Name	Date of Birth	Date of Death	Transcription / Notes	Cemetery Code
Clements	Mary	Louise	1885	1971	Info is from The Historical Society Research located at The College of Southern MD, LaPlata, MD.	SMYNoStone
Clements	Mary		No Date	No Date	Baby / located in Clements Plot	SMY3104
Clements	Maximilian		Oct. 10, 1864	Jan. 7, 1936	His Wife	SIG007
Clements	Neale		Oct. 24, 1893	Dec. 14, 1943		HGH1004
Clements	Rebecca	H.	1903	1979		SIC6073
Clements	Robert	Alvin	Mar. 21, 1882	Nov. 27, 1970		SJO2347
Clements	Robert	Lee	1864	1929	his wife	SMY3088
Clements	Robert	Leon	Dec. 8, 1904	Mar. 4, 1974		SMY3127
Clements	Rose	L.	Oct. 19, 1855	Jan. 23, 1917		SJO3052A
Clements	Susie	P.	Aug. 28, 1882	Nov. 15, 1958		SJO3038
Clements	Thomas	A.	1824	1902		SJO3279
Clements	Unknown		No Date	No Date	Infant son of John O. Clements	HGH1111
Clements	William	B.	Aug. 27, 1874	May 4, 1955		SCL1126
Clements, Jr.	William	Noble	Oct. 5, 1927	No Date		SMY3158
Clements, Sr.	William	Noble	Jun. 17, 1893	Mar. 5, 1982		SMY3101
Clerklee	Jacubus		No Date	No Date	Londini nativus, obit IV Die Marti, Anno Domini, MDCCCXIX, Aetatix Sune LXI (unable to locate graves, info is from the Historical Society Research located at the College of Southern MD, LaPlata, MD) / picture is from the files of J. Richard Rivoire	BRO002
Clerklee	Margaret	Russell, Jacoli	No Date	No Date	Conjux. Obit XXIII Die Novembris Anno Domini MDCCCXXIX Aetatis Suse XLV (unable to locate graves, info is from the Historical Society Research located at the College of Southern MD, LaPlata, MD)	BRONoStone
Cleveland	Dorothy	Jane	Sep. 23, 1909	Aug. 2, 1982		CHR195
Cleveland	Philip	Frederick	Aug. 27, 1902	Jun. 6, 1974		CHR196
Clifford	Gertrude	M.	1886	1980		SJO5018
Clifford	Thomas		Jun. 7, 1944	Jul. 18, 2004	Number 251K inscribed on stone	CLV371
Cline	Olive	Davis	Feb. 8, 1907	Nov. 18, 1990		CMX2114
Clopton	William	W.	Jan. 15, 1941	Apr. 12, 2002	RM2 US Navy Vietnam	SAC1063

Last Name	First Name	Middle Name	Date of Birth	Date of Death	Transcription / Notes	Cemetery Code
Close	Alverta	Eunice	Jan. 5, 1934	No Date	Together Forever June 29, 1957 / Back of Stone: Be not afraid I go before you always Come, follow me and I will give you rest	SAC2055
Close, Sr.	William	Edward	Mar. 7, 1927	Apr. 27, 2006	Together Forever June 29, 1957 / PFC US Army WW II Back of Stone: Be not afraid I go before you always Come, follow me and I will give you rest	SAC2055
Clynes	Charles	T.	Sep. 25, 1931	No Date	In Loving Memory / USAF - CMSGT Korean / Vietnam Veteran	SJO5003
Clynes	Eleanor	M	May 3, 1937	No Date	In Loving Memory / USAF - CMSGT Korean / Vietnam Veteran	SJO5003
Clynes	Kyle	Luis	No Date	Dec. 8, 1990	In loving memory of	NSP713
Coakley	Forrest		1904	1990		SPL5122
Coates	Agnes	I.	Apr. 7, 1960	Jul. 6, 1995		SMC4172
Coates	Arthur	DeSales	10/31/1944	6/15/1963	Burial site is unknown / From the church records	SMCNoStone
Coates	Dora	L.	Oct. 14, 1894	May 11, 1963		ODE223
Coates	Edward	T.	Feb. 8, 1892	Jul. 10, 1950		ODE221
Coates	Irene		Dec. 12, 1903	May 24, 1956		NSP309
Coates	Jessie	M.	1897	1959	Mother	SJE063
Coates	Joseph	Kenneth	1/??/1939	9/??/1972	Burial site is unknown / From the church records	SMCNoStone
Coates	Margaret		1919	1969		ALX070
Coates	Mary	Ann	Sep. 9, 1953	Aug. 19, 1991		SMC4174
Coates	Mary	Frances	May 23, 1925	Apr. 8, 1998		OAK049
Coates	Melvin	C.	1894	1959	Father	SJE063
Coates	Melvin	Lee	1919	1924	Son	SJE055
Coates	Noble	Thomas	Jul. 26, 1917	Apr. 16, 1978	CPL US Army World War II	OAK185
Coates	Paul	E.	1940	1989		SMC3158
Coates	Rachel	M.	1938	1991		SMC3157
Coates	Tearra	L.	Aug. 19, 1991	Aug. 19, 1991		SMC4174
Cobey	Alean		No Date	Apr. 17, 1961	Letters carved into cement cross which is partially sunken.	OAK140
Cobey	Amelia	A.	No Date	Feb. 3, 1837	In memory of / daughter of Wm F & Catharine Rennoe who departed this life / in the 21st year of her age	REN012

Last Name	First Name	Middle Name	Date of Birth	Date of Death	Transcription / Notes	Cemetery Code
Cobey	Ann		No Date	Dec. 25, 195?	letters carved into cement cross which is partially sunken. With Randy Cobey	OAK139
Cobey	Catherine	E.	Sep. 14, 1817	Jan. 20, 1897	w/o William D. Cobey / I know that my redeemer liveth	ODE237
Cobey	Effie	S.	1878	1921		MTR4180
Cobey	Ellen	M.	Oct. 31, 1842	May 4, 1904	The gift of God is eternal life through Jesus Christ our Lord. Rom. VI.IIM	ODE236
Cobey	Ethel	H. Gaines	Feb. 8, 1915	Jul. 18, 2000		OAK039
Cobey	Eugene		Jul. 22, 1920	Nov. 7, 2004	CPL US Army World War II	OAK023
Cobey	Francis	Welby	No Date	Sep. 18, 1887	Father was John Francis Cobey and Mother was Laura Price Cobey (info is from Old Durham Church microfilm pg 79 located at the College of Southern MD, LaPlata, MD)	ODENoStone
Cobey	Fredericka	Rainey	Oct. 13, 1906	Nov. 4, 2008	Lt. Col. U.S. Army Air Force / His Wife	ODE235
Cobey	James	E.	Feb. 9, 1970	Jan. 10, 2001	"Jimmy" / son	OAK037
Cobey	Jermal	A., Chippie	Jun. 15, 1963	Feb. 11, 1972		MHB195
Cobey	John	Alexander	Jan. 4, 1884	Sep. 8, 1887	In memory of our Darling / s/o A.D. & S.C. Cobey / Of such is the Kingdom of Heaven	ODE256
Cobey	John		No Date	Jul. 5, 1889	Buried Jul 7, 1889 age 51 (info is from Old Durham Church microfilm pg 81-82 located at the College of Southern MD, LaPlata, MD)	ODENoStone
Cobey	Margaret		1921	1994	Thornton Funeral Home Marker	OAK150
Cobey, M.D.	Milton	Carpinter	Apr. 24, 1909	Jan. 4, 1983	Lt. Col. U.S. Army Air Force / His Wife	ODE235
Cobey	Randy		No Date	Nov. 7,1959	letters carved into cement cross which is partially sunken. With Ann Cobey,	OAK139
Cobey	Rosa	A.	Dec. 8, 1872	Jul. 5, 1911	Aged 38 yrs. She was beloved by God and man	POM085
Cobey	Samuel		1915	1974	Thornton Funeral Home Marker	OAK142
Cobey	Shaneka	R.	Feb. 23, 1978	May 28, 2001	The Lord is my Shepherd	SJO2234
Cobey, Jr.	Sylvester		Apr. 10, 1933	Sep. 9,1989	In Loving Memory	OAK210
Cobey, Sr.	Sylvester		Aug. 14,1911	Jan. 26,1987		OAK211
Cobey	Troy	E.	Mar. 25, 1977	Feb. 24, 2002	Brother Beloved Son Dad	MHB012
Cobey	William	R.	1871	1926	Info is from church records	MTR4193A

Last Name	First Name	Middle Name	Date of Birth	Date of Death	Transcription / Notes	Cemetery Code
Cobey	William	W.	No Date	Sep. 25, 1906	Age 1 / Buried Sep 27, 1906 (info is from Old Durham Church microfilm pg 85-86 located at the College of Southern MD, LaPlata, MD)	ODENoStone
Coburn	Clyde	Ernest	Feb. 7, 1919	Aug. 15, 1952		CLV422
Cochrane	John	Irving	Nov. 16, 1892	Mar. 24, 1922	May he rest in peace	MTR1196
Cochrane	John	Mitchell	1865	1944		MTR1184
Cochrane	Loretta	Gardiner	1902	1968		MTR1195
Cochrane	Mitchell	Clark	1900	1962		MTR1183
Cochrane	Rebecca	Rice	1869	1950		MTR1185
Cockcroft	Frances	E.	Sep. 16, 1905	Oct. 16, 1970		SCL3222
Cockerham	Charles	D.	Jan. 24, 1924	Jul. 15, 1987		MTR4212
Cockerham	Craft	Enos	Aug. 2, 1896	Apr. 6, 1954		MTR4211
Cocking, Mrs.	Fannie		No Date	Apr. 24, 1896	Buried Apr 26, 1896 (info is from Old Durham Church microfilm located pg 83-84 at the College of Southern MD, LaPlata, MD pg 81)	ODENoStone
Cocking	John		No Date	Jun. 12, 1890	Buried Jun 14, 1890/ s/o Joseph and Ann Cocking (info is from Old Durham Church microfilm pg 81-82 located at the College of Southern MD, LaPlata, MD)	ODENoStone
Cocking	Lottie		Jan. 1889	Jul. 7, 1889	Age 6 mo's. d/o Joseph Cocking and Fannie P. Millar Cocking (info is from Old Durham Church microfilm pg 811, at the College of Southern MD, LaPlata, MD)	ODENoStone
Cocking	Robert		No Date	Jul. 1886	Buried Jul 28, 1886 age 2 weeks (info is from Old Durham Church microfilm pg 79-80 located at the College of Southern MD, LaPlata, MD)	ODENoStone
Cocking, Mrs.	Unknown		No Date	May 10, 1890	Info is from Old Durham Church microfilm pg 81-82 located at the College of Southern MD, LaPlata, MD	ODENoStone
Coe	Fred		1901	1928		SMY3186
Coe, Jr.	Fred		1924	1924		SMY3186
Coe	Margaret	W.	1899	1974		SMY3186
Cofer	Agness	A.	Mar. 16, 1905	Mar. 25, 19( )		SCL2192
Cofer	Celestia	Lucile	Dec. 26, 1907	Sep. 6, 1917		SCL3364
Cofer	Geneva	L.	Dec. 17, 1908	Jan. 15, 1916		SCL3363
Cofer	George	R.	Mar. 26, 1900	Oct. 31, 1900		SCL2191

Last Name	First Name	Middle Name	Date of Birth	Date of Death	Transcription / Notes	Cemetery Code
Cofer	Harriet	A.	Jun. 15, 1840	Jul. 10, 1920	A precious mother from us has gone, the voice we loved is still, a place is vacant in our homes, which never can be filled / by her sons T. F. & J. V. Cofer	SCL2174
Cofer	John	F.	Jan. 16, 1898	Oct. 22, 1918	s/o W.E. & Emma C. Cofer	SCL2188
Cofer	John	W.	Sep. 7, 1910	Feb. 20, 1912		SCL3363
Cofer	Joseph	Z.	Mar. 3, 1899	Mar. 6, 1899		SCL2190
Cofer	Lawrence		Mar. 24, 1917	Aug. 23, 1917	Children of W.E. & E.C Cofer	SCL2189
Cofer	Russell		Oct. 31, 1896	Feb. 22, 1936		SCL2187
Cofer	Veronica		Sep. 1, 1904	Apr. 4, 1944		SCL2186
Cofer	William	C.	Jun. 21, 1905	Aug. 17, 1905		SCL3362
Cofer	Mary	Susie	Jan. 6, 1899	Jan. 3, 1988		NSP235
Coffren	Clara	Louise	Dec. 26, 1910	Apr. 10, 2000	Middle name is from church records	SPL5067
Coffren	Herbert	H.	Jan. 1, 1907	Feb. 18, 1985		SPL5067
Cogley	Charles	G.	1872	1946		CHR576
Cogley	Jean	Brook	No Date	Oct. 11, 1907	Infant - info is from church records	CHRNoStone
Cogley	Mary	Lydia	No Date	Dec. 13, 1907	Name is shown on church records but burial location is unknown, date is the burial date, not death date	CHRNoStone
Cogley	Ruby	R.	1882	1938		CHR576
Colbert	Alphus		No Date	Jun. 16, 1970	Info is from church records	SHINoStone
Colbert	Ellsworth		No Date	Jan. 22, 1971	Info is from church records	SHINoStone
Colbert	Grant		1920	1942		NSP251
Colbert	Gwennette		1879	1947		SHI173
Colbert	James	Cornelius	May 7, 1927	Jun. 20, 2003	PVT US Army World War II	HGH4047
Colbert	Margree		No Date	Jan. 8, 1919	Age 18 / info is from church records	SHINoStone
Colbert	Mattie		1888	1979		SHI280
Colbert	Meredith		No Date	Jun. 4, 1922	Age 69 / info is from church records	SHINoStone
Colbert	Theodore	H.	No Date	Oct. 22, 1926	Infant / info is from church records	SHINoStone
Colbert	Traci	E.	Mar. 10, 1973	Sep. 30, 1980	Son / Love / Peace	HGH4288
Cole	Agnes	E.	Jun. 26, 1924	Jun. 29, 1998		SMY2139
Cole	Agnes	N.	1902	1933		SCL4157
Cole	Alice	L.	1914	1987		SCL3039

Last Name	First Name	Middle Name	Date of Birth	Date of Death	Transcription / Notes	Cemetery Code
Cole	Angela	Lynnet	1981	1981	Arehart Funeral Home located to the left of Rebecca	SAC3075
Cole	Annie	F.	1888	1983	Golladay (found some letters laying on the ground)	SMY2120
Cole	Betty	Joe	Jul. 17, 1931	Nov. 28, 1993		PKH111
Cole	Charles	Clifton	Jan. 26, 1919	Dec. 4, 1957	Rest in Peace	PKH095
Cole	Dan		Sep. 2, 1844	Dec. 1955	Unable to tell if Death Date is Dec. 3 or Dec 31.	SMY2132
Cole	DeSales	Coster	Jan. 2, 1925	Feb. 23, 2005	Pvt US Army WWII	SAC4046
Cole	DeWayne	Wesley	Oct. 30, 1977	Apr. 2, 2003	The great Outdoorsman	PKH094
Cole	Dorothy	Louise	1945	1982	In loving memory	SMC4065
Cole	Frederick		Mar. 20, 1920	Jul. 23, 1997	In loving memory	SMC3116
Cole, Jr.	George		1947	2003	Thornton Funeral Home marker (Dates are from Maryland Independent Newspaper b. Jul 8, 1947 d. Jun 2, 2003)	SMY2102
Cole	Harriet		Jun. 11, 1916	Mar. 4, 1998		SMC1173
Cole	Harry	A.	1895	1975	Info is from The Historical Society Research located at The College of Southern MD, LaPlata, MD.	SMYNoStone
Cole	Helen	Jane	Jun. 8, 1919	No Date		SMY5004
Cole	J.	Freddie	Jan. 18, 1919	Jul. 4, 1982	In Memory of	SAC4044
Cole	James	D.	Mar. 17, 1922	May 15, 1991		SMY2139
Cole	Joseph	DeSales	Jul. 7, 1917	Jul. 14, 2003		SMY5004
Cole, Rev.	Joseph	Gerard	Sep. 6, 1912	Oct. 6, 1997	Ordained: June 9, 1939 / Lord, you gave Joseph, your servant and priest, the privilege of a Holy Ministry in this world. May he rejoice forever in the glory of your kingdom. We ask this through our Lord, Jesus Christ, your Son, who lives and reigns with you and the Holy Spirit, one God, forever and ever. Amen. (located where the Statue is)	SMY1001
Cole, Sr.	Joseph	W	Apr. 15, 1921	Nov. 27, 1994		SAC4040
Cole	Marion	C.	Jun. 2, 1900	May 3, 1992		SMC4097
Cole	Mary	Helen	Jan. 23, 1928	Jan. 22, 1998		SAC4040
Cole	Mary	J.	Feb. 24, 1899	Feb. 28, 1977		SCL3367
Cole	Mary		No Date	1983	Infant daughter of John R and Mary M Cole	SMCI006
Cole	Mary	Ossie, Lee	Jul. 27, 1927	No Date	Beloved Wife	SAC4045

Last Name	First Name	Middle Name	Date of Birth	Date of Death	Transcription / Notes	Cemetery Code
Cole	Mattie		1941	2008	Thornton Funeral Home marker	SMY2101
Cole	Olivea		1878	1949		SMCD291
Cole	Phillip	G.	1904	1997		SAC4047
Cole	Roy	Rogers	1956	1984	Brother	SMY2121
Cole	Sandra	Jean	May 16, 1950	Jun. 7, 1950		PKH096
Cole	Sue	Carol	Jun. 22, 1948	Oct. 22, 1948		PKH096
Cole, Jr.	Thomas	C.	Oct. 21, 1971	Oct. 27, 1990		SMC2028
Cole	Viola	Alzean	1919	1964	Mother	SMC3115
Cole	William	F.	Feb. 5, 1896	Mar. 21, 1975	MATT 1 US Navy	SCL3040
Cole	Winkler		No Date	Jan. 25, 1940		PKH156
Coleman	Baker		Jun. 21, 1907	Sep. 15, 1980	PVT US Army WWII	SCA117
Coleman	Betty	Rae	Oct. 27, 1925	Apr. 22, 2003		SIC9081
Coleman	Charles	F.	Jul. 8, 1930	Mar. 16, 1984	US Air Force Korea	SCL1186
Coleman, Sr.	Clarence	M.	1926	2004	Funeral Home Marker from: J. K. Redmond Shacklefords, VA	DUD006
Coleman	Deborah	A.	Oct. 18, 1957	Jul. 18, 1997		NSP753
Coleman	Emily	Marie	Jun. 29, 1903	Mar. 16, 1984	Beloved wife and mother	SCL1167
Coleman	Harry	Dewey	Feb. 25, 1898	Apr. 10, 1994	Y1 US Navy WW I	SCL1166
Coleman	Henrietta		No Date	Mar. 2, 1927	May she rest in peace	OSP116
Coleman	Henry	Dewey	Jul. 31, 1925	Oct. 27, 2004	SF3 US Navy WW II	SCL1169
Coleman	Janice	Lee, Drinkard	Dec. 24, 1935	May 23, 2004	Beloved wife and mother	SCL1187
Coleman	John	Robert	Nov. 8, 1932	No Date		SIC9081
Coleman	Margaret		1901	1982		SCA118
Coleman	Mary	F.	Aug. 28, 1918	Dec. 21, 1992	"Midge" / My Wife	SCL1168
Coleman	Matilda	C.	Apr. 5, 1919	Sep. 9, 1986		SJO2251
Coleman	Rosa	Ella P.	1929	2002	J. K. Redmond funeral home marker, Shacklefords, VA	DUD013
Coles	Jennie	Jarboe	Aug. 2, 1887	May 5, 1922	w/o N. R. Coles	SIC3140
Coles	Marie	B.	1923	1993		DUD023
Coles	Warren	W.	1917	1999	In Loving Memory	DUD022

Last Name	First Name	Middle Name	Date of Birth	Date of Death	Transcription / Notes	Cemetery Code
Collier	Vanessa	S.	1968	1982	Info missing from funeral home marker (Info is from Historical Society Research located at College of Southern MD, LaPlata, MD	MHB128
Collier	Willie		1917	1993	Thornton Funeral Home Marker	MHB044
Collin	Shaina		No Date	No Date	Funeral home marker / dates are missing from marker	SAC1024
Collinge	George	Jess	1906	1993		HGH4133
Collinge	Helen	Curtin	1912	2000		HGH4133
Collins	Buren	Earl	Feb. 14, 1936	Jul. 24, 1994		NJB317
Collins	Catherine	C.	Dec. 16, 1902	Jan. 2, 1992	In God's Care	SMC2038
Collins	David	H.	Dec. 7, 1929	No Date	At Rest	POM251
Collins	Ella	Evelyn	1912	1983		PIS017
Collins	Ernescine	D.	Dec. 15, 1935	May 10, 2005	In God's Care	POM251
Collins	Francis		Aug. 13, 1920	No Date		SAC5013
Collins, Jr.	Gene	Clark	Dec. 13, 1968	Aug. 19, 1969		NSP948
Collins	Lillian		1890	Jul. 9, 1980	Info is from church records	CLVNoStone
Collins	Lillie	M.	Aug. 8, 1892	Nov. 21, 1962	In loving memory	ODE425
Collins	Maggie	M.	Mar. 15, 1917	Oct. 4, 1987		NZN068
Collins	Margaret	Lucille	Jun. 11, 1940	No Date	Aged 73 yrs / At rest / to my mother by her daughter Josephine	NJB317
Collins	Nancy	Ann	No Date	Dec. 14, 1897	In loving memory	SIC5072
Collins	Roosevelt		Nov. 7, 1911	May 13, 1995		NZN066
Collins	Rosalie		Jul. 23, 1922	May 27, 1999	Francis' Child / Info is from the 1984 church cemetery transcription list	SAC5013
Collins	Unknown		No Date	No Date		SICNoStone
Collins	Walter	M.	Apr. 29, 1890	Jan. 23, 1966		ODE425
Collins	William	G.	Jan. 27, 1915	Apr. 18, 1986	TEC 4 US Army / World War II	SCA143
Collis	Edward	John	No Date	Apr. 21, 1895	Sacred To the memory of / Once of Angelo Stourbridge, England who died at Bel Alton / aged 52 years. Blessed are the dead that die in the Lord. They rest from their labours and their works do follow them. / This stone was sunken and in the woods	SIC2058

Last Name	First Name	Middle Name	Date of Birth	Date of Death	Transcription / Notes	Cemetery Code
Colton	Drusilla	E. M.	No Date	Apr. 7, 1853	In memory of / beloved wife of John T. Colton D. aged 22 yrs 2 mo. & 7 days	CHR388
Combs	Effie	M.	Dec. 17, 1899	Oct. 7, 1961		NSP474
Combs	Marshall	Owen	Jun. 29, 1923	Jun. 26, 1961		NSP473
Comeau	John	A.	Dec. 27, 1937	Sep. 13, 1979		SJO1107
Compton	Alice	R.	1872	1937		MTR2137
Compton	Benjamin	Barnes	Jun. 5, 1873	May 6, 1965	God giveth his Beloved rest	ODE270
Compton, II	Benjamin	B.	Jan. 6, 1943	Dec. 21, 1948	wife of B. B. Compton / Gone but not forgotten / Footstone	SIC6069
Compton	Canie	G.	Dec. 11, 1872	Jul. 9, 1907		BGN006
Compton, Sr.	Calvin	L.	May 23, 1912	Mar. 11, 1988	Devoted h/o Margaret Wade Compton	MTR2136
Compton	Charlotte	Watts	May 30, 1817	Jun. 28, 1864	w/o Wilson Compton / Footstone: C.W.C.	RML002
Compton	Conway		No Date	Jun. 24, 1952	Age 1 - No Marker / info is from church records	CLVNoStone
Compton	Emanuel	M.	Jul. 8, 1907	Jan. 12, 1952		PIS003
Compton	Harriet	Elizabeth	Oct. 1, 1948	Oct. 17, 1948		MTR2134
Compton	Henrietta	M.	Dec. 16, 1901	Jan. 31, 1983		MTR4240
Compton	Henry		Feb. 17, 1898	Oct. 28, 1981		MTR1242
Compton	Irma	E.	Dec. 2, 1910	Jun. 26, 1925	Dau. of R. & B. B. Compton / Asleep in Jesus	PIS001
Compton	John	T.W.	Oct. 16, 1896	Sep. 16, 1973		MTR4240
Compton	Kathryn	Chapman	Apr. 30, 1906	Apr. 25, 1981		MTR1242
Compton	Margaret	Wade	Oct. 27, 1911	Nov. 3, 1986	Beloved w/o Calvin L. Compton, Sr.	MTR2135
Compton	Marjorie	R.S.	1909	1936		MTR2137
Compton	Rachael	Dement	Feb. 14, 1829	Aug. 25, 1902	In loving memory of / w/o Ruel Keith Compton, M.D. / "Oh happy saints forever blest at Jesus feet, how safe your rest"	SJE182
Compton	Rosa	B.	Feb. 10, 1893	Dec. 1, 1965	God giveth his Beloved rest	ODE270
Compton, Dr.	Ruel	Keith	No Date	Apr. 14, 1899	Aged 71 years / Dear Lord remember me.	SJE180
Compy	Elvin	Matthew	1937	No Date		SCA040
Compy	Joanna	Botelho	1941	1978		SCA040
Comstock	Arthur	A.	Oct. 5, 1949	Jul. 13, 1999	I will not fear, for you are ever with me, and You will never leave me to face my perils alone.	SCL3115
Comstock	John	D.	Nov. 2, 1959	Apr. 25, 1999	It is through living that we love and are loved "Boo"	SCL3116

Last Name	First Name	Middle Name	Date of Birth	Date of Death	Transcription / Notes	Cemetery Code
Comstock	Peter	E.	1885	1963		NZN021
Comstock	Ruth	M.	1902	1961		NZN021
Conley	Neil	Henry	Feb. 9, 1925	Jun. 1, 1978	Beloved Uncle	NSP539
Conlyn	Helen	Pearson Chapman	Dec. 13, 1876	Apr. 2, 1951		MTR4151
Conlyn	Louise	Adams	Mar. 1, 1923	May 21, 1980		MTR4152
Conlyn	William	James	Dec. 21, 1869	Mar. 21, 1950		MTR4150
Conlyn, Jr.	William	James	Mar. 3, 1910	Jan. 11, 1997	Capt US Army WW II	MTR4153
Connell	William		No Date	Mar. 1930	Age 68, buried March 15, 1930 Info is from the Historical Society Research located at the College of Southern MD, LaPlata, MD	ODENoStone
Conner or Jameson	Catherine	E.	1909	1953	Not sure if her last name is Conner or Jameson	SMCA213
Connor, S.J.	Joseph	M.	Sep. 22, 1920	Oct. 1, 2005	IHS / NAT. 22 September 1920 / INGR. 7 September 1940 / OBIT. 1 October 2005	SIC1043
Contee					Conjuges difectae hoc testimonuin amoris consecrairt maritus phillippus A.L. Contee, Obit 24 died Maii, Anno Domini MDCCCXIX Aetetes Suae XXIII (unable to locate graves, info is from the Historical Society Research located at the College of Southern MD, LaPlata, MD) / picture is from the files of J. Richard Rivoire	
	Annae	Russell	No Date	No Date		BRO003

Last Name	First Name	Middle Name	Date of Birth	Date of Death	Transcription / Notes	Cemetery Code
Contee	Edmund	W.	Aug. 27, 1799	Jul. 18, 1832	To the memory of Edmund W. Contee whose mortal remains lie buried under this marble, he was cut off in the spring of life but not before his excellent character, his amiable and honorable disposition and his open and benevolant generosity had won the friendship and affection of all his neighbors and acquaintences. As his lived beloved and respected so he died honored and lamented. His memory will be long cherished by his surviving friends who trust that the grave will not forever separate them. He was born on the 27th day of August in the year 1799 and died on the 18th day of July 1832 (unable to locate graves, info is from the Historical Society Research located at the College of Southern MD, LaPlata, MD) / picture is from the files of J. Richard Rivoire	BRO004
Contee	Ellen	Blanche, Neale	Jan. 31,, 1850	Aug. 7, 1936	His wife	HGH2066
Contee	Emma		No Date	Jan. 24, 1926	Info is from church records	SHINoStone
Contee	Peter		No Date	Nov. 22, 1768	Interred the body of / s/o Alexander and Jane Contee, who departed this life the / aged 72 years and 2 months (outside fenced area) (info is from the Historical Society Research located at the College of Southern Maryland, LaPlata, Md)	MUL001
Contee	Phillip		Jun. 21, 1841	Feb. 28, 1899		HGH2066
Contee	Sarah	R.	Jan. 2, 1881	Feb. 2, 1944		SHI013
Conyers	Priestley		1889	1974	Thornton Funeral Home Marker	DUD054
Cook	Gary	Thomas	Mar. 3, 1973	May 4, 1998	Loving Son & Father	SAC5087
Cook	George	Thomas	Mar. 13, 1945	No Date	Loving Son & Father	SAC5087
Cook	James	W.	No Date	Nov. 21, 1926		OFENoStone
Cook, D.D.S.	John	Morgan	Feb. 14, 1876	Nov. 22, 1926	Age 49 / info is from church records	OFE2122
Cook	Laura	B.	1874	1956		OSM030
Cook	Mary	J.	1850	1930		SCL4219
Cook, Jr.	Marion	Davis	Feb. 4, 1949	Apr. 17, 2002	Son / Our guardian angel / NASA	LUM179
Cook, Sr.	Marion	Davis	Jan. 27,1928	Dec. 8, 2010	Father / We will meet / Divers Emblem	LUM180

Last Name	First Name	Middle Name	Date of Birth	Date of Death	Transcription / Notes	Cemetery Code
Cook	Ruth	Griffin	Dec. 5, 1910	Nov. 18, 2003	Dates are from ancestry.com	CHR291
Cook	Victoria	Bowling	Mar. 28, 1930	No Date	Mother / We will meet	LUM180
Cooke	Ernest		Jun. 26, 1885	Nov. 11, 1951		OSP129
Cooke	Gayle	A.	Oct. 6, 1939	Jan. 26, 2000	Loving Mother and Grandmother	SAC2083
Cooke	Gertrude		Jul. 31, 1888	May 4, 1953		OSP129
Cooke	Hazel	B.	1908	1965		SPL1048
Cooke	James	A.	1926	1989	In loving memory	NSP816
Cooke	John	Thomas	Sep. 10, 1849	Dec. 5, 1925		OSP133
Cooke	Louise	G.	Sep. 8, 1912	Apr. 13, 1983	Headstone shows date of death as 3, but footstone shows day of death as 13.	OSP063
Cooke	Mary	E.	Sep. 30, 1854	Dec. 17, 1916	Beloved w/o John T. Cooke / At Rest	OSP131
Cooke	Timothy	C.	1959	1978		NSP817
Cooksey	Agnes	R.	Sep. 14, 1927	No Date	Beloved wife and mother	SMC1114
Cooksey	Alice	P.	1873	1947	Mother / w/o William F. Cooksey / At Rest (Family plot)	SAC1074
Cooksey	Amy	Lee	Nov. 3, 1889	Dec. 21, 1968	footstone: A.L.C.	TRI350
Cooksey	Anna	M.	Jan. 14, 1887	Oct. 26, 1918	Beloved w/o Ferdinand C Cooksey / Loved in life, in death remembered	SMCA186
Cooksey	Annie	V.	Aug. 21, 1874	Jun. 19, 1953		MTR1025
Cooksey	Ashby	S.	Sep. 3, 1870	Sep. 10, 1943		CHR065
Cooksey	Beatrice	E.	Aug. 13, 1910	Mar. 15, 1995		SCL4130
Cooksey	Benjamin	Tilden	Apr. 17, 1918	Nov. 9, 1926	Son of E.L.--A.A. Cooksey (Family plot)	SAC1071
Cooksey	Bessie	Williams	No Date	Dec. 1886	Buried Dec 26, 1886 age 10 mo's. (info is from Old Durham Church microfilm pg 79-80 located at the College of Southern MD, LaPlata, MD)	ODENoStone
Cooksey	C.	M.	Nov. 16, 1818	Dec. 28, 1888	They shall be mine saith the Lord in that day when I make up my jewels / Faith Stonemason was J.F. Manning, Wash D.C.	ODE240
Cooksey	C.	Natalie	1894	1983		SCL3007
Cooksey	Calvin	L.	1938	1989	Son	LUM211
Cooksey	Carlton	W.	1906	1963	Shares stone with M. Viola Cooksey	LUM198A
Cooksey	Caroline	A.	1899	1929		SAC1094

Last Name	First Name	Middle Name	Date of Birth	Date of Death	Transcription / Notes	Cemetery Code
Cooksey	Caroline	T.	1903	1949		MTR3010
Cooksey	Catherine	D.	Jan. 12, 1869	Jun. 5, 1921	At rest / footstone C.D.C.	TRI186
Cooksey	Clarence	Abraham	Apr. 17, 1879	Jul. 11, 1957	Verse on stone: Farewell dear family I am at rest and shall forever be I could not stay with you on earth but you can come to me	LUM205
Cooksey	David	Fairfax	1904	1990		MTR3014
Cooksey	Delphenia	Hancock	Sep. 15, 1880	Jul. 27, 1954	Verse on stone: Farewell dear family I am at rest and shall forever be I could not stay with you on earth but you can come to me	LUM205
Cooksey	Dorothy	B.	May 22, 1924	No Date		LUM083
Cooksey	Dorothy	F.	Dec. 23, 1920	Aug. 25, 1993	Dates are from Ancestry.com	CHR102
Cooksey	Douglas	Tildon	May 8, 1897	Feb. 6, 1978	Footstone: PVT US Army WW I	SCL3007
Cooksey	Edward	F.	Mar. 30, 1930	Nov. 10, 2001		HGH4204
Cooksey	Edwardyna	Budd	Aug. 31, 1912	Sep. 25, 1994		CHR093
Cooksey	Edwin	D.	Oct. 9, 1902	Dec. 24, 1968	Dates are from Ancestry.com	CHR096
Cooksey	Elizabeth	H.	1910	1973		LUM207
Cooksey	Elsie	G.	Oct. 9, 1925	Dec. 5, 2001	When we all get to heaven	NSP571
Cooksey	Emily	C.	Jan. 26, 1871	Mar. 4, 1897	(metal rods are missing and stone is laying on ground)	COO007
Cooksey	Ernest	A.	1901	1984		LUM173
Cooksey	Ethel	Graves	1903	1988		MTR3013
Cooksey	Eva	H.	1875	1944		TRI270
Cooksey	Evelyn	L.	1914	2001		MTR1123
Cooksey	Ferdinand	C.	1928	1952		SMY3148
Cooksey	Ferdinand	C.	Jan. 27, 1881	May 8, 1928	May he rest in peace	SMCA183
Cooksey	Florence	M.	No Date	Sep. 2, 1955	Age 67 / info is from church records	OFENoStone
Cooksey	Florence	M.	1889	1955		MTR1124
Cooksey	Florence	W.	Jul. 23, 1874	Feb. 9, 1946	At Rest	LUM060
Cooksey	Floyd	A.	Nov. 6, 1926	Nov. 26, 2008	Death date is from Maryland Independent Newspaper dated Dec 3, 2008	SAC1102
Cooksey	Frances	A	1894	1974		SAC1070
Cooksey	Francis	M.	Nov. 24, 1865	Mar. 22, 1890		CHR061
Cooksey	Frank	E.	Feb. 9, 1878	Nov. 1, 1960		MTR1024

Last Name	First Name	Middle Name	Date of Birth	Date of Death	Transcription / Notes	Cemetery Code
Cooksey	Frederick	M.	1929	1993	"Shadrack"	SAC1080
Cooksey	George	Merrick	1873	Dec. 20, 1900	Info is from Times Crescent Newspaper dated Jan 4, 1901. Note: b. 1873; d. Dec 20, 1900; s/o Thomas H Cooksey	TRINoStone
Cooksey	Grace	V.	Dec. 28, 1903	Mar. 2, 1982		HGH1202
Cooksey	Grover	Cleveland	Mar. 6, 1885	Jan. 17, 1968		MTR1009
Cooksey	Harold	Roger	Aug. 17, 1925	No Date		TRI349
Cooksey	Harry	S.	Oct. 7, 1909	Apr. 2, 1960		SMY3141
Cooksey	Henry	Graham	No date	Apr. 9, 1850	In Memory of / second s/o Jos. H. and Catherine M. Cooksey who died April 9th 1850 in the 3rd year of his age / Obit notice in the Port Tobacco Times May 1, 1850 Vol 1, pg 58	HDV012
Cooksey	Hester	Penn	1899	1972		LUM082
Cooksey	Howard	R.	Jul. 21, 1922	Feb. 3, 1988		LUM083
Cooksey	Inez		1906	2004		LUM210
Cooksey	J.	Augustus	Dec. 20, 1906	Jul. 11, 1986		SAC1134
Cooksey	J.	F.	Mar. 14, 1875	Jan. 29, 1960		SPL6088
Cooksey	J.	Mark	1917	1930		MTR1125
Cooksey	J.	Reed	1899	1969		SAC1081
Cooksey	James	C.	Mar. 22, 1842	Dec. 5, 1902	h/o Susan E. Cooksey / footstone: J.C.C.	TRI265
Cooksey	James	F.	Sep. 14, 1920	Jul. 3, 1992	When we all get to heaven	NSP571
Cooksey	James	G.	1873	1952	He was beloved by God and man / footstone: J.G.C.	TRI332
Cooksey	James	Norman	No Date	No Date		SMY3147
Cooksey	James	O.	1913	1990	"Teddy"	SCL1147
Cooksey	Jane	R.	Jun. 10, 1932	Sep. 21, 2003		SAC1102
Cooksey	Janice H.	Clark	No Date	Apr. 12, 1919	Info is from Christ Church microfilm Reel 3, Pg 228-229 located at the College of Southern MD, LaPlata, MD	MTRNoStone
Cooksey	Jean	S.	Jul. 18, 1930	No Date		HGH4204
Cooksey	Jeanette	Burroughs	Sep. 19, 1931	Jun. 25, 2001	In God's Care	SAC1082
Cooksey	Jennifer	Lynn	No Date	Mar. 23, 1977		SAC1002
Cooksey	John	D.	1874	1953		TRI270
Cooksey	John	R.	Aug. 23, 1873	Apr. 4, 1955		CHR099

Last Name	First Name	Middle Name	Date of Birth	Date of Death	Transcription / Notes	Cemetery Code
Cooksey	John	S.	Jun. 18, 1906	May 25, 1981	Dates are from Ancestry.com	CHR102
Cooksey	Jos.	H.	Mar. 14, 1817	Oct. 23, 1859	They shall be mine saith the Lord in that day when I make up my jewels / Faith Stonemason was J.F. Manning, Wash D.C.	ODE240
Cooksey	Joseph	D.	Mar. 8, 1927	No Date	Beloved husband, father and Pop Pop / Beloved wife, mother and grandma	SJO5071
Cooksey	Joseph	L.	1921	1985		SCL4007
Cooksey	Joseph	Norman	1901	1929	Beloved h/o Lessie Swann / at rest	SMY3142
Cooksey, Jr.	Joseph	Reed	Aug. 18, 1926	May 29, 2000	In God's Care	SAC1082
Cooksey	Josephine		No Date	Mar. 30, 1899	Buried Apr 21, 1899 (info is from Old Durham Church microfilm pg 85-86 located at the College of Southern MD, LaPlata, MD)	ODENoStone
Cooksey	Lena	C.	1886	1950		LUM059
Cooksey	Loretta	A.	1941	1997	Together forever Married May 11, 1963	SMC3131
Cooksey	Louise	Harrison	Mar. 26, 1933	Feb. 4, 1997		TRI349
Cooksey	Lucille		1922	1999		SMC3154
Cooksey	Lucy	J.	May 13, 1885	Nov. 17, 1973		SMC3219
Cooksey	M.	Grafton	1885	1961		LUM206
Cooksey	M.	Viola	1911	1989	Share stone with Carlton Cooksey	LUM198B
Cooksey	Mamie Ellen	Harrington	Dec. 14, 1884	Apr. 12, 1919	Beloved w/o Grover Cleveland Cooksey / I heard the voice of Jesus say come unto me and rest	MTR1014
Cooksey	Marguerite	K.	May 31, 1906	Apr. 27, 2005	Birth and death dates are from ancestry.com	LUM173
Cooksey	Marie		1891	1948		SMCD319
Cooksey	Mary	Alice	Apr. 14, 1918	Nov. 9, 1926	Daughter of W.F.-A.P. Cooksey (Family plot)	SAC1072
Cooksey	Mary	Ardella	Mar. 11, 1891	Jan. 16, 1971		CHR583
Cooksey	Mary	E.	Jul. 1, 1888	May 6, 1917	Metal rods are missing and stone is laying on the ground	COO006
Cooksey	Mary	E.	Sep. 16, 1858	Jan. 30, 1916		CHR584
Cooksey	Mary	E., Chrismond	Sep. 12, 1875	Jan. 19, 1958		SMY3144
Cooksey	Mary	E. E.	1879	1961		LUM206
Cooksey	Mary	Edith	Oct. 12, 1907	Nov. 18, 1983		SAC1134
Cooksey	Mary	Ellen	No Date	No Date	Infant of J.F. and O.T. Cooksey	SPL6086

Last Name	First Name	Middle Name	Date of Birth	Date of Death	Transcription / Notes	Cemetery Code
Cooksey	Mary	Ginette	Feb. 1853	Jun. 27, 1931	Info is from the Maryland Independent Newspaper dated Jul 3, 1931. Note: Mary Ginette Mattingly; b. Feb 1853; d. Jun 27, 1931	TRINoStone
Cooksey	Mary	V.	Apr. 5, 1874	Apr. 9, 1955		CHR099
Cooksey	Mary Elizabeth	Swann	Nov. 8, 1841	May 15, 1915	His wife	CHR064
Cooksey	Matthias	A.	Feb. 25, 1849	Jan. 23, 1922	Father / Matthias A. Cooksey / Loved in life in death remembered	COO003
Cooksey	Mattie	G.	1897	1964		CHR096
Cooksey	Michael	Earle	No Date	No Date	Small marble stone with a lamb on top	HGH1204
Cooksey	Myrtle	M.	1895	1981		TRI331
Cooksey	Naomi	F.	1921	1961		MTR4075
Cooksey	Nellie	M.	1889	1971		TRI431
Cooksey	Ora	T.	Apr. 7, 1906	Sep. 6, 1960		SPL6085
Cooksey	Pearl	Elizabeth	Sep. 1, 1911	Feb. 4, 1980		SAC1078
Cooksey	Pearl	L.	Apr. 14, 1927	Dec. 19, 2004	Beloved husband, father and Pop Pop / Beloved wife, mother and grandma	SJO5071
Cooksey	Robert	A.	1936	No Date	Together forever Married May 11, 1963	SMC3131
Cooksey	Robert	Budd	Oct. 5, 1934	May 24, 1981	US Air Force Korea	CHR091
Cooksey	Robert	E.	Sep. 3, 1955	Apr. 27, 1989	Bobby	LUM084
Cooksey	Robert	L.	May 11, 1868	Nov. 12, 1949		CHR584
Cooksey	Robert	Lee	Jul. 8, 1911	Aug. 25, 1990		CHR093
Cooksey	Robert	R.	1879	1949		TRI331
Cooksey	Robert	V.	Apr. 29, 1898	Nov. 3, 1988		HGH1202
Cooksey, Jr.	Robert	V.	May 22, 1926	Apr. 19, 1945	Maryland Pvt 32 Inf 7 inf Div World War II	HGH1203
Cooksey	Roger	W.	Aug. 1, 1899	Dec. 15, 1925	Hope / Beloved s/o James G & Mary E / Loved in life, in death remembered	SMY1108
Cooksey	Ruby	Dutton	Nov. 11, 1896	Jan. 1, 1981		CHR582
Cooksey	Rudolph		1914	1991		SMC3154
Cooksey	Rupert	P.	1905	1981		LUM207
Cooksey	Ruth	M.	1917	No Date		SCL1147
Cooksey	Samuel	C.	1888	1961		MTR1124

Last Name	First Name	Middle Name	Date of Birth	Date of Death	Transcription / Notes	Cemetery Code
Cooksey	Samuel	L.	1910	2001		MTR1123
Cooksey	Samuel	T.	Jan. 2, 1876	Jan. 15, 1901	Footstone: S.T.C.	TRI268
Cooksey	Sarah	E.	Feb. 12, 1852	Oct. 12, 1923	Mother / Sarah E. Cooksey B / at rest	COO003
Cooksey	Somersett		Nov. 22, 1838	Apr. 15, 1897	In memory of / "Asleep in Jesus! Blessed sleep"	CHR064
Cooksey	Susie	E.	Aug. 11, 1852	Jun. 22, 1911	w/o James C Cooksey / footstone: S.E.C.	TRI265
Cooksey	T.	Ford	1883	1953		TRI431
Cooksey	Thelma	L.	1925	2004		SCL4007
Cooksey	Thomas	B.	1882	1954		LUM059
Cooksey	Thomas	Dutton	May 5, 1928	Apr. 5, 1983		SAC1069
Cooksey	Thomas	H.	Jun. 4, 1848	Jul. 22, 1930	Hope / At rest / footstone: T.H.C.;	TRI188
Cooksey	Thomas	Kenneth	Jun. 23, 1911	Mar. 10, 1977		TRI190
Cooksey	Thomas	Melvin	Sep. 30, 1899	Jul. 16, 1901	Beloved s/o Clarence & Delphenia / gone but not forgotten (metal rods are broken and stone is laying on the ground)	COO004
Cooksey	Thomas	P.	Nov. 8, 1910	Dec. 27, 1998		SCL4130
Cooksey, Jr.	Thomas	V.	1919	1989		MTR4075
Cooksey	Thomas	Vivian	Feb. 1, 1886	Mar. 29, 1960		SMC3218
Cooksey	Unknown		No Date	No Date	Info is from church records	MTRNoStone
Cooksey	Unknown		No Date	1963	Infant S/o Dutton and Rebecca Cooksey (Family plot)	SAC1073
Cooksey	Unknown		No Date	Dec. 27, 1952	Daughter of Joseph & Jeanette	SAC1079
Cooksey	William	Algie	1900	1991		LUM082
Cooksey	William	Elmer	Apr. 22, 1897	Feb. 26, 1974	Footstone: W.E.C. Note: s/o James G Cooksey	TRI350
Cooksey, Jr.	William	Elmer	No Date	No Date		SMY3146
Cooksey	William	Fairfax	May 10, 1870	May 15, 1961		TRI334
Cooksey	William	Jesse	Apr. 7, 1912	Oct. 2, 2006	TEC 5 US Army World War II	SMC1114
Cooksey	William	Price	Jan. 24, 1863	Aug. 27, 1950		CHR109
Cooksey	William	T.	1892	1983		SAC1070
Cooksey	Wilson		1910	1991		LUM210
Cooley	Jeanne	Brooks	Jul. 17, 1907	Oct. 11, 1907	Infant daughter of Charles G. & Ruby Cooley	CHR604
Coombs	Ana	Maria, Bachur	May 7, 1957	Nov. 28, 2003	"Muito Bonita" / Loving Wife and Mother	SJO5051
Coombs	Beverley	G.	Aug. 20, 1955	Jan. 23, 2002		SJO1128

Last Name	First Name	Middle Name	Date of Birth	Date of Death	Transcription / Notes	Cemetery Code
Coombs	Dorothy	M.	Aug. 21, 1913	Oct. 23, 1985	Mother	SJO1125
Coombs	F.	Marian	Nov. 9, 1934	Jan. 31, 2001	Beloved wife & Mother	SJO1127
Coombs	F.	Roy	Oct. 27, 1897	Feb. 13, 1972	Father - Mother / Our Father which art in Heaven	SJO4186
Coombs	George	O.	1887	1964		SAC4014
Coombs	George		No Date	Jun. 8, 1925	Info is from Christ Church microfilm Reel 3, Pg 232-233 located at the College of Southern MD, LaPlata, MD	MTRNoStone
Coombs	Harry	J.	Jan. 13, 1945	Jan. 8, 2007		SAC4088
Coombs	Helena	Ann	1932	1988		SJO4098
Coombs	J.	Edward	1890	1954		SJO3176
Coombs	James	Edward	Mar. 6, 1919	Dec. 21, 1996		SAC4087
Coombs	Laurence	Edward	May 26, 1934	Oct. 4, 1998	TSGT US Air Force Korea Vietnam	SJO1126
Coombs	Marion	E	1902	1982		SJO3176
Coombs	Mary	G.	1910	1987		SAC4014
Coombs	Michael	Glenn	Jan. 21, 1942	Jul. 5, 1998	Father / At rest	SJO3173
Coombs	Michael		May 22, 1960	Jan. 7, 1961		SJO4154
Coombs	Michelle		May 10, 1958	Dec. 28, 1958		SJO4153
Coombs	Mittie	F.	Mar. 3, 1867	Jul. 7, 1953		SJO3175
Coombs	Nellie	R.	Jul. 27, 1900	Jan. 27, 1968	Father - Mother / Our Father which art in Heaven	SJO4186
Coombs	Reginald	X.	1930	No Date		SJO4098
Coombs	Walter	E.	Oct. 22, 1910	Aug. 23, 1980		SJO3170
Coombs	Walter	H.	Sep. 2, 1863	Sep. 25, 1919		SJO3175
Coomes	Catherine	Ann	1965	1927		SCL3217
Cooney	Aileen	Wrightson	Aug. 21, 1918	Nov. 3, 1988	DAR emblem	CHR253
Cooney	Gerald		No Date	Oct. 14, 1995	Info is from church records	CHRNoStone
Cooney	Jeannie		No Date	Jan. 7, 1982	Info is from church records	CHRNoStone
Cooney	Robert	J.	Aug. 20, 1938	May 7, 2008		SJO2274
Cooper	Annie	E.	1908	1932		SCA021
Cooper	Carl	L.	Jun. 6, 1966	Nov. 10, 1988		SCA127
Cooper, Jr.	Calvin	I.	Jul. 14, 1963	Feb. 21, 2003	Coins left on base of headstone	SCA089
Cooper	Eleanor	W.	Feb. 1, 1918	May 4, 1998	Ellie	MTR3184
Cooper	Ethel	M.	1910	1954		SCA071

Last Name	First Name	Middle Name	Date of Birth	Date of Death	Transcription / Notes	Cemetery Code
Cooper	Ethel	N.	Jul. 25, 1936	No Date		HGH1240
Cooper	Francis	H.	Dec. 12, 1939	Sep. 19, 1996		HGH4154
Cooper	George	S.	1910	1977		SCA072
Cooper	Gregory		Apr. 25, 1953	Apr. 10, 1976		SAC5039
Cooper	Hazel	J.	1895	1982	Back of stone: Nonie	ODE436
Cooper	James	E.	1939	1965		SCA080
Cooper, Jr.	James	H.	1914	1981		SCA094
Cooper, Sr.	James	H.	1883	1954		SCA021
Cooper	John	H.	Sep. 19, 1917	Jul. 25, 1991		SCA059
Cooper	John	M.	1941	1974	Old cement cross	SJO3352
Cooper	Joseph		1918	1959		SJO3319
Cooper	Joseph	I.	Dec. 27, 1922	Aug. 17, 1977		MTR3185
Cooper, Jr.	Joseph	J.	Dec. 4, 1979	May 2, 2003		SJO4042
Cooper	Lawrence	B.	Mar. 6, 1965	Oct. 31, 1980		HGH4127
Cooper	Leonard	Joseph	Nov. 13, 1953	Sep. 4, 1993	SN US Navy Vietnam	SJO3400
Cooper, Jr.	Lloyd	C.	Feb. 24, 1968	Dec. 11, 1995	"Eric" / He had a big heart and was loving and caring	SHI238
Cooper	Lottie	Mary	Aug. 11, 1906	Sep. 28, 1980		SJO3365
Cooper	Louise	J.	1886	1975		SCA021
Cooper	Margaret	A.	Nov. 15, 1916	Oct. 6, 2000		SJO3401
Cooper	Margaret	A.	Sep. 25, 1920	Jun. 6, 1989		SHI235
Cooper	Margaret	M.	1916	No Date		SAC4013
Cooper	Monroe	W.	Jun. 12, 1943	Apr. 1, 1972		HGH1240
Cooper	Rita	U.	Oct. 6, 1960	No Date		SJO4042
Cooper	Teresa		Dec. 2, 1962	Jul. 21, 2007	In loving memory "sugar"	SJO3399
Cooper	Theadore	R.	May 22, 1911	Mar. 24, 1968	Asleep in Jesus / Info is from church records	SHI236
Cooper	Vernon	Wayne	Aug. 23, 1895	Sep. 21, 1970	Back of stone: Pop / Virginia PFC US Army WW I	ODE436
Cooper	William	H.	1913	1993		SAC4013
Coper	Celestia	Lucile	Dec. 26, 1907	Sep. 6, 1917	Info is from the Historical Society Research located at The College of Southern MD, LaPlata, MD	SCLNoStone
Coper	Geneva	L.	Dec. 25, ??	Jan. 15, 1916	Info is from the Historical Society Research located at The College of Southern MD, LaPlata, MD	SCLNoStone

Last Name	First Name	Middle Name	Date of Birth	Date of Death	Transcription / Notes	Cemetery Code
Coper	John	W.	Sep. 7, 1910	Feb. 20, 1912	Info is from the Historical Society Research located at The College of Southern MD, LaPlata, MD	SCLNoStone
Coper	William	C or E	Jun. 21, 1905	Aug. 17, 1905	Info is from the Historical Society Research located at The College of Southern MD, LaPlata, MD	SCLNoStone
Copher	Albert	H.	1872	1955		HGH1148
Copher	J.	Urchea	1901	1975		HGH1125
Copher	Joseph	R.	1904	1955		HGH1126
Copher	M.	Martha	1916	1975		HGH1127
Copher	Sarah	L.	1876	1953		HGH1147
Copher	William	P.	1868	1955		HGH1128
Copsey	Bertha	M.	Sep..14, 1891	Oct.. 29,1950		OFE2026
Copsey	Ida	R.	Jul. 24, 1893	Mar. 7, 1968		SAC1129
Copsey	James	E.	1880	1967		OFE2037
Copsey	James	L.	Sep. 9, 1890	Apr.il 14, 1976		SAC1129
Copsey	Jas	Levi	Jun.e 2,1847	Jul.y 4,1938	In memory / Father / Rom. 8:38-39	OFE2025
Copsey	John	Earl	1910	1931		SIG022
Copsey	Julia	E.	1898	1963		OFE2037
Copsey	Katherine	H.	1880	1906		SIC3137
Copsey	Margaret	L.	Aug. 17, 1953	May 24, 1987		NSP1029
Copsey	Maude	M.	1898	1984	In Loving Memory	OFE4084
Copsey	Phillip	L.	Aug. 11, 1858	Jun. 13, 1911	We will meet again	SIC4040
Copsey	Richard	H.	1853	1916		SIC3137
Copsey	William	A.	No Date	Mar. 26, 1919	Aged 59 years / May he rest in peace	SIC4038
Copsey	William	E.	Dec. 26, 1876	Aug. 2, 1952	Masonic Emblem	OFE2023
Copsey	Zora	Anna Wood	Nov. 10,1853	Feb..12,1917	Mother / Beloved w/o J Levi Copsey Asleep in Jesus	OFE2024
Coradetti	Regina	M.	Mar. 16, 1918	Nov. 3, 1997		NSP721
Corbett	John	F.	No Date	Dep 10, 1829	Aged 16 years / Info is from the 1940 DAR book page 159	SMYNoStone
Corbett	John	F.	No Date	Sep. 10, 1829	Aged 16 years (info is from the 1940 DAR book page 159)	SMYNoStone
Corbett	Mary	M.	Sep. 2, 1904	Jan. 28, 1993		NSP895

Last Name	First Name	Middle Name	Date of Birth	Date of Death	Transcription / Notes	Cemetery Code
Cordell	John	F.	No Date	Sep. 10, 1829	In memory of / who departed this life / in the 16th year of his age	SMY1100
Core	Lisa	Marie	Apr. 16, 1987	Aug. 31, 1991	In God's care but forever in our hearts	MTR3197
Corry	Symphonia	A.	No Date	1873	R.I.P.	SMY1102
Costain	Eloise	Virginia	1906	1975		MTR2019
Costain, Rev.	Herbert	S.	1907	No Date		MTR2019
Costello	Clarence	C.	Sep. 15, 1910	Jun. 25, 1944		SMCD240
Costello	Howard	B.	1917	1999		SMCD238
Costello	Wilfrid	F.	Mar. 26, 1909	Dec. 25, 1990	PFC US Army World War II	SMCD241
Costello	William	C.	May 29, 1915	Jun. 16, 1971		SMCD239
Costen	Jefferson	S.	1901	1973	Rest in peace	SMCD120
Costen	Marie	C.	1894	1992	Rest in peace	SMCD120
Costley, Jr.	Cornelius	A.	Dec. 8, 1924	No Date		SJO3236
Costley	LaDonna	Helen	Jul. 2, 1940	Feb. 6, 1973		SJO3236
Coudon	Jane	Y. H.	Dec. 12, 1880	Jun. 1, 1940		MTR4065
Coulby	Adrian	Morris	Oct. 30, 1933	No Date		CHR462
Coulby	Debra	Lynne	Aug. 24, 1960	No Date		CHR487
Coulby	Edgar	M.	1901	1948		CHR494
Coulby	Elvira	P.	Oct. 24, 1936	Jun. 19, 1997		CHR488
Coulby	Harry		No Date	No Date	Infant - at base of tree (info is from church records)	CHRNoStone
Coulby	Helen	E., Lindsay	Nov. 11, 1933	No Date		CHR462
					Sgt. 1st class Duty Honor Country Our love goes with you Till we meet again D. H. T. K. K. Emblems of US Army and Member of the Sons of the American	
Coulby, Jr.	Howard	Chapman	Dec. 21, 1955	Oct. 24, 1992	Revolution	CHR491
Coulby, Sr.	Howard	C.	1932	No Date	Mother - Father Held in God's loving care	CHR459
Coulby	Irene	A.	Mar. 12, 1915	Oct. 24, 2000	Dates are from ancestry.com	CHR495
Coulby	Mary	Florence	Dec. 29, 1872	Apr. 6, 1938		CHR468
Coulby	Mary	Madelon, Simms	1906	1930	Beloved w/o Edgar M	CHR470
Coulby	Myrtle	L.	1930	2001	Mother - Held in God's loving care	CHR459
Coulby	Richard	A.	Apr. 19, 1964	Dec. 9, 1978	Precious Lord take my hand / The Lord is my shepherd	CHR493

Last Name	First Name	Middle Name	Date of Birth	Date of Death	Transcription / Notes	Cemetery Code
Coulby	Thomas	Jefferson	1863	1946		CHR465
Coulby	William		1867	1947		CHR465
Coulby	John	R.	Feb. 7, 1936	No Date		CHR488
Council	Mary	Rose, Edelen	1925	No Date		SMC3165
Council	Woodrow	Wilson	1920	2002		SMC3165
Countiss	Gertrude	E.	Sep. 23, 1917	No Date	Mom	SMC1075
Courtney	Laura		Oct. 19, 1838	Nov. 3, 1894	Beloved w/o Richard Courtney / Call not back the dear departed anchored safe where storms are o'er	ODE018
Covington	Barbara	A.	No Date	No Date		SAC2014
Covington, Jr.	Cleven		Jun. 19, 1939	Jul. 5, 1974		SAC2014
Covington	Delores	S.	Jan. 24, 1940	Jun. 17, 2003	Loving wife and mother	OAK020
Cox	Alice	Florence	1884	1950		SJO2084
Cox	Alice	M.	Aug. 29, 1852	Apr. 5, 1931	Sacred to the memory of / w/o Samuel H. Cox / Entered into rest Easter Day / The strife is O'er the battle done The victory of life is won The son of triumph has begun Alleluia	SJE197
Cox	Ann	K., Robertson	Nov. 11, 1846	Mar. 4, 1930	w/o Samuel Cox Jr.	MTR2098
Cox	Anna	Spalding	1877	1964	Mother - Son - Daughter	SJO4157
Cox	C.	Russell	1903	1986		SJO4175
Cox	Charles	H.	Sep. 4, 1866	Dec. 5, 1929		MTR4027
Cox	Christie	Sue	1964	1967		MRB002
Cox	Clara	A.	Mar. 25, 1867	Mar. 17, 1907	To the memory of / beloved w/o J. Arthur Cox / d/o late Warren C. Willett / Eternal rest grant to her O Lord and may perpetual light shine upon her. May she rest in peace. Amen	SJO2318
Cox	Dorothy	E.	1904	1990	Mother - Son - Daughter	SJO4157
Cox	Dorothy	M.	1920	1999		MTR1115
Cox	Edwin	C.	Oct. 26, 1855	Apr. 28, 1885	In memory of / "So teach us to number our days that we may apply our hearts unto wisdom"	SJE091
Cox	Ella	M.	Nov. 9, 1849	Nov. 29, 1890	w/o Samuel Cox Jr.	MTR2096
Cox	Emily		No Date	Nov. 9, 1899	Name is shown on church records but burial location is unknown, date is the burial date, not death date	CHRNoStone
Cox	Emma	Jane	Sep. 23, 1874	Mar. 19, 1917		NJB030

171

Last Name	First Name	Middle Name	Date of Birth	Date of Death	Transcription / Notes	Cemetery Code
Cox	Florence	E., Higgs	Nov. 4, 1885	Apr. 28, 1950	Info is from the Times Crescent Newspaper dated, Fri. May 19, 1950 / d/o James M & Alice E Higgs; w/o William A Cox	SICNoStone
Cox	Florence	R.	Aug. 9, 1912	Jan. 9, 1937		NJB027
Cox	G.	Thomas	Oct. 7, 1874	Apr. 19, 1894	s/o J.R. & Carrie Cox / Info is from the 1940 DAR book page 153	SMYNoStone
Cox	Gertrude	R.	1907	2001		SJO4175
Cox	Glovenia		No Date	Apr. 8, 1947	Info is from Christ Church microfilm Reel 4 Pg 270-271 located at the College of Southern MD, LaPlata, MD (Times Crescent newspaper dated Apr 18, 1947 says she died April 10, 1947)	MTRNoStone
Cox	Hannah	Carlin	No Date	Jun. 4, 1900	To our dear mother / aged 73 years "Well done good and faithful servent enter thou unto the joy of thy Lord"	SJE093
Cox	Harold	F.	1909	1973		MTR1115
Cox	Harry	Price	Aug. 29, 1881	May 12, 1962		TRI124
Cox	Helen	Emily	1884	1962		SJE195
Cox	Hugh		Dec. 22, 1779	Dec. 12, 1849	Aged 70 years / info is from the 1940 DAR book page 177 / unable to locate graves	COXNoStone
Cox	James	B.	Nov. 8, 1838	Apr. 6, 1922	Father / In memory of / h/o Mary E. Cox / at rest	PKY030A
Cox, Jr.	James	D.	Apr. 11, 1944	Aug. 17, 1976	I love you now. I'll love you forever. One of these day's we will be together	SJO2227
Cox	James	Cornelius	No Date	Dec. 10, 1922	Sacred to the memory of / departed this life / May he rest in peace	SCL2233
Cox, Sr.	Jesse	A.	Apr. 30, 1913	Dec. 30, 2002		SJO2315
Cox	John	H.	Mar. 29, 1907	Aug. 19, 1907		NJB031
Cox	John	W.	Feb. 15, 1837	Jan. 2, 1884	His wife	NJB515
Cox	John	W.	Oct. 24, 1879	Jan. 4, 1950		NJB388
Cox	John	H.	Aug. 16, 1816	Nov. 12, 1877	In memory of / In the 62nd year of his age. "Come unto me, all ye that labour, and are heavy Laden, and I will give you rest." Matt. 11, 28.	SJE246
Cox	Josephine	J.	No Date	Mar. 12, 1896	In memory of / beloved w/o Wm. J. Cox / in the 48th year of her age / Come unto me all ye that labor and are heavy laden and I will give you rest.	SJO2231

Last Name	First Name	Middle Name	Date of Birth	Date of Death	Transcription / Notes	Cemetery Code
Cox	Julian		Nov. 6, 1868	Feb. 16, 1899	Verse on stone: In my fathers house there are many mansions, go to prepare a place for you. Who shall not say, To die is gain, the spirit thus set free from conflict weariness and pain. Gone home with Christ to be. Sickness & Sorrow all are past, The heart can grieve no more, The frail bark anchored safe at last, Upon the heavenly shore. To die is blessed gain for those, wearied with earthly strife, Tis quiet rest, tis sweet repose Tis entrance into life.	SJE090A
Cox	Kate	G.	1866	1936	w/o Wm. J. Cox	MTR4116
Cox	Landonia	Price	1861	1908		ODE186
Cox	Leonard	S.	1919	1977	Mother - Son - Daughter	SJO4157
Cox	Maria		1864	1885	She is on the back of the stone for George W. Berry Jr.	MTR1177
Cox	Marshall	C.	Jun. 15, 1901	Apr. 11, 1928	Loved in life / remembered in death	NJB028
Cox	Mary	Ann	Apr. 6, 1786	Jan. 28, 1856	wife of Hugh Cox / Info is from the 1940 DAR book page 177 / unable to locate graves	COXNoStone
Cox	Mary	E.	Aug. 4, 1842	Aug. 11, 1909	Mother / In memory of / w/o James B. Cox / At Rest	PKH030
Cox	Mary	W.	Aug. 4, 1842	Mar. 2, 1928	His wife	NJB515
Cox	Milton	B.	Mar. 7, 1877	Sep. 15, 1880	His wife	NJB515
Cox	Philip	H.	Nov. 21, 1906	Jan. 22, 1912	s/o J. Arthur & Clara A. Cox	SJO2318
Cox	Ruth	Marguerite	Sep. 15, 1916	Aug. 4, 2009	Age 92 / d/o the late Joseph Edward Carpenter and the late Ruth Edmonia Cooksey Carpenter / w/o the late Jesse-A. Cox Sr. / info is from Maryland Independent Newspaper Fri. Aug 7, 2009 Page A 11 Col 1	SJO2315
Cox	S.	Margaret	Mar. 20, 1821	Mar. 17, 1887	Sacred to the memory of / Being Justified by Faith we have peace with God, Through our Lord Jesus Christ.	PIS186
Cox, Col.	Samuel		Nov. 22, 1819	Jan. 7, 1880		MTR2101
Cox, Jr.	Samuel		Feb. 8, 1847	May 5, 1906	Lead kindly lights	MTR2097
Cox	Samuel	H.	Nov. 8, 1825	Jun. 18, 1899	Sacred to the memory of	SJE196
Cox	Susanah	C.	No Date	Mar. 5, 1916	w/o J.H. Cox d/ aged 84 years	SJE246B
Cox	Thomas	J.	1863	1939		NJB516
Cox	Thomas	J.	Mar. 5, 1914	Nov. 10, 1937		NJB026
Cox	Virginia	A.	Jul. 4, 1915	Apr. 20, 2005	Beloved Mother / Nannie	NSP449

Last Name	First Name	Middle Name	Date of Birth	Date of Death	Transcription / Notes	Cemetery Code
Cox	Walter	Ann	Jun. 9, 1821	Nov. 9, 1894	w/o Col. Samuel Cox	MTR2100
Cox	Walter	Aubry	Aug. 19, 1886	Aug. 13, 1900	Sacred to the memory of / Entered into Rest / Blessed are the pure in heart for they shall see God.	SJE194
Cox	William	C.	Oct. 4, 1871	Dec. 4, 1942		NJB029
Cox	William	H.	No Date	Mar. 18, 1895	In memory of / Aged 65 years. "The lord gave and the Lord has taken away."	SJE092
Cox	William	Jesse	Nov. 16, 1850	Dec. 2, 1933	Rest in peace	SJO2229
Cox	William		No Date	Dec. 30, 1906	Info is from Christ Church microfilm Reel 3, Pg 220-221 located at the College of Southern MD, LaPlata, MD	MTRNoStone
Coxen	George	R.	1877	1948		SPL3064
Coxen	Sarah	A.	1884	1949		SPL3064
Crabb	Thomas		May 13, 1672	Jan. 4, 1719	Here lyes Thomas Crabb B / had issue by Elizabeth, his wife ? Jane, Elizabeth and Margaret. He departed this life / Aged 46 years	CRB002
Craig	Joseph	E.	May 17, 1919	Apr. 2, 1969		OAK085
Craig	Pauline		May 21, 1922	Jul. 23, 1987		OAK085
Crain, Jr.	Bennett		Oct. 1, 1930	Sep. 3, 2006		CRA014
Crain	Eloise	Miller	Feb. 12, 1921	Nov. 11, 2002		CRA018
Crain	M. Louise	Stone	Sep. 9, 1865	Jun. 7, 1894	w/o Robert Crain / d/o Frederick & Maria Stone	MTR1003
Crain	Mary		Jan. 6, 1832	Dec. 16, 1910	Daughter of Dr. Robert Crain Sr. and his wife Mary Wood	CRA007
Crain	Maxine		Feb. 27, 1907	Apr. 3, 1989	wife of Robert Crain Jr.	CRA019
Crain	Peter	Wood	No Date	Jul. 4, 1868	son of Dr. Robert & Nettie Crain / "Suffer little children to come unto me."	CRA011
Crain	Robert		Nov. 25, 1902	Feb. 17, 1971	son of Robert and Margaret Crain	CRA019
Crain	Robert		Nov. 12, 1865	Aug. 26, 1928		CRA015
Crain, Dr.	Robert		No Date	Mar. 31, 1868	To the memory of / aged 39 years / For earth to good perhaps and loved too much. Heavens early saw and early marked thee for its own.	CRA008
						CRA008A
Crain	W. G.	Bennett	Jun. 20, 1905	Nov. 9, 1978		CRA015
Cramer	Carrie	M.	No Date	Jul. 2, 1950	Name is shown on church records but burial location is unknown, date is the burial date, not death date	CHRNoStone

Last Name	First Name	Middle Name	Date of Birth	Date of Death	Transcription / Notes	Cemetery Code
Cramer	Harry		No Date	Apr. 21, 1943	Name is shown on church records but burial location is unknown, date is the burial date, not death date	CHRNoStone
Cramer	Sharon	A.	Mar. 14, 1949	Apr. 5, 1949		LUM123
Crandall	Ester	L.	Sep. 18, 1940	Apr. 13, 2005	Precious memories	CMX2132
Crandall	Larry	R.	Sep. 27, 1938	No Date	Precious memories	CMX2132
Cravat	Harland	R.	1916	1989	Ace	MTR2090
Cravat	Lula	S., Penn	1902	1987	Lou	MTR2090
Craw	Mary	E.	Apr. 21, 1876	Nov. 23, 1949		NSP378
Craycroft	Benjamin	Franklin	1856	1918		SJE088
Craycroft	Jennie	Celeste, Cox	Mar. 5, 1884	Aug. 16, 1913	w/o B.F. Craycroft	SJE089
Credle	Aline	C.	Jun. 6, 1905	Oct. 29, 1973		NSP488
Credle	Frank	S.	Dec. 26, 1900	No Date		NSP488
Creed	Blanche	H.	Dec. 10, 1898	Mar. 14, 1987	In loving memory	CMX1130
Creed	Edward	E.	Apr. 25, 1895	Mar. 16, 1982	In loving memory	CMX1130
Creed			May 26, 1872	Sep. 7, 1942	His memory is Blessed / No other name in church records or on stone, but ancestry.com shows a Joseph G. Creed	MRB057
Creel	Joseph	Patrick	Aug. 7, 1956	Jun. 14, 1995	Loving Husband & Father	SJO3403
Creighton	Margaret	R.	Dec. 21, 1949	Jan. 3, 1982	Jeanie	CHR112
Creveling	Mary Roby		Sep. 22, 1900	Jul. 3, 1952	w/o W.A. Creveling	MTR3057
Crews	Hazel	L.	Oct. 3, 1920	Dec. 13, 1989	Mother, Grandmother, Great Grandmother our Gammy	MTR3165
Crishi, Sr.	John	Bernard	1918	1977	SGT US Army WW II	SCL3010
Crismond	Anna	M.	Mar. 4, 1921	No Date	The Lord is my Shepherd I shall not want	MRB003
Crismond	Earl	M.	Jun. 5, 1910	Apr. 30, 1966		PKH068
Crismond	Leonard	A.	Aug. 3, 1913	Jul. 24, 1953	The Lord is my Shepherd I shall not want	MRB003
Crismond	Lizzie	R.	Dec. 24, 1881	Oct. 8, 1970		PKH069
Crismond	Otis	W.	May 22, 1876	Jan. 17, 1967		PKH069
Croft	Alfred		1858	1882		MTR4272
Croft	Annie	A.	1907	1953		LUM075
Croft	C.	Marie, Murphy	Dec. 6, 1947	No Date	Not my will but thine be done	LUM089
Croft	Clara		Sep. 23, 1862	Sep. 25, 1925		MTR4273

Last Name	First Name	Middle Name	Date of Birth	Date of Death	Transcription / Notes	Cemetery Code
Croft	Cornelia	G.	Feb. 9, 1867	Apr. 25, 1943	w/o William Croft / Blessed are the pure in heart for they shall see God	MTR4282
Croft	Fannie	Belle, Davis	Feb. 11, 1868	Jul. 24, 1934		MTR4162
Croft	Fannie	Davis	Feb. 11, 1868	Jul. 24, 1934	His Wife (She is buried at Mt Rest Cemetery, LaPlata, MD)	PTC008
Croft	Frederick		Dec. 17, 1885	Dec. 17, 1921		MTR4281
Croft	Georgietta	Lyon	Feb. 20, 1903	Mar. 9, 1999		MTR4160
Croft	Lorena	Belle	Aug. 20, 1899	Sep. 25, 1995	Verse on stone: A loving mentor / Give her of the fruit of her hands and let her own works praise her in the gates, Proverbs 31: 31	MTR4161
Croft	Mary		1827	Aug. 26, 1888	Migrated from Fotherby Lincolnshire, ENG. 1870	MTR4273A
Croft	Russel	G.	1897	1966		LUM075
Croft	Sara		No Date	Sep. 25, 1925	Info is from Christ Church microfilm Reel 3, Pg 232-233 located at the College of Southern MD, LaPlata, MD	MTRNoStone
Croft	Thomas		Aug. 14, 1828	Oct. 25, 1878	Info is from Historical Society Research located at the College of Southern MD, LaPlata, MD	MTRNoStone
Croft	Thomas		Aug. 14, 1828	Oct. 25, 1896	Migrated from Fotherby Lincolnshire, ENG. 1870	MTR4273A
Croft	William	Russell	Aug. 19, 1942	Aug. 13, 1997	Not my will but thine be done	LUM089
Croft	William	Thomas	Aug. 20, 1899	Jun. 12, 1987		MTR4160
Croft	William			Mar. 31, 1930	Co-founder Port Tobacco Baptist Church (1903-1947) Formerly buried in this Baptist Cemetery Not my will but thine be done. (He is buried at Mt Rest Cemetery, LaPlata, MD)	PTC008
Croft	William		Aug. 28, 1855	Mar. 31, 1930	Not my will but thine be done	MTR4163
Croggan	Thos.		No Date	Dec. 21, 1836	A native of Gromy ( ) county Cornwall, England, who departed this life / in the 66th year of his age / Info is from the 1940 DAR book pg 87	NMENoStone
Cromwell	Ashley	Leo	Sep. 26, 1924	May 27, 1987	Married Oct 5, 1946 / PVT US Army WW II	SCL4009
Cromwell	Mary	Geraldine	Jan. 4, 1929	Mar. 17, 1986	Married Oct 5, 1946	SCL4009
Cronk	Bertha	A.	1881	1946		PKH152
Cronk	Carlyle	Mitchell	Oct. 14, 1920	Jun. 16, 1993	T SGT US Army WW II	PKH153
Cronk	Joseph	W.	1873	1960		PKH152
Croom	Velma	L.	Aug. 3, 1937	Apr. 21, 1983		HER023

Last Name	First Name	Middle Name	Date of Birth	Date of Death	Transcription / Notes	Cemetery Code
Croom, Jr.	Wilbert	N.	Jan. 22, 1932	No Date		HER023
Cropley	George	Bird	No Date	Oct. 1839	Son of Richard & Philippa Cropley Born in England	CRP003
Crosby	Patrick	D.	1935	1974		PKH143
Cross	Albert	E.	Feb. 12, 1898	Nov. 6, 1942		OFE2014
Cross	George	William	Dec. 16, 1858	Jan. 7, 1926	Father / Loved in life in death remembered	OFE2013
Cross	Helen		Jun. 27, 1950	No Date	SSGT US Air Force	SMC3016
Cross	Jennings	C.	1927	No Date		SMC2120
Cross	Jos		No Date	No Date		SMCW019
Cross	Joseph	S.	Aug. 27, 1948	No Date	Sgt US Air Force	SMC3016
Cross	Lorraine	G.	1928	No Date		SMC2120
Cross	Margaret	E.	May 15, 1923	Aug. 14, 2003	Loving wife and mother	SMC3021
Cross	Sarah	Elizabeth	Oct. 22, 1859	Mar. 7, 1952	Mother / Loved in life in death remembered	OFE2013
Cross	Stanley	L.	Feb. 17, 1921	Jul. 22, 2004	SSGT US Army WW II	SMC3019
Crouse	Alice	S.	Feb. 19, 1911	Mar. 6, 2004		NJB427
Crouse	Catherine	Inez	Nov. 1, 1923	Mar. 25, 1981	Mother	SIG053
Crouse	Harold	A.	Oct. 25, 1918	Mar. 14, 1976	Father	CMX2071
Crouse	Kessie	V.	Mar. 2, 1896	Dec. 4, 1949		CMX2070
Crowley	Edith	Florimbio	Dec. 16, 1915	Sep. 4, 2001	Married Jul 11, 1942 / Beloved Parents of Kathleen & Anne	SJO3103
Crowley	Joseph	Anthony	Jun. 3, 1910	Aug. 5, 1963	Married Jul 11, 1942 / Beloved Parents of Kathleen & Anne	SJO3103
Crown	Andy	Vernon	Apr. 25, 1973	Apr. 25, 1973	Our Angel Baby	PKH120
Cruikshank	Elizabeth		Aug. 17, 1908	Dec. 22, 1992		MTR4280
Cruikshank	Florence	Patterson, Mitchell	May 23, 1875	Mar. 13, 1909	In loving memory of / beloved w/o Thomas Ward Cruikshank and d/o John H. & Lillie T. C. Mitchell / Faithful unto death	MTR4276
Cruikshank	Harrison		Feb. 11, 1878	Jul. 27, 1925		MTR4267
Cruikshank	McLane		May 30, 1904	Jan. 24, 1981		MTR4280
Cruikshank	Nan, Dabney	Maury, Halsey	Apr. 10, 1889	Jul. 31, 1973	Beloved w/o Harrison Cruikshank	MTR4266

Last Name	First Name	Middle Name	Date of Birth	Date of Death	Transcription / Notes	Cemetery Code
Cruikshank	Thomas	Ward	Dec. 28, 1871	Oct. 24, 1905	In loving memory of / eldest s/o Rev. Harrison & Julia McLane Ward Cruikshank of Cecil Co., MD, and beloved h/o Florence Patterson Mitchell Cruikshank / Blessed are the pure in heart	MTR4277
Cullison	Delores	A.	Nov. 12, 1953	No Date		SMC3169
Cullison	Lindesy	D.	Oct. 9, 1949	No Date		SMC3169
Culver	Clyde	E.	Dec. 21, 1899	May 23, 1964		SPL3039
Cumberland	John	E.	Jul. 22, 1942	Jan. 5, 1996	Beloved son	SIC2071
Cummings	James	C.	1876	1928	Husband	OFE4006
Cummings	Lillie	L.	1877	1934	Wife	OFE4006
Cunningham	Moses		1906	1975	Thornton Funeral Home Marker	OAK114
Cunningham	Peter		No Date	No Date	Rough cement cross with the name painted on in black paint	OAK109
Cunningham	Sarah		No Date	No Date	Info was obtained from the Historical Society Research located at the College of Southern Md, LaPlata, Md	OAKNoStone
Curry	Ardell	Hancock	May 26, 1900	Oct. 15, 1990		OAK157
Curry	Thomas	Ben	Mar. 12, 1919	Aug. 31, 1997	U S Navy World War II	OAK002
Curtis	Ann		Mar. 6, 1955	Jun. 17, 2002		NSP063
Curtis	Anne	Rebecca	Sep. 8, 1913	Jun. 3, 2008		SJO4084
Curtis	James	C.	Oct. 22, 1941	Apr. 17, 1976	At rest	NSP077
Curtis	Jerome		1906	1984	Thornton funeral home marker	SCL3224
Curtis	Joseph	B	Aug. 13, 1907	Dec. 13, 1989		SJO4084
Curtis	Mary	Ellen	1866	1959		SCL3338
Curtis, Sr.	Ralph	C.	1951	1978	We Love You	SJO4081
Curtis	Rosie		1916	1989	Thornton funeral home marker	SCL3223
Curtis	Thomas	Alfred	Jan. 2, 1945	May 25, 1981	SP4 US Army	SJO4082
Curtis	Virginia	H.	Mar. 10, 1916	Dec. 2, 1956		OFE4021
Curtis	Unknown		No Date	Aug. 13, 1882	Info is from church records	OFENoStone
Cushenette	Gary	Jon	Feb. 14, 1965	Jan. 9, 1982	Precious Memories / Beloved son & brother	NSP616
Cusic	Robert	T.	No Date	1962		SAC4004
Cusick	Foley	Leo	Dec. 12, 1911	Dec. 2, 1979		NSP733

Last Name	First Name	Middle Name	Date of Birth	Date of Death	Transcription / Notes	Cemetery Code
Cusick	Frances	Catherine	No Date	No Date	May be a twin to Otis Elmer Cusick / age 1 month / information is from church records	OFENoStone
Cusick	Harry	E.	1901	1979		SMY3052
Cusick	Kathryn	Ann	Apr. 1, 1882	Jul. 28, 1960		NSP684
Cusick	Mary	W. J.	1902	1989	In Wathen Plot	SMY3154
Cusick	Otis	Elmer	No Date	Jun. 11, 1919	May be a twin to Frances Catherine Cusick age 21 days / info is from church records	OFENoStone
Cusick	Philip	Alexander	Sep. 22, 1878	Dec. 8, 1960		NSP684
Cusick	Philip	Everett	Mar. 14, 1908	Mar. 12, 1934		NSP685
Cusick			No Date	Sep. 30, 1930	Infant Cusick stillborn / info is from church records	OFENoStone
D.	A.	E. N.	No Date	No Date	Broken pieces of stone that have the initials A. E. N. D.	OTC014
D.	M.	M.	No Date	No Date	Headstone with no inscription other than the initials	CAR003
Dade	Clayton	F.	1922	1987	Thy Kingdom come, Thy will be done	NSP941
Dade	Mable		Oct. 31, 1922	Nov. 16, 1955		NSP275
Dade	Mary	A.	1926	No Date	Thy Kingdom come, Thy will be done	NSP941
Dade	Nettie	D.	May 13, 1884	Feb. 4, 1976		SMY2061
Dameron	Agnes	H.	1919	2005		SIC3132
Dameron	Della	B.	Sep. 18, 1901	Mar. 17, 1952		CHR349
Dameron	Edith	C.	Jul. 10, 1914	May 18, 2000		HGH1163
Dameron	Florence	L.	Nov. 21, 1908	Jan. 1, 1977	Dates are from Ancestry.com	CHR330
Dameron	J.	Edward	1913	2005		SIC3132
Dameron	John	G.	Feb. 22, 1883	Oct. 7, 1954	Dates are from Ancestry.com	CHR330
Dameron	William	J.	Jun. 26, 1916	Oct. 24, 2003	In loving memory / Army engineer corps	HGH1163
D'Amore	Joseph	Michael	Mar. 26, 1987	Apr. 1, 1987	Our precious baby	NSP343
Dangerfield	Charles	W.	Nov. 25, 1895	Jan. 1972	Military Stone that is sunken, unable to see the dates (info is from web site familysearch.org)	POM209
Dangerfield	Hattie		May 6, 1900	Mar. 1990	Name and dates are painted on stone. Paint is peeling off and unable to read dates (Info came from web site familysearch.org)	POM179
Daniels	Dorothy	E.	Apr. 16, 1960	No Date	In Loving Memory	CLV409
Daniels	J.	David	Dec. 17, 1952	No Date	In Loving Memory	CLV409
Daniels	Mary	E.	Aug. 4, 1921	No Date	In Loving Memory	CLV409

Last Name	First Name	Middle Name	Date of Birth	Date of Death	Transcription / Notes	Cemetery Code
Daniels, Sr.	Richard	A.	Mar. 5, 1920	Jan. 8, 2002	In Loving Memory	CLV409
Danielson	Cyrus	R.	Dec. 20, 1904	May 24, 1915		OSM008
Danielson	Kathleen	A.	May 14, 1935	Jun. 6, 2001	Loving wife, mother and grandmother / Forever in our hearts	PKH011
Darcey	Edward	N.	1880	1958		CHR136
Darden	Percy	Lee	May 21, 1899	Aug. 5, 1975	Rest in Peace	MHB176
Darg	James	H.	Aug. 18, 1898	May 28, 1968		SPL3121
Darg	Jennie	E.	Apr. 16, 1861	May 19, 1931		SPL3101
Darg	John	J.	Apr. 9, 1851	Dec. 20, 1938		SPL3101
Darg	Mary	Gertrude	1902	1963	w/o James H. Darg / God Bless her	SMC3261
Darke	Violet	Hayden	Mar. 9, 1910	Dec. 26, 1994		HGH4173
Darlak	Brenden	A.	May 28, 1973	Dec. 8, 1974		NSP585
Darnall	Eliza	V.	Aug. 15, 1861	Feb. 5, 1940		SCL2126
Darnell	Laura	E.	1869	1964		MRB005
Darnell	Mary	Wright	1912	1956		PKH020
Darnell	Michael	Ray	Aug. 5, 1953	Dec. 29, 1989		MTR4015
Darnell	William	N.	1872	1928		MRB005
Dashielda	Georgia		No Date	Jul. 18, 1961	Info is from church records	SHINoStone
Dashiell	Veronica	M., Green	Aug. 31, 1912	Dec. 12, 1986	Mother	SCL3291
Dashiells	Agnes	Caroline	1894	1978		SJO2248
Datcher	Bernyce	Carroll	Jul. 1, 1915	Mar. 14, 2005	In God's Care	MHB207
Datcher	Carrie	H.	Dec. 12, 1868	Feb. 12, 1913	Beloved w/o J.M. Datcher/ Gone but not forgotten	POM004
Datcher	Chester	Anthony	Apr. 29, 1929	Aug. 3, 1997	US Army Korea	MHB205
Datcher	Fannie	E.	Dec. 8, 1933	Jun. 24, 2003	"Mickey" "GG" Loving Mother and Grandmother	SCL3238
Datcher	Florence		1927	2006	Williams Funeral Home Marker	MHB208
Datcher	Frank	Leroy	Mar. 20, 1917	Jul. 16, 1998	PFC US Army WWII	MHB206
Datcher	Henrietta		1919	2006		MHB203
Datcher	Jane	E.	Dec. 10, 1924	Jun. 7, 1967		POM142

Last Name	First Name	Middle Name	Date of Birth	Date of Death	Transcription / Notes	Cemetery Code
Datcher	Jane	Kathryn, Carter	May 22, 1918	Mar. 24, 2000	Beloved Mother / Back of Stone: Momma, Your body may be gone but your spirit lives on forever in our hearts. The bright rays of the sun reminds us of your smile and the chirping of the birds reminds us of your laugh. Your love is with us everyday and everyday our love is with you. Rest in peace Momma while we await to be together again	SCL4151
Datcher					Daugter / Back of Stone: Momma, Your body may be gone but your spirit lives on forever in our hearts. The bright rays of the sun reminds us of your smile and the chirping of the birds reminds us of your laugh. Your love is with us everyday and everyday our love is with you. Rest in peace Momma while we await to be together again	
Datcher	Lisa	Marie	Nov. 29, 1968	No Date		SCL4151
Datcher	Mary	E.	Jan. 18, 1900	Nov. 16, 1981		MHB201
Datcher	Richard	E.	Jul. 21 1896	Feb. 27, 1914	s/o J. M. & C. H. Datcher / At rest (Stone is Broken)	POM005
Datcher	Ronald	Keith	Jun. 23, 1970	No Date	Son	SCL4151
Datcher	Steven	B.	Jul. 30, 1951	Jan. 1, 2006	In Loving Memory	POM076
Datcher	Sydney		Feb. 3, 1898	Sep. 22, 1988		MHB201
Datcher, Jr.	Sydney	A.	1919	1977		MHB199
Datcher, Sr.	Thomas		1921	1985	STM1 US Navy World War II	MHB203
Datcher	William	F.	1923	1983	PFC US Army WWII	MHB202
Datcher, Jr.	Winston		Jul. 10, 1949	Aug. 6, 1974	SP 5 US Army	MHB197
Daugherty	Ann		Dec. 9, 1927	Apr. 24, 1991		NSP426
Daugherty	Barbara	Jean	May 4, 1955	May 7, 1955		NSP357
Daugherty	Roy	F.	Apr. 11, 1928	No Date		NSP426
Daughhetee	Betty	Howard	May 25, 1925	Feb. 8, 1992	May she rest in peace with God	LUM090
Davenport	Katherine	B.	Oct. 3, 1918	Apr. 8, 2006		SCL4206
Davie	Harriet	G.	No Date	Jul. 22, 1896	Beloved w/o Rev. W. R. Davis / In hope of a glorious Immortality	POM017
Davis	Agnes	M.	1881	1954		NJB036
Davis	Alberta	C.	1913	1987		MTR2164
Davis	Alverter	Dorcas	No Date	Jul. 6, 1840	Infant d/o Peregrine & Ann Davis / Aged 5 mos.	SPL4092

Last Name	First Name	Middle Name	Date of Birth	Date of Death	Transcription / Notes	Cemetery Code
Davis	Ancle	Jack	1931	1993	SGT US Army Korea	MTR2146
Davis	Andrea	Marie	Sep. 30, 1986	Apr. 25, 2008	Age 21 / d/o Lisa Marie Cole and the late Lloyd Douglas Davis. (Info is from the Maryland Independent Newspaper Friday May 2, 2008 page A 10 Column 3)	SACNostone
Davis	Ann	E.	Jul. 10, 1815	Mar. 13, 1860	w/o Peregrine Davis / dates are from the 1940 DAR book page 26	SPL4091
Davis	Anna	Mae	May 26, 1935	May 30, 1989		SCL3329
Davis	Annie	Brookbank	1892	1985		TRI020
Davis	Benjamin		Apr. 13, 1757	Nov. 18, 1818	In memory of / B / D / Stone maker is Gaddeus........ Footstone	DAF023
Davis	Bertram	H.	1904	1963		NJB011
Davis	Beulah	E.	Jan. 5, 1914	Sep. 29, 2002	In loving memory	NJB301
Davis	Blanche	Armor, Rasnick	Feb. 19, 1886	Feb. 20, 1919		MTR4207
Davis	Bradford		Jan. 12, 1877	Nov. 18, 1958		PIS071
Davis	Catherine	D.	Sep. 5, 1921	Apr. 17, 1988		MHB091
Davis	Cecelia	A.	Feb. 4, 1801	Dec. 14, 1862	In memory of / d/o Benjamin & Sarah Davis B / D /	DAF013
Davis	Cecil	Edward	Nov. 19, 1908	Nov. 23, 1976		MTR4203
Davis	Clada	E.	May 31, 1905	Mar. 30, 1979		NJB065
Davis	Colon	I.	1887	1966		CLV126
Davis	Compton	L.	1890	1971		TRI021
Davis	Daniel	D.	Nov. 11, 1878	Dec. 8, 1953		NJB047
Davis	David	Anthony	No Date	Aug. 14, 1986	Our Little Angel	SAC1020
Davis	Delano	R.	Nov. 5, 1932	Jul. 22, 1933		PKH115
Davis, Jr.	Donald	Neil	Oct. 26, 1958	Jul. 16, 2004	SGT US Marine Corps	CMX1112
Davis, Sr.	Donald	Neil	Jan. 19, 1930	May 31, 1991		CMX1114
Davis	Doris	E.	1899	1976		PKH113
Davis	Dorothy	K.	Dec. 12, 1909	Sep. 20, 1912	Our Darling / Budded on earth to bloom in heaven	NJB046
Davis	Dorothy	M.	Nov. 9, 1938	No Date	Devoted wife and mother	NJB348
Davis	Edith	B.	?? 17, 1925	Dec. 6, 1927	info is from the Historical Society Research located at The College of Southern MD, LaPlata, MD	SCLNoStone
Davis	Eleanor	V., Thompson	Nov. 4, 1910	Jun. 27, 1995		MTR4203
Davis	Eliza	R.	Aug. 2, 1854	Apr. 18, 1936		SPL3026

Last Name	First Name	Middle Name	Date of Birth	Date of Death	Transcription / Notes	Cemetery Code
Davis	Elizabeth	Ann	No Date	Aug. 31, 1827	Placed here by maternal love and respect to the memory of a dearly beloved daughter. Sleep on my child and wait the Almigthy's will. Then rise unchanged and be an angel still.	GMC010
Davis	Elizabeth	Grace, Ward	No Date	Oct. 5, 1869	2nd w/o Thomas Andrew Davis. Married May 1, 1810 mother of Elizabeth Ann Davis, Jane Davis, Jane Matilda Davis, Samuel Dyson Davis, Henrietta Davis, Mary Grace Davis and Ann Amanda Davis Possibly buried here next to her husband. She outlived him by 47 years. (Notes from Sister Miriam John at Mt Carmel Monastery, LaPlata, MD)	GMCNo Stone
Davis	Elizabeth	Hagan	No Date	May 18, 1808	First wife of Thomas Andrew Davis, married Nov 18, 1806. Her only child was Dr. Thomas Andrew Davis. (Notes are from Sister Miriam John at Mt. Carmel Monastery, LaPlata, MD)	GMCNo Stone
Davis	Emmer	Zulekia	No Date	Oct. 21, 1843	In memory of / d/o Peragrine & Ann E. Davis	SPL4093
Davis	Emogean		1927	1991	Thornton Funeral Home Marker	ALX083
Davis	Eugene	V.	Jul. 15, 1819	Nov. 25, 1851		SJO3090
Davis	Eva	J.	Mar. 1, 1888	Sep. 7, 1968		NJB045
Davis	Florence	A.	1907	1978		NJB449
Davis	Florence	Ethel	Jun. 14, 1881	May 6, 1930	Wife of James L. Davis, Jr.	NJB013
Davis	Frances	E.	Dec. 9, 1911	Nov. 6, 2003		NJB044
Davis	Frances	M.	1930	No Date	"Rut" "Sis"	SIG093
Davis, Jr.	Frank	A.	Oct. 3, 1923	Jul. 10, 1968		PKH114
Davis	Frederick	E.	No Date	No Date	Fred - Beth (Sheriff badge engraved on stone)	SAC1107
Davis	George	B.	Feb. 7, 1881	Mar. 3, 1919		NJB377
Davis, Jr.	George	T.	Feb. 17, 1928	Dec. 3, 1997		SCL3329
Davis	George	W. H.	Jun. 12, 1903	Dec. 9, 1968		NJB065
Davis	Gladys	S.	Feb. 14, 1907	Oct. 5 1956	I live for those who love me for those who know me true, for the heaven that smiles above me and the good that I can do	NJB037
Davis	Glenn	Allen	Feb. 19, 1935	Mar. 6, 1994	Dad	PKH112
Davis	Gloria	Irene	Mar. 19, 1942	Jul. 24, 2001		MTR4165

Last Name	First Name	Middle Name	Date of Birth	Date of Death	Transcription / Notes	Cemetery Code
Davis	Grover	C.	Nov. 4, 1906	Dec. 8, 1994	Gone home	NJB291
Davis	Grover	Cleveland	Feb. 20, 1885	Jan. 23, 1981		NJB226
Davis	Harriet	Beecher	Dec. 16, 1915	Mar. 10, 1988	Beloved Aunt	SJE030
Davis	Hattie	F.	May 26, 1891	Nov. 7, 1959		TRI122
Davis	Hugh	W.	1883	1943		MTR4208
Davis	Ida	Elizabeth	Jul. 24, 1923	Dec. 22, 2007	d/o Robert Henry Bowie and Fannie Belle Golden Bowie / information is from the Maryland Independent Newspaper dated Dec 22, and 28, 2007	CMXNoStone
Davis	Ida	T.	1890	1962		MTR4209
Davis	Inez		No Date	No Date	Funeral Home Marker	ZBC080
Davis	Inez		1894	1987		MHB080
Davis	Ivan B.		No Date	Jul. 16, 1974	Info is from Christ Church microfilm Reel 4 Pg 292-293 located at the College of Southern MD, LaPlata, MD	MTRNoStone
Davis	J.	Russell	Aug. 21, 1915	Jul. 27, 1916	Our darling one hath gone before to greet us on the blissful shore	NJB378
Davis	James	A.	No Date	No Date	"Father" / aged 78 years (info is from the 1940 DAR book page 30)	SPLNoStone
Davis	James	B.	Jul. 27, 1917	Oct. 27, 1998	In loving memory	NJB301
Davis	James	L.	Nov. 13, 1850	Dec. 31, 1930		NJB178
Davis, Jr.	James	L.	1884	1962		NJB012
Davis	Jane	Catharine	Aug. 22, 1803	Nov. 4, 1845	In memory of / d/o Benjamin & Sarah Davis	DAF015
Davis	Jane		No Date	No Date	infant d/o Thomas Andrew Davis and Elizabeth Grace Ward.	GMCNo Stone
Davis	Jeffrey	L.	Apr. 15, 1960	Jan. 12, 1993	In Loving Memory	SAC1026
Davis	John	L.	No Date	No Date	Entered into rest in the 45 year of his age / May he rest in peace Farewell Mother, thou has left us, we thy loss most deeply feel, but tis God who has bereft us, he can all our sorrows heal	CMX1098
Davis	Joseph	G.	Oct. 12, 1851	Jun. 12, 1928		SPL3026
Davis	Joseph		Apr. 29, 1832	Mar. 21, 1882	Loved in life, in death remembered / Father	OSP088
Davis	Karen	J.	Oct. 24, 1959	Mar. 17, 2000		SCL3328
Davis	Karen	Lee	Nov. 7, 1964	Feb. 6, 2004	Blessed are the pure in heart for they shall see God Matt. 5:18	NJB302

Last Name	First Name	Middle Name	Date of Birth	Date of Death	Transcription / Notes	Cemetery Code
Davis	Katherine	Clagett	Aug. 23, 1942	Nov. 4, 2002	In Loving Memory / "Kay" "Mommy" / There are souls in this world which have the gift of finding joy everywhere and of leaving it behind them when they go	MTR4271
Davis	Kathy	T.	May 25, 1964	No Date		CMX1112
Davis	Katie	V.	Mar. 17, 1887	Aug. 1, 1960		PIS071
Davis	Kenneth	T.	Jul. 12, 1918	Jan. 17, 1989	PFC US Army WWII	MHB092
Davis	Lawrence	Allison	Sep. 19, 1909	Jul. 23, 1991		NJB205
Davis	Leola	Erna	Aug. 23, 1889	Mar. 3, 1973		NJB377
Davis	Leslie	Emory	1912	1979	PFC US Army WWII	NJB227
Davis	Lewis	E.	1922	1987	"Rut" "Sis"	SIG093
Davis	Lillian	G.	Jan. 11, 1910	Dec. 25, 1992	Gone Home	NJB291
Davis	Louise		May 19, 1923	May 4, 2006	Age 83 / Green Funeral Home Marker	NJB349
Davis	Lydia	D.	1875	1944	At rest in God's heavenly home	NJB179
Davis	Maceo	H.	1903	1966		MHB173
Davis	Mack	Delano	Nov. 13, 1932	Jul. 23, 1983		MTR2063
Davis	Mamie		1889	1939		POM090
Davis	Mammie	E.	Nov. 19, 1887	May 3, 1908	w/o W.T. Davis, also infant child aged 3 mos	NJB436
Davis	Margaret	M.	Jul. 12, 1801	Mar. 16, 1884	Entered into rest in the 45 year of his age / May he rest in peace Farewell Mother, thou has left us, we thy loss most deeply feel, but tis God who has bereft us, he can all our sorrows heal Cement Cross Huntt and Ryon Funeral Home Marker / aged 41 (Information is from the Historical Society Research located at the College of Southern MD, in the Southern MD, LaPlata, MD)	CMX1098
Davis	Marie	L.	No Date	Sep. 14, 1951	Thornton Funeral Home Marker	ALX084
Davis	Martina		1898	1979		ALX045
Davis	Mary	E.	Jul. 14, 1853	Nov. 2, 1892	Asleep in Jesus He giveth his beloved sleep	CHR075
Davis	Mary	E., Adams	No Date	No Date	"Mother" / w/o James A. Davis / age 68 years (info is from the 1940 DAR book page 30)	SPLNoStone
Davis	Mary	Elizabeth	No Date	Apr. 4, 1902	Aged 54 years / Gone but not forgotten. Erected by her son Thomas Davis / Footstone: Wife	PIS058
Davis	Mary	Elizabeth	Aug. 6, 1956	Oct. 14, 1998	Beth	SAC1107

Last Name	First Name	Middle Name	Date of Birth	Date of Death	Transcription / Notes	Cemetery Code
Davis	Mary	Jane	( ) 11, 1812	Aug. 30, 1899	IHS / Sacred to the memory of / Beloved w/o the late Dr. Thomas A. Davis / Rest in peace / stone was broken and repaired unable to see birth date	SJO3086
Davis	Mary	Margaret	Dec. 20, 1921	Sep. 25, 1996	In loving memory	NSP119
Davis	Melvin	L.	May 13, 1932	Sep. 16, 2004	SGT US Army Korea	NJB347
Davis	Myra	Lou	Apr. 6, 1944	No Date	But those who wait on the Lord shall renew their strength / They shall mount up with wings as eagles / They shall run and not be weary / They shall walk and not faint. ISA 40:31	NJB302
Davis	Norman	R.	Jun. 5, 1925	Nov. 20, 2004	In Loving Memory / Husband, Father, Grandfather	PGN073
Davis	Orville	W	1913	1969		MTR2164
Davis	R.	T.	Jun. 11, 1842	Nov. 30, 1895		SMY1109
Davis	Ralph	Edward	Oct. 20, 1940	Jul. 4, 1958		MTR4205
Davis	Robert	E.	1901	1966		NJB449
Davis	Robert	H.	1874	1954		NJB036
Davis	Robert	L.	Jan. 8, 1926	Dec. 9, 1973		SCL3064
Davis	Rosa	Lee	1912	1983	Peace be unto you and Praise the Lord	DUD081
Davis	Rose	Marie	1929	1994		ODE210
Davis	Rudolph		Jan. 14, 1845	Oct. 25, 1848	s/o Peregrine & Ann E. Davis 3y, 9m, 11d Aged 74 yrs. Gone but not forgotten. Erected by his son Thomas Davis / Footstone: Husband	SPL4094
Davis	Rufus		No Date	Jul. 11, 1914		PIS056
Davis	Russell	G.	1912	1924		MTR4206
Davis	Sadie	O.	1894	1978		CLV126
Davis	Sarah	E.	Sep. 26, 1850	Oct. 9, 1925		NJB177
Davis	Sarah	Etta	Feb. 17, 1892	May 12, 1965		SPL1070
Davis	Sarah	T.	Mar. 24, 1798	Mar. 9, 1843	In memory of / d/o Benjamin & Sarah Davis Footstone	DAF017
Davis	Sarah		Feb. 28, 1767	Dec. 29, 1833	In memory of / w/o Benjamin Davis	DAF020
Davis	Sarah Jane	Scott	Aug. 28, 1884	Jan. 20, 1947		NJB226
Davis	Stonewall	J.	1872	1935	At rest in God's heavenly home	NJB179
Davis	Thelma	L.	Jun. 20, 1912	Aug. 9, 1976		MTR4204

Last Name	First Name	Middle Name	Date of Birth	Date of Death	Transcription / Notes	Cemetery Code
Davis	Theodore	G.	Dec. 7, 1905	Jan. 26, 1991	I live for those who love me for those who know me true, for the heaven that smiles above me and the good that I can do	NJB037
Davis, Jr.	Theodore	G.	Mar. 4, 1938	Dec. 27, 2001	Sonny	OFE3020
Davis, Dr.	Thomas	A.	May 18, 1808	Aug. 14, 1850	A kind husband, a tender parent a warm friend & an exemplary Christian. May he rest in peace	SJO3088
Davis	Thomas	Andrew	No Date	Oct. 6, 1822	In Memory of / who departed this life / aged 42 years. The father of six children two sons and four daughters	GMC001
Davis	Thomas	B.	1908	1995		MTR3079
Davis	Thomas	Leroy	No Date	Feb. 6, 1965	Info from Md Independent Newspaper Mar 11, 1965	SMYNoStone
Davis	Unknown		No Date	No Date	w/o W.T. Davis, also infant child aged 3 mos	NJB436
Davis	Unknown		No Date	1918	Info is from church records	SHINoStone
Davis	Unknown		No Date	No Date	Unable to read stone, footstone has a sleeping lamb on top	DAF009
Davis	Virginia	Cooksey	Sep. 2, 1915	Jul. 30, 1966		MTR1015
Davis	Virginia	M.	1915	No Date		MTR3079
Davis	William	G.	Jan. 26, 1882	Dec. 19, 1967		SPL1070
Davis	William	R.	Jul. 27, 1941	No Date	Trust in the Lord with all your heart. Lean not to your own understanding. In all your ways acknowledge him and he shall direct your path. Prov 3:5&6	NJB302
Davis	Wilmer		Feb. 1943	Feb. 12, 1943	No Marker / info is from church records	CLVNoStone
Davis	Wm.	T.	No Date	Jul. 12, 1916	Age 73 yrs	CHR075
Dawes	Lillian	C.	Apr. 18, 1931	Nov. 8, 1991		SJO2055
Day	Alexander		1860	1931	Father	SCL2207
Day	Althea	M.	1916	1961		SJE008
Day	Annie	B.	Feb. 9, 1793	May 17, 1845	In memory of Annie B. Day wife of E. W. Day, born in Scotland / aged 52 years. She is not dead whose dear remains lie here entomed beneath this sod, this better to be that death enchains, she lives herself with Christ her God	MUL008A
Day	Annie		Mar. 30, 1903	Feb. 13, 1965		SJO2252
Day	Emma	E.	Dec. 10, 1933	No Date		SCL1044

Last Name	First Name	Middle Name	Date of Birth	Date of Death	Transcription / Notes	Cemetery Code
Day	Joseph		No Date	1899	Info is from Old Durham Church microfilm pg 85 located at the College of Southern MD, LaPlata, MD	ODENoStone
Day	Katherine		1890	1961	Mother	CLV415
Day	Mae	Evonne, Gamble	Jan. 8, 1957	Sep. 27, 2005	If tears could build a stairway and memories a lane. I'd walk right up to heaven and bring you home again / (information is from church records)	MTR3069
Day	Marie		1896	1993	Thornton Funeral Home Marker	MHB043
Day	Mary	Joe	Mar. 1, 1832	May 13, 1927	Rest in Peace	SIC5053
Day	Mary		Jun. 7, 1869	Dec. 4, 1916	May she rest in peace	SCL2205
Day	Owen		Mar. 4, 1954	No Date	If tears could build a stairway and memories a lane. I'd walk right up to heaven and bring you home again	MTR3069
Day, III	Richard	A.	Feb. 28, 1950	Sep. 19, 2005		MTR3017
Day	Valerie	C.	No Date	Jun. 10, 1958		MTR3016
Day	Veronica	A.	Jan. 18, 1927	Aug. 16, 1992		SCL1054
Day	Wilson	J.	Sep. 8, 1919	Mar. 9, 1993		SCL1044
Days	Rosena		Nov. 8, 1894	Jan. 8, 1922		POM060
Days	William	E. M.	Sep. 14, 1890	Jan. 28, 1930	PVT / Co. 28 O.S.C / Gone but not forgotten	POM058
Daywitt	Jeanne		Jan. 31, 1922	No Date	"To everything there is a season."	SPL4063
De Thierry	Louis	A.	1885	1954		SCL1157
Deakins	Agnes	M.	Sep. 18, 1910	Jan. 15, 1946		NJB142
Deakins	Anna		1864	1932	Anna b/ d/ d/o John J. and Ellen Waters. Deakins / Father in thy gracious keeping, Leave we now thy servant sleeping. Many that sleep in the dust of the earth Shall awake. Dan. 12:2 Note: the stone has broken off the base and is laying on the ground.	WAT002
Deakins	Betty		May 11, 1951	Sep. 20, 2006	Age 55 Green Funeral Home Marker	NJB496
Deakins	Carrie	M.	1895	1993		NJB144
Deakins	Edward	B.	Nov. 7, 1809	Jan. 3, 1840	In Memory of / "Thy Word is a lamp under my feet and a light unto my path"	OFE4038
Deakins	Eleanor		1906	1984		NJB143
Deakins	Henry	R.	1902	1989		NJB143
Deakins	John	E.	Mar. 6, 1840	May 4, 1865	In Memory of / Blessed are the dead who die in the Lord	OFE4029

Last Name	First Name	Middle Name	Date of Birth	Date of Death	Transcription / Notes	Cemetery Code
Deakins	Jos	H.	1857	1932		MRB038
Deakins	Laura	V.	1871	1923		MRB038
Deakins	Michael	R.	Sep. 29, 1970	Nov. 3, 2000	In loving memory	NJB149
Deakins	Nellie	C.	Sep. 12, 1941	No Date	In loving memory	NJB147
Deakins	Ruth	Ann, Waters	Mar. 15, 1805	Sep. 26, 1876	Our grandmother / w/o Edward B. Deakins / by J. E. Jay and Sister	OFE4039
Deakins	Sallie	E. V.	1870	1961	Father / Mother	NJB141
Deakins	Thomas	E.	Jun. 2, 1959	Jun. 22, 1973	In loving memory	NJB148
Deakins	Thomas	R.	1891	1955		NJB144
Deakins	Wilbur	B.	1860	1932	Father / Mother	NJB141
Deakins	Wilbur	K.	1906	1977		NJB146
Deakins, Jr.	Wilbur	K.	Apr. 17, 1937	Aug. 20, 1997	In loving memory	NJB147
Dean	Agnes	Philo	1916	1983	In loving memory	SMC1071
Dean	Carolyn	Joyce	Oct. 24, 1941	No Date		LUM023
Dean	Cathrine	O.	May 9, 1913	Jan. 13, 1974		SCL4039
Dean	Ellen	S.	No Date	Jan. 25, 1863	Sacred to the memory of / w/o Obadiah Dean / in the 22nd year of her age / Follow me yonder. / Again we hope to meet her when the day of life is fled then in Heaven to greet her where no farewell is shed	BRD013
Dean	George	A.	1918	1982	(stone is located near the woods)	HGH1241
Dean, III	George	A.	1980	1980	Beloved Son (stone is located near the woods)	HGH1242
Dean	Jerry	Michael	Jun. 23, 1942	May 10, 1996	Thanks for the wings of your laughter	LUM023
Dean	John		No Date	Jul. 13, 1880	Info is from church records	OFENoStone
Dean	Mildred	L.	1912	1989	Stone is located near the woods	HGH1241
Dean	Obadiah		No Date	Mar. 17, 1863	Sacred to the memory of / in his 26th year	BRD015
Dean	Obadiah		No Date	No Date	Sacred to the memory of William Lee & Obadiah / twin children of Obadiah & Ellen S. Dean / aged respectively 12 & 18 months / Lovely flowers plucked from earth to make more beauteous paradise Footstone	BRD010
Dean	Russell		No Date	No Date	Baby / info is from church records	MTRNoStone

Last Name	First Name	Middle Name	Date of Birth	Date of Death	Transcription / Notes	Cemetery Code
Dean	William	Lee	No Date	No Date	Sacred to the memory of William Lee & Obadiah twin children of Obadiah & Ellen S. Dean / aged respectively 12 & 18 months / Lovely flowers plucked from earth to make more beauteous paradise Footstone	BRD010
DeAngelis	Nicola		Feb. 3, 1886	Dec. 28, 1962		SAC2054
Dearing	Anita	M.	Nov. 20, 1887	Jun. 15, 1974	Beloved Husband - Beloved Wife	ODE385
Dearing	James	M.	Jun. 15, 1870	Mar. 5, 1947	Beloved Husband - Beloved Wife	ODE385
DeAtley	William	A.	Mar. 9, 1928	Aug. 4, 1986	"Big Willie" / He was loved by many	NSP593
DeFibaugh	Amy	H.	Oct. 29, 1955	Apr. 10, 2001	If tears could build a stairway and memories a lane, we would walk right up to heaven and bring you back again	SMC4212
Defilippo	Phillip		Jan. 12, 1949	Jun. 5, 2002	In loving memory	NSP008
DeForge	Frances	A.	1898	1962	Mother	OFE3040
DeGirolamo	Assunta	B.	Feb. 24, 1936	Jun. 1, 2007	"Susie"	SAC1119
Degroat	Caitlin	Christine	No Date	Sep. 19, 1988		SMCI005
Dehman	Marion	E.	Jan. 26, 1924	Jan. 13, 1997		NSP091
Dehman	Ralph	J.	Apr. 8, 1920	Nov. 1, 1982		NSP091
DeKoster	Rebecca	Worrell	Dec. 19, 1943	Sep. 21, 1996		SMC2150
Del Fa	Mario	J.	May 20, 1931	Jan. 3, 1997		SMC2153
DeLabar	David	Donald	Jul. 18, 1961	Mar. 28, 2003		SJO5070
Delano	Edward	M.	Jun. 2, 1955	Oct. 21, 1976		NJB203
Delano	Esther	M.	May 3, 1926	Jul. 3, 1978		NJB202
Delashmit	Mary	B.	1904	1952	Mother	PIS209
DeLashmit	Willie	R.	1900	1962		MTR3135
Delgado Jr.	Frank		Sep. 27, 1931	Aug. 23, 1992	"Dad"	NSP263
Della	Ann	Sophia	Apr. 6, 1885	Dec. 18, 1970	Mother (footstone)	LUM077B
Della	Edward	M.	Oct. 15, 1881	May 29, 1953	Father (footstone)	LUM077A
Della	Elizabeth	A.	Jan. 25, 1855	Jun. 5, 1930	Rest in peace	GHB002
Della	Estelle	Cusick	Oct. 12, 1921	Nov. 23, 1985	Wife / m. May 1, 1937	LUM073
Della	George	Morris	May 16, 1912	Feb. 26, 1999		LUM070
Della	Gwynn	E.	1904	1967		LUM074
Della, Jr.	John	William	May 19, 1947	Sep. 7, 1999	At Rest	LUM088

Last Name	First Name	Middle Name	Date of Birth	Date of Death	Transcription / Notes	Cemetery Code
Della, Sr.	John	William	Mar. 7, 1919	Feb. 28, 1983		LUM087
Della	Lillian	A.	1916	1926	Daughter of Edward and Sophia Della / Safe in the arms of Jesus	LUM076
Della	Linda	Marie	Jul. 9, 1948	Dec. 10, 2007		LUM073A
Della	Luther	A.	May 11, 1885	Apr. 15, 1964		GHB041
Della	Luther	Andrew	Sep. 6, 1909	May 25, 1998	Husband / m. May 1, 1937	LUM073
Della	Luther	M.	Mar. 10, 1839	Sep. 4, 1917	Rest in peace	GHB003
Della	M.	Elsie	1912	2003		LUM074
Delozier	Caroline				In Loving Memory Delozier Henry and Caroline Husband & Wife / Lillian - Daughter Mattingly / Children of Emily and Harry Carlton / Son, Veretta C. - Twin to Valetta C. Murdock / Sweetly Resting / Erected 2005 Age 30 in the 1880 census, w/o Henry Delozier (A memorial Stone, not all of them are buried here)	PIS133
Delozier	Clara	Rees	Mar. 16, 1874	Jan. 10, 1915	w/o J. T. Delozier / At Rest	PIS242
DeLozier	Doris	Norman	Nov. 12, 1892	Dec. 14, 1976		NJB199
DeLozier	Evelyn		Nov. 20, 1927	Dec. 14, 1993		SJO3134
Delozier	Henri	Carlyle	May 11, 1906	Dec. 11, 1995	"To everything there is a season and a time to every purpose under the heaven" Ecclesiastes 3.1	CHR418
Delozier	Henry				In Loving Memory Delozier Henry and Caroline Husband & Wife / Lillian - Daughter Mattingly / Children of Emily and Harry Carlton / Son, Veretta C. - Twin to Valetta C. Murdock / Sweetly Resting / Erected 2005 Age 30 in the 1880 census, w/o Henry Delozier (A memorial Stone, not all of them are buried here)	PIS133
Delozier	J.	Thomas	Mar. 17, 1868	Oct. 8, 1936	His toils are past, his work is done, He fought the fight the victory won	PIS241
Delozier	Jane	E.	Nov. 30, 1855	Dec. 23, 1885	In Memory of / Beloved w/o M. A. B. Delozier / Seperated on earth, but hope to be united in heaven. Stone maker was Benner Washington	PIS125
DeLozier	John	Michael	Dec. 23, 1950	Dec. 9, 1993	"Mike" / Gone Fishin	SJO3137
DeLozier	John	T.	Dec. 16, 1927	Apr. 20, 2004		SJO3134
DeLozier	Joseph	Carroll	Nov. 23, 1938	Sep. 21, 2003	"Pop Pop"	SJO3132
DeLozier	Joseph	Thomas	Jul. 11, 1963	Jul. 13, 1997	"Little Joe"	SJO3133

Last Name	First Name	Middle Name	Date of Birth	Date of Death	Transcription / Notes	Cemetery Code
Delozier	Marie	Link	Apr. 1, 1924	No Date		CHR418
Delozier	Mildred	Wright	1909	1999	In Gods Care	PKH026
DeLozier	Naomi		Oct. 21, 1911	Mar. 23, 2001		NJB200
Delozier	Noel		Jun. 12, 1859	Apr. 7, 1887	In Memory of / s/o (info is missing) He is gone but not forgotten. (Stone was broken and then repaired, unable to see parents name but could be Thos. B & Sarah J. E. Delozier)	PIS128
DeLozier	Philemon	M.	Jul. 10, 1886	Apr. 29, 1935	In Memory of Sarah Delozier / Beloved daughter of Thos. B. & Sarah J. E. Delozier / "O Rest, sweet rest"	MRB019
Delozier	Sarah		Feb. 19, 1849	Sep. 20, 1889	In Memory of Sarah Daughter of Thos. B. & Sarah J. E. Delozier / "O Rest, sweet rest" (age 11 in 1860 census)	PIS130
Delozier	Sylvia	W.	1929	1931	Beloved d/o T. E. and D. M. Delozier / Too sweet to live, too loving to stay. God sent an angel and took her away / info is from familysearch.org	PKH027
Delozier, Sr.	Theodore	E.	1900	1989	In Gods Care	PKH026
DeLozier	V.	Carol, Bays	Mar. 6, 1943	Apr. 8, 1999	"Nana"	SJO3143
Delp	Charles	W.	Oct. 31, 1936	Jul. 22, 1948		SPL3077
Delp	Cora	M.	Jul. 2, 1913	Oct. 6, 2001	m. Nov 13, 1935 / Middle name is from church records	SPL3078
Delp	Walter	Charles	Feb. 18, 1914	Jun. 12, 1990	m. Nov 13, 1935	SPL3078
delRosario, M.D.	David	Revilla	1924	1985		SAC3048
delRosario, M.D.	Maria Luisa	Tan, Gatue	1926	No Date		SAC3048
DeLuca	Maria	Rosa	May 10, 1885	Jul. 7, 1959		SAC2051
Demaret	Timothy	J.	Jul. 12, 1960	Aug. 26, 2006	Beloved Son, Brother, Uncle / You knew our hearts and loved each of us	SAC3084
Demaris	Pauline	Mae	Jul. 30, 1933	Mar. 21, 1991		NSP744
Demaris	Robert	William	May 14, 1930	Mar. 25, 1980	AGI US Navy, Korea	NSP744A
DeMarr	Catherine	Louise	1930	1998		CLV367
DeMarr	Dorothy	Anne	Jun. 30, 1973	Feb. 25, 1974	Daughter	SAC1004
DeMarr	William	Roger	Jan. 29, 1930	Oct. 22, 1997	SP3 U S Army	CLV367
DeMaury	Lucille	Elise	Jan. 17, 1914	Feb. 18, 1991	In loving memory / beloved d/o Ballinger S and Elise Boarman Goldsmith	SIC3088
Dement	Achra	E.	1867	1937	Wife	PKH126
Dement	Adrian	Francis	Aug. 6, 1916	Aug. 16, 1933		SCL2129

Last Name	First Name	Middle Name	Date of Birth	Date of Death	Transcription / Notes	Cemetery Code
Dement	Benjamin	F.	Mar. 18, 1843	Sep. 9, 1914		SCL2132
Dement	Charles	F.	Jan. 20, 1869	Sep. 8, 1922	Back of stone: C. F. Dement / Only s/o Capt. Wm. F. Dement & Mary Green Dement / Beloved husband of Bertha Waring Dement	SJO3223
Dement	Elizabeth	Bryan	No Date	Oct. 22, 1826	Erected to the memory of Elizabeth w/o William Dement who died 22 Oct 1826 aged 72 years (info is from Louise Turner's Historic Sites File) w/o William Dement, d/o William Bryan and Dianna Guttride. She is said to have been born in 1755 / Additional info is from the files of J. Richard Rivoire Footstone: with initials E.D.	MKT009
Dement	Gertrude	Teresa	Apr. 20, 1874	Apr. 25, 1940		SJO2328
Dement	John	F.	1859	1937		PKH126
Dement	Mary	A.	Jul. 21, 1868	Jan. 15, 1951		SJO2328
Dement	Mary	A.	1896	1975		NSP902
Dement	Mary	E.	No Date	No Date	Daughter of B.F. & Mary Starbuck Dement / Aged 2 Yrs and 7 Mos / M.E.D.R.S.D.	SCL2130
Dement	Mary	S.	Jan. 19, 1834	Jan. 31, 1925	Rest in peace	SJO2329
Dement	Mary	Starbuck	1847	1938		SCL2133
Dement	Richard	M.	1889	1962		NSP902
Dement	Richard		May 13, 1796	Oct. 17, 1843	Table stones are turned upside down. Info is from the 1940 DAR book page 72 / s/o William and Elizabeth (Bryan) Dement. He was born in 1796 and the Alex. Gaz., dated Oct 26, 1843 shows his age is 47. (Additional info is from the files of J. Richard Rivoire)	MKT012
Dement	Roger	S.	No Date	No Date	s/o B.F. & Mary Starbuck Dement / Aged 4 Months	SCL2131
Dement	William	F.	Mar. 8, 1826	May 31, 1907	Rest in peace	SJO2329
Dement	William		1751	Sep. 18, 1820	Erected to the memory of William Dement who died 18th Sept 1820 aged 69 years (Stonemaker: J. Birth) / h/o Elizabeth (Bryan) Dement. s/o John Dement (ca. 1705-ca. 1775). William was born in 1751 and married Elizabeth Bryan in 1775 (Additional info is from the files of J. Richard Rivoire)	MKT010
Dement	Bertha	Mary, Waring	Nov. 16, 1872	Aug. 27, 1949		SJO3223

Last Name	First Name	Middle Name	Date of Birth	Date of Death	Transcription / Notes	Cemetery Code
Dement	George		No Date	Sep. 25, 1843	Sacred to the memory of / in the 54th year of his age. Death's ruthless shaft asunder tears, The dearest tie we form on earth. But found affection hovers near and bears this tribute to departed worth. A neighbour kind a husband dear in peaceful quiet slumbers here.	SJE177
Demisink	Theodore		1916	1973	Funeral Home Marker / info is from the Historical Society Research located at The College of Southern MD, LaPlata, MD	LUMNoStone
DeMoya, M.D.	Armando	A.	1936	1987		HGH4163
Dempsey	Susan	Marie	1959	1998	Beloved Daugher Plot N12	GMC019
DeNittis	Carol	M.	Apr. 26, 1929	Nov. 30, 2006	Married Oct 28, 1950 / Love Always	SAC1059
DeNittis	Leonard	A.	Jan. 30, 1928	No Date	Married Oct 28, 1950 / Love Always	SAC1059
Dennin	Brian	Edward	Jul. 22, 1970	Sep. 29, 1991	In loving memory / Forever in our hearts / Back of stone: Our son, Our brother, Our friend. We love you, we miss you	SJO3126
Dennin	Margaret	A.	Aug. 26, 1946	No Date	In loving memory / Wed Nov 11, 1967	SJO3125
Dennin	Michael	R.	Oct. 2, 1945	Aug. 6, 2002	In loving memory / Wed Nov 11, 1967	SJO3125
Dennis	Cornelia		No Date	Mar. 2, 1971	info is from church records	SHINoStone
Dennis	Evelyn	Bond	Aug. 18, 1915	Feb. 17, 1957		SAC4011
Denniston, Jr.	Raymond	Steven	Mar. 11, 1897	May 8, 2008	Age 85 s/o the late Raymond S. Denniston, Sr. and the late Eleanor Gilliland Denniston. h/o Marion Berish Denniston. (info is from MD independent Newspaper; Wed May 14, 2008 Pg A10 Col 2) (Additional info is from web site Rootsweb.com)	MTRNoStone
Dent	Alice	M.	Jun. 1, 1906	May 10, 1980	Effie	NSP074
Dent	Ann		Mar. 1692	No Date	Here lyes / of Ann Dent d/o and Eliza Dent / the first / only a piece of the tombstone / info is from DAR book Pg 143, at the College of Southern MD, LaPlata, MD	ODENoStone
Dent	Annie		1888	1935	Mother - Father	ZBC190
Dent	Anthony	Lee	Aug. 20, 1966	Oct. 8, 1990		NSP041
Dent	Audrey	N.	May 25, 1896	Dec. 30, 1963		ODE024
Dent	Augusta	H.	1882	1964		NSP402

Last Name	First Name	Middle Name	Date of Birth	Date of Death	Transcription / Notes	Cemetery Code
Dent	B.	Cecelia	No Date	Jul. 6, 1860	In Memory of / d/o Jos. C. & Drucilla C. Dent D / aged 1 yr. 11 mo. 6 days. Little Cecelia thou hast left us, we thy loss must deeply feel, but tis God that has bereft us. He can all our sorrows heal.	DIN001
Dent	Benjamin	F.	No Date	Mar. 21, 1858	Aged 19 yrs and 9 mos. No headstone only footstone with initials B.F.D. (info is from Historical Society Research located at the College of Southern MD, LaPlata, MD)	DIN006
Dent	Betty	Lou	Jul. 20, 1940	Jul. 26, 1982		MAC065
Dent	Catharine	Petrie	Jul. 10, 1791	Sep. 20, 1838	In Memory of / Rest (Stone is separated from the base and is laying on the ground)	DWH004
Dent	Cecilia		Oct. 2, 1839	Aug. ?th, 1858	In memory of / w/o Jos. C. Dent B / D /. Oh lead me to that Savior fly, whost arm alone can save, then shall my hopes ascent on high and triumph o'er the grave. Footstone: Initials C. D.	DIN002
Dent	Clinton		No Date	Jul. 10, 1897	Name is shown on church records but burial location is unknown, date is the burial date, not death date	CHRNoStone
Dent	Constance	Alberta	No Date	Aug. 18, 1895	Info is from Christ Church microfilm Reel 2 Pg 171-172 located at the College of Southern MD, LaPlata, MD	MTRNoStone
Dent	Cora	M.	Aug. 4, 1870	Mar. 28, 1950		SMCA064
Dent	Doreen	C.	1932	No Date	Beloved Husband - Wife and Mother	SAC3068
Dent	Eddie	D.	1924	1984		ZBC061
Dent	Edith		1880	1914	d/o Frederick L & Lydia S Dent	OFE2031
Dent	Eleanor	A.	1909	1996		NSP413
Dent	Elizabeth	T.	No Date	Dec. 22, 1787	Together are Intered the remains of James Trueman and his granddaughter / He died / aged 47 years. She departed this life / in the 3rd year of her age.	DLV002
Dent	Ella	Lucille	Oct. 18, 1922	Jul. 1, 1996	In Loving Memory / Gone but not forgotten	OAK056
Dent	Elsie	Schultz	May 6, 1921	No Date		SMC4276
Dent	Ersylene		1923	1998	Thornton Funeral Home Marker	MHB022
Dent	Eugene	C.	1933	1992	Beloved Husband - Wife and Mother	SAC3068
Dent	Frederick	L.	1831	1922	Beloved h/o Lydia S.	OFE2030
Dent	Frederick	Lee	1951	1972	Montgomery Brothers Funeral Home Marker	MHB190
Dent, Mrs.	Frederick		No Date	Aug. 14, 1886	Info is from church records	OFENoStone

Last Name	First Name	Middle Name	Date of Birth	Date of Death	Transcription / Notes	Cemetery Code
Dent	Frederick	Phillip	Apr. 12, 1912	Nov. 22, 2006	Age 94. s/o Molly Ward Dent and Sidney Dent / info is from the MD Independent Newspaper	CLVNoStone
Dent	George	S.	1865	1939		TRI007
Dent	George		1843	Oct. 9, 1917	Footstone / Times Crescent Newspaper dated Oct 19, 1917 shows death date	CHR540
Dent	Gerrard		1688	1699	Here lyes ye body of / (info is from DAR book Pg 143 located at the College of Southern MD, LaPlata, MD	ODENoStone
Dent	Glynn	W.	Apr. 23, 1965	Feb. 4, 2005	Son and Loved one "Loved Forever"	OAK025
Dent	Harrison		No Date	No Date	Montgomery Brothers Funeral Home Marker, dates are missing from marker	MHB193
Dent	Henry	Clay	Apr. 11, 1844	May 12, 1898	In Memory of / PVT Co B 2 MD Inf CSA	GHB004
Dent	Henry	Story	No Date	May 29, 1887	In memory of / who departed this life / aged 72 years	ODE354
Dent, Capt.	Hezekiah		No Date	Sep. 8, 1792	Who departed this life / in his 45th year	BDKNoStone
Dent	Howard	M.	1872	1939		NSP403
Dent, Jr.	Howard	Martin	Nov. 17, 1911	Dec. 29, 2003		SMC4276
Dent	James	B.	Apr. 3, 1922	Jan. 24, 1971		MHB143
Dent	James	C.	No Date	Jan. 10, 1841	In memory of / aged 28 yrs. 5 months leaving a loving wife, child, an aged father, brothers and sisters to mourn their loss. Christ took him, he thought best / info is from the Historical Society Research located at the College of Southern MD, LaPlata, MD - No Stone	DIN009
Dent	James	Clinton	Oct. 21, 1917	Jan. 18, 1988		MHB084
Dent, Jr.	John		1947	1995	Thornton Funeral Home Marker	ZBC018
Dent	John	B.	Jul. 10, 1786	Sep. 20, 1841	In Memory of / Rest / Stonemason was J. H. Shelton Wash. D.C. (Stone is laying on the ground)	DWH001
Dent					To my husband / Precious is the sight of the Lord is the death of his saints / Departed this life / aged 47 years 10 months & 1 day. / Farewell dear wife, I am at rest, and shall forever be; I could not stay with you on earth, but you can come to me (metal rods are broken and stone is laying on the ground)	
Dent	John	B.	No Date	Jan. 19, 1877		COO001

Last Name	First Name	Middle Name	Date of Birth	Date of Death	Transcription / Notes	Cemetery Code
Dent	John	B.	No Date	Apr. 24, 1838	In memory of / who departed this life April 24, 1838 aged 79 years 5 months and 9 days / info is from the 1940 DAR Book pg 18A & 19, additional info is from W. Preston Williams list of private Cemeteries and The Historical Society Research, at The College of Southern MD, LaPlata, MD.	DENNoStone
Dent	John	C.	No Date	Jan. 28, 1816	Who departed this life / in the 23rd year of his life	BDKNoStone
Dent	John		1934	2004	Thornton Funeral Home marker	NSP025
Dent	John ???		No Date	Jan. 16, 4898	Info is from Christ Church microfilm Reel 1 Pg 86-87 located at the College of Southern MD, LaPlata, MD	MTRNoStone
Dent, Sr.	John	F.	1909	2003	In Loving Memory "Deacon" "Daddy" / your Family Will Always Love You	MHB232
Dent	Julia		No Date	No Date	Info supplied by a church member	PGONoStone
Dent	Kate	M., Proctor	Jan. 8, 1915	Oct. 18, 1985	In Loving Memory "Sister"	MHB069
Dent	Kate		1868	1934		ZBC185
Dent	Laura	C.	Sep. 1, 1840	May 23, 1924		SMCA063
Dent	Laura	Williams, Maddox	1854	1910	His wife Laura Williams Maddox Dent / Footstone	CHR540
Dent	Lawrence	P.	Apr. 9, 1906	Jul. 5, 1991		NSP177
Dent	Leonard	Leland	No Date	Aug. 1914	Age 21 years	DSP003
Dent	LeRoy	Allynn	No Date	Apr. 1915	Age 25 years	DSP002
Dent	Lily	O.	1910	1975	Beloved Wife	ZBC063
Dent	Lydia	S.	No Date	Aug. 19, 1886	In memory of / the beloved w/o F.L.Dent who departed this life aged 48 years 6 months 1 day Rest in Peace	OFE2032
Dent	Lydia	S.	1838	1886		OFE2030
Dent	Maggie		1923	1971		MHB194
Dent	Mamie		No Date	No Date	Info is from the Historical Society Research located at the College of Southern MD, LaPlata, MD	ZBCNoStone
Dent	Martha		No Date	Jul. 14, 1824	who departed this life / in her 13th year	BDKNoStone
Dent	Martha	A.	1858	1932		OFE2030
Dent	Mary	C.	Sep. 1, 1817	Oct. 6, 1894	A wise and loving mother, a Christian woman, her children arise up and call her blessed	NME002
Dent	Mary	E.	Nov. 25, 1835	Nov. 30, 1919	Stone is laying on the ground	COO010
Dent	Mary	M.	1862	1944		TRI006

Last Name	First Name	Middle Name	Date of Birth	Date of Death	Transcription / Notes	Cemetery Code
Dent	Mary	N.	Jan. 14, 1912	Sep. 3, 1990	Old Stone with Info Etched Into it Thornton Funeral Home Marker	MHB105
Dent	Mary	V.	May 12, 1905	Aug. 12, 2000		SCL3297
Dent	Matilda		Aug. 5, 1822	Nov. 6, 1884	In memory of / Relict of Thomas S. Dent / "Them which sleep in Jesus, will God bring with Him."	ODE356
Dent	Minnie	C.	Nov. 2, 1887	May 15, 1993		NSP193
Dent	Ned		No Date	Oct. 17, 1900	Info is from Christ Church microfilm Reel 1 Pg 86-87 located at the College of Southern MD, LaPlata, MD	MTRNoStone
Dent	Nina	L.	Apr. 21, 1920	Dec. 24, 1970		NSP168
Dent	Priscilla		No Date	May 24, 1845	In memory of / of Maryland who departed this life May 24, 1845, age 84 years 4 months, 25 days. (Her maiden name was also Dent) / info and picture is from the 1940 DAR Book pg 18A & 19, additional info is from W. Preston Williams list of private Cemeteries and the Historical Society Research located at the College of Southern MD, LaPlata, MD	DEN001
Dent	Reginald	G.	Nov. 24, 1917	May 23, 1997	T SGT US Army WW II	ZBC060
Dent	Robert	P.	1920	1998		NSP414
Dent	Robert	Phillip	Mar. 10, 1941	Oct. 24, 2003	In Loving Memory	CLV254
Dent	Robert		1878	1947	Mother - Father	ZBC190
Dent	Roy		Mar. 27, 1911	Mar. 6, 1997		SJO3382
Dent	Rozier	W.	1906	1982	Husband	ZBC062
Dent	Sarah		No Date	Apr. 9, 1795	Under this stone is deposited the body of Sarah Dent d/o Thomas & Elizabeth Marshall. She died April 9th 1795 age 59 years and 6 months. This tribute due to the memory of an excellent mother and good woman is made by G. Dent	MRS005
Dent, Dr.	Stouten	Warren	Jan. 15, 1806	Oct. 7, 1883	In Memory of born in Charles County, MD died in same county. He was not slothful in business. Fervent in spirit serving the lord. Blessed are the dead who died in the Lord	NME003
Dent	Theodore		No Date	Apr. 1, 1900	Info is from Christ Church microfilm Reel 1 Pg 86-87 located at the College of Southern MD, LaPlata, MD	MTRNoStone

Last Name	First Name	Middle Name	Date of Birth	Date of Death	Transcription / Notes	Cemetery Code
Dent	Theophilus		Oct. 22, 1778	Nov. 15, 1867	To the memory of / s/o Gideon Dent, B / D / Aged 89 yrs. 24 days leaving a host of relative and friends to mourn their loss, may he rest in peace. / Info is from the Historical Society Research located at the College of Southern MD, LaPlata, MD / Footstone: Initials T.D.	DIN004
Dent	Thomas	S.	Sep. 19, 1809	Dec. 21, 1878	May be rest in peace	ODE355
Dent	Thomas		1874	1945		ZBC184
Dent	Unknown		1908	1991	Thornton Funeral Home Marker	MHB114
Dent	Unknown		No Date	Aug. 25, 19??	Cement Cross with info etched in the cement	MHB182
Dent	Vivian		1877	1941	At rest	CHR416
Dent	Warren	L.	1871	1957	s/o Frederick L & Lydia S Dent	OFE2029
Dent	William	A.	Dec. 3, 1857	Jan. 1, 1901	In memory of / At rest Footstone	CHR521
Dent	William	Edward	May 20, 1931	Aug. 21, 1976	CPL US Army Korea	NSP076
Dent	William	T.	Jun. 18, 1894	Mar. 17, 1953		ODE024
Dent	William		Dec. 13, 1687	Nov. 18, 1695	Here lyes the body of / s/o William & Elizabeth Dent / info is from DAR book Pg 143 located at the College of Southern MD, LaPlata, MD	ODENoStone
DePew	Amanda	Jane	Mar. 8, 1919	Mar. 4, 1981		LUM052
DePew	Anna	Melinda	Apr. 17, 1971	May 20, 1984	Our Daughter / 13 Years of Love & Joy	SAC1017
DePew	Bissie		1923	1964	Arehart funeral Home Marker / info is from the Historical Society Research located at The College of Southern MD, LaPlata, MD	LUMNoStone
DePew	Charles	E.	May 4, 1940	Nov. 15, 1942		LUM051
DePew	Emory		Jul.y 14, 1886	1955	Arehart funeral home marker / date of birth is from Family search.org	LUM053A
DePew, Sr.	Ray	Clifton	Oct. 10, 1943	Dec. 18, 1990		SAC1027
DePew	Zella	Faye	No Date	1944	Sleep Baby Sleep	LUM053
DeRoode	Mary	Jameson	1870	1950		SMCA067
DeRoode	Rudolf	J. J.	1865	1910		SMCA067
DeRoode, Jr.	Rudolf	J. J.	1890	1890		SMCA067
Derrickson			No Date	Nov. 6, 1891	Our precious angel sweetly sleeps / Infant s/o Wm. B. & Bertha Derrickson	HNT051
Desper	Raymond	C.	1909	1931		MTR3070

Last Name	First Name	Middle Name	Date of Birth	Date of Death	Transcription / Notes	Cemetery Code
Dettor	Frances	Jean	Apr. 23, 1931	Oct. 16, 1985	In Loving Memory	LUM169
Dettor	Lucille	M.	Apr. 13, 1935	No Date		MTR3113
Dettor, M.D.	Vernon	B.	Mar. 11, 1923	May 1, 1989	Deputy State Health Officer for Charles County 1961-1982. He was a gentleman. In Loving Memory	MTR3113
DeVane	Ella	A.	Aug. 26, 1909	Jan. 6, 1996	Married Sep 5, 1934	NJB125
DeVane	George	F.	Jul. 14, 1908	May 5, 1978	Married Sep 5, 1934	NJB125
Diamond	Corrine	Allison	Apr. 17, 1898	May 5, 1977	Mother	LUM032
Dickinson	James	Lovejoy	Mar. 25, 1921	Mar. 3, 2000	US Submarines WW II Veteran Emblem	ODE040
Dickinson	Mardalee	Ely, Bishop	Feb. 13, 1923	No Date	DAR Emblem	ODE040
Dietz	Robert	M.	Jul. 17, 1939	Sep. 3, 1939		SMCD318
Digges	Amy	W.	1878	1954		SIC2193
Digges	Arthur	S.	Jan. 19, 1874	Nov. 16, 1905	s/o Robert & Mary C Digges / Blessed are they that fear the Lord that walk in his ways	SIC2188
Digges	Catherine		Sep. 10, 1802	No Date	w/o M. Digges / Stone is sunken / Info is from the Historical Society Research located at the College of Southern MD, LaPlata, MD	SICNoStone
Digges	Catherine	I.	1870	1954		SIC3010
Digges	Catherine	Mitchell	Aug. 24, 1847	Jun. 14, 1887	In Loving Memory of / beloved w/o John T. Digges and d/o Gen. Walter & Mary Mitchell	MTR4224
Digges	Edward	Simms	Nov. 17, 1916	Sep. 14, 2002	s/o Walter Mitchell Digges and Natalie Jenkins Digges	SIC9029
Digges	Elizabeth		No Date	May 9, 1705	stone is laying on the ground and is broken into 3 pieces / There is a bronze plaque in front of the broken stone. / To the memory of / d/o Henry Darnall and w/o Mr. Edward Digges / deceased May 9, 1705 / May she now enjoy eternal bliss. Amen (this info was also on the broken stone.)	SIC2005
Digges	Eugene	Dudley	Feb. 8, 1885	Apr. 14, 1910	In loving memory of / beloved s/o John T. & Catherine M. Digges	MTR4226

Last Name	First Name	Middle Name	Date of Birth	Date of Death	Transcription / Notes	Cemetery Code
Digges	H.	Taney	No Date	Aug. 13, 1851	To the memory of / s/o Robert & Catherine Digges / who departed this life / aged 16 yrs 10 months 17 days / How vain the hopes that youth and health impart. How ___ our Fathers and Mothers heart How will ___ all the love they bore their darling child a ___ dark days ___ That all may meet in bliss, how they beseech Of heaven be his they aim ___ lone to teach	SIC2117
Digges	Jane	Hortense	May 24, 1840	Jan. 23, 1909	Beloved daughter of John & Mary Digges	SJO6008
Digges	John	Dudley	Jan. 8, 1912	Feb. 25, 1983	Judge / Court of appeals of Maryland / son of Walter Mitchell Digges and Natalie Jenkins Digges	SIC9025
Digges, M.D.	John	Henry	1874	1929	Beloved s/o John T. & Catherine M. Digges	MTR4246
Digges, M.D.	John	T.	Dec. 14, 1841	Jan. 13, 1915	In loving memory of / s/o John H. & Mary Digges / A life crowned in Glory of ministering to the suffering of his fellow man and in the comforting of the sick and needy	MTR4225
Digges	M.		1837	1918	Husband of Walter Ann / R.I.P.	SIC4125
Digges	Maria	McHugh	Jul. 8, 1922	Jun. 10, 2006	Daughter of Dr. William A. McHugh and Gwendolyn Barnes McHugh	SIC9030
Digges	Mary	Catherine	Jun. 2, 1904	Oct. 22, 1904	d/o William Jos. & Catherine Sellman Digges	SIC3012
Digges	Mary	Cecelia, Thompson	Jul. 30, 1834	Sep. 7, 1913	In memory of / w/o Robert Digges / Her children rose up and called her blessed	SIC2113
Digges	Mary	Matilda	Mar. 14, 1879	Mar. 3, 1941		MTR4247
Digges	Mary		May 8, 1864	Feb. 2, 1923	In memory of / d/o Robt.-Mary C. Digges / "Blessed are the dead, who die in the Lord"	SIC2115
Digges	Natalie	Jenkins	May 20, 1875	Aug. 16, 1960	Beloved wife of Judge Walter Mitchell Digges / daughter of John Joseph Jenkins and Antoinette Simms Jenkins	SIC9027
Digges	Ollie		No Date	Jul. 20, 1875	Our little Ollie / This tiny white stone is in front of the stone for Francis Hughes Wills and Mary Digges Wills but 1984 church records show the last name as Digges, so it's probably not in the proper place.	SIC4155
Digges	Robert		Jan. 13, 1828	Feb. 11, 1901	In memory of / s/o Robert & Catherine Digges	SIC2114
Digges, Sr.	Robert		Apr. 18, 1799	May 14, 1877	Our father / rest in peace (stone is broken in half laying on the ground embedded in the grass)	SIC2119
Digges	Robert	I.	Mar. 14, 1867	Mar. 30, 1916	s/o Robert & Mary C. Digges / Blessed are the dead who die in the Lord	SIC2191

Last Name	First Name	Middle Name	Date of Birth	Date of Death	Transcription / Notes	Cemetery Code
Digges	Thos	Hugh	Dec. 20, 1883	Jan. 12, 1884	Beloved s/o J. T. & C. M. Digges	MTR4223
Digges	Walter	Ann	1851	1920	Wife of M. Digges / R.I.P.	SIC4125
Digges	Walter	Mitchell	Feb. 17, 1877	Oct. 15, 1934	Judge / Court of appeals of Maryland / son of John Thomas Digges M.D. and Catherine Mitchell Digges	SIC9026
Digges	William	Joseph	Apr. 18, 1860	Nov. 18, 1915	In loving memory of / s/o Robert & Mary C. Digges	SIC3011
Digges, Jr.	Walter	Mitchell	Jul. 27, 1913	Dec. 15, 1993	s/o Walter Mitchell Digges and Natalie Jenkins Digges	SIC9028
Diggs	Adele		1894	1980	Thornton Funeral Home Marker	MHB119
Diggs	Annie		No Date	No Date	Funeral Home Marker	ZBC161
Diggs	Annie		1863	1949	Mother	SMCD292
Diggs	Bertha		1934	1996	Thornton Funeral Home Marker	ZBC079
Diggs	Bryan	N.	Jul. 29, 1962	Mar. 31, 2001	In Gods care / We love you and will miss you	SMI061
Diggs	Cecelia	A.	Feb. 24, 1932	Mar. 27, 1999	Wife and Mother	MHB019
Diggs	Charles		May 15, 1880	Nov. 30, 1911	Aged 30 years / rest in peace	SIC4122
Diggs	Frank		Mar. 1, 1920	May 14, 1966	Maryland SGT Co A 386 ENGR BN WW II	ZBC162
Diggs	Helen		May 30, 1923	Aug. 29, 1997		ALX107
Diggs	Leonard	E.	1939	1971		ZBC163
Diggs	Mary	C.	Oct. 21, 1926	Sep. 29, 1992		SCL1227
Diggs	Park		Mar. 17, 1896	Nov. 5, 1972		ALX098
Diggs	Paul	Edward	Dec. 4, 1918	Feb. 1, 1985	STMI US Navy WW II	ZBC123
Diggs	Rachel		1896	1992		ALX106
Diggs	Susie		Feb. 11, 1882	Oct. 20, 1977		SIC8076
Diggs	Unknown		No Date	No Date	"Mother" / Info is from the 1984 church cemetery transcription list	SICNoStone
Diggs	William	Alexander	Dec. 31, 1918	Feb. 12, 1995	s/o the late Park and Rachel Diggs / Historian and Educator, Founder of African American Historical Society and Museum of Charles County 1974	ALX105
Diggs	William		1918	1995	Thornton Funeral Home Marker	ALX100
Digtz	Robert	M.	Jul. 17, 1939	Sep. 3, 1939	Info is from the Historical Society Research located at the College of Southern MD, LaPlata, MD	SMCNoStone
Dillon	Robert	Leroy	Dec. 3, 1949	Mar. 23, 1977	Sgt. US Air Force Vietnam	MTR1128
Dinatale	Joseph	J.	Oct. 6, 1921	Sep. 26, 1987		SCL4011
DiNatale	Michele	K.	Sep. 10, 1950	Apr. 10, 1967	Beloved Daughter	SCL3082

Last Name	First Name	Middle Name	Date of Birth	Date of Death	Transcription / Notes	Cemetery Code
DiNatale	Unknown		No Date	Sep. 22, 1957	Infant s/o Joseph and Verna	SCL3081
Dippold	Margaret	G., Stone	Jun. 27, 1911	Jan. 1, 1983		MTR4038
Dippold	Nicholas		Jan. 1, 1908	Sep. 5, 1990		MTR4038
Dirolf, Sr.	Joseph	A.	Feb. 17, 1939	Feb. 10, 1991	Loving memories / A2C US Air Force	NJB217
DiSabatino	Karen	L.	1953	1987		SJO1068
Ditoto	Anthony	J.	Jul. 27, 1928	Sep. 9, 2008	Together forever married Jun 2, 1951	SMC4287
Ditoto	Mary	Lucy	Sep. 18, 1929	Jan. 12, 2006	Together forever married Jun 2, 1951	SMC4287
Dixon, Sr.	Albert	Alexander	Jan. 19, 1901	Mar. 1, 1983	In loving memory	CHR517
Dixon	Aletha	L.	Oct. 16, 1921	May 23, 1978		MAC022
Dixon	America	Mary, Irene	Jul. 27, 1917	Jan. 11, 2007		SIC7019
Dixon	Jennie		No Date	No Date	Stone: 23 / Numbered Stonemarkers have been placed on unmarked graves by church. Metal nameplate is attached to marker	CMX2136
Dixon	Jim		No Date	No Date	Stone: 24 / Numbered Stonemarkers have been placed on unmarked graves by church. Metal nameplate is attached to marker	CMX2135
Dixon	John	W.	1907	1985	I love you angel	NSP837
Dixon	Lillian	T.	1914	1989	I love you angel	NSP837
Dixon	M.	Gerolene	Apr. 6, 1907	Jan. 20, 1944	Beloved Mother and Wife	SHI133
Dixon	W.	H.	No Date	No Date	Stone: 22 / Numbered Stonemarkers have been placed on unmarked graves by church. Metal nameplate is attached to marker	CMX2137
Doane	Betty	Ruth	Jun. 15, 1935	Jun. 15, 1935	God gave, he took, he will restore. He doeth all things well.	MRB054
Doane	Clarence	L.	1911	1987		MRB055
Doane	Dora	C.	1906	No Date		MRB055
Doane	Llewellyn	G.	1878	1958		MRB056
Doane	Nellie	E.	1887	1982		MRB056
Dobbins	Joseph		Apr. 20, 1855	May 17, 1923	May his soul rest in peace / old stone that is laying on the ground and is broken off it's base	SIC5011
Dobbins	Louise		Jun. 9, 1890	Nov. 30, 1915	An old stone laying on the ground and is broken off it's base	SIC5011

Last Name	First Name	Middle Name	Date of Birth	Date of Death	Transcription / Notes	Cemetery Code
Dobbins	Phoebe		Sep. 14, 1881	Oct. 25, 1908	An old stone laying on the ground and is broken off it's base	SIC5011
Dobbins	Rosa	M.	Jun. 3, 1888	Apr. 12, 1908	An old stone laying on the ground and is broken off it's base	SIC5011
Dobry	John	Andrew	No Date	May 25, 1977		SAC1003
Dobson	Annie	B.	1902	1992		SJE112
Dobson	William	J.	1892	1943		SJE113
Dockett	Sarah	H.	Mar. 30, 1912	Oct. 15, 1988	Together Forever	HER011
Dockett	Sydney	E.	Feb. 8, 1904	Apr. 22, 1988	Together Forever	HER011
Dodd	Cleveland	Lee	1909	1993	In loving memory	LUM003
Dodd	Fannie		No Date	Jan. 26, 1892	5 yrs. Info is from Old Durham Church microfilm pg 81-82 located at the College of Southern MD, LaPlata, MD	BASNoStone
Dodd	Lannie	G.	1890	1945		GHB013
Dodd	Lazarus	Peter	1900	1958	Together forever	NJB308
Dodd	Lena	Maria	1907	1993	In loving memory	LUM003
Dodd	Linnie		No Date	Jul. 1875	9 mo.'s info is from Old Durham Church microfilm	BASNoStone
Dodd	Mary Frances	Bowie	1905	1990	Together forever	NJB308
Dodd	Unknown		No Date	1888	Buried 1888 (info is from Old Durham Church microfilm pg 81-82 located at the College of Southern MD, LaPlata, MD)	ODENoStone
Dodge	Dorothy	S.	Mar. 23, 1895	Mar. 12, 1945		NSP658
Dodge	J.	Heath	Mar. 11, 1918	Aug. 11, 1918	s/o J.H. & Dorothy Dodge	OSP091
Dodson	Donie	W.	Apr. 1888	Apr. 1974		SHI271
Dodson	Dorriea		1910	1995	Thornton Funeral Home Marker	ZBC121
Dodson	Fannie	L.	Aug. 11, 1918	Oct. 6, 1993	In God's Care / Mother	SMT048
Dodson	Frances	E.	Jul. 19, 1928	May 16, 2002		MTR3036
Dodson	Louise	Virginia	Mar. 22, 1905	Jan. 12, 1982		HER022
Dodson	Loulie	Dickinson, Pugh	Sep. 28, 1907	Mar. 19, 1991	DAR Emblem	ODE041
Dodson	Margaret	B.	Oct. 22, 1918	Feb. 21, 1989		NSP792
Dodson	Nathaniel	A.	Mar. 27, 1920	Jan. 4, 2003		MTR3036
Dodson	Noel	P.	Dec. 8, 1905	Nov. 27, 1993		NSP792
Dodson	Raymond	I.	Aug. 11, 1892	Dec. 15, 1962		ODE042

Last Name	First Name	Middle Name	Date of Birth	Date of Death	Transcription / Notes	Cemetery Code
Dodson	Walter		No Date	Jan. 19, 1929	Age 52 / info is from church records	SHINoStone
Donahue	Janice	Kathleen, Murray	Feb. 24, 1958	Aug. 28, 2002	"Kate" Beloved wife, mother, daughter, sister and friend to all	SCL3346
Doniver	John		1889	1964	Info is from the Historical Society Research located at The College of Southern MD, LaPlata, MD	SCLNoStone
Donley, Sr.	William	J.	May 19, 1917	Sep. 16, 1954		MTR3107
Donnellon	John	B.	1918	2004		SAC1135
Donohoe	Richard	J.	1917	2005		SIC5010
Donohoe	Virginia	J.	1917	No Date		SIC5010
Dooley	Dorothy	F.	May 2, 1918	Sep. 2, 1985		TRI120
Dorch	Annie	Beatrice	Feb. 2, 1916	Jun. 3, 2003		ZWU010
Dorough	Sammie	D.	Aug. 28, 1944	Jan. 20, 2004	Sea US Navy Vietnam	HGH4056
Dorsett	Charlotte	Matilda, Gray	1888	1964	Abide with me	ODE401
Dorsett	Francis	C.	May 31, 1858	Jan. 8, 1920	Mother	CHR534
Dorsett	James	A.	Jan. 26, 1841	Dec. 29, 1918	Father	CHR534
Dorsett	Joseph	Harris, Maddox	1888	1951	Abide with me	ODE401
Dorsett	Margaret	T. H.	No Date	Feb. 11, 1925	Name is shown on church records but burial location is unknown, date is the burial date, not death date	CHRNoStone
Dorsey	Agnes		1920	1984		SMI065
Dorsey	Albert	B.	Apr. 11, 1932	Mar. 24, 1976	s/o Ann Stine / Footstone: Albert Barton Dorsey ST3 US Navy Korea 1932 1976	CHR587
Dorsey	Alice	E.	1917	No Date		SMC2055
Dorsey	Andre	T.	1982	1987	Beloved	SMY2137
Dorsey	Blanche		Jan. 1, 1923	Dec. 5, 1995		ALX027
Dorsey	Carrie		Aug. 10, 1904	Dec. 30, 1965		SMY2116
Dorsey	Catherine	I.	May 21, 1924	Feb. 13, 1985	Gone but not forgotten	HGH3007
Dorsey	Catherine	J.	Sep. 1, 1953	Sep. 30, 1995		SMY2138
Dorsey	Chantel	M.	Aug. 8, 1987	Sep. 3, 2004	Our beloved daughter, sister and friend	SMC1064
Dorsey	Clinton		Feb. 14, 1952	Nov. 2, 1988		SMY2136
Dorsey	Dale	Alvin	Jun. 30, 1969	Oct. 28, 2002	Beloved Son and Father	SMT040
Dorsey	Elizabeth	C.	1934	1986	In loving memory	SMC2057
Dorsey	Emma	R.	1869	1937		OAK102

Last Name	First Name	Middle Name	Date of Birth	Date of Death	Transcription / Notes	Cemetery Code
Dorsey	Estelle	Henrietta	Aug. 17, 1935	Jan. 6, 1985	Beloved wife and Mother	SMT013
Dorsey	Gale		1959	1988	Thornton Funeral Home Marker	ALX043
Dorsey	Geneva	C.	1928	1997	Our Trust Is In God	SMY2145
Dorsey	Gerald		1969	1970		SMI065
Dorsey	Harriett	A.	Feb. 25, 1910	Dec. 10, 1987		SMC1072
Dorsey	James	B.	1902	1986		SMC2055
Dorsey	James	Carl	Mar. 27, 1920	May 24, 2002	S1 US Navy World War II	HGH4111
Dorsey	James	Elmer	1925	1985	Our Trust Is In God	SMY2145
Dorsey	James		1959	1985	Thornton Funeral Home Marker	SMT012
Dorsey	James		1913	1994	Thornton Funeral Home Marker	OAK071
Dorsey	Janice	J.	Dec. 14, 1972	Dec. 25, 2004		SMC1034
Dorsey	John	V.	1938	1985	Gone but not forgotten	HGH4108
Dorsey	John	W.	Apr. 2, 1928	Dec. 4, 2004		HGH4077
Dorsey	John	E.	Apr. 2, 1927	Apr. 27, 2002		SMY2153
Dorsey, Sr.	John	L.	1930	2001	In loving memory / "Chick"	SMC2056
Dorsey	John	S.	1912	1972	Beloved Husband / Rest in Peace	SMY2111
Dorsey	John	W.	1907	1996		SMY2146
Dorsey	Joseph	G.	Dec. 6, 1956	Jul. 1, 1976	(Baldy)	HGH4109
Dorsey	Joseph	Preston	Jan. 29, 1925	May 15, 1955	Maryland PFC 25 Combat team World War II	HGH3010
Dorsey	Joseph		Jul. 31, 1898	Apr. 8, 1967	PVT US Army WW I	SMCB014
Dorsey	Julie		No Date	No Date	Unmarked stone to right of Benjamin Bond	ALX020B
Dorsey	Margaret	E.	Dec. 22, 1938	No Date		HGH4077
Dorsey	Mary	E.	Jul. 24, 1935	Feb. 4, 1989		SMY2047
Dorsey	Mary	Ellen	Jan. 10, 1943	Oct. 1, 1998	Sodality	SMC1065
Dorsey	Mary	V.	Jan. 3, 1919	Nov. 15, 1999	"Mother"	HGH4107
Dorsey	Melanie	Jean	Oct. 4, 1960	Aug. 26, 1965	Daughter of Albert & Alice Jean Dorsey / Patient Brave and Loving. Remembered by all who loved her	HGH1234
Dorsey	Melanie	Jean	No Date	No Date	Children's Memorial / and all other children buried here	HGH4328
Dorsey, Jr.	Patrick	Fitzgerald	Jul. 2, 1985	Aug. 31, 1998		HGH4316
Dorsey	Paul	LaMont	1971	1980	Our beloved son / Rest in peace	SMC1163
Dorsey	Rubin	A.	Jun. 16, 1898	Sep. 7, 1980		SMY2033

Last Name	First Name	Middle Name	Date of Birth	Date of Death	Transcription / Notes	Cemetery Code
Dorsey	Thomas	P.	No Date	Feb. 4, 1971	Info is from church records	SHINoStone
Dorsey	Thomas		No Date	Apr. 21, 1917	Aged 75 years / May he rest in peace	SIC4096
Dorsey	William	Joseph	Sep. 16, 1884	Dec. 14, 1961		SMY2092
Dorsey	Wills	K.	Jul. 1, 1950	Sep. 28, 1968		HGH3009
Dorwart	Frank	E.	No Date	Dec. 5, 1974		NSP959
Dorwart	Marie	A.	No Date	Feb. 25, 2003		NSP959
Dorwart	Timothy	J.	Aug. 25, 1961	Apr. 22, 2002	"Timmy" / Loving husband and father	SIC9010
Dotson	Charlott	S.	1854	1930		POM056
Dotson	Florence	E.	Feb. 22, 1942	Apr. 25, 1997	"Kitten"	ZBC022
Dotson	Harry	Lee	1861	1939		POM056
Dougherty	Dan	Robert	Jun. 1961	Oct. 1961		SCL4001
Douglas	Lamel	Jerome	Oct. 26, 1991	Feb. 18, 1992		SMCI004
Douglas	Mary	Alice	Sep. 7, 1940	Jul. 10, 1972		SMC4091
Douglas	Unknown		No Date	No Date	Funeral home marker with no info except the name Douglas	SMCW051
Doukas	Peter	James	Jun. 2, 1941	Nov. 1, 2000	In Loving Memory	SAC5119
Doutt	Harold	J.	Aug. 2, 1918	Oct. 29, 1966		SIC7031
Dove	Agatha	R.	1915	1994		SIC7045
Dove	Josephine	Kerr	Mar. 18, 1864	Sep. 5, 1905		CLV263
Dove	Paul	A.	1910	2007		SIC7045

Last Name	First Name	Middle Name	Date of Birth	Date of Death	Transcription / Notes	Cemetery Code
Downey, Mrs.	Bridget			No Date	To My Mother / unto dust thou shall remain Gen. 3rd Chap 19th ver. / Sacred to the memory of / who departed this life, at her residence St. Mary's F. Institute near Bryantown Chas. Co. Md. / Aged 67 years / May she rest in peace. Marble urn preserve the ashes. Treasured in this silent tomb's mark the spot where lies our mother. Till the day of final doom weeping willows, trail your branches. Round the place where rest our dear. Heaven has robed her soul in glory, earth lie gently on her head. / Stonemaker: W. Henderson 33 E. Pratt St. Balt°. / Right of stone: "Favor is deceiptful and beauty is vain, the woman that feareth the Lord, she shall be praised'" Give her of the fruits of her hands; and let her works praise her in the gates." Proverbs 31st Chap. 30 & 31 Vers.	SMCE048 SMCE049
Downs	Bernard	W.	Sep. 19, 1877	Oct. 21, 1946		OSM066
Downs	Bernard		Dec. 7, 1912	Mar. 2, 1970		OSM064
Downs	Edgar	M.	1841	1904		OSM035
Downs	Edith	H.	Aug. 22, 1886	Feb. 2, 1966		OSM065
Downs	Ella	E.	Feb. 8, 1881	Aug. 31, 1912	Beloved w/o Thos F. Downs	SJO2311
Downs	George	F.	May 16, 1926	Dec. 26, 2000	Mary Pray for us / Nov 24, 1951	DOW001
Downs	George	W.	1835	1903	Father	OSM071
Downs	H.	Celeste	Aug. 23, 1931	Oct. 7, 2009	Born in Wash. D.C. She was a retired Orphans Court Judge for Charles County, MD. / Mary Pray for us / In double wedding rings the date Nov 24, 1951	DOW001
Downs	Harry		Jan. 6, 1888	Mar. 1, 1904	Beloved s/o Mary A & Alpheus Downs	OSM078
Downs	Laura	Ann	1834	1906	Mother	OSM070
Downs	Margret	P.	1882	1948		OSM058
Downs	Mary	J.	1838	1894		OSM036
Downs	Roger	L.	May 16, 1910	Apr. 14, 1917	s/o T.F. & Ella E. Downs / Asleep in Jesus Blessed Sleep	OSM060
Downs	Thomas	Fiske	1875	1941		OSM059
Downs	Virginia	Lee	Oct. 11, 1908	Dec. 28, 1911	Virginia Lee Downs / daughter of B.W. and Edith Downs / Asleep in Jesus blessed sleep	OSM067

Last Name	First Name	Middle Name	Date of Birth	Date of Death	Transcription / Notes	Cemetery Code
Dows	Edith	Kate	No Date	May 25, 1872	youngest d/o William and Eleanor Dows, Age 9 mo's./ died at Rosemary Lawn. / Not sure if she is buried here / info is from Port Tobacco Abstracts Vol. 3 Pg 88 and appeared in the newspaper June 7, 1872 Vol XXVIX # 6	RMLNoStone
Doyne, P.S.J.	Josephus		No Date	Nov. 12, 1803	IHS / O.B. 12 Nov 1803 / AET 69 (In Priests Plot)	SIC1004
Drake	Gustella		1925	1981		POM236
Drake	Thomas	C.	1925	1972		POM210
Draper, III	William	C.	Apr. 2, 1940	Nov. 11, 1992	Dearest husband, father, grandfather & friend / We Love You	MTR3166
Drapp	Marcella	D.	1904	1979		SMC1179
Drapp	Matthew	A.	1896	1985		SMC1179
Dries	John		May 13, 1909	Nov. 12, 1992	If a grain of wheat falls on the ground and dies, it yields a rich harvest	SJO4103
Drinkard	Ada	Pearl, Williams	Oct. 10, 1889	Sep. 28, 1934		MRB010
Drinkard, Sr.	Dennis	Robert	Feb. 27, 1943	Oct. 23, 1997	"Denny" / Loving father, son, brother & grandfather / The world without Denny will not be as exciting, interesting, or fun. / SP4 US Army Vietnam	NZN007
Drinkard	Lawrence	R.	Mar. 9, 1913	Aug. 18, 1998	Masonic Emblem	CHR277
Drinkard, Jr.	Lawrence	Robert	Aug. 3, 1939	Mar. 10, 1942		NZN005
Drinkard	Mary		Mar. 15, 1949	Mar. 15, 1949	"Larry" / Safe in the arms of Jesus	NZN041
Drinkard	Mildred	L.	Aug. 8, 1915	Nov. 8, 2005		CHR277
Drinkard	Volney	Howard	Apr. 19, 1889	May 24, 1947		MRB010
Drinks	Alberta	C.	Feb. 24, 1911	Feb. 3, 1973		CHR132
Drinks	Ann	Katherine	No Date	Feb. 9, 1901	Name is shown on church records but burial location is unknown, date is the burial date, not death date	CHRNoStone
Drinks	Catherine		No Date	Oct. 10, 1925	Name is shown on church records but burial location is unknown, date is the burial date, not death date	CHRNoStone
Drinks	Charles	J.	1913	1980		SIC6010
Drinks	Charles		No Date	Mar. 22, 1910	Name is shown on church records but burial location is unknown, date is the burial date, not death date	CHRNoStone
Drinks	E.	Paul	1879	1955		CHR324
Drinks	Edna	Earl	1886	1972		CHR324

Last Name	First Name	Middle Name	Date of Birth	Date of Death	Transcription / Notes	Cemetery Code
Drinks	Harry		No Date	1923	Name is shown on church records but burial location is unknown, date is the burial date, not death date	CHRNoStone
Drinks	John	F.	1883	1957	Capt	CHR367
Drinks	Joyce	Ellen	No Date		Name is shown on church records but burial location is unknown	CHRNoStone
Drinks	Lester	J.	Dec. 18, 1906	Mar. 26, 1958		CHR131
Drinks	Margaret	E.	1914	Sep. 20, 1974		SIC6010
Drinks	Rae	M.	1946	2007		SJO3309
Drinks	Robert	L.	No Date	1987	Flat marker is located at base of cedar tree	CHRNoStone
Drinks	Unknown		No Date	Jul. 14, 1943	Name is shown on church records but burial location is unknown, date is the burial date, not death date	CHRNoStone
Drummond	Patricia		Aug. 10, 1967	Oct. 4, 1941	Name is shown on church records but burial location is unknown, date is the burial date, not death date	CHRNoStone
du Mas	Dorothy	V.	Dec. 9, 1927	Jun. 29, 2005	Number 230-E inscribed on marker info is from church records	CLV427
Dubois	Julia		Jan. 13, 1874	Jul. 16, 1992	In loving memory	NJB292
Duckett	Clanzy		1876	Jul. 2, 1880	Info is from DAR book pg 16 located at The College of Southern MD, LaPlata, MD	PAT014
Duckett	Ernest	L.	1908	1938		OSP145
Duckett	Janie		1883	1973		NSP147A
Duckett	Lillie		No Date	1927		OSP145
Duckett	Mabel	E.	1926	Nov. 26, 1936	Age 26 / Info is from the Historical Society Located at the College of Southern MD, LaPlata, MD	BRCNoStone
Duckett	Mary	Goldring	Feb. 11, 1929	1999		SMT050
Duckett	Russell	A.	No Date	Oct. 23, 2005	On earth / In Heaven	SMC4206
Duckett	Viola	E.	1946	Jul. 17, 1977	Aged 38 / Info is from the Historical Society Located at the College of Southern MD, LaPlata, MD	BRCNoStone
Duckett	Virgie	Lee	1922	1993	In God's Care / Mother	SAC1116
Dudley	Addie	K.	1896	No Date		NSP147A
Dudley	Belle	Robey	1867	1976	Info is from the Historical Society Research located at the College of Southern MD, LaPlata, MD	ZBCNoStone
Dudley	Edith	R.	Oct. 14, 1889	1954		SPL1035
Dudley	Hazel	C.	Jul. 28, 1913	Dec. 26, 1934	Woodman of the World memorial Dum Tace Telamat	OFE2008
Dudley				Sep. 15, 1971		CLV054

Last Name	First Name	Middle Name	Date of Birth	Date of Death	Transcription / Notes	Cemetery Code
Dudley	James	Arthur	Feb. 29, 1888	Oct. 11, 1968	Arehart Funeral Home, Inc. Funeral Home Marker and ground marker	PIS053
Dudley	Jeremiah		May 8, 1820	Apr. 18, 1901		SMCD116
Dudley	John	D.	Sep. 17, 1871	Apr. 17, 1932	Woodman of the World memorial Dum Tace Telamat	OFE2008
Dudley, Jr.	John	Sullivan	1918	1968		SJE185
Dudley, Sr.	John	S.	Jan. 23, 1889	Apr. 30, 1967	Father	SJE188
Dudley	Louis	P.	Aug. 31, 1854	Feb. 17, 1910		OFE2011
Dudley	Lucy	Jennie	No Date	Nov. 4, 1878	Beloved d/o Jeremiah and Jennie H Dudley D/Aged 7 years	OFE2009
Dudley	Wilton	K.	Nov. 25, 1925	May 24, 1977	PFC US Army WW II	MTR2021
Dudley	Lillian	M.	Feb. 7, 1889	Jan. 2, 1958		SJE187
Duffy	J.	Philip	Sep. 9, 1957	Feb. 16, 1979		NSP996
Duffy	James	H.	Aug. 28, 1924	No Date		NSP996
Duffy	James	Hubert	No Date	Apr. 15, 1915	In the 69th year of his age. (Info is from the Historical Society Research located at the College of Southern MD, LaPlata, MD)	SCLNoStone
Duffy	James	Hubert	1887	1925	(Info is from the Historical Society Research located at the College of Southern MD, LaPlata, MD)	SCLNoStone
Duffy	Joseph	H.	No Date	May 25, 1893	In memory of / beloved h/o Alice Duffy / aged 48 years / May he rest in peace / What to me is life without thee. Darkness & despair alone. When with sighs we seek to find thee. This tomb proclaims that thou art gone.	SJO3053
Duffy	Margaret	B.	Nov. 4, 1926	No Date		NSP996
Duffy	Mary	Alice, Welch	Mar. 1, 1861	Mar. 13, 1935	Info is from the Historical Society Research located at the College of Southern MD, LaPlata, MD	SCLNoStone
Dugan	Albert	W.	Dec. 7, 1874	May 16, 1959	Pvt 44 Co. Coast Arty. Spanish American War	SPL4033
Dugan	Mary	W.	1870	1948		SPL4033
Dugan	Richard	E.	Oct. 13, 1928	Feb. 1, 2002		LUM004
Duke	Martha	R.	1913	1981		SCL1184
Duke	William	S.	1909	1960		SCL1184
Dulabahn	John	William	Nov. 11, 1916	Apr. 22, 1991	In loving memory	MTR1224
Dulcey	Jeffrey	Michael	Oct. 23, 1985	Dec. 7, 1985	Child of God	NSP711
Duley, Sr.	Joseph	Alvin	Sep. 21, 1906	Mar. 20, 1995		ODE067

Last Name	First Name	Middle Name	Date of Birth	Date of Death	Transcription / Notes	Cemetery Code
Dulcey	Laura	Marie	No Date	Nov. 20, 1987	Angel of the Lord	NSP709
Dulcey	Michael	Joseph	Dec. 7, 1983	Mar. 3, 1984	Child of God	NSP710
Dunbar	Elsie	M.	1922	2001	Our Father Which Art In Heaven	SCA116
Dunbar	Frederick		1883	1948	Father (under a bush)	SCA069
Dunbar	James	R.	1918	1995	Our Father Which Art In Heaven	SCA116
Dunbar	Marion	A.	1885	1950	Mother (under a bush)	SCA070
Dunemore	Sarah		No Date	No Date	Info is from the Historical Society Research located at the College of Southern MD, LaPlata, MD	ZBCNoStone
Dunn	Eula	P.	1930	1971	Our Beloved sister / Rest in Peace	SCL4120
Dunnington	Ada		1892	1951		SCL4226
Dunnington	Ann	Courtright	Jul. 5, 1928	No Date		ODE088
Dunnington	Annie	Gantt	Sep. 21, 1852	Sep. 2, 1927	At rest	ODE098
Dunnington	Audrey	M.	Dec. 6, 1944	Jul. 27, 1952		SCL4225
Dunnington	Beulah	C.	1935	1999	In Loving Memory Wife Mother "Boo"	MHB020
Dunnington	Edith	Regina	Nov. 6, 1928	Jun. 25, 2010	Thornton Funeral Home Marker / age 81 d/o the late Frank and the late Minnie Thomas. w/o William McKinley Dunnington. Obit was in the Maryland Independent Newspaper dated July 7, 2010	PGN089
Dunnington	Elgin	A.	Mar. 18, 1897	May 21, 1960		ODE087
Dunnington	Elgin	Adams	Dec. 20, 1924	Feb. 4, 2001		ODE088
Dunnington	Eric	Francis	Mar. 24, 1970	Aug. 29, 2007	Age 37, s/o William Francis "Bonie" Dunnington and Catherine Annette Day Dunnington Diggs / info is from the MD Independent Newspaper Sept 5, 2007 Pg A-14	CLVNoStone
Dunnington	Francis	E.	Sep. 12, 1852	Oct. 18, 1940		ODE093
Dunnington	Frank		Aug. 20, 1819	Feb. 1, 1894	A good name is rather to be chosen than great riches, and loving favor rather than silver and gold	ODE097
Dunnington	George		No Date	Jan. 18, 1894	Info is from Old Durham Church microfilm pg 83-84, at the College of Southern MD, LaPlata, MD	ODENoStone
Dunnington	George		1743	1804	In memory of / 1791 / church planter, trustee, benefactor for Nanjemoy Baptist Church, the first Baptist Church in Charles County, Md. To God be the glory.	NJB494

Last Name	First Name	Middle Name	Date of Birth	Date of Death	Transcription / Notes	Cemetery Code
Dunnington	Hettie	May	May 8, 1907	Oct. 7, 1907	Infant d/o B. F. & Adele Dunnington / Of such is the kingdom of heaven	PIS043
Dunnington	Howard	M.	Apr. 17, 1913	May 21, 1967		SCL4225
Dunnington	Marcellous		1889	1991		SCL4226
Dunnington	Margaret	Rebecca	Dec. 25, 1828	Aug. 9, 1892	Beloved wife of Francis Dunnington. / "Give her of the fruit of her hands, and let her own works praise her in the gates"	ODE096
Dunnington	Mary	E.	Dec. 12, 1864	Jun. 27, 1943		ODE092
Dunnington	Ruhamah	Dean	Mar. 1, 1840	Jun. 6, 1878	w/o Walter W. Dunnington	ODE090A
Dunnington	Ruhamah	Dean	Oct. 20, 1902	Jun. 25, 1997	Ruby	ODE086
Dunnington	Stanislaus	B.	Jun. 23, 1856	Feb. 23, 1891	Sacred to the memory of / He giveth his loved ones sleep	ODE094
Dunnington	Unknown		No Date	Jan. 1901	Age 70 (info is from Old Durham Church microfilm pg 85, at the College of Southern MD, LaPlata, MD)	ODENoStone
Dunnington	Walter	W.	Jan. 6, 1828	Jan. 6, 1901	h/o Ruhannah Dean Dunnington	ODE090A
Dunnington	William		1927	1994	Thornton Funeral Home Marker	PGN042
Dunphy	George	W.	Nov. 28, 1929	Aug. 5, 2006		SCL4166
Dunphy	Mary	M.	Oct. 21, 1929	Mar. 10, 1988		SCL4166
Dupree	Jonathan	Risteau	Mar. 10, 1972	Oct. 3, 2005	Mother - Son	MTR4177
Dupree	Sarah	Craik	Feb. 14, 1943	Jul. 4, 2005	Mother - Son	MTR4177
Durn	Lillian	Mary, Adams	Aug. 30, 1900	May 31, 1987	Loving Tender Mother Faithful Friend	SJO2009
Durner	Barbara	A.	Aug. 5, 1932	Feb. 23, 1995	Never to part	TRI422
Durner	Wm.	Eric	Dec. 7, 1925	Mar. 17, 1985	Never to part	TRI422
Dusenberry	Dorothy	S.	1920	1987		SJE001
Dusenberry	William	G.	1916	1994		SJE001
Dutton	Alice	J.	1851	1889	Mother	GHB009
Dutton	Caroline	Elizabeth	Apr. 24, 1878	Dec. 17, 1947	Wife of Edwin Lancaster / Rest	HGH1180
Dutton	Donna	Card	Oct. 30, 1957	Jun. 16, 1976	Wife of Christopher R. Dutton / Mother of Lisa Ann Dutton	SMC3203
Dutton	Edwin	C.	Sep. 10, 1849	Feb. 26, 1890		GHB005
Dutton	Edwin	L.	Feb. 14, 1883	Jul. 15, 1934	Father / Husband of C. E. Simpson / May he rest in peace	HGH1179

Last Name	First Name	Middle Name	Date of Birth	Date of Death	Transcription / Notes	Cemetery Code
Dutton	Eliza	A.	Feb. 16, 1819	Dec. 20, 1886	w/o J.H.M. Dutton	SIC3029
Dutton	James	Willard	May 4, 1919	Dec. 28, 1995		SJO1054
Dutton	John	T.	1841	1920	Father	GHB039
Dutton	Lucy	Colton	Mar. 7, 1857	Aug. 26, 1933		GHB006
Dutton	Mary	Roberta	Dec. 12, 1895	Jan. 29, 1977	w/o Notley T. Dutton	SJO1055
Dutton	Maybelle		No Date	1886	Baby / Information was obtained from the Historical Society's transcription from 1980	GHBNo Stone
Dutton	Melanie	S.	Jun. 10, 1964	No Date	In loving memory	SJO1040
Dutton	Myrtle	Marguerite	Jul. 8, 1906	Jul. 6, 1907	In memory of / Gone but not forgotten	CHR280
Dutton	Notley	Thomas	Nov. 10, 1915	Jun. 7, 2002		SJO1053
Dutton	Notley	Thomas	No Date	Apr. 28, 1935	Maryland Pvt US Marine Corps	GHB007
Dutton	Richard	C.	Apr. 21, 1930	Mar. 21, 1991	In loving memory	SJO1040
Dutton	Richard	C.	Jun. 2, 1885	Jul. 12, 1911		GHB008
Dutton	Rita	V.	Jan. 21, 1934	No Date	In loving memory	SJO1040
Dutton	Sally	Anne	Mar. 15, 1963	Jun. 16, 1976	Beloved d/o Richard & Rita Dutton	SJO1057
Dutton	Sarah	M.	Jul. 12, 1872	Nov. 1, 1899	W/o C.P., d/o Geo. O. & Anna D. Hensel	MTR1020
Dutton	Unknown		No Date	No Date	Our babys-Infant daughter & son of C.P. & F.B. Dutton	MTR1019
Dutton	Unknown		No Date	No Date	Our babys-Infant daughter & son of C.P. & F.B. Dutton	MTR1019
Dutton	William	Edwin	Feb. 27, 1906	Oct. 15, 1906	In loving remembrance of / Gone but not forgotten / footstone	CHR281
Dutton	William	Lancaster	Mar. 28, 1909	Apr. 4, 1941	"Rest"	HGH1178
Dwyer	Eric	Shaun	1979	1980		SJO2264
Dyer	Austin	Miles	Sep. 26, 1841	Mar. 25, 1911	Pvt / Co B 1 MD Cav CSA	SMCC023
Dyer	Beatrice	G.	Oct. 28, 1884	Feb. 4, 1940		SMCC038
Dyer	Bernadetta		1880	1950		HGH2116
Dyer	Dorothy		Mar. 19, 1794	Sep. 2, 1843	In remembrance of / w/o George Dyer	OSP125
Dyer	Eugene	S.	1905	1987		SJO4005
Dyer	George	E.	Nov. 5, 1813	Aug. 2, 1863	In memory of / Info is from The Historical Society Research located at College of Southern MD, LaPlata, MD	OSPNoStone
Dyer	George		Mar. 12, 1790	Oct. 10, 1822	Lying on ground	OSP126
Dyer	Gladys	Lee	Jul. 5, 1943	No Date	In Loving Memory	SAC1041

Last Name	First Name	Middle Name	Date of Birth	Date of Death	Transcription / Notes	Cemetery Code
Dyer	James	A.	Sep. 24, 1902	Jun. 17, 1992		HGH2108
Dyer	James	T.	1846	1899		SMY1122
Dyer	James	T.	1878	1956		HGH2116
Dyer	John	B.	1875	1940		NSP351
Dyer	Joseph	Ralph	Jul. 9, 1936	Aug. 25, 2005	In Loving Memory / Dates are from website familysearch.org	SAC1040
Dyer	Julia	Gates	Aug. 9, 1925	No Date	In God's care	SMC2188
Dyer	Julian	Gardiner	Aug. 23, 1916	Dec. 16, 1996	Footstone: SGT US Army WW II	SIC3039
Dyer	Julian		Oct. 7, 1874	Nov. 8, 1948		SMCC037
Dyer	Katharine	R.	Jul. 15, 1903	Oct. 31, 1988		HGH2108
Dyer	Mary	A.	1858	1907		SMY1122
Dyer	Mary	Agnes	No Date	Jul. 5, 1873	d/o Jere & M C Dyer / aged 1 year & 12 ds	SMCA117
Dyer	Mary	Cecelia	1846	1933	w/o Miles Dyer	SMCC026
Dyer	Mary	Ellen	1903	1969		SJO4005
Dyer	Mary	Queen	1872	1952		HGH1067
Dyer	Mathelene		May 30, 1899	No Date	To our baby / beloved d/o M.A. & J.T. Dyer Note: Unable to read death date	SMY1123
Dyer	Miles		1841	1911	Rest in peace	SMCC024
Dyer	Naomi	R.	1886	1939		NSP351
Dyer	Nettie	R.	Sep. 6, 1893	Mar. 5, 1979		LUM078
Dyer	Sophia		No Date	Oct. 2, 1831	IHS / Scared to the memory of / w/o Edward Dyer of Washington City who, departed this life on Sunday the 2nd day of Oct 1831 in the 31st year of her age. Fond husband, innocent child, pastors solicitious for the suffering among your flock, well may you weep near this tomb! But mourn not; think of the crown secured above and example left below, by her whom you have lost / May she rest in peace, Amen	SMCD273
Dyer	Theresa	E.	Mar. 31, 1928	No Date	w/o Julian G. Dyer	SIC3039
Dyer	Thomas	Austin	Mar. 28, 1920	Jun. 15, 2009	In God's care	SMC2188
Dyer	Thomas	B.	No Date	Mar. 25, 1835	In the 29th year of his age	OSP162
Dyer	Webster	Wilburn	Dec. 23, 1912	Apr. 4, 1963		SMT010

Last Name	First Name	Middle Name	Date of Birth	Date of Death	Transcription / Notes	Cemetery Code
Dyson	Alexander	Thomas	No Date	Dec. 1941	Age 80, buried December 5, 1941 (Info is from the Historical Society Research located at the College of Southern MD, LaPlata, MD)	ODENoStone
Dyson	Amanda		No Date	No Date		SHI272
Dyson	Anna	Christina	Apr. 5, 1890	May 12, 1971		SIC8017
Dyson	Anne	E.	1922	1994		TRI091
Dyson	Annie	Ward	1894	1932		TRI093
Dyson	Benjamin		1876	1939		SHI283
Dyson, M.D.	Bennet		No Date	Jun. 29, 1855	To the memory of our revered father / who departed this life / Aged 62 years/and our beloved mother / Aged 26 years / This monument is affectionateyly inscribed by their devoted children / May God give their precious Souls the rest of his beloved	CAR004
Dyson	Bertha	M.	Jan. 30, 1937	No Date	Together Forever	MAC042
Dyson	Catherine	B.	1852	1935		SHI268
Dyson	Catherine	M.	Dec. 4, 1918	Dec. 31, 2001	Kate / Wed Mar 6, 1935	SCL1037
Dyson	Catherine	Moran	1858	1931		TRI319
Dyson	Cecelia		No Date	No Date		SHI272
Dyson	Clara	V.	Jan. 29, 1876	Feb. 18, 1913		TRI054
Dyson	Columbia	J.	Sep. 30, 1863	Apr. 2, 1945		NSP362
Dyson	Cornelia	A.	1909	1990	Together forever.	TRI343
Dyson	Cornelia		No Date	No Date	Age 30 in the 1920 census, info from ancestry.com	SHI272
Dyson	Edna	Martha	1886	1978		TRI056
Dyson	Edward	E.	1921	1998		TRI090
Dyson	Elbt	H.	No Date	Dec. 9, 1912	Back of stone says Elbt. Dyson died Dec 9, 1912	POM039
Dyson	Elizabeth	Bowie	Nov. 15, 1903	Apr. 26, 1973	To live in the hearts we leave behind is not to die	ODE272
Dyson	Ella		No Date	No Date	Information is from the Historical Society Research located at The College of Southern MD, LaPlata, MD	SIGNo Stone
Dyson	Esther	C.	Feb. 1, 1926	Jun. 24, 1993	Rest in Peace	POM159
Dyson	Fannie		No Date	Sep. 22, 1922	Info is from church records	SHINoStone
Dyson	Frank		No Date	Feb. 26, 1956	Info is from church records	SHINoStone
Dyson, Sr.	George	Albert	Mar. 14, 1898	Dec. 7, 1972	Father / In loving memory	MAC036

Last Name	First Name	Middle Name	Date of Birth	Date of Death	Transcription / Notes	Cemetery Code
Dyson	George	Conrad	Jun. 18, 1894	Feb. 9, 1955	In Thee O' Lord have I put my trust	ODE271
Dyson	George	H.	Jul. 14, 1914	Apr. 4, 2002	Harry / Wed Mar 6, 1935	SCL1037
Dyson	George	L.	Apr. 23, 1935	Apr. 12, 1991	In loving memory from your family	SAC3025
Dyson	George		No Date	No Date	age 32 in 1920 census, info from ancestry.com	SHI272
Dyson	George	Preston	Aug. 22, 1896	May 23, 1984	PFC US Army WWI.	TRI344
Dyson	H.	Wayne	Jul. 4, 1934	Dec. 3, 1985		NSP385
Dyson	Harriet		No Date	Apr. 21, 1922	Info is from church records	SHINoStone
Dyson	Harris	R.	1874	1956	Info is from church records	SHI269
Dyson	Harry	Jerome	Jan. 3, 1965	Apr. 28, 2007	May The Works I've Done Speak For Me	SCL1069
Dyson	Helen	Thersa	Jun. 11, 1925	Sep. 23, 1973		SIC8029
Dyson	Henry		No Date	No Date	Age 40 in the 1920 census, info from ancestry.com	SHI272
Dyson	James	G.	Apr. 10, 1921	Nov. 25, 1996	Wed Dec 25, 1941	SJO3378
Dyson	James	H.	No Date	Nov. 12, 1924	Age 84 / info is from church records	SHINoStone
Dyson	James	W.	May 8, 1952	Mar. 24, 1967		SJO1151
Dyson	John	Francis	Jan. 15, 1874	Jul. 13, 1924		HNT028
Dyson, Jr.	John	Francis	1911	1965		HNT025
Dyson	John	Samuel	1849	1923		TRI042
Dyson, Sr.	Joseph	Marvin	Sep. 11, 1955	Nov. 17, 2001	In Loving Memory / "Joe" / We Love you Joe	SAC2110
Dyson	Judith	Ophelia	1918	1918		TRI092
Dyson	Laura	Louvenia	Jun. 25, 1923	Mar. 6, 1999	Together forever	NJB273
Dyson, II	Lawrence	Lowell	Mar. 15, 1967	Jun. 3, 1967		SJO3317
Dyson	Lena	Smith	Sep. 29, 1904	Nov. 20, 1994	An inspiration to all who knew her / info is from church records	SHI270
Dyson, III	Leon	James	Mar. 16, 1988	Apr. 10, 1993	Son of Leon James, Jr. and Cindie Johnson	OAK065
Dyson	Louis	David	Apr. 9, 1959	May 26, 1992	He is our only need	SMC2042
Dyson	Lucille	B.	1928	1995		TRI088
Dyson	M.		No Date	No Date	Writing was done by hand	SJO1138
Dyson	Mary	Catherine	No Date	No Date	Info is from Maryland Independent Newspaper dated Jan 18, 2002. Note: Mary Catherine (Kitty) Dyson; b. Nov 19, 1930; d. Jan 11, 2002; d/o George Preston & Minnie Cooksey Dyson	TRINoStone

Last Name	First Name	Middle Name	Date of Birth	Date of Death	Transcription / Notes	Cemetery Code
Dyson	Mary	Elizabeth	1854	1945		TRI041
Dyson	Mary	Helen	Mar. 10, 1889	May 30, 1898	d/o W.W.-Catherine Dyson.	TRI323
Dyson	Mary	I.	1932	1982		SAC4019
Dyson	Mary	J.	1875	1951		SHI284
Dyson	Mary	L., Lewis	Oct. 2, 1921	Aug. 13, 2000	Wed Dec 25, 1941	SJO3378
Dyson					To the memory of our revered father / who departed this life / Aged 62 years / and our beloved mother / Aged 26 years / This monument is affectionateyly inscribed by their devoted children / May God give their precious	
Dyson	Mary	M.	No Date	May 1833	Souls the rest of his beloved	CAR004
Dyson	Mary		No Date	No Date		SHI272
Dyson	Matthew	Allen	Apr. 7, 1934	Aug. 18, 1995	Pvt US Army	SIC8018
Dyson	Minnie	Cooksey	Nov. 21, 1904	Jan. 10, 1994	In loving memory.	TRI345
Dyson	Miriam	E.	Apr. 24, 1898	Jul. 11, 1978		NSP361
Dyson	Molly		1886	1941	Name and Dates are painted on a cement cross	POM167
Dyson, Rev.	Norvel	W.	1843	1929		SHI268
Dyson	Rebecca		No Date	1948		POM170
Dyson	Robert	P.	No Date	Jun. 7, 1925	Age 50 yrs / info is from church records	SHINoStone
Dyson					Sacred to the memory of / who departed this life / in the 34th year of his age. May he rest in peace. Amen. I am the resurrection and the life: he that beliveth in me although he be dead, shall live St. John 11 C. 25 V Blessed are the clean of heart: for they shall see God St. Matthew 4C. 8V / This stone is located on the left side of	
Dyson, M.D.	Robert		No Date	Oct. 24, 1860	the church and is inside an iron fence.	SIG170
Dyson	Robert		No Date	Oct. 13, 1964	Info is from church records	SHINoStone
Dyson	Roberta	O.	No Date	No Date	Cement cross	MAC025
Dyson	Rosie	C.	Jan. 24, 1909	Jul. 8, 1968	Mother	MAC029
Dyson	Russell	H.	Nov. 25, 1915	Jun. 23, 1981		SJO2237

Last Name	First Name	Middle Name	Date of Birth	Date of Death	Transcription / Notes	Cemetery Code
Dyson	S.	Justin	Nov. 21, 1978	Jun. 5, 2001	Loving Son and Father / ALJA / Back of Stone: To those I love and those who love Me. I won't be far away, for life goes on. So if you need me, call and I will come. And if you listen with your heart, you'll hear all my love around you soft and clear	SAC3005
Dyson	Samuel	Edgar	1888	1957		TRI094
Dyson, Mrs.	Sarah		No Date	Sep. 1, 1857	Sacred to the memory of / consort of the late Doctor John Dyson who departed this life/in the 77th year of her age / and even to your old age I am He and even to hoar hairs will I carry you / Isaiah 46 Chapter 4th Verse / for if you believe that Jesus died and rose again, even so them also which sleep in Jesus will God bring with him / 1 Thesalonians 4 Chapter 14 Verse / She passed from a life of grace through a death of peace to an immortality of Glory	CAR005
Dyson	Susie	Huntt	Sep. 8, 1872	Jan. 28, 1939		HNT029
Dyson	Thomas	Bernard	Mar. 8, 1921	May 9, 2000	Together forever	NJB273
Dyson	Thomas	R.	1909	1966	Old cement cross painted white	POM252
Dyson	Unknown		1978	1978	Baby girl Dyson (Info is from the Historical Society Research located at The College Of Southern MD., LaPlata, MD)	SCLNoStone
Dyson	Virgie		No Date	May 26, 1956	Info is from church records	SHI272
Dyson	William	A.	Aug. 18, 1894	May 7, 1974		NSP360
Dyson, Sr.	William	A.	Jun. ??	Jun. 15 ?	Father	POM166
Dyson	William	Herbert	1925	1929	Beloved s/o Elbert & Julia A Dyson At Rest	OFE2064
Dyson	William	O.	Sep. 3, 1844	May 24, 1928	At rest / footstone W.O.D.	TRI035
Dyson	William	W.	Jul. 17, 1849	Apr. 7, 1919	Hope / Beloved h/o Katherine Moran / Loved in life, in death remembered / footstone: W.W.D.	TRI321
Dyson, Jr.	William	W.	1891	1979	Together forever.	TRI343
Dyson	William		No Date	No Date		SHI272
Dyson	William		No Date	No Date	Name is written with wire	POM168
Dyson	Woodrow	J.	Mar. 11, 1938	Sep. 1, 1994	Together Forever	MAC042
Dyson	Yates		No Date	Mar. 20, 1964	Age 39 in the 1920 census, info from ancestry.com death date is from church records	SHI272

Last Name	First Name	Middle Name	Date of Birth	Date of Death	Transcription / Notes	Cemetery Code
Eagee	Frances A	Bailey	1909	1944		MTR3027
Eagen	Frances	Cecelia	Jul. 16, 1874	Mar. 7, 1953	No Stone / Info is from Historical Society Research located at the College of Southern MD, LaPlata, MD	MTRNoStone
Early	Naomi	Huntt	1880	1958		MTR1079
Early	Richard	Brandt	1883	1963		MTR1078
Earnshaw	Christy	Lynn	No Date	Oct. 5, 1957	Our Baby / Age 2 weeks	NSP730
Earnshaw	Pamela	Kay	Jun. 1958	Aug. 1958		NSP731
Eastman	Unknown		No Date	Mar. 21, 1956	Infant	NSP756
Eaton	Edward	H.	Jun. 9, 1902	Oct. 6, 1990	Capt	CHR125
Eaton	Frances	L.	1937	No Date		HER030
Eaton	James	R.	1916	1994		HER030
Eaton	Unknown		No Date	No Date	No Dates name carved in cement brick	GIL007
Eaton	Unknown			Aug. 16, 1831	broken stone pieces	OSB005
Echols	Catherine	E.	1918	1995		SCL3321
Echols	Elmo	G.	1915	1986		SCL3321
Echols	Juanita	Ann	Aug. 26, 1937	No Date		SCL3320
Eck	Bernard	H.	1913	1968	Dad	SCL4089
Eckman	Unknown		No Date	Sep. 25, 1966	Infant child of Doloris and William Eckman	MTR3149
Eckstein	Christina	Marie	Apr. 19 1863	Jun. 24, 1917	Beloved w/o Emil A. Eckstein / Rest in peace	SJE249
Ecton, Mrs.	Unknown		No Date	Feb. 27, 1890	Info is from church records	OFENoStone
Edelen	Alice	G.	Aug. 23, 1863	Nov. 1, 1914	May she rest in peace	SJO2326
Edelen	Alma	G., Mudd	Oct. 27, 1889	Nov. 8, 1972	Wife	SMCE017
Edelen	Anne	Wiley	No Date	No Date	Daughter	SIC4013
Edelen, III	Benjamin	M.	Sep. 14, 1904	Sep. 16, 1975		SMC2138
Edelen, Jr.	Benjamin	M.	1871	1947	On the back of this headstone is the name Boarman	SMCD174
Edelen	Benjamin	Marcellus	1834	1915		SMCD145
Edelen	Bernard	H.	1852	1916	Husband	SMCA044
Edelen	C.	Grantly	Jan. 28, 1863	Dec. 27, 1910		SMCE017
Edelen	Camilla	Lancaster	1824	1904		HGH1053
Edelen	Carol	A.	1945	No Date	Together forever	SMC2111
Edelen	Carrie	R.	1900	1965		SMY2086

Last Name	First Name	Middle Name	Date of Birth	Date of Death	Transcription / Notes	Cemetery Code
Edelen	Charles	Barromeo	1894	1894		SMCD144
Edelen	Claude	O.	1908	1989		HGH4192
Edelen	David		No Date	Jan. 18, 1929	Age 80 / info is from church records	OFENoStone
Edelen, Sr.	David	L.	Nov. 10, 1941	Feb. 10, 2003	In loving memory	NSP828
Edelen	Delle	A.	Oct. 25, 1903	Aug. 7, 1989	Mother / Gone but not forgotten	HGH4279
Edelen	Dora	Alieen, Thomas	Oct. 30, 1938	No Date	In Loving Memory	SMY2006
Edelen	E.	Leigh	Jul. 9, 1884	Mar. 30, 1970	Married Dec 8, 1909	SJO4068
Edelen	E.	V.	Apr. 14, 1825	Aug. 26, 1888	Our father / Sacred to the memory of our father / R I P	SMCD287
Edelen	Edward	Benjamin	Jul. 2, 1906	Mar. 19, 1995		SMC2095
Edelen	Edward	G.	Feb. 25, 1880	Jul. 28, 1967		SMCD235
Edelen	Edward	G.	1905	1981		HGH2005
Edelen	Edward	J.	Dec. 27, 1887	Dec. 1, 1946		SMCE017
Edelen, M.D.	Edward	Joseph	Mar. 16, 1912	Feb. 1, 1982		SIC4013
Edelen	Eliza		No Date	May 14, 1857	Sacred to the memory of Eliza Edelen who departed this life on / in the 30th year of her age. Remember thou blissful soul, Thy widowed husband and thy three orphan children whilst they lament thy lost in this dreary vale of years.	SMY1090
Edelen	Elizabeth	F.	May 17, 1875	Sep. 26, 1959		SMCD235
Edelen	Elizabeth	June	1830	1898	w/o Thomas David Stone died at Ellenborough / information is from Betty Lybrook to the Historical Society Research located at the College of Southern MD, LaPlata, MD	ELLNo Stone
Edelen	Elizabeth	M.	1862	1948	Mother	SMCA149
Edelen	Elzear	Gardiner	1869	1891		SMCD144
Edelen	F.	Louis	Feb. 22, 1916	Nov. 15, 1992		NSP572
Edelen	Frances	L.	Dec. 5, 1924	Apr. 7, 1992		SJO4067
Edelen	Francis	H.	No Date	Apr. 15, 1869	Aged 79 years / May he rest in peace	SMY1092
Edelen	George	A.	1940	1974		SAC3095
Edelen	George	F.	Dec. 20, 1919	Feb. 23, 1920		SMCD234
Edelen	George		No Date	Nov. 13, 1855	In memory of / in the 78th year of his age / "Requiescat in pace" / Stone maker was: A Gaddess, Balto., MD	SMCD313A

Last Name	First Name	Middle Name	Date of Birth	Date of Death	Transcription / Notes	Cemetery Code
Edelen	George		1889	1975		NSP105
Edelen	Jacqueline		1941	2000	Thornton Funeral Home Marker	SHI020
Edelen	James		1918	1980	Info is from The Historical Society Research located at The College of Southern MD, LaPlata, MD.	SMYNoStone
Edelen	James	A.	1857	1909	Father	SMCA148
Edelen, Jr.	James	Francis	Apr. 13, 1927	May 4, 1986	PVT US Army World War II	HGH4191
Edelen	Jane	T.	No Date	Sep. 10, 1858	Consort of Alexis Edelen died in the 95th year of her age. / Info is from the 1940 DAR book page 159	SMYNoStone
Edelen	Jane	T.	No Date	Sep. 10, 1858	Consort of Alexis Edelen died in the 95th year of her age (info is from the 1940 DAR book page 159)	SMYNoStone
Edelen	Joan	R.	Feb. 22, 1941	No Date	In loving memory	NSP828
Edelen	John	F.D.	1911	1991	Margaret Green Edelen is on the back of this stone	HGH3022
Edelen	John	M.	1934	1974		SMC4017
Edelen	John		No Date	Feb. 17, 1852	Sacred to the memory of John Edelen who died at Annapolis / Then a Member of the General Assembly of Maryland / Aged 41 years / Back of stone: Mr. Edelen was a man who had no Enemies, Modest, unassuming, energetic, fulfilling the relations of Life, as a friend, a citizen, and a Magistrate. He secured the full affection of those around him and the unqualified approval of His Fellow Citizens. To his Christian Friends he has left the consolation derived from the assurance, that he is now Happy.	ELL0003
Edelen	Joseph	A.	Apr. 7, 1898	Feb. 12, 1900	In memory of / s/o J A & Lizzie M Edelen / "Suffer little children to come unto me"	SMCA155
Edelen	Leola	A.	1916	1999		HGH4192
Edelen	Louis	A.	1906	1996		SMC4033
Edelen	Louis	Adolphus	1892	1894		SMCD144
Edelen	Mamie	A.	1922	1991		SAC3076
Edelen	Margaret	E.	Dec. 15, 1922	No Date		NSP572
Edelen	Margaret	Green	1884	1952	She is on the back of the stone for John F.D. Edelen	HGH3023
Edelen	Margaurite		May 18, 1936	Dec. 11, 2004	"Grace" / (Handmade Wood marker)	SMY2154
Edelen	Marguerite	W.	Oct. 27, 1893	Mar. 28, 1978	Married Dec 8, 1909	SJO4068

Last Name	First Name	Middle Name	Date of Birth	Date of Death	Transcription / Notes	Cemetery Code
Edelen	Marie	C.	1896	1993		NSP105
Edelen	Marie	Doris	Aug. 30, 1913	Jun. 24, 1991	Right side of stone	SMCE017
Edelen	Martha	C.	Oct. 15, 1938	Dec. 8, 1971	We love you mother / Judy and Henry	HGH3020
Edelen	Martha	E.	1916	1970		HGH3021
Edelen	Martha	O.	Jan. 27, 1920	Dec. 29, 1983		SMY2109
Edelen	Mary	B.	1872	1949	On the back of this headstone is the name Boarman	SMCD174
Edelen	Mary	B.	May 3, 1887	Dec. 26, 1894	Our beloved / d/o James A & Lizzie M Edelen	SMCA153
Edelen	Mary	B.	No Date	Feb. 14, 1899	w/o R.H. Edelen / aged 62 years / Blessed are the pure in heart for they shall see God	SIC2173
Edelen	Mary	Bernice	Jul. 28, 1945	Mar. 12, 1992	He has risen / Beloved Mother	SMC4236
Edelen	Mary	Boarman	Sep. 14, 1904	Oct. 14, 1990		SMC2130
Edelen	Mary	Ellen	Oct. 8, 1940	Mar. 5, 2005	Together forever	SMC2137
Edelen	Mary	Gladys	1896	1896		SMCD144
Edelen	Mary	Henrietta	No Date	Jan. 30, 1858	w/o L.C. Edelen / aged 24 / info is from the Historical Society Research and the 1940 DAR book pg 188 located at the College of Southern MD, LaPlata, MD.	SMCNoStone
Edelen	Mary	Keech	Aug. 19, 1908	Nov. 4, 1990	w/o Edward Joseph Edelen	SIC4013
Edelen	Mary	T., Gardiner	1849	1923	w/o Benjamin Marcellus Edelen	SMCD145
Edelen	Mary	Catherine	3/28/1913	2/28/1970	Burial site is unknown / info is from the church records	SMCNoStone
Edelen	Mary	Louise, Butler	Jan. 12, 1941	Sep. 12, 2005		SIC9013
Edelen	Nancy	Denise	Jan. 27, 1953	Oct. 30, 1962		NSP858
Edelen	Nora	L.	1913	No Date		SMC4033
Edelen	Nora		1863	1890	Wife	SMCA043
Edelen	Philomena		Jan. 23, 1858	Aug. 12, 1925	Wife	SMCE017
Edelen	Raphael	Hamilton	1890	1899		SMCD144
Edelen	Raphael	W.	No Date	Sep. 13, 1845	IHS Sacred to the memory of / who departed this life / in th 33rd year of his age / Requiescat in pace	SMCD286
Edelen	Richard	H.	No Date	May 2, 1898	Aged 69 years / He loved justice and mercy and walked humbly with his God	SIC2175
Edelen	Richard	Henry	Aug. 16, 1922	Feb. 1, 1995	AS US Navy WWII	SMCE021
Edelen	Rosalie	B.	May 19, 1908	Feb. 16, 2000		SMC2138
Edelen	Sarah	Marie	1873	1880		SMCD144

Last Name	First Name	Middle Name	Date of Birth	Date of Death	Transcription / Notes	Cemetery Code
Edelen	Sarah	Q.	No Date	Nov. 8, 1878	In memory of / relict of George Edelen / aged 80 years / Requiescat in Pace	SMCD283
Edelen	Thomas	Earl	Jul. 26, 1927	Oct. 13, 2001	In Loving Memory	SMY2006
Edelen	Turner	A.	Jan. 19, 1939	No Date	Together forever	SMC2137
Edelen	Vivian	Bounds	Jul. 28, 1917	No Date		SMC2095
Edelen	Wallace	E.	Apr. 9, 1917	Feb. 27, 1982		SJO4067
Edelen	Wilbur	X.	Jul. 27, 1964	May 19, 2002	Beloved Husband and Father / "Whimpy" / "I love you Whimpy, We love you daddy"	SMC4241
Edelen	William	A.	1917	1975		SAC3076
Edelen	William	B.	1942	No Date	Together forever	SMC2111
Edelen	William	Theodore	May 5, 1913	Jun. 9, 1974	Beloved Husband / Rest in Peace	SMY2110
Edelin	Annie	Gertrude	Apr. 29, 1890	Jun. 13, 1890	Infant d/o Jas A & Lizzie M Edelin	SMCA151
Edelin	Dorothy		No Date	No Date	Old cement stone with names etched by hand.	CMX2121
Edelin	Harris		No Date	No Date	Old cement stone with names etched by hand.	CMX2121
Edelin	Joseph	W.	No Date	Sep. 24, 1876	May they rest in peace / Loved in life remembered in death by their devoted son John Burke Edelin	SMCD019
Edelin	Matilda		No Date	Sep. 13, 1881	May they rest in peace / Loved in life remembered in death by their devoted son John Burke Edelin	SMCD019
Edgar	Courtney	Anne	Nov. 29, 1990	Apr. 24, 1994	In God's care / "Silly Goose" / d/o John & Tina Edgar / Our little angel	NSP340
Edmond	Viola	G.	Sep. 15, 1887	Jan. 21, 1973	Info is from church records	SHI113
Edwardes	Elizabeth	R.	1913	2005		SIC5009
Edwardes	Vance	P.	1916	2008		SIC5009
Edwards	Barbara	May	1927	1928		CLV233
Edwards	Bernadette		1877	1970	Infant d/o Hattie & Robert Edwards	HGH1054
Edwards	Cornelia	R.	Jul. 27, 1909	Mar. 13, 1989		SCL3120
Edwards	David	Perry	Apr. 20, 1922	Jul. 14, 1984	Major, US Air Force, WW II & Korea	SPL4146
Edwards	Edward	Moore	No Date	Jun. 17, 1894	Infant / info is from church records	OFENoStone
Edwards	Frank	Stanley	Oct. 23, 1924	Feb. 26, 1990	F1 US Navy World War II	CHR256
Edwards	Harry	E.	1879	1957		HGH1054
Edwards	Hattie	Iola	Apr. 4, 1895	Dec. 18, 1987	Stone is located near the woods	CLV232
Edwards	Katherine	I., Robey	Jun. 21, 1923	No Date		SPL4146

Last Name	First Name	Middle Name	Date of Birth	Date of Death	Transcription / Notes	Cemetery Code
Edwards	Robert	Harrison	Nov. 10, 1880	Mar. 17, 1959		CLV231
Edwards	Thomas	C.	Jul. 10, 1906	Nov. 3, 1999		SCL3120
Egan	M.	Angela	No Date	Sep. 7, 1896	Sister / Mission Helper of the Sacred Heart / Professed on her deathbed / R.I.P.	SIC3013
Egan	Madeline		Jul. 13, 1897	Apr. 10, 1993		SCL4204
Ehlers	Elizabeth	B.	Apr. 15, 1883	Nov. 19, 1965	Arcadia	MTR1075
Ehlers	Laura	Cooksey	Feb. 4, 1891	Jan. 7, 1929		CHR062
Ehrenreich	Derrek		1987	1998	Arehart funeral home marker	SJO2277
Eilbeck	Sarah		No Date	Dec. 11, 1780	Sarah Eilbeck, Born Edgar. And Wife of William Eilbeck. Died the 11th of December 1780. Aged 76 years. Footstone: Initials S. E.	EIL005
Eilbeck	William		No Date	Jul. 26, 1765	William Eilbeck of Charles County, Merchant died the 26th of July 1765. / Aged 69 years. / Stone looks like it had been broken and was repaired. Footstone: Has the Initials W. E.	EIL002
Eing	George	H.	Apr. 16, 1879	Nov. 23, 1936		SMCD188
Eing	Gertrude	C.	May 21, 1925	Mar. 28, 1979		SMC2123
Eing	Henry	M.	Mar. 1, 1906	May 18, 1996		SMC2123
Eing	Mary	M.	Aug. 4, 1883	Sep. 14, 1953		SMCD188
Eisert	Viola		No Date	Jul. 18, 2005	Number 230-F inscribed on marker info is from church records	CLV428
Elder	Albert	L.	1894	1954		SIC1104
Elder, Jr.	Albert	Leo	1925	1998	Charles Richard / Karen Crosley / Beloved Husband and Father	SAC2102
Elder	Aloysius	A.	1852	1934	This person is also shown on pictures 4003-4004 with his wife Elizabeth Darsey 1852-1926	SIC1104
Elder	Charles	Richard	1953	1987		SAC2118
Elder	Dolores	Carr	1927	No Date	Charles Richard / Karen Crosley	SAC2102
Elder	Doutt		No Date	1966	Infant	SIC1104
Elder	Elizabeth	F., Darsey	1852	1926	His wife	SIC4003
Elder	Frances	D.	1852	1926		SIC1104
Elder	Genevieve	H.	1902	1988		SIC1104
Elder	Henriette	Arnold	1814	1911	His Wife	SIC4003

Last Name	First Name	Middle Name	Date of Birth	Date of Death	Transcription / Notes	Cemetery Code
Elder	J.	Hampton	1892	1954		SIC3075
Elder	Jos	H.	1883	1957	His Wife	SIC4003
Elder	Mabel	B.	1904	1976		SIC3075
Elder	Mary	B.	1882	1886		SIC4003
Elder	Mary	Elizabeth	1882	1931	w/o Joseph H. Elder	SIC3083
Elder	Mary	H.	1848	1922		SIC4003
Elder	R.	Guy	1887	1889		SIC4003
Elder	Wm.	P.	1810	1892		SIC4003
Elgin	Edna	Mae	Aug. 30, 1913	Jan. 1, 2004		ODE353
Elgin	Richard		Nov. 2, 1911	Sep. 23, 1993		ODE353
Ellerbe	Viola		1907	1999	Thornton Funeral Home Marker	SCL1107
Elliott	Lydia (?)		No Date	No Date		CHR378
Elliott, Col.	David	Hamilton	No Date	No Date	Col. David Hamilton British Royal Artillery 370929 Lydia Elliott Austria (Script writing)	CHR378
Ellis	Edna	L.	1934	2005		SAC1075
Ellis	Helen	D.	1908	1986		SAC1075
Ellis	James	R.	1930	1973		SAC1075
Ellis, Sr.	Kenneth	J.	Sep. 13, 1940	Dec. 15, 1994	PFC US Army	SAC4075
Ellwanger	Virginia	R.	Dec. 10, 1900	Oct. 13, 1992		SMC3139
Elmore	Alice	M.	1877	1939		POM049
Emerson, III	Milan	O.	Mar. 9, 1939	May 5, 2003	Daddy / "Bud" / "Daddy-Pop"	NSP047
Emley	Michael	Barry	Jan. 10, 1964	Jul. 25, 1991	Beloved son	SIC6004
Engels	Michael	F.	Oct. 1, 1957	May 20, 2000		HGH4311
Engels	Susan	C.	No Date	No Date		HGH4311
English	Cornell		1951	1985	In Loving Memory / cardboard painted black	SJO2222
English	Emma	E.	Jul. 3, 1932	Jan. 6, 1996	Mother / We love you	SJO2220
Ennis	India	A.	Feb. 24, 1886	Nov. 24, 1974		ALX040
Ennis	Violene		Mar. 6, 1929	Sep. 13, 2004	In loving memory	ALX026
Entwisce	Unknown		No Date	Oct. 5, 195?	Baby / Unable to locate a stone	SJENoStone
Epp	Agatha	C.	1903	1980	Mother we love you	NSP390
Epp	Agnes		Feb. 18, 1930	Sep. 20, 1946	"Dolly"	SMCA009

Last Name	First Name	Middle Name	Date of Birth	Date of Death	Transcription / Notes	Cemetery Code
Epp	Bertha	Therres	Jan. 13, 1897	Nov. 25, 1978	In loving memory	SMC3234
Epp, Sr.	Edmond	Alfred	Sep. 26, 1920	Feb. 2, 1985	CM 3 US Navy WW II	SMC3255
Epp	George	Leonard	1887	1961	Son	SMCA009
Epp	Harold	Simon	Apr. 21, 1923	Oct. 13, 1945	Maryland PFC Transportation Corps WW II	NSP392
Epp	John	S.	1900	1978	A loving father, tender and kind. What a beautiful memory you left behind	NSP391
Epp	Kenneth	L.	1934	1984	Loving Memory	NSP389
Epp	Margaret	Florence	Apr. 24, 1933	Jun. 7, 1973	Mother	SMC3233
Epp	Philip	Daniel	Apr. 12, 1889	Dec. 16, 1968	Maryland CPL 1 Mech Regt Air Svc WW I	SMC3235
Epp	Rosa		1866	1935	Mother	SMCA009
Epp	Simon		1863	1958	Father	SMCA009
Erwin	Eleanor	Malida	Feb. 16, 1915	Aug. 27, 2002		SJO6067
Estep, Sr.	A.	Victor	Feb. 13, 1888	Feb. 1, 1972		SMCD084
Estep	Arline	Mae	Mar. 17, 1888	Nov. 18, 1969		SMC1195
Estep	B.	Lucille	Aug. 30, 1896	Nov. 6, 1985	Daughter of James T & Blanche N Estep	SMCD078
Estep	Benjamine	N.	Jun. 29, 1863	Apr. 4, 1913		OFE1038
Estep	Blanche	N.	Jul. 19, 1857	Jan. 8, 1938		SMCD080
Estep	Christine	B.	Jul. 10, 1904	Jan. 24, 1910	d/o B.N. & E.A. Estep	OFE1039
Estep	Clara	B.	Feb. 6, 1893	Nov. 10, 1978		SMCD084
Estep	Clarence	N.	Jan. 27, 1893	Nov. 19, 1967		SMC1254
Estep	Clarence	T.	Nov. 28, 1885	Jul. 19, 1933		SMCD059
Estep, Jr.	Earl	Francis	Aug. 31, 1956	Feb. 6, 1998		SMC3129
Estep	Elizabeth	A.	Sep. 26, 1864	Jan. 28, 1948		OFE1038
Estep	Etta	J.	Jan. 20, 1898	Dec. 4, 1969		SMC1254
Estep	Francis	E.	No Date	Dec. 23, 1969	Father	SMCB008
Estep, Sr.	George	Walter	Nov. 23, 1883	Dec. 4, 1967		SMC1195
Estep	Henry	C. N.	May 15, 1890	Aug. 11, 1891	s/o R. A. and J. E. Estep	OFE4089
Estep	J.	Leo	1909	1989	Together Forever	SMC3297
Estep	James	Andrew	No Date	No Date	Infant s/o B.N. and E. A. Estep / marker placed at bottom of stone for Acton	OFE4088
Estep	James	E.	Sep. 24, 1955	Sep. 11, 1992		SMC1198

Last Name	First Name	Middle Name	Date of Birth	Date of Death	Transcription / Notes	Cemetery Code
Estep	James	Houston	Mar. 22, 1882	Oct. 26, 1898	s/o J T & Blanche N Estep / May he rest in peace	SMCD054
Estep	James	P.	Oct. 4, 1932	Dec. 30, 2007	SP3 US Army	SMC3062
Estep	James	Thomas	Feb. 22, 1857	Mar. 31, 1935		SMCD079
Estep	Jennie	A.	Jan. 4, 1901	Dec. 18, 1962	Beloved Mother & Grandmother / Forever in our hearts	SMCB009
Estep	Joseph	A.	Jan. 13, 1948	May 3, 1979	Forever in our hearts	NSP107
Estep	Joseph	Milton	Jan. 1, 1891	Jan. 18, 1913	s/o James T & Blanche N Estep / May he rest in peace	SMCD054
Estep	Louisa		Aug. 4, 1792	Jul. 18, 1853	In memory of / (She was the d/o Philemon and Margaret Estep / info is from familysearch.org)	RND009
Estep	M.	Lillian	1912	1983	Together Forever	SMC3297
Estep	Marie	R.	Aug. 2, 1909	Aug. 26, 1989		NSP294
Estep	Philemon		1744	Nov. 25, 1801	Departed this life / in the 37th year of his age (married Margaret Barber B: Aug 21, 1770 / info is from familysearch.org)	RND002
Estep	Richard	C.	Jan. 21, 1799	Mar. 19, 1816	Departed this life / in the 18th year of his age (Son of Philemon and Margaret Estep / info is from familysearch.org)	RND001
Estep	Sarah	R.	No Date	Dec. 24, 1865	d/o J.C. & E.E. Estep / aged 9 years	OFE2118
Estep	Sharon		No Date	Aug. 10, 1967	Age 10y / Information acquired from the Historical Society's 1983 transcription	ZWUNoStone
Estep	Unknown		No Date	No Date	Infant s/o B.N. and E. A. Estep / marker placed at bottom of stone for Acton	OFE4088
Estep	Viola		Jun. 30, 1897	Jul. 20, 1984		SMCD060
Estes, Sr.	Edwin	E.	1910	1994	Forever in our hearts	NSP835
Estes	Marie	E.	1914	No Date	Forever in our hearts	NSP835
Estevez	Alan	H.	Dec. 24, 1947	Aug. 1, 1978	Peace / Kip / In loving memory	SJO4143
Estevez	Argentina	M.	1920	1945	In loving memory	SIC6050
Estevez	Betty	J.	Feb. 28, 1927	Sep. 30, 1994	James / Yonkers, NY / Married June 25, 1944 / Betty / Wise, VA.	SAC2111
Estevez	Daniel	L.	Jul. 6, 1885	Sep. 8, 1973	Born-Lugo. Spain	SIC6071
Estevez	E.	Carola	Sep. 4, 1921	No Date	In loving memory	NSP936
Estevez	George		Dec. 7, 1920	May 4, 2003	In loving memory	NSP936
Estevez	Henry		Sep. 15, 1915	May 6, 1994		SJO4187

Last Name	First Name	Middle Name	Date of Birth	Date of Death	Transcription / Notes	Cemetery Code
Estevez	James		Jun. 4, 1926	Apr. 22, 1997	James / Yonkers, NY / Married June 25, 1944 / Betty / Wise, VA.	SAC2111
Estevez	M.	Teresa	Feb. 3, 1918	Aug. 31, 1991		SJO4187
Estevez	Marina	M.	Nov. 19, 1899	Sep. 21, 1994	Born-Logrono, Spain	SIC6071
Estevez	Mario	Lawrence	Apr. 6, 1933	Feb. 11, 1956	Footstone: Maryland Sgt. HQ Co 29 Infantry Regt	SIC6072
Estevez	N.	Marina	Mar. 16, 1945	Aug. 4, 2006		SAC1088
Estevez	Unknown		No Date	1955	Small flat stone to the ground that has no first name or birth date on it	SIC6048
Eugenia	Mariam		No Date	Jul. 23	Age 2 years / info is from Christ Church microfilm reel 1 Pg 315 located at the College of Southern MD, LaPlata, MD (Unable to read death year, listed as Mariam Eugenia)	STENoStone
Evans	Joseph		No Date	1898	Info is from Old Durham Church microfilm pg 83-84 located at the College of Southern MD, LaPlata, MD	ODENoStone
Evans	Richard		Aug. 18, 1868	Apr. 4, 1916	Gone but not forgotten, nor ever shall he be as long as life within me lasts I will remember thee	POM115
Evans	Susie	M.	Jan. 23, 1915	Feb. 13, 1976		MHB198
Evans	Virginia	Millar	Dec. 25, 1893	Jun. 8, 1973		ODE198
Everett	Harry	E.	No Date	No Date	Info is from church records	MTRNoStone
Everett	Joseph		No Date	Mar. 18, 1839	Memory of / aged 47 years (Stone is no longer there)	NME009
Fairall	Wilson	L.	Aug. 14, 1916	Nov. 2, 1961	Maryland PVT 284 ORD Tank Maint Co WW II	NSP874
Fairfax	Elmo	B.	Sep. 22, 1915	Aug. 18, 1983	YI US Navy WW II	PKH146
Fairfax	Florence	L.	Aug. 17, 1909	Jun. 3, 2001		CHR315
Fairfax	Franklin	W.	Mar. 2, 1907	Jul. 16, 2002		CHR315
Fairfax	Ray	Edgar	1919	1982		PKH133
Fairfax	Raymond	E.	1919	1982	EMI US Navy WW II	PKH145
Fairfax, Sr.	Rudolph	Rudy, K.	Feb. 11, 1916	May 15, 1994		HER026
Falkinburg	Deborah		Jul. 17, 1943	Aug. 25, 2001	Merrick - Falkinburg	LUM091
Fambro	Brent	M.	1905	1977		SCA057
Fanelli	Elizabeth		Oct. 12, 1929	No Date	"Betty" / For Eternity	NSP610
Fanelli	Irene	E.	Dec. 2, 1902	Mar. 20, 1993		NSP611
Fanelli	Leonard		Jul. 26, 1928	Feb. 17, 2003	For Eternity / "Len"	NSP610

Last Name	First Name	Middle Name	Date of Birth	Date of Death	Transcription / Notes	Cemetery Code
Fannon	Robert		Oct. 11, 1919	Dec. 19, 1962	Mama	NSP859
Fantel	Catherine	M.	Oct. 20, 1907	Apr. 10, 1975	Father	MTR3153
Fantel	Morris	M.	Aug. 8, 1901	Mar. 4, 1964		MTR3152
Farmer	Carrie	M.	Apr. 27, 1911	Aug. 27, 1997		SMC1261
Farmer	Doris		1925	2002	Funeral home marker	PGN065
Farmer	Elizabeth	M.	Oct. 14, 1925	No Date		SIC8087
Farmer	Francis	A.	Nov. 23, 1913	Dec. 20, 1986		SMC4083
Farmer	George	F.	Jul. 23, 1913	Apr. 20, 1985	With love to pops	NSP052
Farmer	Hortense	M.	Aug. 19, 1916	Mar. 13, 1986	Rest in Peace / (Skeeter)	SMY2030
Farmer	James	Barry	1963	2004	Beloved Husband and Father	PGN072
Farmer, Sr.	John	Francis	Jul. 19, 1940	Apr. 16, 2005	Beloved Father	SAC1045
Farmer	John	W.	Mar. 8, 1921	Jul. 18, 2000		SIC8087
Farmer	Joseph	Vincent	1915	1985	TEC 5 US Army WW II	SIC8088
Farmer	Kerry	Lee	Jan. 25, 1967	Oct. 23, 1980	We Love You	SMY2089
Farmer	Lucy	A.	Nov. 4, 1876	Apr. 29, 1959		SMC4013
Farmer	Mary	Florence	Aug. 15, 1885	Jul. 7, 1962		SMC3086
Farmer	Mary	Reginia	Sep. 29, 1929	No Date		SAC1034
Farmer	Mary	Burnice	Apr. 8, 1913	Aug. 16, 1952		SAC4066
Farmer	Naomi	C.	Jul. 23, 1919	Jun. 11, 1992	Rest in Peace / Mother / We Love You	SAC5081
Farmer	Samuel	A.	1874	1959		SMC3327
Farmer	Susan	E.	Sep. 14, 1942	Jun. 15, 2006	Beloved mother	SJO1064
Farmer	Susie	Regina	1930	2006	Arehart-Echols Funeral Home Marker	SMY3212
Farmer, Sr.	Thomas	A.	Dec. 3, 1925	Dec. 12, 2006		SAC1034
Farmer	William	Joseph	No Date	May 28, 1977	Aged 72 (info is from Historical Society Research located at The College of Southern MD, LaPlata, MD)	SACNostone
Farmer	Wm.	Herman	May 30, 1899	Nov. 11, 1973		SMC1261
Farr	Agnes	C.	1898	1982		HGH1022
Farr	David	Algernon	Apr. 8, 1891	Jan. 1, 1979		HGH1017
Farr	Eugene	F.	Mar. 8, 1913	Jan. 5, 1994		SMY3094
Farr	Francis	C.	1895	1974		HGH1022
Farr	John	Fenley	Jul. 19, 1884	Dec. 29, 1918	PVT. D.C. Fire Dept.	HGH1016

Last Name	First Name	Middle Name	Date of Birth	Date of Death	Transcription / Notes	Cemetery Code
Farr	John	Gregory	Dec. 4, 1919	Dec. 9, 1919		HGH1017
Farr	John	Gregory	Feb. 13, 1860	Mar. 11, 1927		HGH1021
Farr	Katherine	I.	Aug. 23, 1862	Apr. 24, 1945		HGH1021
Farr	Lorrine		1920	No Date		SMY3113
Farr	Margaret		Nov. 15, 1890	Mar. 25, 1986		HGH1017
Farr	Mary	H.	Jan. 12, 1888	Dec. 19, 1932		HGH1015
Farr	Mary	Katherine	Nov. 25, 1919	Nov. 28, 2001		HGH1023
Farr	Mary	N.	Sep. 14, 1914	Sep. 15, 2006		SMY3094
Farr	Minnie	E.	1880	1962		SMY3095
Farr	Thomas	I.	1872	1950		SMY3095
Farr	Thomas	L.	1920	1968		SMY3113
Farr	Thomas	R.	Sep. 28, 1911	Aug. 4, 1944	Maryland Staff SGT 115 Inf 29 Inf DIV WW II	SMY3096
Farrall	Adelaide	Manning	Sep. 23, 1893	Jul. 15, 1996	Mother / In loving memory	SIC3070
Farrall	Adrian	E.	1910	199	Death date on stone only shows 199 / Ancestry.com has an Adrian E. Farrall born Nov 10, 1910 died Dec 25, 2000 in Pearl Harbor, Pinellas, Fl.	SMC2140
Farrall	Ann	Rebecca	Oct. 18, 1832	Jan. 5, 1893	info is from the 1940 DAR book pg 185	SMCNoStone
Farrall	Catherine	C.	1856	1934		MTR4251
Farrall	Cecelia	Elizabeth	1916	1972		SIC7053
Farrall	Elias		1843	1916		MTR4221
Farrall	Elizabeth	Queen	Oct. 9, 1902	Aug. 19, 1991	Together forever	SMC2103
Farrall	Hilda	C.	1893	1952		SIC3072
Farrall	James	E.	1860	1939		SMCA158
Farrall	James	Emanuel	Feb. 19, 1938	Aug. 21, 1995	D.D.S.	SMC2106
Farrall	James	G.	Sep. 16, 1903	Oct. 14, 1972		SMC2139
Farrall	Jane	C.	1872	1960		SMCA157
Farrall	John	R.	Jul. 9, 1861	Oct. 15, 1958		SMCA032
Farrall	John	W.	No Date	No Date	Erected to the memory of / by his devoted wife. He is not dead but sleepeth	SMY1054
Farrall	Julia	E.	Mar. 10, 1863	Jul. 15, 1935		SMCA025
Farrall	Leo	K.	1885	1959	Father / In loving memory	SIC3071

Last Name	First Name	Middle Name	Date of Birth	Date of Death	Transcription / Notes	Cemetery Code
Farrall, III	Leo	K	Sep. 22, 1945	Feb. 13, 1997	Footstone L.K. - Dad - PA	SIC4060
Farrall	Louis	Ansel	1887	1892		SIC3014
Farrall	Mary	Lee	1917	1992		SMC2140
Farrall	Pansy	Warfield	1880	1882		SIC3014
Farrall	Reginald	A.	Jul. 13, 1877	Jun. 2, 1941		SIC3073
Farrall	Richard	Earl	Jan. 10, 1902	Dec. 22, 1991	Together forever	SMC2103
Farrall	Sara	Elizabeth	Mar. 17, 1814	Jan. 26, 1851	Beloved w/o Richard Farrall / info is from the Historical Society Research and the 1940 DAR book pg 185 located at the College of Southern MD, LaPlata, MD.	SMCNoStone
Farrall	Sarah	Briscoe	1846	1908		SIC3014
Farrall	Stoughton		1880	1939		MTR4219
Farrall	Thomas	Richard	1843	1926		SIC3014
Farran	Dorathy	Elizabeth	Feb. 16, 1913	Jul. 25, 1913		SIC4027
Farran	F.	M.	Jul. 24, 1844	May 25, 1923	Father / At Rest (old stone that is shaped like a cross at the top. A large crack at the base of the cross)	SIC4028
Farran	Martha	Ann	1844	Jul. 24, 1901	In memory of my mother / beloved w/o Francis M. Farran / Gone but not forgotten / May she rest in peace	SIC4026
Farran	Thomas	Marion	Feb. 2, 1904	Mar. 18, 1906		SIC4027
Farrar	Cachita	E.	Feb. 7, 1945	Feb. 22, 2003		NSP1009
Farrar	Sean	M.	Mar. 4, 1970	No Date		NSP1009
Farrar	Vashti	N.	Dec. 23, 1975	No Date		NSP1009
Farrell	Alice		Sep. 4, 1917	Jan. 15, 1984		SPL5076
Farrell	Belle	Louise, Robey	Sep. 25, 1925	Sep. 28, 2006	No Stone but is located to the right of James F. Robey (info is from church records) Dates are from Ancestry.com	PIS038
Farrell	Catherine	L.	1889	1971		HGH1129
Farrell, S.J.	F.	Michael	1823	Oct. 13, 1873	IHS / OB. 13 Oct. 1873 / AET. 53 (In Priests Plot) Birth date is from church records	SIC1040
Farrell	Harry	H.	1918	1937	At rest / Son	HGH2083
Farrell	Hattie	L.	Nov. 2, 1921	Aug. 11, 1992	We love you	CMX2002
Farrell	J.	Arthur	1914	1983		HGH2074
Farrell	James	L.	Aug. 20, 1924	Mar. 1, 2005		HGH1215

Last Name	First Name	Middle Name	Date of Birth	Date of Death	Transcription / Notes	Cemetery Code
Farrell	James	M.	1913	1978		HGH1249
Farrell	John	D.	Apr. 14, 1890	May 7, 1951		HGH1250
Farrell	John	S.	Sep. 17, 1883	Jul. 7, 1948		SMCA021
Farrell, Jr.	Joseph	Arthur	Dec. 24, 1939	Dec. 30, 1989	SP4 US Army / Stone bench with In loving memory "Hoppy" on it.	HGH2077
Farrell	Joseph	D.	May 19, 1892	Sep. 4, 1953	Maryland PFC HQ Co 313 Infantry World War I	HGH1205
Farrell	Joseph	H.	Sep. 27, 1882	Aug. 21, 1966		HGH2085
Farrell	Julia	M.	1915	2002		HGH4203
Farrell	M.	Ethel, Mattingly	1918	No Date		HGH2074
Farrell	Mamie	H.	Sep. 25, 1894	Oct. 30, 1986		HGH1250
Farrell	Mary	M.	Feb. 18, 1903	Aug. 9, 1996		HGH1216
Farrell	Mattie	B.	Jan. 5, 1907	Dec. 27, 1985		CHR200
Farrell	Nellie	E.	Feb. 24, 1886	Dec. 25, 1964		SMCA020
Farrell	Peter	J.	Nov. 4, 1894	Oct. 15, 1965		CHR200
Farrell	Sara	H.	Feb. 27, 1887	Jan. 10, 1975		HGH2085
Farrell	Stephen	L.	Jun. 7, 1898	Dec. 11, 1977		HGH1216
Farrell	Unknown		No Date	No Date	one stone with this name was erected. See Carmel In America 1890 by Bishop Charles Warren Currier (Notes from Sister Miriam John at Mt Carmel Monastery, LaPlata, MD)	GMCNo Stone
Farrell	Violet	A.	1913	1965		HGH2084
Farrell	Wilbur	J.	1910	1992		HGH4203
Farrell	William		No Date	Nov. 1898	Age 35 years	SIC4107
Fassel	Agnes	A.	1902	1983	Together forever	SMC1242
Fassel	George	G.	1889	1969	Together forever	SMC1242
Faucett	Edith	D.	Dec. 23, 1883	Feb. 20, 1961		SMC1066
Faucett	George	M.	Oct. 8, 1882	Jan. 3, 1966		SMC1066
Faunce	Taylor	Jacqueline	No Date	May 4, 2000	Our Beloved Daughter / Playing in God's Garden	SMC4240
Fava	Alice	M.	Jun. 26, 1918	Nov. 30, 1999	nee Gilroy / Beloved aunt	NJB275

Last Name	First Name	Middle Name	Date of Birth	Date of Death	Transcription / Notes	Cemetery Code
Fe???	Mary	Ann			Sacred to the memory of / my beloved s_____ / In life lamented, in death ____ May she rest in peace Note: The church has placed parts of stones and loose stones in a plot by themselves.	SMY1003 SMY1004
Feimster	Algie	Metcalfe	No Date	No Date	In loving memory	SIC7044
Feimster, Jr.	Maurice	B.	May 29, 1931	Nov. 26, 2001	In loving memory	SIC7044
Felton	Brenda	C.	May 2, 1927	Nov. 9, 1990	We will always love you	NSP022
Fennell	James	A.	Dec. 26, 1970	1968		SIC7074
Fennell	Michael	G.	1896	May 11, 1989	We Love You Always / Back of Stone: Be not afraid I go before you always come follow me and I will give you rest.	SAC1101
Fennell	Rosalie	Stone	Jul. 27, 1961	1973		SIC7075
Fentress, Sr.	Michael	Leo	1907	Nov. 2, 2003	You were loved	CMX2178
Fentress	Pearlene	M.	Jul. 25, 1948	Nov. 12, 1987	May she have the endless love she gave - He will long be remembered by many	CMX2177
Fentress	William	F.	Jul. 17, 1922	Sep. 3, 1976	May she have the endless love she gave - He will long be remembered by many	CMX2177
Fenwick	Alice	J.	Oct. 9, 1919	Jan. 30, 1998		SMY2007
Fenwick	Charles	F.	Nov. 10, 1946	May 27, 1979		SMY3152
Fenwick	David	L.	Dec. 14, 1904	1997	Now It Is Time for You to Rest / Your Family and Friends Loved You Best	SMY2028
Fenwick	Doris	A.	1963	Jul. 17, 2003	IHS / Love always, Buck & Sharon	SJO3316
Fenwick	Edward		Dec. 22, 1949	Jun. 4, 1824	To the memory of / who departed this life upon the / the thirty sixth year of his age. This stone is erected by his sisters. In the morning man shall grow up like grass; in the morning he shall flourish and pass away Psalm LXXX (90:6)	
Fenwick	Elsie	Mae	No Date	Dec. 10, 1965		FEN012
Fenwick	Henrietta	Maria	Oct. 28, 1905	Feb. 14, 1794	In memory of / wife of James Fenwick and daughter of John Lancaster	SMY3151
Fenwick	James	Leroy	No Date	Jan. 11, 2005		FEN007
Fenwick	James	Theodore	May 19, 1940	Nov. 20, 1952	In Loving Memory	SMY2073
Fenwick			Nov. 14, 1916			SMY2090

Last Name	First Name	Middle Name	Date of Birth	Date of Death	Transcription / Notes	Cemetery Code
Fenwick	James		No Date	Sep. 3, 1823	Sacred to the memory of James Fenwick who departed this life / in the 60th year of his age. He was the eldest son of Ignatius Fenwick & Sarah Taney his wife. May he rest in peace	FEN005
Fenwick	John	Ceslays	1759	Aug. 20, 1815	IHS / O. P. Nat. C 1759 / OBIT. 20 Aug. 1815 (In Priests Plot)	SIC1015
Fenwick	John	Maxwell	1905	1984		SJO3344
Fenwick	Louisiana		Mar. 1, 1829	Sep. 15, 1830	To the memory of / who was born upon the 1st of March 1829 and died at Pomonkey Charles County, MD / aged one year, six months and thirteen days. This stone is erected by her affectionate parents William L. Brent and Maria Fenwick, his wife, "The Lord bless thee and keep thee" Numbers Chapt. VI V183 Stone maker was J. Birth Fecit	FEN009
Fenwick	Margaret		No Date	No Date	Information acquired from the Historical Society's 1983 transcription	ZWUNoStone
Fenwick	Mary	E.	Mar. 15, 1924	Feb. 24, 2005		SMY2074
Fenwick	Mary	Margaret	Apr. 29, 1921	Nov. 15, 2003	In Loving Memory	SMY2090
Fenwick	Richard	Alden	May 19, 1953	Apr. 14, 1988		NSP175
Fenwick	Rokita	Michelle	Oct. 9, 1984	Sep. 23, 1991	Dedicated by Dr. Brown P.T.O. and Staff	SJO3342
Fenwick	Sarah	Ann	No Date	Sep. 22, 1815	In memory of Sarah Ann, daughter of James Fenwick and Teresa his wife, daughter of Robert Brent, who died Sep 22, 1815 (grave is next to tree, and stone is broken in half)	FEN014
Fenwick	Tina	Marie, Wells	Dec. 28, 1966	Dec. 1, 2008	Info is from church records	SHINoStone
Ferguson	Jennie	Speake	No Date	Jun. 6, 1896		ODE178
Ferguson	Robert		No Date	May 25, 1903	Info is from Christ Church microfilm Reel 1 Pg 90-91 located at the College of Southern MD, LaPlata, MD	MTRNoStone
Fergusson	Adele	C.	1849	1922		MTR3084

Last Name	First Name	Middle Name	Date of Birth	Date of Death	Transcription / Notes	Cemetery Code
Fergusson	Amelia		Apr. 12, 1829	Dec. 18, 1852	Virtue records its own Eulogy. / Sacred to the memory of / youngest daughter of Gen'l John Matthews and Wife of James Fergusson. Who was born / and died / A husbands love has erected this monument, as an affectionate tribute of respect to the memory of her who when living was to him so good so kind and so devoted a wife / If a character made up of those qualities which adorn the Christian, the daughter, the sister, the mother and the wife, can give assurance of a state beyond the grave of blissful immortality; then such truly is her inheritance. / Farewell. I feel deserted and alone. My home is drear and reft of joy. I've nothing left me now to love. Save one our darling sprightly boy. May God Bless our child. Footstone: Initials A.J.	FER002 FER003
Fergusson	Blanch		No Date	No Date	Info is from church records	MTRNoStone
Fergusson	Eleanor	Jones	Apr. 1, 1923	May 21, 2007	In Loving memory	SIC4052
Fergusson	Elizabeth	Davis	No Date	Apr. 5, 1897	w/o Robt. Fergusson /Aged 51 years / ( ) who die in the Lord / stone has been broken and repaired making part of the verse unreadable	SJO3094
Fergusson	Elizabeth	R.	1875	1951		MTR3083
Fergusson	Elizabeth		Sep. 15, 1821	Jan. 18, 1833	Sacred to the memory of / d/o John and Eliz'th Fergusson	MUL044
Fergusson	Elizabeth		Jul. 23, 1785	Nov. 11, 1848	Sacred to the memory of /, relict of John Fergusson who was born in this county on the /, Mild in her temper gentle in her manners and a meek Christian, she was a rare example to her sex in the several relative duties of life, she lived without reproach and died a Christian, moved by filial reverance and love, her children have erected this tablet (Some writing is unlegible (Info is from the Historical Society Research, at the College of Southern Md, LaPlata, Md)	MUL021
Fergusson	James		Sep. 22, 1878	Nov. 21, 1922	Brother / James, s/o Robert C. and Katharine Fergusson	MUL037

Last Name	First Name	Middle Name	Date of Birth	Date of Death	Transcription / Notes	Cemetery Code
Fergusson	James		Mar. 11, 1816	Oct. 28, 1854	Sacred to the memory of / s/o John and Elizabeth Fergusson who was / He graduated at Yale College in 1836, honest as a lawyer and faithful as a legislator, he died in the midst of his usefulness, sincerely mourned by his numberous friends, he was a man of high literary attainments, amiable and gentle in his disposition, devoted as a husband, father and friend	MUL024
Fergusson	Jane	C.	Dec. 29, 1811	Aug. 15, 1813	Sacred to the memory of / d/o John and Eliz'th Fergusson	MUL009
Fergusson	Jessie		Dec. 29, 1881	Jun. 9, 1901	Jesus said unto her, I am the resurrection and the life, he that believeth in me though he were dead, yet shall he live John 11:25	MTR3085
Fergusson	John		Jan. 18, 1773	Nov. 8, 1847	Sacred to the memory of /, who was born in Dumfries Co. Scotland on the / and died in this county / He was a merchant upright and honest, his strict integrity and strong of cultivated intellect gave him a commanding position in the community of his choice, he discharged the duties of Judge, Chief Judge of the Orphans court of Charles County with singular fidelity and ability, filial love has erected this tablet. (Information is from the Historical Society Research located at the College of Southern Md, LaPlata, Md)	MUL019
Fergusson	John	B. T.	Dec. 19, 1813	Dec. 6, 1855	Sacred to the memory of /, s/o John and Elizabeth Fergusson who was born / and died /, honest and upright as a merchant, dutiful and affectionate as a son, attached and sincere as a brother, honourable and candid in his dealings with his fellow men. Beloved and respected by all for his many manly virtues. He lived without guile and died without an enemy (writing wraps all around stone) no pics	MUL026
Fergusson	John Beale	Turner	Jun. 23, 1889	Feb. 14, 1897	s/o Robert C. and Katharine Fergusson, / Brother	MUL012
Fergusson	Katharine	J.	Jan. 6, 1887	Feb. 26, 1955	Beloved niece of L. Allison & Mary E. Wilmer	MTR2126
Fergusson	Katharine		Oct. 16, 1852	Sep. 5, 1896	Mother, Katharine, w/o Robert Cutler Fergusson	MUL014
Fergusson	M	Josephine	Aug. 1, 1843	Sep. 10, 1930		MUL013

Last Name	First Name	Middle Name	Date of Birth	Date of Death	Transcription / Notes	Cemetery Code
Fergusson	Matilda	J.	Aug. 23, 1825	Aug. 17, 1831	Sacred to the memory of / d/o John and Eliz'th Fergusson	MUL011
Fergusson, Dr.	Oscar		Mar. 12, 1827	Feb. 18, 1864	Sacred to the memory of / s/o John & Elizabeth Fergusson / As a physician he was eminent and useful, as a man, generous and noble, as a husband, brother and friend he was affectionate kind and true	MUL015
Fergusson, Dr.	Robert		Nov. 18, 1806	Apr. 4, 1879	Sacred to the memory of Dr. Robert Fergusson aged 72 years, 4 mos. & 16 days, Blessed are the merciful for they shall obtain Mercy	MUL023
Fergusson	Robert	Cutler	Aug. 14, 1883	Dec. 20, 1918	Brother / s/o Robert C. and Katharine Fergusson	MUL036
Fergusson	Robert	Cutler	Mar. 26, 1851	Mar. 2, 1894	Father, Robert Cutler, s/o James & Amelia Fergusson	MUL014
					Sacrd to the memory of Robert Fergusson who died / aged 72 years, he was a native of Dumfries County, Scotland, but America was early the country of his choice and Maryland for 50 years the theatre of his useful honourable and virtous actions. He was a merchant of the first rank and talents, Chief Justice of the Orphans Court of Charles County and in every relation of society an upright and benevolent man, as in life he was respected and esteemed, so in death he was justly lamented. In testimony of their affection and gratitude for a kind and magnificent Uncle, this monument is erected by his nephews Robert, John and James Fergusson (Crypt top is leaning against the fence. Crypt sides are laying on the ground) (Info is from the Historical Society Research located at the College of Southern Md. LaPlata, Md).	
Fergusson	Robert		No Date	Sep. 1, 1812		MUL041
Fergusson	William	B.	1844	1931		MTR3084
Fergusson	William	C.	Jan. 16, 1877	Jul. 31, 1933	Brother / William C., s/o Robert C. and Katharine Fergusson	MUL038
Fergusson	William	Merrill	Aug. 8, 1911	Jan. 14, 1994	In loving memory	SIC4052

Last Name	First Name	Middle Name	Date of Birth	Date of Death	Transcription / Notes	Cemetery Code
Fergusson	William		Aug. 15, 1808	Jan. 17, 1857	Sacred to the memory of /, second s/o John and Elizabeth Fergusson born / died /...He was a merchant of intelligence and integrity, a man "just and upright in all his dealings, quiet and peaceable; full of compassion, and ready to do good to all man, in the relations of son, brother, husband, father and friend, he acted with rigid fidelity and love, his untimely death was sincerely mourned by the community in which he spent his virtuous and useful life." (Writing is wrapped all around the stone, no pictures)	MUL017
Fergusson	William		1874	1948		MTR3083
Fergusson	Zephaniah	T.	Sep. 29, 1819	Jul. 30, 1823	Sacred to the memory of / s/o John and Eliz'th Fergusson	MUL010
Fernandez	Louise		1914	1987		SCL3051
Ferrall	Ethel	H.	1917	No Date		NSP706
Ferrall, Jr.	Francis	I.	Sep. 20, 1945	Sep. 21, 1988	"Chip"	SMC4073
Ferrall	John	Dent	Feb. 6, 1947	Jul. 26, 1988	Loving father	SMC4102
Ferrall	William		1913	1998	"Sandy"	NSP706
Ferris	Carl		Jul. 7, 1930	No Date	Nina and Pop make life better for their children, grandchildren and great grandchildren	SCL3242
Ferris	Elaine	L.	1930	No Date		SMY3165
Ferris	Regina		Apr. 9, 1929	May 25, 2001	Nina and Pop make life better for their children, grandchildren and great grandchildren	SCL3242
Ferris	William	J.	1913	1984	"Our World Lil Daddy"	SMY3165
Ficklin	Benjamin	Slaughter	Sep. 4, 1898	Jan. 22, 1988	h/o Madeline B Ficklin	LUM127
Fielder	Olga	Edith	Dec. 31, 1908	Feb. 24, 2003	In Loving Memory	SAC1118
Fields	Laverne	D.	Jan. 24, 1917	Jan. 2, 1993		SPL6071
Fields	Rev. Walter	Garrett	Nov. 1, 1914	Apr. 9, 1981	A Priest forever.	SPL6071
Fifield	Sarah		No Date	Apr. 22, 1897	Info is from Old Durham Church microfilm pg 83-84 located at the College of Southern MD, LaPlata, MD	ODENoStone
Filgueiras	Joseph		May 5, 1940	May 29, 1991		SMC1231
Finall	Bessie	V.	May 15, 1897	Nov. 19, 1983	Mother	NJB192
Finall	Boyd	M.	Feb. 26, 1900	Jul. 12, 1979		NJB163

Last Name	First Name	Middle Name	Date of Birth	Date of Death	Transcription / Notes	Cemetery Code
Finall	Ida	Grace	Oct. 31, 1911	Mar. 6, 1935	Gone but not forgotten	NJB166
Finall	Lilly	May	May 25, 1880	Aug. 30, 1944	Gone but not forgotten	NJB168
Finall	Martha	J.	Sep. 16, 1907	Jan. 18, 1961	Gone but not forgotten	NJB164
Finall	Roy	W.	Dec. 7, 1904	Sep. 3, 1945	Gone but not forgotten	NJB169
Finall	Samuel		Apr. 6, 1870	Dec. 24, 1937		NJB167
Finall	Willie	G.	Jun. 2, 1895	Sep. 23, 1940	God is love	NJB165
Fine	Christopher	S.	Mar. 5, 1979	Apr. 4, 1979	Our Son / Little ones to Him belong	NSP995
Fine	D.	Angela	May 18, 1953	No Date		NSP995
Fine	Mark	S.	Jul. 3, 1953	No Date		NSP995
Fischer	Doris	June	Mar. 5, 1927	Dec. 28, 1987	Our Loving Mother / "Grandma"	MTR3151
Fischer	Myles	S.	Oct. 24, 1922	Nov. 10, 1982	M. Sgt US Air Force, Korea	NJB268
Fish	Phyllis	B.	Jul. 17, 1920	Feb. 10, 2004		SCL4216
Fish	William	E.	Sep. 6, 1921	Oct. 1, 1998		SCL4216
Fisher	Amos		No Date	Apr. 24, 1945	Age 57 - No Marker / info is from church records	CLVNoStone
Fisher	Eugene	J.	1926	1970		SIC7081
Fisher	Gail	F.	1928	No Date		SIC7081
Fisher	George	H.	Oct. 19, 1888	Dec. 28, 1929		TRI123
Fisher	Jeanette	L.	Jul. 16, 1943	Mar. 9, 1996	Mother by chance, friend by choice	SCL4092
Fisher	Jonathan	Lamont	May 15, 1972	Oct. 30, 1993	PFC US Marine Corps	SCL4093
Fisher, Sr.	John	E.	Dec. 12, 1924	No Date		NJB333
Fisher, II	Laurence	E.	No Date	Jun. 9, 2001	s/o Laurence and Deborah / We love you	SIC7082
Fisher	Mary		No Date	1881		MTR4298
Fisher, Jr.	Raymond	William	Nov. 19, 1927	Nov. 10, 1972		CHR374
Fisher	Thomas		No Date	1884		MTR4298
Fisher	Violet	M.	Jul. 9, 1924	Jun. 25, 2001		NJB333
Fjellheim	Alan	K.	1953	2009	Brinsfield-Echols Funeral Home Marker	SMC1006
Fladung	Joseph	F.	Nov. 20, 1881	Feb. 27, 1906	Beloved s/o J & M Fladung / May his soul rest in peace	SMCA031
Fladung	Martin	B.	Jan. 22, 1886	Aug. 10, 1897	Beloved s/o J & M Fladung / Rest in peace	SMCA030
Flaim	Dario		Dec. 31, 1912	Jul. 7, 1962	Be united together	NSP820
Flaim	Lina		Aug. 14, 1912	Jul. 2, 1999	Be united together	NSP820
Flanary	William	C.	1979	2007	Raymond Funeral Home Marker	NJB521

Last Name	First Name	Middle Name	Date of Birth	Date of Death	Transcription / Notes	Cemetery Code
Flathman	Christen	A.	Oct. 13, 2001	Mar. 27, 2006	Forever Young and Always Together	SAC5007
Flathman	Paula	M.	Apr. 29, 1972	Mar. 27, 2006	Forever Young and Always Together	SAC5007
Flerlage	August	H.	Oct. 20, 1915	Sep. 26, 1974	PFC US Army	SMCD182
Flerlage	August	H.	Nov. 15, 1945	Jul. 1, 1997	In loving memory	SMCD1045
Flerlage	August		Aug. 26, 1877	May 12, 1930		SMCD191
Flerlage	Clara	M.	Nov. 13, 1919	Nov. 24, 1922		SMCD191
Flerlage	Helen	M.	Jul. 19, 1886	Jan. 30, 1965		SMCD191
Flerlage	William	W.	Dec. 29, 1951	Nov. 26, 1985		SMC1096
Flerlage, Jr.	William	Walter	1977	1979		SMC1097
Flesher	Rebecca	Louise	No Date	Mar. 14, 1993	d/o Jeff & Susan Flesher	NSP337
Fleshman	Cecil		Aug. 26, 1909	Jun. 19, 1975		NSP537
Fleshman	Nora	C.	Dec. 23, 1910	Jun. 19, 1985		NSP537
Fletcher	George	Briscoe	1836	1837	s/o George and Lucinda Fletcher, who died at Catawba when the property was occupied by his Uncle, Dr. Richard S. Briscoe. Info was supplied by J. Richard Rivoire Jul 2009	MACNoStone
Fletcher	Jonathan	M.	Mar. 15, 1984	Feb. 11, 2001	Father - Son Johnny Forever 16 Back of Stone: Dear Johnny, Your are my angel, my brightest star in the sky. I will love you always and forever until I take my last breath. Your mom; We all love and miss you	SCL2004
Fletcher	Mary	Theodose	No Date	Oct. 3, 1825	Age 2 yrs. 2 mos. 11 days. She was the d/o George and Lucinda Briscoe Fletcher. / Info is from the 1940 DAR book Page 98	MACNoStone
Fletcher	William	E.	Aug. 5, 1952	Apr. 12, 1993	Father - Son Johnny Forever 16	SCL2004
Flibbert	Matthew	James	1974	1986	In loving memory of our son	NSP1016
Flint	James		No Date	May 1, 1899	Info is from church records	OFENoStone
Flint, Mrs.	James		No Date	Jan. 23, 1901	Info is from church records	OFENoStone
Flint	Lester	Thompson	Jun. 1, 1926	Apr. 17, 1994		SAC2067
Flint	Margaret	Eulalia	Jul. 5, 1928	Sep. 1, 1983		SAC2066
Flint	Ruth	Frances	Oct. 8, 1957	Mar. 1, 1973		SAC2065
Flower	Gustavus		No Date	Jul. 19, 1906	Age 63 (info is from Old Durham Church microfilm pg 85, at the College of Southern MD, LaPlata, MD)	ODENoStone

Last Name	First Name	Middle Name	Date of Birth	Date of Death	Transcription / Notes	Cemetery Code
Floyd	Anne	Olivia	Jul. 2, 1826	Dec. 8, 1905	In loving remembrance of / d/o the late David I & Sarah Semmes Floyd / Eternal rest grant unto her O Lord and let perpetual light shine upon her / Sacred heart of Jesus have mercy on her	SIC2007
Floyd	Marguerite	V.	Jun. 18, 1918	Sep. 25, 1996	"Peggy" / In loving memory	NJB286
Floyd	Robert	Semmes	No Date	Apr. 3, 1863	the only s/o a widowed Mother / who departed this transitory life / in the 34th year of his age. His sun went down while it was yet day, but unto the just there ariseth everlasting light. May he rest in peace.	SIC2009
Floyd	Sarah	Semmes	Dec. 27, 1796	Nov. 7, 1882	To our Mother Sarah Semmes Floyd / Sacred heart of Jesus have mercy on her	SIC2011
Floyd	T.	Gilbert	1878	1952		SJE011
Fluharty	Helen	C.	1926	No Date	Together forever / Married Sep 14,1957	SMC2001
Fluharty	Walter	Joe	1930	2000	Together forever / Married Sep 14,1957	SMC2001
Flynn, Jr.	Charles	H.	May 17, 1936	Mar. 30, 2001		SJO1097
Flynn	Charles	Henry	Apr. 10, 1904	Apr. 8, 1985	Rest in Peace	SJO1095
Flynn	Edith	R.	Feb. 5, 1911	Oct. 4, 2003	Rest in Peace	SJO1095
Flynn	Evelyn	M.	Mar. 20, 1915	May 20, 2002		SPL7011
Flynn	Francis	Gerald	Dec. 31, 1952	Apr. 29, 1973		SJO1094
Flynn	James	F.	Jan. 30, 1912	Jan. 10, 1987	Sgt US Army WW II	NSP845
Flynn	Paul	E.	May 2, 1937	Oct. 23, 1993	In Loving Memory	SJO1096
Flynn	William	J.	Dec. 14, 1917	Oct. 25, 1919	s/o Patrick & Mary Flynn	SCL3220
Folkers	Lillian	M.	1921	1996		MTR3108
Foote	Juliette	E.	Jun. 29, 1919	Oct. 26, 2003		CHR126
Foote	Vernon	C.	Oct. 2, 1915	Feb. 21, 2001		CHR126
Forbes	Bernadette	L.	Oct. 14, 1919	Feb. 6, 2007		SAC3001
Forbes	Margaret	L.	Mar. 4, 1842	Mar. 8, 1934		OSP115
Ford	Agnes	L.	Jul. 31, 1930	Oct. 1, 2002		SAC5016
Ford	Ahmad		1982	2005	Thornton Funeral Home Marker	PGN075
Ford	Alice	Ann	Jul. 2, 1886	Mar. 13, 1974	Loving parents of the Ford Family of Shiloh	SHI197
Ford	Angus	James	Mar. 10, 1910	Aug. 4, 1980	The Lord is light and my salvation	SHI201
Ford	Ann	Elizabeth	Dec. 5, 1937	Dec. 20, 2001	"From your loving sister and family"	HGH4270

Last Name	First Name	Middle Name	Date of Birth	Date of Death	Transcription / Notes	Cemetery Code
Ford	Ashley	S.	1993	1993	In loving memory / Love Mom and Dad	ZBC102
Ford	Bennie		No Date	Apr. 1966	Info is from church records	SHINoStone
Ford	Bessie		No Date	May 10, 1965	Info is from church records	SHI207
Ford	Catherine	C.	Dec. 27, 1920	Mar. 25, 1995	Her many acts of kindness uplifted family and friends	SHI203
Ford	Diane		1945	2005	Thornton Funeral Home Marker	MHB246
Ford	Dorothy	Lorraine, Waugh	Apr. 14, 1934	Oct. 24, 1992	In Loving Memory / info is from church records	SHI169
Ford	Dorothy	M.	Apr. 7, 1923	Jan. 16, 2001	In loving memory	NSP049
Ford	Elizabeth	Jane	Mar. 8, 1909	Sep. 11, 1995	"From your loving daughter and family"	HGH4308
Ford	Ella	Mae	1933	1979	Wife and Mother	NSP286
Ford	Elsie	C.	Mar. 21, 1927	Apr. 10, 1988		HGH4216
Ford	Emma	L.	Jun. 4, 1935	Feb. 3, 1991	w/o John E. Ford, Sr.	NSP305
Ford	Ernest	F.	Feb. 28, 1933	No Date		SJO3373
Ford	Esebell		No Date	No Date	Can only see a small part of the stone	SHI171
Ford	Florence	A.	Mar. 10, 1881	Mar. 27, 1951		NSP254
Ford	Frances	L.	Feb. 21, 1937	No Date		SJO4079
Ford	George	Albert	Mar. 9, 1912	Jan. 28, 1997	In loving memory	SMCB012
Ford	George		No Date	Jan. 30, 1960	Info is from church records	SHINoStone
Ford	George		No Date	No Date	Funeral Home Marker (dates missing from marker)	OAK068
Ford, Sr.	George	Mac	Apr. 1, 1883	Jan. 3, 1961	Loving parents of the Ford Family of Shiloh	SHI197
Ford	Henrietta	G.	Apr. 8, 1915	Aug. 30, 1992		SJO3375
Ford	Isabelle		No Date	Sep. 1971	Info is from church records	SHINoStone
Ford	James	A.	Jul. 13, 1936	Jan. 22, 1985		SJO3361
Ford	James	Calvin	1949	1989	Thornton Funeral Home Marker, Pomonkey, MD	SCA144
Ford	James	H.	1913	1966		POM195
Ford	Jennie	R.	1895	Aug. 15, 1975	Info is from Historical Society Research located at The College of Southern MD, LaPlata, MD	SACNostone
Ford	Jno	William	No Date	Oct. 9, 1923	Info is from church records	SHINoStone
Ford	John	Edward	Nov. 12, 1927	Jan. 1, 1998	In Loving Memory	SHI169
Ford	John		No Date	Aug. 16, 1968	Info is from church records	SHI207
Ford, Jr.	John	E.	Jul. 2, 1950	May 19, 1979	Son	NSP306
Ford, Sr.	John	H.	May 27, 1935	Jul. 7, 2008		SJO4079

Last Name	First Name	Middle Name	Date of Birth	Date of Death	Transcription / Notes	Cemetery Code
Ford	John	W.	No Date	Oct. 6, 1974	Info is from Historical Society Research located at The College of Southern MD, LaPlata, MD	SACNostone
Ford	Joseph	P.	No Date	No Date	Info is from Historical Society Research located at The College of Southern MD, LaPlata, MD	SACNostone
Ford	Joseph	Philip	Oct. 3, 1952	Mar. 24, 1972		SJO3362
Ford	Joseph	S.	Oct. 10, 1893	Jan. 30, 1987	Pvt. US Army WW I	SMI017
Ford	Julia		No Date	Jun. 5, 1927	Info is from church records	SHINoStone
Ford	Justine	J.	1955	1993	In loving memory / Love Mom and Dad	ZBC102
Ford	Leroy	F.	No Date	No Date		SHI207
Ford	Louise	E.	1910	1989	In loving memory	HGH2013
Ford	Marie	Christine	Nov. 10, 1940	Mar. 11, 2000	"Puddin" / Gone but not forgotten	ZBC021
Ford	Martha	Y.	No Date	Mar. 13, 1882	Gone but not forgotten / Footstone but no picture of it	GRY007
Ford	Mary	Hortense	Feb. 25, 1927	Feb. 19, 2002	Beloved Grandmother	SHI050
Ford	Mary	Jessie	Aug. 14, 1921	May 4, 1970	In loving memory	SMCB012
Ford	Mary	V.	Jul. 8, 1911	May 12, 2002	(Jennifer)	SMY2063
Ford	Minnie	E.	Mar. 30, 1952	Dec. 27, 1975		SMI117
Ford	Ronnie	A.	Feb. 4, 1968	Jul. 7, 2002		NSP1012
Ford	Rosalee		1930	2002	Thornton Funeral Home Marker	SCL4073
Ford	Thomas	W.	1942	1977	Info was obtained from the Historical Society Research located at the College of Southern Md, LaPlata, Md)	OAKNoStone
Ford	Thomas	W.	Oct. 29, 1924	May 13, 2004		HGH4216
Ford	Thomas		No Date	Dec. 16, 1973	Info is from church records	SHINoStone
Ford	Viola	M.	Oct. 18, 1920	Feb. 18, 1985	Beloved Mother	OAK191
Ford	William	Taylor	Jul. 20, 1900	Apr. 4, 1975	Middle name is from church records	SHI101
Ford	William		1928	2000	Thornton Funeral Home Marker	MHB028
Ford	Wilson	W.	Jun. 10, 1912	Jul. 12, 1971		HGH2013
Forde	Veronica	Chase	Jul. 9, 1908	Feb. 8, 2003	At Rest	SJO1162
Forest	Edward		Apr. 22, 1923	Mar. 6, 2002	Married July 17, 1947 / Tec 5 US Army WW II	DUD004
Forest	James		No Date	Sep. 25, 1884	Age 75 (Information is from The records of Christ Church Episcopal located on microfilm at the College of Southern MD, LaPlata, MD)	HDVNoStone

Last Name	First Name	Middle Name	Date of Birth	Date of Death	Transcription / Notes	Cemetery Code
Forest	Mary	Frances	Oct. 10, 1922	Dec. 27, 2003	Married July 17, 1947	DUD004
Forester	Anna		1901	1970		SCA005
Forney	Marion	Elizabeth	May 22, 1910	No Date	Beloved aunt	CHR417
Forrest	Fenwick	W.	No Date	Mar. 22, 1906	Name is shown on church records but burial location is unknown, date is the burial date, not death date	CHRNoStone
Forrest	Mylie		1907	1990		DUD055
Foster	Hargest	Marion	Aug. 30, 1958	Jul. 22, 1984	Rick / Loving husband and devoted father	NJB316
Foster	Pauline	J.	No Date	Feb. 6, 1950	Infant	SCL2106
Foster	Sabor		1968	1975	Information is from the Historical Society Research located at the College of Southern MD, LaPlata, MD	SMINoStone
Fowke	Agnes	Woollen	Sep. 10, 1894	Sep. 3, 1984	Beloved h/o Agnes Woollen Fowke	MTR2154
Fowke	Jennie	F. S.	Feb. 23, 1859	Mar. 2, 1896	In memory of / beloved w/o Wm A. Fowke	MTR2024
Fowke	William	Augustus	Jun. 4, 1892	Dec. 3, 1967	Beloved h/o Agnes Woollen Fowke	MTR2154
Fowke	William	Augustus	No Date	Feb. 9, 1857	Sacred to the memory of / only son of Gerard and Mary Fowke d / aged 25 years. High moral worth and all the sweet Virtues adorned his exemplary life and endeared him to all his aquaintances. His death has left a void in the hearts of his two surviving sisters which time can never fill, and as a token of their love, they raise this memorial. Green be the turf above thee . Friend of my better days. None knew thee but to love thee. None named thee but to praise.	GUN002
Fowke	Wm	A.	1846	1924		MTR2024
Fowler	Agnes	Rosalie	Sep. 20, 1936	Sep. 16, 2008	Loving mother & nan	SMC1060
Fowler	Annie	Mae	May 30, 1928	Jun. 20, 2000	Sister	SHI092
Fowler	Charlotte	A.	Oct. 9, 1913	Apr. 5, 1991		SMC4192
Fowler	Coy	Wayne	1918	1979	1st Sgt. US Army WW II	NSP663
Fowler	Eliza		No Date	Dec. 24, 1898	Name is shown on church records but burial location is unknown, date is the burial date, not death date	CHRNoStone
Fowler	Hilda	C., Woods	Jul. 19, 1934	Aug. 12, 2008	On earth / In Heaven	HGH4137
Fowler	J.	Henry	Nov. 25, 1914	Aug. 18, 1990		NJB289
Fowler	John		Aug. 13, 1924	Sep. 14, 2003	Dates are from internet site familysearch.org	SHI094

Last Name	First Name	Middle Name	Date of Birth	Date of Death	Transcription / Notes	Cemetery Code
Fowler	Joseph	Archer	No Date	Nov. 7, 1958	(Info is from the Times Crescent Newspaper Thus. Nov 13, 1958 Pg 7)	SICNoStone
Fowler	Joyce	Ann	Oct. 21, 1947	Nov. 13, 2002	Daughter	SHI093
Fowler, IV	Zach	M.	Jul. 25, 1959	Dec. 26, 1978	Fire Department Emblem	SMC3069
Fowler, Jr.	Zach	M.	Jun. 27, 1933	Nov. 29, 1987		SMC3068
Fox	Brandy	Nicole	1985	1985	Arehart Funeral Home marker	SAC1018
Franke	Louise		No Date	Feb. 9, 1907	Info is from Christ Church microfilm Reel 3, Pg 220-221 located at the College of Southern MD, LaPlata, MD	MTRNoStone
Franklin	Agnes		Apr. 5, 1870	Aug. 31, 1875	Left side: d/o Alex & Cornelia Franklin; Backside: They are gone but not forgotten	CMX1099
Franklin	Alexander		Apr. 6, 1838	Jan. 3, 1895		CMX2119
Franklin	Alvert		No Date	Jun. 11, 1961	Letters carved into cement cross stone that is sinking into the ground	OAK135
Franklin	Ben		Jul. 30, 1870	Oct. 13, 1904	At Rest / Our only son / By his parents	PIS041
Franklin	Bessie		May 24, 1889	May 27, 1972		PIS033
Franklin	Charlotte	C.	Mar. 3, 1867	May 22, 1952	Aged 85 years	NJB465
Franklin	Clarence	Peter	May 25, 1943	Jul.y 10, 1969	Maryland SP4 U.S. Army Vietnam	OAK116
Franklin	Clarence		1918	1982	Thornton Funeral Home Marker	OAK112
Franklin	Cornelia	D.	Sep. 22, 1844	Jan. 30, 1899		CMX2119
Franklin	Dave		Jan. 6, 1917	Feb. 15, 1986	m. Dec 23, 1944	LUM092
Franklin	Edwin	H.	1885	1959	Stonemaker: Keystone Memorials	CMX2142
Franklin, Miss.	Elizabeth		No Date	Nov. 1920	Buried Nov 11, 1920 age 73 (info is from Old Durham Church microfilm pg 159 located at the College of Southern MD, LaPlata, MD)	ODENoStone
Franklin	Elsie	R.	Jan. 22, 1894	Apr. 30, 1986	At Rest	PIS039
Franklin	Emma	Irene	1893	1947		NJB195
Franklin	Emma	V.	1895	1965		CMX2142
Franklin	Ethel		1923	1980	Thornton Funeral Home Marker	OAK113
Franklin	Evelyn	Scott	Apr. 21, 1912	Feb. 17, 1981	She will live in a mansion in heaven	NJB219
Franklin	Grace		Apr. 13, 1925	No Date	m. Dec 23, 1944	LUM092
Franklin	Harry	J.	Jul. 29, 1888	Jan. 5, 1967		NJB196
Franklin	Hezekiah		No Date	Mar. 8, 1911	Age 85 years / Rest in peace	PIS176

Last Name	First Name	Middle Name	Date of Birth	Date of Death	Transcription / Notes	Cemetery Code
Franklin	Hyland		Apr. 1, 1874	Sep. 9, 1876	Right side: S/o Alex & Cornelia Frankin; Backside: They are gone but not forgotten	CMX1099
Franklin	Irene	Posey	No Date	No Date		NJB424
Franklin	Irving	Alexander	1891	1960		CMX2140
Franklin	James	W.	Jun. 12, 1819	Jan. 4, 1865	Footstone to right of Franklin stone: W. F. (initial J. appears broken off)	FKE002
Franklin	John	A.	No Date	Mar. 22, 1923	In Memory of / Lead kindly light / departed this life / aged 69 years - May he rest in peace	NJB466
Franklin	Johnny		1947	1997	Funeral Home Marker	OAK001
Franklin	Josephine		Oct. 29, 1837	Oct. 12, 1869	In memory of / An old stone that is broken off the base and laying on the ground	SJO6065
Franklin	Julia	E.	Aug. 8, 1851	Oct. 12, 1929	w/o Wesley Franklin (info is from the Historical Society Research located at The College of Southern MD, LaPlata, MD)	FRANoStone
Franklin	Katie	M.	1899	1957	Mother	NJB490
Franklin	Margaret		No Date	Jul. 1906	Sacred to the memory of Margaret Franklin Beloved w/o Hezekiah Franklin / In her 83rd year / Blessed are the dead who die in the Lord (Stone was broken and has been repaired)	PIS177
Franklin	Mary	S.	May 22, 1892	May 22, 1977		PIS033
Franklin	Morris		1899	1976	Info is from Historical Society Research located at the College of Southern MD, LaPlata, MD	MTRNoStone
Franklin	Myrtle		1920	1991	Thornton Funeral Home Marker	MHB055
Franklin	Penny	Cornell	No Date	Jul. 31, 1959	Cement stone with name carved in it	OAK155
Franklin	Thomas	Wesley	Jun. 13, 1899	Oct. 6, 1899	Brother (info is from the Historical Society Research located at The College of Southern MD, LaPlata, MD)	FRANoStone
Franklin	Thomas		Dec. 6, 1844	Apr. 27, 1921	Info is from The Historical Society Research located at the College of Southern MD, LaPlata, MD	SICNoStone
Franklin, Mrs.	Unknown		No Date	May 1888	Info is from Old Durham Church microfilm pg 79-80 located at the College of Southern MD, LaPlata, MD	ODENoStone
Franklin	Walter		Jul. 4, 1895	Feb. 7, 1988	At Rest	PIS039
Franklin	Wesley		Apr. 26, 1838	Jun. 26, 1929	info is from the Historical Society Research located at The College of Southern MD, LaPlata, MD	FRANoStone
Frankline	Thos.	Benj.	No Date	Apr. 6, 1876	Infant / info is from church records	OFENoStone

Last Name	First Name	Middle Name	Date of Birth	Date of Death	Transcription / Notes	Cemetery Code
Franlin	Philip		May 17, 1901	Feb. 28, 1971		MTR3134
Frederick	Alfred		No Date	Nov. 20, 1894	Info is from Christ Church microfilm Reel 2 Pg 171-172 located at the College of Southern MD, LaPlata, MD	MTRNoStone
Frederick	Charles		No Date	No Date	His wife	CHR390
Frederick, Rev.	J.	Arthur	No Date	No Date	Don't know why he is on the stone with the Brown family. Found a J Arthur Frederick, Priest in the 1880 census from ancestry.com	SHI109
Frederick	Lillian		Jan. 22, 1895	May 17, 1971		SAC4068
Frederick	Mary	B.	Mar. 6, 1905	Nov. 24, 1997		SAC4084
Frederick	Minnie		No Date	No Date	His Wife	CHR390
Frederick	Robert	Lee	1895	1972	Arehart Funeral Home Marker	SMT053
Freeman	Abner		1901	1923		SJO2288
Freeman	Alexander	Marshall	Mar. 18, 1837	Sep. 6, 1904	Back of stone: J.A., B.L., M.J. Freeman & K.F. Lyon; footstone: C.A.F.	TRI403
Freeman	Aurella		1922	1997		NJB439
Freeman	B.	L.	1882	1951		TRI404
Freeman	Catherine	Ann	Sep. 2, 1849	Jul. 1, 1943	Back of stone: J.A., B.L., M.J. Freeman & K.F. Lyon; footstone: C.A.F.	TRI403
Freeman	Consuella		1902	1902		SJO2288
Freeman	Dorothy	Veronica	Mar. 10, 1907	Sep. 13, 1991	TEC 4 US Army WW II	SJO2225
Freeman	Elizabeth	D.	Dec. 19, 1822	Feb. 22, 1879	In memory of / w/o John H. Freeman B / D / "Weep not, she is not dead, but sleepeth."	DAF007
Freeman	Flora	Elizabeth	Oct. 29, 1858	May 1, 1915	In memory of Flora Elizabeth Freeman d/o John H.-Elizabeth D. Freeman B / D / Until the day break and the shadows flee away. (stone has fallen off the base, but is intact. The gravesite has been disturbed by animals leaving a a hole, the hole was filled in by the Charles County MD Genealogical Society) (There is probably a footstone but it may be sunken)	DAF011
Freeman	Harold	Bernard	Mar. 14, 1930	Oct. 3, 1998	"Slim" / Loving son and father / "Easy, friendly" / Middle name is from church records	SPL6042

Last Name	First Name	Middle Name	Date of Birth	Date of Death	Transcription / Notes	Cemetery Code
Freeman	Henry	C.	Oct. 3, 1856	Apr. 22, 1915	In memory of / s/o John H.-Elizabeth D. Freeman B / D / Not my will but thine oh God be done. There is a footstone but it has been disturbed by animals and is sunken.	DAF001
Freeman	J.	A.	1876	1949		TRI404
Freeman	J.	Marion	Nov. 9, 1839	Dec. 21, 1911		NME001
Freeman	John	H.	Aug. 16, 1830	Mar. 25, 1908	In memory of / B / D / His servants shall serve him and they shall see his face. Footstone	DAF004
Freeman	Joseph		1919	1919		SJO2288
Freeman	Lawrence		1904	1955		SJO2288
Freeman	Louis		1910	1911		SJO2288
Freeman	M.	J.	1895	1972		TRI404
Freeman	Margaret	S.	Jan. 25, 1935	Sep. 20, 1996	Loving Mom and friend. We'll miss you. / "Mother" / "Peggy"	SPL6043
Freeman	Marshall	Thomas	Feb. 2, 1880	Nov. 11, 1909	back of stone, J.A. B.L M.J. Freeman & K. F. Lyon / footstone: M.T.F	TRI403
Freeman	Mary	E.	Apr. 22, 1857	Mar. 8, 1883	To the memory of / Beloved wife of E. M. Freeman / Thy will be done	TUB007
Freeman	Mary	Elizabeth	1914	1980	Information is from the 1984 church cemetery transcription list	SICNoStone
Freeman	Mary	S.	Aug. 1, 1840	Jun. 23, 1890	d/o Dr. S. W. and M.C. Dent / A faithful servant of God	NME004
Freeman	Mary	McClain	1882	1932		SJO2288
Freeman	Nathaniel		1908	1958		SJO2288
Freeman	Ronald	F.	1959	1978	Our beloved son / rest in peace	NJB438
Freeman	Samuel		1876	1955		SJO2288
Freeman	Sherman		Aug. 25, 1920	Aug. 13, 2005	Age 84	NJB439
Freeman	Wilfred		1914	1928		SJO2288
Freeman	William	H.	1870	1904		TRI040
Freeman	Z...	Francis	Nov. 5, 1840	Feb. 23, 1890	Back of Stone: Francis Philmon, Mary Vivian, and Stanislaus. Children of Z. F. and Mary A. Freeman	SMY1082
Freer	Effie	Brace	No Date	Aug. 8, 1948	Info is from Christ Church microfilm Reel 4 Pg 272-273 located at the College of Southern MD, LaPlata, MD	MTRNoStone

Last Name	First Name	Middle Name	Date of Birth	Date of Death	Transcription / Notes	Cemetery Code
Freer	Eleanor	Sellman, Fowke	Jan. 20, 1926	Jul. 1, 1947	Beloved w/o Romeo H. Freer Jr / To live in the hearts of those we Love is not to die	MTR2155
French	Albert		1890	1973	Information was obtained from the Historical Society Research located at the College of Southern MD,. LaPlata, MD	EMO001
French	Ethel		1896	1994	Thornton Funeral Home Marker	OAK129
French	Gloria		1933	1987	Funeral Home Marker / info is from church records	PGN027
Frender	Ann	R.	Feb. 28, 1940	No Date	Together Forever	SMC4232
Frender	James	W.	Jul. 10, 1938	Nov. 13, 2005	Together Forever	SMC4232
Frere, Capt.	Barrow		Apr. 1820	Apr. 1884	Born at Herdordshire England	HGH166
Frere	Charles	P.	1891	1935		HGH1158
Frere	Charles	Richard	Dec. 10, 1925	No Date		SIC4053
Frere	Charlotte	Spalding	Nov. 9, 1925	No Date		SIC4053
Frere	F.	Marie	1887	1936		HGH1159
Frere	Francis	Joseph	1900	1974		HGH1137
Frere	Helen	R.	1884	1973		HGH1136
Frere, Sr.	James	Merrick	Nov. 19, 1931	Mar. 31, 1991	Husband of Muriel	HGH1135
Frere	James	Robert	No Date	No Date	Children's Memorial / and all other children buried here	HGH4328
Frere	James	Robert	Jan. 30, 1929	Jun. 29, 1930		HGH1156
Frere	John	E.	Oct. 5, 1920	May 2, 1985	Our Trust is in God / Footstone: Capt US Army WW II	SIC3001
Frere	John	Edward	Dec. 31, 1894	Feb. 27, 1939	Father	HGH1142
Frere	Josephine		1859	1941		HGH1168
Frere	M.	Phyllis	Sep. 16, 1898	Apr. 18, 1984	Mother	HGH1142
Frere	Margaret	Ann	Jul. 17, 1836	Jan. 13, 1905	Sacred to the memory of / Wife of Barrow Frere / May she be resurrected to the glory of God	HGH1165
Frere	Marian	Louise	Nov. 10, 1927	May 6, 1994		HGH1145
Frere	Marie	E.	May 21, 1893	Oct. 10, 1979		SIC7018
Frere	Marion	Eliza	Sep. 29, 1904	Jun. 3, 1918	Daughter of Wm J. & Josephine Frere	HGH1167
Frere	Marion	G.	1886	1886	Children of Wm J. & Josephine Frere	HGH1166
Frere	Mary	Jane	Jun. 27, 1923	Jan. 12, 2009	Our Trust is in God	SIC3001
Frere	Muriel	Jean	Apr. 7, 1933	Mar. 17, 1972		HGH1134

Last Name	First Name	Middle Name	Date of Birth	Date of Death	Transcription / Notes	Cemetery Code
Frere	Robert	Lee	1898	1899	Children of Wm J. & Josephine Frere	HGH166
Frere	Rose	Byrne	1891	1968		HGH1137
Frere	William	J.	1884	1981		HGH1136
Frere	William	J.	Apr. 12, 1922	Feb. 10, 2004	In loving memory	HGH1146
Frere	William	J.	1861	1922		HGH1168
Friedberg	A.		No Date	No Date	Stone: 60 / Numbered Stonemarkers have been placed on unmarked graves by church. No metal nameplate is attached to marker/ info is from church records	CMX2052
Friedberg	D.		No Date	No Date	Stone: 61 / Numbered Stonemarkers have been placed on unmarked graves by church / No metal nameplate on marker (info is from church)	CMX2030
Friedrich	Chandler	Bailey	Mar. 17, 2004	Jan. 6, 2007	"Our Loving Son" "We held your hand for just a short while / but we hold your heart forever"	SMY4004
Friedrich	Emily	G.	Apr. 2, 1941	Sep. 17, 1941	Our Darling	GHB001
Friedrich	Robert	Anthony	Oct. 14, 1982	Jul. 2, 2004	My son / "I love and miss you always and will be by your side forever"	SIC9094
Fritter	Audrey	A.	Apr. 8, 1925	No Date		CMX2064
Fritter	Dollie	D.	1894	1964		CMX2068
Fritter	Edith	Louise	1925	1995	In loving memory	CMX2066
Fritter	M.	Clyde	1890	1963		CMX2068
Fritter, Jr.	Marion	Clyde	Feb. 10, 1923	Mar. 15, 1987	Tec 5 US Army WWII	CMX2067
Fritter	Richard	Elsworth	Feb. 23, 1921	Jun. 1, 1999	PFC US Army WWII	CMX2064
Froman	Richard	Allen	Oct. 25, 1953	Apr. 20, 1974	Beloved s/o Earl C. & Mildred Burgess Froman	ODE424
Fuchs	Arnold	W.	Feb. 21, 1893	Apr. 5, 1965		SCL1150
Fuchs	Barbara	M.	Nov. 27, 1893	Jul. 25, 1972		SCL1150
Fuchs	Mildred	H.	Sep. 28, 1921	No Date	Thy Kingdom come, thy will be done / Mother	SCL1252
Fuchs	Paul	J.	Mar. 23, 1921	Dec. 18, 1989	Thy Kingdom come, thy will be done / Father	SCL1252
Fulk	Janie	K.	Mar. 4, 1957	Apr. 30, 1957		CMX2038
Fuller	Catherine	A.	Sep. 8, 1958	Aug. 28, 2004		SMC4137
Fuller	Catherine	Louise	1914	1952		SCL2080
Fuller	Catherine	M.	1905	1992		LUM132
Fuller	Ernest	A.	1901	1972		LUM132

LastName	First Name	Middle Name	Date of Birth	Date of Death	Transcription / Notes	Cemetery Code
Fuller	William	Edward	1902	1986		SCL2082
Fuller	William	Thomas	Sep. 14, 1935	Oct. 30, 1989	SP 3 US Army Korea	PKH029
Fultz	Edward	R.	1935	No Date	Together Forever	SCL3394
Fultz	Ruth	Ann	1937	1999	Together Forever	SCL3394
Funkhouser	Elva	M.	Jan. 16, 1922	No Date	Mother	NZN071
Funkhouser	Winfield	S.	Jun. 25, 1914	Aug. 11, 1996	Father	NZN071
Furbush	Eligah		1856	1908	Age 85 d/o the late Louise and Anthony Chirieleison. (info is from MD Independent Newspaper Wed. April 2, 2008 Page A-10 Column 1) Raymond Funeral Home Marker	HGH1181
Furbush	Jane	Frances	Dec. 28, 1922	Mar. 31, 2008		SAC2132A
Furbush	John	H.	Nov. 6, 1919	Nov. 18, 1922		HGH1183
Furbush	John	W.	1882	1963		HGH1182
Furbush	Mary	B.	1887	1969		HGH1182
Furbush	Mary	Jane	1857	1940		HGH1181
Furey	Randolph		Aug. 18, 1899	Dec. 15, 1960	Maryland SDC US Navy WW I & II	POM233
Fusco	Anthony	Peter	Jun. 29, 1920	No Date	Back of stone: Loving Parents of / William Elliott Crown April 17, 1941 - Jul 29, 1997 / Daryl Bruce Crown Dec 30, 1943	PKH025
Fusco	Esther	Sullivan, Crown	Jul. 24, 1910	Jul. 28, 1999	Back of stone: Loving Parents of / William Elliott Crown April 17, 1941 - Jul 29, 1997 / Daryl Bruce Crown Dec 30, 1943 (info is from a family relative)	PKH025
G.	I.	C.	No Date	No Date	Footstone (unable to located headstone)	MTR2224
G.	G.		No Date	No Date	Footston, G.G. (in Woods) Probably for George Gardiner, died 1873	OSP070A
G.	Unknown	A.	No Date	No Date	Footstone, ( ) A.G. (Could be for Catherine A. Gardiner) (In woods)	OSP170
Gacad	Agripino	R.	Nov. 8, 1911	Jan. 18, 2000		NSP038
Gacad	Leonora	L.	Jan. 11, 1913	May 10, 1986		NSP038
Gagliardi	Carl	A.	Oct. 27, 1920	Feb. 19, 2002	Capt US Army WW II / Beloved Husband (There is a headstone with the name Gagliardi on one side and Clarke on the other)	MTR3128
Gail	Bobby		No Date	Oct. 4, 1997	Age 51 / info is from church records	OFENoStone

Last Name	First Name	Middle Name	Date of Birth	Date of Death	Transcription / Notes	Cemetery Code
Gaines	Anthony	Donald	Mar. 1968	Jan. 1970	Funeral Home Marker	OAK162
Gaines	Bertha		No Date	No Date	Funeral Home Marker	OAK134
Gaines	Clara		1925	1986	Cement Cross	OAK096
Gaines	James		No Date	No Date	Funeral Home Marker	OAK147
Gaines	Robert	William	1942	1975	Info was obtained from the Historical Society Research located at the College of Southern Md, LaPlata, Md)	OAKNoStone
Gaines	Robert		No Date	No Date	Funeral Home Marker	OAK148
Gaines	Robert		1919	1998	Funeral Home Marker	OAK003
Gaines	Rosie	J.	1876	1964		OAK076
Gaines	Samuel		No Date	No Date	Funeral Home Marker	OAK146
Gaines	Smith		1891	No Date	Thornton Funeral Home Marker	OAK138
Gaines - Wilson	Emma	Line	Jan. 31, 1908	May 17, 2005	Grandmother	OAK029
Gaiser	Rose	F.	Sep. 21, 1913	No Date		SAC1035
Gaither	Mary	J.	1909	1974		SAC2114
Gaither	William	I.	1912	1983		SAC2113
Galanti	Anne	Laura, Clark	Apr. 26, 1960	No Date		SJO4022
Galanti	John	Michael	Nov. 20, 1949	Jun. 10, 2002		SJO4022
Gales	Frances	Ann	1875	1957	Mother	SHI273
Galvin	Austin	Charles	No Date	Oct. 3, 1997	Our Baby / "Gone to be an Angel"	SAC1025
Gam or Jameson	Frances	J.	1918	No Date	Not sure if last name is Gam or Jameson	SMCA216
Gamble	Alvey	Denton	Aug. 30, 1867	Oct. 7, 1942		MTR3105
Gamble, Jr.	Alvey	Denton	Oct. 9, 1903	Feb. 6, 1955	Those who have passed from this world, die only when we whom they loved forget them	MTR3124
Gamble	Charles	William	Mar. 17, 1918	Feb. 10, 1990	"Bill" Do not stand at our graves and weep, we are not here. We do not sleep. We are a thousand winds that blow. We are the diamond glint on snow. We are the sunlight on ripened grain. We are the gentle autumn rain. When you wake in the morning hush we are the swift, uplifting rush of quiet birds in circling flight. We are the soft starlight at night. Do not stand at our graves and weep. We are not here, we do not sleep, Loving Parents and Grandparents	MTR3065

Last Name	First Name	Middle Name	Date of Birth	Date of Death	Transcription / Notes	Cemetery Code
Gamble	Christine	Irene	No Date	Mar. 5, 1955	"Sandy"	MTR3038
Gamble	Earl	Chester	Jul. 14, 1919	Nov. 6, 1985	"Teen"	MTR3072
Gamble	Harry	J.	Apr. 23, 1906	Sep. 9, 1946		MTR3102
Gamble	Ida	E. C.	Jun. 12, 1871	Mar. 29, 1945		MTR3104
Gamble	Irene	Mae	Dec. 20, 1908	Jan. 18, 1974		MTR3125
Gamble	James	Harvey	Aug. 17, 1893	Mar. 3, 1971	"Happy"	MTR3101
Gamble	Leroy	Benjamin	No Date	May 16, 2008	Age 82 s/o the late Alvey Dent Gamble and the late Irene Mae Grimm Gamble. h/o Olga Ann Gamble. Raymond Funeral Home (info is from the MD Independent Newspaper; Wed. May 21, 2008 Pg A10)	MTRNoStone
Gamble	Lula	M.	May 19, 1885	Feb. 18, 1936		MTR3071
Gamble	M.	Delree	Dec. 4, 1933	Jan. 31, 1990	"Bill" Do not stand at our graves and weep, we are not here. We do not sleep. We are a thousand winds that blow. We are the diamond glint on snow. We are the sunlight on ripened grain. We are the gentle autumn rain. When you wake in the morning hush we are the swift, uplifting rush of quiet birds in circling flight. We are the soft starlight at night. Do not stand at our graves and weep. We are not here, we do not sleep, Loving Parents and Grandparents	MTR3065
Gamble	Roy	E.	Sep. 17, 1908	Nov. 8, 1943	At Rest	MTR3103
Gambrell	Bennett	V.	Jan. 9, 1911	Mar. 8, 1975	Our beloved brother, rest in peace	MTR1066
Gambrell, Sr.	William	Bennett	May 16, 1949	Apr. 14, 1986	In loving memory	MTR1067
Gambrill, Jr.	Bennett		No Date	No Date	Info is from church records	MTRNoStone
Gamp	Sarah		No Date	Apr. 4, 1875	Info is from church records	OFENoStone
Gant	Margaret	Lenora	Jul. 10, 1916	Nov. 18, 1991		SAC5020
Gant, Jr.	James	A.	Sep. 16, 1947	Sep. 26, 2002	Daddy	SAC5118
Gant, Jr.	William	E.	Feb. 6, 1956	Aug. 4, 1999	We Will Always Love You	SMY2067
Garcia, M.D.	Ignacio	T.	Aug. 3, 1926	Oct. 18, 1991	They Who Have Done Good Shall Come Forth Unto Resurreciton of Life	SAC4085
Gardiner	A.	Elbert	1894	1984	Brother	NSP530
Gardiner	Adele	deBarth, Walbach	Sep. 2, 1815	Jan. 6, 1904	His wife (Right side of stone)	SMCE057

Last Name	First Name	Middle Name	Date of Birth	Date of Death	Transcription / Notes	Cemetery Code
Gardiner, Sr.	Adrian	P.	Mar. 21, 1893	Mar. 31, 1972	Maryland PVT HQ CO 19 FLD Arty WW I	SIC3057
Gardiner, Jr.	Adrian	Posey	Jun. 5, 1923	Sep. 3, 1990		SIC4108
Gardiner	Albert	J.	Sep. 10, 1903	Apr. 5, 1978		NSP921
Gardiner	Albert		Sep. 29, 1847	May 13, 1934		NSP421
Gardiner	Alberta	Burch	1866	1922		NSP368
Gardiner, Sr.	Aloysius	B.	1866	1946		NSP367
Gardiner, Jr.	Aloysius	Bowling	1911	1926		NSP381
Gardiner	Andrew	Carl	1885	1969		SIC3039
Gardiner	Ann	T.	No Date	Oct. 22, 1844	Sacred to the memory of / Who died / Aged 31 years / She was taken away lest wickedness should alter her understanding or deceit beguile her soul for her soul pleased God, therefore He hastened to bring her out of the midst of iniquities. Wisdom IV (Unable to read No. of verse) May she rest in peace, Amen / stone maker: A Merideth maker Balt	SMCD245
Gardiner	Anna	Howard	1860	1939		SIC3049
Gardiner	Anna	L.	No Date	No Date	Age 48 / info is from the Historical Society Research and the 1940 DAR book pg 192 located at the College of Southern MD, LaPlata, MD.	SMCNoStone
Gardiner	Annie	Frances	Sep. 19, 1837	Jul. 18, 1901	IHS / In memory of / Rest in peace / Daughters of Ignatius F & Catherine Gardiner (Sister to Margaret Helen Gardiner)	SMCD252
Gardiner	Arthur	E.	Feb. 17, 1882	May 25, 1966		NSP509
Gardiner	B.	Franklin	1882	1941		NSP352
Gardiner	Beatrice		Apr. 23, 1836	Mar. 24, 1912	R I P	SMCD229
Gardiner	Benjamin	D.	No Date	Sep. 27, 1832	Sacred to the memory of / second son of J F and C Gardiner / died in the 23rd year of his age / May he rest in peace / This stone has been placed here, by his Brother and Sister, In grateful remembrance	SMCD305
Gardiner	Benjamin	Franklin	No Date	May 10, 1831	eldest s/o Ig's & Catharine Gardiner who departed this life / In the 11th year of his age / May he rest in peace	SMCC005
Gardiner	Benjamin	Walter	Jan. 10, 1820	Oct. 1894		OSPNoStone
Gardiner	Berdinia	L.	Oct. 26, 1922	No Date	In loving memory	NSP885

Last Name	First Name	Middle Name	Date of Birth	Date of Death	Transcription / Notes	Cemetery Code
Gardiner	Bernadette	Norris	Aug. 6, 1895	Jul. 1, 1968		NSP626
Gardiner	Bessie		Jan. 4, 1883	Aug. 27, 1909	Daughter of Lorenza J & Rhoda M Gardiner / Blessed are the pure of heart for they shall see God	SMCD236
Gardiner	C.	Elsie	Dec. 27, 1903	Mar. 6, 1988		NSP527
Gardiner	Catharine	A.	No Date	Jul. 4, 1851	d/o S. F. Gardiner / Catharine A. Gardiner departed this life / in the 34th year of her age / Info is from The Historical Society Research located at College of Southern MD, LaPlata, MD	OSPNoStone
Gardiner	Catharine	C.	Nov. 13, 1829	Mar. 22, 1897	In memoram / d/o Ignatius F. & Catharine Gardiner / rest in peace	SMCC006
Gardiner	Catharine		No Date	Sep. 27, 1823	Sacred to the memeory of / consort of John F Gardiner who departed this life / in the 52nd year of her age. Leaving 3 sons & 2 daughters to mourn her irreparable loss. Dear mother thou hast left here thy loss we deeply feel. But tis God who hath bereft he can our sorrow heal / Stone maker: F Sisson, Balto.	SMCD303
Gardiner	Catharine		No Date	Oct. 24, 1864	Consort of Ignatius F. Gardiner / In the 65th year of her age	SMCC001
Gardiner	Catherine	C.	1891	1963		SIC3049
Gardiner	Cecelia	Cox	Feb. 9, 1912	Nov. 1, 1986	My request was denied	SMC4075
Gardiner	Clara	A.	Jul. 10, 1930	No Date	Beloved wife and mother	SMC1038
Gardiner	Clara		Feb. 21, 1923	Mar. 15, 1924	Beloved d/o Mary E and Arthur E Gardiner	NSP511
Gardiner, Jr.	David	C.	Mar. 5, 1965	Sep. 5, 1998	Treasured son / Beloved husband / Devoted father / Forever in our hearts	SIC6027
Gardiner	Doris	E.	Aug. 22, 1925	No Date	In loving memory	NSP735
Gardiner	Dorothy	Eleanor	Dec. 20, 1922	Mar. 16, 2002		NSP447
Gardiner	Edith	M.	1918	1995		SMC1100
Gardiner	Edward	L.	No Date	1861	In memory of / There is only one date on the stone	SMCD224
Gardiner	Edward	S.	1880	1935		SIC3049
Gardiner, Sr.	Edward	W.	May 13, 1925	Apr. 8, 1998	In loving memory	NSP735
Gardiner	Edwin	M.	1869	1955		NSP480
Gardiner	Elizabeth	Ann	Oct. 18, 1903	Apr. 8, 1978		NSP424
Gardiner	Emanuel	Simms	Jul. 3, 1853	Apr. 9, 1904	May he rest in peace / top of stone is missing	SMCD266

Last Name	First Name	Middle Name	Date of Birth	Date of Death	Transcription / Notes	Cemetery Code
Gardiner	Emily	Carrico	Aug. 13, 1864	Apr. 29, 1925	Eva Geraldine Gardiner Infant of A.W. & Mary J. Gardiner / Aged 3 months & 10 days (Stone is laying on the ground and broken in half)	SMCE057
Gardiner	Eva	Geraldine	No Date	Jul. 30, 1856		SMCE070
Gardiner	Evangeline	L.	1915	1958	Beloved w/o George I Gardiner	SMC3246
Gardiner	Frances	Edith	Apr. 22, 1929	No Date		NSP425
Gardiner	Frances	Sophia	No Date	No Date	Also his eight little children, Teresa, Frances Sophia, Joseph Henry, Richard Thomas and four without names (child of George H. Gardiner)	SMCD264
Gardiner	Genevieve	M.	1879	1949		NSP408
Gardiner	George	H.	Jul. 6, 1804	Sep. 8, 1854	Also his eight little children, Teresa, Frances Sophia, Joseph Henry, Richard Thomas and four without names	SMCD264
Gardiner	George	H.	No Date	Feb. 6, 1892	In the 77 yr of his age May he rest in peace	OSP023
Gardiner	George	H.	Dec. 7, 1929	Jan. 14, 1938		NSP683
Gardiner	George	Ignatius	May 17, 1879	Apr. 28, 1946		SMCA141
Gardiner	George	S.	Oct. 17, 1906	Aug. 4, 1997	Per website Ancestry.com his last name is Gardiner	NSP883
Gardiner	George		No Date	Sep. 21, 1873	aged 91 yrs	OSP069
Gardiner	Gerald	J.	No Date	Mar. 8, 1854	Son of A.W. & M.E. Gardiner / Aged 5 Months & 23 Days	SMCE068
Gardiner	Helena	Seifert	Jun. 8, 1913	May 25, 2000		SMC2173
Gardiner	Henry		No Date	Apr. 17, 1909	In the 83 yr of his age "May he rest in peace" / stone is lying on the ground	OSP025
Gardiner, Sr.	Hugh	C.	1875	1952		NSP640
Gardiner, III	Hugh	C.	Apr. 23, 1933	No Date		SIC6026
Gardiner, Jr.	Hugh	C.	Feb. 1, 1906	Apr. 17, 1991		SIC6025
Gardiner	Idalia	L.	1878	1973		NSP480
Gardiner	Ignatius	F.	No Date	Apr. 26, 1841	Sacred to the memory of / who departed this life / In the 52nd year of his age. / This stone has been placed here by his widow in grateful remembrance / also his daughter Mary Rose who departed this life / in the 17th year of her age / May they rest in peace. Amen	SMCC003
Gardiner	Ignatius	Francis	No Date	Sep. 1832	infant s/o Ig's F & Catharine Gardiner	SMCC003
Gardiner	Imogene	M.	1872	1952		SMCE022

Last Name	First Name	Middle Name	Date of Birth	Date of Death	Transcription / Notes	Cemetery Code
Gardiner, Sr.	J	Leo	Sep. 23, 1907	Aug. 20, 1980		SMC4075
Gardiner	J.	Nolan	Mar. 21, 1930	Dec. 11, 1938		NSP734
Gardiner, M.D.	J.	deB W.	Dec. 1, 1841	Feb. 5, 1907	Captain U. S. Army	SMCE057
Gardiner	James	deB, Walbach	Nov. 11, 1859	May 23, 1905	Left side of stone	SMCE057
Gardiner	James	R.	1911	1986		SMC1100
Gardiner	James		No Date	Jun. 27, 1909	At rest / In the 67th year of his age / R I P	SMCD227
Gardiner	Jane	Marie	1946	1995		SMC2133
Gardiner	John	Benedict	Jan. 20, 1839	May 19, 1861	Sacred to the memory of / third s/o John F and Mary Gardiner / In the 23d year of his age / "May he rest in peace" / Side of stone: This humble tribute of a fathers love not only marks the spot where now he lies, But warning gives to all who hither rove, To seek in death, a home beyond the skies.	SMCA105
Gardiner	John				IHS / Sacred to the memory of / who departed this life / in the 78th year of his age. Leaving 3 sons and 2 daughters to mourn his irreparable loss. He was modest, meek & good indeed courteous to all, helpful to those in need, a careful father, and a loving friend, peaceable was his life, and calm his end, his body here in grave composed is his soul now rests with Christ in endless bliss	
Gardiner	John	F.	No Date	Sep. 12, 1831		SMCD309
Gardiner	John	F.	Aug. 8, 1803	Jul. 7, 1877	IHS / To our father / Requiescat in Pace	SMCA103
Gardiner	John	F.	1877	1958		NSP382
Gardiner	John	Percival	Jan. 28, 1877	Oct. 10, 1902	s/o Thos. R. & Lucy A. Gardiner	SIC3039
Gardiner, Sr.	Joseph	Bernard	Aug. 12, 1916	Feb. 25, 1992		NSP446
Gardiner, Sr.	Joseph	Cecil	Jun. 26, 1895	Sep. 12, 1958		NSP626
Gardiner	Joseph	D.	1862	1930		SMCE022

Last Name	First Name	Middle Name	Date of Birth	Date of Death	Transcription / Notes	Cemetery Code
Gardiner	Joseph	D.	No Date	Apr. 26, 1863	Sacred to the memory of / In the 41st year of his age. / Leaving a wife, two daughters, and an infant son to mourn their irreparable loss. / Side of stone: This monument has been placed here by a devoted wife in grateful remembrance / Other side of stone: Go fair example of untainted life, of modest wisdom, firmness without strife; Composed in sufferings and joy sedate. Good without noise, without pretentions great. Just to thy word; in every thought sincere, Who knew no wish but what the world might hear. Of softest manners, unaffected mind, lover of peace, and friend of human kind. Go live! for Heaven's eternal year is thine. Go and exalt thy moral to divine; Go' then where only bliss sincere is known. Go where to love, and to enjoy are one. / May he rest in peace	SMCA093
Gardiner	Joseph	Henry	No Date	No Date	Also his eight little children, Teresa, Frances Sophia, Joseph Henry, Richard Thomas and four without names (child of George H. Gardiner)	SMCD264
Gardiner, Jr.	Joseph	Leo	Jul. 16, 1937	Nov. 30, 1996	A2C US Air Force / A kind and gentle man / Married Oct 20, 1962 / There are 2 emblems on the stone for Assistant Chief Hughesville Fire Dept. and U.S. Mail	SMC2161
Gardiner, Sr.	Joseph	Llewellyn	Nov. 22, 1913	Aug. 9, 1969		SMC2173
Gardiner	Joseph	Warren	Jun. 14, 1915	Feb. 9, 1936		NSP659
Gardiner	L.	S.	No Date	1851	Age 45 / info is from the Historical Society Research and the 1940 DAR book pg 19 located at the College of Southern MD, LaPlata, MD.	SMCNoStone
Gardiner	Lillian	V.	1880	1968		NSP352
Gardiner	Lillie	A.	Feb. 20, 1852	Jun. 29, 1876		SMCE057
Gardiner	Louise	Parlett	Dec. 17, 1923	Nov. 5, 2001	Back of stone	SIC4108
Gardiner	Lucy	Ann	Feb. 9, 1846	Aug. 11, 1936	w/o Thomas R Gardiner	SIC3039
Gardiner	Margaret	Frere	Oct. 28, 1906	Nov. 19, 1986		SIC6024
Gardiner	Margaret	Helen	No Date	Feb. 25, 1905	IHS / In memory of / Rest in peace / Daughters of Ignatius F & Catherine Gardiner (Sister to Annie Frances Gardiner)	SMCD252
Gardiner	Margaret	I.	1923	1991	Mother	SPL5095

Last Name	First Name	Middle Name	Date of Birth	Date of Death	Transcription / Notes	Cemetery Code
Gardiner	Margaret	K.	Mar. 2, 1920	Nov. 17, 2002	Mother / In Loving Memory	CLV379
Gardiner	Margaret	Summers, Bowling	May 10, 1848	Sep. 28, 1900	To the memory of / Beloved w/o Francis D. Gardiner / Requiescat in pace	SMCA077
Gardiner	Marguerite	Geraldine	Dec. 13, 1895	Sep. 3, 1983		SIC3056
Gardiner	Maria	Theresa	1878	1968		SMCA142
Gardiner	Mary	A.	No Date	Jul. 4, 1877	Our Aunt / Age 76 years	SMCD301
Gardiner	Mary	Angela	Sep. 25, 1914	Aug. 27, 1979	per website Rootsweb.com her last name is Gardiner	NSP883
Gardiner	Mary	Catharine	Oct. 24, 1828	Oct. 6, 1892	To our mother Mary Catharine Gardiner w/o Jos. D. Gardiner / May she rest in peace	SMCA097
Gardiner	Mary	Catherine	Jun. 22, 1827	May 29, 1863	w/o Benj. W. Gardiner Mary Catherine Gardiner Old stone that is difficult to read / Info is from the Historical Society Research located at the College of Southern MD, LaPlata, MD	OSP158
Gardiner	Mary	E.	Nov. 14, 1883	Apr. 7, 1966		NSP510
Gardiner	Mary	Eliza, Mudd	1813	1869	In loving memory / Back of Stone: Erected by the family 2001	SMCD225
Gardiner	Mary	Ellen	No Date	Jul. 1854	w/o George Gardiner / Departed this life In the 64 yrs of her age / May she rest in peace	OSP071
Gardiner	Mary	I.	1878	1960		NSP641
Gardiner	Mary	Imogene	Jan. 23, 1934	Jul. 24, 1935		NSP639
Gardiner	Mary	Imogene	Aug. 18, 1911	Dec. 3, 2002		NSP638
Gardiner	Mary	Lou	Sep. 11, 1875	Apr. 5, 1928		SMCA140
Gardiner	Mary	M.	1889	1957		SIC3049
Gardiner	Mary	Marjorie	1914	1992		NSP419
Gardiner	Mary	Regina	No Date	Apr. 15, 1901	In the 57 year of her age / "May she rest in peace"	OSP021
Gardiner	Mary	Rose	No Date	1838	Our sister / d/o Francis I. & Catharine Gardiner / aged 17 years. / May she rest in peace. (Top part of the stone with her name on it is broken off and laying up against the rest of the headstone. / Info is also from the 1940 DAR book pg 199	SMCC007A
Gardiner	Mary	Rose	No Date	Jun. 24, 1838	d/o Ignatius F. Gardiner / In the 17th year of her age. May they rest in peace. Amen	SMCC003

Last Name	First Name	Middle Name	Date of Birth	Date of Death	Transcription / Notes	Cemetery Code
Gardiner	Mary		Mar. 22, 1801	Feb. 5, 1861	Sacred to the memory of / consort of John F. Gardiner / Leaving one Daughter and three Sons, to mourn their irreparable loss / "May she rest in peace" / Side of stone: This monument has been placed here by a devoted husband in grateful remembrance / side of stone: May her exemplary piety and many virtues never fade in the memory of her husband, children and friends	SMCA099
Gardiner	Mildred	Mae	Nov. 1, 1913	Jan. 1, 1998	Loving wife and mom	SMC2007
Gardiner	Nancy	Jo	1936	1939		SIC6023
Gardiner	Paul	Robert	Jan. 11, 1931	May 12, 1994		NSP425
Gardiner	Peggy		Nov. 14, 1934	Nov. 14, 2006		SIC6026
Gardiner	Philip	I.	Aug. 25, 1922	No Date	In loving memory	NSP885
Gardiner	Richard	H.	Dec. 27, 1836	Nov. 1, 1877	To our brother / Requiescat in Pace	SMCA079
Gardiner	Richard	Thomas	No Date	No Date	Also his eight little children, Teresa, Frances Sophia, Joseph Henry, Richard Thomas and four without names	SMCD264
Gardiner	Rose	DeLima	Oct. 8, 1875	Mar. 15, 1943		NSP422
Gardiner	Rubey		Jan. 10, 1877	May 18, 1881	s/o T.L. & Fannie Gardiner	SMCE005
Gardiner	Samuel	Jerome	Nov. 9, 1901	Aug. 13, 1967		NSP424
Gardiner	Sarah	C.	Jul. 12, 1848	Oct. 8, 1932	May she rest in peace	OSP021
Gardiner	Sarah	Frances	1907	1992		NSP423
Gardiner	Sarah	M.	1834	1893	In memory of	SMCD224
Gardiner	Sophia	A.	No Date	May 31, 1874	To our mother / Relict of George H Gardiner / Aged 65 years / May she rest in peace	SMCD262
Gardiner	Sophia		No Date	Feb. 19, 1901	In the 76 yr of her age / "May she rest in peace"	OSP023
Gardiner	T.	Percy	Nov. 17, 1903	Nov. 25, 1994		NSP527
Gardiner	T.	Elzear	May 23, 1813	Oct. 9, 1886	His wife (Right side of stone)	SMCE057
Gardiner	Teresa		No Date	No Date	Also his eight little children, Teresa, Frances Sophia, Joseph Henry, Richard Thomas and four without names (child of George H. Gardiner)	SMCD264
Gardiner	Thelma	K.	Sep. 28, 1905	Aug. 1, 1981		NSP921
Gardiner	Thomas	Cecil	1878	1961		NSP407

Last Name	First Name	Middle Name	Date of Birth	Date of Death	Transcription / Notes	Cemetery Code
Gardiner, Col.	Thomas	I.	No Date	Dec. 29, 1874	Col. / youngest son of John E & Catharine Gardiner departed this life / at the hour of 8 o'clock P.M. In the 62nd year of his age / Requiescat in Pace / This momument placed here by his Brother, Sister and Nieces, in grateful remembrance	SMCD307
Gardiner	Thomas	R.	Aug. 17, 1845	Jan. 31, 1931		SIC3039
Gardiner	Thomas	Samuel	1806	1859	In loving memory / Back of Stone: Erected by the family 2001	SMCD225
Gardiner	Unknown		No Date	Jul. 11, 1956	Infant s/o Thomas and Ann Gardiner	NSP528
Gardiner	Unknown		No Date	No Date	Per Sister Miriam John at Mt. Carmel Monastery two special plots to south of crucifix are on an angle, north to south, 1 and 2 are for two Gardiner sisters	GMCNo Stone
Gardiner	William	M.	1835	1916		SIC3049
Gardiner	William	Paul	Feb. 28, 1918	No Date		SMC2158
Gardiner, Jr.	William	P.	Mar. 28, 1923	Feb. 1, 1951	Death date on stone was changed from 1953 to 1951	NSP680
Gardiner	William	Ralph	Oct. 5, 1908	Jul. 12, 1985		NSP637
Gardiner	Wm.	Purcell	May 15, 1891	Jan. 25, 1946		NSP681
Gardner	Patricia	Irene	1933	2001	Thornton Funeral Home Marker / info is from Catholic Cemeteries	HGH4261
Garett	William		No Date	Sep. 7, 1934	Info is from Christ Church microfilm Reel 3, Pg 238-239 located at the College of Southern MD, LaPlata, MD	MTRNoStone
Garland	Clifton		No Date	No Date	Name only	SPL2038
Garland	Harriet		No Date	No Date	Name only	SPL2038
Garner	Adelaide	Gray	Nov. 2, 1909	Sep. 5, 1986		MTR3011
Garner	Ann	C.	1869	1945	Mother	SJO2112
Garner	Arthur	Richard	1909	1963		CLV227
Garner	Audrey	C.	Nov. 21, 1931	Aug. 24, 1974	Wife - Mother / Beloved One	SJO4144
Garner	Augustus		No Date	Dec. 10, 1929	Info is from Christ Church microfilm Reel 3, Pg 236-237 located at the College of Southern MD, LaPlata, MD	MTRNoStone
Garner	Benjamin	Franklin	Jan. 23, 1902	Apr. 27, 1949		CLV245
Garner	Bernard	E.	Feb. 2, 1913	Feb. 9, 1913		SAC1006
Garner	Blanche	Davis	Dec. 4, 1918	Jan. 17, 2004	Married Apr 12, 1941	MTR4105
Garner	Celestial	G.	Aug. 3, 1863	Jun. 16, 1901	w/o Geo. L. Garner	MTR4100

Last Name	First Name	Middle Name	Date of Birth	Date of Death	Transcription / Notes	Cemetery Code
Garner	Celestial	R.	Nov. 30, 1884	Feb. 17, 1953		MTR4102
Garner	Charles	Beverly	Jun. 16, 1860	Mar. 13, 1934		MTR2116
Garner	Charles	H.	1900	1975		SAC1077
Garner	Charles	R.	1889	1963	Wife / Husband	MTR2131
Garner	Charles		1902	1971	Beloved h/o Louise T. Garner	SCA006
Garner	Chloe	Ellen	Nov. 16, 1841	Sep. 17, 1929		MTR2115
Garner	Daniel	Ginn	Jun. 24, 1948	Feb. 4, 2000	They That Wait Upon The Lord Shall Renew Their Strength They Shall Mount Up With Wings as Eagles Isaiah 40:31	SMY2152
Garner	Edmonia		1877	1968		SCA004
Garner	Elizabeth	H.	1872	1955		SAC1096
Garner	Elsie	L.	1903	1994		SAC1077
Garner	Estelle	E.	Nov. 1, 1900	Oct. 26, 1963		SIC7031A
Garner	Evelyn	Genevieve	Jun. 30, 1923	Dec. 13, 2006	Info is from Maryland Independent Newspaper Dec 20, 2006	SACNostone
Garner	Frances	M.	1860	1927		SCL2091
Garner	Frances	V.	1887	1950	Mother	SJO6036
Garner	Francis	C.	Jan. 26, 1930	No Date		MTR4218
Garner	Francis		1913	1918	son	SCA002
Garner	G.	Sellman	May 15, 1890	Aug. 15, 1974		MTR4104
Garner	Geo	Sellman	Oct. 6, 1912	Jan. 17, 1913	Infant s/o Geo. Sellman and Ormye Isadora Garner	MTR4103
Garner	George	L.	Nov. 12, 1921	Oct. 11, 1980		MTR4253
Garner	George	L.	Jun. 12, 1858	Jun. 11, 1911		MTR4100
Garner	George	L.	Apr. 11, 1925	Apr. 1, 1927		SAC1005
Garner	George	Washington	1824	Jun. 25, 1891	In memory of / Aged 67 years. An honest man, the noblest work of God. None knew him but to love him. None named him but to praise Note: The church has placed parts of stones and loose stones in a plot by themselves	SMY1003 SMY1004
Garner	George	Edward	Jun. 3, 1870	Mar. 25, 1949		CLV248
Garner	Georgia	V.	1900	No Date	Wife / Husband	MTR2131

Last Name	First Name	Middle Name	Date of Birth	Date of Death	Transcription / Notes	Cemetery Code
Garner, Sr.	Harold	Brent	Jul. 16, 1926	Aug. 5, 2005	In loving memory / Feb 25, 1950 / S SGT US Army WW II / Purple Heart	SAC3111
Garner	Harris	Beverly	No Date	No Date	Info is from church records	MTRNoStone
Garner	Hazel	C.	1915	No Date		SPL6083
Garner	Isabella		Apr. 26, 1840	Nov. 7, 1892	In memory of / Old stone that is broken off base and is laying on the ground. It is also cracked in half	SJO6061
Garner	Ivernette	C.	May 15, 1890	Oct. 25, 1891		MTR4100
Garner	J.	Enoch	1875	1960		CLV228
Garner	James	Heber	1889	1940		MTR4099
Garner, Sr.	James	Leonard	Feb. 23, 1924	No Date	Married Nov. 24, 1946	MTR4050
Garner	Jane	Catherine	Jul. 25, 1875	Sep. 19, 1946	Beloved Mother / May She Rest in Peace	CLV247
Garner	John	Ollie	Mar. 22, 1915	Jul. 11, 1984		SCA009
Garner	John	Wm.	Jan. 7, 1840	May 31, 1923		SAC2027
Garner	Joseph	A.	1894	1963		SJO2083
Garner	Joseph	Sidney	Feb. 8, 1908	Sep. 6, 1982		SCA007
Garner	Julia	Beverly	Jun. 24, 1895	Jan. 5, 1967		MTR2114
Garner	Julia	Cecelia	Jan. 17, 1856	Sep. 4, 1932		MTR2117
Garner	L.	Roberta	Jun. 24, 1932	Sep. 19, 1986	Lillian / First name is from church records	MTR4218
Garner	Laurence	S.	Jul. 17, 1925	Dec. 7, 1929		MTR4057
Garner	Lelia	B.	Jun. 18, 1905	Aug. 12, 1984		MTR4056
Garner	Lillian	Beatrice	Mar. 18, 1936	Sep. 1, 1936		SIC5098
Garner	Lillian	Cox	May 5, 1904	May 9, 1922	If I could have my dearest wish fulfilled and take my chance of all earth's treasures too or choose from whatever I will I would ask for you. Loved in life in death remembered by her loving husband & mother	SJO2111
Garner	Lyon	S.	Jun. 6, 1895	Nov. 21, 1966		MTR4056
Garner	M.	Ida	May 2, 1876	Oct. 5, 1939	Mother	ZBC168
Garner	Marbury	Edward	Mar. 23, 1896	Jul. 1, 1963	Maryland PVT BTRY B 33 Field Arty WW I	SJO2113
Garner	Marie	Kelly	May 20, 1926	No Date	Married Nov. 24, 1946	MTR4050
Garner	Mary	B.	No Date	No Date	And family	HGH3090
Garner	Mary	Beatrice	Jul. 22, 1937	Jun. 6, 1975		SCA001
Garner	Mary	R Murphy	Feb. 1, 1892	Sep. 25, 1981	In loving memory of	SIC4114

Last Name	First Name	Middle Name	Date of Birth	Date of Death	Transcription / Notes	Cemetery Code
Garner	Mary	Tynan	1914	1951		SIC7052
Garner	Minnie	E.	Aug. 15, 1865	Feb. 10, 1946		SAC1076
Garner	Miranda	E.	1882	1962		CLV228
Garner	Ormye	I.	Feb. 16, 1889	Oct. 11, 1969		MTR4104
Garner	Pearl	E.	Nov. 12, 1895	May 18, 1968	Maryland PVT Co G 313 Infantry WWI	SAC1097
Garner, Jr.	Reginald	Ralph	Jun. 24, 1949	Oct. 30, 1962	Son	SPL6084
Garner, Sr.	Reginald	Ralph	Jul. 18, 1906	Oct. 24, 1991	Middle name is from church records	SPL6083
Garner	Richard	A.	1852	1921		SCL2091
Garner	Richard	A.	1865	1928		SAC1096
Garner	Robert	Edward	Feb. 17, 1933	Mar. 27, 1984	PVT US Army Korea	SJO2078
Garner	Robert	L.	1878	1935		SCA004
Garner	Robert	M.	Apr. 25, 1899	Jul. 30, 1967		SIC7031A
Garner	Robert	S.	Feb. 19, 1868	Aug. 23, 1946		SAC1076
Garner	Robert	W.	1906	1918	Son	SCA003
Garner	Roland	F.	1907	1999	23rd Psalm	ZBC130
Garner	Rosebelle		Jul. 21, 1895	Dec. 29, 1994	Birth date on stone was changed, ancestry.com shows birth as 1895	SIC8037
Garner	Rudolph	L.	Jan. 3, 1920	Oct. 1, 2005	Married Apr 12, 1941	MTR4105
Garner	Rudolph	L.	May 30, 1944	Nov. 26, 2000	"Sonny"	MTR4082
Garner	Russell	Louis	Dec. 1, 1914	Aug. 22, 1950	Maryland / Pfc 18 infantry WWII / BSM	SIC8004
Garner	Ruth	C.	1913	2003	23rd Psalm	ZBC132
Garner	Shirley	Mae	Sep. 11, 1930	No Date	In loving memory / Feb 25, 1950	SAC3111
Garner	Thomas	A.	Mar. 28, 1889	Dec. 29, 1957		SIC8037
Garner	Walter	R.	Aug. 7, 1898	Oct. 28, 1932		CLV246
Garner	William		No Date	Feb. 12, 1960	Info is from Christ Church microfilm Reel 4 Pg 280-281 located at the College of Southern MD, LaPlata, MD	MTRNoStone
Garner	William	Samuel, Gilbert	Feb. 19, 1885	Mar. 26, 1902	In memory of / beloved s/o Charles B and Julia Albrittain Garner	MTR2118
Garner	Wilson	Samuel	Oct. 29, 1917	Jan. 31, 1992	Sgt US Army WW II	SIC8038
Garner	Winifred	M.	1897	1974		MTR4099

Last Name	First Name	Middle Name	Date of Birth	Date of Death	Transcription / Notes	Cemetery Code
Garner	Wm.	F., McP	Sep.t 22, 1830	Sep. 23, 1885	Wm. F. McP Garner / Old stone with the top right corner missing that shows the last name / last name is from the 1940 DAR book page 83, located at The College of Southern MD, LaPlata, MD	SJO6062
Garner, Jr.	Xavier	W.	1914	1971		MTR3012
Garner	Xavier	Worthington	Oct. 22, 1891	Dec. 10, 1963	In loving memory of	SIC4114
Garnette	Robert		No Date	Nov. 7, 1896	Info is from Christ Church microfilm Reel 2 Pg 173-174 located at the College of Southern MD, LaPlata, MD	MTRNoStone
Garret	Robert		No Date	Nov. 5, 1896	Info is from Christ Church microfilm Reel 2 Pg 173-174 located at the College of Southern MD, LaPlata, MD	MTRNoStone
Garrett	Annie	S.	1918	1989		POM218
Garrett	Bert	W.	1916	1992		POM218
Garrett	Joseph	Francis	Jun. 19, 1906	Jul. 29, 1994	US Navy World War II	HGH4169
Garrett	Verlinda	Ann	Jun. 9, 1904	Apr. 15, 1995		HGH4169
Garvey	Florence	Anna	1922	No Date	In loving memory	SIC9096
Garvey, Jr.	William	E.	1922	2009	In loving memory	SIC9096
Gassaway, Jr.	Arthur		May 5, 1916	Mar. 17, 1969	Maryland STM2 USNR World War II	OAK125
Gatchell	Hazel	Frances	Aug. 19, 1911	Oct. 17, 2005	"Nana"	SJO2278
Gates	Amelia	A.	No Date	No Date	Age 77 years. Gone but not forgotten	SPL5082
Gates	Andrew	M.	Jul. 24, 1863	Apr. 14, 1932	A stone bench is grave marker	CLV235A
Gates	Anna	C.	Apr. 26, 1923	No Date	True Love / m. Jul 31, 1948	SPL5104
Gates	Benson	W.	Nov. 3, 1893	Dec. 17, 1944	Md. Pvt., US Army WWI	SPL5083
Gates, Jr.	Benson	W.	Feb. 20, 1930	Jul. 31, 2005	TSCT US Air Force Korea	SPL5086
Gates	Catherine	Irene	Jan. 19, 1933	Apr. 21, 1991	Our Beloved Momma	SPL2022
Gates	Clyde		1894	1945		SPL6190
Gates	Consuelo	V.	1895	1967		SPL5103
Gates, Jr.	Earl	P.	Dec. 18, 1923	Apr. 9, 2005	True Love / m. Jul 31, 1948	SPL5104
Gates, Sr.	Earl	P.	1898	1956		SPL5103
Gates	Ellen	Matildia	Nov. 1, 1902	Nov. 28, 1988	Additional info is from church records	SPL2023
Gates	Florence	Inez	Nov. 2, 1913	Jun. 29, 1914	d/o Ovelton and Ruth Gates / Our darling baby budded on earth to bloom in heaven	SPL6185
Gates	Florence	V.	1863	1917	Rest sweet rest	OFE1040

Last Name	First Name	Middle Name	Date of Birth	Date of Death	Transcription / Notes	Cemetery Code
Gates	George	E.	Jun. 26, 1890	Jul. 29, 1960		CMX2036
Gates	Grace	Lee	May 6, 1888	Aug. 19, 1888	d/o Pliny & Ida C. Gates	SPL1021
Gates	Ida	C.	1866	1941		SPL5079
Gates	Jennings	L.	1897	1964		SPL2023
Gates	Margaret	Alice	Aug. 18, 1922	Dec. 5, 1964		SPL5088
Gates	Margaret	M.	1910	1994	Buried at Sea	SPL5084
Gates	Mary	Isabel	Oct. 22, 1897	Feb. 10, 1984	Additional info is from church records	SPL6190
Gates	Mitchell	O.	1887	1942		SPL6191
Gates	Naomi	C.	Apr. 19, 1887	Mar. 20, 1963		SIG058
Gates	Naomi	I.	1893	1938		MRB022
Gates	Patricia		No Date	Aug. 29, 1953	An Angel	SPL2024
Gates	Peter	P.	1857	1954		SPL5079
Gates	Randolph		Sep. 16, 1902	Dec. 16, 1962		SPL5049
Gatt	Mary	E.	Oct. 6, 1935	Jan. 27, 1989		CLV017
Gatt, Sr.	Robert	W.	Dec. 10, 1930	Jul. 23, 2005	Metal marker with 12 A.B on it / info is from church records	CLV018
Gatton	Betty	Ann	Apr. 11, 1932	No Date		SMCD185
Gatton	Delphine		1861	1928	Peace perfect peace by the ongoing duties pressed to do the will of Jesus, this is rest	OFE3013
Gatton	James	Calvin	Mar. 11, 1930	Jun. 9, 2006		SMCD185
Gatton	Joseph	B.	1865	1951		OFE3014
Gaumond	Robert	Louis	Dec. 18, 1983	Dec. 12, 2002	Sealed by the spirit and marked as Christ's own forever (Baby) / Info is from the Historical Society Research located at The College of Southern MD, LaPlata, MD	SPL3085
Gauthier	Unknown		No Date	Apr. 7, 1965		SCLNoStone
Gaynor	Agnes		1927	1989		SMI011
Gayon	Anna	Lee	Jul. 15, 1932	Jan. 26, 1935	Our darling	NJB139
Gehring	Barbara	C.	Mar. 31, 1901	Feb. 11, 1987		SMC4061
Gehring	Herman		Oct. 28, 1901	Apr. 12, 1962		SMC4060
Gehring	James	Elwood	Jul. 19, 1931	Nov. 12, 1988	SGT US Army Korea	SMC4093
Gehring	Martha	A.	Sep. 6, 1935	No Date	Beloved wife and mother	SMC4094
Geib	Hazel	Mitchell, Geib	Aug. 3, 1935	Oct. 16, 2005		LUM219
Gentilcore, Jr	Anthony	Michael	May 28, 1967	Jun. 30, 1988	Beloved son and brother "Tony"	SCL1217

Last Name	First Name	Middle Name	Date of Birth	Date of Death	Transcription / Notes	Cemetery Code
George	Frances	Brooke	Nov. 9, 1917	Nov. 4, 1994		SJE163
George	Henry	Wardelly	Jan. 20, 1914	Jul. 5, 1990		SJE163
George	Pauline		1917	1986		POM107
George	Henry	Wardelly	Jan. 20, 1914	Jul. 5, 1990	US Army SSG US Air Force WWII Korea	SJE184
George, III	Richard		Jul. 14, 1991	Jun. 8, 2006	Age 14 Green Funeral Home Marker	NJB495
Geremia	Andrew	D.	1927	1996	Together forever / Married Jun 14, 1952	SMC4255
Geremia	Mary	P.	1931	No Date	Together forever / Married Jun 14, 1952	SMC4255
Gerhardt	Carin	Aileen	May 19, 1978	May 27, 1978	Our beautiful daughters/ Full of love and courage. / Asleep in Jesus / Our Baby	NSP719
Gerhardt	Lorin	Ann, Ellen	Aug. 24, 1981	Aug. 2, 2000	Our beautiful daughters/ Full of love and courage.	NSP719
Gernhardt	Gary	K.	Dec. 3, 1945	No Date	Col. USAF	LUM009
Gernhardt	Seli	Marie	Oct. 20, 1965	Jun. 18, 1994	Veterinarian / They loved horses	LUM009
Gernhardt	Vicki	L.	May 15, 1945	No Date	Equestrienne	LUM009
Geuder	Cassandra		Jan. 30, 1984	Feb. 28, 1985	Back of stone: God's special child	SJO1101
Gholson	Thelma		Apr. 14, 1929	Apr. 3, 2011	Thornton Funeral Home Marker / Age 81 d/o the late Robert Butler and the late Marie Thomas Butler. Obit appeared in the Maryland Independent Newspaper dated Apr 8, 2011	PGN093
Gibbon	Liza	Ellen	Apr. 17, 1862	Dec. 23, 1865	In Memory of Liza Ellen Gibbon Eldest d/o Warner & M. Rebecca Gibbon / Aged 3 years 8 mos & 6 days. She was lovely. She was fair and for awhile was given; An Angel came and claimed his own and bore her home to heaven	OFE2077
Gibbons	Alexander		No Date	Jul. 18, 1877	Info is from church records	OFENoStone
Gibbons	Clara	Cecelia	1881	1959	Sister of Jane Rosalie Bowie	MTR4169
Gibbons	Dorothy	J.	1922	1997		CHR122
Gibbons	Elaine	S.	1929	No Date		OFE4118
Gibbons	Elizabeth	A.	Jun. 4, 1860	Jan. 30, 1897	Age 36 yrs and 8 mos (She is on side 3 of the stone)	SMY1110
Gibbons	Frances	Buckley	1908	July 1963	info is from church records	OFENoStone
Gibbons	Francis	J.	1918	2001		CHR122
Gibbons	Glodie	U.	Dec. 5, 1856	Mar. 7, 1907	w/o J.P. Gibbons / She was a kind and affectionate wife, a fond mother and a friend to all	SJO3128

Last Name	First Name	Middle Name	Date of Birth	Date of Death	Transcription / Notes	Cemetery Code
Gibbons	Henry	A.	1859	1930		OFE2104
Gibbons	Hezekiah	M.	Dec. 4, 1861	Dec. 27, 1889	h/o Eliza D. Gibbons	OFE1056
Gibbons	Ida	V.	1865	1935		OFE2103
Gibbons	James	H.	Aug. 4, 1785	Feb. 6, 1863	Sacred to the memory of James H. Gibbons "Requiescat in pace" / From every eye he wipes the tear All sighs and sorrows cease / More alternate hope or fear But everlasting peace	OSP075
Gibbons	James	H.	Apr. 25, 1838	Feb. 17, 1921	Rest in peace	OSP020
Gibbons	John	H.	Apr. 5, 1818	Oct. 18, 1843	IHS / In memory of / The sweet remembrance of the Just Shall flourish when they sleep in dust	OSP076
Gibbons	John		No Date	Jul. 21, 1966 ?	Aged 79 years / Information is from the Historical Society Research located at The College of Southern MD, LaPlata, MD	SIGNo Stone
Gibbons, Sr	Louis	Ralph	1903	Jan. 4, 1970	Age 66 / info is from church records	OFENoStone
Gibbons	Lucille	Mae	No Date	Jun. 22, 2004	Age 84 "Sis" / info is from church records	OFENoStone
Gibbons	Margaret	D.	Nov. 23, 1795	Dec. 31, 1832	In Memory of	GIB002
Gibbons	Mary	A.	No Date	Apr. 6, 1859	In Memory of / w/o Warner Gibbons / in the 26th year of her age. Blessed are the dead who die in the lord	OFE2105
Gibbons	May	Angela	Jan. 23, 1897	Jul. 1897	She is on side 2 of the stone	SMY1110
Gibbons	Ollie	L.	1925	1986	"Cotton"	OFE4118
Gibbons	Oswell		Oct. 30, 1791	No Date	In Memory of (stone is broken, can only locate 1 piece of the stone) Birth Date is from The Historical Society Research located at The College of Southern MD, LaPlata, MD	GIB001
Gibbons	Susan	E.	Jul. 9, 1957	Nov. 15, 1978		SMCA252
Gibbons	Thomas	M.	No Date	Sep. 6, 1915	Age 47 yrs (He is on side 1 of the stone)	SMY1110
Gibbs	Anthony	Addison	Nov. 4, 1960	Jul. 4, 1992	Always and forever / Love you / Bessy, Deanna and Alex	PGN038
Gibbson	Viola		No Date	No Date	Info is from church records	SHINoStone
Gibson	Ellen	Anne	Apr. 26, 1944	Jul. 22, 1998		SIC4001
Gibson	George	Roland	Jan. 11, 1918	Sep. 13, 1983	A gentle man	SIC4002
Gibson	George	William	Apr. 5, 1971	Apr. 14, 1986		SMC1068
Gibson	Glenn	Michael	Mar. 15, 1953	Apr. 17, 1972	Honor, courage, sacrifice / Our Beloved Son	NSP724

Last Name	First Name	Middle Name	Date of Birth	Date of Death	Transcription / Notes	Cemetery Code
Gibson	Mary	Anne, Mudd	Jul. 26, 1916	Feb. 22, 1996		SMC1068
Gifford	Kathy	Beth	Oct. 8, 1953	Apr. 28, 1999		OSM150
Gifford	Robert	A.	Apr. 16, 1925	Jul. 30, 2001		OSM149
Gilbert	Florence	E.	1904	1991		NSP226
Gilbert	Mae	Eidson	Nov. 15, 1919	Mar. 20, 1956	Nee Collins	ODE426
Gilka	Jennifer	E.	Mar. 19, 1973	Mar. 19, 1973	Born and died on same day	SJO3213
Gilka	Jodie	M.	Mar. 19, 1973	Mar. 19, 1973	Born and died on same day	SJO3213
Gillespie	Ann	M.	Jun. 3, 1929	No Date	In loving Memory	NSP752
Gillespie	Anne	M.	Apr. 8, 1942	No Date		SIC9016
Gillespie	Arnold	E.	Aug. 16, 1926	Nov. 5, 2001	In loving Memory	NSP752
Gillespie	Frank	Joseph	1886	1963		NSP856
Gillespie	James	J.	Feb. 28, 1941	Oct. 28, 2005		SIC9016
Gillespie, Jr.	Julian	Edgeworth	Mar. 9, 1931	Aug. 7, 1982	Gilly / In Posey Plot	SIC1049
Gilliam	Margaret	Mary	Aug. 27, 1918	May 14, 1995		SIG096
Gilliam	Millie	Ann	Jun. 18, 1935	Sep. 28, 1956		SPL4152
Gilliam	Richard	D.	Aug. 13, 1954	Sep. 21, 1999		SIG097
Gilliam	Tiffany	Nicole, Rose	Feb. 18, 1986	Jan. 11, 2006	Back of Stone: Like an angel, I came from heaven above, I shared my compassion, my pain, my love, I only stayed long enough to teach you how to love, to share and your goals to reach. / Tiffany / Annie / Missing you until we're together again	CMX2106
Gillilan	Edgar	Grover	Apr. 6, 1909	Apr. 29, 1978	Private US Marine Corps / WWII / Masonic Emblem	SPL4150
Gillilan	Grace	Louise	Jul. 31, 1910	May 5, 2003	Eastern Star Emblem / Obit appeared in Maryland Independent Newspaper May 7, 2003	SPL4150
Gillispie	Mary	E.	Apr. 18, 1943	Jan. 20, 2001		SIG103
Gillogly	Helen	B.	Jul. 9, 1924	Feb. 12, 2003	My wife and best friend	SCL3356
Gillogly, Sr.	William	P.	Dec. 16, 1931	No Date	My wife and best friend	SCL3356
Gillooly	John	Thomas	1923	1985	PFC US Army WW II	SCL3066
Gillott	Catherine	M.	Jun. 27, 1916	Feb. 13, 1996		SMCE045
Gilroy	Albert	B.	1860	1929		ODE181
Gilroy	Annie	M.	1886	1942		CMX2005
Gilroy	Arvilla	G.	Dec. 25, 1918	Jan. 15, 2005		SJE064

Last Name	First Name	Middle Name	Date of Birth	Date of Death	Transcription / Notes	Cemetery Code
Gilroy	Bernard		1905	1976		CMX2008
Gilroy	Beverly	M.	Mar..26, 1935	Feb. 4,1998	"Tookie" - In Loving Memory	GIL003
Gilroy	Catherine	Naomi	No Date	Nov. 1921	Buried Nov 28, 1921 age 15 (info is from Old Durham Church microfilm located at the College of Southern MD, LaPlata, MD)	ODENoStone
Gilroy	Charles	E.	1902	1972		NZN015
Gilroy	Charles	J.	1868	1939		NZN013
Gilroy	Clifton	Lee	Nov..22,1932	Nov..8,1989	Wooden Cross with painted letters and Arehart Funeral Home Marker	GIL006
Gilroy	Cora	B.	1878	1960		NZN013
Gilroy	Dorothy	M.	Jan. 19, 1930	No Date	Book of Life, married Sun. Feb 5, 1950	MTR1100
Gilroy, Sr.	Edward	L.	Jul. 4, 1904	Feb. 22, 1955		SJE068
Gilroy	Emily		Apr. 8, 1853	Apr. 2, 1917	A precious one from us has gone	SJE070
Gilroy	Ernest	S.	Oct. 25, 1906	Nov. 12, 1906	Twins / Twin to John W Gilroy	SJO2295
Gilroy	Florence	M.	1867	1939		ODE181
Gilroy	Floyd	C.	Oct. 27, 1926	Nov. 29, 1975	Book of life, married Sun. Feb 5, 1950 / PVT US Army WWII / From family And Loved Ones / Wife Dorothy, Sons Monty & Russell, Daughters Becky & Robin	MTR1100 MTR1102
Gilroy	Frank	L..	Sep. 24, 1910	Mar. 22, 1998	In loving memory	NJB209
Gilroy	George	W.	Feb. 22, 1903	Jun. 30, 1903		SJO2295
Gilroy	Gertrude	A.	Feb. 27, 1899	Aug. 25, 1961	Gone but not forgotten	ODE124
Gilroy	Gordon	M.	Sep. 6, 1950	Jan. 15, 2005	Forever in our hearts	CMX2011
Gilroy	Grace	M.	Mar. 4, 1912	Sep. 19, 1990	Rest now in heaven, time cannot dim the love you gave	CMX2010
Gilroy	Ida	Florine	Mar. 29, 1917	Nov. 6, 1985		CMX2160
Gilroy	J.	Berry	Mar..8,1908	Jul..26,1981		GIL016
Gilroy	James	Albert	No Date	Sep. 25, 1898	Age 4 yrs. (info is from Old Durham Church microfilm pg 83-84 located at the College of Southern MD, LaPlata, MD)	ODENoStone
Gilroy	James		Dec. 20, 1928	Jun. 2, 2009	James Gilroy / s/o the late James Barry Gilroy and the late Josephine Gilroy. h/o Joice Gilroy. Info is from the MD Independent newspaper dated Friday Jun 5, 2009 pg A10 Col 4	GILNo Stone
Gilroy	John	W.	Oct. 25, 1906	Nov. 12, 1906	Twins / Twin to Ernest S. Gilroy	SJO2295

Last Name	First Name	Middle Name	Date of Birth	Date of Death	Transcription / Notes	Cemetery Code
Gilroy	John	Lewis	May 18, 1913	Aug. 1, 1981		CMX2160
Gilroy	Josephine	M.	Apr. 5, 1912	Jul. 5, 1991		GIL016
Gilroy	Lollie	B.	Sep. 27, 1899	Feb. 14, 1980		GIL021
Gilroy	Maggie	E.	Sep. 28, 1882	Jan. 17, 1959		GIL023
Gilroy	Mary	Augusta	Jul. 21, 1879	Jan. 28, 1909	In Memory of	SJO2309
Gilroy	Mary	E.	Mar. 14, 1949	Jul. 19, 2006	In Loving Memory	GIL026
Gilroy	Mary	V.	1873	1945		NJB411
Gilroy	Maynard	Lloyd	Apr. 10, 1931	Jul. 15, 1993	In loving memory	CMX2077
Gilroy, Jr.	Maynard	M.	Jun. 27, 1946	No Date	In Loving Memory	GIL026
Gilroy, Sr.	Maynard	Mitchell	Apr. 29, 1910	Jan. 8, 1978	Tec 4 US Army WWII	CMX2161
Gilroy	Maynard	N.	1875	1964		CMX2005
Gilroy	Minnie	M.	1896	1963		CMX2008
Gilroy	Norman	J.	Aug. 25, 1898	Aug. 6, 1968		GIL019
Gilroy, Sr.	Paul	B.	Mar. 17, 1917	Jul. 23, 1995	Rest now in heaven, time cannot dim the love you gave	CMX2010
Gilroy	Paula	J.	No Date	No Date	Forever in our hearts	CMX2011
Gilroy	Pauline	Mary	Jul. 9, 1896	Feb. 16, 1980		SJE066
Gilroy	Pearl	Davis	Apr. 5, 1912	Dec. 7, 1996	In loving memory	NJB209
Gilroy, Sr.	Perry	W.	Jan. 21, 1876	Sep. 2, 1957		SJE067
Gilroy, Jr.	Perry	Wilmer	Jan. 19, 1916	Dec. 29, 1987	TEC 5 US Army WWII	SJE064
Gilroy	Ruby	M.	1906	1974		NZN015
Gilroy	S. J.	Sabina	Nov. 2, 1867	Nov. 18, 1895	d/o R. L. & J. C. Wedding / w/o A. B. Gilroy / By her parents	PIS134
Gilroy	Sandra	Robin	May 31, 1956	Jun. 26, 1957	We miss you darling	MTR1106
Gilroy	Shirley	L.	Sep. 7, 1935	May 15, 1936		GIL020
Gilroy	Stacy	Sue	Nov. 1, 1982	Aug. 30, 1984	Daughter	CMX2176
Gilroy, Sr,	Thomas	Clark	Aug. 28, 1934	Feb. 5, 1991	Wooden Cross with painted letters and Arehart Funeral Home Marker	GIL001
Gilroy	Unknown		No Date	No Date	Unknown who the parents are, name is painted on a white stone (Baby)	GIL028
Gilroy	Unknown		No Date	No Date	Painted White Brick Paver - unknown who the parents are (Baby)	GIL015

Last Name	First Name	Middle Name	Date of Birth	Date of Death	Transcription / Notes	Cemetery Code
Gilroy	Unknown		No Date	No Date	Painted White Brick Paver - unknown who the parents are (Baby)	GIL014
Gilroy	Unknown		No Date	No Date	Painted White Brick Paver - According to Betty Gilroy, this is a child of Wm.S and Margaet "Maggie" Gilroy (this is a second baby)	GIL013
Gilroy	Unknown		No Date	No Date	Painted White Brick Paver - According to Betty Gilroy, this is a child of Wm.S and Margaet "Maggie" Gilroy	GIL012
Gilroy	Unknown		No Date	Nov. 1942	Twin Babies / Buried Nov 22, 1942 (info is from Old Durham Church microfilm pg 162 located at the College of Southern MD, LaPlata, MD)	ODENoStone
Gilroy	Violet	G.	1900	1987		NZN014
Gilroy	Wayne	Albert	May 15, 1958	Jan..14,2000	Wooden Cross with painted letters and Arehart Funeral Home Marker	GIL002
Gilroy	William	J. B.	Nov. 17, 1900	Jul. 22, 1952		SJE069
Gilroy	William	M.	1870	1935		NJB412
Gilroy	William	S	Apr. 14, 1877	Dec. 6, 1935		GIL024
Gilroy	Zeland	T.	May 5, 1904	Aug. 30, 1988	Home at last	ODE123
Gilroy	Zella	F.	1919	1980		CMX2161
Gilroy	Zuleima	F., Johnson	Nov. 17, 1910	Aug. 10, 1993	Loving mother	NJB279
Giltner	Elva	Groves	Jan. 28, 1915	Jun. 22, 1989		CMX2156
Gimmel, Sr.	Michael	D.	1960	1978	To know him was to love him	OSM009
Gingell	Barry	E.	1891	1965		MTR4291
Gingell	Mary	V.	1905	1983		MTR4290
Gleason	George	H.	Jan. 30, 1858	Jan. 31, 1925		HNT032
Gleason	Mamie	M.	Aug. 13, 1878	Apr. 21, 1958		HNT031
Glista	Vincent	M.	Sep. 19, 1975	Jan. 16, 2005	"Vinnie" / Beloved Son And Brother	SCL1053
Gloden	George	L.	Nov. 18, 1907	Sep. 6, 1952		PIS027
Gloden	Isabelle	Carmichael	Dec. 21, 1861	Jul. 17, 1945	Asleep in Jesus	PIS005
Gloden	John	L.	1901	1983		PIS002
Gloden	Louis	L.	1904	1973		PIS002
Glovan	Marjorie	T.	Nov. 25, 1935	No Date	Together Forever	SJO6023
Glovan	Richard	L.	Jul. 14, 1959	May 3, 2000	Together Forever	SJO6023

Last Name	First Name	Middle Name	Date of Birth	Date of Death	Transcription / Notes	Cemetery Code
Glovan	Walter	E.	Jan. 28, 1930	No Date	Together Forever	SJO6023
Glover	Ida	Jean	Jul. 3, 1930	No Date		LUM010
Glover	Joseph		May 28, 1927	Apr. 13, 1994		LUM010
Gobble	Ruth	D.	Nov. 4, 1921	Jun. 18, 1981		SAC3089
Goelling	Sue	Ellen	Sep. 2, 1956	Apr. 23, 1991		SMC4166
Goggi	Joan	M.	Nov. 4, 1922	No Date	Married Aug. 10, 1943	SJO3102
Goggi	Louis	J.	May 16, 1920	May 23, 2004	Married Aug. 10, 1943	SJO3102
Golaboski	Leon	P.	Feb. 16, 1908	Jun. 11, 1989	MM 2 US Navy	SIG119
Golden	Addie	L.	Aug. 28, 1885	Mar. 5, 1967		CMX2092
Golden	Alexander	R.	1887	1952		CMX2092
Golden	Arthur		No Date	No Date	Stone: 19 / Numbered Stonemarkers have been placed on unmarked graves by church. Metal nameplate is attached to marker	CMX2063
Golden	Eugenia	Rennoe	Jun. 8, 1865	Mar. 11, 1927	His wife / May they rest in peace / Footstone: Mother	CMX2097
Golden	Hazel	A. Mills	1918	1944		CMX2092
Golden	Irene		Feb. 1873	No Date	w/o Sidney Golden / info is from Preston Williams list of Private Cemeteries in Charles County, located at the College of Southern MD, LaPlata, MD, and the 1900 census	GOLNoStone
Golden	John	A.	1898	1970		NJB426
Golden	John	W.	1918	1984	Father / Truly thine	CMX2112
Golden	John	W.	May 3, 1845	Mar. 6, 1926	His wife / May they rest in peace / Footstone: Father	CMX2097
Golden	Kate	M.	Aug. 13, 1844	Jul. 20, 1870	Sacred to the memory of / w/o Robert A. Golden She is not dead but sleepeth. Stone Maker is J. Jouvenal Wash'n D.C. Footstone: initials K.M.C.	CHG013
Golden	Katie	Adella	1888	1957		CMX2111
Golden, Mrs.	Lizzie	H.	Jul. 28, 1855	Sep. 23, 1880	d/o J. B. & V. Carpenter	PIS111
Golden	Maggie	M.	Jun. 1887	No Date	Infant d/o Sidney Golden / info is from Preston Williams list of Private Cemeteries in Charles County, located at the College of Southern MD, LaPlata, MD, and the 1900 census	GOLNoStone
Golden	Mamie	E.	1899	1984		NJB070
Golden	Mary	E.	1926	No Date	Mother / Truly thine	CMX2112

Last Name	First Name	Middle Name	Date of Birth	Date of Death	Transcription / Notes	Cemetery Code
Golden	Nora		May 10, 1879	Mar. 7, 1943		CMX2110
Golden	P.	W.	No Date	No Date	Stone: 18 / Numbered Stonemarkers have been placed on unmarked graves by church. No metal nameplate on marker. (info is from church records)	CMX2073
Golden	Richard	Cornelius	Apr. 25, 1925	May 19, 1988	S1 US Navy WWII / Masonic emblem on stone	NJB068
Golden	Richard	M.	1889	1960		NJB070
Golden	Robert	A.	May 9, 1921	May 19, 1921		NJB353
Golden	Sarah	P.	1900	1950		NJB426
Golden	Sidney		Oct. 1862	No Date	Info is from Preston Williams list of Private Cemeteries in Charles County, located at The College of Southern MD, LaPlata, MD, and the 1900 Census	GOLNoStone
Golden	Sylvia	Louise	Nov. 4, 1919	Oct. 3, 1981		CMX2113
Golden	William	A.	1916	1933		CMX2092
Golden	William	C.	1892	1969		CMX2111
Goldey	Ashley	Marie	May 11, 1998	Sep. 16, 1998	I Now Have Perfect Winds	SMY2046
Goldey	Donna	M., Bowling	Jan. 25, 1965	No Date		SMY2046
Goldey, Jr.	Howard	T.	May 6, 1969	No Date		SMY2046
Golding	Dorothy	Grinder	May 1, 1917	No Date		PKH132
Golding	William	D.	Aug. 16, 1915	Dec. 22, 1997		PKH132
Goldman	Anne	P.	1936	1970		CHR129
Goldring	Annie	Mae	Sep. 25, 1916	Mar. 8, 1996		SMY2068
Goldring	Blanche		Dec. 22, 1924	May 28, 1987	Ancestry.com website shows her last name is Goldring and she died in St Mary's County, MD	SMCD098
Goldring	Charles	Lindburgh	Aug. 31, 1936	Dec. 1, 2004	In loving memory of	SMC1033
Goldring	Donald	A.	May 20, 1959	Dec. 19, 1999	Pv1 US Army	SMY2098
Goldring	Emma	V.	Jul. 9, 1927	Jan. 22, 2000	Beloved Mother	SAC2096
Goldring	Erma	C.	Apr. 1, 1900	Dec. 19, 1987		SMC3022
Goldring, Sr.	James	Albert	Apr. 30, 1933	No Date		SMC4180
Goldring, Sr.	John	B.	Apr. 9, 1931	Mar. 16, 2001		SMC4207
Goldring	John	F.	Jun. 11, 1913	Feb. 19, 1983	Husband	SMY2039
Goldring, Jr.	Joseph	A.	Apr. 1, 1947	Feb. 9, 1968		SMC3023
Goldring	Margaret	T.	1933	1989	Mother	SMY2097

Last Name	First Name	Middle Name	Date of Birth	Date of Death	Transcription / Notes	Cemetery Code
Goldring	Mary	C.	Jan. 9, 1934	Aug. 29, 1990		SMC4092
Goldring	Mary	Ethel	Sep. 19, 1938	Apr. 12, 2002		SMC4180
Goldring	Mary	Frances	Dec. 25, 1925	Jan. 16, 1990		SMC4144
Goldring	Mary	Lucille	Jan. 14, 1951	Dec. 20, 1966		SMY2117
Goldring	Mary	V.	Aug. 22, 1931	Sep. 13, 1999	"Nana"	SMC4139
Goldring	Romaine	H.	1908	1973		SMC3294
Goldring	Thomas	R.	Jul. 28, 1906	Dec. 28, 1991		SMY2068
Goldring	William	J.	Feb. 26, 1945	Apr. 10, 1980		SMY2051
Goldring, Sr.	William	J.	May 7, 1925	Nov. 29, 2002	PFC US Army WW II	SMC4140
Goldring	William	R.	1902	1977		SMC3295
Goldsmith	A	Vertie	Apr. 25, 1934	Dec. 20, 1990		SMC1106
Goldsmith	A.	L.	1909	1924		OSP064
Goldsmith	Alexander		No Date	Apr. 16, 1883	Info is from church records	OFENoStone
Goldsmith	Anna	Frances	1904	Aug., 26, 1995	Per church records	OFE4117
Goldsmith, Jr.	Archie	Harold	Oct. 8, 1960	Feb. 3, 1992	We love you with all our heart	LUM020
Goldsmith, Sr.	Archie	Harold	Aug. 23, 1935	Mar. 4, 2004	"Buddy"	LUM021
Goldsmith	Archie	T.	1905	1948	Father	SIC6087
Goldsmith	Arlen	E.	No Date	Dec. 29, 1943	Name is shown on church records but burial location is unknown, date is the burial date, not death date	CHRNoStone
Goldsmith	Arlene	E	1892	1934	Mother	SIC1102
Goldsmith	B.	George	May 1, 1932	Jan. 25, 1992		SMC1106
Goldsmith	B.	Leroy	1905	1986		SMCA262
Goldsmith	Ballenger	S.	Nov. 28, 1884	May 1, 1945	s/o Robert B. and Georgeanna Hill Goldsmith / also has a small stone in front of the headstone with his name and dates on it	SIC6088
Goldsmith	Barbara	Ann	1952	1959	Baby / Our darling	CHR424
Goldsmith	Barbara	C.	Mar. 18, 1936	No Date	Together forever / Married Apr 19, 1954	SMC4258
Goldsmith	Benj	A.	1876	1954		SMCA264
Goldsmith	Bettie	Ellen	No Date	Aug. 11, 1934	Age 8 months / Buried Aug. 13, 1934 / info is from church records	OFENoStone
Goldsmith	Bunnie		No Date	Oct. 8, 1898	Info is from church records	OFENoStone

Last Name	First Name	Middle Name	Date of Birth	Date of Death	Transcription / Notes	Cemetery Code
Goldsmith	Caroline		No Date	No Date	Grave is marked with a cinderblock per the church records	CHRNoStone
Goldsmith	Chesley		1882	1913		SMY3027
Goldsmith	Chester	J.	Apr. 5, 1906	Oct. 23, 1977		NSP947
Goldsmith	Cora	M.	1876	1948		SMCA265
Goldsmith	Cora		1888	1951		OFE2003
Goldsmith	Dallas	S.	1906	1945	At Rest	OFE3021
Goldsmith	Dallise	A.	May 9, 1895	Apr. 25, 1914		OFE4114
Goldsmith	Donald	E.	Sep. 18, 1933	Mar. 8, 2007	Together forever / Married Apr 19, 1954	SMC4258
Goldsmith	Elise	B.	Feb. 1, 1893	Jun. 10, 1970	d/o John M and Belle Simms Boarman	SIC6088
Goldsmith	Ella	Elizabeth	Mar. 13, 1863	Feb. 27, 1929	w/o Townley Goldsmith / May she rest in peace / Stone shows the day of birth as 12, small flat stone to the ground shows day of birth as 13	SIC1100
Goldsmith	Emily	T.	Nov. 30, 1904	Dec. 14, 1988	In Memory of Emily Goldsmith / d/o Benj. H. Goldsmith / Farewell dear parents, brother and sisters too. I must depart from you. My saviour calls and I must go in heaven to take my view	NSP775
Goldsmith	Emily		Sep. 3, 1829	Dec. 3, 1859		OFE4017
Goldsmith	Estelle	H.	Sep. 5, 1930	Jul. 29, 1993	Loving wife & mother	CHR421
Goldsmith	Frances		1927	1946		SIC7054
Goldsmith	Francis	Roger	No Date	Jun. 6, 1959	Name is shown on church records but burial location is unknown	CHRNoStone
Goldsmith	G.	L.	1903	1904		OSP064
Goldsmith	Garfield		Aug. 25, 1908	Feb. 14, 1976		SMC1221
Goldsmith	George	A.	1902	1958		SMCA263
Goldsmith	George	Alton	No Date	Aug. 12, 1970	Name is shown on church records but burial location is unknown	CHRNoStone
Goldsmith	George	J.	Nov. 1, 1938	Apr. 21, 1987	In loving memory	CHR172
Goldsmith	Georgianna		1854	1946	Mother	SMY3031
Goldsmith	Grace	L.	Mar. 29, 1900	Jan. 15, 1971	Dates are from ancestry.com	CHR403
Goldsmith	Henry	S.	Apr. 13, 1913	Mar. 2, 1993	In loving memory / Together forever / Married Dec 21, 1940	SMC1050
Goldsmith	Hooker		No Date	Apr. 3, 1884	Info is from church records	OFENoStone

Last Name	First Name	Middle Name	Date of Birth	Date of Death	Transcription / Notes	Cemetery Code
Goldsmith	Isabelle	C.	Dec. 12, 1925	Apr. 27, 1999	In loving memory / Together forever / Married Dec 21, 1940	SMC1050
Goldsmith	James	Albert	1902	1944		OFE4117
Goldsmith	James	Archie	No Date	Aug. 3, 1929	Age 6 weeks / info is from church records	OFENoStone
Goldsmith	James	B.	1900	1950		NSP764
Goldsmith	James	T.	Jul. 5, 1956	Oct. 16, 2006		CHR171
Goldsmith	Jas	A.	Jul. 1, 1833	Oct. 6, 1898		OFE4026
Goldsmith	Jesse	H.	Oct. 24, 1911	Nov. 3, 1979		OFE2005
Goldsmith	Jim		1919	1997	Pop	HGH4297
Goldsmith	John	D.	1892	1918	Daddy	SMY3032
Goldsmith	John	T.	Jan. 1, 1882	Jan. 7, 1954		CHR402
Goldsmith	Joseph	E.	1947	1949		SIC7012
Goldsmith	Kathleene		1912	1940	Mother	SIC6087
Goldsmith	Katrina	Lynn	No Date	Jan. 12, 1983	God's little angel	SMC1194
Goldsmith, Mrs.	L.	D.	No Date	Feb. 28, 1866	In Memory of / w/o B. H. Goldsmith / aged 70 years (bottom of stone is broken off, rest of stone is set into the ground)	OFE4027
Goldsmith	Lewis	E.	Jul. 11, 1904	Dec. 23, 1948		OFE4116
Goldsmith	Lillian	Margaret	Feb. 10, 1908	Oct. 29, 1978		SIC7035
Goldsmith	Lorraine	M.	1911	1984		NSP765
Goldsmith	Lucy	Cora	Oct. 14, 1886	Jun. 30, 1966		SIC7056
Goldsmith	M.	Agnes	1910	1994		SMCA261
Goldsmith	M.	Dorothy	Nov. 9, 1908	Jan. 15, 1956	(Dottie)	SIC6066
Goldsmith	M.	Gertrude	1905	1992		SMC1130
Goldsmith	M.	L.	1897	1910		OSP064
Goldsmith	Margaret	E.	1925	No Date		NSP619
Goldsmith	Margaret	S.	May 11, 1869	Mar. 31, 1955		NSP772
Goldsmith	Marian	L.	Nov. 30, 1923	Apr. 9, 1989	Momma rest in peace Morris Sonny and Delores	SMC1188
Goldsmith	Martha		Sep. 17, 1914	Dec. 11, 2002		SMC1221
Goldsmith	Mary	C.	Sep. 14, 1840	Dec. 25, 1898	Mother / Rest in peace	SMCA184
Goldsmith	Mary	E.	1918	1993	At rest	OFE3021

Last Name	First Name	Middle Name	Date of Birth	Date of Death	Transcription / Notes	Cemetery Code
Goldsmith	Mary	Lucretia	No Date	Jul. 28, 1958	Name is shown on church records but burial location is unknown	CHRNoStone
Goldsmith	McEllen	G.	1901	1991		NSP619
Goldsmith	Olive	W.	Oct. 12, 1912	Jan. 29, 1982		NSP947
Goldsmith	Osema		1896	1920		SMY3013
Goldsmith	Parran	Leonard	1931	1954	Brother	CHR407
Goldsmith	Ralph	L.	Jan. 20, 1924	Aug. 6, 1997	Loving father & husband	CHR421
Goldsmith	Richard	M.	Apr. 29, 1947	May 31, 1990	Morris / Love you always, Delores	SMC3170
Goldsmith	Robert	D.	Mar. 4, 1869	May 18, 1949		NSP774
Goldsmith	Robert		1854	1916		SMY3029
Goldsmith	Roy		No Date	No Date		SMY3014
Goldsmith	Russell	B.	Dec. 19, 1909	Sep. 23, 1976		OFE2004
Goldsmith	Ruth		1923	1991	Mom	HGH4297
Goldsmith	Sam		1875	1938		OFE2003
Goldsmith	Sarah	Elizabeth	No Date	Mar. 31, 1919	Aged 92 years	OFE4115
Goldsmith	T.	Elmer	Apr. 7, 1906	Nov. 15, 1972	(The Horse)	SIC6066
Goldsmith	T.	Albert	1895	1986		NSP619
Goldsmith, II	Thomas	F.	1918	1959	In memory of	SIC7078
Goldsmith	Thomas	Francis	Sep. 23, 1880	Nov. 27, 1962		SIC7056
Goldsmith	Thomas	J.	Dec. 22, 1863	Jul. 20, 1934		NSP773
Goldsmith	Thomas	R.	Jan. 23, 1928	Dec. 1, 1959	Maryland PFC US Marine Corps WWII	SPL4048
Goldsmith	Thomas		No Date	Jan. 17, 1929	Age 55 / info is from church records	OFENoStone
Goldsmith	Townley	James	No Date	Jan. 25, 1971	Name is shown on church records but burial location is unknown	CHRNoStone
Goldsmith	Townley		Oct. 27, 1855	Jun. 29, 1944		SIC1099
Goldsmith	Unknown		No Date	No Date	Unmarked grave per church records	CHRNoStone
Goldsmith	Unknown		No Date	Nov. 29, 1923	Baby, Stillborn / info is from church records	OFENoStone
Goldsmith	Wilfred	A.	1923	1977		SIC7079
Goldsmith	William	A.	Apr. 8, 1899	Feb. 21, 1952		NSP771
Goldsmith	William		No Date	No Date	Plain Marker, cinder block, per church records	CHRNoStone
Goldsmith	Wilson	John	Aug. 2, 1914	Oct. 11, 1976	Hart	SMC1188

Last Name	First Name	Middle Name	Date of Birth	Date of Death	Transcription / Notes	Cemetery Code
Goldsmith	Winifred		No Date	Dec. 17, 1882	Info is from church records	OFENoStone
Golladay	Rebecca	D.	Jul. 13, 1979	Oct. 23, 1979	She is asleep not dead	SAC3073
Goncalves	Manuel		Jan. 31, 1928	No Date	Married Jul 13, 1952 / Devoted Father / Loving Mother / Together Forever	SMY3213
Goncalves	Maria	S.	Feb. 11, 1932	Feb. 5, 2008	Married Jul 13, 1952 / Devoted Father / Loving Mother / Together Forever	SMY3213
Gonzalez	Shirley	Marie	Sep. 8, 1956	Mar. 6, 1983	Loving Wife and Mother / "She know not the word selfish"	SMC4181
Good, Jr.	Arthur	Gorman	Feb. 8, 1944	Feb. 16, 1944	Gone to be an Angel	SIG081
Good	Arthur	P. G.	Apr. 7, 1896	Mar. 11, 1985		SIG080
Good	Blanche	E.	1898	1963		CHR085
Good	Carrie	Lena	1877	1966	"Nannie"	NJB263
Good	Charles	S.	Nov. 9, 1868	Jan. 25, 1938	Gone but not forgotten (writing on bottom of stone is from church records)	CHR023
Good	Diann	Reklis	Aug. 22, 1935	Feb. 3, 1987	"Sugar"	SCL3310
Good	Frances	D.	Nov. 16, 1908	May 5, 1961	Saint	OFE4086
Good	Hazel	C.	Mar. 16, 1914	Sep. 16, 1991		SIG080
Good	Henry		No Date	Jan. 12, 1873	In Memory of / age 73 years 4 mos & 5 days. / When those we love are snatched away, By deaths listless hand, Our hearts the mourned tribute pay that friendship must ( ) Oh let us to our saviour fly, whose arms alone can save: Then will our hopes ascend on high and triumph over the grave.	GOS003
Good	Henry		No Date	Jun. 12, 1873	In Memory of / age 73 years 4 mos & 5 days. / When those we love are snatched away, By deaths listless hand, Our hearts the mourned tribute pay that friendship must deny. Oh let us to our saviour fly, whose arms alone can save: Then will our hopes ascend on high and triumph over the grave.	GOS003
Good	James	E.	1886	1955		CHR084
Good	Maria		May 16, 1813	Mar. 27, 1894	In memory of / Footstone: M.G.	GOS006
Good	Maria		May 16, 1813	Mar. 27, 1894	In memory of / Footstone: M.G.	GOS006
Good	Robert	Wayne	Feb. 15, 1953	Feb. 18, 1953	Gone to be an Angel	SIG102

Last Name	First Name	Middle Name	Date of Birth	Date of Death	Transcription / Notes	Cemetery Code
Good	Robin	L.	Sep. 28, 1972	Jan. 20, 1973		NZN051
Goode	Albert	S.	1916	1975		CHR021
Goode	Ernest	Dudley	No Date	Jan. 7, 1909	Name is shown on church records but burial location is unknown, date is the burial date, not death date	CHRNoStone
Goode	George	P.	1867	1927		SMCD216
Goode	John	C.	May 28, 1918	Nov. 4, 1996	Wed Dec 7, 1940 / "Our Hero" / "The wind beneath our wings"	PKH147
Goode	Joseph	C.	1913	1963		SCL1164
Goode	M.	Helen	1905	1928		SMCD215
Goode	Mary	D.	1870	1968		CHR022
Goode	Mary	E.	1872	1923		SMCD217
Goode	Virginia	M.	Apr. 17, 1920	No Date	Wed. Dec 7, 1940 / "Our Hero" / "The wind beneath our wings"	PKH147
Goodier	Margaret	Tubman	Dec. 20, 1897	Feb. 27, 1931	Dear Father Thy Will not mine be done	SCL2163
Gooding	Margaret	R.	No Date	Sep. 1965	Age 69, buried September 11, 1965 / Info is from the Historical Society Research located at the College of Southern MD, LaPlata, MD	ODENoStone
Goodman	David		Nov. 27, 1947	Dec. 16, 2003	In loving memory of / "Billy" / Sunrise / Sunset	PGN069
Goodrich	Delbert	C.	Nov. 30, 1882	May 28, 1957		TRI105
Goodrich	Richard		1866	1959		OFE3002
Goodrich	Tumus		No Date	Mar. 4, 1914	Age 46 / info is from church records	OFENoStone
Goodrich	Unknown		No Date	Aug. 28, 1874	Child of Mr. Goodrich / info is from church records	OFENoStone
Goodrich	Unknown		No Date	Aug. 28, 1874	Brother of Mr. Goodrich / info is from church records	OFENoStone
Goodwin	Ann	D. F.	Jan. 13, 1836	No Date	Stone is sunken, unable to read death date / Footstone: Initials A.D.P.	PAR003
Goodwin	John	F.	Sep. 2, 1838	Oct. 3, 1842		PAR001
Gooseberry	Joseph	Richard	1904	1962	In loving memory / Your children Thomas Leonard, Mary Virginia, Joseph Richard Jr., James Paul, Mary Luverta, Francis Proctor / Gone but not forgotten	HGH3035
Gooseberry	Margaret		1907	1985	In loving memory / Your children Thomas Leonard, Mary Virginia, Joseph Richard Jr., James Paul, Mary Luverta, Francis Proctor / Gone but not forgotten	HGH3035
Gordan	William	A.	1843	1915		ALX093

Last Name	First Name	Middle Name	Date of Birth	Date of Death	Transcription / Notes	Cemetery Code
Gordon	Bertha	Berry	Dec. 26, 1879	Apr. 7, 1942		OSM001
Gordon	Earle	F.	Mar. 15, 1897	Aug. 2, 1979		SPL6105
Gordon	James		Apr. 3, 1870	Nov. 17, 1948		OSM003
Gordon	Mae	Pearson	Jan. 20, 1913	Sep. 16, 1986	Middle name is from church records	SPL6105
Gore	Edward	P.	1910	1996	Married Nov 10, 1945	SCL1180
Gore	Marie	M.	1914	1989	Married Nov 10, 1945	SCL1180
Gorham	Emory	L.	1898	1985		NJB247
Gorham	Violet	B.	1898	1978		NJB247
Gorman	Robert	J.	Sep. 5, 1943	No Date	Together Forever / Married Sept. 18, 1965	SMC4216
Gorman	Roseann	M.	Oct. 28, 1944	Aug. 20, 2000	Together Forever / Married Sept. 18, 1965	SMC4216
Gosnell	Berenice	Howard	Jul. 2, 1911	Dec. 26, 1995		NSP505
Gossett, Jr.	Jesse	Edward	Aug. 23, 1948	Mar. 11, 1999	Rest in Peace	PKH091
Gough	Aaron	Blaine	Oct. 8, 1971	May 17, 2002	Beloved Father, Son and Brother	LUM176
Gough	Alice		No Date	Jun. 5, 1912	Age 5 years	SPL3047
Gough	Anna		No Date	Jun. 5, 1848	d/o Wm H & Lucy Gough / departed this life / aged 5m, 27d	TRI211
Gough	Annie	Lee	Mar. 18, 1887	Jul. 29, 1887	Infant d/o Richard & Annie Lee Gough	TRI237
Gough	Annie	Reeder	Sep. 16, 1847	Dec. 24, 1889	Beloved w/o James H Gough / In memory of / My faith looks up to thee/ Mother	TRI248
Gough	Annie	S.	1867	1940		TRI238
Gough	Annie		Jan. 8, 1848	Jun. 5, 1848	Front of stone William H Gough stone; footstone: A.G., L.G., H.G.	TRI243
Gough	Cheryl	Arleen	No Date	Sep. 9, 1962		NSP550
Gough	Clarence	Richmond	Feb. 18, 1910	Jun. 12, 1983	Note: He is the Sr.	CHR086
Gough, Jr.	Clarence	Richmond	Feb. 19, 1937	No Date	Masonic Emblem	CHR274
Gough	Dorothy	Keech	Dec. 29, 1904	Jan. 12, 1906	Infant d/o George R & Mattie Bell Gough / Suffer little children to come unto me, and forbid them not, for of such is the kingdom of heaven	TRI284
Gough	Ellen	Elizabeth	Sep. 29, 1917	Feb. 24, 1990	Additional info is from church records	SPL5110
Gough	Harry		1868	1940		SPL3044
Gough	Hezekiah		Oct. 8, 1860	Oct. 17, 1860	Front of stone William H Gough stone; footstone: A.G., L.G., H.G.	TRI243

Last Name	First Name	Middle Name	Date of Birth	Date of Death	Transcription / Notes	Cemetery Code
Gough	James	Henry	Sep. 15, 1845	Dec. 6, 1901	h/o Annie Reeder Gough / In memory of / Father	TRI248
Gough	James	Pinckney	Feb. 4, 1877	May 5, 1964	Cpl Co D 1 Regt MD Inf Sp. Am. War / back of stone Jenness Frieze.	TRI250
Gough	Janet	Jones	Jan. 6, 1944	Jan. 3, 1997		CHR274
Gough	Jenness	Frieze	Feb. 2, 1887	Nov. 22, 1971	w/o James Pinckney Gough	TRI251
Gough	Joseph	R.	1910	1992		SIC5068
Gough	Louis		May 7, 1919	Dec. 17, 1919	s/o Mr & Mrs L G Gough / Darling we miss thee	TRI213
Gough	Lucinda	Bean	Jan. 9, 1824	Apr. 23, 1896		TRI245
Gough	Lucy		Oct. 26, 1855	Jun. 8, 1856	Front of stone William H Gough; footstone: A.G., L.G., H.G.	TRI243
Gough	Lucy		No Date	Jun. 9, 1853	d/o Wm H & Lucy Gough / departed this life / aged 7m, 13d	TRI212
Gough	Mary	A.	1908	1983		SIC5068
Gough	Mary	E.	Sep. 10, 1854	Sep. 2, 1931		TRI209
Gough	Mary	V.	1884	1959		SPL3044
Gough	Richard		1856	1922		TRI238
Gough	Robert	C.	Nov. 28, 1937	Feb. 3, 1973	Maryland SP 5 US Army	NSP546
Gough	Thomas	B.	Dec. 3, 1846	Feb. 24, 1900	Beloved husband; my faith looks up to thee.	TRI210
Gough	Walter	G.	May 25, 1914	Mar. 6, 1994	Additional info is from church records	SPL5110
Gough	William	H.	Sep. 24, 1819	Jan. 24, 1863	Simply to thy cross I cling / to my husband / back of stone Annie, Lucy & Hezekiah Gough.	TRI242
Grabis, Sr.	Andrew	J.	Apr. 5, 1932	Jul. 22, 2002		SCL3414
Grabis	Anna	M.	1891	1980		SCL3414
Grabis	Barbara		1893	1964		SMCE029
Grabis	Donald	Allen	1964	2002		SMC1015
Grabis, Sr.	Edward	James	Apr. 30, 1927	Mar. 13, 2000	PFC US Army WW II	SCL3414
Grabis	Frank	J.	Jun. 7, 1888	Jul. 14, 1953		SCL3414
Grabis	John	P.	1890	1982		SMCE029
Grabis	Leo	J.	Mar. 10, 1918	Jul. 3, 1918		SCL3414
Grabis	Mary	E.	1914	1984		SCL3414

Last Name	First Name	Middle Name	Date of Birth	Date of Death	Transcription / Notes	Cemetery Code
Grabis	Mary		No Date	Sep. 23, 1938	Aged 69 yr 9 mos. / info is from the Historical Society Research and the 1940 DAR book pg 188 located at the College of Southern MD, LaPlata, MD.	SMCNoStone
Grabis	Sophronia	Elizabeth	No Date	Mar. 11, 1937	Aged 46 years / info is from the Historical Society Research located at the College of Southern MD, LaPlata, MD, and the 1940 DAR book pg 188	SMCNoStone
Graff	Mary	Elizabeth	Sep. 30, 1922	Mar. 4, 1990	We Love you Memaw	SIG134
Gragan	Anna	E.	Jul. 14, 1912	Jul. 5, 1981		SIC8090
Gragan	George	C.	May 23, 1909	Jun. 17, 1988		SIC8090
Gragan	Linda	H.	Mar. 29, 1938	No Date	Wed. Oct 21, 1961	SIC9015
Gragan	Mary	Z.	Oct. 27, 1942	Sep. 25, 1980	"Dolly"	MTR4055
Gragan	Paul	D.	Jul. 19, 1934	Feb. 2, 2001	Wed Oct 21, 1961	SIC9015
Graham	Eric	R.	Jan. 15, 1984	Mar. 11, 2002	In loving memory	SCL3296
Graham	Estelle	V.	Apr. 8, 1927	Jul. 14, 1945		NSP248
Graham	Florence	Agatha	1910	1938		NSP273
Graham	Frances	A.	Aug. 27, 1890	Apr. 21, 1967		NSP277
Graham	Henry	Robert	1917	1939		NSP247
Graham	Jeanette	Chatham	Mar. 20, 1916	May 12, 1996	Sister of Elizabeth Chatham Wheeler	ODE390
Graham	Qawaun	Daray	Apr. 20, 1985	Jul. 3, 1986	Son / Forever in Our Hearts	SMY2026
Graham	William	R.	Jun. 8, 1880	Feb. 19, 1966		NSP278
Grandison	Mary	Helen	May 14, 1920	Feb. 29, 1984		SCA008
Grant	Charlott	L.	1938	1965		SAC5022
Grant	Helen		1906	1942		SHI123
Grant	Myron	E.	1959	1996		DUD027
Grant	Sarah	Elizabeth	Aug. 25, 1986	May 23, 2003	Forever Loved	SAC5098
Graves	Aloysius	I.	1917	1981		SMC1226
Graves, Rev. D.D.	Alvan		Sep. 15, 1851	Mar. 8, 1929	He is not dead but Sleepeth in the arms of Jesus / Footstone	GHB014A
Graves	Carol	Lynn	Jun. 12, 1965	Feb. 19, 2005		SMC1005
Graves	Edna	R.	1925	1997		SMC1226
Graves	Eva		1867	1944		MTR3059
Graves	Landonia	D.	Unknown	1938		GHB014

Last Name	First Name	Middle Name	Date of Birth	Date of Death	Transcription / Notes	Cemetery Code
Graves	Mary	P.	No Date	Dec. 1, 1881	In memory of / w/o Capt. Geo. W. Graves Died Dec 1st 1881 in the 49th year of her age	HGH2072
Graves	Sarah McKee		No Date	May 23, 1944	Info is from Christ Church microfilm Reel 4 Pg 268-269 located at the College of Southern MD, LaPlata, MD	MTRNoStone
Graves	Thomas	J.	Jan. 9, 1867	Dec. 7, 1956	"Robey"	SMY3015
Gray	Ada	B.	Jul. 7, 1920	No Date		SCL4061
Gray	Alberta		May 22, 1900	Aor 5, 1985		ALX080
Gray, Capt.	Alexander		May 30, 1788	Jul. 25, 1839	Here lies the body of Captain Alexander Gray who was / and departed this life / Footstone	GRA027
Gray	Alexander	Price	Oct. 2, 1914	Nov. 24, 1919	s/o J. Parker & Effie H. Gray	ODE422
Gray	Alton	J.	Nov. 4, 1924	Apr. 16, 1983	PFC US Army WW II	SCL1143
Gray	Amanda	Carter	No Date	Mar. 30 1930	Mother	SCL2211
Gray	Ann	Matilda	1858	1931	His wife / There hath pass'd away a Glory from the Earth	ODE361
Gray	Annie	B.	May 9, 1929	Feb. 2, 1981		SCL4143
Gray	Annie	M.	1890	1965		SCL1144
Gray	Benedictor	E.	No Date	Mar. 13, 1866	Consecrated to the memory of / who departed this life / In the 48th year of her age. Sustained by the grace of God: In her pilgrimage. The end of her strife with death, is everlasting life. The righteous hath hope in his death: Glory be to God Footstone	GRA004
Gray	Bertha	A.	1880	1949		NSP196
Gray	Blanche	Poole	Jun. 3, 1895	Jul. 8, 1978		ODE406
Gray	Brian	Darrick	1956	1989	Our Love forever "Moving Fox"	SCL4110
Gray	Carlyle	G.	1907	1947		NSP222
Gray	Carolyn	Crum	Mar. 15, 1917	Jul. 11, 1983	In loving memory of / w/o J. Arthur Gray	ODE134
Gray	Charles	Aubrey	1901	1902		ODE360
Gray	Charles	C	1914	1974		SCL1145
Gray	Charles	Henry	Jul. 8,1929	May 7,1995	PFC US Army	MHB037
Gray	Charles	M.	1880	1948		NSP195
Gray	Charles	S.	1947	1965		SCL1146
Gray	Charles		1886	1964		SCL1144

Last Name	First Name	Middle Name	Date of Birth	Date of Death	Transcription / Notes	Cemetery Code
Gray	Cheryl	Rosier	Sep. 21, 1962	Mar. 23, 1995	"Rest in Peace" / Loving Daughter & Sister, Devoted Mother	SAC4038
Gray	Clair	A.	No Date	Sep. 17, 1905	Buried at Mansion Hall grave yard. / Information is from the records of Durham Church microfilm pg 85 located at the College of Southern MD, LaPlata, MD	GRANo Stone
Gray	Cora		No Date	Aug. 4, 1895	Info is from Christ Church microfilm Reel 2 Pg 171-172 located at the College of Southern MD, LaPlata, MD	MTRNoStone
Gray	Dorothy	C.	Dec. 27, 1907	Sep. 21, 1966		NSP322
Gray	Dorothy	M.	Dec. 5, 1914	Jul. 24, 1977		SCL4026
Gray	Edna	I.	Sep. 20, 1920	Apr. 12, 1958	Number 12 is inscribed on the lower left of stone	CLV014
Gray	Effie	Haislip	Nov. 14, 1871	Oct. 30, 1959	In Memoriam	ODE420
Gray	Elizabeth		Jun. 1, 1796	Nov. 6, 1824	w/o Robert Gray / and departed this life / Footstone	GRA040
Gray	Elizabeth		Jul. 15, 1793	Aug. 6, 1857	In memory of / w/o Capt. Alexander Gray / I know that my redeemer liveth. Stonemaker was C.L. Neale, Alex. VA	GRA022 GRA023
Gray	Elizabeth		Jan. 28, 1821	Mar. 27, 1863	In memory of / w/o Joseph C. Gray	GRA011
Gray	Elizabeth		Dec. 18, 1917	No Date		SAC5021
Gray	Ella	Louise	Jul. 2, 1915	Jun. 13, 1999	Mother / John, Richard, Austin, Leonard, James / Shirley, Tillie, Lorraine, Ruth, Grace / Mother	SCA121
Gray	Fannie	Temple	Mar. 30, 1895	Oct. 8, 1895	Age 6 mo's. d/o George William Gray (info is from Old Durham Church microfilm pg 83-84 located at the College of Southern MD, LaPlata, MD)	ODENoStone
Gray	Fannie	Temple, Davis	1861	1939		ODE455
Gray, Jr.	Francis	A.	1922	2000		MTR4046
Gray, Rev.	Francis	Alexander	1893	1950	Priest of the church Twenty Three years	MTR4049
Gray	Francis	P.	1909	1940		OSP147
Gray	Frank	Douglas	1951	1994		MTR4058
Gray	Gary	Gregory	Aug. 28, 1953	Apr. 14, 1974		SCL1120
Gray	Genneieve		1928	2005	Thornton funeral home marker	SCL4085A
Gray	George		1919	1976	Info is from the Historical Society Research located at the College of Southern MD, LaPlata, MD	ZBCNoStone

Last Name	First Name	Middle Name	Date of Birth	Date of Death	Transcription / Notes	Cemetery Code
Gray	George	F.	No Date	Feb. 1940	Buried Feb 11, 1940 (info is from Old Durham Church microfilm pg 161 located at the College of Southern MD, LaPlata, MD)	ODENoStone
Gray	George	Guy S.	1900	1962	Info is from Historical Society Research located at the College of Southern MD, LaPlata, MD	MTRNoStone
Gray	George	M.	Dec. 26, 1878	Nov. 6, 1968	Married May 14, 1917	SCL4139
Gray	George	Truman	1897	1897		ODE359
Gray	George	Truman, Clagett	1852	1940	His Wife / There hath pass'd away a Glory from the Earth	ODE361
Gray	George	William	1862	1930		ODE455
Gray	Gladys		Jul. 1890	Aug. 1970		NSP301
Gray	Harold	Lowell	Feb. 5, 1933	Dec. 3, 1971	ME2 US Navy Korea	SCL4025
Gray	Harriett		No Date	No Date	funeral home marker	SCL4065
Gray	Helen	B., Stark	1919			MTR4045
Gray	Helen	Davis	Dec. 29, 1889	Jan. 27, 1902	In memory of	ODE454
Gray	Irene		1923	2000	Thornton Funeral Home Marker	OAK010
Gray	J.	Arthur	Mar. 13, 1913	Sep. 19, 1996	s/o Margaret & James	ODE135
Gray	James	A.	Dec. 24, 1873	Dec. 25, 1952	s/o Jane and Alexander Gray	ODE132
Gray	James	F.	No Date	Sep. 5, 1862	Sacred to the memory of / who departed this life / in the 40th year of his age "Blessed are the pure in heart, for they shall see God" / Footstone / Stonemaker was A. Gaddess, Balto.	GRA036
Gray	James	R.	Feb. 8, 1899	Jan. 16, 1964		SCL4082
Gray, Jr.	James	Russell	Jun. 3, 1925	Mar. 8, 1968		SCL4085
Gray	James	W.	Nov. 11, 1951	Jul. 2, 1991	Peace Forever	SCA091
Gray	James	Wm.	Jun. 22, 1894	Nov. 12, 1980		CLV016
Gray	Jane	Young	Feb. 29, 1832	Jan. 12, 1899	Beloved w/o Joseph Alexander Gray	ODE131
Gray	Jerome	W.	1914	1996		SCL3407
Gray	John		No Date	Sep. 25, 1927	Age 51 yrs.	SCL4062
Gray, Capt	John	F.	Nov. 24, 1771	Jun. 26, 1830	Here lies	GRA031
Gray	John	Parker	Oct. 13, 1864	Nov. 9, 1933	Beloved h/o Effie H. Gray /Gone but not forgotten	ODE421
Gray, Jr.	John	Parker	1909	1940	How desolate our home. Bereft of Thee	ODE419

Last Name	First Name	Middle Name	Date of Birth	Date of Death	Transcription / Notes	Cemetery Code
Gray	John	Robert	Sep. 1861	Mar. 1928		MTR4059
Gray	Joseph	Alexander	May 24, 1830	Feb. 16, 1902	Footstone	GRY009
Gray	Joseph	C.	May 18, 1820	Jun. 1, 1880	In memory of / Ye sinners seek the grace of God, whose wrath ye cannot bear. Fly to the shelter of his cross and find salvation there. Footstone	GRA008
Gray, Sr.	Joseph	C.	Dec. 30, 1912	May 27, 1985		SAC5021
Gray	Joseph	Edwin	1893	1899		ODE358
Gray	Joseph	G.	Dec. 31, 1933	Jan. 19, 2001		SCA122
Gray, Sr.	Joseph	Sherman	Jul. 7, 1952	Dec. 9, 2005	PVT USMC Loving Father And Grandfather We'll Love You Always	SCL1113
Gray	Joseph		1901	1978		SCA141
Gray	Josephine	Clagett	May 28, 1855	Jun. 18, 1918	His wife / asleep in Jesus	ODE403
Gray	Katherine	S.	Sep. 12, 1859	Jul. 10, 1941		MTR4060
Gray	Lawrence	L.	Feb. 28, 1918	Jul. 16, 2004		SCL4061
Gray	Lawrence	E.	Mar. 1, 1903	Oct. 10, 1966		NSP322
Gray	Leon	Terrell	Jul. 15, 1978	Jul. 10, 1999	I Love You	SAC5063
Gray	Leroy	V.	Aug. 24, 1910	Oct. 25, 1968		SCA100
Gray	Leroy	V.	Aug. 24, 1910	Oct. 25, 1968	Info was obtained from the Historical Society Research located at the College of Southern Md, LaPlata, Md)	OAKNoStone
Gray	Leroy	B.	1939	1986		SCA142
Gray	Linda	M.	1950	1972	Wife	SCL3063
Gray	Louisa	Hall	Dec. 26, 1862	Jul. 14, 1915	In memory of / d/o Thomas P. and Sarah E. Gray / "Asleep in Jesus"	ODE370
Gray	M.	Madeline	1917	1981		SCA141
Gray	Mamie	M.	1915	1999		SCL3407
Gray	Margaret	C.	Oct. 10, 1929	Oct. 24, 1998		SCL1114
Gray	Margaret	Scott	Jun. 10, 1884	Apr. 5, 1957		ODE133
Gray	Marion	Elizabeth	Jun. 15, 1942	Jan. 19, 2001	"June" / We Love and Miss You / RN	SPL1073
Gray	Marshall	Clagett	Feb. 26, 1900	Feb. 2, 1980	s/o George William Gray and Fannie Davis Gray	ODE465
Gray	Marshall	H.	No Date	No Date		ALX089
Gray	Marshall	Harrison	1889	1942		ODE405
Gray	Mary	Belle	Feb. 26, 1905	May 9, 1981		SCL4082

Last Name	First Name	Middle Name	Date of Birth	Date of Death	Transcription / Notes	Cemetery Code
Gray	Mary	Beverley	1896	1993		MTR4048
Gray	Mary	Edna	Oct. 20, 1888	Nov. 30, 1971		ODE374
Gray	Mary	Madaline	Apr. 18, 1918	May 28, 1989		SCL1073
Gray	Mary	S.	Sep. 24, 1887	Aug. 17, 1975	Married May 14, 1917	SCL4139
Gray	Mary		No Date	Feb. 13, 1930	Aged 48 years	SCL4062
Gray	Mary		No Date	Aug. 15, 1902	Age 7 days (info is from Old Durham Church microfilm pg 85 located at the College of Southern MD, LaPlata, MD)	ODENoStone
Gray	Mary	Anne, Tucker	1919	1959		MTR4047
Gray	Miriam	Chandler	Sep. 11, 1902	Nov. 1, 1938	w/o Joseph A. Gray / She gave her all for others	ODE457
Gray	Paul	R.	Jun. 6, 1922	Nov. 21, 1996		SCL1114
Gray	Paul		Feb. 24, 1885	Nov. 12, 1947		ODE456
Gray	Paula Louise	Clark, Marshall	Sep. 16, 1924	Jan. 24, 2003		MTR3031
Gray	Preston	A.	Apr. 28, 1906	Mar. 19, 1970	Dear daddy, gone but not forgotten	SCL4088
Gray	Price		Dec. 9, 1853	Oct. 9, 1925	His wife / asleep in Jesus	ODE403
Gray, Jr.	R.	L.	No Date	Jan. 29, 1972		PIS136
Gray	Ralph		No Date	Apr. 5, 1928	Age 21 years	SCL4062
Gray	Raymond	V.	Dec. 4, 1922	Jan. 5, 1991		SCL4143
Gray	Robert	Walter	1919	1993	T SGT US Army WW II	MTR3030
Gray	Robert		Dec. 8, 1792	Dec. 26, 1851		GRA034
Gray	Roland	Vincent	Jan. 4, 1951	Sep. 26, 1969		SCL1119
Gray	Russell	Drake	Apr. 17, 1964	Aug. 24, 1986		SCL4071
Gray	Samuel		1939	2001	In loving memory - Father / "Sonny"	SCL4050
Gray	Sara	Brown	Apr. 1868	Jul. 1948		MTR4059
Gray	Sarah	E.	Jul. 23, 1829	May 14, 1922		ODE372
Gray	Sarah Wallace		No Date	Jan. 31, 1912	Info is from Christ Church microfilm Reel 3, Pg 222-223 located at the College of Southern MD, LaPlata, MD	MTRNoStone
Gray	Shirley	A.	Dec. 8, 1936	Aug. 15, 1967		SCA119
Gray	Sondra	M.	1941	No Date	Mother / In loving memory	SCL4050
Gray	Susan	Elizabeth	No Date	Feb. 6, 1929	Info is from Christ Church microfilm Reel 3, Pg 234-235 located at the College of Southern MD, LaPlata, MD	MTRNoStone

Last Name	First Name	Middle Name	Date of Birth	Date of Death	Transcription / Notes	Cemetery Code
Gray	Sylvester		Oct. 22, 1896	Mar. 7, 1980		ALX081
Gray	Theodore	W.	Dec. 27, 1917	Oct. 31, 1944		NSP199
Gray	Thomas	Everett	Sep. 27, 1934	Dec. 31, 1977	PFC US Army	SCL4024
Gray	Thomas	H.	Mar. 4, 1909	Dec. 24, 1967		SCL4026
Gray	Thomas	Price	May 8, 1828	Nov. 24, 1902	In memory of	ODE371
Gray	Thomas	Price	Aug. 21, 1889	Dec. 20, 1892	In memory of / s/o Geo. T.C. & Ann Matilda Gray / When Christ who is our life shall appear there shall ye also appear with him in Glory	ODE357
Gray	Unknown		1911	2001	Thornton Funeral Home	ZBC109
Gray	Vera	L.	Mar. 25, 1943	Jan. 9, 1972		POM201
Gray	Veronica	G.	No Date		Info is from the Historical Society Research located at the College of Southern MD, LaPlata, MD, and the 1940 DAR book pg 188	SMCNoStone
Gray	Walter	H.	Nov. 25, 1866	Jul. 7, 1937		MTR4060
Gray	Welby	Turner	Aug. 9, 1924	Jan. 24, 1943	Blessed are the pure in heart for they shall see God / middle name is from church records	SPL7005
Gray	William	Alexandria	1867	Sep. 4, 1985		ODE373
Gray	William	H.	No Date	1942	To my Husband aged 47 years... "He is not dead but sleepeth"	GRA001
Gray	Wm.	H.	No Date	Feb. 29, 1888	Age 48 / info is from Old Durham Church microfilm located at the College of Southern MD, LaPlata, MD	ODENoStone
Greathouse	R.	Wayne	Dec. 25, 1958	Feb. 29, 1988	Beloved Son, Brother & Friend	HER008
Green	Allison	Dawne	1970	Feb. 26, 1995		SJE086
Green	Cecelia	Viola	No Date	2002	Infant / info is from church records	SHINoStone
Green	Clara	A.	1870	May 21, 1927		SJO3252
Green	Edna	F.	Apr. 21, 1918	1933	Forever in our hearts	SJO2087
Green	Edward		1908	Mar. 5, 2001		SJO3376
Green	Eleanor	M.	Aug. 9, 1904	1988	d/o Joseph W. - Eleanor E. Green / R.I.P.	SJO3273
Green	Elizabeth	B.	1910	Oct. 13, 1918		NSP276
Green	Elizabeth	T.	No Date	1951	D.O.M. / In memory of / who departed this life / in the 45th year of her age / R.I.P.	SJO3270
Green	Francis	B.	1832	Jul. 30, 1851		SJO3251
Green				1907		

Last Name	First Name	Middle Name	Date of Birth	Date of Death	Transcription / Notes	Cemetery Code
Green	Francis	C.	No Date	May 15, 1851	D.O.M. / In memory of / who departed this life / in the 56th year of his age R.I.P.	SJO3268
Green	Gertrude	A., Cooke	Jun. 22, 1880	May 1, 1920	beloved w/o Albert V. Greene	OSP132
Green	Hattie	T.	Nov. 4 1924	No Date		HGH3054
Green	Hazel	P.	1911	1987	Mother and Sister	SAC3072
Green	James	A.	Aug. 29, 1923	Oct. 31, 1980		HGH3054
Green	James	K.	1881	1966		HGH3005
Green, Sr.	James	T.	1916	1992	Beloved husband, father and grandfather	SJO2239
Green	John	Allen	1905	1980	Use to have an Arehart Funeral Home Marker (Info is from Irma Simpson research located at The College of Southern MD, LaPlata, MD)	SMYNoStone
Green	Joseph	W.	1867	1950		SJO3253
Green	Kevin	J.	Mar. 19, 1968	Apr. 2, 2003	Beloved son	SJO2238
Green	Louisa	Virginia	1842	Jun. 28, 1897	Age 60 years / info is from DAR 1939-1940 Book pg 78	SJO3272
Green	Margaret	G.	May 19, 1845	Jun. 10, 1940		SCL2182
Green	Mary	Della	1893	1976		HGH3006
Green	Mary	E.	No Date	Dec. 9, 1924	Age 85	SHINoStone
Green	Mary	Helen	1869	1950		SJO3254
Green	Mary	Louise, Dent	Dec. 22, 1927	Mar. 4, 1991		NSP042
Green	Mary	Roberta	1873	1955		SJO3255
Green	Ronald	F.	1957	1987	Beloved father, brother and son	SJO2240
Green	Ruby	Elizabeth	No Date	Mar. 20, 1961	Info is from church records	SHINoStone
Greenard	Lillian	C.	Nov. 27, 1914	Oct. 17, 1970	Beloved Mother	OAK219
Greenard	Rudolph	John	Jan. 12, 1938	Sep. 28, 1995	In Memory of	OAK063
Greene	Mary	Lillian	5/11/1930	10/24/1967	Burial site is unknown / from the church records	SMCNoStone
Greenfield	Elsie		Jan. 28, 1894	Nov. 9, 1968		NSP218
Greenfield, Sr.	Eugene	B.	Dec. 17, 1926	No Date		NSP062
Greenfield	Francis	D.	1923	2008		SMC3106
Greenfield	H.	Roosevelt	1904	1940		NSP240
Greenfield, Sr.	James	A.	Nov. 18, 1946	Sep. 2, 1993		SMC3291
Greenfield	James	E.	1886	1957		NSP295

Last Name	First Name	Middle Name	Date of Birth	Date of Death	Transcription / Notes	Cemetery Code
Greenfield	James	E.	Apr. 22, 1945	Jan. 9, 1987	"Butch"	NSP137
Greenfield	James	Rudolph	Feb. 28, 1949	Jun. 30, 1968		SMC4193
Greenfield	John	A.	Dec. 7, 1947	Apr. 22, 1968	Maryland SP4 CO B 39 INF 9 INF DIV Vietnam ARCOM	SMC3290
Greenfield	John	H.	Apr. 26, 1927	May 11, 1948		NSP208
Greenfield	Joseph	L.	1923	1989	Married Jan. 18, 1944	SMC3298
Greenfield	Madeline	Novella	Jun. 3, 1915	Jun. 21, 1995		SMC4224
Greenfield	Mary	B.	Dec. 1, 1930	Oct. 28, 2000		NSP062
Greenfield	Mary	E.	1924	1988	Married Jan. 18, 1944	SMC3298
Greenfield	Mary	Lillian	1891	1978		NSP080
Greenfield	McKinley		May 24, 1896	Oct. 7, 1967		NSP218
Greenfield, Jr.	Nathan	Irwin	Jun. 16, 1972	Mar. 11, 1992	In loving memory	NSP061
Greenfield	Robert		No Date	Dec. 7, 1879	Info is from church records	OFENoStone
Greenfield	Shanika	S.	Sep. 4, 1984	Nov. 6, 2004		SAC5110
Greenfield	Wayne	M.	Apr. 18, 1955	Jun. 2, 1989	In loving memory	NSP216
Greenfield	William	H.	Jan. 28, 1949	Feb. 20, 2004	On Earth / In heaven	SMC4222
Greenhow	Carolyn	Rosalie	Apr. 9, 1907	Feb. 7, 1998		SCL3390
Greenhow	John	R.	Dec. 15, 1937	Apr. 27, 1974	SN US Navy	SCL3389
Greenhow	Thomas	L.	Feb. 24, 1926	May 12, 1929	White stone that is laying on the ground	SCL3398
Greer	Beulah	C.	1916	1979		SIG128
Greer	Beulah	Jean	1946	1947		CMX2026
Greer III	Carlisle		No Date	Feb. 6, 1960		SIG129
Greer	Daphne	Jo	1948	1950		CMX2027
Greer	Geraldine	L.	Nov. 23, 1928	Feb. 23, 1934	Darling We Miss Thee	SIG122
Greer	Hannah	V.	1898	1986		SIG074
Greer	Harriet	Anna	1903	1977		SMI118
Greer, Sr.	J.	Carlisle	Mar. 28, 1902	May 30, 1982	Forever in our hearts & mind	SIG125
Greer	John	Raymond	Feb. 28, 1919	Apr. 14, 1996	CPL US Army WW II	SMI018
Greer	John	S.	1879	1933		SIG121
Greer	John	W.	1896	1977		SIG074
Greer, Jr.	John	S.	1903	1969		SIG123

Last Name	First Name	Middle Name	Date of Birth	Date of Death	Transcription / Notes	Cemetery Code
Greer	Joseph	Leroy	May 20, 1901	Jun. 19, 1986	Forever in our hearts and mind	SIG076
Greer	Katie	M	Sep. 6, 1905	Apr. 28, 1984		NJB507
Greer	Linda	Marie	No Date	Jul. 6, 1947	Infant	SIG076
Greer	M.	Sally	No Date	Dec. 10,	Sacred to the memory of / Relic of W. T. Stoddert & Consort of Alexander Greer who departed this life December 10, ? in the 63 year of her age / In Deed and in truth she was a Christian (above ground crypt)	ODE005
Greer	Margaret	C.	Feb. 7, 1918	Oct. 31, 1986	In Loving memory	SMI019
Greer	Margaret	Marie	Sep. 27, 1906	May 23, 1995		SIG076
Greer	Mary	C.	1881	1954		SIG121
Greer	Mary	E.	1867	1923		SIG015
Greer	Mary	E., Copsey	1878	1937	Mother	SIG016
Greer	Mary	Jenkins	Apr. 24, 1900	Feb. 10, 1930		SCL2180
Greer	McCarthy	S.	1914	1974		SIG128
Greer	Olive	G.	1890	1958		SIG015
Greer	Richard	A.	1868	1935		SIG015
Greer	Susanne	M.	1895	1972	Inscription on back of stone for G. Montgomery	SPL2017
Greer			No Date	No Date	No other names or dates on stone	SIG130
Gregan, III	Martin		Sep. 12, 1966	Sep. 13, 1997	"Marty" / I live not in myself but I become portion of that around me	SJO3100
Gregory	Helen	G.	May 22, 1909	Aug. 27, 1979		SMC2124
Gregory	Lester		1932	1977	Thornton Funeral Home Marker	DUD051
Gregory	Patricia	Faye	Nov. 26, 1933	Jun. 27, 1996	Mother wife friend	SCL3001
Gregory	Thomas	B.	May 7, 1908	Jun. 25, 1973		SMC2125
Gretes	Randolph	Henry	Jan. 12, 1927	Aug. 5, 1984	US Navy WW II	SIC9022
Griffin	Cora	May	No Date	Aug. 1918	Buried Aug 22, 1918 / info is from Old Durham Church microfilm pg 159 located at the College of Southern MD, LaPlata, MD	ODENoStone
Griffin	Emma	B.	1922	1995		DUD041
Griffin, M.D.	John	Henry	May 19, 1914	Oct. 18, 1988	Mary Louise McDonagh Griffin is on the other side of this stone / CDR US Navy WW II / Medical Corps	SIC1077
Griffin	Mary, Louise	McDonagh	Aug. 23, 1920	Nov. 26, 1995	John H. Griffin is on the other side of this stone	SIC1076

Last Name	First Name	Middle Name	Date of Birth	Date of Death	Transcription / Notes	Cemetery Code
Griffith	Annie		1874	1960		MRB004
Griffith	Katherine	Dement, Padgett	Nov. 12, 1892	Nov. 21, 1965	O God thou has given so much to us, give one more thing, a grateful heart. Amen	MTR1080
Griffith	Madelyn June	Powell	Jun. 17, 1930	No Date	Lord thou hast been our refuge from one generation to another	MTR1269
Griffith	Philip	Lawrence	Jan. 28, 1927	Jan. 7, 2002	Good night sweet prince and flights of angels sing thee to thy rest	MTR1268
Grigg	Lillian	Maurice	Apr. 2, 1895	Apr. 17, 1986		MTR1164
Grigg	Martha	Livdahl	Jun. 28, 1935	No Date	Twas heaven here with you	MTR1166
Grigg, Jr.	Robert	Dinwiddie	Jun. 3, 1893	May 29, 1978		MTR1164
Grigg	William Thomas	Maurice	Mar. 22, 1934	No Date	Twas heaven here with you	MTR1166
Griggs	Amy	Gray	1904	1996		ODE430
Griggs	Paul	D.	1901	1985		ODE430
Griggs, Jr.	Paul	Dallas	Sep. 12, 1929	Sep. 19, 1929		ODE423
Griggs	Unknown		No Date	Jul. 1933	Baby / buried Jul 28, 1933 age 2 days / info is from Old Durham Church microfilm pg 161 located at the College of Southern MD, LaPlata, MD	ODENoStone
Grigsby	Bertie	T.	Jun. 13, 1887	Dec. 20, 1948	At Rest	OSM102
Grigsby	Dorothy	Sperlbaum	Apr. 1, 1922	Dec. 11, 1988	Age 50 / info is from Old Durham Church microfilm pg 79-80, at the College of Southern MD, LaPlata, MD	SMY2150
Grigsby	Mary	Ellen	No Date	Dec. 9, 1888		ODENoStone
Grigsby	Virgie	M.	Aug. 7, 1890	Aug. 8, 1948		OSM102
Grimes	Hilda	C.	Aug. 9, 1918	Aug. 5, 1988		NSP599
Grimes	Nadine	Mae	Aug. 28, 1916	May 6, 1982	In Loving Memory / Number 246 B inscribed on the lower left of stone	CLV394
Grimes	Walter	Emory	Jan. 25, 1943	Mar. 23, 1995	In Loving Memory / Pop Pop / Number 246-1 inscribed on the lower left of the stone	CLV364A
Grimm	Bertha	V.	Sep. 29, 1913	Nov. 13, 1980		MTR3073
Grimm	Carl	L.	Aug. 17, 1906	Sep. 27, 1988		MTR3064
Grimm	Eleanor	Swann	Apr. 10, 1929	Jan. 20, 2006	Mother / Always in our hearts	CHR118
Grinder	Atha	Wheeler	Nov. 7, 1913	Apr. 25, 1928	At rest / Children of W.F. & Sadie Grinder	CMX1046
Grinder	Barney	A.	Mar. 2, 1895	Nov. 3, 1984	Footstone: Father	CMX2102

Last Name	First Name	Middle Name	Date of Birth	Date of Death	Transcription / Notes	Cemetery Code
Grinder	Beulah	R.	1892	1982	Married Oct 30, 1917	CMX2028
Grinder	Catherine	E.	Sep. 29, 1901	Apr. 27, 1985		SCL3259
Grinder	Harry	Irvin	Jan. 7, 1908	Sep. 1, 1982		CMX2025
Grinder	James	E.	1891	1977	Married Oct 30, 1917	CMX2028
Grinder	Jane	E.	Feb. 9, 1869	Mar. 6, 1950		CMX2024
Grinder	Janie	Gertrude	Dec. 27, 1912	Nov. 14, 1913	At rest / Children of W.F. & Sadie Grinder	CMX1046
Grinder	John	C.	Sep. 18, 1898	May 24, 1983		SCL3259
Grinder	John	P.	Mar. 13, 1949	Aug. 21, 1951	Mother / Marion Bowie	ODE049
Grinder	Julia	Lee	No Date	Nov. 1966	Age 27, buried November 17, 1966 / Info is from the Historical Society Research located at the College of Southern MD, LaPlata, MD	ODENoStone
Grinder	Louise	Bowie	1904	1990	In Loving Memory	PIS080
Grinder	Malcolm	Russell	Sep. 13, 1923	Nov. 29, 1942	To him we trust a place is given among the Saints with Christ in Heaven	MRB058
Grinder	Minnie	E.	1897	1960		PKH136
Grinder	Roberta	G.	Aug. 17, 1898	Jan. 13, 1985	Footstone: Mother	CMX2102
Grinder	Sadie	L.	1889	1932	We shall meet again	CMX1045
Grinder	Thomas	E.	1893	1971		PKH136
Grinder	Vernon	A.	Jun. 4, 1942	Aug. 22, 2005	"Buddy" / Loving Father, Granddaddy, Brother, Uncle, Friend	ODE056
Grinder	W.	C. C.	Jun. 1, 1861	Jan. 23, 1945		CMX2024
Grinder	William	F.	1889	1959	We shall meet again	CMX1045
Grisett	Martha	S.	No Date	Aug. 1886	Info is from Old Durham Church microfilm pg 79-80 located at the College of Southern MD, LaPlata, MD	ODENoStone
Grissett	Catherine	A.	1898	No Date		HGH1139
Grissett	Richard	L.	1896	1973		HGH1139
Groeger	Jeremy	Michael	No Date	Mar. 17, 1986	Baby / Our little Angel	MTR4300
Groenwoldt	Ella	J.	Aug. 21, 1938	Sep. 11, 1976	Rest in peace No one was more loved	SJE123
Groenwoldt	Mark	Andrew	Jan. 16, 1971	Mar. 9, 1972	Our gift from God	SCL4131
Gross, Sr.	Albert		1893	1979		SAC4031
Gross	Bernard	James	1931	1983	CPL US Army Korea	SMT052
Gross	Charles	J.	Feb. 17, 1955	Oct. 14, 1975	PVI US Army	NSP304

Last Name	First Name	Middle Name	Date of Birth	Date of Death	Transcription / Notes	Cemetery Code
Gross	Charles	N.	Mar. 1, 1925	Feb. 22, 1994		SMC3060
Gross	Elizabeth		No Date	Oct. 3, 1875	Info is from church records	OFENoStone
Gross	Georgeanna		1930	2006		SMC3047
Gross, Jr.	James	B.	1930	2004		SMC3047
Gross, Sr.	James	B.	1894	1998		SMC3044
Gross	James	S.	Oct. 20, 1922	Jul. 4, 1989		SMC3136
Gross	Joseph	Edward	1942	1964		SMC3043
Gross	Margaret	Ann	1892	1984	"Maggie"	SMC3287
Gross	Margaret	C.	Feb. 13, 1920	Jun. 15, 1976	In memory - wife and mother	SMC4038
Gross	Marie	E.	1903	1993		SMC3046
Gross	Mary	Ella	Jul. 25, 1934	Jul. 25, 1995	"Grandmer" / Loving Mother and Grandmother	SMT051
Gross	Mary	Sadie	1924	2008	Brinsfield Echols funeral home marker	SMC3064
Gross	Richard	B.	Jan. 25, 1909	Aug. 4, 2004	TEC 5 US Army	SMC4037
Gross	Ruth	M.	Sep. 16, 1923	Sep. 24, 1978		SMC3137
Gross	Sarah	S.	1880	1947		NSP188
Gross	Sarah		Feb. 20, 1929	Mar. 30, 1995	On Earth / In Heaven / Our Mother "Puddin"	SMC4215
Grote	Helen	Joyce	Dec. 13, 1941	No Date		SIC9045
Grote	Herbert	F.	Apr. 4, 1944	Aug. 31, 2003		SIC9045
Grove	Bernard	L.	1900	1995		SIC9073
Grove	Catherine	B.	1907	No Date		SIC9073
Grove	Dolores	L.	Aug. 26, 1960	Sep. 22, 1991	In loving memory	SIC8062
Grove	Eric	J.	Nov. 27, 1984	Sep. 22, 1991	In loving memory	SIC8062
Grove	Walter	Brand	Jan. 8, 1973	Mar. 17, 1999	Beloved son "Too" With an awe & wonder of all things D/o M.T. & Elvie Groves / She was the sunshine of our home	MTR1194
Groves	Agnes	Mable	Feb. 26, 1911	Aug. 15, 1911		CMX1047
Groves	Benjamin	Douglas	Jul. 13, 1864	May 20, 1951	Death is eternal life	SPL4050
Groves	Elizabeth	Monroe	Aug. 7, 1871	May 27, 1916	Death is eternal life	SPL4050
Groves	Emily	Jaeger	Oct. 8, 1946	Mar. 18, 1989		CMX1145
Groves	George	Raymond	Oct. 17, 1899	May 25, 1968	Death is eternal life	SPL4050
Groves	J.	Louis	Oct. 12, 1897	Dec. 3, 1966		NSP624

Last Name	First Name	Middle Name	Date of Birth	Date of Death	Transcription / Notes	Cemetery Code
Groves	James	Robert	No Date	Jun.e 3, 1978	Aged 1 day (info is from Historical Society Research located at The College of Southern MD, LaPlata, MD)	SACNostone
Groves	James	Thomas	1925	1979	Together forever / Married Jul 9, 1946 / CPL US Army WWII	CMX1146
Groves	Janice	K.	1927	1996	Together forever / Married Jul 9, 1946	CMX1146
Groves	Josephine	Amelia	A.D. 1844	Oct. 23, 1864	Sacred to memory of / W/o A. Judson Groves / Professed Christ in baptism Sep 4, 1864 / and died in peace "Thou art gone to the grave; but 'twere wrong to deplore thee, for GOD was thy ransom, thy guardian and guide. He gave thee, he took thee, and soon will restore thee, where sin hath no sting, for Jesus hath died." / "The memory of the just is blessed"	CMX1075
Groves	Katie		No Date	No Date	Identified on church's unmarked grave list as Stone: 51	CMXNoStone
Groves	Leonard	A	May 25, 1912	Mar. 24, 1990	Pvt US Army WWII	CMX2163
Groves	Lina		1892	1955	Mother - Father - Son	CMX1052
Groves	Mary	H.	Apr. 14, 1914	Dec. 20, 1990		CMX2164
Groves	Mary	V.	1850	1933	She lived in peace with mankind, she died in peace With God / Footstone: Grandmother	CMX1049
Groves	Mary	Virgie	Sep. 6, 1919	Jul. 29, 1926	Our Angel / Daughter of Thomas P & Fannie C Groves	ONZ003
Groves	Maude	E.	Apr. 8, 1897	Jul. 10, 1996		NSP623
Groves	Maynard	H.	Apr. 8, 1904	Mar. 5, 1981		CMX2164
Groves	Morty	T.	Oct. 28, 1877	Jul.l 11, 1914	We do not know the pain you bore, we did not see you die, we only know you went away (Rest of stone is in the ground, unable to see if there is any more writing on the stone)	CMX1048
Groves	Morty		1915	1935	Mother - Father - Son	CMX1052
Groves	Mrs. Elenor		Apr. 23, 1801	Oct. 3, 1866	Sacred to the memory of / Baptized Jun 1834 / A happy Christian. Let me die the death of the righteous and my last days like his.	NJB406
Groves	Pat		1886	1937	Mother - Father - Son	CMX1052
Groves	Rosie	B.	May 19, 1917	Dec. 12, 1922	Our darling / beloved d/o Thomas P. and Fannie C. Groves. Info is from the Historical Society Research located at the College of Southern MD, LaPlata, MD	ONZ005
Groves	Ruth	Flowers	Oct. 18, 1893	Oct. 8, 1963	Requiescat in Pace	SPL4124

Last Name	First Name	Middle Name	Date of Birth	Date of Death	Transcription / Notes	Cemetery Code
Groves	Thomas		Jun. 8, 1799	Aug. 1, 1869	In memory of / May he rest in peace	NJB407
Groves	William	Alvie	Feb. 18, 1890	Nov. 25, 1971	Requiescat in Pace	SPL4124
Grubic	Anthony	William	1909	1975	Rest in peace	SJO1100
Grubic	Joseph	W.	1915	1983	Our loving father	SJO1099
Grubic	Ruth	Stewart	1910	1982	Rest in peace	SJO1100
Gruss	Hedwig		1877	1964		NSP797
Gruss	Joseph	Aloysius	Jun. 16, 1905	May 8, 1993	"Uncle Al"	NSP795
Gruss	Joseph	Leo	Apr. 23, 1918	Mar. 5, 2005	In loving memory	NSP882
Gruss	Joseph	M., Leo	1869	1952		NSP796
Gruss	Martha	Eugenia	Jul. 31, 1928	No Date	In Loving Memory	NSP882
Guckert	Mary	Rowe	1879	1974		PIS188
Guenzel	Julius		No Date	Jan. 18, 1882	Info is from Christ Church microfilm Reel 1 Pg 318-319 located at the College of Southern MD, LaPlata, MD	MTRNoStone
Gullett	Mildred	Swann	1921	2003		MTR3063
Gunley			No Date	Jan. 27, 1890	Son of Mr. Gunley / info is from church records	OFENoStone
Gunnell	Jeanne	Lorraine	Jan. 10, 1931	Apr. 29, 2008	Age 77, born in Wash. D.C., d/o Ruth Ward and Mercier Lowe / info is from the MD Independent Newspaper May 1, 2008	CLVNoStone
Gushee	M.	Helen	No Date	No Date	No information on the marker	PIS064
Gutrick	Azell		Nov. 10, 1922	Jun. 14, 1999	Beloved Mother "Azie"	SCL3237
Gutrick	Ben		1907	1986		MHB075
Gutrick	Charles	Ricardo	Aug. 30, 1964	Oct. 26, 1996	"Ricky" / Beloved son & brother, father	SCL3245
Gutrick	Clarence		1934	1999		SCL3225
Gutrick	Donald	Maurice	Mar. 16, 1948	Apr. 24, 1968	MD CPL Co D 503 INF 173 Abn Div Viet Nam PH	MHB186
Gutrick	Dorothy	R.	1919	1992		DUD028
Gutrick	Helen		1938	1991		SCL3225
Gutrick	Jessie	E.	1912	1990		DUD030
Gutrick	Marjorie		1961	1979	Thornton Funeral Home Marker	MHB133
Gutrick	Mitchell		1910	1986	Thornton Funeral Home Marker	DUD029
Gutrick	Reginald	S.	1984	1991		DUD024
Gutrick	Walter		Jan. 7, 1920	Mar. 21, 2004	Husband and Father	MHB235

Last Name	First Name	Middle Name	Date of Birth	Date of Death	Transcription / Notes	Cemetery Code
Gutrick, Sr.	Wayne		Sep. 30, 1949	May 12, 1993	Beloved Brother and Son / Thornton funeral home marker	SMI046
Gutridge	Joseph	Hampton	No Date	Dec. 15, 1908	Info is from Christ Church microfilm Reel 3, Pg 220-221 located at the College of Southern MD, LaPlata, MD	MTRNoStone
Gutridge	Lillian	R.	Mar. 31, 1884	Feb. 7, 1967		MTR3144
Guy	Charlotte	D.	Jun. 19, 1930	Dec. 21, 1999	John 3:16 / "Shoshie" Our mom......Our friend	SPL1022
Guy	Frank	R.	1899	1975	Louise C Guy	TRI225
Guy	Jo Ann	T.	1933	2001	RN Emblem	OFE2099
Guy	Lousie	C.	1904	1993	Frank R Guy	TRI225
Guy	Steven	F.	1932	No Date		OFE2099
Gwinn	Allan	Burch	1882	1958	Hungerford plot	CHR051
Gwynn	Anthony		1912	1960		NSP678
Gwynn	Charles	B.	Apr. 27, 1893	Oct. 19, 1968	Maryland PFC CO A 306 Engineers World War I	CHR334
Gwynn	Dorothy	Emlen	Aug. 27, 1905	Dec. 22, 1976		CHR333
Gwynn	Elizabeth	Ida	Aug. 9, 1888	Nov. 13, 1954		SMC2094
Gwynn	Francis	Bernard	Jul. 26, 1886	Apr. 25, 1975		SMC2093
Gwynn	Jane	C.	1815	Aug. 11, 1886	To our devoted mother / Requiescat in pace / Unable to read the month and day of birth on stone	SMCD283
Gwynn	Joseph	Edwin	Sep. 24, 1910	Mar. 17, 1965		SMC2092
Gwynn	Nellie	L.	1882	1945		SCL4157
Gwynn	Polly		Sep. 19, 1914	Mar. 22, 2002		SMC2091
H.	A.	C.	No Date	No Date	There is a footstone in the bushes and no headstone to go with it.	SMY1102A
H.	K.	C.	No Date	No Date	Footstone with initials K.C.H.	LUM222
H.	M.		No Date	No Date	Footstone with the initials M.H., no headstone	SMCA172
H.	W.	C.	No Date	No Date	Footstone with initials W.C.H.	SMCW043
H.	W.				Old Small footstone with initials W.H.	SCL1259
H, Jr.	P.	C.	No Date	No Date	Small stone with initials P.C.H., Jr. / Masonic Emblem on stone	OFE4010A
H.	A.	C.	No Date	No Date	Not a footstone	SJE060
H.	G.		No Date	No Date	Not a footstone	SJE062
H.	L.		No Date	No Date	Not a footstone	SJE061

Last Name	First Name	Middle Name	Date of Birth	Date of Death	Transcription / Notes	Cemetery Code
Haas	J.	Marian	1872	1964		TRI057
Haas	Raymond	J.	1885	1948		TRI057
Habliston	Charlotte		Dec. 9, 1928	No Date	Our beloved mother	SMC1152
Hachem	G.	L.	Aug. 19, 1953	Jul. 17, 1981	"Larry"	ODE060
Hackerson	Aline	F.	Feb. 13, 1909	Apr. 7, 1988		SCL3234
Hackerson	Eva	E.	1925	2001		SCL1192
Hackerson	Harriet	A.	1847	1903	In Memory of	SMI072
Hackerson	John	Ed	No Date	Jul. 18, 1958	Aged 82 years / Information is from the Historical Society Research located at the College of Southern Md, LaPlata, MD	SMINoStone
Hackerson	Joseph	E.	Nov. 6, 1908	May 27, 1987		SCL3234
Hackerson	William	R.	1907	1972		SCL1192
Hagan	Audrey	E.	Jan. 6, 1924	May 11, 1994		CLV390
Hagan	Jesse	T.	Oct. 7, 1915	Nov. 28, 1995		CLV390
Hagens	Elizabeth		1922	1947		NSP253
Hagens	Hester		1926	No Date		NSP039
Hagens	Mary	L.	1927	2001		NSP043
Hagens	Mary	Louise	Mar. 18, 1947	Dec. 27, 2007		SMC3101
Hagens	Raymond		1914	1995		NSP043
Hagens	William	A.	1912	1987		NSP039
Hahn	John	Miller	Dec. 9, 1971	Nov. 20, 1990		NSP023
Haines	Eliza Eleanor	Padgett	Jul. 22, 1904	May 30, 1995		MTR1069
Hair	Dorothy	Elizabeth	Mar. 1, 1924	Apr. 4, 2000	"Warwick" (info is from church records)	MTR3023
Hairston	Brian	Andrew	1951	1994	Brian Andrew Hairston / Beloved husband & Father / Rest in Peace "Real World"	SCL4117
Hairston	Lorraine	B.	1963	1984	In loving memory	SJO1043
Haislip	Alexander		Apr. 2, 1843	Apr. 26, 1911	Gone, but not forgotten	ODE323
Haislip	Alice	Lucretia	Dec. 4, 1914	Oct. 15, 1915	d/o Philemon A - Virginia E Haislip	ODE309
Haislip	Alpheus		No Date	Sep. 1921	Age 77 / buried Sep 4, 1921 / info is from Old Durham Church microfilm pg 159 located at the College of Southern MD, LaPlata, MD pg 159	ODENoStone

Last Name	First Name	Middle Name	Date of Birth	Date of Death	Transcription / Notes	Cemetery Code
Haislip	Alpheus		Sep. 10, 1899	Oct. 9, 1960		ODE144
Haislip	Ann	H.	May 2, 1816	Apr. 14, 1887	In memory of Ann H. Haislip daughter of Robt. and Annie Slye Hall / The Lord is good to all and his tender mercies are over all his works. Psalms CXLV9 / footstone A.H.H / stone lying down	TRI095
Haislip	Anna	Lucretia	Jan. 14, 1884	Jul. 3, 1888	d/o Alexander & Josephine Haislip	ODE321
Haislip	Edward	R.	No Date	Aug. 12, 1895	Info is from Old Durham Church microfilm pg 83-84 located at the College of Southern MD, LaPlata, MD	ODENoStone
Haislip	James		No Date	Apr. 1923	Age 75 Buried Apr 13, 1923 (info is from Old Durham Church microfilm pg 159 located at the College of Southern MD, LaPlata, MD)	ODENoStone
Haislip	Jane	Elizabeth	Oct. 14, 1854	Mar. 25, 1855	Sacred to the memory of / the beloved d/o Walter A. Haislip who was born / and departed this life / age 34 years 11 mos. 2 days Note: familysearch.org shows her to be the d/o Walter & Lucretia Haislip	HAINoStone
Haislip	Josephine	Elizabeth	Sep. 12, 1875	Sep. 23, 1904	d/o Alexander & Josephine Haislip	ODE324
Haislip	Josephine		Sep. 10, 1846	Jun. 26, 1893	Beloved w/o Alexander Haislip / "Asleep in Jesus."	ODE322
Haislip	Lucretia		Nov. 22, 1820	Oct. 24, 1855	Sacred to the memory of Lucretia the beloved wife of Walter A. Haislip who was born the 22d day of November 1820 and departed this life 24th day of October 1855, aged 34 years, 11 mos., 2 days (This stone is buried and no one knows the location. Pictures are courtesy from Mike Mazzeo's Collection)	HAI001
Haislip	Lucy	Hooe, Barnes	No Date	No Date	w/o Alpheus Haislip	ODE157
Haislip	Pearl	C.	1901	1982		ODE313
Haislip	Philemon	A.	1870	1951	Father	ODE310
Haislip	Priscilla		Mar. 9, 1853	Aug. 28, 1853	d/o Walter & Lucretia Thompson Haislip / info is from the website familysearch.org and from The Historical Society Research located at The College of Southern MD, LaPlata, MD. Note: familysearch.org shows her to be the Dau. Of Walter & Lucretia Haislip	HAINoStone

Last Name	First Name	Middle Name	Date of Birth	Date of Death	Transcription / Notes	Cemetery Code
Haislip	Rufus		Jul. 19, 1851	Oct. 2, 1873	s/o Walter & Lucretia Thompson Haislip / info is from the website familysearch.org and from The Historical Society Research located at The College of Southern MD, LaPlata, MD Note: familysearch.org shows him to be the son of Walter & Lucretia Haislip	HAINoStone
Haislip	Sarah	Francis	Nov. 5, 1839	Nov. 29, 1860	info is from the website familysearch.org and from The Historical Society Research located at The College of Southern MD, LaPlata, MD Note: familysearch.org shows her to be the Dau. Of Walter & Lucretia Haislip	HAINoStone
Haislip	Thomas	Henry		Aug. 6, 1895	Age 48 (info is from Old Durham Church microfilm pg 83-84, at the College of Southern MD, LaPlata, MD)	ODENoStone
Haislip	Virginia	E.	1904	1985		ODE313
Haislip	Virginia	E.	1875	1966	Mother	ODE310
Haislip	Walter	A.	Oct. 6, 1892	Feb. 22, 1975	Pvt. US Army WW I	ODE145
Haislip	Walter	Alexander	Nov. 11, 1812	No Date	s/o Hezekiah & Priscilla B. Franklin / info is from the website familysearch.org and from The Historical Society Research located at The College of Southern MD, LaPlata, MD (He is listed as age 48 in the 1860 census, and not in any census records after that)	HAINoStone
Haislip	William	Francis	May 1, 1838	Nov. 5, 1862	s/o Walter & Lucretia Thompson Haislip / info is from the website familysearch.org and from The Historical Society Research located at The College of Southern MD, LaPlata, MD	HAINoStone
Haisly	Anna	Lucretia	No Date	Jul. 3, 1888	4 yrs old (info is from Old Durham Church microfilm pg 79-80 located at the College of Southern MD, LaPlata, MD)	ODENoStone
Haley	Doris	L.	1921	1962		SJE243
Halkerston	Ann		No Date	Aug. 11, 1774	Here lieth ye body of / d/o Robert & Ann Halkerston who departed this life / info is from DAR book Pg 142, at the College of Southern MD, LaPlata, MD	ODE019
Hall	Bernie	DeHaven	Mar. 6, 1927	Dec. 6, 1997	Baptized in the Catholic Faith on Dec 4, 1997 / m. Jun 12, 1950 / Elizabethtown, KY	NSP822
Hall	Bobby	E.	Jan. 31, 1943	Oct. 4, 1997		OFE5004
Hall	Douglas		1957	Feb. 25, 1957	Info is from church records	CLVNoStone
Hall	Eugene	A.	Apr. 17, 1931	Feb. 21, 1999	Married Jan 28, 1956	SMY2045

Last Name	First Name	Middle Name	Date of Birth	Date of Death	Transcription / Notes	Cemetery Code
Hall	George	I.	1867	1940	To his memory this monument is erected by H. Holland Hawkins as a token of affection and respect for his loyalty as a servant and his trustworthiness as a man. / Footstone lying next to a tree.	BRC006
Hall	Grace	E.	No Date	No Date		SCL1161
Hall	James		No Date	Jan. 16, 1968	Info is from Christ Church microfilm Reel 4 Pg 288-289 located at the College of Southern MD, LaPlata, MD	MTRNoStone
Hall	Joan	M.	Apr. 24, 1936	Mar. 16, 2000	Married Jan 28, 1956	SMY2045
Hall	Julia		1904	1952		SMY2135
Hall	Kathryn	S.	1905	No Date		MTR3182
Hall	Martha	Geraldine, Boothe	May 1, 1929	No Date	"Jerry" / Elizabethtown, KY / m. Jun 12, 1950	NSP822
Hall	Mary	Ann	Jan. 6, 1938	Oct. 3, 1990		GIL004
Hall	Naomi	Wilson	1910	1938		HGH2070
Hall	Shirley	A.	Sep. 29, 1936	Dec. 14, 2000	"We Love You"	POM207
Hall	Theresa	Johnson, Niessen	1899	1989		SIC6011
Hall	Wallace	L.	1897	1975		MTR3182
Hall	William	T.	1905	1975	Info is from the Historical Society Located at the College of Southern MD, LaPlata, MD	BRCNoStone
Hallahan	Roberta	Greer	Dec. 24, 1921	Feb. 16, 2007	Info is from the Catholic Cemetery Assoc	SIG117
Haller	James	D.	1907	1986		SJO3168
Haller	Louise	C.	1907	1992		SJO3168
Hallett	Cynthia		Mar. 22, 1971	May 4, 2007	Cynthia Hallett / "Cindy" / Mommy Back of Stone: If tears could build a stairway and memories were a lane, we would walk right up to heaven and bring you back again. Love Morgan	SMY5002
Halley	Donald		Feb. 3, 1905	Dec. 14, 1979		MTR3142
Halley	Edna	Golden	1889	1963		OSM108
Halley	Ella	Virginia	1855	1939	His Wife	OSM084
Halley	George		Jun. 20, 1878	Aug. 28, 1914	At rest	OSM081
Halley	Inez	Gutridge	Jun. 24, 1905	Dec. 31, 1981		MTR3142
Halley	Irene		May 22, 1911	Apr. 13, 1917	d/o Geo. & Lydia Halley. / God himself our loved ones keep giving his beloved sleep	OSM080

Last Name	First Name	Middle Name	Date of Birth	Date of Death	Transcription / Notes	Cemetery Code
Halley	Irving		Sep. 20, 1884	Jul. 18, 1916	son	OSM049
Halley	J.	W.	Sep. 30, 1836	Apr. 16, 1888	Stone is missing from base. Footstone with initials JWH info is from the 1940 DAR book page 92	OSM068
Halley	James	Thomas	1844	1908		OSM020
Halley	John	Emmett	1880	1964		OSM109
Halley	John	Monroe	1843	1930		OSM084
Halley	Julia	I.	May 25, 1866	Oct. 1, 1887	In memory of / Her happy soul has winged its way to one pure bright eternal day	OSM034
Halley	M.	Lillian, Harris	Oct. 16, 1855	Mar. 9, 1892		SJE165
Halley	Maria		No Date	Feb. 1883	In the 74th year of her age	OSM050
Halley	Mary	Catherine	1850	1928		OSM021
Halley	Richard	Henry	Aug. 27, 1875	Nov. 10, 1967		OSM022
Halley	Rose		1834	1905		OSM037
Halley	Thomas	Richard	No Date	Jun. 1892	In the 85th year of his age	OSM050
Halley	Unknown		No Date	No Date	Infant of J.T. & Mary C.	OSM019
Halley	Virginia	E.	Sep. 15, 1853	Apr. 27, 1894	w/o Winfield Halley	OSM049
Hamann	Jan	Marie	Nov. 4, 1948	Feb. 7, 1995		LUM008
Hamer	Olga	Swann	1916	2000		SMY2013
Hamersley	Helen		No Date	Feb. 4, 1836	Aged 65 years / R.I.P.	HGH1221
Hamersly	Glorvenia	M.	No Date	Dec. 30, 1884	In memory of / aged 79 years (stone is sunken)	HGH1207
Hamersly	John		No Date	May 5, 1880	In memory of / Aged 75 years / May he rest in peace	HGH1206
Hamilton, Rev.	Albert	W.	1883	1950		PIS051
Hamilton	Albert		1874	1949		CLV047
Hamilton	Alice	C.	Sep. 28, 1919	No Date	The wind beneath my wings	SPL5044
Hamilton	Alvie		1895	1954		CLV046
Hamilton	Amanda	Viora	Nov. 1, 1890	Sep. 28, 1973	In Loving Memory	CLV051
Hamilton	Anne	Offutt	Aug. 23, 1912	Nov. 15, 1988	Beloved w/o Francis P. Hamilton	SIC2122
Hamilton	Augusta	T.	1881	1949		SPL2006
Hamilton	C.		No Date	No Date	Number 36-B inscribed on lower left of stone	CLV076
Hamilton	Carl	H.	Oct. 17, 1926	Dec. 3, 1974	Beloved Husband and Father	CLV077

Last Name	First Name	Middle Name	Date of Birth	Date of Death	Transcription / Notes	Cemetery Code
Hamilton	Catherine	Dyer	No Date	Jun. 26, 1924	Catherine Dyer Hamilton / w/o John P. Hamilton / aged 73 years / I have finished my course, I have kept the faith in thee is all I will or desire	SIC2126
Hamilton	Catherine	M.	Nov. 15, 1927	No Date	Additional info is from church records	SPL5111
Hamilton	Cecelia	Plowden	Sep. 21, 1854	Apr. 16, 1917	w/o J. Edward Hamilton / Eternal rest grant unto her O Lord and let perpetual light shine upon her	SIC2168
Hamilton	Charles	E.	May 7, 1870	Sep. 27, 1951		CLV107
Hamilton	Charles	Leo	1908	1980	Middle name is from church records	SPL2001
Hamilton	Clarence	H.	Jul. 27, 1904	Jun. 16, 1983	In Loving Memory	CLV080
Hamilton	Daisy		1884	1953		CLV033
Hamilton	Delbert	M.	1889	1949		SPL5048
Hamilton	Doris	Jacqueline	Jul. 13, 1936	Jul. 6, 2001	"Jackie" / m. Apr 21, 1956	SPL6082
Hamilton	Dorothy	Mae	May 28, 1936	Mar. 13, 1995	In Loving Memory	CLV079
Hamilton	Earl	E.	Jul. 4, 1899	Dec. 15, 1980	Also has a marker, number 110-A	CLV123
Hamilton, Jr.	Earl		Jul. 16, 1926	Jun. 22, 2004	Stauffer Funeral Home PA Fredrick MD / Age 78	CLV115
Hamilton	Ed		No Date	No Date	Number 79 inscribed on lower right of stone Information is from church records	CLV109
Hamilton	Edith	E.	Feb. 26, 1927	Jun. 21, 1976	Moose Waldorf Chapter 1387 / Jesus called	PKH127
Hamilton	Edward	J.	No Date	Dec. 13, 1841	Sacred to the memory of / Our affectionate father who departed this life / in the 44 year of his age: May he rest in Peace. Amen	SJO4178
Hamilton, Sr. LT.	Edward		1762	May 27, 1824	In memory of / who departed this life / aged 65 Maryland's Continental Line. The American Revolution / Exhumed and reinterred at St. Joseph's, Pomfret, Md on March 26, 1981. (Notes from Sister Miriam John at Mt Carmel Monastery)	SJO4177
Hamilton	Elanor		1825	Sep. 17, 1831	d/o John Hamilton and Nancy Hamilton	GMCNo Stone
Hamilton	Eleanor	H.	1799	Aug. 26, 1818	In memory of / d/o Edward Hamilton Sr. who departed this life / aged 19	GMCNo Stone
Hamilton	Eleanor	Hawkins	1778	Nov. 13, 1807	IHS in memory of / consort of Edward Hamilton, Sen. Who departed this life d/ Exhumed and reinterred at St. Joseph's in Pomfret, Md on March 26, 1981 (Notes from Sister Miriam John at Mt Carmel Monastery)	SJO4177

Last Name	First Name	Middle Name	Date of Birth	Date of Death	Transcription / Notes	Cemetery Code
Hamilton	Elizabeth		No Date	Jan. 22, 1915	With abiding faith, patient courage and sweet charity. She lived that she might serve	HWK003
Hamilton	Ella		1880	1946		CLV048
Hamilton	F.	Hill	Mar. 9, 1891	Apr. 13, 1974	Youngest s/o John P. & Catherine D. Hamilton	SIC2124
Hamilton, MA.	F.	Lamar	1913	2002	Author of Pike Connections and Alexander Hamilton of Spy Park. The first Hamiltons of Old Portobacco MD	SJO4176
Hamilton	Francis	P.	Jun. 11, 1884	Oct. 11, 1955	s/o John P. & Catherine D. Hamilton	SIC2125
Hamilton	Francis	P.	May 31, 1902	Nov. 27, 1985	Eldest s/o James Neale and Mary Emily Matthews Hamilton	SIC2123
Hamilton	Francis	P.	Oct. 22, 1838	Nov. 1, 1896	We met with courage the duties of life and faithfully performed them, and when death came he was not afraid.	SIC2016
Hamilton, Jr.	Francis	P.	Jul. 7, 1865	Aug. 27, 1870	This stone is in a hexagontal shape	SIC2099
Hamilton	George	Alston	1902	1991	Middle name is from church records	SPL2002
Hamilton	George	H.	1869	1932		SPL2005
Hamilton	George	Orlando	Aug. 12, 1909	Jun. 20, 1985		SPL7016
Hamilton	Gerald	Allen	Dec. 19, 1932	Mar. 8, 2003	US Army / m. Apr 21, 1956 / Middle name is from church records	SPL6081
Hamilton	Guy	J.	1893	1971		SPL5108
Hamilton	Gwynette		Dec. 6, 1916	Aug. 29, 1996		CLV121
Hamilton	Hanson		1888	1951		CLV033
Hamilton	Helen	Marie	Feb. 15, 1921	Feb. 26, 1926		SPL5047
Hamilton	Henrietta		Feb. 14, 1803	Dec. 12, 1834	IHS Sacred to the memory of / who departed this life / aged 31 years 9 months and 28 days. May she rest in peace / Stonemaker A. Gaddess, Balt Notes from Sister Miriam John at Mt Carmel Monastery)	GMC004
Hamilton	Henry	H.	1929	1970	Father	SJO6006
Hamilton	Ida	Elizabeth	Mar. 26, 1909	Sep. 16, 1984	Burial transit permit reads Ida Elizabeth Hamilton d/o George	SPL6078
Hamilton	Irma	Elizabeth	Feb. 16, 1915	Jan. 18, 1917	Our Darling Baby Irma Elizabeth Hamilton d/o George H. & Augusta T. Hamilton / Our precious angel has gone but not forgotten.	SPL2007

Last Name	First Name	Middle Name	Date of Birth	Date of Death	Transcription / Notes	Cemetery Code
Hamilton	J.	Edward	May 25, 1845	Jul. 12, 1899	Verse on stone: He met death bravely and with an abiding faith went to meet his maker, leaving to his sorrowing family the arom of a good name and the incense of a blameless life	SIC2170
Hamilton, Jr.	J.	Lloyd	May 13, 1948	Apr. 18, 1966		CLV337
Hamilton	James	Neale	1867	1946	His wife	SIC2100
Hamilton	James	O.	Feb. 24, 1901	Mar. 21, 1966		SPL6078
Hamilton	James	P.	Sep. 23, 1929	Jul. 23, 1967	MD PVT 172 Sta Hospital	SPL6095
Hamilton	James	E.	1914	1967		CLV053
Hamilton	Jane	E.	Sep. 17, 1837	Feb. 23, 1926		SPL2010
Hamilton	Janie	S.	Aug. 6, 1905	Aug. 13, 1997	Also has a marker, number 110-A	CLV123
Hamilton	Jennings	L.	Mar. 25, 1897	Nov. 11, 1949	WW I	SPL6005
Hamilton	Jerry	Lalia	Oct. 7, 1936	Apr. 19, 2002		SPL5111
Hamilton	John	D.	1860	1941	Additional info is from church records	SPL6009
Hamilton	John	L.	Oct. 17, 1872	Jan. 23, 1940		CLV218
Hamilton	John	P.	No Date	Apr. 18, 1923	Aged 74 years / In truth sublime words make not a man holy and just, but a virtuous life maketh him dear to God (This was a tall obelisk stone, however the top is broken into 2 pieces and are laying on the ground next to the base)	SIC2128
Hamilton	John	R.	Apr. 5, 1909	Apr. 12, 1982		SPL4149
Hamilton	John		No Date	Feb. 2, 1883	Aged 85 years / He trusted in God, loved truth practiced virtue and left to his children a priceless inheritance of a good name.	SIC2182
Hamilton	John		No Date	No Date	Death probably after his wife's. May be buried next to his wife Nancy Hamilton (Notes from Sister Miriam John at Mt Carmel Monastery)	GMCNo Stone
Hamilton	June	Lee	Jan. 1, 1929	Aug. 1929		SPL6005
Hamilton	Kate		No Date	Mar. 25, 1916	Her life's great treasure was God's gift of faith	SIC2180
Hamilton	Laura	B.	1869	1949		SPL6010
Hamilton	Leroy		Jan. 2, 1886	Apr. 30, 1980	In Loving Memory	CLV051
Hamilton	Lewis	Levie	Aug. 6, 1919	Jan. 28, 1986	In Loving Memory	CLV078
Hamilton	Lloyd		1902	1948		CLV338

Last Name	First Name	Middle Name	Date of Birth	Date of Death	Transcription / Notes	Cemetery Code
Hamilton	Lydia	C.	1899	1978		SPL5048
Hamilton	Margaret	Julia	1901	1986	First name is from church records	SPL5108
Hamilton	Maria	E.	May 14, 1800	Oct. 1, 1830	Sacred to the memory of / Consort of Edw'd J. Hamilton who was / Requiescat in pace, Amen. / Info is from the Historical Society Research, at the College of Southern MD, LaPlata, MD. / Large flat stone on the ground and is hard to read.	SJO4180
Hamilton	Mary	Emily	Feb. 28, 1862	Jul. 1, 1945	d/o Francis P. and Priscilla Neale	SIC2015
Hamilton	Mary	Emily	No Date	Aug. 13, 1876	w/o John Hamilton / aged 65 years. I have fought the good fight. I have finished my course. I have kept the faith	HWK004
Hamilton	Mary	Emily, Matthews	1870	1943	His wife	SIC2100
Hamilton	Mary	A.	Apr. 25, 1870	Jul. 24, 1921	w/o John T. Hamilton / Loved in Life in Death Remembered	CLV217
Hamilton	Mary	F.	Aug. 19, 1868	Jan. 12, 1957		CLV107
Hamilton	Mary Ann	Boarman	No Date	1796	First w/o Edward Hamilton Sr. (Burial verified by descendants (Notes from Sister Miriam John at Mt Carmel Monastery)	GMCNo Stone
Hamilton	Mitchell	Morgan	Oct. 29, 1922	Oct. 2, 1997	The wind beneath my wings / middle name is from church records	SPL5044
Hamilton	Myrtle	I.	1893	1902		CLV066
Hamilton	Nancy	M.	1905	1906		CLV067
Hamilton	Nancy	W.	1834	1919		CLV059
Hamilton	Nancy		1801	Dec. 7, 1827	IHS In the Memory of / the w/o John Hamilton who departed this life / in the 26th year of her age. May she rest in peace. Stone no longer exists	GMCNo Stone
Hamilton	O.	Preston	Jun. 21, 1911	Feb. 23, 1986		CLV121
Hamilton	Ovelton	M.	Jan. 18, 1919	Jul. 9, 1959	Maryland SGT CO C ENGR AVN BR WWII	SPL2003
Hamilton	P.	Arthur	1898	1898		CLV065
Hamilton	Perrie	E.	1876	1952		CLV108
Hamilton	Priscilla	Neale	Jun. 4, 1840	Mar. 20, 1907	In memory of / widow of Francis P. Hamilton / Eternal rest give to her O Lord	SIC2017
Hamilton	Rebekah	Wilmer	Nov. 27, 1889	Jun. 15, 1979		MTR1206

Last Name	First Name	Middle Name	Date of Birth	Date of Death	Transcription / Notes	Cemetery Code
Hamilton	Robert				In loving memory / beloved son, brother & friend / Back of stone: Bobby, My life has been touched because we have walked a special walk together, Because you mattered to me, Because you have given me courage, Because you cared so much, Because we are friends	SJO3117
Hamilton	Robert	E.	Mar. 7, 1969	May 12, 1990		CLV049
Hamilton	Roger	Taney	1898	1921		SIC2014
Hamilton	Ruth	A.	1905	1956		CLV063
Hamilton	S.	Henry	1894	1896		SIC2178
Hamilton	Stella	M.	No Date	Apr. 8, 1881	Aged 30 years / Loved in life in death remembered	SPL6005
Hamilton	T.	Belt	Mar. 8, 1900	Jan. 31, 1989		CLV068
Hamilton	Thelma	L.	1907	1907		SPL4149
Hamilton	Thelma	N.	Jul. 31, 1911	Apr. 11, 1968	In Loving Memory	CLV080
Hamilton	Timothy	S.	Apr. 15, 1911	May 3, 1990	Beloved s/o James and Mary	SPL6097
Hamilton	Unknown		Aug. 8 1955	Jan. 1, 1983	Infant Boy	CLV064
Hamilton	Wallace	W.	1896	1896	Maryland Pvt. Co. A 23 Inf 2 Inf Div WW II PH and OLC	CLV052
Hamilton	William	Curtis	Feb. 18, 1920	Mar. 19, 1971		CLV062
Hamilton	William	Noble	1903	1995		CLV058
Hamilton	William	Richard	1814	1899	Dum Tacet Clamet / Woodmen of the World	CLV060
Hamilton	Wilmer	M.	1862	1945		SPL5121
Hamilton	Wm.	Rufus	Dec. 6, 1906	Aug. 1, 1976	Jesus wept	CLV269
Hamm	Julia	A., Boyer	1847	1918		SJE036
Hammack	Alpheus	Wilson	Apr. 16, 1919	Aug. 31, 1963		CMX1040
Hammack	Anna		Mar. 21, 1895	Jun. 9, 1979		MRB037
Hammack	Clarence		1923	1924	d/o B. M. and E. A. Hammack	CMX1039
Hammack	Emma	A.	No Date	No Date	Our Mother / O Mother thou hast left us, none but God knows our loss. Thou canst never more return, but dear Mother we will come to thee / Footstone	HAM002
Hammack	H.	Bryan	1816	Jan. 12, 1884		CMX1037
Hammack	Homer	B.	May 26, 1900	Oct. 21, 1966		CMX1038
			1847	1927		

Last Name	First Name	Middle Name	Date of Birth	Date of Death	Transcription / Notes	Cemetery Code
Hammack	John	D.	Apr. 17, 1846	Dec. 15, 1863	Our Brother / None knew him but to love him, none named him but to praise / H. Rutherford / Footstone	HAM005
Hammack	John	L.	1815	Dec. 7, 1861	Our Father / Asleep in Jesus / Footstone	HAM008
Hammack	Lucy	M.	Mar. 30, 1902	Apr. 7, 1986		CMX1037
Hammack	Mary	Frances	1857	1947		CMX1038
Hammack	Recarda	L.	No Date	Mar. 10, 1888	In Memory of Recarda L. Hammack beloved d/o John L. & Emma A. Hammack / aged 25 years. Dearest loved one we have laid thee in the peaceful graves imbrace with thy memory will be cherished till we see thy heavenly face Footstone	HAM011
Hammersley	Henry		Oct. 10, 1750	May 28, 1833	In memory of /Aged 83 / His sorrowing children put this Long was my voice in serving God. Full eighty odd years did I spend. Follow the path children I trod and blest as mine will be your end. R. I.P.	HGH1218
Hammersly	Alice	A.	No Date	Aug. 2, 1912	Rest in peace	HGH1208
Hammett	Catherine	S.	1863	1930		HGH1115
Hammett	Dianah		No Date	Jun. 11, 1876	Info is from church records	OFENoStone
Hammett	Ellen	E.	1891	1975		SIC7008
Hammett, Sr.	J.	Gibbons	1905	1985		NSP728
Hammett	Joseph	S.	1899	1991		SIC7009
Hammett	M.	Blondell	1913	1997		NSP728
Hammond	Harley	Thomas	No Date	Nov. 13, 1976	Info is from The Historical Society Research, Located at The College of Southern MD, LaPlata, MD.	NZNNoStone
Hamor	Helen	L.	Jul. 24, 1938	No Date	Victory in Jesus / Masonic emblem on stone	NJB313
Hamor, Sr.	Hoyt	H.	Oct. 10, 1935	Dec. 24, 1992	Victory in Jesus / Masonic emblem on stone	NJB313
Hampton	Carl	Craighead	1913	2002	A big head and a heart to match, a great father, a friend to everyone, he never met a stranger. Home at last in the house of the Lord. Always in my life Love, Babe	ODE343
Hampton	Dorothy	E., Davis	Mar. 19, 1921	No Date	Precious Lord take my hand	CMX1111
Hampton	Lloyd	Winthrop	Aug. 7, 1915	May 22, 1988	Precious Lord take my hand	CMX1111
Hamrick	Ann		No Date	Mar. 14, 1972	Infant	SCL3280
Hanbert	Joseph		No Date	Oct. 9, 1927	Info is from church records	OFENoStone
Hancock	Alice	R.	Aug. 1876	Nov. 1959		OAK156

Last Name	First Name	Middle Name	Date of Birth	Date of Death	Transcription / Notes	Cemetery Code
Hancock	Anna	L.	Oct. 28, 1928	No Date	Gone but not forgotten / There is an Eastern Star emblem engraved on stone	NJB324
Hancock	Betty	E.	Jan. 8, 1924	No Date	Married Jul 21, 1944	SIC2076
Hancock	Bryan		1912	No Date		ODE163
Hancock	Budd	A.	1875	1961		ODE162
Hancock	Carroll	C.	Aug. 8, 1908	Jul. 28, 1996		OFE3047
Hancock	Catherine	Elaine	1932	1958		NSP766
Hancock	Catherine	Elyobeer	No Date	Jan. 25, 1910	Age 80 / info is from church records	OFENoStone
Hancock	Catherine	Ruth	Apr. 26, 1855	Feb. 24, 1909	At rest / Mother / Erected by her daughters	SJO2343
Hancock	Chester	W.	Nov. 28, 1928	No Date		LUM095
Hancock	Chloe	Ann	Jun. 5, 1883	Nov. 22, 1887	Info is from The College of Southern MD, LaPlata, MD	HAN006
Hancock	Christopher	Allan	1980	1994	s/o Melda Hancock Ryce	NJB111
Hancock	Cicero		Sep. 4, 1918	Sep. 29, 2004	Married Jul 21, 1944 / Footstone: AEM3 US Navy	SIC2076
Hancock	Cline	W.	Mar. 29, 1917	May 14, 1983		NJB326
Hancock	Dennis		1954	1979	First name is from church records / Thornton Funeral Home Marker	PGN013
Hancock	Dola	G.	Aug. 16, 1910	Aug. 5, 1972		OFE3047
Hancock	E.	Galen	Aug. 30, 1892	Jan. 15, 1920	In loving Remembrance s/o James D. & Mary C. Hancock	OFE1070
Hancock	Eleanor	T.	Apr. 10, 1931	No Date	Roy and Toogie	SCL3258
Hancock	Ernest	Lee	No Date	Feb. 18, 1918	Age 18 months / info is from church records	OFENoStone
Hancock	Esther	L.	Aug. 31, 1897	Dec. 17, 1954		LUM099
Hancock	George	A.	1921	1962		LUM057
Hancock	Georgia		1911	1978	Slab and Funeral Home Marker	MHB136
Hancock	Gerald	S.	Sep. 7, 1924	Sep. 19, 2005	Age 81 / Gone but not forgotten / Masonic emblem engraved on stone	NJB324
Hancock	Gerard	Hancock	May 6, 1818	Aug. 7, 1848	Old Abandoned Episcopal burying ground near Newtown, in woods of about 50 years growth. Many other graves in this tract, not marked (info is from the 1940 DAR book page 89)	NMENoStone
Hancock	Hannah	L.	Oct. 23, 1938	Apr. 21, 1988		LUM095
Hancock	Harold	Lee	Mar. 9, 1926	Jul. 27, 2010	Into thy hands we commend our spirit	LUM097

Last Name	First Name	Middle Name	Date of Birth	Date of Death	Transcription / Notes	Cemetery Code
Hancock	Harold	Rodger	Jan. 7, 1925	Jul. 18, 1949	TEC 5, U.S. Army World War II	OAK144
Hancock	Harry	C.	Feb. 8, 1929	Oct. 16, 1992		OFE3048
Hancock	Harry	Stanley	1911	1939	Asleep in Jesus	LUM063
Hancock	Helen	V.	Oct. 25, 1920	Apr. 25, 1998	Gone but not forgotten	NJB327
Hancock	Inez	Virginia	Dec. 5, 1886	Nov. 12, 1967		NJB156
Hancock	J.	Clayton	1885	1969		OFE1074
Hancock	J.	Samuel	Aug. 31, 1862	Nov. 8, 1879	In memory of J. Samuel, s/o John H. and Mary A. Hancock / age 17years, 2mo's, 8days (stone has been repaired but a piece is missing) Birth date is from church records	SPL4145
Hancock	James	A.	1921	1979		LUM209
Hancock	James	D.	1856	1927	Our father - mother / His Wife	OFE1071
Hancock	James	H.	Nov. 25, 1939	Jan. 23, 1993		OFE3048
Hancock	James	Louis	Apr. 19, 1925	Sep. 23, 1990		PKH066
Hancock	James	M.	Apr. 23, 1859	Oct. 5, 1935	Asleep in Jesus	LUM114
Hancock	James	Thomas	Oct. 9, 1868	Dec. 5, 1949	Info is from The College of Southern MD, LaPlata, MD. / family member has birth year as 1867 and middle name is Thomas	HAN011
Hancock	Jane	E.	1871	1959		HAN012
Hancock	John	Cochrane	1922	1988		MTR1190
Hancock	John	David	Nov. 1941	Dec. 1959	Beloved son of Wilmer and Anna Hancock	SMCD270
Hancock, Sr.	John	Edward	Aug. 28, 1942	Dec. 23, 2002	Info is from stone and church records	OFE5002
Hancock	John	H.	Dec. 23, 1830	Oct. 5, 1911	Erected by his daughter / At rest	SPL4144
Hancock	John	P.	1896	1947		MTR1186
Hancock	John	T.	Apr. 10, 1840	Aug. 11, 1904	Info is from The College of Southern MD, LaPlata, MD (family member says middle name is Judson, but it says T on the stone	HAN009
Hancock	John	R.	No Date	May 29, 1900	Info is from Christ Church microfilm Reel 1 Pg 86-87 located at the College of Southern MD, LaPlata, MD	MTRNoStone
Hancock	Josias	D.	May 8, 1853	Feb. 8, 1854	Old Abandoned Episcopal burying ground near Newtown, in woods of about 50 years growth. Many other graves in this tract, not marked (info is from the 1940 DAR book page 89)	NMENoStone

Last Name	First Name	Middle Name	Date of Birth	Date of Death	Transcription / Notes	Cemetery Code
Hancock	Josias		Apr. 28, 1807	Apr. 3, 1853	Old Abandoned Episcopal burying ground near Newtown, in woods of about 50 years growth. Many other graves in this tract, not marked (info is from the 1940 DAR book page 89)	NMENoStone
Hancock	Joyce	M.	Jan. 29, 1929	No Date		LUM098
Hancock	Kenneth	Cooksey	Sep. 15, 1932	Feb. 5, 1934	Baby Darling	LUM101
Hancock	L. Pauline	Kendrick	Mar. 20, 1886	Nov. 8, 1971	Mother	NJB110
Hancock	Lily	Ellen	Sep. 24, 1918	No Date	Erected in loving remembrance by Mary F. Davis Turpin	NJB107
Hancock	Louis	W.	Jul. 30, 1912	Apr. 9, 1919	s/o J.C. & E.M. Hancock	OFE1073
Hancock	Luellen		1873	1873		HAN014
Hancock	Lummie	S.	1871	1941		LUM197
Hancock	Luvinia	Marian, Cooksey	May 8, 1819	Jan. 22, 1892	Info is from The College of Southern MD, LaPlata, MD	HAN002
Hancock	M.	Henrietta	Nov. 29, 1840	Oct. 20, 1872	In memory of / beloved w/o T.T. Hancock and d/o Allison and Henrietta Roberts	SPL1060
Hancock	Mabel	Catherine	Jul. 4, 1920	Jan. 29, 1945		LUM100
Hancock	Mable		1902	1976	Montgomery Bros. Funeral Home Marker	PGN009
Hancock	Mamie	E.	1887	1961		OFE1074
Hancock	Mamie	E.	Feb. 20, 1895	Dec. 28, 1917	Loving memory / d/o J.D. & Mary C. Hancock	OFE1069
Hancock	Margaret	Ann	1936	Dec. 9, 1999	Info is from stone and church records	OFE5003
Hancock	Margaret		1852	1937	Thornton Funeral Home Marker	MHB264
Hancock	Margaretta	C.	1898	1978		MTR1187
Hancock	Mark	Anthony	No Date	Jan. 27, 1963		NJB323
Hancock	Mary	A.	1890	1964		OFE1075
Hancock	Mary	C.	1863	1959	Our father - mother / His wife	OFE1071
Hancock	Mary	E.	1875	1964		ODE162
Hancock	Mary	E.	1925	1996		LUM057
Hancock	Mary	Jo	1928	1993	w/o John C.	MTR1191
Hancock	Mary	M.	Mar. 26, 1876	Sep. 8, 1881	Info is from The College of Southern MD, LaPlata, MD	HAN008
Hancock	Mary	Priscilla, Cooksey	May 31, 1845	Jun. 6, 1885	His wife / info is from The College of Southern MD, LaPlata, MD	HAN007

Last Name	First Name	Middle Name	Date of Birth	Date of Death	Transcription / Notes	Cemetery Code
Hancock	Mathew	M.	Mar. 27, 1874	Jun. 10, 1937	When the toil is over, then comes rest and peace / Footstone	LUM062
Hancock	Matilda	L.	Nov. 23, 1872	Apr. 10, 1950	Footstone	LUM061
Hancock	Matthew	Lee	Dec. 3, 1907	May 13, 1976	Erected in loving remembrance by Mary F. Davis Turpin	NJB107
Hancock	Matthew	Melvin	Jun. 16, 1844	Nov. 26, 1898	Info is from The College of Southern MD, LaPlata, MD	HAN007
Hancock	Matthew	Wm.	Oct. 29, 1968	Oct. 27, 1987	Gift of God	LUM096
Hancock	Minerva	Jordan	Feb. 1, 1881	Aug. 26, 1974		ALX096
Hancock	Nolia	V.	1895	1961	Family stone with spouse on it	OAK143
Hancock	Norma	McDonagh	Feb. 15, 1928	No Date	Into thy hands we commend our spirit	LUM097
Hancock	Oscar	S.	Sep. 15, 1905	Jul. 4, 1925		NJB112
Hancock	Pauline	Smith	1916	2003		ODE163
Hancock	R.	Bradford	1868	1943		LUM197
Hancock	R. L.	Cooksey	Jul. 3, 1878	Sep. 8, 1945	Father	NJB109
Hancock	Randolph	Smoot	Jan. 1, 1798	Mar. 15, 1867	Info is from The College of Southern MD, LaPlata, MD	HAN001
Hancock	Reginald		1900	1934	Thornton Funeral Home Marker	MHB265
Hancock	Rennie	A.	1924	2007		LUM209
Hancock	Richard	S.	No Date	Oct. 12, 1913	Name is shown on church records but burial location is unknown, date is the burial date, not death date	CHRNoStone
Hancock	Ricie	O.	Nov. 11, 1907	Jan. 30, 1993	Gone but not forgotten	NJB327
Hancock	Robert	Rice	Oct. 11, 1841	Jun.e 22, 1907	Info is from The College of Southern MD, LaPlata, MD	HAN003
Hancock	Robert		1855	1923	Thornton Funeral Home Marker	MHB263
Hancock	Roy	S.	Sep. 8, 1927	No Date	Roy and Toogie	SCL3258
Hancock	Rudy	M.	1881	1928	Our son at rest	OFE1072
Hancock	Ruth		1913	1929		PKH063
Hancock	Sarah	Anne	No Date	Apr. 30, 1905	Name is shown on church records but burial location is unknown, date is the burial date, not death date	CHRNoStone
Hancock	Sarah	Ellen, Bradshaw	Jul. 19, 1854	Apr. 25, 1938		HAN003
Hancock	Sherwood		1897	1979	Slab and Funeral Home Marker	MHB134
Hancock	Thomas	T.	Apr. 4, 1839	Jan. 24, 1905		MTR2082
Hancock	Truman	C.	1887	1966		OFE1075
Hancock	Uan	Sidney	Jan. 14, 1882	Jul. 13, 1967	Masonic emblem engraved on stone	NJB156

Last Name	First Name	Middle Name	Date of Birth	Date of Death	Transcription / Notes	Cemetery Code
Hancock	Unknown		No Date	Feb. 6, 1943	Baby	LUM102
Hancock	Unknown		No Date	No Date	Baby Boy	NJB105
Hancock	Unknown		No Date	No Date	Baby Girl	NJB106
Hancock	Unknown		No Date	No Date	Info missing from Funeral Home Marker	OAK159
Hancock	Unknown		No Date	No Date		EMO002
Hancock	Unknown		No Date	No Date	Owner of property says "a neighbor told them that Little Dish Hancock was buried on the property" but there isn't a headstone	ARANoStone
Hancock	Virgil		Aug. 17, 1869	Feb. 25, 1899	s/o Thos. T & M. Henrietta Hancock / Love is left alone	MTR2083
Hancock	Walter		1890	1967	Family stone with spouse on it	OAK143
Hancock	Wilbur	E.	Aug. 16, 1922	Apr. 1, 1979		LUM098
Hancock	William	W.	Dec. 27, 1890	Oct. 18, 1970		LUM099
Handley	Harry	Benedict	1885	1955		SIC7002
Hands	Erma	E.	Jul. 3, 1912	Sep. 8, 1993		HGH4275
Hands, Sr.	Joseph	A.	May 10, 1912	Jul. 7, 1997		HGH4275
Hands	R.	Gayle	Oct. 10, 1946	Jun. 4, 2000		HGH4274
Hanline	Bonnie	M.	1946	No Date	m. Oct. 23, 1976 / Love, Laughter, & Music	SJE222
Hanline, Sr.	Steve	T.	1949	1990	m. Oct. 23, 1976 / Love, Laughter, & Music	SJE222
Hannah	William	Kenneth	May 1, 1974	May 3, 1974	Infant son buried in Goldsmith plot per church records	CHR425
Haney	Catherine	Lawson, Digges	1821	1900		ODE386
Hannon	Charles	E.	Sep. 29, 1834	Nov. 9, 1896	h/o Sarah C Hannon, obit notice for Sarah is in the Times Crescent Paper Fri. Jan 7, 1916	SJE153
Hannon	Edwin	E.	1864	1947		SJE155
Hannon	J.	Stanley	1877	1959		SJE156
Hannon	Sarah	C.	Jan. 27, 1843	Jan. 3, 1916	Thou art gone but not forgotten (Times Crescent Newspaper Fri Jan 7, 1916: She was the widow of the late Charles E. Hannon and a d/o the late Isaiah Posey. Sister of C.H. Posey. Children were: Mr. E.E. Hannon, Ella Hannon, Sallie C. Hannon, Charles B Hannon, Walter G. Hannon and John S. Hannon.	SJE154

Last Name	First Name	Middle Name	Date of Birth	Date of Death	Transcription / Notes	Cemetery Code
Hannon	Sarah	Valetta, McDaniel	Sep. 8, 1870	Mar. 17, 1897	Only goodnight dear one, not farewell. Beloved w/o Edwin E. Hannon / "Calm on the bosom of thy God. Fair spirit, rest thee now!" / Footstone: S.V.Mc.D. H. (Obit from the Port Tobacco Times Newspaper dated Mar 19, 1897 Vol LIII No. 42: died at 8:30 O'clock Wednesday evening at the home of her mother, Mrs. Nannie McDaniel, near Waldorf. Valetta died of consumption. She was the youngest daughter of the late George R. McDaniel. She leaves behind her husband and two little babies, 18 month old baby girl and a baby girl only a few weeks old.)	MRH013 MRH013A
Hannon	Unknown		Aug. 20, 1894	Aug. 20, 1894	Our Darling, infant d/o Edwin E. & S. Valetta McDaniel Hannon / aged 4 hours / Safe in the arms of Jesus	MRH016 MRH016A
Hannon	Valetta	McDaniel	Feb. 25, 1897	Sep. 4, 1911	In loving memory of Valetta McDaniel daughter of E. E. & S.V. McD. Hannon / God takes our loved ones from our homes, but never from our hearts	MRH011 MRH011A
Hanson	A.	Lee	No Date	Mar. 25, 1947		ODE138
Hanson	Agnes	P.	1870	1962		ODE301
Hanson, Sr.	Albert	L.	Dec. 1, 1899	Mar. 25, 1981		SJO1106
Hanson	Alvan	B.	1903	1970	Peace be with you	PKH139
Hanson	Eleanor	L.	Dec. 31, 1906	Mar. 27, 1998		SJO1106
Hanson	Elizabeth		No Date	Oct. 12, 1763	Here lyes the body of / d/o John and Jane Hanson who departed this life on the / aged one year and ten months (outside fenced area) (Writing is no longer legible on stone), Info is from the Historical Society Research located at the College of Southern Maryland, LaPlata, Md)	MUL003
Hanson	Ernest		No Date	Jan. 25, 1892	Info is from Christ Church microfilm Reel 2 Pg 167-168 located at the College of Southern MD, LaPlata, MD	MTRNoStone
Hanson	F.	Roberta	Nov. 1, 1912	Jun. 16, 1984	Beloved Mother to all	SAC2016
Hanson	Francis	A.	Nov. 10, 1843	Feb. 19, 1890	Lead kindly light / Also went by Alvin F. Hanson	ODE300
Hanson, Sr.	Hobert	L.	Oct. 15, 1921	Jul. 31, 2000	Masonic Emblem	LUM034
Hanson	Janet	Leigh	Aug. 4, 1956	Mar. 16, 1961		SJO3208
Hanson	Jennie	Millar	Sep. 14, 1845	Jan. 4, 1918		ODE299

Last Name	First Name	Middle Name	Date of Birth	Date of Death	Transcription / Notes	Cemetery Code
Hanson, Sr.	John	Dudley	Feb. 6, 1925	Mar. 27, 2004	In loving memory	SJO3207
Hanson	John		No Date	Mar. 6, 1760	Here lyes buried the body of / s/o John and Jane Hanson who departed this life the / aged 6 years (outside fence) Writing is no longer legible on stone), (Info is from the Historical Society Research located at the College of Southern Maryland, LaPlata, Md)	MUL004
Hanson	Joseph	Allen	Jul. 30, 1953	Oct. 29, 1972	Maryland PFC CO C 2 BN 508 Infantry Vietnam	SJO3209
Hanson	Julia	H.	No Date	Feb. 21, 1924	Info is from Christ Church microfilm Reel 3, Pg 232-233 located at the College of Southern MD, LaPlata, MD	MTRNoStone
Hanson	Marjorie	Louise	Jan. 1, 1927	No Date	In loving memory	SJO3207
Hanson	Mary	Anna	1923	1964		CHR520
Hanson	Mary	Charlotte, Barnes	No Date	Feb. 25, 1908	Age 32 (info is from Old Durham Church microfilm located at the College of Southern MD, LaPlata, MD) / w/o A. Lee Hanson	ODE139
Hanson	Mary	Elizabeth	Oct. 3, 1883	Sep. 23, 1971		SJO3205
Hanson	Mary	W.	Apr. 22, 1910	Apr. 18, 1979		SJO3204
Hanson	Michael	T.	1958	1991		CHR519
Hanson	Reba	June	Dec. 19, 1922	No Date		LUM034
Hanson	Robert	W.	1873	1934		ODE301
Hanson	Samuel		No Date	Oct. 26, 1740	Here lyes the body of / who departed this life the 26th day of Oct 1740 in the fifty sixth year of his age	ROB018 ROB019
Hanson	Samuel		No Date	Nov. 14, 1894	Age 78 (info is from Old Durham Church microfilm pg 83 located at the College of Southern MD, LaPlata, MD)	ODENoStone
Hanson	Tammy	Louise	1960	1961	Baby	SJO3210
Hanson	Theophilus		1743	1808	Here lies the body of Theophilus Hanson (Bronze Plaque) Theophilus Hanson Revolutionary War Soldier and Patriot dedicated by Port Tobacco Chapter NSDAR Thomas Stone Chapter NSSAR May 2005	ODE007
Hanson, Jr.	Thomas	Bayard	Oct. 20, 1919	Apr. 8, 1989		SJO3203
Hanson, Sr.	Thomas	Bayard	May 11, 1880	Jan. 30, 1964		SJO3206
Hanson	William		May 22, 1854	Nov. 4, 1917	IHS / May his soul rest in peace / Beloved h/o Josephine Hanson	SIC4024

Last Name	First Name	Middle Name	Date of Birth	Date of Death	Transcription / Notes	Cemetery Code
Harbin	Catharine	A.	Dec. 4, 1796	Jun. 26, 1853	and his wife	SMCD040
Harbin	Elizabeth		No Date	Sep. 25, 1854	IHS / Sacred to the memory of / widow of Rezin Harbin / who departed this life / In the 80th year of her age. / "May she rest in peace. Amen"	SMCA113
Harbin	Jack	Desmond	1918	1970		CHR255
Harbin	James	A.	No Date	Jun. 21, 1852	Sacred to the memory of James A. Harbin who departed this life / In the 23d year of his age / May the Lord be merciful to him	SMCD038
Harbin	Joseline		No Date	May 1, 1997	Cremated	CHRNoStone
Harbin, Mrs.	Maria		No Date	Jan. 31, 1837	In memory of / who departed this life / aged 38 years / May she rest in peace. Amen / Stone is laying on the ground just outside the Posey Plot / Historical Society records say this stone was found in church wall and is buried in cemetery	SIC1120
Harbin	Rezin		No Date	Jan. 3, 1854	IHS / Sacred to the memory of / who departed this life / in the 70th year of his age / May he rest in peace Amen / Note: stone is laying on the ground and is embedded in the grass	SMCA112
Harbin	Walter		Feb. 16, 1785	Jul. 28, 1853	And his wife	SMCD040
Hardesty	Anna	M.	Apr. 7, 1905	Nov. 11, 1978	w/o Wilford R Hardesty / Gone but not forgotten.	TRI1109
Hardesty	Annie	M.	1889	1951	In Hardesty Plot	SMY3119
Hardesty, Sr.	Carroll	Edward	Nov. 24, 1931	No Date	Pop / In loving memory (Stone has the name Carroll Hardesty Sr. on one side and the other side has the name Margaret Hardesty)	CLV412
Hardesty, II	Carroll	Edward	No Date	Apr. 24, 2007	Info is from church records	CLVNoStone
Hardesty	Cleveland	F.	1892	1960	In Hardesty Plot	SMY3119
Hardesty	Don	Wayne	Jun. 15, 1946	Jan. 19, 2000	In Hardesty Plot	SMY3119
Hardesty	Dudley	R.	No Date	Feb. 8, 1940	Maryland Sgt Base Hosp 53.	TRI282
Hardesty	Ernest	Frederich	Nov. 11, 1911	Jan. 18, 1977		TRI026
Hardesty	Esther	L.	Apr. 1, 1903	Apr. 26, 1992		TRI358
Hardesty	Frederick	John	1923	1952	In Hardesty Plot	SMY3119
Hardesty	H.		No Date	No Date	Number 251 inscribed on the lower left of the stone	CLV383
Hardesty	Harry	Davis	Jul. 19, 1909	Oct. 6, 1978		TRI027

Last Name	First Name	Middle Name	Date of Birth	Date of Death	Transcription / Notes	Cemetery Code
Hardesty	Irene		Nov. 20, 1866	Dec. 30, 1943		TRI283
Hardesty	James	F.	1900	1950		TRI278
Hardesty	Jean	C.	Feb. 14, 1940	No Date		SCL4055
Hardesty	John	F.	1889	1963		SMC4124
Hardesty	Joseph	Wilford	Apr. 2, 1903	Dec. 24, 1948		TRI024
Hardesty	Joseph	Wilford	Jan. 4, 1871	Feb. 28, 1931		TRI281
Hardesty	Leonard	Wilson	Nov. 9, 1912	Apr. 10, 1971		HGH1173
Hardesty	Lillian	Agnes	Oct. 10, 1920	Aug. 29, 1993		HGH1174
Hardesty	Lydia	Marie	1880	1963		TRI023
Hardesty	Margaret	Ann	Aug. 17, 1940	Jan. 24, 2002	Maggie / Mother In Loving Memory (Stone has the name Carroll Hardesty Sr. on one side and the other side has the name Margaret Hardesty)	CLV412A
Hardesty	Mary	E.	1915	1994		SCL4056
Hardesty	Mary	P.	Jul. 21, 1917	Sep. 28, 1991	In Hardesty Plot	SMY3162
Hardesty	Mytle	A.	1900	1971		TRI278
Hardesty, Sr.	Robert	C.	Apr. 21, 1916	Dec. 20, 1976	In Hardesty Plot	SMY3161
Hardesty	Thomas	Francis	1873	1942		TRI023
Hardesty	Thomas	Zachariah	Feb. 2, 1907	Sep. 11, 1973		TRI025
Hardesty, Sr.	Vernon	F.	Jun. 11, 1914	May 3, 1997		SMY3163
Hardesty	Wilford	R.	Apr. 9, 1897	Jul. 12, 1973	h/o Anna M Hardesty / May he rest in peace.	TRI109
Hardesty	William	J.	Feb. 25, 1938	Apr. 23, 1997	"Jimmy"	SCL4055
Hardesty, Jr.	William	J.	1914	1986		SCL4056
Hardey	Elizabeth	C.	No Date	Aug. 31, 1855	d/o Charles H. & E. Melvina Hardy / Aged 8y, 8m, 19d / She was lovely. It was ( ) And ( ), An angel came and ( )And here her home to heaven. / Unable to read verse on stone	SPL1002
Hardey	Henry	W.	1792	1835	To the memory of / Who departed this life in the 43rd year of his age. / Footmarker: H.W.H. / Birth date is from church records	SPL1079
Hardey	Malvina		Sep. 5, 1819	Aug. 26, 1895	Beloved w/o Charles Hardey / At Rest / Blessed are the dead who die in the Lord.	SPL1003
Harding	Amy		No Date	Dec. 11, 1947	Age 74 / info is from church records	OFENoStone

Last Name	First Name	Middle Name	Date of Birth	Date of Death	Transcription / Notes	Cemetery Code
Harding	Elwood	Lee	1918	1998		LUM119
Harding	Gertrude	May	No Date	Mar. 7, 1917	Age 49 / Info is from church records	OFENoStone
Harding	Reese		No Date	Nov. 23, 1941	Age 73 / info is from church records	OFENoStone
Harding	Thelma	Bowling	1919	No Date		LUM119
Harding	Timothy	Brian	1959	1974		LUM119
Hardy	Catharine	P.	Jan. 8, 1805	Dec. 29, 1855	Info is from the Historical Society Research located at the College of Southern MD, LaPlata, MD, and the 1940 DAR book pg 193	SMCNoStone
Hardy, Sr.	Charles	B.	1876	1966		SJE081
Hardy, Jr.	Charles	B.	1914	1989		SIC9035
Hardy	Charles	C.	Oct. 26, 1821	Jun. 24, 1914	A warden of Port Tobacco Parish for over 50 years.	SPL1004
Hardy	Clifford		Jun. 28, 1876	Jul. 10, 1876	s/o Clinton & Emma Hardy.	SPL1010
Hardy	Debera Lynn		No Date	Aug. 27, 1963	Info is from Christ Church microfilm Reel 4 Pg 284-285 located at the College of Southern MD, LaPlata, MD	MTRNoStone
Hardy, Sr.	Donald	L.	Oct. 17, 1943	Feb. 20, 2007	Donnie / Love you always and forever	SIC9099
Hardy	Elizabeth	L.	Nov. 24, 1946	No Date	Betty Lou / Love you always and forever	SIC9099
Hardy	Emma		Apr. 6, 1857	May 14, 1904	w/o William Clinton Hardy.	SPL1013
Hardy	George	V.	Nov. 3, 1891	Oct. 27, 1918	Lo, I am with you always, Even unto the end of world.	SPL1009
Hardy	John	H.	Aug. 2, 1800	Mar. 26, 1827	Info is from the Historical Society Research located at the College of Southern MD, LaPlata, MD, and the 1940 DAR book pg 193	SMCNoStone
Hardy	Margaret	L.	1921	1954		SIC7003
Hardy	Mary	E.	1922	2008		SIC9035
Hardy	Mary	E.	1906	1980		NSP109
Hardy	May		Nov. 14, 1880	Oct. 4, 1889	d/o Clinton & Emma Hardy.	SPL1011
Hardy	Nettie		1874	1961		SJE081
Hardy	William	Clinton	Jan. 19, 1849	Jan. 17, 1930		SPL1013
Hardy	Wilmer		May 25, 1877	Oct. 7, 1889	s/o Clinton & Emma Hardy.	SPL1012
Hargraves	George		No Date	Apr. 24, 1805	In memory of / who departed this life on the / aged 75 (addt'l info is from website usgwtombstones.org)	HSMNoStone
Hargraves	Margaret		No Date	Apr. 23, 1799	"In memory of Margaret Hargraves Who departed this life On the 23rd day of April 1799 Aged 31"	HSM0003

Last Name	First Name	Middle Name	Date of Birth	Date of Death	Transcription / Notes	Cemetery Code
Hargraves	Mary		No Date	Nov. 1, 1848	"In memory of Mary Hargraves who departed this life on the 1st Nov 1848, Aged 73" (This stone is lying on the ground face up near An(ne?) Smoot's stone	HSM0008
Hargraves	Mary			Sep. 1, 1793	"Memory of _____ Hargraves who departed this life 1st day September, 1793, Aged 53" / Addt'l info is from website usgwtombstones.org	HSM0004
Hargraves	Theophilus		No Date	Aug. 1818	"In memory of Theos Hargraves Who departed this life Aug _____ 1818 Aged 12? Years" (Face of stone is starting to split) (behind this stone is a footstone with the initials T.H., have no picture of it) (Addt'l info is from website usgwtombstones.org)	HSM0002
Harley	Agnes	V.	Sep. 10, 1927	Mar. 7, 2004		NSP145
Harley	Angie		Dec. 25, 1886	Apr. 23, 1958	Mother / Rest in peace	SJO3262
Harley	Bernard		1890	1965		NSP185
Harley	Birdie		Mar. 6, 1856	Aug. 30, 1934		SIC5034
Harley	Dorothy	B.	1925	1960		NSP319
Harley	Gerald		Jul. 27, 1952	Jan. 19, 1956	Our son	NSP245
Harley	Grace	Eugenia	Mar. 9, 1925	Sep. 5, 1963		NSP146
Harley	Iola	A.	1922	1990		NSP155
Harley	James	M.	Jan. 29, 1921	Sep. 27, 1978		SCL4199
Harley, Sr.	John	Alton	Apr. 7, 1920	Sep. 5, 1963		NSP146
Harley	John	M.	1916	No Date		NSP155
Harley, Sr	John	W.	Jul. 25, 1950	Jan. 3, 2002	In loving memory / Woody / Pat / Together forever	SJO1116
Harley	John		No Date	Jun. 29, 1925	Age 82 / Old cement cross with the right arm missing and the iron exposed.	SIC5083
Harley	Joseph	G.	Sep. 13, 1940	Oct. 14, 1990		SJO3259
Harley	Joseph		No Date	Oct. 18, 19	Age 62 / death year might be 1915	SIC6030
Harley	Joseph	Oscar	May 9, 1893	Apr. 16, 1961	Footstone shows name as Oscar and birth year as 1899 but headstone says Joseph Oscar born 1893	SJO2039
Harley	Keneisha	M.	No Date	Oct. 8, 1987	Only one date on stone	SJO4110
Harley, Jr.	Lester	M.	No Date	1975		NSP319
Harley	Martha		1894	1949		NSP186
Harley	Mary	E.	Jul. 24, 1896	Oct. 18, 1949	In Loving Memory	SJO2040

Last Name	First Name	Middle Name	Date of Birth	Date of Death	Transcription / Notes	Cemetery Code
Harley	Mary	G.	1928	1984	Nearer my God to thee	NSP083
Harley	Mary	L.	Aug. 3, 1928	Jun. 12, 1988		SCL4199
Harley	Milton	L.	1930	1997	Nearer my God to thee	NSP083
Harley	Shirley	Lee	Jun. 20, 1958	Aug. 27, 1965		NSP128
Harley	Thomas	Louis	May 27, 1941	Dec. 28, 1965		NSP156
Harley	Wanona	P.	Sep. 4, 1951	No Date	In loving memory / Woody / Pat / Together forever	SJO1116
Harley	William	I.	Oct. 18, 1927	No Date		NSP145
Harley	William	M.	Jan. 11, 1950	Oct. 22, 2000	In loving memory / Beloved Dad, Son and Brother / Forever in our hearts	SCL4217
Harley	Wilmer	C.	1923	1979		NSP319
Harlisson	George		No Date	Mar. 31, 1940	Aged 67 years, 10 mos., 10 days / Information is from the Historical Society Research located at the College of Southern MD, LaPlata, MD	SMINoStone
Harlisson	May		No Date	Jul. 25, 1939	Aged 67 years, 3 mos., 78 days / Information is from the Historical Society Research located at the College of Southern Md, in the Southern MD, LaPlata, MD	SMINoStone
Harmon	John	W.	No Date	Jul. 9, 1928	Age 56 / info is from church records	OFENoStone
Harmon	Roland		Sep. 26, 1909	Dec. 16, 1966	Info is from church Records	CLVNoStone
Harmon	Thelma		No Date	1978	Info is from church Records	CLVNoStone
Harris	Ann		No Date	Dec. 10, 1814	In memory of / Wife of Thomas Harris, who departed this life on the / aged 70 years 7 months & 19 days	HAR006
Harris	Anna	Louisa	Sep. 25, 1823	May 25, 1829	In memory of / daughter of Doct. Morgan & Anna Louisa Harris She was B / and D /	WAV1048
					Sacred to the memory of / a native of the Island of Antigua w/o Doctor Morgan Harris She died / aged 29 years. The graces and fruits of a Christian life, shown eminently in her character, conduct and sanctified the virtues of the wife and woman - a stranger in a strange land - she lived beloved and lamented by all who knew her.	
Harris	Anna	Louisa	No Date	Sep. 25, 1825		WAV1046
Harris	Catherine		1913	2005	Thornton funeral home marker	SCL1267

Last Name	First Name	Middle Name	Date of Birth	Date of Death	Transcription / Notes	Cemetery Code
Harris, Dr.	Chapman		No Date	Nov. 28, 1858	In memory of / who departed this life in the 28th year of his age / Left side of stone: "The Lord is my Shephard I shall not fear" Right side of stone: Remember thy Creator in the day of thy youth. Back of stone: "Calm in the bosom of thy God" Dear Spirit rest thee now E'en while with us thy footsteps trod His seal was on thy brow. Dust to its narrow home on earth. Soul to its God on high Who are like thee has conquered death No man need fear to die" Footstone: C.H.	WAV1034
Harris	Elizabeth	Grant	Jul. 20, 1827	Mar. 7, 1855	In memory of / Eldest daughter of Dr. Morgan & Etheldra J. Harris	WAV1031
Harris	Elizabeth		Aug. 23, 1841	Jun. 8, 1842	d/o Nathan & Mary Harris	HRD002
Harris	Elizabeth		No Date	Apr. 22, 1818	In memory of / Daughter of Thomas & Ann. Who departed this life on the 22nd April 1818, aged 46 years & 10 months	HAR002
Harris	Emma	V.	Feb. 17, 1915	Dec. 2, 1974	Eastern Star Emblem	PGN006
Harris	Etheldra	Jane	Jul. 25, 1796	Sep. 28, 1867	Sacred in the memory of / who "slept in Jesus" / Age 71 years after a long life of usefulness and honor in the Christian faith and in the communion of the Catholic Church / "Them that sleep in Jesus shall God bring with him" 1 Thes 4:14 / Blessed are the dead who die in the Lord from henceforth Yea saith the Spirit that they may rest from their labours and their works do follow them Rev XIV 13 / The graves of all his Saints he blessed when in the grave he lay and rising thence their hopes he raised to everlasting day. (Family member gave birth date. She is the 2nd w/o Dr. Morgan Harris)	WAV1030
Harris, Sr.	George	R.	Mar. 10, 1913	Jun. 25, 1995	Father	PGN045
Harris, Jr.	George	Robt	Aug. 22, 1941	Aug. 9, 1964		PGO008
Harris	Gloria	A.	Sep. 30, 1944	Aug. 19, 1994		HER020

Last Name	First Name	Middle Name	Date of Birth	Date of Death	Transcription / Notes	Cemetery Code
Harris	Gwinn		Apr. 27, 1780	Aug. 12, 1837	Sacred to the memory of / who was born on the / and after long and useful service in the Navy of the United States, died on the / whilst President of the Executive Council of his native state having won for himself in both Stations as he did in all the varied scenes of life. The respect, confidence and affection of all with whom he acted. Correct in his principles, just in his transactions and humane in his feelings, his heart was the seat of manly virtue, disinterested and generous, he never knew a "joy but friendship might divide."	HAR008 HAR009
Harris	Henry	Chapman	Jun. 20, 1829	Feb. 24, 1855	In memory of / Eldest son of Doc. Morgan & Etheldra J. Harris He was B / and D / of scarlet fever	WAV1041
Harris	Henry		No Date	Feb. 28, 1926	Age 65 years / info is from church records	SHINoStone
Harris	India		Nov. 6, 1864	Sep. 4, 1892		SJE165
Harris	John	Grant	1833	Jul. 13, 1860	Sacred to the memory of / Who with his nieces Ursula & Nannie Harris was drowned while Yachting on the Potomac near this place D / In the 27th year of his age Left side of stone: In the pride & strength of early manhood by nature noble, ... loving and beloved by all and with bright hope of happiness life, he was called at a moment's warning to appear before him without whom not a sparrow falleth to the ground. And let as humbly trust that he found acceptance with him, who hath said "Lo I am with you always even unto the end. Watch therefor, for in such an hour as ye think not, the son of man cometh." The Lord gave and the Lord hath taken away blessed be the name of the Lord" Right side of stone: It is not death to die To leave this weary road And with the brotherhood on high To be at home with God...... Footstone: J.G.H.	WAV1025
Harris	John	Gwynn	Jun. 13, 1837	Sep. 27, 1867	Departed this life / A member of Christ / This child of God An inheritor of the kingdom of Heaven / Footstone: J.G.H.	HRD005 HRD006

Last Name	First Name	Middle Name	Date of Birth	Date of Death	Transcription / Notes	Cemetery Code
Harris	John		No Date	Mar. 18, 1831	In memory of / Son of Thomas and Eleanor, who departed this life on the / aged 34 years 7 months and 10 days	HAR004
Harris	Kitty	R.	1819	1904	Footstone	CHR510
Harris	Louise		No Date	Mar. 8, 1976	Info is from church records	SHINoStone
Harris	Mary	L.	Feb. 12, 1929	Feb. 21, 2004	In loving memory Mom	SHI021
Harris	Mary		Nov. 3, 1802	Dec. 20, 1843	w/o Nathan Harris & d/o Horatio Clagett	HRD016
Harris	Menchen	H.	Mar. 6, 1924	Nov. 24, 1988	Funeral Home Marker / info is from church records	SHI068
Harris	Morgan		Dec. 17, 1850	Dec. 21, 1855	In memory of / Second son of Doc. Morgan & Etheldra J Harris He was B / and D / of scarlet fever	WAV1020
Harris	Morgan		Nov. 23, 1835	Jan. 17, 1856	s/o Nathan & Mary Harris	HRD010
					Sacred to the memory of / Respected and beloved by all who knew him Though life he maintained with unblemished integrity the character of a physician, a gentleman, & a Christian and died humbly trusting in the atonement of his Savior and with the full assurance of acceptance through his merits	
Harris, Dr.	Morgan		Nov. 16, 1787	Jun. 2, 1856		WAV1039
Harris	Nathan		Sep. 5, 1785	Oct. 23, 1842		HRD022
Harris	Philip		Sep. 29, 1845	Mar. 26, 1876		CHRNoStone
Harris	Rose	Roberts, Padgett	No Date	Apr. 5, 1916	Info is from Christ Church microfilm Reel 3, Pg 226-227 located at the College of Southern MD, LaPlata, MD	MTRNoStone
Harris	Roy	Lester	Oct. 6, 1939	Jan. 4, 1993	"Kidd" God's greatest gift returned to God -- our father	CHR273
Harris	Thomas	H.	Mar. 10, 1840	Jan. 23, 1855	s/o Nathan & Mary Harris	HRD013
Harris	Thomas		No Date	Feb. 22, 1815	In memory of / who departed this life, on the / aged 73 years 6 months & 22 days	HAR012
Harris	Violet	A.	1904	1983	Mother	OFE4023
Harris	Walter			Aug. 21, 1817	In memory of / Son of Morgan & Ann L. who departed this life on the / aged 2 years & 8 months. (pieces of the stone are missing his age is from the 1939-1940 DAR Research located at the College of Southern MD, LaPlata, MD)	HAR014
Harris	William	H.	No Date	Apr. 7, 1926	Age 7 years / info is from church records	SHINoStone
Harrison	Ann	Catherine	No Date	Aug. 17, 1912	Name is shown on church records but burial location is unknown, date is the burial date, not death date	CHRNoStone

325

Last Name	First Name	Middle Name	Date of Birth	Date of Death	Transcription / Notes	Cemetery Code
Harrison	Anna	O.	No Date	No Date	Name is shown on church records but burial location is unknown, date is the burial date, not death date	CHR529
Harrison	Annie	S.	No Date	Jul. 1914	Name is shown on church records but burial location is unknown, date is the burial date, not death date	CHRNoStone
Harrison	Caroline		No Date	Dec. 2, 1901		CHRNoStone
Harrison	Dabney	Carr	Mar. 4, 1885	Jun. 14, 1936	At rest	ODE367
Harrison, Jr.	Dabney	Carr	May 23, 1922	Sep. 21, 1991	Riverside	ODE369
Harrison	Dorothy		Sep. 19, 1721	Mar. 5, 1751	In memory of Dorothy Harrison / A sincere Christian who was the d/o Col. Robert Hanson and Dorothy his wife of Port Tobacco - and wife of Col. Richard Harrison of Nanjemoy - who was / aged 30 years, 3 mos. & 25 days. Had issue Robert Hanson, William Walter Hanson Harrison. Her children arise up and call her blessed her husband also and he praiseth her. Many daughters have done virtuously but thou excelleth them / info is from Historical Society research, located at the College of Southern MD, LaPlata, MD	ODENoStone
Harrison	Elizabeth		Apr. 28, 1718	Aug. 1743	Memonto Morte, Here lyes the remains of / The w/o Richard Harrison of Nanjemoy who was / aged ? Years. Had issue Wirlinda, Joseph and Mary Wade Harrison. Mary wade Harrison died and infant of 12 days. A large flat stone that is cracked / Info is from the DAR book Pg 142, at the College of Southern MD, LaPlata, MD	ODE012
Harrison	John	Benjamin	No Date	Mar. 21, 1906	Name is shown on church records but burial location is unknown, date is the burial date, not death date	CHRNoStone
Harrison	John	Edward	Mar. 1, 1930	Jan. 21, 1957	Maryland FN USNR	CHR533
Harrison	Judy	D.	Apr. 2, 1939	No Date	In Loving Memory	SCA043
Harrison	Kimberly	Yvonne	Apr. 9, 1968	Jul. 27, 2001	Verse on stone: I am the resurrection and the life, He that believeth in me, though he were dead yet shall he live. St John II Verse 25	POM211
Harrison	Logan		No Date	Sep. 20, 1943	Name is shown on church records but burial location is unknown, date is the burial date, not death date	CHRNoStone
Harrison	Louise	V.	1911	1987	Buried Apr 13, 1987 per church records	CHR529
Harrison	Mary	Marbury	Mar. 9, 1889	May 31, 1962	At rest	ODE368

Last Name	First Name	Middle Name	Date of Birth	Date of Death	Transcription / Notes	Cemetery Code
Harrison	Mary	Regina	1913	1986		SCA093
Harrison	Mary		No Date	No Date	Note: child of Elizabeth and Richard Harrison that only lived 12 days. / info is from the DAR book Pg 142 located at the College of Southern MD, LaPlata, MD	ODENoStone
Harrison	N.	Wood	No Date	Sep. 22, 1900	Name is shown on church records but burial location is unknown, date is the burial date, not death date	CHRNoStone
Harrison	Nellie	M.	May 9, 1884	Sep. 23, 1969	The name Powell is on one side of this headstone and Harrison is on the other side.	OFE1022A
Harrison	Patrick	L.	No Date	No Date		CHR529
Harrison	Philip	Stanley	Mar. 2, 1878	Mar. 26, 1956	The name Powell is on one side of this headstone and Harrison is on the other side.	OFE1023
Harrison	Philip		Sep. 23, 1845	Mar. 26, 1876	Located behind the church	CHR620
Harrison	Samuel	W.	No Date	1921	Name is shown on church records but burial location is unknown, date is the burial date, not death date	CHRNoStone
Harrison	Shirley	Ann	No Date	No Date		CHR529
Harrison	Shirley	C.	No Date	Jan. 27, 1935	Name is shown on church records but burial location is unknown, date is the burial date, not death date	CHRNoStone
Harrison	Susan	R.	No Date	Jul. 26, 1906	Name is shown on church records but burial location is unknown, date is the burial date, not death date	CHRNoStone
Harrison	Sydney		1880	1975	Boxwood in memory of /	CHR376
Harrison	Virginia	Bell	No Date	No Date		CHR529
Harrison	Virginia		No Date	Sep. 14, 1939	Name is shown on church records but burial location is unknown, date is the burial date, not death date	CHRNoStone
Harrison	William	M.	Dec. 6, 1935	Oct. 24, 1995	In Loving Memory	SCA043
Hart	Alice	M.	1903	1971	Mother	ALX112
Hart	Bertha	Mae	Nov. 2, 1879	Oct. 23, 1961	Illinois / Y2 USNRF WWI	NJB322
Hart	Carole	Schaefer	Jan. 8, 1942	No Date	Memories remain to touch us once again / Love Always	SIC9005
Hart	Churchill		1907	1973	Information is from the Historical Society Research located at the College of Southern MD, LaPlata, Md.	ALXNo Stone
Hart	Clifton		1853	1973	Information is from the Historical Society Research located at the College of Southern MD, LaPlata, MD	ALXNo Stone
Hart	Daisy		No Date	No Date		ALX047
Hart	Elizabeth	Callister	Apr. 18, 1915	Jan. 9, 2004	Beloved parents of Barbara, Susan and Franklin	MTR4164

Last Name	First Name	Middle Name	Date of Birth	Date of Death	Transcription / Notes	Cemetery Code
Hart	Ella	D.	May 5, 1934	Jul. 5, 1975	Gone but not forgotten	ZBC007
Hart	Francis	Joseph	Sep. 2, 1942	Oct. 15, 1999	Memories remain to touch us once again / Love Always	SIC9005
Hart	Gertrude		1921	1940		ALX049
Hart	Gilbert		No Date	No Date		ALX048
Hart	Godwin	Waring	Dec. 8, 1913	Jul. 12, 1962	Beloved parents of Barbara, Susan and Franklin	MTR4164
Hart	James	Hadlock	Apr. 15, 1910	Sep. 21, 1992	Bessie Earl	ALX006
Hart	Joseph	M.	1897	1975	Cement Cross, Thornton Funeral Home Marker	ALX001
Hart, Jr.	Joseph	M.	Apr. 27, 1916	May 11, 1974	CPL US Army	SCL3041
Hart	Joyce	Atlee	Sep. 15, 1938	Aug. 18, 1962		POM184
Hart	Louise		Sep. 20, 1922	No Date		SCL3422
Hart	Marilee	E.	May 5, 1955	Apr. 13, 1999	In God's Loving Care Beloved Wife and Mother	MHB017
Hart	Melanie	N.	1972	1972	Information is from the Historical Society Research located at the College of Southern MD, LaPlata, Md.	ALXNo Stone
Hart	Parfine		1912	2006	Funeral Home Marker	ALX024
Hart	Ramon	Sidney	Feb. 27, 1921	Jun. 29, 1997	Pop Pop / Both Enjoyed family gatherings	LUM011
Hart	Randolph		Jul. 9, 1913	Aug. 27, 1999	"Basil"	SCL3422
Hart	Rebekah	Drummond	Mar. 5, 1923	Oct. 4, 2007	"Beppy" / Mom Mom / Both Enjoyed family gatherings	LUM011A
Hart	Thelma	V	No Date	1977	Thornton Funeral Home Marker	ALX003
Hart	Thomas	Wilson	No Date	No Date	Thornton Funeral Home Marker	ALX004
Hart, Jr.	William	H.	May 12, 1969	Sep. 10, 2000	We love you Junior	SCL4212
Hartmann	Barbara		Oct. 2, 1867	Jun. 23, 1952		SMCD135
Hartmann	Leona	M.	Mar. 13, 1912	Jan. 5, 1988	Mother	NSP798
Hartmann	Martin		Apr. 28, 1867	Feb. 5, 1943		SMCD136
Hartnett	Daniel	W.	Dec. 27, 1934	Oct. 4, 1983	YN3 US Navy Korea	SCL1251
Hartnett	Katherine	R.	1935	No Date		SCL1251
Harvey	Bessie	C.	1900	1965		SCL3101
Harvey	Charles	Edward	Jun. 18, 1947	Jan. 24, 2000		NSP171
Harvey	Elizabeth	J.	Sep. 1, 1828	Aug. 2, 1903		NJB392
Harvey	James	M.	Oct. 4, 1843	Dec. 20, 1891		NJB394
Harvey	John	M.	1895	1963		SCL3101
Harvey	John	S.	Sep. 10, 1925	Mar. 3, 2002	In loving memory	SCL3102

Last Name	First Name	Middle Name	Date of Birth	Date of Death	Transcription / Notes	Cemetery Code
Harvey	Judith	A.	Jun. 16, 1800	Dec. 23, 1883	Our mother	NJB395
Harvey	Margarette	B.	Jul. 25, 1837	May 7, 1911		NJB391
Harvey	Mary	Annie	1924	1984	Mother / In loving memory	SIC9024
Harvey, Jr.	Paul	Phylistine	Oct. 7, 1969	Aug. 19, 1996	Beloved brother & son	SHI149
Harvey	Rosalie		No Date	Jul. 15, 1975	Info is from Shiloh Church Records	SMTNo Stone
Harvey	Ruth	Willett	1912	1994		SPL4075
Harvey	William	P.	Dec. 13, 1834	Dec. 1, 1901	In memory of	NJB393
Haspert	Adam	J.	Jun. 21, 1914	Oct. 26, 1998	Together forever	SMC2041
Haspert	Marion	A.	May 11, 1918	Mar. 20, 2006	Together forever	SMC2041
Hatchett	Carlethea	L.	1959	1995		DUD019
Hatton	William	Sylvester	1947	1981	Sgt. U.S. Army Vietnam	OAK103
Haviland	Abigal	A.	Apr. 2, 1836	Sep. 15, 1911		PAT020
Haviland	Carrie	E.	Jan. 26, 1867	Oct. 1?, 1951		PAT019
Haviland	Daniel	P.	Sep. 18, 1809	Aug. 12, 1871	18th of 9 mo 1809 / 12th of 8th mo 1871	PAT026
Haviland	Lewise	M.	Jul. 3, 1882	May 21, 1960		PAT016
Haviland	Lillias	A.	Jan. 7, 1808	Aug. 30, 1875	7th of 1st mo. 1808. 30th of 8 mo. 1875 No Marker (Information obtained from the 1940 transcriptions of The Latter Day Saints Church Microfiche 6047,990-1) Age 74 (Henry A. Penn Funeral Director LaPlata, MD, an old funeral home marker that is laying loosely on the ground)	PATNoStone
Hawkins	??as		No Date	Jun. 2,		SMY3197
Hawkins	A.	Ursulena	1925	1982	Sister	SJO3292
Hawkins	Agnes	V.	Jan. 3, 1922	Jun. 4, 1987		SPL7001
Hawkins	Alberta		1914	1998	Rock marks the spot / info is from church records	PGN052
Hawkins	Alice	R.	Aug. 9, 1945	Jan. 16, 2001		NSP1008
Hawkins	Alice		1876	1929	Rest in Peace	POM007
Hawkins	Allie		1906	No Date	Blest be the tie that binds our hearts in Christian Love	SMY3188
Hawkins	C.	W.	Aug. 16, 1887	Nov. 6, 1921		SHI065
Hawkins	Calvin	H.	Dec. 16, 1927	Jul. 9, 1990		SMC4153

Last Name	First Name	Middle Name	Date of Birth	Date of Death	Transcription / Notes	Cemetery Code
Hawkins	Catharine		No Date	Aug. 1, 1901	She was buried at Fair Fountain on Aug 3, 1901, which was also her residence. / Info is from Christ Church microfilm Reel 1 page 88-89 located at the College of Southern MD, LaPlata, MD	HAWNo Stone
Hawkins	Catherine	E.	May 4, 1915	Jan. 16, 1935	Sunken cross painted gray / Mother	NSP104
Hawkins	Cecelia		1909	1971	Montgomery Bros. Funeral Home Marker	OAK178
Hawkins	Charles	J	1888	1947	Father	SJO5032
Hawkins	Charles	P.	Apr. 9, 1904	Feb. 28, 1942		NSP205
Hawkins	Corey	Dion	Aug. 4, 1986	Sep. 2, 1994	In God's Care	SAC5076
Hawkins	Diane	M.	1955	1983		SMC4062
Hawkins	Edward	D.	1875	1979	Father	SAC4036
Hawkins, Jr.	Edward	G.	Oct. 22, 1915	Jan. 27, 1996		SAC4035
Hawkins	Edward	William	Apr. 26, 1924	May 4, 2005	TEC 5 US Army World War II	SMC4006
Hawkins	Eleanor	Marshall	Aug. 8, 1887	Mar. 1, 1888	Our little darling / d/o J. Henry and Jemmie Hawkins / Suffer little children to come unto me	HWK011
Hawkins	Eleanor	T.	Sep. 16, 1916	No Date		SAC4035
Hawkins	Elizabeth	Holland	Oct. 24, 1925	Jul. 8, 1941	Verse on stone: In the beauty & Loveliness of her youth she passed away	MTR4089
Hawkins	Elizabeth	Lloyd, Powell	Oct. 8, 1885	Aug. 24, 1943	In Loving Memory of Elizabeth Lloyd Powell Hawkins Beloved w/o William Pinkney Hawkins, d/o John & Elizabeth Lewis Powell / Her love is not tethered by time or eternity	MTR4090
Hawkins	Elizabeth		No Date	Dec. 27, 1906	Elizabeth eldest d/o Josias Henry and Sarah Weems Hawkins D / Aged 75 years / Peace perfect Peace	HWK014
Hawkins	Ella	L.	Mar. 11, 1911	Dec. 25, 1985	Mother	SMT014
Hawkins	Elsie	Neale	Sep. 20, 1935	Apr. 25, 2002		SMC1035
Hawkins	Florence	Greenfield	Dec. 18, 1867	Feb. 2, 1934	She gave her all without measure	MTR4066
Hawkins	Fran ??		No Date	No Date	Funeral Home Marker	OAK173
Hawkins	Frances	V.	Aug. 30, 1932	Jan. 28, 2004		SMC2032
Hawkins	Francis	L.	Aug. 15, 1927	Mar. 25, 1999	"Butch"	NSP938
Hawkins	Francis	Thomas	No Date	Jun. 23, 1889	Info is from Christ Church microfilm Reel 2 Pg 165-166 located at the College of Southern MD, LaPlata, MD	MTRNoStone
Hawkins	Fredrick	M.	Mar. 14, 1901	Feb. 17, 1955		NSP255

Last Name	First Name	Middle Name	Date of Birth	Date of Death	Transcription / Notes	Cemetery Code
Hawkins	Geo.	W.	No Date	Jan. 6, 1922	Info is from Christ Church microfilm Reel 3, Pg 230-231 located at the College of Southern MD, LaPlata, MD	MTRNoStone
Hawkins	George	F	Oct. 7, 1940	Sep. 14, 2002	Love Margaret	SMC3050
Hawkins	George	Henry	Aug. 21, 1914	Sep. 4, 1987	Father	NSP058
Hawkins	George	M (?)	No Date	Aug. 31, 1890	Info is from Christ Church microfilm Reel 2 Pg 165-166 located at the College of Southern MD, LaPlata, MD	MTRNoStone
Hawkins	Grace	V.	Feb. 11, 1908	Aug. 15, 1988		SMC1207
Hawkins	Helen	E.	1916	1977	Blest be the tie that binds our hearts in Christian Love	SMY3188
Hawkins	Henry	Holland	Jul. 31, 1870	Nov. 3, 1951	Beloved h/o Mary Chapman Hawkins, s/o Peter & Rebecca M. Hawkins / His name was pure gold.	MTR4068
Hawkins	Henry	Holland	No Date	Nov. 28, 1750	Here lieth the body of Henry Holland Hawkins who departed this life on the 28th day of Nov. in the year of our Lord 1750 / aged 67 years	HWK017
Hawkins	Henry	Holland	Dec. 31, 1727	Mar. 11, 1770	Here lieth the body of / son to Henry Holland Hawkins and Joan his wife	HWK015
Hawkins	Ione	Heigham	1906	1928	Located in Hawkins Plot	MTR3175
Hawkins	James	Ellen, Marshall	Oct. 11, 1859	Nov. 30, 1932	Age 72 / Info is from Christ Church microfilm Reel 3 page 238-239, at the College of Southern MD, LaPlata, MD (She was the wife of Josias Henry Hawkins)	HWK012
Hawkins	James	Henry	May 10, 1925	Jul. 5, 1977	CPL US Army WWII	NSP332
Hawkins	Jamesanna	T.	Jul. 10, 1918	Oct. 29, 2004	Precious Lord take my hand....In Loving memory	SMI030
Hawkins	Jane	Robertson	Jan. 23, 1841	May 16, 1929	His Wife	MTR4065
Hawkins	Jane		No Date	Mar. 1, 1913	Age 80, Unmarried / She was buried Mar 3, 1915 at Fair Fountain which was her residence / Info is from Christ Church microfilm Reel 3 pg 224-225 located at the College of Southern MD, LaPlata, MD	HAWNo Stone
Hawkins	Joe		1873	1925		POM008
Hawkins	John	Leroy	Feb. 3, 1947	Apr. 12, 2004	Brother	ZBC086
Hawkins	John	Norman	1896	1969		POM198
Hawkins	John	Vernon	1908	1978	US Army WWII	NSP260

Last Name	First Name	Middle Name	Date of Birth	Date of Death	Transcription / Notes	Cemetery Code
Hawkins, M.D.	John	Weems	1839	Apr. 12, 1925	Age 85 / John's residence was listed as Baltimore, MD. (Info is from Christ Church Records reel 3 pg 232-233 microfilm located at the College of Southern MD, LaPlata, MD)	HWK001
Hawkins	John	S.	No Date	Mar. 6, 1924	Info is from Christ Church microfilm Reel 3, Pg 232-233 located at the College of Southern MD, LaPlata, MD	MTRNoStone
Hawkins	Joseph	E.	1900	1948		SCL3366
Hawkins, Jr.	Joseph	L.	Oct. 2, 1968	Mar. 24, 1989		SJO3374
Hawkins	Joseph	Roy	Mar. 16, 1919	Dec. 30, 1978	STMI US Navy WWII	NSP289
Hawkins	Josias	Henry	1889	1952	Located in Hawkins Plot	MTR3174
Hawkins	Josias	Henry	Aug. 8, 1850	Mar. 23, 1917	Age 66 / Info is Christ Church microfilm Reel 3 pg 226-227, at the College of Southern MD, LaPlata, MD	HWK012
Hawkins	Josias	Henry	Sep. 21, 1800	Dec. 18, 1889	In memory of Josias Henry Hawkins / his wife / Numbered with thy saints in Glory Everlasting. Age 89 yrs. 2 mo & 15 dys of old age. / Info is from Christ Church microfilm Reel 2 pg 165-166 located at the College of Southern MD, LaPlata, MD	HWK009
Hawkins	Josias		No Date	Sep. 10, 1916	Age 77 / Info Is from Christ Church microfilm Reel 3 page 226-227 located at the College of Southern MD, LaPlata, MD	HWKNoStone
Hawkins	Katie		1894	1954	Mother	SAC4037
Hawkins	Laura	S.	Oct. 27, 1887	Aug. 27, 1899	Asleep in Jesus / there are 2 names on the stone but only 1 birth and death date	MTR4133
Hawkins	Laura		No Date	Sep. 7, 1910	Info is from Christ Church microfilm Reel 3, Pg 222-223 located at the College of Southern MD, LaPlata, MD	MTRNoStone
Hawkins	Lemuel	S.	Jan. 6, 1910	Apr. 12, 1948		NSP154
Hawkins	Lena	U.	1890	1958	Mother	SJO3291
Hawkins	Letty		No Date	Apr. 1909	Info is from Christ Church microfilm Reel 3, Pg 222-223 located at the College of Southern MD, LaPlata, MD	MTRNoStone
Hawkins	Lorenzo		Apr. 24, 1899	Oct. 26, 1987		SIC7043A
Hawkins	Lucille	Simms	1899	1955		NSP176

Last Name	First Name	Middle Name	Date of Birth	Date of Death	Transcription / Notes	Cemetery Code
Hawkins	Luke	W. B.	1809	1869	In Memory of / his wife, their children Francis Thomas, John Weems, Jane Yates, Elizabeth Eleanor, Mary Holiday, Margaret Amelia, Wilhemina, Laura, George McClellan - Peace	MTR1095, MTR1095A
Hawkins	Mabel		May 28, 1878	Sep. 13, 1881	d/o Samuel & Jane Hawkins / "Suffer little children to come unto me, and forbid them not, for of such is the Kingdom of Heaven." / Info is from Christ Church microfilm Reel 1 Pg 318-319 located at the College of Southern MD, LaPlata, MD	MTRNoStone
Hawkins	Madeline		1940	1977	Blest be the tie that binds our hearts in Christian Love	SMY3188
Hawkins	Margaret	Amelia	Dec. 15, 1863	Mar. 22, 1926	In loving memory of / entered into the great beyond. After a life of noble service kind deeds and loyal friendships / Rest	MTR1096A
Hawkins	Margaret	V.	Oct. 1, 1932	No Date	"Ronnie"	NSP938
Hawkins	Margaret	Amelia, Smoot	1830	1919	In Memory of / his wife, their children Francis Thomas, John Weems, Jane Yates, Elizabeth Eleanor, Mary Holiday, Margaret Amelia, Wilhemina, Laura, George McClellan - Peace	MTR1095
Hawkins	Margaret	Amelia	Dec. 15, 1863	Mar. 22, 1926	In loving memory of - entered into the great beyond - after a life of noble service & noble deeds and loyal friendship / Rest / Info is from Historical Society Research located at the College of Southern MD, LaPlata, MD	MTRNoStone
Hawkins	Maria		Oct. 26, 1886	Jul. 7, 1971		SMC4016
Hawkins	Martin	L.	Oct. 3, 1952	Apr. 2, 1957		NSP314
Hawkins	Mary	A.	Mar. 23, 1915	Jul. 31, 1992		SMC4005
Hawkins	Mary	Chapman	Jul. 9, 1865	Oct. 26, 1926	Beloved w/o Henry Holland Hawkins, d/o Marshall-Ellen Stockett Chapman / In life Beloved, in death sweet memories linger	MTR4069
Hawkins	Mary	E.	Jun. 28, 1866	May 12, 1940		POM110
Hawkins	Mary	Emily	Jul. 27, 1841	Jul. 12, 1883	In memory of / d/o Josias H. and Sarah W. Hawkins / She hath done what she could. / Info is from Christ Church microfilm Reel 1 pg 320-321 located at the College of Southern MD, LaPlata, MD	HWK002
Hawkins	Mary	H.	1850	1937	At rest	SPL2041

Last Name	First Name	Middle Name	Date of Birth	Date of Death	Transcription / Notes	Cemetery Code
Hawkins	Mary	Holliday	No Date	Nov. 14, 1891	Age 86. / buried Nov 16, 1891 at Fair Fountain. / Info is from Christ Church microfilm Reel 2 pg 167-168, at the College of Southern MD, LaPlata, MD	HAWNo Stone
Hawkins	Mary	Margaret	Apr. 28, 1909	May 3, 1998		SIC9069
Hawkins	Mary	V.	Jun. 2, 1873	Aug. 29, 1968		SJO3366
Hawkins	Mary		Mar. 26, 1778	Dec. 19, 1852	Here reposes the body of the late / w/o Col Saml Hawkins / in the 74th year of her age	HWK006
Hawkins					Age 76 / buried at Fair Fountain. / Info is from Christ Church microfilm Reel 3 page 224-225 located at the College of Southern MD, LaPlata, MD / additional info is from J. Richard Rivoire: Mary Eleanor Hawkins, unmarried, dau of Josias and Caroline Clerklee Hawkins, sister of Jane Hawkins and Josias Hawkins.	
Hawkins	Mary (Mollie)	Eleanor	No Date	Mar. 4, 1913		HAWNo Stone
Hawkins	Matilda		No Date	Nov. 7, 1922	Age 67 / info is from church records	SHINoStone
Hawkins	Michael	Norman	Oct. 22, 1937	Feb. 8, 1990	SN US Navy	SCL1226
Hawkins	Nathaniel	M.	Feb. 6, 1912	Feb. 16, 1971	Info is from church records	SHI015
Hawkins	Peter	W.	No Date	Sep. 17, 1908	Info is from Christ Church microfilm Reel 3, Pg 220-221 located at the College of Southern MD, LaPlata, MD	MTRNoStone
Hawkins, M.D.	Peter	W.	Feb. 17, 1830	Sep. 17, 1908	In Memoriam / Peter W. Hawkins / Ene Placida Combsstus Face Quiescet Let me go for the day breaketh-Her children rise up and call her blessed. Her husband also, and he praiseth her	MTR4067
Hawkins	Ray	T. J.	Jan. 19, 1917	May 3, 1979	PFC US Army WW II	SMI031
Hawkins	Rebecca	W.	Mar. 18, 1839	May 20, 1910	In Memoriam / Rebecca W. Hawkins / Ene Placida Combsstus Face Quiescet Let me go for the day breaketh. / Her children rise up and call her blessed. Her husband also, and he praiseth her	MTR4067
Hawkins	Renada	T.	Oct. 13, 1955	Apr. 1, 1957		NSP314
Hawkins	Samuel	Weems	Oct. 27, 1897	Aug. 27, 1899	Second son of Walter & Laura S. Hawkins / Rest in Peace	MTR4133A
Hawkins	Samuel		Feb. 11, 1836	Apr. 7, 1913		MTR4065
Hawkins, Col.	Samuel		Feb. 28, 1766	Jun. 23, 1833	Aged 66 years / In honor of service in the war of 1812 N.S. U.S.D. 1812	HWK007

Last Name	First Name	Middle Name	Date of Birth	Date of Death	Transcription / Notes	Cemetery Code
Hawkins	Sarah	J., Weems	Jun. 7, 1806	Sep. 2, 1896	In memory of / Numbered with thy saints in Glory Everlasting.	HWK009
Hawkins	Sarah	W.	May 20, 1912	Jun. 20, 1972	Sally	MTR3186
Hawkins	Sarah	Weems	1896	1986	Located in Hawkins Plot	MTR3173
Hawkins	Sidney		No Date	Feb. 18, 1913	Aged 9 mos / Information is from the Historical Society Research located at the College of Southern Md, LaPlata, MD	SMINoStone
Hawkins	Theo	J.	No Date	1910	stone sunken	MAC049
Hawkins	Theodore	L.	Aug. 9, 1902	Dec. 17, 1958		NSP256
Hawkins	Theophilus		No Date	Mar. 3, 1921	Age 86 / He was buried Mar 5, 1921 at Fair Fountain. Info is from Christ Church microfilm Reel 3 pg 230-231 located at the College of Southern MD, LaPlata, MD	HAWNo Stone
Hawkins	Unknown		No Date	No Date	Old cement upright stone on a base	SHI214
Hawkins	Unknown		No Date	No Date	No name or date	POM006
Hawkins	Walter		Oct. 27, 1887	Aug. 27, 1899	Asleep in Jesus (there are 2 names on the stone but only 1 birth and death date	MTR4133
Hawkins	Washington		1848	1936	At rest	SPL2041
Hawkins	William	Pinkney	Nov. 24, 1872	Nov. 28, 1957	In Loving Memory of / Beloved h/o Elizabeth Lloyd Powell s/o Peter W. & Rebecca Morton Hawkins / "Thus not otherwise a soul goes forth none knowest whither and there are they who shall receive it."	MTR4091
Hawkins	Willie	Marshall	1899	Sep. 6, 1900	s/o J. Henry and Jemmie E. Hawkins. / Age 15 months. / Info is from Christ Church microfilm Reel 1 pg 86-87, at the College of Southern MD, LaPlata, MD	HWK010
Hawkins	Wm	E.	No Date	No Date	Old cement upright stone on a base	SHI216
Hawkins	Zenobia	M.	May 19, 1923	Jan. 10, 1983	Mother	SCL3021
Hayden	Alice	C.	Jun. 3, 1886	Mar. 10, 1963		TRI028
Hayden	Aloysius	A.	1867	1927	Footstone	SIC1079
Hayden	Aloysius	L.	1897	1931		SIC1079
Hayden	Aloysius		No Date	No Date		HGH2099
Hayden	Anna	Mae	Aug. 9, 1936	Mar. 18, 1997	Mother	SAC3009
Hayden	Bernard	E.	Mar. 11, 1904	Aug. 6, 1976		SMC2100
Hayden	Bernardine	H.	1913	1993		SIC1079

Last Name	First Name	Middle Name	Date of Birth	Date of Death	Transcription / Notes	Cemetery Code
Hayden	Bernice	M.	1909	1983		SIC1079
Hayden	C.	Rita	1916	1949		SIC1089
Hayden	Charles	F.	Apr. 15, 1839	Sep. 7, 1911		SIC3030
Hayden	Charlotte	Gough	1851	1943		TRI241
Hayden	Columbia		1872	1946		HGH2115
Hayden	Doris	E.	1921	2004		SIC1091
Hayden	Eliza	A C.	1851	1941		SIC3030
Hayden	Eliza	C.	1841	1910	His wife / Erected by Columbia Hayden	HGH2114
Hayden	Ella	G.	Nov. 4, 1879	Jan. 1, 1928	Stone is broken off base and is laying on the ground	HGH1098
Hayden	Emma	Carrick	No Date	Nov. 1942		HGH1170
Hayden	Ethel	Roby	No Date	Aug. 12, 1954		SJO4142
Hayden	Eva	M.	Sep. 20, 1911	Apr. 28, 1983		HGH2011
Hayden	Evangeline	C.	1921	1992		SIC2042
Hayden	Frances	L.	1889	1975		HGH1001
Hayden	Frances	Lyon	1913	1969		SIC2052
Hayden	Francis	T.	1940	1999	Children: Steven & Crissy / Grandchildren: Ryan, Samantha & Kelcy	HGH4138
Hayden	G.	Kenneth	1918	1999		SIC1092
Hayden					Stone is broken / info is from The Historical Society Research located at the College of Southern MD, LaPlata, MD	HGHNoStone
Hayden	George	C.	May 14, 18 ( )	Nov. 24, 1857		HGH2012
Hayden	Helen	C.	Aug. 4, 1913	Apr. 10, 2007		HGH2012
Hayden	Henry	A.	Mar. 9, 1908	Sep. 2, 1986		HGH2033
Hayden	Henry	A.	Oct. 8, 1877	Mar. 31, 1961		SIC1088
Hayden	J.	Earl	1906	1942		SIC1090
Hayden	J.	Marion	1904	1954		HGH2114
Hayden	James	C.	1839	1927	Erected by Columbia Hayden	SIC2069
Hayden	Joseph	M.	Dec. 4, 1878	Dec. 18, 1943		HGH2011
Hayden	Joseph	R.	Sep. 26, 1902	Dec. 2, 1965		SIC1079
Hayden	Kathleen		1909	1970		SIC1093
Hayden, Jr.	Keith	Gregory	Jan. 2, 1976	Jan. 6, 1976	Daddy's little boy / Bronze marker is placed in front of stone for Maurice and Mary Hayden	

Last Name	First Name	Middle Name	Date of Birth	Date of Death	Transcription / Notes	Cemetery Code
Hayden	Laura	A.	Apr. 13, 1879	Apr. 19, 1915	In loving memory of our dear Mother / By her children	HGH2111
Hayden	Lewis	Marion	No Date	Sep. 10, 1950		SJO4142
Hayden	Luke	B.	1888	1961		HGH1002
Hayden	M.	Annabelle	Feb. 8, 1935	No Date	Mother	HGH1171
Hayden	Marie	S.	Sep. 28, 1907	Jun. 28, 1987		SMC2101
Hayden	Mary	A.	Feb. 2, 1888	Jun. 22, 1923		HGH1085
Hayden	Mary	Ada	1873	1964		NSP700
Hayden	Mary	Cordelia	1878	Jul. 19, 1962	Added info is from the Maryland Independent Newspaper Thurs. Jul 26, 1962, d/o Joseph & Fannie Simpson; w/o Maurice Dutton Hayden	SIC1087
Hayden	Mary	E.	1870	1962	Footstone	SIC1079
Hayden	Mary	E.	Dec. 24, 1879	May 6, 1964		HGH2033
Hayden	Mary	E.	No Date	No Date		HGH2099
Hayden	Mattie	B.	Aug. 21, 1906	May 9, 1960		HGH2109
Hayden	Maurice	D.	1873	1945		SIC1087
Hayden	Monica		No Date	No Date		HGH2099
Hayden	Oma		1941	1998	"Cindy" / Children: Steven & Crissy / Grandchildren: Ryan, Samantha & Kelcy	HGH4138
Hayden	Philip	E.	Jul. 29, 1935	No Date	Father	SAC3009
Hayden	R.	Harvey	Nov. 19, 1980	Jun. 7, 1963		HGH1169
Hayden, III	Robert	H.	Oct. 14, 1953	Sep. 7, 2007	Son / Husband of Linda Schwartz	HGH1171
Hayden, Jr.	Robert	H.	Jan. 6, 1930	Jun. 4, 1975	Father / PFC US Army	HGH1171
Hayden	Robert	K.	1902	1975		HGH4018
Hayden	Rose	J.	1865	1938		SIC1079
Hayden	Sadye	M.	May 2, 1886	Feb. 15, 1960		SIC2068
Hayden	Teresa		No Date	Jul. 2, 1925	Info is from church records	SHINoStone
Hayden	Thomas	C.	1919	1998		SIC2042
Hayden	Thompson	D.	No Date	No Date		HGH2099
Hayden	Walter	B.	1894	1964	Info is from The Historical Society Research located at the College of Southern MD, LaPlata, MD	HGHNoStone
Hayden	Webster	P.	Jun. 15, 1874	Aug. 3, 1949	In loving memory of my father by Margaret	HGH2110
Hayden	Wendell		Dec. 18, 1913	May15, 1917	Our Baby / s/o J.M. & Sadye Hayden	SIC2066

Last Name	First Name	Middle Name	Date of Birth	Date of Death	Transcription / Notes	Cemetery Code
Hayden	William	Maurice	1910	1955		SIC2052
Hayes	Barbara	Ann	June 29, 1941	July 5, 1987	Rest in peace / Beloved daughter and mother	HGH3033
Hayes	Bessie	Fay	Jun. 20, 1908	Dec. 6, 1992	Loving Mother	MTR4020
Hayes	Carol	J.	Aug. 9, 1960	Sep. 15, 2002	Loved Mother Grandmother Sister & Daughter	MTR2221
Hayes	Charles	Daniel	Feb. 29, 1904	Jul. 29, 1966		MTR4021
Hayes	Claude		Mar. 23, 1902	Dec. 6, 1981		CLV373
Hayes	Donald	C.	Jun. 27, 1929	No Date		NSP889
Hayes	J.	B.	Apr. 22, 1928	Aug. 6, 1979		MTR4022
Hayes	Mary	M.	Oct. 14, 1904	Oct. 11, 1972		CLV373
Hayes	Maryann	J.	Nov. 13, 1934	Dec. 18, 2002		NSP888
Hayes	Nancy	L.	Jun. 25, 1946	Feb. 2, 2000	In God's Care	MTR3035
Hayes	Rosemarie		No Date	Nov. 15, 1962	Infant	NSP890
Hayes	Steven	N.	1966	1998	In memory	HGH3034
Hayes	Teresa	M.	Aug. 23, 1930	Nov. 16, 1962		NSP890
Hayes	Wilmer	Dean	Jul. 28, 1969	Dec. 16, 1993		MTR3034
Hayman, Sr.	Gerald	W.	Sep. 9, 1946	Oct. 6, 1997	"Jerry"	NSP738
Haynes	Charlene	E.	Nov. 6, 1940	No Date	Always in our hearts / m. Nov 21, 1959	NSP824
Haynes	Josephine	E.	No Date	1997	Name is shown on church records but burial location is unknown	CHRNoStone
Haynes, Sr.	Roger	A.	Jan. 19, 1938	Oct. 7, 2002	Together Forever / m. Nov. 21, 1959 / US Marine Corps / Always in our hearts	NSP824
Haywood	Edgo		No Date	Nov. 30, 1860	painted on bottom of stone of Henretta R. Haywood painted in black paint on this stone is Edgo Haywood died Nov 30, 1860	OAK100
Haywood	Henretta	R.	Oct. 29, 1870	Feb. 10, 1953		OAK100
Heard	Albert	David	Jun. 5, 1953	Dec. 1975	"Rickey" / We Love you and miss you	ZBC010
Heard	Helen		Oct. 25, 1899	Aug. 15, 1987		ZBC114
Heard	Sheldon		1962	1990	Thornton Funeral Home Marker	MHB110
Heat	Gertrude		No Date	Aug. 7, 1940	Age 18 / Information is from the Historical Society Research located at the College of Southern MD, LaPlata, MD	ALXNo Stone
Heathcote	Mary	C.	Nov. 2, 1918	Jun. 9, 2002		SCL4213
Heathcote	Thomas	B.	Oct. 21, 1921	Jul. 20, 2004		SCL4213

Last Name	First Name	Middle Name	Date of Birth	Date of Death	Transcription / Notes	Cemetery Code
Hebert	Claire	C.	1921	2009		SMCD237
Hedden	Clarence	W.	Jun. 6, 1931	Feb. 9, 2006	Married July 30, 1950	SIC9076
Hedden	Doris	M.	May 22, 1934	No Date	Married July 30, 1950	SIC9076
Hedges	Lloyd	L.	1937	2003	We will always love you your loving family	OSM054
Hedges	Myrtle	E.	Jun. 9, 1904	Jun. 23, 1987	Together forever	OSM056
Hedges	Tilton	E.	Jan. 16, 1897	Jun. 22, 1987	Together forever	OSM056
Hedges	Willard	W.	1945	1981	We will always love you. Your wife Janice and daughter Hope. / "Wally"	OSM055
Hedrick	Mary	Anna	Sep. 5, 1898	Oct. 25, 1987	Ancestry.com website shows her last name as Hedrick	SMCD020
Heffernan	Josephine	C.	1905	1975		NSP530
Hegens	Queen	E.	1916	1994		DUD017
Heier	Robert	A.	Mar. 12, 1947	Nov. 18, 2006	Wed. Dec 15, 1976	SMC4223
Heilmeier	Frances	Mary	1931	1951		NSP574
Heilmeier	Frances		1898	1975		NSP576
Heilmeier	Ludwig		1901	1971		NSP575
Hein	Genevieve	Gibson	Apr. 1, 1952	Mar. 19, 2006		SMC1069
Heinze, III	Frederick	George	Nov. 7, 1933	Jul. 27, 1990		SIC8055
Heise	Henry	L.	Aug. 2, 1901	Oct. 18, 1902		SJE131
Heise	Katherine	Edith	1891	1981		SCL2068
Heise	Margaret	L.	Jul. 18, 1864	Dec. 10, 1908	w/o J.C. Heise	SJE133
Heise	Richard	Edward	1892	1940		SCL2070
Heiston	Destin	James	No Date	Jun. 22, 1993	"Baby B" (9 precious hours) / Back of stone: We will always have a guardian Angel	SJO3163
Helmick	Amanda		Nov. 1, 1982	Nov. 1, 1982	flat marker to the ground that is close to the woods and is located to the right of Johnathan Wells	HGH1260
Helmuth	Joseph	F.	May 6, 1900	May 18, 1900	Info is from the Historical Society Research located at The College of Southern MD, LaPlata, MD	FRANoStone
Helwig	Gerald	H.	Aug. 13, 1921	No Date	The worlds best wife	ODE375
Helwig	Mary	D. Gray	Mar. 6, 1917	Nov. 24, 1994	The worlds best wife	ODE375
Hemming	Albert	A.	Apr. 2, 1914	Oct. 6, 1979		SMC3172
Hemming	Brian	Michael	Oct. 28, 1978	Dec. 21, 1978	In Loving memory of our Son	NSP994
Hemming	Catharine		1849	1923	Rest in peace	SMCD163

Last Name	First Name	Middle Name	Date of Birth	Date of Death	Transcription / Notes	Cemetery Code
Hemming	Catherine	U.	Jan. 20, 1920	Aug. 3, 1991	Mother	SMC3171
Hemming	Clara		Feb. 9, 1890	Mar. 11, 1969		SMC3206
Hemming	Henry	A.	Aug. 16, 1967	Aug. 17, 1967		SMCD314
Hemming	Henry		Feb. 22, 1882	Mar. 6, 1959	Father	SMC3205
Hemming	John	A.	Aug. 16, 1967	Aug. 17, 1967		SMCD314
Hemming	Joseph		1893	1931	Rest in peace	SMCD163
Hemming	Paul	L.	Jun. 1, 1929	Jan. 8, 2003		SMC3103
Hemming	Paul	Lawrence	Jun. 1, 1929	Jan. 8, 2003	SSGT US Air Force Korea	SMC3105
Hemphill	Charles	J.	1929	2005		SIC9101
Hemsley	Andrew	D.	Nov. 6, 1984	Sep. 19, 1985		SAC1019
Hemsley	Annie	Mae	Oct. 18, 1945	No Date	In loving memory of our parents	HGH4269
Hemsley	Anthony	R.	Feb. 4, 1967	Nov. 7, 2001		SCL4111
Hemsley	Cecil	B.	1956	2006	Cedell Brooks Funeral Home Marker	HGH4305
Hemsley	Charles		Apr. 28, 1924	May 9, 1994	"Eddie" / Gone but not forgotten	HGH4309
Hemsley	Donna	B.	Aug. 15, 1964	No Date		SCL4111
Hemsley	Donna	R.	Nov. 5, 1961	Sep. 21, 2003	Mike / Love and Peace	SAC1086
Hemsley	Dorothy	A.	Feb. 24, 1936	Feb. 12, 2002	Beloved Sister	SAC3067
Hemsley	Francis	B.	No Date	Nov. 23, 1926	Infant / Info is from church records	SHINoStone
Hemsley	H.	A.	1898	1979	Hattie	SAC5001
Hemsley	Henry	H.	Apr. 12, 1920	Mar. 7, 1973	Maryland Tec 5 US Army WWII	SAC5002
Hemsley	Hillery		No Date	May 30, 1922	Info is from church records	SHINoStone
Hemsley	James	M.	1897	1969		SAC5001
Hemsley	John	S.	Sep. 26, 1938	Apr. 6, 2002		HGH4132
Hemsley	John		No Date	Feb. 21, 1923	Info is from church records	SHINoStone
Hemsley	Larnel	D.	Jan. 21, 1963	Feb. 14, 2006	Loving Son, Brother, Uncle	SAC1087
Hemsley	Lenora		No Date	Aug. 1955	Info is from church records	SHINoStone
Hemsley	Lewis	L.	Sep. 21, 1976	Mar. 18, 1998		HGH4214
Hemsley	Louis	John	Apr. 5, 1930	Jun. 2, 2002	In loving memory of our parents	HGH4269
Hemsley	Lucy	Ann	1900	1996	Mother / You are always in our hearts	SHI017
Hemsley	Mary	M.	No Date	May 2, 1960		HGH3018

Last Name	First Name	Middle Name	Date of Birth	Date of Death	Transcription / Notes	Cemetery Code
Hemsley	Mary	V.	Jan. 24, 1941	Jul. 11, 1981		HGH4131
Hemsley	Mary		No Date	Oct. 24, 1926	Info is from church records	SHINoStone
Hemsley	Matilda		No Date	Jan. 17, 1963	Info is from church records	SHINoStone
Hemsley	Peter		Oct. 10, 1933	Aug. 7, 1970		HGH3053
Hemsley	Sidney		No Date	Dec. 2, 1926	Info is from church records	SHINoStone
Hemsley	William	?	Oct. 11, 1916	Sep. 24, 1975	(Billy)	SHI096
Hemsley, Jr.	William		No Date	Mar. 13, 1957	Info is from church records	SHINoStone
Henderson	Althea	H.	Feb. 28, 1856	Jun. 23, 1927	w/o B. F. Henderson	OFE4022
Henderson	Alton	V.	Jul. 16, 1930	Aug. 2, 2002	PFC US Army	NJB212
Henderson	B.	F.	Dec. 25, 1847	Feb. 11, 1929		OFE4022
Henderson, Jr.	B.	F.	Dec. 2, 1889	Apr. 26, 1938		OFE4018
Henderson	Catherine	M.	Nov. 3, 1950	Oct. 30, 2005	Devoted wife and Mother	ODE167
Henderson	Cecil	E.	Aug. 1, 1909	Jan. 23, 1953		NJB497
Henderson	Charles	H.	1866	1957		NJB365
Henderson	Charlie	M.	Jul. 20, 1939	Feb. 24, 1990	Beloved Husband and Father / there is a verse on the front and back of his stone. Footstone: U.S. Army	ODE167
Henderson	E.	N.	Sep. 16, 1879	Mar. 23, 1951	Church records show first name as Ernest	NJB499
Henderson	Elizabeth		No Date	No Date		NJB244
Henderson	Eva		Aug. 3, 1891	Jan. 1, 1980		SMC2159
Henderson	Frances		1845	1926		NJB450
Henderson	G.	W.	Jul. 1, 1855	Oct. 29, 1929	Church records show first name as George	NJB049
Henderson	George	Gilbert	Jul. 28, 1898	Jun. 11, 1987		PKH024
Henderson	Hattie	A.	No Date	Jan. 1946	Age 64, buried January 19, 1946 Info is from the Historical Society Research located at the College of Southern MD, LaPlata, MD	ODENoStone
Henderson	Herbert	P.	Feb. 12, 1903	Sep. 15, 1968		NJB369
Henderson	Ida	Matilda	No Date	No Date		NJB416
Henderson	Kate	N.	Feb. 15, 1857	May 24, 1921	w/o G.W. Henderson	NJB049
Henderson	Lottie	Monroe	May 2, 1888	Oct. 22, 1958	Church records show middle name as Monroe	NJB498
Henderson	Louise	R	Nov. 23, 1889	Mar. 11, 1971		OFE4020
Henderson	Louise	Sullivan	Apr. 6, 1904	Dec. 24, 1995		PKH024

Last Name	First Name	Middle Name	Date of Birth	Date of Death	Transcription / Notes	Cemetery Code
Henderson	Mary	F.	1872	1908		NJB365
Henderson	Mary	Frances	May 22, 1927	Oct. 15, 1927		NJB366
Henderson	May		No Date	No Date		NJB415
Henderson	Melvin	M.	May 26, 1936	Jul. 26, 1992	PFC US Army	NJB213
Henderson	Meredith	H.	Sep. 18, 1928	Oct. 11, 1982	He cared	NJB211
Henderson	Norman	M.	Feb. 23, 1907	Jul. 23, 1907	At rest (stone is sunken)	NJB050
Henderson	Peter	C.	Mar. 22, 1888	Jun. 7, 1973		OFE4020
Henderson, Jr.	Peter	C.	Aug. 17, 1916	Mar. 6, 1954		OFE4021
Henderson	Phillip	Oliver	Feb. 6, 1905	Sep. 19, 1972		NJB367
Henderson	Richard		1839	1914		NJB451
Henderson	Samuel		No Date	No Date		NJB243
Henderson	William	E.	Nov. 22, 1918	Oct. 24, 1998		NZN011
Hendricks	Ann	Louise	No Date	Dec. 20, 1865	In Memory of / Beloved Wife Of George W. Hendricks / Aged 22 Years / Under the shadow of His wing I'll take my rest an sleep / Rest in Peace / C.L Neale Alex. Va	SCL2088
Hendricks	James		No Date	Apr. 15, 1890	Aged 61 years / A precious one from us is gone. A voice we loved is still. A place is vacant in our home ( ) Never ( ) Be filled thy soul is safe in heaven	SJE072
Henley	Inez	M.	1908	1993	In loving memory	CMX1071
Henley	Leonard	L.	1905	1971	In loving memory	CMX1066
Hennigan	Tracy	Rene	Feb. 19, 1968	Jan. 3, 2000		ODE081
Henry	Clarence	Alan	No Date	No Date	Name painted in black letters on stone	OAK115
Henry	Patricia	Lee	Jul. 8, 1946	Feb. 23, 2001	Verse on stone: It takes both rain and sunshine to make a rainbow / Back of stone: Henry 2 Timothy 4:07 I have fought a good fight. I have finished my course. I have kept the faith.	NJB298
Hensley	Maudie		1887	No Date	w/o Robert Hemsley	PGONoStone
Henson	Annie	K.	1915	1975	Daughter	SCL3339
Henson	Buenell	Craig	Jun. 8, 1889	May 2, 1989		OAK122
Henson	Charles		Dec. 31, 1894	May 5, 1898	Name is etched on stone by hand	SMI001
Henson	Charles		No Date	Apr. 21, 1953	Old Cement Cross - stone sunken into ground	MAC017
Henson	George	Rodney	Sep. 8, 1946	Sep. 11, 1994	Sgt. U. S. Marine Corps / Viet Nam	OAK073

Last Name	First Name	Middle Name	Date of Birth	Date of Death	Transcription / Notes	Cemetery Code
Henson	Ida	B.	1898	1973	Thornton Funeral Home Marker	OAK206
Henson	Joseph	S	1867	1937		POM053
Henson	Josephine		No Date	No Date	A very small stone with the name Josephine behind plastic embedded in the stone / info was supplied by church member	PGO009
Henson, Jr.	Lemuel	H.	Mar. 3, 1930	Jan. 10, 1988	Funeral Home Marker (info is from web site Familysearch.org)	ZBC029
Henson	Mabel	A.	Apr. 10, 1899	Nov. 16, 1982	Forever in our hearts	SMI054
Henson	Mary	F.	1870	1932		POM053
Henson	Mary		1881	1972	Thornton Funeral Home Marker	SMI039
Henson	Michael	Anthony	Aug. 27, 1960	May 30, 2003	God let the perpetual light shine on me forever. Amen	SCL4183
Henson	Sarah		No Date	Dec.	Cement cross	OAK189
Henson	Solomon		No Date	Jun. 28, 1916	Age 16 / info is from church records	OFENoStone
Henson, Jr.	Sydney	H.	Jul. 12, 1933	Nov. 14, 2003	Eternally resting in the care of our Divine Lord	SCL4170
Hepburn	Edith	Booth	Jun. 18, 1917	Feb. 23, 1960		SMC3303
Herbert	Ada	Gertrude	Nov. 6, 1887	Apr. 17, 1904		OFE4060
Herbert	Agnes	Sivillia	1886	1982	Wife & mother / rest in peace	OFE1067
Herbert	Amelia		1871	Mar. 19, 1904	Death date is from church records	HAN010
Herbert	Annie	G.	Feb. 27, 1880	Nov. 25, 1953		SMY2144
Herbert	Archie	H.	1891	1972		OFE2016
Herbert	Bertie	P.	1870	1961		OFE2053
Herbert	Bessie	M.	Jan. 4, 1904	Sept 25, 1998		OFE3026
Herbert	Blanche	B	Dec. 12, 1870	Jul. 30, 1968		SAC2039
Herbert	C.	Webb	Jan. 20, 1905	Mar. 4, 1986		OFE3026
Herbert	Charles	P.	Jan. 16, 1860	Apr. 20, 1949		OFE4057
Herbert, Sr.	Charles	Webster	1906	1971	s/o Peter G. & Agnes S.	OFE1066
Herbert	Dorothy	H.	1908	1969		NSP628
Herbert	Edna	Irene	1877	1942		TRI379
Herbert	Elizabeth	Jane	1881	1961		TRI377
Herbert	Elizabeth		No Date	Nov. 13, 1895	Name is shown on church records but burial location is unknown, date is the burial date, not death date	CHRNoStone

Last Name	First Name	Middle Name	Date of Birth	Date of Death	Transcription / Notes	Cemetery Code
Herbert	Ernest		No Date	Sep. 13, 1913	Name is shown on church records but burial location is unknown, date is the burial date, not death date	CHRNoStone
Herbert	Eva	Mae	1916	1986		TRI381
Herbert	F.	Cleveland	1888	1972		OFE2055
Herbert	George	Elmer	1905	1970		TRI380
Herbert	George	P.	Oct. 7, 1877	Dec. 3, 1926		CHR549
Herbert	James	E.	Jun. 23, 1897	Mar. 6, 1933		OFE4059A
Herbert	James	Edward	Jul. 26, 1902	Sep. 3, 1902	Headstone: Herbert; s/o Mr. & Mrs. Ollie N. Herbert	TRI382
Herbert	James	W.	No Date	Oct. 23, 1971	Age 18 / info is from church records	OFENoStone
Herbert	James	W.	1880	1958		OFE2052
Herbert	Jennie	May	Feb. 5, 1887	Nov. 16, 1915	w/o Jesse M. Herbert	OFE2051
Herbert	Jesse	M.	1883	1972		OFE2053
Herbert	John	Allen	Aug. 26, 1896	Apr. 13, 1931	Beloved h/o Ruth Ridgely Waters	SMY3076
Herbert	John	P.	Jun. 15, 1835	Oct. 25, 1917	Rest in peace	CHR548
Herbert	John	V.	1869	1942	Father / Rest in Peace / Erected to the memory of my loving Father and Mother by their daughter	HGH1090
Herbert	Jos	T.	Dec. 24, 1827	Aug. 22, 1893		SMY1103
Herbert	Joseph	E.	1898	1952	Father	SMCD282A
Herbert	Julia	F.	Jun. 29, 1927	Jul. 16, 2006	In loving memory	HGH1044
Herbert	Leon	Sheirburn	No Date	Mar. 17, 1944	Info from Times Crescent Newspaper Mar 24, 1944	SMYNoStone
Herbert	Leonard	F.	Oct. 19, 1904	Aug. 1, 1974	L.F.H.	SIC7055
Herbert	Leonard	S.	No Date	Nov. 26, 1936	Info from St Mary's Beacon Newspaper Dec 4, 1936	SMYNoStone
Herbert	Lucy	C.	1903	1982		OFE2055
Herbert	Madeline		Sep. 19, 1898	Jun. 25, 1903	In loving remembrance of / d/o J.V. and M.C. Herbert / Budded on earth to bloom in Heaven	HGH1089
Herbert	Maggie	C.	1872	1946		HGH1090
Herbert	Maggie	V.	1892	1986		OFE2016
Herbert	Malinda	C.	Apr. 1, 1842	Feb. 6, 1912	In Loving remembrance of / Beloved w/o John P. Herbert / Gone but not forgotten	CHR547
Herbert	Marguerite	G.	Jul. 31, 1907	Sep. 8, 1988		SIC7055
Herbert	Mary	Ann	Aug. 8, 1865	Aug. 23, 1866	Stone is hard to read	SMY1061

Last Name	First Name	Middle Name	Date of Birth	Date of Death	Transcription / Notes	Cemetery Code
Herbert	Mary	C.	May 10, 1834	Jul. 3, 1894	Mother / Rest in Peace / Erected to the memory of my loving Father and Mother by their daughter	SMY1103
Herbert	Mary	E.	1903	1994		SMC1127
Herbert	Mary	L.	1883	1983		OFE4008
Herbert	Mary	Lancaster	Sep. 9, 1897	Mar. 6, 1932		HGH1043
Herbert	Mary	O.	Sep. 12, 1888	Jul. 25, 1968	Mother	SMCD268
Herbert	Mary	Woodburn	Jan. 27, 1883	Dec. 31, 1911	w/o J.W. Herbert	OFE2049
Herbert	Ollie	Neal	1873	1950		TRI378
Herbert	P.	Addison	1899	1983	In God's care	LUM170
Herbert	Peter	G.	1875	1941		OFE1068
Herbert	Philip	Claudius	No Date	Apr. 15, 1907	In Loving Memory of our darling baby Infant s/o W. M. and M. E. Herbert Fell Asleep in Jesus / aged 5 months and 13 days (footstone)	OFE4010
Herbert	R.	Theodore	Nov. 7, 1881	Jun. 10, 1956	Father	SMCD269
Herbert	Richard	O.	1899	1969		SMC1127
Herbert	Robert	Lee	1864	1909	By R. W. / T. D. Swann	HGH3084
Herbert	S.	Webster	1879	1948		OFE2054
Herbert	Samuel	P.	Mar. 27, 1853	Jul. 19, 1941		OFE2056
Herbert	Sarah	S.	Apr. 14, 1863	Mar. 6, 1946		OFE4058
Herbert	Sophia	D.	1906	1999	In God's care	LUM170
Herbert	Victor	M.	1900	1954		NSP629
Herbert	William	Chicester	Feb. 11, 1937	Dec. 13, 1969	Rest in Peace	OFE2050
Herbert	William	L.	1880	1957		SMY2144
Herbert	William	M.	1882	1946		OFE4009
Herd	Agnes	Graham	Sep. 6, 1924	Nov. 8, 1945		NSP249
Herd	Cecelia	Victoria	1916	1976	In Loving Memory	SAC5065
Herd	Isabell	Jackson	1902	1994	In Loving Memory	SAC5065A
Herd, Sr.	James	F.	1908	1994	In Loving Memory	SAC5065A
Herd	Priscilla	Herd, Proctor	1879	1962	In Loving Memory	SAC5065
Herd, Sr.	Thomas	L.	Aug. 9, 1947	Jul. 21, 1981	Our Loving Brother & Father / US Army	SAC5058
Herman	Carolyn	E.	May 25, 1894	Apr. 2, 1986		NSP675

Last Name	First Name	Middle Name	Date of Birth	Date of Death	Transcription / Notes	Cemetery Code
Herman	Katherine		No Date	1927	76 years old (Lomax & Penn Undertakers) info is from W. Preston Williams list of Private Cemeteries)	BGN001
Herman	Lottie	Emma	Apr. 2, 1906	Mar. 25, 1993	In loving memory of our Mother	NSP932
Herndon	Mary	Rita	No Date	Dec. 11, 1939		HGH4256
Hershberger	Christine	M.	Feb. 6, 1909	Apr. 22, 1974		NSP699
Hervey	Joseph	W.	Jun. 16, 1913	Sep. 2, 2002	Masonic emblem	CHR363
Hess	Mary	E., Mattingly	Mar. 24, 1864	Jan. 25, 1932	Wife of John J. Hess / Rest in peace	HGH1100
Hess	William	H.	No Date	Aug. 1914	Name is shown on church records but burial location is unknown, date is the burial date, not death date	CHRNoStone
Hickey	George	Hussman	No Date	Mar. 20, 1926	4 years 10 months / Name is shown on church records but burial location is unknown, date is the burial date, not death date	CHRNoStone
Hickey	James	D.	Jan. 29, 1919	Jun. 25, 1919	Their grandson / Footstone	CHR534
Hickey	Margaret	Dorsett	No Date	Feb. 6, 1961	Name is shown on church records but burial location is unknown	CHRNoStone
Hickey	William	Henry	No Date	Aug. 21, 1948	Name is shown on church records but burial location is unknown, date is the burial date, not death date	CHRNoStone
Hickmann	Herbert	Walter	Mar. 18, 1921	Dec. 11, 2002	We miss you Dad, Barbara, Steve, Gigi, David / Angel's Charlie / Back of stone: Grandchildren, Jennifer, Julia, Robert, Abbey, Drew	SJO3230
Hickmann	N.	Ann, Hanson	Jan. 25, 1923	Jul. 2, 2000	Charlie's Angels / We miss you Momma, Barbara, Steve, Gigi, David Back of stone: Grandchildren Jennifer, Julia, Robert, Abbey, Drew	SJO3228
Hicks	A.	W., Scott	Sep. 9, 1852	Dec. 17, 1921	Hope. His toils are past. His work is done. He has fought the fight the victory won, and entered into rest. Then let our hearts in every move still say "thy will be done:.	SPL3108
Hicks	Alice	C.	Dec. 13, 1939	Mar. 2, 2002		SMY5005
Hicks	Alice	L.	Sep. 28, 1923	Jul. 10, 1970	Info is from church records	SHI275
Hicks	B.	LeeRoy	1882	1932	Father	SPL5077
Hicks	Benjamin	Holliday	No Date	No Date	At rest	SPL1024
Hicks	Benson	Neal	Jan. 30, 1895	Jul. 18, 1966		SPL4009
Hicks	Bryant	Antron	Jan. 18, 1976	Jun. 23, 1999	"Brian" / We all love and miss you, Mom, Mike, Family and Friends / info is from church records	SHI259

Last Name	First Name	Middle Name	Date of Birth	Date of Death	Transcription / Notes	Cemetery Code
Hicks	Carlton		1875	1931	Woodmen of the World marker / Headstone in side of the building.	SPL4156
Hicks	Catharine	Eloise	No Date		Info is from Christ Church microfilm Reel 1 Pg 90-91 located at the College of Southern MD, LaPlata, MD	MTRNoStone
Hicks	Charles	H.	Jun. 13, 1913	Jun. 29, 1903		SAC4008
Hicks	Charles	Henry, Bush	May 15, 1902	Jul. 26, 1994		SIC6014
Hicks	Charlotte	Dorothy, Ohm	Aug. 24, 1911	Jun. 27, 1981	Verse on stone: They that wait upon the Lord shall renew / Strength, mount up wings as angels, run and not faint. Isaiah 40:31	SPL1023
Hicks	Clarrissa	M.	Nov. 10, 1884	Oct. 9, 1985	Number 341 inscribed on lower right of stone	CLV300
Hicks	Dora	C.	1902	Apr. 2, 1963		SIC8073
Hicks	Edna	M.	Aug. 5, 1911	1980	Ancestry.com website shows her birth date as Aug 5, 1911 and her date of death as Sep 4, 1999	SMC3178
Hicks	Elizabeth	C.	Sep. 18, 1854	Sep. 4, 1999	Peace, perfect peace with loved ones far away	SPL3107
Hicks	Elizabeth	J.	Jun. 20, 1817	May 9,1931	Aged 69y, 10m, 12d / Asleep in Jesus	SPL4122
Hicks	Ella	Louise	Mar. 5, 1922	May 2, 1887	Beloved d/o Luther C & Clarrissa M Hicks	CLV270
Hicks	Ethel	Greer	1908	Dec. 26, 1928	Married Apr 13, 1925	SIG124
Hicks	Florence			2000		SPL4157
Hicks	Francis	E.	1898	Feb. 1, 1983	Person was identified by church record plat	SPL4011
Hicks	George	A.	Jun. 25, 1952	1962		SAC1126
Hicks, Jr.	George	A.	Aug. 10, 1980	Aug. 11, 2000	The Cadillac King	SHI124
Hicks	George	Adrian	Aug. 24, 1907	Aug. 12, 1980	Verse on stone: They that wait upon the Lord shall renew / Strength, mount up wings as angels, run and not faint. Isaiah 40:31	SPL1023
Hicks	George	E.	Jul. 1872	Apr. 16, 1990	Gone But Not Forgotten	CLV266
Hicks	George	M.	Oct. 27, 1878	Feb. 1901	"My lambs" / s/o Washington & Mary A. Hicks	SPL4125
Hicks, Jr.	George	S.	Mar. 20, 1918	Dec. 14, 1884	In Memory of / We Love You (Metal plaque attached to stone)	SAC5079
Hicks	Grace	E.	Aug. 21, 1882	Dec. 27, 1996	d/o Washington & Mary A. Hicks / My Lambs	SPL4127
Hicks	Harry	C.	Dec. 19, 1878	Dec. 11, 1884	At rest	SPL3106
Hicks	Harry	T.	Mar. 6, 1931	Apr. 4, 1928		SAC1127
Hicks	James	E.	Aug. 9, 1880	Dec. 8, 1991	s/o Washington & Mary A. Hicks / My Lambs	SPL4126
Hicks	James	Edwards	1906	Dec. 13, 1884	Married Apr 13, 1925	SIG124

Last Name	First Name	Middle Name	Date of Birth	Date of Death	Transcription / Notes	Cemetery Code
Hicks	James	L.	Jan. 25, 1812	Jul. 12, 1892	"I know that my Redeemer Liveth."	SPL4123
Hicks	James	M.	1928	1994	In God's care / son / In loving memory of Harriett Hicks Hawkins & family	TRI030
Hicks	James	P.	1851	1930		SPL4010
Hicks	James	R.	Dec. 27, 1837	Mar. 26, 1917	Father / Loved in life in death remembered	CLV265
Hicks	John	H.	Apr. 16, 1913	Feb. 17, 1972	Info is from The Historical Society Research located at The College of Southern MD, LaPlata, MD.	SMYNoStone
Hicks	Josephine		1859	1906		SPL4010
Hicks	Lelia	T.	Apr. 6, 1918	No Date		SAC4008
Hicks	Luther	C.	Jun. 17, 1883	Aug. 2, 1965		CLV299
Hicks	Margaret	Ann	Jan. 2, 1923	Jul. 24, 2006	Sunrise / Sunset / We Love You	SMY2072
Hicks	Maria	C.	Mar. 22, 1840	Dec. 10, 1929	Mother / Loved in life in death remembered	CLV265
Hicks	Marion	Cordelia	No Date	No Date	At rest	SPL1024
Hicks	Maurice	C.	Mar. 25, 1954	Nov. 26, 2000	In Memory of	SHI276
Hicks	Nancy	M.	1914	1995	In God's care / Mother / In loving memory of Harriett Hicks Hawkins & family	TRI030
Hicks	P.	Miranda	Mar. 13, 1828	Feb. 3, 1892	"Blessed are the dead that die in the Lord"	SPL5105
Hicks	Paul		Jun. 29, 1888	Aug. 22, 1888	Our baby / Infant s/o A.W.S. & E.C. Hicks	SPL3109
Hicks	Samuel		No Date	Sep. 20, 1938	Aged 69 - No Marker / info is from church records	CLVNoStone
Hicks	Thomas	F.	Feb. 15, 1847	Sep. 15, 1878	Aged 31y, 7m / "I wait for the Lord, my soul doth wait, and in his word do I hope."	SPL5106
Hicks	Unknown		No Date	No Date	Number 342 inscribed on lower right of stone / Info is from church records	CLV291
Hicks	Verbena	A. W.	Sep. 19, 1883	Feb. 8, 1968	Mother	SPL5078
Hicks	William	Lee	1955	1986		SAC2115
Hiett	Unknown		No Date	Mar. 25, 1916	Infant d/o J.E. - E.C. Hiett	SJE034
Higdon	Ann	M.	Jan. 25, 1815	Oct. 3, 1838	Sacred to the memory of / Consort of John E. S. Higdon who was born / departed this life / aged 23 years 8 months & 9 days. She lived without no doubt. She was pious. She is gone to a better life. May she rest in peace (very old piece of stone that is laying on the ground).	SJO5084

Last Name	First Name	Middle Name	Date of Birth	Date of Death	Transcription / Notes	Cemetery Code
Higdon	B	L.		Dec. 22, 1888	My beloved Husband / aged 53 years / May he rest in peace / Wisdom conducted the just man through right ways and showed him the kingdom of God, and made him honorable in his labours and accomplished his works, and gave him everlasting glory. WIS. X	SIC4010
Higdon	Benedict	Leonard	Nov. 3, 1793	Jul. 12, 1833	To the memory of / His distressed wife and brothers put this. It pleased God to use his rod and take my friend away, lone here I weep Till deaths last sleep, me nearby then shall lay. R.I.P.	SMY1130
Higdon	Eleanor	R.	Jun. 26, 1919	Aug. 13, 2000	In Loving memory	SMY3012
Higdon	Elizabeth	Ann	Sep. 4, 1815	Oct. 17, 1843	To the memory of / consort of John F.S. Higdon / Married Oct 8, 1839 / info is from the 1940 DAR book page 84, at The College of Southern MD, LaPlata, MD	SJONoStone
Higdon	Ella	R.	1877	1971	In loving memory	SMY3010
Higdon	Florence	M.	1851	1911	In memory of	SMCD224
Higdon	Francis	J.	1873	1956		PKH017
Higdon	Francis	W.	Apr. 1, 1863	Mar. 13, 1937	In memory of / Rest in peace	HGH2106
Higdon	Frederick	M.	Feb. 16, 1874	Oct. 12, 1939	In memory of / Rest in peace (stone is near the woods)	HGH2102
Higdon	J.	S.	No Date	Apr. 25, 1909	Sacred to the memory of / Age 72 yrs / May he rest in peace. Amen	HGH2103
Higdon	James	B.	Oct. 19, 1861	Dec. 1, 1942	In memory of / Rest in peace	HGH2107
Higdon	James	Edgar	Nov. 8, 1839	Jan. 2, 1897		SMCD001
Higdon	Jas	W. S.	Jun. 19, 1815	Jan. 31, 1832	IHS / to the memory of / His sorrowing brother / stone is sunken, unable to read the rest	SMY1131
Higdon	John	H. S.	No Date	Jul. 28, 1858	Sacred to the memory of / who departed this life in the 47 year of his age. / May he rest in peace / Dearest husband thou hast left us thy loss most deeply felt. But tis God who has bereft us, he can all our sorrows heal.	SJO5078
Higdon	John	T.	1837	1899	In memory of	SMCD224
Higdon	Kate	C. Lloyd	Sep. 1, 1840	Feb. 3, 1931	w/o J. S. Higdon / Rest in peace	HGH2105

Last Name	First Name	Middle Name	Date of Birth	Date of Death	Transcription / Notes	Cemetery Code
Higdon	Loretta	Burroughs	Oct. 6, 1921	Apr. 29, 2008	Born in Wash D.C., Died in LaPlata, MD d/o the late James A Burroughs & Blanche M. Norris Burroughs / w/o the late Thomas L. Higdon. (Info is from Maryland Independent Newspaper twice: Wed Apr 30, 2008 pg A12 column 6 and on Friday May 2, 2008 Pg A-11 Column 1)	SAC3062
Higdon	Margaret	E.	Jun. 2, 1822	Feb. 13, 1904	Mother / w/o John F.S. Higdon	SIC3039
Higdon	Mary	C.	1849	1912		SIG040
Higdon	Mary	E.	Sep. 9, 1891	Apr. 10, 1932		TRI299
Higdon	Mary	Ellen	May 25, 1885	May 28, 1885	Infant d/o B.L. & S.C. Higdon / Dates came from notes made while transcribing the cemetery (stone is partially buried)	SIC4009
Higdon	Mary	Unoine	Aug. 16, 1900	Jul. 29, 1901	Our little baby / Infant daughter of Dr. Thomas L. & Ella R. Higdon	SMY3011
Higdon	Mary	Zora, Burch	May 17, 1860	May 7, 1926	His wife	SMCD001
Higdon	Stanislaus	T.	No Date	No Date	Son of J. S. & Kate Higdon Aged 7 yrs & 5 Mos.	HGH2104
Higdon	Thomas		1839	1918		SIG040
Higdon, M.D.	Thomas	L.	1868	1957	In loving memory	SMY3010
Higdon, Sr.	Thomas	L.	May 18, 1914	Apr. 17, 2002		SAC3062
Higges	Bessie	L.	Feb. 21, 1895	Jul. 24, 1895		SIC2047
Higges	George	T.	No Date	Jun. 10, 1946	Name is shown on church records but burial location is unknown, date is the burial date, not death date	CHRNoStone
Higges	John	H.	No Date	Jan. 23, 1924	Name is shown on church records but burial location is unknown, date is the burial date, not death date	CHRNoStone
Higges	Unknown		No Date	No Date	Infant d/o Wm. H. & Mary M. / death may have been 1877 per church records	CHR385
Higges	Unknown		No Date	No Date	Stone installed but lots not usable per church records	CHR508
Higges	William	H.	No Date	Oct. 13, 1877	In the 42nd year of his age / Brother / Footstone	CHR386
Higginbotham	Jeannette	Tolson	May 6, 1910	Apr. 20, 1987		SMC3254
Higgins	Richard	M.	1934	1990		SCL4215
Higgs	Alice	E.	1850	1922		SJO2108
Higgs	Andrea	D.	Dec. 20, 1944	No Date	"Peanut" / Married Aug 5, 1962	SMY2125

Last Name	First Name	Middle Name	Date of Birth	Date of Death	Transcription / Notes	Cemetery Code
Higgs	Ann	Catherine	No Date	May 14, 1904	(info from St Mary's Beacon Newspaper dated May 19, 1904)	SMYNoStone
Higgs	Bessie	Mae	Oct. 23, 1900	Aug. 15, 1958		SMC3145
Higgs	Denton		1875	1937		OFE2047
Higgs	Elizabeth	Ann	Sep. 2, 1874	Nov. 27, 1934	Mother Dear / Prepare to meet me in Heaven	SIC2056
Higgs	Gertrude		1877	1968		OFE2047
Higgs	James	Bertram	May 23, 1894	Nov. 4, 1970	Maryland Sea USNRF WW I	SMC3146
Higgs	James	L.	Jan. 9, 1938	Sep. 2, 2006	"Jimmy" / Married Aug 5, 1962	SMY2125
Higgs, Sr.	James	L.	1900	1970		SAC1095
Higgs	James	Lloyd	Sep. 17, 1917	Mar. 1, 1966	Maryland OM2 US Navy WW II	SMC3144
Higgs	James	W.	1845	1917		SJO2108
Higgs	James	Walter	Feb. 26, 1874	Jan. 21, 1936	Father Dear / Rest in peace	SIC2057
Higgs	Johnson		1866	1930		TRI324
Higgs	Joseph	Walter	Dec. 25, 1944	Feb. 11, 1950	Son	SIC7028
Higgs	Joseph		No Date	No Date	Child / Info is from the 1984 church cemetery transcription list	SICNoStone
Higgs	Lillian	M.	1907	1993		SAC1095
Higgs	Maria	J.	Aug. 23, 1915	No Date	Back of Stone: Wed Feb 18, 1935	SIC7029
Higgs	Mary	M.S.	1861	1899		TRI324
Higgs	Sarah	A.	Sep. 6, 1887	Mar. 5, 1974		CLV029
Higgs	Sarah	M.	May 15, 1865	Sep. 22, 1923		SMCA235
Higgs	T.	Jefferson	Mar. 17, 1852	Feb. 15, 1908		SMCA234
Higgs, Jr.	Walter	A.	Mar. 29, 1914	Nov. 24, 1996	Back of Stone: Wed Feb 18, 1935	SIC7029
Higgs, Sr.	William	A.	1911	1989		NSP1018
Highby	Sara	Louise, Jameson	Apr. 26, 1919	No Date		SJE028
Highby	William	Erwin	Aug. 26, 1914	Jul. 24, 1995		SJE028
Highfield	Atha	P.	1846	1916		NJB384
Highfield	Katie	N.	Jan. 26, 1877	Sep. 29, 1882	In memory of Little Katie	NJB383
Highfield	Thomas	N.	1845	1917		NJB382
Hilderbrand	M.	Estelle	Jun. 15, 1916	Mar. 24, 1984		SAC2004
Hileman, Jr.	Larry	Eugene	Nov. 26, 1968	Sep. 24, 1989	"Bubby" / Beloved Son and Brother	NSP966

Last Name	First Name	Middle Name	Date of Birth	Date of Death	Transcription / Notes	Cemetery Code
Hill	Ammie	B.	1899	1943		HGH3061
Hill	Annie	Elizabeth, Talbot	Apr. 18, 1923	Dec. 1, 2003		NSP117
Hill	Basil	Guy	Jun. 25, 1930	May 8, 1999		SMC1077
Hill	C.	Frank	Dec. 16, 1903	Jul. 4, 1984		SMC1247
Hill	Carrie		Dec. 2, 1878	Jan. 16, 1948	In remembrance of / beloved w/o Alexander Hill	SCL3283
Hill	Celeste		1928	1996		HGH4238
Hill	Charles	Augustus	Jan. 24, 1925	Jan. 24, 1991		SAC2126
Hill	Charles	H.	Feb. 10, 1898	Oct. 20, 1985		SAC3085
Hill	D.	Esalesm	1918	1976	Info is from The Historical Society Research located at the College of Southern MD, LaPlata MD	HGHNoStone
Hill	Dee		1902	1972		HGH3026
Hill	Doris	L.	Jan. 19, 1927	Jun. 3, 1999		SAC3085
Hill	E.	C.	No Date	Feb. 5, 1957		HGH3065
Hill	Ellen Bruce	Rutherford, Sadler	No Date	No Date	Info is from church records	MTRNoStone
Hill	Frederick	D.	Mar. 16, 1929	Feb. 4, 2001	SGT US Army Korea	HGH4106
Hill	J.	Bruce	1924	1984		HGH4238
Hill	J.	Earl	Nov. 19, 1912	May 15, 1971		HGH1119
Hill, Sr.	J.	Randy	Jul. 1, 1965	Feb. 27, 2005		HGH4081
Hill	J.	W.	1888	1940	Info is from The Historical Society Research located at the College of Southern MD, LaPlata, MD	HGHNoStone
Hill, Sr.	James	Elmer	Jul. 26, 1923	Jun. 13, 1988	PVT US Army World War II	SMC1169
Hill	James	Henry	Feb. 22, 1921	May 20, 2002	Father	EMO010
Hill	James	W.	Jan. 20, 1932	May 13, 2003	Wed June 16, 1956	SMC1076
Hill	James	Walter	Apr. 5, 1923	May 2, 2004	"Jimmy"	NSP117
Hill	Jane	Ruth	Apr. 30, 1926	Jul. 9, 1999	Beloved wife, Mother & Grandmother / better known as Mom Ruth	HGH4019
Hill	John	F.	Jan. 12, 1925	Mar. 4, 1998		SMC1143
Hill	John	W.	Feb. 5, 1894	Apr. 10, 1984	Father	HGH3027
Hill	Joseph	Clarence	Aug. 14, 1926	Aug. 16, 2000		HGH4054
Hill	Joseph	Earl	1890	1956		SIC6065
Hill	Joseph	Harry	Oct. 26, 1900	Mar. 21, 1970	Maryland PFC US Army World War I	HGH2029

Last Name	First Name	Middle Name	Date of Birth	Date of Death	Transcription / Notes	Cemetery Code
Hill	Joseph		No Date	Oct. 23, 1963		HGH1121
Hill, Jr.	Julian	Dale	No Date	No Date	Info is from church records	MTRNoStone
Hill	Kathryn	J.	Oct. 4, 1957	Oct. 22, 1995	Together forever / Married Jun 27, 1981	SMC1199
Hill	Katie	M.	1906	1966		SMC1246
Hill	Margaret	J., Johnson	Oct. 28, 1934	Jan. 13, 2001		SAC5090
Hill	Martina		Aug. 1, 1927	Jan. 24, 2007	Mother	SMC1142
Hill	Mary	A.	No Date	Jul. 14, 1865	Consort of the late / Stanislaus Hill / who departed this life / In the 65th year of her age / May she rest in peace, Amen / Stone maker: A Gaddess, Balto	SMCD028
Hill	Mary	E.	Aug. 21, 1943	No Date		HGH4006
Hill	Mary	L.	Jun. 20, 1925	No Date	Beloved wife and mother	SMC1169
Hill	Mary	L.	Mar. 25, 1887	Mar. 30, 1923	In memory of my devoted wife	SCL1265
Hill	Mary	Truxillo	Dec. 12, 1910	Dec. 24, 1990	Rest in Peace	SAC2094
Hill	Mary	Y.	Jun. 15, 1927	Mar. 25, 1993		SCL4005
Hill	Nannie	M.	1896	1967		SIC6065
Hill	Patrick		1941	1955		HGH3026
Hill	Peggy	Ann	Sep. 29, 1959	Oct. 25, 2000		HGH4045
Hill	Raymond	C.	Jan. 28, 1894	Jan. 23, 1979	Our Dad	HGH3060
Hill	Robert	Leo	Sep. 24, 1918	Jun. 24, 1998	US Army World War II / better known as Steppie	HGH4020
Hill	Ronald	A.	Feb. 29, 1952	No Date	Together forever / Married Jun 27, 1981	SMC1199
Hill	Ruth		1898	1946		SHI282
Hill	Shirley	A.	Feb. 4, 1940	No Date	Wed. June 16, 1956	SMC1076
Hill	Stanislaus		No Date	Jun. 18, 1831	Sacred / to the memory of / who departed this life / In the 28th year of his age / May he rest in peace, Amen info is from The Historical Society Research located at the College of Southern MD, LaPlata, MD	SMCD026
Hill	Unknown		No Date	1970		HGHNoStone
Hill	Victoria	M., Cooper	1964	1993	"Beaver"	SCA044
Hill	Viola	E.	May 22, 1918	No Date		HGH1119
Hill	Wilmont		1902	1978	Info is from The Historical Society Research Located at the College of Southern MD, LaPlata, MD	HGHNoStone
Hilleary	Mary	A.	No Date	Dec. 16, 1963	Name is shown on church records but burial location is unknown	CHRNoStone

Last Name	First Name	Middle Name	Date of Birth	Date of Death	Transcription / Notes	Cemetery Code
Hills	Daisy		1953	2008		SMC4178
Hills	Dorothy	A.	1928	1991		SMC4175
Hills	Kim		1953	No Date		SMC4178
Hills	Norman	R.	1928	2005		SMC4175
Hillyard	Anthony	W.	1938	1997	"You are my Sunshine"	SMC4165
Hilton	Dorothy	Virginia	Feb. 16, 1917	Nov. 5, 2003		HGH4307
Hilton	James	A.	No Date	Sep. 18, 1938	Only one date on stone	HGH2015
Hilton	John	H.	No Date	No Date	No dates on stone	HGH3015
Hilton	Marie	F.	No Date	No Date	No dates on stone	HGH3016
Hilton	Mary	A.	No Date	Nov. 2, 1970	Only one date on stone	HGH2015
Hilton	Mary	C.	No Date	No Date	Info is from The Historical Society Research Located at the College of Southern MD, LaPlata, MD	HGHNoStone
Hilton	Mary	L.	No Date	No Date	No dates on stone	HGH3017
Hilton	William	Augustine	Sep. 1, 1926	Mar. 10, 2000	PVT US Army World War II	HGH4306
Hinchliffe	Christine	Wallace	No Date	No Date		CHR378
Hinchliffe	Richard	Ward	No Date	No Date		CHR378
Hindle	Bunny		Jun. 17, 1924	May 20, 1944		SIG051
Hindle	Cordelia		Dec. 26, 1882	May 29, 1968		SIG078
Hindle	Jacqueline	E.	Nov. 23, 1914	Mar. 18, 1986		ODE278
Hindle	John	A.	Aug. 24, 1829	Jul. 2, 1885	Info is from the Historical Society Research located at the College of Southern MD, LaPlata, MD, and the 1940 DAR book pg 197	SMCNoStone
Hindle	John	E.	Jun. 23, 1852	May 30, 1884	Sacred to the memory of my beloved husband / Stone is broken off the base and is sunken. / Info is from The Historical Society Research located at the College of Southern MD, LaPlata, MD	SMCD093
Hindle	John	Thomas	Sep. 14, 1872	Feb. 27, 1945		SIG079
Hindle	Lillie	M.	1894	1950		SIG050
Hindle	Mary	E.	Apr. 3, 1824	Nov. 21, 1903	Wife of John A Hindle / Rest in peace	SMCD095
Hindle	Thomas	E.	Mar. 23, 1914	Mar. 31, 1980		SIG052
Hindle	William	A.	1891	1959		SIG049
Hindle	William	E.	Aug. 6, 1912	Nov. 24, 2006		ODE278

Last Name	First Name	Middle Name	Date of Birth	Date of Death	Transcription / Notes	Cemetery Code
Hinton	Helen	R.	1913	2004	Devoted Daughter	MTR4149
Hintze	Arthur	L.	Jun. 10, 1926	No Date	Together Forever	NSP668
Hintze	Herbert	F.	Jan. 6, 1898	Jul. 7, 1997	Together Forever	NSP956
Hintze	Mary	A.	Feb. 4, 1937	May 24, 2004	Wed Oct 27, 1956	SMC2136
Hintze	Pearl	E.	Apr. 2, 1905	Nov. 15, 1980	Together Forever	NSP956
Hintze	Russell	F.	Mar. 28, 1930	No Date	Wed Oct 27, 1956	SMC2136
Hintze	Sadonia	V.	Nov. 11, 1921	Sep. 6, 1985	Together Forever	NSP668
Hinze	Gertrude	Eileen	Nov. 8, 1946	No Date	"Trudi" / In loving memory	NSP827
Hinze	Herbert	Paul	Jul. 13, 1938	Jun. 23, 2000	In loving memory / "Herb" / Humble Texan	NSP827
Hitch	Dorothy	E.	Apr. 15, 1909	May 27, 1998	In Loving Memory	OFE4007
Hitch	Martha	H.	Apr. 5, 1915	Nov. 23, 1995		NSP438
Hitch	Martha	M.	Mar. 13, 1884	Aug. 18, 1952		OFE4015
Hitch	Mary	Margaret	Nov. 22, 1919	No Date	In Loving Memory "Ottie"	SCL2001
Hitch	Milton	L.	Sep. 10, 1913	Apr. 1, 1966		NSP438
Hitch	Raymond	J.	Jun. 23, 1882	Nov. 15, 1929		OFE4016
Hitch	William	Elton	Sep. 10, 1913	Oct. 2, 2006	In Loving Memory	SCL2001
Hixson	Elizabeth	Ackerson	Mar. 31, 1941	Oct. 28, 1997	Middle name is from church records	SPL5068
Hockett	Malcolm	C.	Jul. 18, 1906	Nov. 11, 1980		MTR2196
Hockett	Susie	B.	Sep. 9, 1906	Oct. 8, 2002		MTR2196
Hodge	Shirley	Natalie	Sep. 26, 1922	Jul. 3, 1972		SCL3006
Hodges	Benjamin		1842-1843	No Date	Is he buried at St John's with his wife Georgianna? s/o Eliz M. Hodges	SJENoStone
Hodges	Elva	M.	Feb. 1915	Nov. 1936		MTR1113
Hodges	Georgianna	N. Brown	Dec. 1846	Apr. 28, 1920	Times Crescent newspaper May 7, 1920 says she died at her home near Marshall Hall. She is survivd by four daughters and two sons: Annie Hodges, Loulie Hodges, Mrs. H.B. Elliott of Washington, Mrs. J.P. Marshall of Pomonkey, James T. Hodges and William M. Hodges of Marshall Hall. Interment was in Bumpy Oak Cemetery. / per J. Richard Rivoire she was the d/o John Marshall Brown and Elizabeth Clagett.	SJENoStone
Hodges	James	T.	Feb. 1874	Nov. 1961		MTR1116

Last Name	First Name	Middle Name	Date of Birth	Date of Death	Transcription / Notes	Cemetery Code
Hodges	Mary	A.	Nov. 19, 1842	Mar. 5, 1919		ODE396
Hodges	Mary	M.	1878	1946		SJE082
Hodges	May	G.	May 21, 1885	Nov. 13, 1963		MTR1118
Hodges	Thomas	O.	1871	1960		SJE082
Hodges	Thomas	O.	1840	Oct. 12, 1877	Serg / Co F 2 MD INF CSA	SJE080
Hodges	W.	Maurice	Feb. 1909	Jul. 1940		MTR1114
Hodges	William	M.	Feb. 1878	Jan. 1962		MTR1117
Hoefler	Eva	A.	No Date	No Date	Daughter	SMCD170
Hoelke	Peter		Sep. 21, 1880	Mar. 28, 1928		OSM033
Hoelscher, Sr.	George	C.	Jan. 3, 1926	Aug. 9, 1987	SH2 US Navy WW II Korea	HER027
Hoffman	A.		No Date	Mar. 1887	Info is from church records	OFENoStone
Hoffman	Ann	Croft	Jun. 6, 1935	May 19, 1991	Blessed are the pure of heart for they shall see God	LUM086
Hoffman	Charles	Thomas Oda	May 23, 1902	Jun. 29, 1917	In Memoriam / s/o Charles & M.E. Hoffman Rest in Peace	SMY3019
Hoffman	Emma	V.	1900	1965		MRB012
Hoffman	Frances	Rae	May 21, 1936	Dec. 30, 1986		SIC9019
Hoffman	Francis	L.	1935	1935	Info is from church records	MRB011
Hoffman	George	F.	1897	1940		MRB012
Hoffman	Henry	Herman	Apr. 3, 1908	Jul. 18, 1985		OFE4048
Hoffman	Joseph	Francis	No Date	Aug. 3, 1933	Age 68 / info is from church records	OFENoStone
Hoffman	Julia	Annie	No Date	Mar. 17, 1947	Age 71 / info is from church records	OFENoStone
Hoffman	Margaret	Peggy	Oct. 12, 1948	Feb. 17, 2006	Nanny	SAC3002
Hoffman	Melvin	Marcellas	May 14, 1927	Feb. 22, 2000	Beloved Father	SHI167
Hoffman	Naomi	A.	Jun. 9, 1923	Feb. 13, 1963	Beloved Mother	SHI125
Hoffman	Ruby	Virginia	Dec. 19, 1917	Aug. 28, 1991		OFE4048
Hoffman	Thomas	A.	Oct. 4, 1938	No Date	Pop Pop	SAC3002
Hogan	Dolores	J.	Aug. 24, 1932	Mar. 8, 1990	Blessed are the husband and wife in heaven	SCL1218
Hogan	Edward	F.	Jul. 22, 1932	Jul. 31, 1996	Blessed are the husband and wife in heaven / You are my friend, husband and my life. I will always love you. Faye One stone shows death month as July and the other stone says August	SCL1218

Last Name	First Name	Middle Name	Date of Birth	Date of Death	Transcription / Notes	Cemetery Code
Hogan	James	J.	Jul. 25, 1929	Oct. 17, 1993		NSP968
Hogg	Emma	L.	1886	1974	Small flat stone that has been painted white	SJO6025
Hogg	Levi		1875	1965	Small flat stone that has been painted white	SJO6024
Hogge	David	L.	Jan. 5, 1939	No Date	In God's Care	NSP973
Hogge	Elizabeth	M.	1908	1974		SIC7032
Hogge, Jr.	George	W.	1906	1992		SIC7032
Hogge	Rita	B.	Nov. 12, 1940	No Date	In God's Care	NSP973
Hogge	Vincent	A.	1933	1969		SIC7032
Hogges	Mary	Ann	No Date	July 9, ( )	Consort of ( ) Hogges / info is from The Historical Society Research Located at the College of Southern MD, LaPlata, MD	HGHNoStone
Holl	Frank	A.	Jan. 15, 1934	Aug. 23, 1999	PFC US Army	NSP006
Holl	Mark	S.	Feb. 27, 1959	May 26, 1999	Beloved son	NSP007
Holland	Jossie		1908	1975	Thornton Funeral Home Marker	DUD059
Holland	Newton	Elwood	Oct. 8, 1908	Nov. 14, 1977	PFC US Army WW II	SCL3009
Hollaway	Carolyn		Jul. 2, 1952	Aug. 14, 1952		NSP356
Hollifield	Shane	D.	Apr. 21, 1959	May 13, 1980	In Loving Memory	MTR4252
Hollingsworth	Dwight		No Date	Oct. 1941	Info is from church records	CLVNoStone
Hollingsworth	Mae	C.	May 18, 1915	Aug. 19, 1975		CLV414
Hollingsworth	Ray	C.	Apr. 1, 1903	May 26, 1965		CLV414
Hollows	Edward	W.	1913	2002		NZN017
Holly	James	Quarles	1925	No Date		MTR4166
Holman	Laura		Jul. 25, 1900	Nov. 17, 1954	Erected by Husband and Children	SHI217
Holmes	Annie		Oct. 13, 1872	Oct. 23, 1934		OAK132
Holmes	Carlos		Dec. 24, 1867	Dec. 3, 1943		OAK131
Holmes	Emory		1900	1982		OAK133
Holmes	Magdalene		Sep. 21, 1907	Jun. 19, 1998		SAC1044
Holmes	Mary		1910	2000	Thornton Funeral Home Marker	OAK041
Holmes	Ruth	E.	1910	1988		SMC2037
Holmes	Sherry	Gehman	Nov. 5, 1963	Feb. 2, 1996	Loved in life, loved in spirit	SPL7004
Holmes, Jr.	Thomas	D.	1930	1992		SMC2037

Last Name	First Name	Middle Name	Date of Birth	Date of Death	Transcription / Notes	Cemetery Code
Holson	Charles	A.	1940	1968		SMC1089
Holt	Eliza		Aug. 29, 1942	Dec. 6, 1998	Footstone & small headstone funeral home marker / birth and death dates are from website Ancestry.com	MAC066
Holt	Frances		1907	1971	Mother	POM204
Holt, Jr.	John	G.	Oct. 10, 1923	Feb. 19, 2003	PFC US Army WWII / Purple Heart	CMX2076
Holt	Julie	Ann	Jan. 25, 1985	Feb. 5, 1985	Our little Angel	NSP740
Holt	Lucy		1855	1944	Funeral Home Marker	MAC058
Holt	Mary	Ann K.	Sep. 2, 1954	Oct. 3, 1999		NSP739
Holt	Nancy	C.	1907	1984	Cement stone with funeral home marker	MAC051
Holt	Richard	C.	Jun. 6, 1904	Mar. 17, 1971		CMX2165
Holt	Vesta	V.	Aug. 15, 1905	Nov. 9, 1979		NJB325
Holton	Delores	Ann	Mar. 15, 1944	May 19, 1987	Wife and Mother	SMC4088
Holton	Hannah	M.	1906	Nov. 22, 1979	Montgomery Brothers Funeral Home Marker	SHI142
Holton	Hester	G.	Dec. 27, 1886	Sep. 10, 1936		SHI204
Holton	Joseph		Mar. 12, 1912	Jun. 6, 1973		HGH3001
Holton	Mary	Virginia	Apr. 30, 1914	No Date		HGH3001
Holton	Theodore	Axzel	1964	1992	Thornton Funeral Home Marker / info is from church records	SHI192
Holton	Theodore		1907	May 25, 1975	Info is from church records	SHI143
Holtz	Ann		No Date	Apr. 29, 1929	Age 90 / info is from church records	OFENoStone
Holtz	Isaac		No Date	Jun. 1, 1899	Info is from church records	OFENoStone
Homa	Unknown	Agnes	No Date	No Date	Info is from Historical Society Research located at The College of Southern MD, LaPlata, MD	SACNostone
Homan	Carolyn	Ann	Sep. 6, 1900	Dec. 19, 1983	Beloved wife and mother	OSM053
Homan	Roy	M.	May 8, 1897	Oct. 26, 1982	US Navy WWII	OSM051
Hood	Burmah	Broome	Oct. 10, 1888	Jun. 26, 1937	Mother	MRB021
Hood	Donald	Lee	Feb. 6, 1945	Jun. 15, 1957		SPL6104
Hood, Jr.	James	Pearson	Sep. 24, 1962	Nov. 18, 1990	Beloved son & father	HGH2058
Hood	William	Carlos	Jan. 8, 1900	Jan. 13, 1928		MRB020
Hook	John	Russell	Oct. 13, 1900	Dec. 2, 1976		NSP855
Hook	Martha	Marie	Feb. 28, 1898	Jan. 2, 1975		NSP855

Last Name	First Name	Middle Name	Date of Birth	Date of Death	Transcription / Notes	Cemetery Code
Hooper	Anne	Matthews	Sep. 4, 1912	May 24, 1967		SIC7060
Hooper, III	Timothy	J.	Mar. 4, 1937	Jul. 30, 2004		SIC9007
Hooper, Jr.	Timothy	J.	Nov. 2, 1911	May 23, 1975		SIC7060
Hoopes	Dillwyn		Mar. 2, 1858	Oct. 1, 1911	h/o Lydia J. Hoopes B: 3 mo. 2nd 1858 D: 10 mo. 1st 1911	SJE059
Hope	Linda	Elizabeth	Jun. 5, 1958	Jan. 10, 1959	Stone is leaning	ALX042
Hopkins	Lee	F.	Jun. 25, 1903	Nov. 16, 1969		NJB267
Hopkins	Lucy	M., Chase	Oct. 19, 1930	Feb. 15, 2004	In memory of	SMC4141
Hopkins	Marion	L.	Dec. 24, 1911	Sep. 1, 1994		NJB267
Hopkins	Unknown		Jan. 29, 1944	Jan. 29, 1944	No Marker / info is from church records	CLVNoStone
Hopper	Francis	Waters	May 20, 1862	Sep. 22, 1940	Beloved h/o Julia Stonestreet Muschette	MTR2036
Hopper	Julia	Stonestreet	Feb. 22, 1865	Jul. 4, 1951	Beloved w/o Francis Waters Hopper	MTR2035
Horan	Julie	Marie	Apr. 20, 1969	Jun. 19, 1982		NSP965
Horseman	Clifford		No Date	Oct. 17, 1918	Age 8 months / info is from church records	OFENoStone
Horseman	George	T.	No Date	Jan. 31, 1915	Info is from church records	OFENoStone
Horseman	Nellie	L.	No Date	Nov. 8, 1923	Age 40 / info is from church records	OFENoStone
Horsman	George	Townshend	1888	1962		OFE3044
Horsman	Joeann		May 5, 1856	May 19, 1900	Beloved w/o Geo. W. Horsman / Her end was Peace	OFE3042
Horsman	Louisea	Ellen	1864	Feb. 8, 1935	"Wife" / Info is from the church records	OFENoStone
Horsman	Mildred	Shorter	1899	1976		OFE3043
Horsmon	James	H. M.	1859	1931	Capt. Bob	OFE4101
Hortch	Faye	E.	May 14, 1919	Sep. 21, 2005	Beloved wife and mother	SMC4278
Horton	Edward	Lee	Apr. 1, 1955	Mar. 21, 1989	Daddy / We love you	SCL3243
Horton	Effie	Berry	1875	1969	His wife	MTR1168
Horton	Margarett	A.	1810	1900	She is listed on the same stone as Geo. And Elizabeth Berry	MTR1171
Horton	William	Malcolm	1874	1938	his wife	MTR1168
Host	Nannie		No Date	Dec. 20, 1886	Info is from Old Durham Church microfilm pg 79-80 located at the College of Southern MD, LaPlata, MD	ODENoStone
Hottle	James	Edward	1915	1974		SJE029
Hottle	Margaret	Brown	1918	1996		SJE029

Last Name	First Name	Middle Name	Date of Birth	Date of Death	Transcription / Notes	Cemetery Code
Houck	Elizabeth	R.	No Date	No Date	In loving memory / and mother	NJB342
Houston	Ada	L.	1925	1980	Nee Key	SCL1001
Houtz	Angela	M.	Sep. 6, 1974	Sep. 11, 2001	(Back of stone): "I am carrying on a great project and cannot go down" Nehemiah 6:30	SAC1110
Howard	Angel	Sydney	Jan. 8, 1883	Apr. 22, 1895	d/o Wm. M.-Lizzie Seemes Howard	SIC3111
Howard	Bernard	A.	Oct. 5, 1870	Jul. 4, 1936	Beloved h/o Nelley DeLashmutt	SIC3107
Howard, Sr.	Bernard	M.	Jun. 4, 1918	No Date	In Loving Memory / Wed May 13, 1939	SJO5037
				Apr. 19, 1853	To the memory of / who departed this 19th April 1853 in the 51 year of her age. Kind Angels watch the silent dust. Whilst Jesus comes to call the just. And may she wake in sweet surprise. And in her saviors image rise. (located behind the church)	CHR616
Howard, Mrs.	Catharine		No Date	Feb. 16, 1904	AE 72 yrs.	SIC3096
Howard	Catherine	C.	No Date	Jul. 22, 1993		PKH130
Howard	Dora	K.	Dec. 19, 1914	Feb. 12, 1924	w/o Wm. M. Howard / Mercy my Jesus Mercy	SIC3109
Howard	Elizabeth	R., Semmes	Oct. 28, 1849	Oct. 3, 1989	Father	SCL1100
Howard	Eugene	R.	May 24, 1908	Sep. 13, 1953		NSP632
Howard	George	Wilbur	May 11, 1914	1974		SMC4027
Howard	Gladys	M.	1905	Jul. 11, 1974		NSP631
Howard	Helen	L.	Dec. 3, 1914	No Date	Small piece of stone laying on the ground / No Dates	SIC3113
Howard	J.	Camillus	No Date	Feb. 23, 1932		NSP503
Howard	J.	H.	Apr. 13, 1873	1986		NSP602
Howard	James	C.	1898	Sep. 15, 1879	AE 51 yrs	SIC3095
Howard	John	E. A.	No Date	Nov. 7, 1933		NSP542
Howard, III	Joseph	H.	Apr. 25, 1933	Nov. 21, 1999	BU2 US Navy Korea / Pray for me	SMC1037
Howard	Joseph	R.	Feb. 12, 1930	Apr. 16, 1911	Thy trials ended, thy rest is won	SJE122
Howard	Josie	L.	May 11, 1881	1986		NSP602
Howard	Loretta	G.	1898	Jun. 22, 1955	There is rest in Heaven	PIS008
Howard	Marion	R.	Apr. 21, 1902	No Date	Infant children of William M. and Lizzie Semmes Howard / Mary Aloise and Mary Camile Howard	SIC3112
Howard	Mary	Aloise	No Date	No Date	Infant children of William M. and Lizzie Semmes Howard / Mary Aloise and Mary Camile Howard	SIC3112
Howard	Mary	Camille	No Date			

Last Name	First Name	Middle Name	Date of Birth	Date of Death	Transcription / Notes	Cemetery Code
Howard	Mary	Eleanor	No Date	No Date	This small flat stone can easily be overlooked as it may be covered with grass. It is located next to the stone for Catherine C. Howard	SIC3096A
Howard	Mary	Irma	Sep. 2, 1880	Sep. 1, 1952		NSP504
Howard	Nanie	M.	No Date	May 27, 1900	Beloved w/o Wm. Howard / aged 48 years. / Sacred Heart of Jesus, have mercy on her	SIC4105
Howard	Patricia	A.	Apr. 21, 1935	Jan. 6, 1996		NSP601
Howard	Pauline		May 9, 1920	Jul. 16, 2008	In Loving Memory / Wed May 13, 1939	SJO5037
Howard	Richard	Allan	Jan. 15, 1918	Dec. 16, 1928	Beloved s/o Jos H. and Irma Howard / Loved in life in death remembered	NSP501
Howard	Robert		No Date	No Date	Info is from church records	PISNoStone
Howard	Rose	C.	Jun. 4, 1928	Jan. 3, 2006	Mother	SCL1100
Howard	Russell	T.	1905	1945		NSP635
Howard	Selby	L.	Jun. 21, 1912	Aug. 6, 1976		PKH130
Howard	Thomas	A.	1904	1965		SMC4027
Howard	Wilhelmina	G.	1907	1979		NSP634
Howard	William	Lester	Dec. 26, 1909	Jun. 28, 1988	"Bird" / Middle name is from church records	SPL7002
Howard	William	M.	Sep. 30, 1852	Aug. 18, 1917	Oh, sacred heart of Jesus, Mercy	SIC3110
Howarth	Louisa	C.	1892	1969	Eastern Star emblem	CHR197
Howarth	Reginald		1891	1970	Masonic emblem	CHR197
Howe	Anna	Cecelia	Feb. 13, 1927	May 17, 2007	Beloved wife	SMC1073
Howe	Edward	Lewis	Oct. 6, 1959	Mar. 5, 1960	Small piece of black marble with info etched on it	SMCC049B
Howe	George	Henry	Aug. 21, 1930	Apr. 21, 1993	MSGT US Air Force / Beloved husband father and opa	SMC1119
Howe	Joseph		Sep. 23, 1934	No Date		SMC1122
Howe	Mary	C.	1855	1935		HGH2020
Howe	Shirley		Jul. 31, 1937	Nov. 14, 1976		SMC1122
Howe	Thomas	J.	1890	1943		HGH2019
Howe, Sr.	Thomas	William	Jul. 15, 1923	Aug. 9, 1995	PFC US Army World War II	SMC1073
Howe	Unknown		Nov. 3, 1964	Nov. 3, 1964	Born-Died (small piece of black marble with the info etched on it)	SMCC049A
Howe	Vernon	Anthony	Mar. 13, 1959	May 5, 2009		SMC1074
Howell	Charlotte	Anne	1954	1983		SAC3033

Last Name	First Name	Middle Name	Date of Birth	Date of Death	Transcription / Notes	Cemetery Code
Howell	Lorraine		1981	1983		SAC3033
Howell	Robert	Martin	1979	1983		SAC3033
Hoyle	Thelma	Louise, Berry	Jun. 28, 1909	Aug. 19, 2003	Loving mother and nana	OSM043
Hoyme	Henry	H.	No Date	Jan. 9, 1948	Name is shown on church records but burial location is unknown, date is the burial date, not death date	CHRNoStone
Hoyt	Emma	L., Lothrop	No Date	May 18, 1895	She was born in Boston, Mass / w/o Timothy Hoyt / info is from the research of John E. Lothrop	HOY002
Hoyt	Timothy		Oct. 5, 1826	Aug. 16, 1904	And his wife Emma L. Lothrop. He was born in Cato, NY / info is from the research of John E. Hoyt	HOY002
Hruska	A.	Louise	Feb. 4, 1921	Aug. 14, 2007	Married Sep 28, 1982	SIC8003
Hruska	Leo	G.	Jan. 18, 1914	Feb. 25 2004	Married Sep 28, 1982	SIC8003
Hubbard	Gertrude	M.	1897	1986		CLV032
Hubbard	Marie	Ward	Nov. 3, 1920	Oct. 30, 1990	Loving Mom, Grandma & Granny	MTR2223
Hubbard	Thomas	W.	1889	1950		CLV031
Huber	Betty		1876	1958		CHR579
Huber	George	W.	1876	1934		CHR579
Huber	Lora	Lee	1900	1969		ODE429
Huber	Walter	B.	1903	1982		ODE429
Huber, Jr.	Walter	B.	Jun. 22, 1942	Mar. 18, 2002	"Corky" / Husband - Father - Friend Note: There is a bronze plaque attached to the brick wall on the inside of the cemetery	ODE234
Hudson	Caleb		No Date	Aug. 12, 1798	In memory of / who departed this life / in the 55 Year of his age. Who liv'd Beloved and ???? (stone has been repaired unable to read last few words)	ODE016
Hudson, Sr.	Charles	Irvin	Nov. 11, 1965	Sep. 19, 2008	Info is from church records	SHINoStone
Hudson	Lola	B.	Mar. 3, 1911	Nov. 9, 2001	Forever in our hearts	ZBC046
Hudson	Mary	C.	Jun. 10, 1938	Aug. 24, 2004	In loving memory	SMC4268
Huffman	Connie	R.	1907	1992		NZN069
Huffman	Cornelius		1888	1975	In loving memory	NZN019
Huffman	Daisy	V.	1916	1976		NZN069
Huffman	Ella	C.	1896	1965	In loving memory	NZN020
Hughes	??ette		No Date	Jan. 19, 1919	Age 75 / Info is from church records	SHINoStone

Last Name	First Name	Middle Name	Date of Birth	Date of Death	Transcription / Notes	Cemetery Code
Hughes	Anna		No Date	Nov. 11, 1924	Age 50 yr's. 2 mo's. and 7 days / info is from church records	SHINoStone
Hughes	Edward	Lee	Feb. 3, 1955	Dec. 30, 1995	We love and miss you	SCL1216
Hughes	Elizabeth	H.	Jul. 2, 1786	May 17, 1853	Relict of Col Jno Hughes / May she rest in peace	SMCD232
Hughes	John	J.	No Date	No Date	h/o Victorine R	SIC4055
Hughes, Col.	John		Jan. 30, 1799	Sep. 17, 1848	Col. / May he rest in peace	SMCD271
Hughes	Maria		No Date	Apr. 23, 1836	In her 36th year / w/o Col. John Hughes / info is from the Historical Society Research located at the College of Southern MD, LaPlata, MD, and the 1940 DAR book pg 191	SMCNoStone
Hughes	Victor		Jun. 19, 1878	Sep. 9, 1896		CHRNoStone
Hughes	Victorine	R.	1834	1919		SIC4054
Humphreys	Charles	Raymond	May 2, 1853	Nov. 18, 1906	Asleep in Jesus / His middle name came from a family member	WAV1009
Humphreys	Elizabeth	Chapman, Hungerford	Aug. 30, 1854	Jan. 30, 1938	Asleep in Jesus (family member supplied additional info: Elizabeth Chapman Hungerford Humphreys Born Aug. 30, 1854 Died Jan 30, 1908.) Footstone: C.H.	WAV1009
Humphreys	Jessie	Page	Jul. 31, 1878	Mar. 19, 1963	Info for Jessie is on the back of the stone for Charles & Elizabeth Humphreys, her parents. (Info is from a family member)	WAV1012
Humphreys	Nannie		Mar. 4, 1880	1959	Info for Nannie is on the back of the stone for Charles & Elizabeth Humphreys, her parents. (Birth date is from a family member)	WAV1012
Hungerford	Allan	Gwinn	Sep. 16, 1927	Jan. 12, 1995	Hungerford plot	CHR121
Hungerford	Annie	H.	1854	1936		POM049
					Our dear little Chappie / Of such is the kingdom of Heaven / Back of Stone: God in his wisdom has called the precious boon his love had given And though the casket moulders here The gem is sparkling now in Heaven (Only name on stone is Chappie; Info is from a family member: he died At Barnums Hotel, Baltimore, MD of Scarlet Fever. He was 1 year old. The son of Gerald & Nannie Hungerford) Footstone: C. H. H.)	
Hungerford	Chapman	Harris	May 22, 1858	May 22, 1859		WAV1016
Hungerford	Frank		1875	1939		SIC6101

Last Name	First Name	Middle Name	Date of Birth	Date of Death	Transcription / Notes	Cemetery Code
Hungerford	Gerard	Wood	Feb. 15, 1862	Feb. 25, 1922	Footstone: G.W.H. (family member says he was married to Laura Dent who was much younger. Laura is buried at Mt. Rest Cemetery, LaPlata, MD)	WAV1043
Hungerford	Gerard	Wood	Mar. 31, 1819	Mar. 9, 1871	His wife / "Until the day break and the shadows flee away"	WAV1005
Hungerford	Gwinnette	Reeder	Mar. 20, 1860	Jan. 1, 1935	Hungerford plot / church records say last name is Hungerford	CHR012
Hungerford	Harrison	R.	Aug. 20, 1896	Nov. 30, 1982	Info is from church records / Ancestry.com shows date of birth as Aug 20, 1896 / Hungerford Plot	CHR120
Hungerford	I.	Norman	Jun. 4, 1925	Apr. 16, 1976	S 2 US Navy WW II	SMC4036
Hungerford	Jane	Toole	Apr. 24, 1902	Jul. 17, 1970	Hungerford plot	CHR016
Hungerford	John	Gwinn	Mar. 23, 1929	Apr. 26, 1997	Hungerford plot	CHR142
Hungerford	John	Gwinn	Feb. 29, 1856	Apr. 12, 1938	Hungerford plot (church records show last name as Hungerford)	CHR050
Hungerford	John	Gwinn	Jul. 28, 1887	Aug. 4, 1968	Hungerford plot (church records show last name as Hungerford)	CHR015
Hungerford	Julia	Dent	Dec. 4, 1907	Mar. 14, 2007	Death Date is from Maryland Independent Newspaper Mar 16, 2007	SCL2224
Hungerford	Lizzie		1875	1965	His wife / old upright stone that has been repaired	SIC6101
Hungerford	Margaret	T.	Apr. 21, 1908	Feb. 20, 1999	Hungerford plot (church record shows last name as Hungerford)	SCL2036
Hungerford	Marion	Blunt	Aug. 4, 1904	Sep. 14, 1946	Hungerford plot; no surname on stone (church records show last name as Hungerford)	CHR052
Hungerford	Mary	Louise	1880	1887	Hungerford plot	CHR014
Hungerford	Mary	Susan, Price	1855	1894	His wife / "Until the day break and the shadows flee away"	CHR013
Hungerford	Nannie	Gwinn, Harris	Mar. 31, 1832	Jan. 27, 1913		WAV1005
Hungerford, Sr.	R.	Adelbert	Aug. 13, 1898	Sep. 18, 1983	"I believe in Music"	SCL2224
Hungerford, III	Robert	A.	Jun. 25, 1953	Jul. 10, 1976		SCL2221
Hungerford	Robert	E.	May 20, 1901	Oct. 21, 1976	Back of Stone	SCL2034
Hungerford	Sidney	Kent	Dec. 1, 1938	Jan. 5, 1940	Hungerford plot (church record shows last name as Hungerford)	CHR053
Hungerford	Victoria	Copping	May 24, 1898	Jun. 17, 1987	Hungerford plot (church records show last name as Hungerford)	CHR119

Last Name	First Name	Middle Name	Date of Birth	Date of Death	Transcription / Notes	Cemetery Code
Hungerford	Vivienne	Hoffman	Nov. 6, 1893	May 16, 1960	Hungerford plot	CHR048
Hungerford, Sr.	William	Barton	Feb. 22, 1934	Dec. 26, 2000	Death is shown in the Maryland Independent Newspaper dated Dec 29, 2000	CHRNoStone
Hunt	Amelia	Myrtle	1904	1965		NSP865
Hunt	Henrietta	Marie	No Date	Jul. 20, 1905	Name is shown on church records but burial location is unknown, date is the burial date, not death date	CHRNoStone
Hunt, Sr.	John	Henry	1906	1952		NSP864
Hunt	Matilda		Dec. 31, 1827		In memory of / consort of George A Hunt / stone broken, no death year (info is from the Historical Society Research located at the College of Southern MD, LaPlata, MD, and the 1940 DAR book pg 182	SMCNoStone
Hunt	Miriam	M.	Mar. 6, 1908	Dec. 9, 1990		SMY3111
Hunt	Nathan	Haines	Sep. 30, 1900	Feb. 13, 1976		SMY3111
Hunt	William	Washington	No Date	Sep. 22, 1822	Sacred to the memory of / s/o William and Elizabeth Hunt who departed this life in the 26 year of his age.	SPL3124
Hunter, Fr. S.J.	Geo.		Jul. 6, 1713	Jun. 16, 1779	IHS / Entered Jesuit Order 1730 Professed 1748 / Prospere Procede Et Regna Founded St. Joseph Feb 22, 1763 (in Priests Plot)	SIC1005
Hunter	Mary	A.	1868	1945	w/o Milton O Hunter	OFE4067
Hunter	Mary	E.	No Date	Oct. 13, 1857	In Memory of / aged 1 year and 4 months (there are 2 stones in the cemetery with the same name	OFE4064
Hunter	Mary	E.	Jun. 16, 1828	Feb. 22, 1903		OFE4063
Hunter	Milton	O.	Jun. 19, 1855	Jan. 17, 1924	At Rest	OFE4066
Hunter, Rev.	Moses	Hoge	No Date	Jan. 10, 1899	Aged 84 years, his wife Nannie / The souls of the righteous are in the hands of God	HWK013
Hunter	Nannie		No Date	No Date	Aged 84 years / The souls of the righteous are in the hands of God	HWK013
Hunter	Nannie	Hawkins	No Date	May 20, 1922	Info is from Christ Church microfilm Reel 3, Pg 230-231 located at the College of Southern MD, LaPlata, MD	MTRNoStone
Hunter	Thomas	I.	Apr. 5, 1822	Feb. 27, 1892	In memory of	OFE4062
Hunter, P.S.J.	William		No Date	Aug. 15, 1723	Buried Under Sacristy (In Priests Plot)	SIC1001
Huntt	Bernadette	Ann	Sep. 15, 1923	Oct. 17, 1923		HNT042
Huntt	Bernadette	C.	Dec. 10, 1896	May 13, 1983		NSP790

Last Name	First Name	Middle Name	Date of Birth	Date of Death	Transcription / Notes	Cemetery Code
Huntt	Bessie		1887	1972		SPL4003
Huntt	Catherine	L.	Dec. 31, 1912	Jun. 19, 1997		SJO4101
Huntt	Charlie		No Date	No Date	To our darling / only s/o T.J. and E.J. Huntt / Aged 9m, 18d	SPL6052
Huntt	Constance	E.	May 4, 1894	May 30, 1958		HNT008
Huntt	Edward	L.	Feb. 28, 1839	Aug. 12, 1912	At rest	HNT073
Huntt	Eleanor		1909	1961		SJO3323
Huntt	Eliza	A.	1833	Oct. 18, 1868	In memory of / w/o George A. Huntt, who departed this life / in the 35th year of her age / Birth date is from church records	SPL1044
Huntt	Elizabeth	J.	Sep. 11, 1837	Jul. 15, 1877	In memory of / w/o Theodore J. Huntt / Asleep in Jesus peaceful rest whose making is supremely blest.	SPL6051
Huntt	Elizabeth		No Date	Sep. 24, 1843	Sacred to the memory of / w/o William Huntt / who departed this life / aged 67 years	SPL3123
Huntt	Ernest		No Date	No Date	infant son of Robt. & Martha Huntt Footstone	SJO4147
Huntt	Gabrielle	A.	Apr. 13, 1843	May 23, 1907	Gate ajar / Aged 35 years / My faith looks up to thee	OSM121
Huntt	George	J. R.	1849	Mar. 26, 1924	Loved in life, in death remembered / Father	HNT010
Huntt	George	R.	Dec. 20, 1884	1915		MTR1074
Huntt	George		1908	Feb. 24, 1956		HNT001
Huntt	J.	L.		1976		SPL4002
Huntt	Joseph	A.	Dec. 21, 1910	Jul. 3, 1968		HNT074
Huntt	Joseph	Eli	Feb. 6, 1837	Oct. 26, 1897	In loving memory of / Father	SJO4101
Huntt	Joseph	R.	Oct. 19, 1805	Jul. 23, 1882	Sacred in the memory of / Come wife come / Footstone: Father	HNT014
Huntt	Julia	A.	Feb. 1, 1810	Dec. 10, 1888	Husband I come / Footstone: Mother	HNT017
Huntt	Julia	A.	Apr. 13, 1845	Jul. 4, 1926	Loved in life, in death remembered / Footstone: Mother	HNT019
Huntt	June	Theresa	Dec. 19, 1925	Jun. 5, 1994		HNT010
Huntt	Kansas	E.	Dec. 29, 1855	Jun. 9, 1882	w/o G.J.B. Huntt	NSP788
Huntt	Laura	Susannah	Nov. 6, 1841	May 17, 1914	You though I walk through the valley of the shadow of death, I will fear no evil. / Mother	SIC3009
Huntt						HNT013

Last Name	First Name	Middle Name	Date of Birth	Date of Death	Transcription / Notes	Cemetery Code
Huntt	Lizzie		Jul. 29, 1860	May 13, 1873	Beloved d/o Theo. J. & Elizabeth J. Huntt / Loved in life, in death remembered.	SPL6053
Huntt	Martha	Caroline	No Date	Apr. 24, 1904	Beloved wife of Robert Huntt / Aged 79 years / Rest in Peace	SJO4150
Huntt	Mary	A.	No Date	Jun. 27, 1894	In loving remembrance of / beloved w/o Edward L. Huntt / age 53y, 10m, 12d / Through all pain at times she'd smile, A smile of Heavenly birth; And when the angels called her home, she smiled farewell to earth.	HNT072
Huntt	Mary	A.	Apr. 19, 1841	Dec. 29, 1922	I shall be satisfied when I awake, with thy likeness	HNT030
Huntt, Sr.	Patrick	W.	Jun. 11, 1940	May 21, 2007	Beloved husband of Dianne Huntt / Back of stone: Loving father of Tracy & Chip (carbon Copy) Poppy of Deanna & Brent / Uncle Pickle - Tickle Tickle Friend to all he met	SJO3324
Huntt	Philip	Edward	Jan. 14, 1892	Nov. 24, 1953		NSP789
Huntt, Jr.	Philip	Edward	Aug. 19, 1924	Dec. 20, 1924		HNT042
Huntt	Robert		No Date	May 10, 1867	Beloved husband of Martha Caroline Huntt, aged 45 years / Rest in Peace	SJO4150
Huntt	Robert		No Date	No Date	Infant son of Robt & Martha Huntt	SJO4149
Huntt	Theodore	J.	Dec. 23, 1830	Jan. 25, 1897	Blessed are the dead who die in the Lord	SPL6050
Huntt	Thomas	F.	1912	1985		SJO3323
Huntt	Thomas	J.	Jun. 14, 1937	Apr. 28, 1991	In loving memory	SJO3310
Huntt	Tracy	Rebecca	Apr. 17, 1963	Jul. 17, 1980	Beloved daughter of Patrick and Dianne Huntt / Back of stone: Our daughter was a special gift from God above. She was warmth, laughter, thoughtfulness and love. Though from our earthly presence she was called to depart. She remains with us in loving memory to be forever cherished in our hearts.	SJO3121
Huntt	William	E.	Apr. 24, 1880	Jun. 29, 1939		HNT009
Huntt	William		No Date	Feb. 11, 1826	Sacred to the memory of / who departed this life / aged 61 years / and Elizabeth his wife	SPL3123
Hupp	Ella	Bryan	1897	1982		SJE141
Hurd	Anna	Elizabeth	Apr. 11, 1941	Mar. 16, 1999		SJO4035
Hurd	Carrie	M.	Apr. 19, 1924	Oct. 29, 2003	In loving memory / Lady Bug"	ZBC110
Hurd, Sr.	Charlie	Morton	Aug. 16, 1938	Aug. 30, 2007		SJO3146

Last Name	First Name	Middle Name	Date of Birth	Date of Death	Transcription / Notes	Cemetery Code
Hurd	Cloray	Ann	1837	May 20, 1896	In Memory of / w/o Hillery Hurd B / D / Aged 65 yrs. This stone is located on the left side of the church	SIG162
Hurd	Elizabeth	A.	1943	1987	In Loving Memory	ZBC115
Hurd	Elizabeth	Savoy	May 14, 1888	Dec. 8, 1964		SCA079
Hurd	Marilyn	Jeanette	Jun. 23, 1999	Mar. 3, 2009		SJO3146
Hurd	Martha	C.	Oct. 27, 1875	Aug. 5, 1962	Mother	SCL3400
Hurd, Sr.	Robert	Harry	Feb. 10, 1959	Dec. 27, 1999	A loving son, brother, husband and father. "Hey Bud, what's happening"	SJO3146
Hurlburt	Edward	M.	Mar. 11, 1923	Feb. 19, 2002	Lord make me an instrument of your peace where there is hatred let me sow love / SGT US Army WW II	SJO4096
Hurlburt	Eric	Michael	No Date	Feb. 5, 2003		SJO4095
Hurlburt	Lloyd		Mar. 5, 1890	Aug. 29, 1962		SJE016
Hurlburt	Margaret	Willett	Apr.il 10, 1927	No Date	Lord make me an instrument of your peace where there is hatred let me sow love	SJO4096
Hurlburt	Rachael	Warren	Jun. 9, 1889	Mar. 16, 1960		SJE017
Hurley	Annie	L.	No Date	Aug. 5, 1901	Info is from church records	OFENoStone
Hurley, Mrs.	Unknown		No Date	Mar. 28, 1884	Buried the husband, brother, sister and son of Mrs. Hurley at Trinity Chapel / info is from church records	OFENoStone
Hurst	George	Eric	Apr. 30, 1970	Mar. 9, 2001	(Back of stone): Our angel, always and forever Love Kristin & Angel Face	SAC4091
Hurst	Kristin	D.	Mar. 30, 1973	No Date	(Back of stone): Our angel, always and forever Love Kristin & Angel Face	SAC4091
Hurt	Elijah	D.	Jun. 2, 1994	Feb. 14, 1998	Our Beloved Son	SJO5028
Hurt	Gladys	M.	1919	1977	Montgomery Brothers funeral home marker	ZBC166
Hurysh	Loretta	A.	1934	No Date		SMC4229
Hurysh, Sr.	Nicholas	L.	1933	No Date		SMC4229
Husar	Anasta		Sep. 10, 1913			SMC4026
Husar	Ostap		Oct. 3, 1889	Jan. 18, 1965		SMC4025
Hutchins					They loved in life and in death were not divided Mother Footstone: E.H.H..(family member gave death date and says she died a few hours apart from her husband Richard Philemon Hutchins and there was a double funeral)	
	Ethel	Hungerford	1860	May 3, 1929		WAV1022

Last Name	First Name	Middle Name	Date of Birth	Date of Death	Transcription / Notes	Cemetery Code
Hutchins	Richard	Philemon	1862	May 3, 1929	They loved in life and in death were not divided Father Footstone: R.P.H. ...family member gave death date and says he died a few hours apart from his wife Ethel Hungerford Hutchins and there was a double funeral	WAV1022
Hutchinson	Scott	Justin	Sep. 26, 1981	Jul. 16, 2001	Loving son and brother / Lieutenant JRYDE	SMC1008
Huth	Carl	Daniels	1931	2000	Beloved Father	SAC2077
Huth	Daniel	Aaron, Karos	1976	1995	"Dan Doody"	SAC2076
Hutton	Joseph		No Date	Jun. 27, 1869	In memory of / in the 76th year of his age	SIC2196
Hyatt	Richard	W.	1935	1990		SMC1250
Hybo, Mrs.	M.	A.	No Date	Mar. 15, 1928	Age 45 years old / Old cement cross with a piece of glass covering paper that has info on it (information is from The Historical Society Research located at the College of Southern MD, LaPlata, MD)	SIC5101
Hyde	Albert	Augustine	Jul. 8, 1915	Mar. 19, 1966	flat stone behind upright stone	SIC2043
Hyde, Jr.	Albert	Augustine	Oct. 28, 1947	Oct. 14, 1974	Has a large headstone and a flat stone to the ground	SIC2074
Hyde	Elizabeth	B.	1869	1963		SIC6074
Hyde	L.	Southgate	Dec. 2, 1892	Dec. 27, 1971		PIS247
Hyde	Laura	Mattingly	Apr. 11, 1916	Jun. 15, 1989	Flat stone behind upright stone	SIC2043
Hyde	Louis	M.	1864	1948		SIC6074
Hyde	Mabel	A.	Jun. 6, 1892	Mar. 3, 1975		PIS247
Hyde	Mary	Florine, Burch	1858	1898	In loving memory / wife and mother / Rest in peace	SIC2001
Illick	Frederick	S.	Jan. 19, 1933	Sep. 29, 2001	Back of Stone: There is now no condemnation for those who are in Christ Jesus, Romans 8:1	MTR2199
Impellizzeri, Sr.	Frank	C.	Nov. 21, 1926	May 22, 2004	Beloved husband, Father, Grandfather / US Army WW II	SAC3106
Ingle	Jeanie	McGuire	Feb. 15, 1892	Jul. 31, 1995	D/o Julian Ingle and Melville McGuire Ingle	CHR434
Ingle	William	Pechin	Nov. 1, 1887	Jul. 19, 1964		CHR433
Irwin	Agnes	Roberta, Jarboe	May 8, 1895	Oct. 20, 1922	w/o Mathew W. Irwin	SIC2152
Irwin	Alice	R.	Feb. 10, 1896	Feb. 14, 1987		SIC2062
Irwin	Elizabeth	A.	May 1, 1887	Aug. 7, 1899	Eldest d/o Matthew M. & Elizabeth A. Irwin	SIC2050
Irwin	Jerome	P.	Sep. 27, 1921	Feb. 1, 1969	"Pat" / Footstone: District of Columbia Y2 USNR WW II	SIC2072

Last Name	First Name	Middle Name	Date of Birth	Date of Death	Transcription / Notes	Cemetery Code
Irwin	Mary	Zaiac	Oct. 19, 1920	Nov. 5, 2005		SIC2072
Irwin	Matthew	M.	Jan. 21, 1861	Apr. 7, 1924		SIC2063
Irwin	Matthew	W.	Aug. 26, 1888	Jul. 26, 1945		SIC2151
Irwin	Robert	M.	Apr. 16, 1927	Aug. 21, 1977	Gone but not forgotten…TEC 5 US Army WW II	MTR2211
Irwin	Sarah	Susanna	Feb., 19, 1871	Jul. 23, 1900	Beloved w/o John J. Irwin / stone is broken and is leaning up against the base	SIC2048
Irwin	William	Henry	Jul. 12, 1894	Aug. 6, 1979	Pvt US Army WW I	SIC7004
Irwin	Elizabeth	Alice	Jan. 7, 1864	Oct. 23, 1901	Beloved w/o Matthew M. Irwin	SIC2064
Iserman	RoseMarie	F.	Jun. 28 1936	May 16, 1996		SCL1122
Isreal	Veronica	M.	Oct. 31, 1938	Jan. 31, 1987	Wife / At Rest	ZWU013
Istvan	Cleo	Helen	Jun. 16, 1934	No Date		SMC4227
Istvan	Dorothy	L.	1917	2000		SMC3301
Istvan	Elizabeth	Haus	Jul. 12, 1896	Dec. 8, 1918	w/o Joseph Istvan / Rest in peace	SMCA222
Istvan	Ignatz		Dec. 19, 1877	Sep. 27, 1973		SMC3286
Istvan	James	R.	Jun. 14, 1935	Oct. 16, 2007		SMC4227
Istvan, Sr.	John	M.	Sep. 21, 1921	Nov. 29, 1974	TEC 4 US Army	SMC3272
Istvan	Joseph	L.	1916	1951		SMCA224
Istvan	Joseph		1893	1959		SMCA223
Istvan	Leopold	W.	1912	1990		SMC3301
Istvan	Mamie		1899	1952		SMCA221
Istvan	Mary	Teresa	Mar. 19, 1934	Jan. 22, 1935	In loving memory / Our first Angel	SMC3302
Itayem	M. Louise	Dillinger, Wathen	Dec. 1, 1910	Oct. 7, 1988		LUM001
Ivins	John	Lloyd	1820	1904		SJE096
Ivins, Jr.	John	Lloyd	1868	1911		SJE095
Ivins	Julia	S.	1827	1908	Mother	SJE097
Ivins	Mary	Olivia	1866	1940		SJE101
Ivins	Samuel	F.	1859	1916	Brother	SJE094
Ivins	William	L.	1865	1932		SJE100
J.	E.		No Date	No Date	Stone with initials E.J. (looks like the J is backwards)	SCL1272
J.	G.	W.	No Date	No Date	Small Footstone with initials GWJ	SMCW026
Jackson	A.	Dudley	1876	1958		TRI156

Last Name	First Name	Middle Name	Date of Birth	Date of Death	Transcription / Notes	Cemetery Code
Jackson	Albert	Charles	May 8, 1924	Feb. 25, 1991	Beloved Father	MHB112
Jackson	Alberta		1901	1985		OAK213
Jackson	Alease			1984	The "J" may be missing from the funeral home marker, so it is listed twice under the last name of Ackson and as Jackson	DUD036
Jackson	Alexander	S.	1894	Nov. 16, 1947	s/o Rebecca Hawkins & Alexander S. Jackson of KY	SPL2040
Jackson	Alfred	T.	1910	1982		HGH4290
Jackson	Alfred	T.	1937	No Date		HGH4302
Jackson	Alice	E.	1924	1971		SCL4205
Jackson	Allen	Bennett	Oct. 5, 1950	Sep. 23, 2006	Chaplain	HGH4271
Jackson	Amanda	Shorter	1847	1914		MTR1090
Jackson	Annie	Virginia	1892	1993		MHB039
Jackson	Anthony	Daniel	Aug. 10, 1957	Aug. 29, 2002		SJO2235
Jackson	Bailey		Mar. 25, 1888	Dec. 30, 1954		MHB268
Jackson	Benjamin	E.	Dec. 15, 1894	Feb. 15, 1977		SJO2247
Jackson	Bernice		Jan. 19, 1924	Sep. 6, 1994	Mother	MHB038
Jackson	Bunny		No Date	No Date		EMO003
Jackson	Carroll	E.	Nov. 7, 1923	Dec. 14, 1972		SCL3062
Jackson	Catharine	Turner	May 8, 1839	Apr. 18, 1927	His Wife	OFE4107
Jackson	Cecelia	Ann	No Date	Jan. 21, 1964	Aged 29 years / Information is from the Historical Society Research located at the College of Southern Md, in the Southern MD research Room, LaPlata, MD	SMINoStone
Jackson	Charles	Potter	Jun. 7, 1890	Nov. 14, 1947		SCL2043
Jackson	Clarice	B.	1940	2008		HGH4302
Jackson	Clifton	.	1929	1988	US Army Thornton Funeral Home Marker	MHB093
Jackson, Sr.	Clinton		1915	2006	Thornton Funeral home marker	SCL3067
Jackson, Jr.	Curtis	Randolph	Dec. 3, 1986	Jun. 13, 1999	Beloved Son / Forever In Our Hearts	ZBC045
Jackson	Dorothy	M.	Oct. 10, 1931	No Date		HGH4231
Jackson	Dorothy	Marie	1925	1993	In loving memory	SMC3135
Jackson	Dorothy	Short	Nov. 25, 1916	Jul. 2, 2000	In Loving memory	ZBC024
Jackson	Emma	M.	Dec. 10, 1884	Jan. 5, 1955		HGH2043

Last Name	First Name	Middle Name	Date of Birth	Date of Death	Transcription / Notes	Cemetery Code
Jackson	Esther	Regina	Aug. 5, 1948	Aug. 7, 1964	At Rest	MHB164
Jackson	Eubie	I.	1912	2004		HGH4290
Jackson	Evangeline	D.D.	Apr. 14, 1970	Oct. 22, 2003	"Dee Dee"/Beloved Daughter, Mother, Sister and Friend / Forever In Our Hearts	MHB234
Jackson	Evelyn	N.	1920	1972	In Loving Memory of Our Parents	MHB163
Jackson	Fannie	Chandler	1870	1947		ODE463
Jackson	Florine	Thomas	May 26, 1928	Jun. 19, 1976		PGN008
Jackson	Francis	V.	Jul. 4, 1910	Aug. 7, 1976		HGH4276
Jackson	Gail		1951	2006	Funeral home marker	SCL3104
Jackson	George	Irwin	Jan. 16, 1897	Apr. 4, 1982	Sweethearts forever, Married 60 yrs. 10-20-21 / Back of stone: Your garden is filled with the flowers of all the kindness you've shown. Each blossom looks up with the sweetness of all of the friends you have known. The pathway you walked has been gladdened, the song of the brook made more clear. The whole of life has been brightened because of your presence here / Footstone: Pvt US Army WW I	SIC5001
Jackson	Gladys	M.	1904	1971		SMC3148
Jackson	Henry		Feb. 8, 1916	Apr. 6, 1980	Beloved Husband and Father "Totts" Gone But Not Forgotten B /Sunrise D / Sunset	MHB158
Jackson	Isaac	Bernard	1904	1991		MHB113
Jackson	James	Anthony	Apr. 2, 1956	Jul. 4, 1991	PFC US Army	SMI022
Jackson	James	D.	1930	1986	Our trust is in God	SJO2241
Jackson	James	Harold	1929	2009	Brinsfield-Echols funeral home marker	SMC3134
Jackson	James	S.	Feb. 4, 1897	Dec. 28, 1962		HGH2048
Jackson	James	S.	Jan. 26, 1928	No Date		HGH4231
Jackson	Janet	Marie	Mar. 6, 1954	Sep. 12, 1970		SJO2236
Jackson	Jean	E.	May 19, 1944	Jun. 4, 1999	Sister	MHB016
Jackson	John	C.	May 12, 1844	Apr. 27, 1899	Co. G 3rd Regt	POM119
Jackson	John	C.	1866	1951		HGH2046
Jackson	John	Turner	No Date	Sep. 12, 1957?	Huntt Ryon Funeral Home Marker / 75 years	SMT033
Jackson	Joseph	A.	Jan. 10, 1870	Mar. 6, 1926	In memory of	SMCD151

Last Name	First Name	Middle Name	Date of Birth	Date of Death	Transcription / Notes	Cemetery Code
Jackson	Joseph	Albert	Feb. 14, 1867	Nov. 30, 1932	Info is from the Historical Society Research located at the College of Southern MD, LaPlata, MD, and the 1940 DAR book pg 190	SMCNoStone
Jackson	Joseph	Bassie	1893	1962		SMC3147
Jackson	Julia	B.	Sep. 7, 1914	Dec. 15, 1994	Married July 6, 1941	SJO5004
Jackson	Katie	A.	1917	1987	An inspiration to all who knew her w/o Maxwell A. Jackson m/o Irene, Marshall, Henrietta, Joseph, William, Edward and Leroy	SMT023
Jackson, Rev.	Lewis	H.	Jan. 23, 1838	Dec. 6, 1910		OFE4107
Jackson	Louise	M.	Jun. 28, 1910	Jun. 22, 1948	d/o Rebecca Hawkins & Alexander S. Jackson of KY	SPL2039
Jackson	Madeline		Oct. 4, 1913	May 5, 1991		SJO4078
Jackson	Maggie		No Date	No Date	Thornton Funeral Home Marker dates are missing from marker	MHB068
Jackson	Margaret	A.	No Date	No Date	Our trust is in God	SJO2241
Jackson	Marian	O.	1882	1955		TRI157
Jackson	Marie	Theado	Feb. 11, 1901	Dec. 5, 1982	Sweethearts forever, Married 60 yrs. 10-20-21 / Back of stone: Your garden is filled with the flowers of all the kindness you've shown. Each blossom looks up with the sweetness of all of the friends you have known. The pathway you walked has been gladdened, the song of the brook made more clear. The whole of life has been brightened because of your presence here	SIC5001
Jackson	Mary	A.	No Date	1963	Cement Cross	SMT032
Jackson	Mary	B.	Apr. 28, 1918	Jan. 14, 1997		HGH4276
Jackson	Mary	E.	1878	1946	Loving wife of Luther A. Price / stone is laying on the ground	HGH1185
Jackson	Mary	Eliza	No Date	Oct. 23, 1875	In Memory of Mary Eliza Jackson / Beloved w/o Rev. L. H. Jackson Entered the rest of Paradise / in the 46th year of her age. "There his servants shalt serve him and they shall see his face:	OFE4093
Jackson	Mary	M.	Jun. 14, 1900	Oct. 25, 1999		SJO2247
Jackson	Molly	L.	No Date	No Date	Mother	SMCD170
Jackson	Natalie		1926	2005	Arehart Funeral Home	HGH2045

Last Name	First Name	Middle Name	Date of Birth	Date of Death	Transcription / Notes	Cemetery Code
Jackson	Nelson	W.	Apr. 13, 1870	Nov. 19, 1910	At Rest / h/o Alice E. Jackson / Aged 41 yrs.	POM030
Jackson	Ocie	C.	Apr. 2, 1921	No Date	Married July 6, 1941	SJO5004
Jackson	Raymond		1920	1972	In Loving Memory of Our Parents	MHB163
Jackson	Richard	A.	1945	1948		HGH2042
Jackson	Richard	E.	1935	1975	Info is from the Historical Society Research located at the College of Southern MD, LaPlata, MD	ZBCNoStone
Jackson	Robert	A.	Feb. 20, 1947	Apr. 15, 2005	Bobo	MHB241
Jackson	Robert	T.	Feb. 16, 1921	Dec. 2, 2005	Father	MHB247
Jackson	Rosa	L.	No Date	Jun. 3, 1900	Info from Times Crescent Newspaper Jun 8, 1900	SMYNoStone
Jackson	Rose	Milstead	1869	1973	Mother / Gone But Not Forgotten / The Lord Is My Shepherd I Shall Not Want	MHB162
Jackson	Sankston	W.	Nov. 7, 1884	May 28, 1969		HGH2043
Jackson	Sarah	Estella	1888	1919		SJO2115
Jackson	Shalisha	Kiana	Jan. 21, 1988	Sep. 3, 2006	Thornton Funeral home marker / middle name and dates are from ancestry.com	SCL3068
Jackson	Susan	A.	Feb. 16, 1869	Jan. 7, 1941		SMCD184
Jackson	Thelma	L.	Mar. 6, 1909	Nov. 17, 1993	In Loving memory "Sis"	SMI060
Jackson	Theresa	O.	Apr. 22, 1914	May 23, 1979		SJO4074
Jackson	Thomas		1923	1972		SCL4205
Jackson	Unknown		No Date	No Date	No other name or date on stone	POM118
Jackson	Unknown		1909	1977	Thornton Funeral Home Marker (first name is missing from marker)	DUD050
Jackson	Walter	L.	Jan. 17, 1862	May 16, 1934	Beloved husband of Susan A	SMCD183
Jackson	Walter	L.	Aug. 12, 1912	Aug. 28, 1974	BM 1 US Navy World War II	HGH2044
Jackson	William	L.	Jul. 31, 1912	Mar. 12, 1959		SJO4075
Jackson	William	T.	No Date	No Date		EMO004
Jacobs	Agnes	L.	Dec. 28, 1886	Jan. 1977	Dates are from ancestry.com	CHR133
Jacobs	Den	Howe	1927	1928		ODE084
Jacobs	Dennis	Howe	1905	1932		ODE084
Jacobs	Eleanor	M.	Oct. 24, 1928	Sep. 11, 1978		SMC1144
Jacobs	Eleanor	Ramsden	1919	1997	Beloved Mother & Grandmother	MTR4003
Jacobs	Hughes	Loxley	1909	1982	TEC 3 US Army WW II	MTR4002

Last Name	First Name	Middle Name	Date of Birth	Date of Death	Transcription / Notes	Cemetery Code
Jacobs	John	H.	1874	1956		CHR133
Jaeger	Mary	Susan, Edelen	Jan. 20, 1943	Feb. 1, 1997	Find faith, peace, strength, laughter and inspiration in the memory of Sue who loved us so	SIC3078
James	Corrine	Taylor	Nov. 11, 2000	Feb. 5, 2001		SIC9006
James	Dorothy	D.	1916	1979		HGH4073
James	Edna	Canter	1908	1975		OFE1030
James	Mary	Magdalene, Greenfield	Jan. 5, 1945	Aug. 19, 1988		SMC4194
James	Paul	A.	1911	1991		HGH4073
Jameson	A.	Queen	1915	1964		SMCA214
Jameson	Agnes	Gertrude	Jun. 7, 1925	May 3, 2007		SMC3197
Jameson	Alice	Mary	1878	1961		SMCA014
Jameson	Andrew	J.	Jan. 11, 1904	Apr. 25, 1948	Son	SMCD064
Jameson	Anna	Estelle	Apr. 5, 1914	Oct. 7, 1914	Beloved d/o J.A.K.E. Jameson	SMCA215
Jameson	Anna		1923	No Date		NSP745
Jameson	Anne	Skone	May 3, 1930	No Date		MTR1026
Jameson	Annie	C.	Sep. 30, 1850	Feb. 18, 1933	Mother / Eastern Star Emblem	OFE2006
Jameson	Annie	U.	1854	1927		SCA020
Jameson	Aubrey	B.	1907	1983	Together forever	SMC1149
Jameson, Jr.	Aubrey	B.	1933	2008	Forever together / Married Oct 20, 1956	SMC1155
Jameson	Austenous		Jan. 18, 1857	Dec. 17, 1912	His wife Elizabeth Irene	SMCA197
Jameson	Benjamen		No Date	Aug. 30, 1870	Aged 58 years / May he rest in peace / This stone is located on the left side of the church	SIG167
Jameson	Bennett		Apr. 27, 1888	Dec. 27, 1975		SMCD098
Jameson	Beulah		1906	1931		SIG013
Jameson	C.	Mabel	1891	1941		SIC6055
Jameson	Catharine		No Date	May 22, 1868	In Memory of / w/o B. W. Jameson D. / In the 32 year of her age. Blessed are they that hunger and thirst after justice for they shall be filled. Matthew 5 C, 6 V / This stone is located on the left side of the church	SIG168
Jameson	Catherine	E.	1883	1931		SMCA212
Jameson	Catherine	Lloyd	Feb. 21, 1873	Aug. 7, 1962		SIG011

Last Name	First Name	Middle Name	Date of Birth	Date of Death	Transcription / Notes	Cemetery Code
Jameson	Charles	H.	1850	1923	In memory of	SMCD187
Jameson	Charles	H.	1862	1949		SAC1111
Jameson	Cleopatra		Apr. 10, 1886	Nov. 14, 1965		SMC1022
Jameson	E.	Lee	1861	1937		SIC2046
Jameson	E.	Raymond	May 9, 1927	May 3, 1982	TEC 5 US Army WW II	SMCA233
Jameson	Edward		1891	1971		SCA019
Jameson	Edward	L.	1924	No Date		NSP745
Jameson	Eliza		No Date	Jun. 2, 1853	IHS To the memory of / Consort of Wm Jameson who departed this life / In the 39th year of her age / May she rest in peace	SMCD256
Jameson	Elizabeth	Irene	Apr. 29, 1860	No Date		SMCA197
Jameson	Elizabeth		No Date	May 12, 1864	IHS In memory of / w/o B. W. Jameson / in the 54 year of her age. May she rest in peace / This stone is located on the left of the church	SIG165
Jameson	Emily	O.	Sep. 15, 1892	Jan. 7, 1984		TRI263
Jameson, Jr.	Ernest	M	Oct. 15, 1899	Mar. 6, 1956		SMC1167
Jameson	Ernest	M.	1876	1952		SMCA014
Jameson	Estelle	B.	Jul. 26, 1907	Dec. 24, 1973		SMCA2167
Jameson	Evelyn	T.	May 5, 1912	Jan. 11, 1975	Asleep in Jesus	SJO3200
Jameson	F.	Leo	May 23, 1917	Dec. 18, 1975		SMC1099
Jameson	F.	Napoleon	1855	1928		SIC4019
Jameson	Frances	S.	1901	1991		SMC3179
Jameson	Francis	L.	Aug. 29, 1886	Jun. 6, 1920	At rest	SMCD118
Jameson	Frederick	Bennett	Nov. 21, 1952	Nov. 18, 2000		MTR1026
Jameson	Frederick		1889	1891	Son of R J C Jameson	SMCD159
Jameson	George	W.	No Date	Nov. 3, 1823	In memory of / s/o Luke F Jameson, who departed this life / aged 2 years and 15 days	SCL1182
Jameson, Dr.	George	W.	No Date	Oct. 5, 1821	IHS Doctor / Sacred to the memory of / who departed this life / in the 23rd year of his age / May he rest in peace, Amen Stonemaker: Jct. Birth Fecit Washington	SMCD289

Last Name	First Name	Middle Name	Date of Birth	Date of Death	Transcription / Notes	Cemetery Code
Jameson	George		No Date	Apr. 23, 1857	s/o Wm. And Eliza Jameson / in his 24th year / info is from the Historical Society Research located at the College of Southern MD, LaPlata, MD, and the 1940 DAR book pg 191	SMCNoStone
Jameson	George		Aug. 11, 1888	Jan. 11, 1956		SMC1225
Jameson	George	Curtis	Jul. 17, 1901	Mar. 9, 1968		SIG137
Jameson	Hazel	P.	Oct. 17, 1921	Jan. 7, 1990		SMC1145
Jameson	Helen	A.	1899	1963		MTR3150
Jameson	Helen	Esleep	Oct. 21, 1880	Oct. 7, 1928	w/o Walter A Jameson info is from the 1940 DAR book pg 191	SMCNoStone
Jameson	Helen	L.	May 31, 1919	Jun. 17, 1989		SMC1099
Jameson	Helene	E.	Oct. 21, 1880	Oct. 7, 1928	Rest in peace	SMCD218
Jameson	Henrietta		Jan. 24, 1795	May 19, 1826	IHS In memory of / w/o Dr. Luke F. Jameson who departed this life on / aged 31 years 3 months 25 days, the mother of George Washington & Thos. Andrew Jameson / Info is from Sister Miriam John at Mt Carmel Monastery	GMC007
Jameson	Irma	A.	1915	2003	Together forever	SMC1149
Jameson, Jr.	J.	A.rchie	Apr. 8, 1911	Apr. 22, 1990		SMC2167
Jameson	J.	Archie	1879	1941		SMCA212
Jameson, Jr.	J.	Clarence	1896	No Date	In God's loving care	SMC1166
Jameson	J.	Emmanuel	1889	1912		SIC3067
Jameson	J.	Grantly	1901	1990		SMC1125
Jameson	J.	Leroy	May 23, 1895	Jul. 15, 1954		TRI262
Jameson	J.	Norbert	1895	1964		SMC3179
Jameson	J.	Warren	Feb. 21, 1884	Feb. 24, 1976		SMC1022
Jameson, Jr.	J.	Warren	Apr. 26, 1927	No Date		SMC1013
Jameson	James	C.	1915	1988		SMC1146
Jameson	James		No Date	Nov. 5, 1822	In memory of / second s/o Walter Jameson who died 5th day of November 1822 aged 28 years	SCL1174
Jameson	Jane	C.	Jun. 10, 1842	No Date	his wife	SMCD153
Jameson	Jane	Elizabeth	Jul. 13, 1911	May 4, 1968		SMCD020

Last Name	First Name	Middle Name	Date of Birth	Date of Death	Transcription / Notes	Cemetery Code
Jameson	Joan	S.	Mar. 19, 1933	Aug. 10, 2000		SMC1013
Jameson	John	Francis	1907	1967		SMCA014
Jameson	John	Grant	Nov. 21, 1865	May 15, 1941	Father	SMCD020
Jameson	Jos	Milton	1920	1921	Son of W A & H E Jameson / Rest in peace	SMCD219
Jameson	Joseph	Adelbert	Feb. 14, 1867	Nov. 30, 1932		SMCD173
Jameson	Joseph	D.	Mar. 21, 1918	Mar. 23, 1945	Maryland / Captain, Infantry WW II	SMCA014
Jameson, Sr.	Joseph	F.	Dec. 24, 1907	Jul. 29, 1968		SMC1257
Jameson	Katherine		1879	1953		SCA019
Jameson	Kenneth	A.	1917	1967		SMC1269
Jameson	Leon		1898	1980		SIC2070
Jameson	Lewey	Woodrow	Sep. 11, 1918	Feb. 14, 1936		SMCA182
Jameson	Lewis	Edwin	Nov. 13, 1900	Jun. 28, 1962		SMCD064
Jameson	Lucy	B.	1911	1993		SMC1125
Jameson, Dr.	Luke	F.	No Date	No Date	Birth unknown. Death probably after his wife's. May 19, 1826 (Notes from Sister Miriam John at Mt. Carmel Monastery)	GMCNo Stone
Jameson	Lydia	Mills	1899	1990	In God's loving care	SMC1166
Jameson	M.	Adelaide	1902	1956		SAC1111
Jameson	M.	Gladys	1900	1980		SIG014
Jameson	M.	Louise	May 17, 1892	Aug. 9, 1987		SMC1225
Jameson	M.	Margaret	No Date	Feb. 13, 1910	w/o W.M. Jameson / aged 73 years	SMCA068
Jameson	Magdalen	B.	1906	1992		SIC2070
Jameson	Magruder		No Date	Feb. 10, 1906	Aged 6 years In loving remembrance of / Children of ? And ? Jameson / This stone is located on the left side of the church	SIG156
Jameson	Margaret	A.	1858	1930	In memory of	SMCD187
Jameson	Martha	E.	Feb. 3, 1872	Feb. 17, 1951	Mother	SMCD020
Jameson	Mary	Bernice	Apr. 14, 1904	Sep. 4, 1964		SMCA229
Jameson	Mary	C.	1918	2001		SMC1146
Jameson	Mary	Eliza	No Date	Nov. 5, 1852	To the memory of / Daughter of Wm & Eliza Jameson who departed this life / In the 11th years of her age / May she rest in peace	SMCD254

Last Name	First Name	Middle Name	Date of Birth	Date of Death	Transcription / Notes	Cemetery Code
Jameson	Mary	Emily	Jan. 14, 1894	No Date	No death date is shown on stone	SMCA074
Jameson	Mary	Henrietta	No Date	No Date	w/o Thomas Andrew / info is from the Historical Society Research located at the College of Southern MD, LaPlata, MD, and the 1940 DAR book pg 199	SMCNoStone
Jameson	Mary	K.	Mar. 17, 1885	Mar. 26, 1960	At rest	SMCD118
Jameson	Mary	Louise	1906	1912		SMCA190
Jameson	Mary	M.	1888	1963		SMCA190
Jameson	Mary	Margaret, Middleton	Nov. 2, 1934	No Date		NSP1035
Jameson	Mary	N.	1922	2001		SMC1269
Jameson	Mary	P.	1936	No Date	Forever together / Married Oct 20, 1956	SMC1155
					In memory of / consort of the Late Dr. Samuel D. Jameson who departed this life / in the 36th year of age. When I can read my title clear to mansions in the skies I bid farewell to many dear and wipe my weeping cries. (stone under a tree laying on ground & broke in half is not in the original place)	
Jameson	Mary	S.	No Date	Sep.t 24, 1861		OFE2046
Jameson	Maude	H.	1858	1953		SIC4018
Jameson	Milton		1914	1933		SIG010
Jameson	Nobert		1892	1892		SMCD157
Jameson	Oscar	Bennett	Jul. 2, 1929	Nov. 5, 1995		MTR1026
Jameson, II	Paul		1891	1893	Son of R J C Jameson	SMCD156
Jameson	R.	Bernard	1888	1890	Son of R J C Jameson	SMCD158
Jameson	Rebecca		1859	1904	Son of R J C Jameson	SIC3129
Jameson	Regina	Posey	Mar. 28, 1863	Dec. 4, 1946		SIC2003
Jameson	Richard		Feb. 8, 1842	Jun. 1, 1913		SMCD153
Jameson	Robert	M.	Sep. 25, 1858	Jun. 29, 1927	Father / Masonic Emblem	OFE2006
Jameson	Robert	S.	1890	1970		MTR3150
Jameson	Rose	C.	Jun. 10, 1910	May 27, 1960		SMC1168
Jameson	Rudy	F.	1881	1961		SMCA190
Jameson, Dr.	Sam'l	D.	No Date	May 6, 1853	Who departed this life / In the 31st year of his age. / "Not my will but thine O Lord be done"	SMCC012

Last Name	First Name	Middle Name	Date of Birth	Date of Death	Transcription / Notes	Cemetery Code
Jameson	Sara	Warren	Jul. 25, 1892	Jun. 30, 1978		SJE018
Jameson	Sarah	E.	1869	1957		SIC2046
Jameson	Sothern	Key	Sep. 4, 1891	Feb. 10, 1967	California EMC US Navy World War I & II	SMCD186
Jameson	Stanie		No Date	Apr. 5, 1903	Aged 6 years In loving remembrance of / Children of ? And ? Jameson / This stone is located on the left of the church	SIG156
Jameson	Stanley	Wingate	Jul. 10, 1925	May 21, 2002	US Army Air Forces WW II	NSP1034
Jameson	Sudie	Agusta	Dec. 8, 1881	Aug. 20, 1916	May she rest in peace	SMCD154
Jameson	T.	Paul	1892	1965		SIC6055
Jameson	Thelma	M.	Jan. 10, 1910	Nov. 3, 1963		SMCD064
Jameson	Theresa		No Date	Jul. 15, 1812	"In the 47th year of her age, the mother of 12 children- five sons and seven daughters" (info is an excerpt from The Rambler-Washington Star Aug 13, 1916 sent by Mike Marshall via e-mail)	SCLNoStone
Jameson	Thomas	A.	1884	1932		SMCD155
Jameson	Thomas	Irvin	Dec. 8, 1912	Mar. 29, 1970		SMCA256
Jameson	Thomas	Jefferson	1895	1988		SAC1111
Jameson	Thomas	Magruder	Mar. 11, 1863	Mar. 30, 1927		SIG012
Jameson	Thomas	Rudolph	Dec. 22, 1933	Mar. 1941		SMCA255
Jameson	Unknown		No Date	No Date	In loving memory of children of J. M. and Mary Catherine Jameson This stone is located on the left side of the church	SIG156
Jameson	Veronica	M.	Feb. 11, 1980	Nov. 3, 2005		SMC2014
Jameson	W.	Claude	1902	1970		SIG014
Jameson	W.	M.	No Date	May 19, 1922	Aged 88 years	SMCA069
Jameson, Jr.	Walter	A.	Sep. 24, 1912	Aug. 11, 1981		SMC1145
Jameson, Sr.	Walter	A.	Apr. 21, 1882	Oct. 24, 1968	Rest in peace	SMCD218
Jameson	Walter	T.	1883	1951		SAC1111
Jameson	Walter		Sep. 13, 1808	Feb. 24, 1868	In memory of / Requiescat in pace	SMCD171
Jameson	Walter		No Date	Mar. 12, 1814	Aged 54 years (info is an excerpt from The Rambler- Washington Star Aug 13, 1916 sent by Mike Marshall via e-mail)	SCLNoStone

Last Name	First Name	Middle Name	Date of Birth	Date of Death	Transcription / Notes	Cemetery Code
Jameson	William	C.	No Date	Dec. 16, 1902	Sacred to the memory of my dear husband / aged 45 years / May he rest in peace	SIC3043
Jameson	William	E.	1879	1913		SMCD152
Jameson, Rev.	William	Harold	Nov. 14, 1905	Aug. 19, 1973	Rev	SMCD025
Jameson	William	Penn	Jun. 26, 1891	Dec. 11, 1968		SJE025
Jameson	William	V.	1865	1923	May he rest in peace	SMCA070
Jameson	William		No Date	Oct. 8 1846	In his 46th yr. / info is from the Historical Society Research located at the College of Southern MD, LaPlata, MD, and the 1940 DAR book pg 191	SMCNoStone
Jameson	Wm.	Raymond	1918	1918	Son of W A & H E Jameson / Rest in peace	SMCD220
Jameson	Yong	Chin	Mar. 11, 1952	No Date		MTR1026
Jamieson	Anita	V.	Mar. 28, 1936	Aug. 16, 1981	"Peace Forever"	SCA066
Jamieson	Harris	S.	Jun. 11, 1893	Dec. 20, 1956	"Peace Be Yours" / Maryland PVT US Army WWI	SCA060
Jamieson, Jr.	Joseph	M.	Jul. 24, 1965	Oct. 22, 1977		SJO5024
Jamieson, Jr.	Joseph	M.	Jul. 24, 1965	Oct. 22, 1977		SJO4029
Jamieson	Margaret	B.	1907	1978	"Peace Be Yours"	SCA061
Jamison	Marie	Peterson	No Date	May 24, 1997	Info from church records	OSMNoStone
Janifer	Preston		1891	1978	PVT US Army World War I	MHB261
Janifer	Sallie	B.	Sep.t.14,1887	Aug..27,1952	Beloved w/o Preston Janifer	MHB260
Janifer	Unknown		1974	1974	Baby Janifer, don't know if Janifer is the first or last name. (info is from the Historical Society Research located at the College of Southern MD, LaPlata, MD)	ZBCNoStone
Janschek	Anna		1875	1940		NSP349
Janschek	Elizabeth	M.	Aug. 26, 1906	Sep. 29, 1994		NSP672
Janschek	Gladys	R.	Jun. 19, 1913	Jul. 2, 1992		SPL6011
Janschek	John	Joseph	Jan. 21, 1911	Mar. 24, 1984	F1 US Navy WW II	SPL6011
Janschek	Mary	L.	Nov. 15, 1912	Feb. 1, 2001	Married Oct 4, 1932	NSP671
Janschek	Michael		1868	1935		NSP348
Janschek	Nicholas	J.	Jul. 22, 1909	No Date	Married Oct 4, 1932	NSP671
Janschek	Teresa	Ann	Mar. 13, 1958	Jul. 13, 1972	In loving memory of our daughter	NSP673
Jansen	Christean		Apr. 29, 1868	Nov. 21, 1919		SJE129
Jansen	Edna	Louise	Nov. 26, 1901	Jul. 4, 1902		SJE132

Last Name	First Name	Middle Name	Date of Birth	Date of Death	Transcription / Notes	Cemetery Code
Jansen	Laura	Alice	Apr. 8, 1882	Dec. 26, 1950		SJE129
Jansen	Leroy	C.	Oct. 1, 1912	Jul. 31, 1913		SJE130
Jansen	Mildred	Robie	Jun. 24, 1901	Jan. 29, 1979		MTR2194
Jansen	Thomas	P.	Aug. 26, 1900	Jan. 30, 1976		MTR2193
Janssen	Della	M.	1925	No Date	Wed. July 15, 1942 / In loving memory	NSP495
Janssen	Lloyd	F.	1918	No Date	Wed. July 15, 1942 / In loving memory	NSP495
Jarboe	Jessie	D.	1893	1956		SIC3142
Jarboe	Joseph	B.	1891	1955		SIC3142
Jarboe	Joseph	B.	Aug. 18, 1851	Sep. 20, 1920		SIC3138
Jarboe	Mary	E.	Oct. 4, 1860	May 8, 1932	Dates for Mary are hard to read on the stone	SIC3138
Jarboe	Mathew	Cajetan	Aug. 7, 1888	Mar. 13, 1918	At rest / s/o J.B. & M.E. Jarboe May he rest in peace	SIC3061
Jarboe	Unknown		No Date	Jan. 28, 1916	Infant d/o Jos. R. Jr., & Jessie D. Jarboe	SIC3084
Jarrett	Dorothy	Lee, Lederer	1909	1985		ODE469
Jarrett	John	Wallace	1933	No Date		ODE448
Jarrett	Virginia	Lee	1944	No Date		ODE447
Jarrett	Wallace	Orion	1906	1993		ODE468
Jasper	Georgia	Butler	Mar. 18, 1906	Aug. 7, 1998		SCL1246
Jeneski	Unknown		No Date	April 27, 1971	Baby girl	SCL4046
Jenifer	Agnes	L.	May 24, 1920	Mar. 18, 1999	Until We Meet Again	SMY2065
Jenifer	Annie	R.	Apr. 19, 1919	Aug. 30, 2000		SMC2063
Jenifer	Benjamin		1925	1979	CPL US Army WWII	SMY2036
Jenifer	Catherine	C.	May 30, 1915	Aug. 12, 1972		SJO1149
Jenifer, Sr.	Eli	S.	Aug. 20, 1919	Jul. 11, 2001	Until We Meet Again	SMY2064
Jenifer	George	E.	1904	1977	Info is from The Historical Society Research located at The College of Southern MD, LaPlata, MD.	SMYNoStone
Jenifer	George	K.	Nov. 4, 1900	Dec. 5, 1986		SMC3310
Jenifer	James	A.	May 31, 1915	Mar. 19, 1985	In loving memory	SJO1148
Jenifer	James	Alfred	No Date	Aug. 14, 1976	Aged 71 (info is from Historical Society Research located at The College of Southern MD, LaPlata, MD)	SACNostone
Jenifer	James	Dennis	Oct. 25, 1948	Sep. 17, 1993	We Love You	SMY2066
Jenifer	Jennie		Mar. 25, 1866	Mar. 25, 1951		TRI015

Last Name	First Name	Middle Name	Date of Birth	Date of Death	Transcription / Notes	Cemetery Code
Jenifer	John	Kousps	1876	1963		SMC3311
Jenifer	Louis	H.	Apr. 21, 1905	Feb. 29, 1980		SMC3273
Jenifer	Mary	Julia	1904	1976		SMC3309
Jenifer	Rachel	C.	1875	1930	In Memory Husband and Children	MHB258
Jenifer	Sarah	E.	Feb. 26, 1904	Feb. 24, 1989		SMY2055
Jenifer	Susanna	Banks	1883	1958		SMC3311
Jenifer	William	D.	Jan. 17, 1924	Jul. 24, 1996	"Sloppy Joe"	SMC2065
Jenifer	William		1922	1995	Thornton Funeral Home marker	SMY2037
Jenkins	Adelaide	R.	1876	1955	Footstone: Mother	SAC1104
Jenkins	Albert	L.	1864	1927	His wife - At Rest	SMY3018
Jenkins	Albert	L.	No Date	Mar.ch 31, 1930	Only one date shown on the stone	SJO3004
Jenkins	Amy	G.	1894	1978		SMY3086
Jenkins	Andrew	R.	1877	1950	Together forever	HGH1013
Jenkins	Anna	Mae	Feb. 22, 1927	Mar. 19, 1927	Our Darling / infant daughter of E.A. & O.H. Jenkins "Gods Angel"	SJE247
Jenkins	Arthur	J.	Apr. 18, 1911	May 6, 2004		SCL2033
Jenkins, Sr.	Benedict	E.	Feb. 27, 1919	May 20, 1985	TEC 5 US Army WW II	SJO6019
Jenkins, Jr.	Benedict	Edward	Oct. 25, 1953	Mar. 25, 1977		SJO6022
Jenkins	Benedict		1851	1928	Small flat stone that is painted white	SJO6031
Jenkins	Benjamin	J.	1909	1991		SIC8060
Jenkins	Benjamin	M.	Sep. 27, 1889	Nov. 28, 1972		SJO6029
Jenkins	Benjamin	T.	1893	1969		SMY3086
Jenkins	Bertha	Mae	1913	1979		HGH4031
Jenkins	Bertha	Simms	Mar. 5, 1861	Feb. 3, 1944		SIC4034
Jenkins	Bessie	P.	1894	1968		LUM058
Jenkins	Catherine	R.	Dec. 11, 1926	No Date	Beloved wife and mother	SJO6019
Jenkins	Catherine	R.	1897	1958		SCL2079
Jenkins	Catherine		Feb. 28, 1886	Jun. 15, 1966		HGH2024
Jenkins	Clarence	N.	Aug. 24, 1899	Feb. 23, 1980		TRI424
Jenkins	Clarence	Roy	Jun. 6, 1923	Sep. 26, 1979	Pvt US Army WWII	TRI426

Last Name	First Name	Middle Name	Date of Birth	Date of Death	Transcription / Notes	Cemetery Code
Jenkins	Delbert	A.	1905	1980		SCL3016
Jenkins	Donald	O.	1934	1979		CMX2017
Jenkins, Jr.	Donald	Oscar	Jun. 16, 1960	Aug. 7, 2004	A loving son and brother	SCL3391
Jenkins	Donnie		Apr. 21, 1900	Nov. 19, 1969		MRB018
Jenkins	Dorothy	Hefner	Apr. 11, 1908	Dec. 17, 1959	Footstone	SIC6056
Jenkins	Dorothy	Kitchen	May 14, 1923	No Date		HGH4032
Jenkins	Edward		No Date	Dec. 7, 1913	Aged 25 yrs.	SIC3145
Jenkins	Elizabeth		No Date	Apr. 13, 1777	Grandfather of John J. Jenkins / his wife / R.I.P.	SJO3081
Jenkins	Elmer	Butch	1943	1987	Brother	SCL3019
Jenkins	Elsie	Lee	1891	1970		MTR4011
Jenkins	Elsie	Lucille	1914	2005	Wife	SMCA088
Jenkins	Emily	A., Gardiner	No Date	Aug. 3, 1877	Sacred to the memory of / in the 64 year of his age and his wife Emily A. Gardiner Jenkins in the 56th year of her age / R. I. P.	SJO3008
Jenkins	Emily		No Date	May 2, 1928	Info is from church records	SHINoStone
Jenkins	Emma	Carter, Swann	Feb. 19, 1877	May 9, 1956	Rest In Peace	SCL2199
Jenkins	Etta	M.	1898	1987	In loving memory	SMC3231
Jenkins, Jr.	Eugene	A.	Aug. 6, 1928	Jul. 9, 2003		SJO3011
Jenkins	Eugene	Augustine	Mar. 8, 1897	Jan. 3, 1986	Requiescat in Pace	SJO3005
Jenkins	Eugene	M.	1890	1942		SJO1143
Jenkins	Florence	M.	Mar. 25, 1917	Dec. 31, 1958		SJO6027
Jenkins	Frank	Plowden	Jul. 20, 1887	Mar. 1, 1975		SIC6056
Jenkins	Frank	Plowden	May 29, 1855	May 24, 1906		SIC4034
Jenkins	George	A.	1843	1929		HGH2010
Jenkins	George	E.	1875	1948		HGH2023
Jenkins	George	Plowden	1810	1889	Thy live in the hearts of those who love them best.	SIC3019
Jenkins	George	Plowden	1913	1969		SCL2184
Jenkins	George	R.	1904	1982		SMY3217
Jenkins	George	R.	May 29, 1922	Jul. 5, 1962		SJO6026
Jenkins, Jr.	George	R.	1932	1966		SMY2158

Last Name	First Name	Middle Name	Date of Birth	Date of Death	Transcription / Notes	Cemetery Code
Jenkins	George		No Date	1830	Father of J.J. Jenkins, aged 70 years / his wife / R.I.P.	SJO3081
Jenkins	Gladys	Mallory	Jan. 7, 1936	No Date		SIC3136
Jenkins	Gladys V.	Deakins	Feb. 10, 1918	Jan. 28, 1988	Love and tender care 1939-1988	NJB145
Jenkins	Grace	May	Nov. 9, 1940	Dec. 19, 2002	A loving mother	SCL3392
Jenkins	Henrietta	Davis	1818	1898	Thy live in the hearts of those who love them best.	SIC3019
Jenkins	James	B.	1868	1941	Husband	SMCA176
Jenkins	James	E.	Oct. 15, 1936	Feb. 21, 1997	Beloved husband	SMC4138
Jenkins	James	W.	1892	1918	This is a small flat marker sinking and covered with grass. It is located to the right of James B. Jenkins	SMCA176
Jenkins	James	W.	1911	1997	(Jimmy)	HGH4029
Jenkins	Jason	Javon	Jan. 16, 1976	Jun. 13, 1998		HGH4310
Jenkins	Jennie	Simms	Nov. 26, 1886	May 24, 1969		SIC4036
Jenkins	Jesse	C.	Mar. 6, 1906	Aug. 6, 1976		SAC1106
Jenkins	Jessie	I.	Jan. 18, 1900	May 25, 1972		TRI424
Jenkins	Jessie	W.	Mar. 22, 1913	Jul. 10, 1988		SCL2033
Jenkins	Jo	Ann, Wilkinson	Oct. 9, 1933	No Date	(Jody)	SCL2232
Jenkins	John	Ashbury	No Date	Jul. 28, 1913	Whose ever liveth and believeth in me shall never die / Beloved son of Thos Canfield and Nellie Compton Jenkins / Aged 22 Years	SCL2121
Jenkins	John	H.	Mar. 15, 1873	Nov. 15, 1932	At Rest / Masonic Emblem	POM052
Jenkins	John	J.	No Date	Jan. 2, 1845	In his 59 year / His wife / in her 43 year / R.I.P. / This stone was erected to the memory of / and / his wife / by their children. Who pray that God may be merciful to their souls	SJO3081
Jenkins	John	J.	Aug. 14, 1842	Apr. 19, 1921		SIC3125
Jenkins	John	W.	No Date	Oct. 22, 1882	Sacred to the memory of / in the 64 year of his age and his wife Emily A. Gardiner Jenkins in the 56th year of her age / R. I. P.	SJO3008
Jenkins	John	W.	1894	1965		SCL2171
Jenkins	John	William	Nov. 29, 1858	Jan. 6, 1928		SCL2185
Jenkins	Joseph	Harry	1885	1977		MTR4011
Jenkins	Joseph	J.	1896	1989	Beloved father	SMC4084

Last Name	First Name	Middle Name	Date of Birth	Date of Death	Transcription / Notes	Cemetery Code
Jenkins	Joseph	L.	Feb. 6, 1933	May 25, 1999	SP4 US Army	SMC4086
Jenkins	Joseph	M.	1890	1959		SCL2115
Jenkins	Joseph	S.	1880	1933	In Wathen Plot	SMY3155
Jenkins	Julia		No Date	1937	Died: 1937	SJO6030
Jenkins	Katie		1898	1982	Info is from the 1984 church cemetery transcription list	SICNoStone
Jenkins	Kester	F.	Oct. 3, 1916	Apr. 8, 1975	TEC 3 US Army World War II	HGH4032
Jenkins	Lauren	Ann	Jul. 4, 1990	Jun. 25, 2003	D/o Ronald and Jennifer / Back of stone: Dear Lauren, You've shown us courage, compassion and beauty, through your eyes we learned so much. You were wiser than your twelve years. God sure did get a good girl. Always daddy's little Angel and mommy's special friend, forever now, go up thee and ride your horses! Love Daddy and Mommy / To Lauren, In sunshine, rain, I will always remember the greatest sister in the world, you will be with us always. Love Tyler / To Lauren, Live in peace my dear sister. Love Jeffrey	SJO5052
Jenkins	Lee	Joseph	1900	1951		SMY2159
Jenkins	Lewis	E.	1877	1951	Footstone: Father	SAC1105
Jenkins	Lottie	I.	Oct. 14, 1902	Aug. 2, 1992		SAC1106
Jenkins	Louis	Plowden	Mar. 29, 1926	May 6, 2006		SIC3136
Jenkins	Lucille	T.	Aug. 25, 1892	Apr. 4, 1967		SCL2112
Jenkins	Lula	A.	1878	1945	Mother	SMCA088
Jenkins	Luther	C.	1889	1953		LUM058
Jenkins	Lydia	M.	1909	1991		SMY3217
Jenkins	M.	Courtney	Nov. 28, 1862	Jan. 7, 1945		SCL2116
Jenkins	Mable	L.	1909	1972		SCL2171
Jenkins	Margaret	C.	1841	1913		HGH2021
Jenkins	Margaret		1917	1958	Info is from The Historical Society Research located at The College of Southern MD, LaPlata, MD	SJONoStone
Jenkins	Marguerite	Plowden	Dec. 3, 1892	Oct. 24, 1961		SIC4035
Jenkins	Marie	Antionette	Dec. 21, 1889	Aug. 22, 1896	Old stone with a cross etched at the top	SIC3069

Last Name	First Name	Middle Name	Date of Birth	Date of Death	Transcription / Notes	Cemetery Code
Jenkins	Marie	Antoinette, Simms	Apr. 3, 1851	Sep. 18, 1941	w/o John J. Jenkins	SIC3125
Jenkins	Mary	Alice	Oct. 18, 1903	Dec. 3, 1999	Mother	SMC4085
Jenkins	Mary	Beecher	1917	1990		SCL2183
Jenkins	Mary	E.	1871	1942	Mother	SMCA176
Jenkins	Mary	Ellen	1866	1916	His wife - At Rest	SMY3018
Jenkins	Mary	Eva	Aug. 24, 1892	Sep. 11, 1963		SJO6029
Jenkins	Mary	F.	1876	1973	Together forever	HGH1013
Jenkins	Mary	Wright	Aug. 22, 1877	Mar. 17, 1931		SCL2179
Jenkins	Mary		No Date	Jun. 27, 1827	In his 59 year / His wife / in her 43 year / R.I.P. / This stone was erected to the memory of / and / his wife / by their children. Who pray that God may be merciful to their souls	SJO3081
Jenkins	Mary		No Date	Oct. 5, 1787	Father of J.J. Jenkins, aged 70 years / his wife / R.I.P.	SJO3081
Jenkins	Mary		No Date	Nov. 11, 1821	IHS / In memory of Mary Jenkins / the wife of Capt Tho. Jenkins ( ) / This memorial has been placed here by their children as a token of their love and respect. Crowned in virtue esteemed and in they gone to eternal rest. Age 70 (stone is broken and sunken.)	HGH1087
Jenkins	Maye	Simms	Jul. 9, 1893	Dec. 23, 1974		SIC3135
Jenkins	Morris	Leo	1911	1980	Husband	SMCA088
Jenkins	Naomi	L.	Sep. 7, 1931	No Date		SMC1136
Jenkins	Nellie	Compton	Aug. 19, 1860	Jul. 9, 1943	Beloved wife of Thomas Canfield Jenkins / In thee, O Lord, Have I put my trust	SJE190
Jenkins	Olga	H., Thee	Nov. 9, 1901	Dec. 18, 1986	Requiescat in Pace	SJO3005
Jenkins	Renee				Front of home made wood cross painted white says Renee, back of cross says Jenkins	HGH4048
Jenkins	Richard	S.	Apr. 15, 1882	Jun. 25, 1926	Beloved Husband of Mary M. Farrall	HGH2009
Jenkins	Ruby	L.	Jun. 8, 1908	Dec. 21, 1985		MRB018
Jenkins	Russell	Norris	Jul. 4, 1916	No Date	Love and tender care 1939-1988	NJB145
Jenkins	Ruth	C.	Jan. 2, 1878	Nov. 10, 1883	d/o John I & Antoinette Jenkins / Of such is the kingdom of God / Old stone and writing is hard to read	SIC3068
Jenkins	Ruth	E.	1916	No Date		SIC8060

Last Name	First Name	Middle Name	Date of Birth	Date of Death	Transcription / Notes	Cemetery Code
Jenkins	Sidney	A.	1898	1969	In loving memory	SMC3232
Jenkins	Stephen	T.	1946	2002	Devoted son	HGH4030
Jenkins	Sylvester		1880	1925	Small flat stone that is painted white	SJO6032
Jenkins	Sylvia	Garrett	Oct. 11, 1904	Oct. 10, 2002	Always In Our Hearts	SAC5091
Jenkins	Thomas	C.	Mar. 10, 1894	Oct. 12, 1972		SCL2112
Jenkins	Thomas	Canfield	No Date	Feb. 12, 1916	Son of Thomas Courtney and Caroline Piatt Jenkins / Beloved Husband of Nellie Compton Jenkins / Aged 51 Years / The Cup Which My Father Hath Given Me, Shall I Not Drink It / REQUIESCAT IN PACE	SCL2119
Jenkins	Thomas	Keith	May 10, 1888	Dec. 3, 1923	In blessed memory of / Beloved h/o Edith Jenkins and Eldest s/o Thomas Canfield and Nellie Jenkins / Even so, Father, for so it seemed good in thy sight. Requiesat In Pace	SJE191
Jenkins, Sr.	Thomas	Keith	Sep. 27, 1930	Jan. 12, 1984		SCL2231
Jenkins, Jr.	Thomas	Keith	Apr. 6, 1954	Nov. 11, 1972		SCL2230
Jenkins	Thomas	R.	1894	1976		SCL2077
Jenkins	Thomas	W.	Mar. 21, 1924	Mar. 9, 1945	Maryland PVT 47 INF 9 Div WW II	SJO6028
Jenkins, Capt.	Thomas		No Date	Nov. 14, 1821	IHS / In memory of / This memorial has been placed here by their children as a token of their love and respect. Crowned in virtue esteemed and in they gone to eternal rest. Age 70 (stone is broken and sunken)	HGH1087
Jenkins	Unknown		Sep. 7, 1972	Sep. 7, 1972	Twin sons of Patrick and Ann Jenkins	SMCA120
Jenkins	Vincent	R.	Sep. 24, 1928	Jun. 9, 2004		SMC1136
Jenkins	Viola	C.	1907	1991		SCL3016
Jenkins	Virginia		No Date	No Date		NJB338
Jenkins	Walter	V.	Apr. 12, 1933	Oct. 7, 2002		SMY3055
Jenkins	William	M.	Jul. 3, 1910	Aug. 4, 2000	From your loving family and wife	NSP132
Jenkins	William	W.	1874	1947	Father	SMCA088
Jenkins	William		No Date	Jul. 26, 1782	Grandfather of John J. Jenkins / his wife / R.I.P.	SJO3081
Jenkins	Wilmer	T.	Mar. 24, 1907	Feb. 21, 1979	In loving memory	SMC1139
Jenkins	Unknown		Oct. 26, 1943	Oct. 26, 1943	Info is from church records	CLVNoStone

Last Name	First Name	Middle Name	Date of Birth	Date of Death	Transcription / Notes	Cemetery Code
Jennifer	Alfred		Oct. 10, 1841	Jan. 28, 1919	Beloved husband of Jennie Jennifer / May he rest in peace	SMCD317
Jennings	Betty		Nov. 24, 1940	Sep. 2, 1995	Rest in Peace	POM213
Jennings	Rynette	Worthy	Apr. 8, 1991	Jun. 2, 2008	Age 17 / Born in Wash D.C. and Died in LaPlata, MD. (info is from Maryland Independent Newspaper dated Friday Jun 6, 2008 Pg A-12 Column 2)	HERNoStone
Jensen	Charles	J.	Aug. 15, 1960	May 13, 2003	Beloved Son / Plot S7	GMC044
Jeter	Arthur		Aug. 27, 1918	Oct. 4, 1968		NJB372
Jodeit	John	Paul	Jun. 30, 1969	Sep. 2000	Cremated and buried in the St Francis Memorial Garden / No Marker	SPL9001
Johns	Dorothy	Edelen	1938	1990		SAC3076
Johns	Margaret	Boggs	Oct. 23, 1919	Apr. 30, 1998	In Loving Memory	MTR4023
Johnsen	Chad	S.	Apr. 20, 1986	May 28, 1998	Loving son - caring brother / forever our angel / God was his strength / He never gave up / Life is eternal / love is immortal	SIC9043
Johnsen	Rachel	E.	Oct. 9, 1989	Apr. 6, 2008	Together forever / Ray Ray Live, Love, Laugh	SIC9044
Johnson	A.	T.	No Date	Apr. 15, 1914	Husband / Aged 54 years	POM087
Johnson	Agnes	M.	Feb. 2, 1925	Mar. 4, 2005		SCL4086
Johnson	Albert	A.	1866	1952		SMCA084
Johnson	Alexander		No Date	Jun. 13, 1816	Sacred to the memory of / who departed this life / in the 49th year of his age, info is from the 1940 DAR book pg 186	SMCNoStone
Johnson	Alfred	Grima	1919	Oct. 29, 2008	New York City 1919 / Branitan 1949- 20 / Age 89, from pneumonia. h/o Francine Johnson / Additional info came from an Article in the Washington Post Newspaper dated Nov 27, 2008 Pg B 6	LOC005
Johnson	Alice	E.	Jul. 20, 1913	Sep. 26, 1976		NSP705
Johnson	Alice		Mar. 17, 1854	Jan. 31, 1941		POM088
Johnson	Alonza	T.	1897	1984		MAC008
Johnson	Alonzo	T.	Feb. 27, 1883	Feb. 27, 1970		POM203
Johnson	Alonzo		Jul. 22, 1846	Oct. 14, 1924	PVT. CO F 45 US CLD INF	MAC073
Johnson	Alvin	A.	Apr. 7, 1935	Apr. 14, 2004	Father	MHB237
Johnson	Amelia	Booth	1897	1956		SMC3307

Last Name	First Name	Middle Name	Date of Birth	Date of Death	Transcription / Notes	Cemetery Code
Johnson	Andre	Hubert		1953 2002	Per occupant of the property, He was buried somewhere else and his remains were relocated to this site. / His name appears in the Washington Post Newspaper dated Nov 27, 2008 Pg B 6 as the son of Alfred and Francine Johnson	LOC008
Johnson	Angel	Monique	1982	1982		DUD032
Johnson	Anna	N.	Jun. 18, 1899	May 5, 1962		POM109
Johnson	Anna E.	Swann, Wills	Feb. 19, 1906	Jul. 19, 1970		SIC3024
Johnson	Annie	Bailey	1848	1881		SCL2215
Johnson	Annie	K.	No Date	No Date	She is mentioned on the stone with Joseph M. Johnson. Don't know if she is buried with him.	ODE036
Johnson	Annie	L.	1907	1963	stone with name and dates carved in it	OAK184
Johnson	Annie	Robinson	1916	1970		OFE2084
Johnson	Archie	L.	Jun. 26, 1905	Dec. 16, 1966	(Pat)	ODE228
Johnson	Beatrice	E.	Jun. 12, 1920	Feb. 14, 2004	In loving memory	SJO3099
Johnson	Benedict		Apr. 16, 1888	Oct. 6, 1963	Maryland Pvt US Army WW 1	SMC3268
Johnson	C.	R.	May 4, 1839	Sep. 17, 1907	In memory of my beloved husband / his wife	SMY1136
Johnson	Camille	Louise	No Date	Jan. 28, 1987	Nee Dameron, Died LaPlata, MD, Info is from church records	CHRNoStone
Johnson	Cardinal	B.	Jan. 20, 1936	Sep. 17, 1998	In loving memory	SMC3250
Johnson	Carolan		No Date	Jun. 4, 1899	Info is from Christ Church microfilm Reel 1 Pg 86-87 located at the College of Southern MD, LaPlata, MD	MTRNoStone
Johnson	Caroline	Elizabeth	No Date	Jan. 5, 1899	Info is from Christ Church microfilm Reel 1 Pg 84-85 located at the College of Southern MD, LaPlata, MD	MTRNoStone
Johnson	Carroll	A.	Jul. 8, 1920	May 4, 1992		SCA086
Johnson	Charles	I.	1902	1977	Info is from the Historical Society Research located at the College of Southern MD, LaPlata, MD	SCLNoStone
Johnson	Charles		1919	1992	Thornton Funeral Home Marker	OAK188
Johnson	Charlotte	A.	May 27, 1892	Apr. 23, 1981		SPL2026
Johnson	Charlotte	E.	May 26, 1869	Dec. 23, 1964	Gone but not forgotten	SCL2073
Johnson	Clare	Lawangina	Nov. 1985	Mar. 10, 1988	Washington Post Newspaper dated Nov 27, 2008 Pg B 6 says a child of Alfred and Francine Johnson	LOC010
Johnson	Clarence	C.	Feb. 8, 1896	Sep. 1, 1984	Missed and Loved For Eternity	SCL2096

Last Name	First Name	Middle Name	Date of Birth	Date of Death	Transcription / Notes	Cemetery Code
Johnson, Sr.	Clifford	A.	Jan. 2, 1951	Jul. 6, 2002	We Love you and miss you	ZBC099
Johnson	Columbus		No Date	Oct. 17, 1874	Info is from church records	OFENoStone
Johnson	Cora		Apr. 9, 1899	May 28, 1988		SCL1062
Johnson	Cornelius		Feb. 17, 1864	Dec. 23, 1927	Beloved h/o Elizabeth Johnson / Gone but not forgotten	ODE230
Johnson	Cornell	Curtis	Oct. 21, 1948	Feb. 20, 1996	"C J" Best Husband and Father	POM178
Johnson	Curtis		1927	1976	PFC US Army WW II	SJO2116
Johnson	Darnell		1959	1989	Cement stone with decorative top and Thornton Funeral Home Marker	OAK192
Johnson	Densil	Lee	No Date	No Date	s/o William Mitchell & Jennie Grigsby Johnson (info is from the Historical Society Research located at The College of Southern MD, LaPlata, MD)	FRANoStone
Johnson	Derrick		1968	1968		SPL2020
Johnson	E.	H.	Jun. 24, 1890	Dec. 25, 1900		POM086
Johnson	E.	Layton	1888	1958		SPL2025
Johnson	Earl		Nov. 15, 1927	Apr. 12, 2001	In loving memory, the Johnson family (church records show his name as Joseph Earl)	MTR1108
Johnson	Effie	O.	Oct. 30, 1879	Mar. 27, 1934		BRC010
Johnson	Elizabeth	Mae	May 4, 1931	Jul. 27, 1964	Blessed are the pure in heart	NSP898
Johnson	Elizabeth		1779	Mar. 29, 1831	Religious name, Mary Magdalen of St. Joseph. Professed April 25, 1800. d/o John Johnson and Ann Seville. Nun buried at Mt. Carmel but don't know where	GMCNo Stone
Johnson	Ella		Dec. 22, 1870	Jun. 16, 1950		OFE4045
Johnson	Ellen		1861	1943		SIG056
Johnson, Jr.	Ernest	M.	Apr. 2, 1961	Feb. 8, 1983	"Bunny"	HGH4175
Johnson	Eugene	L.	1911	1962		SIC7020
Johnson, Jr.	Eugene	L.	Mar. 28, 1943	Sep. 4, 1948		SIC7021
Johnson	Eva	A.	1868	1916		SMCA084
Johnson	Florence	F.	Aug. 5, 1879	May 5, 1968		ODE316
Johnson	Florence	G.	Nov. 1895	Feb. 1930		POM066
Johnson	Florence	Marie	Apr. 13, 1908	Dec. 23, 1989	We Love you Nana / Sis, Nieces, Nephews and Family	SMI007
Johnson	Florence		No Date	No Date		NJB318
Johnson	Frances	M.	Jul. 2, 1925	Jun. 28, 2004	In Loving Memory	SAC5008

Last Name	First Name	Middle Name	Date of Birth	Date of Death	Transcription / Notes	Cemetery Code
Johnson	Francine	Buffet	1924	No Date	Paris, France 1924 - Branitan 1949 - 20	LOC005
Johnson	Francis	Leroy	Mar. 14, 1934	Jan. 14, 1976	AB U.S. Air Force	SPL2018
Johnson	Francis		Sep. 22, 1921	Mar. 17, 1973	US Army	SMC3088
Johnson	Frank		No Date	Jan. 1952	Aged 65 yrs / Huntt & Ryon Funeral marker	BRC018
Johnson	Garry		Jul. 31, 1960	Jul. 19, 1978	Rest in peace	HGH4126
Johnson	Gary	Allen	May 26, 1966	Mar. 12, 1994	His tenderness and kindness will never fade from our hearts and memory. / Beloved son, brother & friend / "459"	SPL7012
Johnson	Geo.	R.	Jul. 15, 1868	Apr. 1, 1898	In memory of	OFE4097
Johnson	George	A.	1882	1957		SAC4081
Johnson	George	C.	Dec. 16, 1835	Nov. 18, 1927		SMCA057
Johnson	George	Clarence	No Date	Sep. 7, 1900	Info is from Christ Church microfilm Reel 1 Pg 86-87 located at the College of Southern MD, LaPlata, MD	MTRNoStone
Johnson	Gertrude	Asandra	Dec. 5, 1947	Aug. 28, 1975		SMC3087
Johnson	Gertrude	T.	Jan. 18, 1894	Jul. 22, 1973		POM196
Johnson	Grace	Bean	No Date	Jul. 2, 1861	In Memory of / aged 4 mos and 24 days Infant d/o Wm & Ellen Johnson / In starry wings from earth to heaven, has borne a spirit to its home. An added Cherubim there given. The parents heart was left alone	OFE2116
Johnson	Grace	L.	May 22, 1881	Sep. 3, 1976	Rest in peace	OFE1035
Johnson	Grace		No Date	Jun. 16, 1950	Age 79 / info is from church records	OFENoStone
Johnson	Gregory	D.	Aug. 18, 1955	Jul. 31, 2003	Love and Peace	SAC1086
Johnson	Gurnies	Ely	No Date	Nov. 1962	Age 35, buried November 25, 1962 (Info is from the Historical Society Research located at the College of Southern MD, LaPlata, MD)	ODENoStone
Johnson	Harry	Theodore	1920	1978	STM1 US Navy WWII	SAC5040
Johnson, Jr.	Harry	Theodore	Jun. 7, 1941	Jun. 25, 1990	SP4 US Army Vietnam	SAC5009
Johnson	Harry		1913	1990	Thornton Funeral Home Marker	MHB108
Johnson	Helen	L.	1900	1979		ODE180
Johnson	Henry	W.	1880	1957		POM234
Johnson	Herman	Leroy	Apr. 5, 1941	1983	Pointed stone with a cross and info painted on it, Thornton Funeral Home Marker	OAK196

Last Name	First Name	Middle Name	Date of Birth	Date of Death	Transcription / Notes	Cemetery Code
Johnson	Herman	Paul	May 7, 1940	No Date	Our Son / Dad & Mom / Father of Kayla & Paul / In loving Memory / Together forever	SJO3307
Johnson	Ida		Oct. 9, 1901	Apr. 2, 1935	At rest in heaven with God	MTR1107
Johnson	Isaac	Leroy	Nov. 24, 1924	Apr. 23, 1976	SC2 US Navy WWII	SAC5042
Johnson	Iver	M.	May 29, 1916	Jan. 11, 1982		SPL2027
Johnson	J.	Ardy	1899	1983		ODE180
Johnson	James	Carl	1919	1968		HGH1177
Johnson	James	David	Mar. 28, 1951	Aug. 7, 1994	Sgt US Army Vietnam / Our Beloved Donnie	SAC5010
Johnson	James	E.	Mar. 3, 1917	Dec. 25, 1978		SMC3066
Johnson	James	F.	Jan. 23, 1935	Jun. 22, 2003	Together forever	SCL3244
Johnson	James	H.	1883	1951		SJO6007
Johnson	James	Vincent	No Date	No Date	s/o Cornelius & Charlotte Simmons Johnson(info is from the Historical Society Research located at The College of Southern MD, LaPlata, MD)	FRANoStone
Johnson	James		No Date	Nov. 1929	Buried November 19, 1929 (Info is from the Historical Society Research located at the College of Southern MD, LaPlata, MD)	ODENoStone
Johnson	Jefferson		Aug. 27, 1931	2002	Thornton Funeral Home Marker & Homemade Marker	OAK013
Johnson	Jennie	D.	No Date	Mar. 5, 1917	Aged 22 yrs	BRC013
Johnson	Jenny	Virginia	No Date	Dec. 15, 1939	w/o Wm. Mitchell Johnson / Information is from the Historical Society Research located at The College of Southern MD, LaPlata, MD	SIGNo Stone
Johnson	Jerome	S.	Jul. 15, 1944	Jun. 5, 1987	SP 4 U.S. Army	OAK195
Johnson	Jewish	S.	Apr. 9, 1950	Oct. 3, 1952		ODE036
Johnson	John	C.	No Date	? 24, 1963	Age 55 / info is from church records	OFENoStone
Johnson	John	H.	1840	1914	His son John S. Johnson / at rest	SMCB013
Johnson	John	S.	1870	1925	s/o John H. Johnson / at rest	SMCB013
Johnson	John	W.	Jun. 14, 1887	Apr. 21, 1969		ODE316
Johnson	Johnny	Leroy	Feb. 3, 1956	Mar. 24, 1997	I Love You Always, "Jelly"	MHB026
Johnson	Joseph	L. C.	1906	1978	Together forever	SMC3159
Johnson	Joseph	M.	1902	1954	In Memory of Annie K. Johnson (Don't know if Annie is buried here)	ODE036

Last Name	First Name	Middle Name	Date of Birth	Date of Death	Transcription / Notes	Cemetery Code
Johnson, Sr	Joseph	S.	Jan. 3, 1906	Feb. 20, 1998	Father / in loving memory	CHR283
Johnson	Josephus	M.	Jan. 27, 1883	Nov. 7, 1973	IHS / NATUS 27, Jan. 1883 / ING 6 Sept. 1906 / OB. 7, Nov 1973 / R.I.P. (In Priests Plot)	SIC1039
Johnson	Julia	A.	Feb. 28, 1886	Feb. 10, 1971		SAC4080
Johnson	Julian	F.	Mar. 23, 1893	Mar. 1, 1974	At rest in heaven with God	MTR1107
Johnson	Julius	T.	Jun. 3, 1875	Jun. 6, 1896	Our Children	SMY1138
Johnson	Larry	P.	Jun. 26, 1952	Jul. 5, 2000	"Big Brother"	SAC1085
Johnson	Lawrence	Stanley	Sep. 25, 1932	Feb. 7, 2002	CS3 US Navy Korea	SPL7013
Johnson	Lena	E.	1882	1959		HGH1176
Johnson	Lewis	A.	Jul. 11, 1891	Jun. 28, 1896	s/o George C & Nellie Johnson / No bitter tears had he to weep / No sins to be forgiven / but closed his loving eyes in sleep to open them in heaven	SMCA059
Johnson	Lillian	A.	Jul. 31, 1913	Nov. 3, 2000		SAC3058
Johnson	Lillian		Sep. 2, 1919	Mar. 7, 2001		ALX082
Johnson	Lizzie		1926	No Date	Funeral home marker	MAC070
Johnson	Lloyd	Elroy	Oct. 22, 1959	1980	Info was obtained from the Historical Society Research located at the College of Southern Md, LaPlata, Md)	OAKNoStone
Johnson	Louie		1906	1980		ALX109
Johnson	Louis	M.	Nov. 6, 1926	Nov. 15, 1975	US Navy WWII	SAC5041
Johnson	Louis		1914	1984		SAC5082
Johnson	Louise		No Date	No Date	Arehart Funeral Home Marker	SMT031
Johnson	Madeline		1927	1992	Thornton Funeral Home Marker	MHB048
Johnson	Margaret	A.	No Date	Mar. 29, 1886	In Memory of / Beloved w/o George C. Johnson / aged 50 years / May she rest in peace	SMCA055
Johnson	Margaret	Alice	Aug. 29, 1904	Sep. 20, 1997	PO Dept. USA 43 years service	OFE1033
Johnson	Marie	L.	Nov. 21, 1886	1887	Our Children	SMY1138
Johnson	Marion		1917	1968		SJO3286
Johnson	Martha	L.	1920	1990		SAC5003
Johnson	Martha	R.	Nov. 8, 1941	No Date	Married Apr 22, 1966	SCL1051
Johnson	Mary	L.	Mar. 5, 1925	Dec. 6, 2002		SJO3110
Johnson	Mary	Lorraine	Sep. 9, 1918	Mar. 28, 1997		SPL4069
Johnson	Mary	M.	Sep. 22, 1922	Jan. 30, 1976		SMC3114

Last Name	First Name	Middle Name	Date of Birth	Date of Death	Transcription / Notes	Cemetery Code
Johnston	Mary	M.	Feb. 28, 1836	Dec. 22, 1908	w/o Henry H. Johnston	SJO3060
Johnson	Mary		No Date	Feb. 11, 1923	Age 75 / Info is from church records	SHINoStone
Johnson	Mary		No Date	No Date	s/o William Mitchell & Jennie Grigsby Johnson (info is from the Historical Society Research located at The College of Southern MD, LaPlata, MD)	FRANoStone
Johnson	Mary	E.	Apr. 8, 1884	Nov. 4, 1902	Our Children	SMY1138
Johnson, Sr.	Matthew	Jack	Aug. 1, 1910	Feb. 26, 1995	Father / info is from church records	SHI019
Johnson	Melissa	V.	No Date	No Date	Children's Memorial / and all other children buried here	HGH4328
Johnson	Melissa	V.	Mar. 1, 1969	Apr. 13, 1977	Our little angel / Gone but not forgotten	HGH3024
Johnson	Melvin	Thomas	No Date	Aug. 29, 1959	Age 93 / info is from church records	OFENoStone
Johnson	Millie		No Date	Aug. 9, 1964	Huntt Funeral Home Marker 80 yrs	SMT020
Johnson, Mrs.	Unknown		No Date	No Date	Probably buried next to her husband. m/o Symphronia L. Johnson Spalding (Notes from Sister Miriam John at Mt Carmel Monastery)	GMCNo Stone
Johnson	Nancy	A.	Jan. 6, 1936	No Date		SPL7015
Johnson	Nathalie		No Date	1950	There is an unmarked stone in the cemetery located in the vicinity of the Johnson Family. This could be for Nathalie. / d/o A. Grima Johnson / Info on this child is from The Washington Post Newspaper dated Nov 27, 2008 Pg B 6	LOCNoStone
Johnson	Nellie	C.	1876	1941		SCL2216
Johnson	Ophelia	M.	Dec. 15, 1918	Aug. 23, 1986	Mother	SHI162
Johnson	Ose		No Date	No Date	Info supplied by a church member	PGONoStone
Johnson	Paul	Christopher	Jan. 14, 1970	May 4, 2008	Our Son / Dad & Mom / Father of Kayla & Paul / In loving Memory / Together forever	SJO3307
Johnson	Philip	J.	1868	1940		HGH1176
Johnson	Philip	Morris	Mar. 31, 1948	Aug. 16, 1996	"Pee Wee" / In Loving Memory	OAK055
Johnson	Phillip	O'Donald	Jan. 14, 1928	Jul. 1, 1974	CPL Army Air Forces	SCL3004
Johnson	Purnell	C.	Oct. 21, 1948	Jul. 17, 1977		SAC3088
Johnson	Rachel	Eva	No Date	No Date	d/o Cornelius & Charlotte Simmons Johnson (info is from the Historical Society Research located at The College of Southern MD, LaPlata, MD)	FRANoStone
Johnson	Raymond	A.	Dec. 16, 1916	Jul. 6, 1968	Maryland SGT US Army WWII	SAC5004

Last Name	First Name	Middle Name	Date of Birth	Date of Death	Transcription / Notes	Cemetery Code
Johnson	Rebecca		Jan. 5, 1900	Jan. 22, 2002		MAC068
Johnson	Regina	Reintzell	Sep. 8, 1919	Sep. 5, 2004	Pres. Fire Dept. Aux., Charter members, Hughesville Volunteer Fire Dept. Married Oct 6, 1946	OFE1034
Johnson	Richard	David	Jun. 2, 1940	Dec. 27, 1978		SAC3083
Johnson	Richard		No Date	May 7, 1934	Info is from Christ Church microfilm Reel 3, Pg 238-239 located at the College of Southern MD, LaPlata, MD	MTRNoStone
Johnson	Robert	H.	No Date	Jun. 25, 1907	Aged 68 years	MTR3218
Johnson	Robert	J.	Sep. 20, 1869	Jun. 5, 1927		BRC011
Johnson, Sr.	Robert	L.	Sep. 27, 1922	Oct. 23, 1993		SJO3110
Johnson	Robert	K.	1961	1985		SAC4071
Johnson	Roland	E.	May 9, 1918	May 6, 1963		SPL2021
Johnson	Rose		1902	1963		HGH1117
Johnson	RoseMary	E.	Aug. 18, 1914	Mar. 26, 1981	Missed and Loved For Eternity	SCL2096
Johnson	Roy	S.	Jan. 15, 1924	Oct. 7, 2002	In God's Care / Husband & Father	POM148
Johnson	Russell	Calvin	May 25, 1926	Apr. 10, 1998	Pvt. U. S. Army / World War II	OAK048
Johnson, Sr.	Russell	L.	Feb. 17, 1943	May 13, 2004	Married Apr 22, 1966	SCL1051
Johnson	S.	Wallace	Jun. 27, 1912	Mar. 7, 1996		NSP705
Johnson	Sadie		1917	1994	Mom / From her loving family	OAK054
Johnson	Samuel	C.	Feb. 20,1904	1984	Pointed stone with a cross and info painted in black on the stone	OAK198
Johnson	Sandra	T.	Feb. 29, 1948	No Date	Together forever	SCL3244
Johnson	Sarah	A.	Feb. 27, 1845	Jan. 4, 1921	In memory of my beloved husband / his wife	SMY1136
Johnson	Sarah	Elizabeth	1886	1979		POM234
Johnson	Sarah	Louise	Dec. 24, 1930	Feb. 11, 1999	Beloved Wife, Mother, and Grandmother / Forever in our hearts	OAK047
Johnson	Sarah	S.	Dec. 27, 1903	Jul. 13, 1972		SMT028
Johnson, Miss	Sarah		No Date	Aug. 1873	Info is from church records	OFENoStone
Johnson	Shirley	Ann	Jun. 7, 1946	No Date	Our Son / Dad & Mom / Father of Kayla & Paul / In loving Memory / Together forever	SJO3307
Johnson	Susie	S.	Oct. 9, 1909	Aug. 16, 1986		SMT027
Johnson	Tammy		1967	1985	Thornton Funeral Home Marker	MHB067
Johnson	Tammy		1968	2001	Thornton Funeral Home Marker	MHB010

Last Name	First Name	Middle Name	Date of Birth	Date of Death	Transcription / Notes	Cemetery Code
Johnson	Thelma	T.	1904	1985		SCL3003
Johnson	Thomas	Harold	Jun. 30, 1937	Aug. 17, 2002	US Army	SMC3097
Johnson	Thomas	M.	Nov. 11, 1930	Jun. 12, 1956	Maryland PFC Co B 981 Engr Cons Bn	SMY2091
Johnson	Thomas	N.	Nov. 15, 1874	Jun. 28, 1928	Rest in peace	OFE1036
Johnson	Thomas	Warren	Jun. 12, 1921	Sep. 17, 1997	Pres. Fire Dept. Aux, Charter members, Hughesville Volunteer Fire Dept. Married Oct 6, 1946 / US Army WW II	OFE1034
Johnson	Thomas		1934	1993	Thornton Funeral Home Marker	OAK066
Johnson	Thomas		No Date	1955	Funeral Home Marker	MAC062
Johnson	Tiney	E.	1896	1949		OAK190
Johnson	Unknown		No Date	No Date		NJB319
Johnson	Unknown		No Date	Oct. 1922	Baby / age 8 mo's. Buried Oct 17, 1922 (info is from Old Durham Church microfilm pg 159 located at the College of Southern MD, LaPlata, MD)	ODENoStone
					Died before 1829 (the death of his first grandchild, Basil Marcellus Spalding.) f/o Symphronia L. Johnson Spalding. John Spalding, her husband, recorded in his family Bible that he buried his wife and two infants next to their "grandpa" at Mount Carmel. Since his parents are buried at St. Joseph's in Pomfret, he meant his first wife's father. John Spalding and his second wife, Mary Carroll, are buried at Pomfret. (Notes from Sister Miriam John at Mt Carmel Monastery)	
Johnson, Mr.	Unknown		No Date	No Date		GMCNo Stone
Johnson	Van	Allen	Jan. 2, 1963	Apr. 6, 2007	My Son, Our Brother	PIS095
Johnson	Victorine	M.	May 23, 1929	Apr. 19, 1985	Mother	SMC3267
Johnson	Viola	A.	Apr. 24, 1860	Dec. 27, 1948	Mother of Etta P. Robinson	SPL5062
Johnson	Wallace	H.	Dec. 14, 1923	Nov. 14, 1981	Absent from the body present with the Lord the family	MAC009
Johnson	Walter	Melvin	No Date	Feb. 14, 1962	Age 60 / info is from church records	OFENoStone
Johnson	William	A.	1874	1945		SCL2216
Johnson	William	A.	1848	1933	His Wife Annie Bailey Johnson	SCL2215
Johnson	William	A.	1912	1975	Info is from Historical Society Research located at The College of Southern MD, LaPlata, MD	SACNostone
Johnson, Sr.	William	B.	Apr. 19, 1907	May 11, 1939	Father	SCL1040

Last Name	First Name	Middle Name	Date of Birth	Date of Death	Transcription / Notes	Cemetery Code
Johnson	William	Carrico	No Date	Jul. 13, 1894	Infant / info is from church records	OFENoStone
Johnson	William	Francis	1901	1979	Info is from church records	SPLNoStone
Johnson	William	Francis	Dec. 21, 1920	Jan. 31, 1968	Maryland TEC5 US Army WWII	SPL2029
Johnson	William	M.	No Date	Sep. 1, 1956	Age 63, buried September 1, 1956 (Info is from the Historical Society Research located at the College of Southern MD, LaPlata, MD)	ODENoStone
Johnson	William	Perry	No Date	No Date	s/o William Mitchell & Jennie Grigsby Johnson (info is from the Historical Society Research located at The College of Southern MD, LaPlata, MD)	FRANoStone
Johnson	William		No Date	Jun. 27, 1901	Info is from church records	OFENoStone
Johnson	William		No Date	Jun. 1927	Age 80, buried June 24, 1927 (Info is from the Historical Society Research located at the College of Southern MD, LaPlata, MD)	ODENoStone
Johnson, Mrs.	William		No Date	Mar. 28, 1884	Info is from church records	OFENoStone
Johnson	Willie	M.	No Date	Feb. 26, 1875	Son of William and Ellen Johnson aged 12 years and 4 mo's.	OFE2115
Johnson	Willie		No Date	No Date	Arehart Funeral Home Marker / Willie and Louise Johnson Headstone	SMT030
Johnson	Willie		No Date	Sep. 18,1969	Aged o years / Arehart Funeral Home marker, LaPlata, MD	DUD074
Johnson	Wilmer	Bernard	1905	1991		HGH1175
Johnson	Zephaniah	Guy	Aug. 10, 1894	Jul. 25, 1980	MM2 US Navy World War I	HGH1118
Jone	I.	L.	1/7/1866	Mar. 18, 1921	I. L. JONE Bo. Jan. 7, 1866 die. Mar. 18, 1921	SMCW029
Jones	Ada		1919	1994	Thornton Funeral Home	ZBC087
Jones	Albert	Golden	No Date	Sep. 13, 1960	Age 76 / info is from church records	OFENoStone
Jones	Albert	Golden	Nov. 5, 1883	Jul. 13, 1960	Info is from website ancestry.com / last name is from church records	OFE2106
Jones	Alice	V.	May 4, 1921	Mar. 14, 1966		SMC3089
Jones	Almon		Apr. 25, 1917	Jul. 22, 1999	"Bill" / Beloved muma and pupa	NSP170
Jones	Alva	E.	Jan. 6, 1914	No Date		SCL1178
Jones	Anna	Silas	1855	1952		SHI151
Jones	Arthur	Elwood	Dec. 4, 1868	Aug. 5, 1871	4th of 12 mo 1868 / 5th of 8 mo 1871	PAT004
Jones	Azaraih	F.	1877	1947		SHI151

Last Name	First Name	Middle Name	Date of Birth	Date of Death	Transcription / Notes	Cemetery Code
Jones	Beatrice	Nelson	Oct. 9, 1912	No Date		SPL3043
Jones	Beverly	Joyce	1934	2004	Sweetie Pie	HGH4147
Jones	Blanche		No Date	Feb. 21, 1919	Info is from Christ Church microfilm Reel 3, Pg 228-229 located at the College of Southern MD, LaPlata, MD Small round stone with the letters CFJ and numbers 11 75 on it (could last name be Jones) / Info is from church records	MTRNoStone
Jones, Sr.	Carl	F.	No Date	1975		CHR292
Jones	Catherine	V. Wills	Mar. 14, 1918	May 14, 1998	In loving memory of	SAC3026
Jones	Charles	L.	Jul. 4, 1839	Feb. 21, 1903		SCL1022
Jones	Charles	R.	Nov. 11, 1894	Jul. 16, 1969	Maryland PVT 11 CO 3 DEV BN WW I	CHR312
Jones, Maj.	Chester	A.	1921	1992	In Plot for Archibold family	OFE2079
Jones	Chloe	H.	1857	1940		PAT006
Jones	Cleveland	C.	1886	1977	US Army World War I	CHR293
Jones	Cloteal		1906	1970	Thornton Funeral Home Marker / C. Loteal or Cloteal	PGN002
Jones	Doris	Alice	No Date	Oct. 22, 1932	Info is from Christ Church microfilm Reel 3, Pg 238-239 located at the College of Southern MD, LaPlata, MD	MTRNoStone
Jones	Dossie	H.	1926	1958	US Army Korea	ZBC143
Jones	E.	Elwood	1910	1995	Together Forever	SMC3216
Jones	Edith	L.	1928	2001	In God's Care / Mother	SCA045
Jones	Edward	L.	1948	1954		SMC3241
Jones	Edward	Mitchell	Dec. 17, 1927	Apr. 6, 1990	Verse on stone: Beloved husband and father / On back of stone: Do not stand at my grave and weep. I am not there, I do not sleep. I am a thousand winds that blow, I am the diamond glint on snow. I am the sunlight on ripened grain, I am the gentle autumn rain. When you wake in the morning hush I am the swift, uplifting rush of quiet birds in circling flight, I am the starlight at night. Do not stand at my grave and weep, I am not there. I do not sleep.	CHR295
Jones	Elisha	D.	1856	1935		PAT007
Jones	Elizabeth	I.	1918	1988	Together Forever	SMC3216
Jones	Elizabeth	R.	Mar. 5, 1884	Dec. 6, 1958		CHR313
Jones	Ellen	Gross	May 29, 1882	Jul. 24, 1916	May she rest in peace	SIC4101

Last Name	First Name	Middle Name	Date of Birth	Date of Death	Transcription / Notes	Cemetery Code
Jones	Elwood	E.	1880	1884		PAT005
Jones	Enoch		Jul. 7, 1819	Mar. 31, 1886	7th of 7 mo. 1819 / 31st of 3 mo. 1886	PAT002
Jones	Ethel		1948	1998	Name is painted on a small stone / info is from church records	PGN051
Jones	Frances	Posey	Dec. 27, 1912	Sep. 9, 1995	In loving memory	SMCA194
Jones	Frank	Thomas	Oct. 5, 1880	Mar. 22, 1966		CHR314
Jones	Geneva	J.	Jul. 6, 1923	Dec. 6, 2005	Beloved Wife	SIC9100
Jones	Genevieve	L.	Nov. 20, 1918	Nov. 28, 1998	Loving Children	SMC3051
Jones	George	E.	1946	1952		SMC3242
Jones	George	M.	1927	1984		CLV234
Jones	Gladys	B.	No Date	Dec. 29, 1990	Info is from church records	CLVNoStone
Jones	Helen	Anna	1914	1996	Beloved Mother and Grandmother	SAC2075
Jones, Sr.	Henry	R.	Aug. 15, 1907	Aug. 7, 1975		SMC3192
Jones Jr.	Jack		1948	1949	My Beloved Son	CLV057
Jones, Dr.	Jacob	James	Oct. 16, 1888	Apr. 10, 1970	Info is from Christ Church microfilm Reel 4 Pg 288-289 located at the College of Southern MD, LaPlata, MD	MTR4109
Jones	Jacob	James	No Date	Apr. 10, 1970		MTRNoStone
Jones	James	S	1947	2003	In God's Care/ Brother / "Dusty"	SCA030
Jones	Johnson	W.	1918	1983		SAC2088
Jones	Joseph		No Date	No Date	Info is from church records	SHINoStone
Jones	Julie	A.	1887	1952		SHI151
Jones	Katharyn	S.	Mar. 30, 1916	Mar. 16, 2004		SCL1178
Jones	Keith	L.	Aug. 10 1964	Aug. 26, 2001	Brother / In Loving memory of	ZBC011
Jones	Kellie	Mae	May 22, 1969	May 22, 1986	(Back) To one who suffered so much, gave so much & asked so little, love to all who cared to receive	NJB278
Jones	Lambert	J.	Sep. 17, 1859	Jun. 29, 1882	17th of 9 mo 1859 / 29th of 6 mo 1882	PAT003
Jones	Leroy		No Date	Aug. 6, 1974	Funeral Home Marker 74 years. / Info is from Shiloh Church records	SMT047
Jones	Louise		1897	1960		NSP379
Jo	M.	T.	1900	1994	(Wood Cross) This could possibly be Mary T. Jones born in 1900	SAC5031
Jones	Mabel	Gibson	Jan. 27, 1899	Sep. 3, 1966		MTR4108

Last Name	First Name	Middle Name	Date of Birth	Date of Death	Transcription / Notes	Cemetery Code
Jones	Marian	C.	1919	1919		PAT008
Jones	Mary	A.	1926	1985	In Plot for Archibold family	OFE2080
Jones	Mary	Helen	Apr. 23, 1921	Jun. 22, 2003	Mother / Always in Our Hearts / Your Daughters	SAC5035
Jones	Mary	Keith, Bean	Apr. 16, 1884	May 8, 1972		SPL3042
Jones	Mary	M.	No Date	Nov. 1, 1922	Age 51 / info is from church records	SHINoStone
Jones	Naomi		1911	1995		SMT024
Jones	Otis	Conway	Nov. 9, 1893	Jun. 25, 1963	IHS / May He Rest in Peace	CLV056
Jones	Patricia	A.	1927	1991		SAC2088
Jones	Pearl	Dent	Jul. 30, 1899	Jul. 19, 1984		ODE038
Jones	Richard	G.	No Date	Dec. 15, 1935	Name is shown on church records but burial location is unknown, date is the burial date, not death date	CHRNoStone
Jones	Rita	Veronica	Jan. 19, 1919	Jul. 16, 1996	Beloved muma and pupa	NSP170
Jones	Robert	Arthur	Aug. 17, 1911	Dec. 26, 1982		SPL3043
Jones	Roy		1887	1952		NSP379
Jones	Ruth	Ethel, Gibbons	Feb. 20, 1887	May 7, 1957	Info is from website Ancestry.com / last name is from church records	OFE2106
Jones	Ruth	Gibbons	No Date	May 18, 1957	Age 70 / info is from church records	OFENoStone
Jones	Sammie	L.	1884	1961		MTR3132
Jones	Samuel	McDowell	May 20, 1966	Jan. 6, 2004	In God's Loving Care	DUD009
Jones	Sandy		No Date	Mar. 29, 1928	info is from church records	SHINoStone
Jones	Stephen	Robert	Mar. 14, 1955	Apr. 23, 2000		SMC3084
Jones	Thomas	A.	Oct. 2, 1820	Mar. 5, 1895	Signal Corps Norris Co CSA..Chief Agent	SMY1133
Jones	Thomas	E.	Nov. 13, 1923	Apr. 12, 1985		ODE038
Jones	Thomas	Earl	1958	1976	In loving memory	SMC3243
Jones	Thomas		Aug. 1, 1906	Oct. 25, 1978		NSP535
Jones	Unknown		No Date	1944	Name is shown on church records but burial location is unknown, date is the burial date, not death date (Baby) webb site familysearch.org shows Walter Jones born Dec. 13, 1889 and died Jul 1969 in Bryantown, Charles Co., MD	CHRNoStone
Jones	Walter	L.	1889	No Date		MTR3132
Jones	Walter		1897	1982		SMT024
Jones	Wesley		No Date	Apr. 12, 1931	Aged 80 yrs / Erected by the Rowe Family	SMI131

Last Name	First Name	Middle Name	Date of Birth	Date of Death	Transcription / Notes	Cemetery Code
Jones	Wilbur	Harper	Jun. 1, 1914	Feb. 18, 1973	In loving memory	SMCA194
Jones	William	J.	1923	2001	Thornton Funeral Home marker	SAC5036
Jones	William	McG	No Date	Feb. 14, 1922	Infant / Name is shown on church records but burial location is unknown, date is the burial date, not death date	CHRNoStone
Jones	William	Wilson	No Date	May 14, 1943	Name is shown on church records but burial location is unknown, date is the burial date, not death date	CHRNoStone
Jones	Woodrow		Sep. 22, 1912	Jan. 5, 1985		CHR294
Jordan	Alice	E.	Jan. 12, 1914	Jan. 18, 1938		POM092
Jordan	Carol	I.	Apr. 26, 1937	Jan. 16, 1950		POM091
Jordan	Cleopas	H.	Aug. 16, 1928	Sep. 22, 1950		POM094
Jordan	Donald	Garnell	Oct. 5, 1945	Apr. 24, 1993	CPL US Army / Aged 48 yrs, 6 mos & 19 dys (J B Jenkins Funeral Home, 7474 Landover Rd. Landover, MD)	ZBC073
Jordan	Edward		Jan. 2, 1899	May 30, 1955	Beloved wife Lucy	ALX102
Jordan	Emory	Wilmer	Apr. 19, 1934	Dec. 7, 1995	Age 62 years / J B Jenkins Funeral Home Marker, 7474 Landover Rd. Landover, MD	ZBC075
Jordan	Estelle	E.	Sep. 6, 1891	Mar. 2, 1973		POM099
Jordan	Francis		1912	1982	Info is from the 1984 church cemetery transcription list	SICNoStone
Jordan	George	T.	Jan. 26, 1919	Jul. 27, 1971		POM205
Jordan	James	H.	Jun. 4, 1912	Feb. 28, 1963		POM095
Jordan	James	Rudolph	1935	1980	PVT US Army Korea	POM100
Jordan	John	W.	Feb. 5, 1916	Mar. 23, 1975	PFC US ARMY (death date came from web site familysearch.org)	POM175
Jordan	Martha		1846	1926		ALX094
Jordan	Ralph		1894	1981	Thornton Funeral Home Marker	ALX095
Jordan	Virginia		1909	1989	In Loving Memory	ZBC182
Jordan	Wesley	S.	Feb. 23, 1884	Mar. 16, 1949		POM093
Jordan	William		No Date	Sep. 9, 1976	Aged 63 years (info is from the Historical Society Research located at the College of Southern MD, LaPlata, MD)	ZBCNoStone
Jordan	William		1905	1969	In Loving Memory	ZBC182

Last Name	First Name	Middle Name	Date of Birth	Date of Death	Transcription / Notes	Cemetery Code
Josephs	Donald	E.	No Date	No Date	Cremated and buried in the St Francis Memorial Garden / No Marker	SPL9001
Josephs	Eileen	Kelly	Oct. 28, 1941	Jul. 16, 1999	Cremated and buried in the St Francis Memorial Garden / No Marker	SPL9001
Josephs	Michael	Richard	No Date	No Date	Cremated and buried in the St Francis Memorial Garden / No Marker	SPL9001
Joson	Noida	S.	Nov. 16, 1928	No Date		LUM107
Joson, Jr. M.D.	Tirso	E.	Aug. 28, 1926	Mar. 30, 1990	Physician of the Year Mar 30, 1990	LUM107
Jowers	May	Wright	1910	1955		MRB043
Joyce	John	Caroll	1915	1976	Info is from The Historical Society Research Located at the College of Southern MD, LaPlata, MD	HGHNoStone
Juhle	Bernward	C.	1900	1955	Dr. of Geology, Lost in Alaska, Valley of Ten Thousand Smokes	ODE127
Juhle	Hans	Bodo	1933	1961		ODE126
Juhle	Lisa	M.	1901	1994	Dr. of Geology, Lost in Alaska, Valley of Ten Thousand Smokes	ODE127
Juhle	Werner		1929	1953	Dr. of Geology, Lost in Alaska, Valley of Ten Thousand Smokes	ODE127
Jupiter	Annie	E.	Dec. 14, 1921	Dec. 30, 2003	Always in our hearts	HGH4053
Jupiter	Arthur		No Date	Dec. 29, 1972	Info is from church records	SHINoStone
Jupiter	Charles		No Date	Dec. 17, 1924	Info is from church records	SHINoStone
Jupiter	David	M.	Aug. 30, 1963	Jun. 7, 1984	Son	HGH3031
Jupiter	Elizabeth		No Date	1957	There is only one date on the Funeral Home Marker	SHI132
Jupiter, Jr.	Ernest		Apr. 11, 1916	Dec. 22, 1975	Pfc US Army WW II	SHI237
Jupiter	Emma		No Date	Jul. 22, 1923	Info is from church records	SHINoStone
Jupiter	Harry	Edward	1927	Jun. 16, 1985	Middle name and death date are from the church ledger book	SHI239
Jupiter	Kate		No Date	Apr. 3, 1928	Age 80 / info is from church records	SHINoStone
Jupiter	Lucinda		1897	Sep. 14, 1966	Info is from church records /	SHI233
Jupiter	Mel		No Date	Apr. 8, 1957	Info is from church records	SHINoStone
Jupiter	Robert		No Date	Jul. 6, 1926	Age 97 years	SHINoStone
Jupiter	Thomas	Edward	1952	1984	LCPL US Marine Corps	HGH3030
Jupiter	Thomas		No Date	Sep. 9, 1922	Info is from church records	SHINoStone

Last Name	First Name	Middle Name	Date of Birth	Date of Death	Transcription / Notes	Cemetery Code
Jupiter	Thomas		Oct. 12, 1922	May 8, 1985	Info is from church records	SHINoStone
Jupiter	William	A.	Feb. 7, 1917	Aug. 26, 2003	We Love you	SHI240
Justice	C.	Mitchell	May 27, 1918	No Date	Keep the whole world singing	MTR4147
Justice	Cecelia	Chapman	Feb. 20, 1920	Jan. 26, 1996		MTR4148
Justice	Clarence	Mitchell	Mar. 12, 1886	Feb. 10, 1978	B: LaPlata, MD / Whom God Hath Joined" B: Asheville, NC	MTR4146
Justice	Cynthia	King	May 21, 1940	No Date	Keep the whole world singing	MTR4147
Justice	Leola	Elmore, Chapman	Jul. 18, 1884	Jul. 17, 1974	B: LaPlata, MD / Whom God Hath Joined" B: Asheville, NC	MTR4146
K.	J.	O.	No Date	No Date	A footstone with the initials J. O. (K) ?	NME006
K..	M.	R.	No Date	No Date	Painted marker	MAC041
Kaiser	Unknown		No Date	No Date	Number 257 inscribed on the lower left of the stone / Name came from church records	CLV376
Kane	James		No Date	Mar. 26, 1805	Here lieth the remains of / Native of the Waterside of Londonderry Ireland who departed this life / aged 22 years	OFE2036
Kane	Lillian	E.	May 7, 1936	Feb. 26, 1978	"Betty" d/o John F & Mary E McGinn / She had earned her crown and her heavenly rest	NSP800
Kannapell	Charles	Carter	Jun. 23, 1932	Nov. 17, 2008	"Poppy" / In loving memory	SIC9041
Kannapell	Patricia	Mudd	Apr. 14, 1938	Dec. 18, 2003	In loving memory	SIC9040
Kans	Steven	Harmon	Nov. 23, 1961	Dec. 25, 1998	Forever in our hearts	HGH4085
Karlsson	Anna	J.	1924	1996		ODE128
Karlsson	Arthur		1891	1975		ODE129
Karlsson	Erich	P.	1920	2004		ODE128
Karlsson	Rita		1899	2000		ODE129
Karmiloff	A.		1897	1962		MTR3137
Karpuk	Anna	H.	Nov. 6, 1923	No Date		SMC4024
Karpuk	Fedor		May 23, 1913	No Date		SMC4024
Kastroba	Andrew	R.	1912	1973		SCL4049
Kastroba	Mildred	C.	1919	2001		SCL4049
Katsouros	Emmanuel		Mar. 25, 1945	Nov. 6, 2003	In loving memory, forever in our hearts / "Mike" / PFC US Army Viet Nam / Purple Heart	NSP133

Last Name	First Name	Middle Name	Date of Birth	Date of Death	Transcription / Notes	Cemetery Code
Katsouros	Joseph	Daly	Jul. 14, 1971	Jan. 6, 2003	"Kats" / "Butchie Boy" / We live as long as we're remembered / Biggest Boy / Back of Stone: Loving you always. Cherishing your memory and keeping you in our hearts forever / E=MC^2	SAC2100
Kaufmann	Eleanor	M.	Jan. 4, 1927	Sep. 17, 2009	Beloved wife and mother (Death date is from Ancestry.com)	SMC4291
Kavlick	Ronald	W.	Oct. 24, 1964	Aug. 4, 1987	Beloved son and brother	SCL4002
Kear III	Frank	Gregg	Jun. 4, 1941	Jun. 2, 1991	In Loving Memory	SAC1141
Kearney	Kevin	M.	1956	2003		NSP453
Keating, S.J.	Daniel	A.	Nov. 10, 1855	Jan. 14, 1873	IHS / Schel / NAT. die 10 Nov. 1855 / Obit die 14. Jan 1873 / R.I.P. (In Priests Plot) Dates are from church records	SIC1029
Keech	Anne	S.	1869	1934	other sides of stone / James A, Frank B, Emily Keech, Mizpah / footstone A.S.K.	TRI203
Keech	Annie	Dyer	1878	1970	Mizpah / footstone E.B.K. / w/o James A Keech	SMCD006
Keech	Emily		1834	1889	Other sides of stone: Annie S, Frank B Keech, Mizpah; footstone E.B.K. / w/o James A Keech	TRI200
Keech	Emma	C.	No Date	Mar. 19, 1861	d/o Dr. Wm. S. & Olevia T. Keech	OFE2121
Keech	Estelle		May 12, 1868	Aug. 23, 1893	d/o William S and Eva T Keech; Headstone: Estelle; footstone: E.K.; plotstone: K	TRI194
Keech	Frank	B.	1866	1937	other sides of stone: Annie S, James A, Emily Keech, Mizpah / Lieut Col footstone F.B.K.	TRI205
Keech	James	A.	1809	1879	Other sides of stone: Annie S, Frank B Keech, Mizpah; His wife Emily; footstone: J.A.K.	TRI200
Keech	James	E.	No Date	Jan. 9, 1851	In the 40th year of his age	BDKNoStone
Keech	Laura	J.	Oct. 3, 1848	Jul. 8, 1849	d/o James and Martha A. Keech	BDKNoStone
Keech	Lois	Hamilton	Nov. 26, 1932	No Date		SPL6028
Keech	Martha	A.	Aug. 1, 1815	Jul. 30, 1859	w/o James E. Keech and d/o John C. and Ann Dent	BDKNoStone
Keech	Olevia	Tinsdall	Nov. 19, 1839	Feb. 22, 1916	d/o the late Rev John & Sarah Wiley; widow of the late Doctor William S. Keech; grant to her oh Lord eternal rest and let light perpetual shine upon her; may she rest in peace / Mother	TRI163
Keech	Roland	Leigh	Aug. 25, 1934	Mar. 13, 2000	SP4 US Army / middle name is from church records	SPL6028
Keech	William	Wiley	1858	1940		SMCD006

Last Name	First Name	Middle Name	Date of Birth	Date of Death	Transcription / Notes	Cemetery Code
Keech, M.D.	William	S.	Feb. 21, 1804	Nov. 19, 1885	M.D. / To giveth his beloved sleep / Father / W.S.K.	TRI160
Keegan	Jennie	Rose Meier	Jul. 4, 1890	Feb. 16, 1977		ODE043
Keemer	Robert	M.	1956	1991	In Loving Memory (All info is painted on white marker flush to the ground, can be found in front of grave for Shee Tong Ching)	HER014
Keenan	Doris	G.	Nov. 27, 1911	No Date		SMC3042
Keese	Constance		Feb. 21, 1917	Aor 16, 1991		ALX079
Keirn	Guy	Milton	No Date	Jun. 20, 1941	Virginia Corp. 13 Regt. U.S.M.C.	SCL3396
Kellam, Jr.	Jack	T.	1959	1976	Our Beloved son and brother. / Ever close in mind and heart	PKH073
Keller	Ellen	Robinson	Jun. 11, 1965	Jun. 17, 2002	Beautiful wife and mother	SMC3247
Keller	Ernest		1902	1984		SMC3258
Keller	Grace	S.	Dec. 6, 1894	Jun. 23, 1993		SMC3256
Keller	Leonard	J.	Oct. 3, 1896	Nov. 16, 1966		SMC3257
Keller	Mary	E.	1911	No Date		SJE076
Keller	Paul	R.	1910	1962		SJE076
Keller	Perry	Rennoe	No Date	May 1910	Baby / age 6 mo's. 28 dys. Buried May 4, 1910 (info is from microfilm pg 158 located at the College of Southern MD, LaPlata, MD)	ODENoStone
Keller	Rosina		1910	2005		SMC3258
Kelley	Mary Jo	Salzman	Nov. 28, 1932	Mar. 8, 2004		CHR108
Kelley	Rex	Eugene	1926	1996		SIC9090
Kelley	Robert		No Date	Aug. 25, 1887	In memory of / Bottom part of this stone is broken off. It is leaning up against another headstone	SIC4162
Kellis	Randy	Antonio	Sep. 10, 1963	Oct. 14, 1989	L Cpl US Marine Corp	ALX025
Kelly	Charles	Alexander	No Date	May 4, 1891	Info is from Christ Church microfilm Reel 2 Pg 167-168 located at the College of Southern MD, LaPlata, MD	MTRNoStone
Kelly	Dorothy	M.	May 22, 1912	Dec. 22, 1999		SAC2121
Kelly	Edward	J.	Sep. 24, 1907	Apr. 17, 1997		SAC2121
Kelly	Ethel		1923	1991	Thornton's Funeral Home Marker	MAC005
Kelly	Jacques	Michael	May 20, 1921	May 3, 1988	In Posey Plot	SIC1050
Kelly	John	H.	Sep. 13, 1912	May 29, 1975		SIC8064

Last Name	First Name	Middle Name	Date of Birth	Date of Death	Transcription / Notes	Cemetery Code
Kelly	Joseph	Hyde	Aug. 6, 1912	Oct. 16, 1978	Masonic Emblem / EM2, US Navy WWII	OFE1005
Kelly	Louise	H.	1910	1995	Eastern Star	OFE1005
Kelly	Louise	Henderson	Sep. 10, 1910	Mar. 15, 1995		OFE1011
Kelly	Madeline		Jun. 7, 1910	Jan. 5, 1967		SIC8058
Kelly	Mary		No Date	Oct. 3, 1941		SIC4094
Kelly	Veronica	Agnes	No Date	Jan. 22, 1995	Cremated and buried in the St Francis Memorial Garden / No Marker	SPL9001
Kelly	William	J.	Dec. 9, 1917	Jan. 17, 1983		SJO3360
Kelton	Anita	T.	Sep. 2, 1945	Feb. 2, 2003	Mother / At Rest	DUD010
Kelton	Anna	L.	1915	1975	Info is from the Historical Society Research located at The College of Southern MD, LaPlata, MD	SCLNoStone
Kelton	Harry	William	May 26, 1926	Dec. 23, 2006	Right of Stanley Berry / Obit appeared in the MD Independent Newspaper dated Dec 27, 2006	ALX111A
Kelton	Leroy		Aug. 28, 1930	Dec. 19, 2007	s/o the late Archie Swann and the Late Mamie Kelton. / Info is from MD Independent Newspaper, Friday Dec 28, 2007 Pg A-13 Col 2	SCLNoStone
Kemp	B.	B.	1926	2002		SIC7077
Kemp	Catherine	L., Wills	1897	1980		SIC7036
Kemp	Ellen	Bennet	1930	1989		SIC7077
Kemp, M.D.	J.	McKendree	Feb. 5, 1837	Feb. 18, 1916		MTR3088
Kemp	John	Jay	Dec. 26, 1875	Mar. 16, 1941	Beloved h/o Ula Fay Kemp	MTR3089
Kemp	Mary		Mar. 28, 1886	Mar. 8, 1944		MTR3097
Kemp	Ralph	W.	Sep. 1, 1877	Aug. 21, 1951	Located in Kemp plot	MTR3096
Kemp	S.	Worthington	1893	1960		SIC7036
Kemp	Sarah	Ann	Nov. 17, 1851	Nov. 1, 1949		MTR3088
Kemp	Ula	Fay	Apr. 19, 1891	Aug. 6, 1951	Beloved w/o John Jay Kemp	MTR3090
Kendall	Lawrence	R.	May 6, 1930	No Date	In Loving Memory	ODE288
Kendall	Nola	Pauline	Apr. 1, 1928	Feb. 12, 1997	In Loving Memory	ODE288
Kendig	Marcella		Apr. 6, 1917	Jul. 27, 2001	Info is from church records	MTRNoStone
Kendig, Jr.	Omer	B.	Apr. 17, 1917	Oct. 2, 1981	US Army WW II	MTR2213
Kendrick	Annie	E.	Feb. 13, 1863	Jan. 12, 1941	Tender Mother, Faithful friend	MRB031
Kendrick	Carlton	Rye	Feb. 21, 1896	Oct. 8, 1898		NJB032

Last Name	First Name	Middle Name	Date of Birth	Date of Death	Transcription / Notes	Cemetery Code
Kendrick	Isabella	C.	Dec. 15, 1862	Oct. 16, 1944	Gone but not forgotten	NJB034
Kendrick	Josephine	I.	Apr. 19, 1859	Feb. 18, 1919		SCL2181
Kendrick	Lessie		No Date	No Date		NJB337
Kendrick	Peter	W.	Sep. 21, 1858	Sep. 16, 1921	Gone but not forgotten	NJB033
Kendrick	Sarah	C.	May 10, 1829	Sep. 11, 1906	Our beloved mother-may her soul rest in peace / Amen	NJB474
Kendrick	Selena		Mar. 26, 1860	Jan. 20, 1941		NJB476
Kendrick	Singie	V.	Oct. 20, 1874	Jul. 6, 1958		NJB336
Kendrick	Stephen	W.	Mar. 7, 1902	Jun. 14, 1931		MRB029
Kendrick, Jr.	Stephen	W.	Dec. 20, 1922	Apr. 28, 1923		MRB028
Kendrick	Theresa	A.	May 25, 1933	Apr. 20, 1996	Our Beloved mother	SIC9084
Kendrick	Thomas		Aug. 10, 1848	Jul. 31, 1924	His wife Josephine I. Kendrick	SCL2181
Kendrick	Virlinda	Ann	Dec. 30, 1780	Dec. 30, 1808	Verse on stone: The reward of her virtue we trust are Heaven. We are born to live that we may die. And to die, that we may live.	SCL1111
Kendrick	William	Henry	1856	1939	His memory is Blessed	MRB030
Kenley	Lucille	M.	Oct. 15, 1924	Mar. 30, 2000	Loving and Beloved Nana	NSP723
Kenlon	Bernard	L.	Jul. 7, 1911	Nov. 9, 1994		LUM192
Kenlon	Emma	H.	1921	1968		OSM153
Kenlon	Gus		No Date	No Date	Buried in same grave as Joseph Alan Kenlon / info is from church records	OSM142
Kenlon	John	Wilbur	May 20, 1917	Sep. 25, 1964	Maryland MMI USNR WWII	OSM152
Kenlon	Joseph	Alan	Oct. 11, 1944	Nov. 6, 1946	Our darling / Now I lay me down to sleep	OSM142
Kenlon	Rennie	V.	Oct. 8, 1917	No Date		LUM192
Kennedy	James	J.	1942	1990	In Loving Memory / Our Father which art in Heaven	SJO4007
Kennedy	Loretta	Marie	Mar. 23, 1910	Feb. 19, 1980		SJO4102

Last Name	First Name	Middle Name	Date of Birth	Date of Death	Transcription / Notes	Cemetery Code
Kennedy	Lydia		No Date	Dec. 1, 1795	In memory of / who departed this life / in the 41 years of her age. Condoled by a husband and child, Beauty, Virtue, she did possess, Her pious life faith exress that the is gone to realms above thene to live in endless love. Below this stone is written: Life 24th May 1812 aged 64 years. / Is this Lydia's husband? / Info is from DAR Book Pg 143 and Historical Society research located at the College of Southern MD, LaPlata, MD	ODE004
Kennedy	Mary		No Date	Feb. 11, 1825	In memory of / consort of Daniel Kennedy who departed this life / in the 40th-year of her age	ODE003
Kennedy	Patricia	G.	1959	No Date		SJO4007
Kent, III	Kenneth	Howe	Feb. 19, 1981	Apr. 22, 2001	In Loving Memory / Our Father which art in Heaven	NSP718
Keokuk	Minyon		Nov. 28, 1967	Aug. 25, 1988	Kenny / Gift from God / Return to Heaven	SCL1247
Kermit	Unknown		No Date	No Date	Tweedy - Sunshine	CHR410
Kerr	Benjamin	Dunn	Jan. 16, 1833	Mar. 11, 1900	White statue of an Angel	CLV260
Kerr	Frank	D.	Jan. 24, 1906	Jun. 07, 1943	Masonic Emblem on headstone	CLV313
Kerr	Ida	Robinson	Sep. 21, 1881	Aug. 14, 1961		CLV314
Kerr	Mabel	Blakeway	Mar. 8, 1885	Jul. 26, 1885	Mother	CLV259
Kersey	Eleanor	S.	1924	1987	Mother / In loving memory	NSP978
Kersey, Sr.	James	T.	1922	2001	Father / In loving memory	NSP978
Kersey	Margaret	C.	1899	1990		SAC2002
Kersey	Melvin	J.	1918	1968		SAC2003
Kersey	Rachael	M.	1921	1990		SAC2003
Kersey	Thomas	V.	1897	1954		SAC2002
Kershaw	Pattie	E.	1869	1956	Mother	OFE2007
Kesley	Evelyn	W.	Jan. 17, 1906	Nov. 1, 1970	Blessed are the pure of heart	CMX2018
Kestle	Nancy		May 12, 1910	Dec. 9, 2005	In Loving Memory of Mom & Nana	SAC1028
Key	Annie	C.	Mar. 22, 1922	Feb. 17, 1988	Mother	POM096
Key	Annie	Rosana	No Date	Dec. 1889	Info is from Christ Church microfilm Reel 2 Pg 167-168 located at the College of Southern MD, LaPlata, MD	MTRNoStone
Key	arl		1918	1996	Part of first name is missing on Thornton Funeral Home Marker	SMI044

Last Name	First Name	Middle Name	Date of Birth	Date of Death	Transcription / Notes	Cemetery Code
Key	Benjamin	L.	Mar. 12, 1916	Feb. 23, 2006	Daddy / "Best checker player in Charles County"	POM243
Key	Bertha	Arzena, W.	Dec. 3, 1915	Apr. 17, 2005	Asleep in Jesus	POM246
Key	Bertha	Florence	Jan. 11, 1918	Mar. 30, 2003	In loving memory	SCL3307
Key	Carroll		1898	1920		POM015
Key	Charles	H.	1866	1920		POM013
Key	Charles	Robert	Aug. 9, 1914	Nov. 19, 1979	TEC 5 US Army WW II	POM247
Key	Charles	S.	Feb. 11, 1884	Jun. 3, 1958	Beloved Husband and Father	POM249
Key	Clara	Elizabeth	No Date	Aug. 13, 1939	Age 34 / Info is from the Historical Society Located at the College of Southern MD, LaPlata, MD	BRCNoStone
Key	Elsie		Oct. 24, 1912	Jul. 3, 1992	w/o J. Wesley Key Jr.	POM018
Key	Emma	Cecelia	1905	1981		POM172
Key	Ethel	M.C., Gales	Dec. 31, 1910	May 10, 1995	Sunrise-Sunset / But they that wait upon the Lord shall renew their strength Isaiah 40:31	SHI285
Key	Frances	A.	1890	1971	At Rest	SCL1049
Key	Frank	J.	Jan. 15, 1913	May 25, 1969	Asleep in Jesus	POM246
Key	Grant		No Date	No Date		SHI207
Key	Harriet		1868	1928		POM014
Key	Harriet		No Date	May 14, 1876	Info is from Christ Church microfilm Reel 1 pg 314-315 located at the College of Southern MD, LaPlata, MD	HWKNoStone
Key	J.	Wesley	Oct. 11, 1875	Jul. 1, 1957	Our Father / The Word of the Lord endureth forever	POM020
Key, Jr.	J.	Wesley	Jan. 29, 1911	Nov. 21, 1974		POM025
Key	Jahmar or Jahnar				Funeral Home Marker / Unable to make out first name	SCL3049
Key	James	Brooks	1921	1978	Cpl US Army Korea	DUD047
Key	James	Warren	1908	Jan. 21, 1977	Info is from church records	SHI206
Key	Jane	Elnora	1881	1976		POM114
Key	Jeremiah		1901	1963	Cement cross painted white	POM173
Key	Joseph		1946	1997	Thornton Funeral Home Marker	SMI047
Key	Julia	Victoria	1857	1932	Mother	POM010
Key	June	H.	May 28, 1913	Mar. 2, 1980		POMNoStone
Key	Leon		Jan. 17, 1935	Jun. 15, 1952		POMNoStone

Last Name	First Name	Middle Name	Date of Birth	Date of Death	Transcription / Notes	Cemetery Code
Key, Jr.	Louis		1884	1936		POM033
Key	Marbury	D.	1898	1948	Husband	POM023
Key	Martha		1910	1981	Thornton Funeral Home Marker	SCL1249
Key	Mary	Elizabeth	No Date	No Date	Our Mother / I know that my redeemer liveth	POM022
Key	Mary	J.	1887	1918	Name etched on a cement cross	POM031
Key	Mollie	C.	Apr. 13, 1884	Dec. 14,	Stone is partially sunken, unable to read death date	POM064
Key	Nathan	T.	1903	1954		POM026
Key	Parrie	Lee	No Date	Dec. 1889	Info is from Christ Church microfilm Reel 2 Pg 167-168 located at the College of Southern MD, LaPlata, MD	MTRNoStone
Key	Philip		Jul. 4, 1859	Jul. 17, 1905	Info is from the Historical Society Located at the College of Southern MD, LaPlata, MD	BRCNoStone
Key	Susie		No Date	No Date		SHI207
Key	Unknown		1974	1974	Baby Boy	POM174
Key	William		No Date	Jun. 2, 1927	Death date is from church records	SHINoStone
Key	William		No Date	Jun. 2, 1927	Death Date is from church records	SHI207
Key	Wm	Louis	1853	1923	Father	POM010
Keye	Dorothy		Oct. 4, 1898	Feb. 17, 1976		SHI145
Keye, Jr.	Walter	C.	Oct. 29, 1925	Apr. 3, 1958	s/o Dorothy F. Keye / At Rest	SHI130
Keyes	Catherine	C.	Aug. 31, 1957	No Date		SMC4155
Keyes	Donald	E.	Jun. 30, 1954	Dec. 9, 1996		SMC4155
Keys	Alice	M.	Jul. 18, 1957	May 15, 2001	In Loving Memory / Mother	OAK012
Keys	Alice		1913	1991	old cement cross and Thornton Funeral Home Marker	MHB115
Keys	Audrey	B.	Apr. 17, 1929	Dec. 18, 1992	In Loving Memory	MHB047
Keys	Beulah M.	Wheeler, Hoffman	Sep. 9, 1908	Oct. 23, 1972		CMX2134
Keys	Carlin		1954	1989	Thornton Funeral Home Marker	OAK093
Keys	Charles		No Date	No Date	Info is from the Historical Society Research located at the College of Southern MD, LaPlata, MD	ZBCNoStone
Keys	David	Randolph	1956	1991	Thornton Funeral Home Marker	MHB056
Keys	Elizabeth	Proctor	1888	1925		ZBC194
Keys	Elsie	Marie	1900	1984	Thornton Funeral Home Marker	SMI045
Keys	Fredericka	E.	May 6, 1899	Mar. 6, 1997	"Sissy" / She was the sunshine of our home	POM126

Last Name	First Name	Middle Name	Date of Birth	Date of Death	Transcription / Notes	Cemetery Code
Keys	George	Harrison	Dec. 14, 1933	Aug. 24, 1959	Veteran of WWII	SCA083
Keys	Gregory	J.	Jun. 26, 1952	May 1, 1993		MHB042
Keys	Harris	Augustus	Jan. 31, 1940	Feb. 13, 1996	Pvt US Army	MHB029
Keys	James	H.	Jul. 2, 1868	Jan. 20, 1906		POM084
Keys, Sr.	John	Francis	May 16, 1905	Nov. 18, 1970		ZBC049
Keys	John	W.	1942	1972	Funeral home marker / info is from Historical Society Research located at the College of Southern MD, LaPlata, MD	ZBC051
Keys	John		No Date	No Date	Info is from the Historical Society Research located at the College of Southern MD, LaPlata, MD	ZBCNoStone
Keys, Jr.	Joseph	H.	1930	1990	Montgomery Brothers Marker	MHB103
Keys	Josephine		Apr. 6, 1918	Dec. 11, 2000	Beloved Mother / "Josie"	ZBC055
Keys	Maggie	Y.	Dec. 11, 1935	No Date	Pvt US Army	MHB029
Keys, Jr.	Marbury	Domver	Nov. 11, 1926	Nov. 25, 1988	MAM 3 US Navy WW II	POM120
Keys	Regina		No Date	No Date	At Rest / Old cement marker	ZBC157
Keys	Richard	William	Oct. 1, 1945	May 18, 1975	PFC U.S. Army Viet Nam	OAK080
Keys	Rufus	H.	Oct. 19, 1931	Sep. 11, 1992	In Loving Memory / Psalm 27	OAK208
Keys	Shirley	Ann	Feb. 21, 1946	Jan. 5, 1995	"Shirlann" / An Inspiration to all who knew her / Wed Mar 31, 1978	SCA145
Keys	Theodore		1938	1992	Thornton Funeral Home Marker	MHB046
Keys	Tresa	M.	Jul. 21, 1960	May 9, 1991		MHB060
Keys	Unknown		No Date	No Date	Cement cross with Keys painted on it in black letters	OAK092
Keys, Sr.	Unknown		No Date	Nov.. 9,1958	Old Cement Cross that is sinking into the ground	MHB175
Keys	Unknown		1917	1993	Thornton Funeral Home Marker	ZBC048
Kidwell	Inez	Eva	Sep. 6, 1913	Aug. 20, 2000	Beloved Mother	CLV250
Kidwell	Samuel	Wesley	Jan. 1, 1914	Jan. 13, 1985		CLV249
Kidwell	Wesley	S.	Feb. 13, 1934	Jun. 2, 2005	I wasn't the man I meant to be / Death Date is from June 8, 2005 Maryland Independent Newspaper	CLV304
Kilhoffer	A.	Cecelia	May 4, 1925	Jul. 29, 1991		SMC2132
Kilhoffer	Carl	G.	1907	1986		SMC2142
Kilhoffer	Charles	B.	Oct. 2, 1883	Apr. 18, 1974		SMC2156
Kilhoffer	Clara	Louise	Dec. 4, 1878	Mar. 13, 1953		SMC2157

Last Name	First Name	Middle Name	Date of Birth	Date of Death	Transcription / Notes	Cemetery Code
Kilhoffer	Helen	M.	Feb. 15, 1911	May 7, 1969		SMC2141
Kilinski	Alexander		1914	1971		SIC7068
Kilinski	Dorothy	L.	1916	1974		SIC7068
Kilinski	James		1939	2000	"Buzzy"	SMY2042
Kilinski	Marc	A.	Oct. 15, 1972	Feb. 14, 1999	Loving son brother & friend	HGH4317
Kilson	Jennette	Long	1931	1998	Beloved d/o Eben & Arintha Long	ZBC138
Kilson	William		1923	2007	Thornton Funeral Home	ZBC137
Kim	Young	Sun	Jan. 21, 1898	Jan. 18, 1979		SJO3023
King	Amelia	Ann, Grimes	Jan. 7, 1936	Aug. 10, 2007	Age 71, d/o John Emory Grimes and Nadine Williams Grimes / info is from the MD Independent Newspaper, Aug 14, 2007 / Together Forever / Number 246-C inscribed to the right of the name on the stone	CLV391
King, Sr.	Barry	A.	Jun. 16, 1958	Nov. 23, 2002	In loving memory	SCL3111
King	Benjamin		No Date	Sep. 6, 1946	Info is from church records	CLVNoStone
King	Betty		No Date	No Date	Number 249 inscribed on the lower left of the stone info is from church records	CLV384
King	Catherine		No Date	Jan. 20, 1950	Number 18 inscribed on the lower left of the stone / info is from church records	CLV454
King	Charles	Edward	Mar. 6, 1935	Jan. 4, 1998	Together Forever Number 246-D inscribed to the right of the name on the stone	CLV391
King	David		No Date	Sep. 2, 2006	Info is from church records	CLVNoStone
King	Earl	S.	1914	1984		PGN037
King	Eleanor	A.	Mar. 6, 1934	Sep. 29, 2001		NSP972
King	Essie	Lelia	Mar. 27, 1912	Aug. 15, 1983	Number 246-A inscribed to the right of the name on the stone	CLV396
King	Flora	Lorraine	Jan. 31, 1941	Oct. 14, 1995	Wood letters spell out the word Mom, but some letters are missing	CLV363
King	Gladys	V.	Mar. 19, 1934	Apr. 12, 1981	"Rest in Peace"	SJO5056
King	Hellen	Young	Dec. 5, 1908	Oct. 23, 1991		CRA013
King	Hylind	G.	No Date	No Date	Old cement cross engraving etched by hand	SCL1056
King	J.		No Date	No Date	Number 250 inscribed on the lower left of the stone	CLV386
King	Jacqueline	M.	Oct. 20, 1955	Apr. 10, 1969		MAC028
King, Sr.	James	A.	Jan. 19, 1930	No Date		NSP972

Last Name	First Name	Middle Name	Date of Birth	Date of Death	Transcription / Notes	Cemetery Code
King	James		Oct. 23, 1947	Oct. 26, 1947	Number 208 inscribed on the lower left of the stone info is from church records	CLV445
King	Joseph	E.	1892	1953		NSP207
King	Julia	A.	No Date	Mar. 6, 1967	Age: 87 years	SJO3275
King	L.		No Date	No Date	Number 247 inscribed on the lower left of the stone	CLV399
King	Margaret	T.	1890	1979		SCL4187
King	Mary	C.	1923	1997	"Goldie"	SCL3112
King	Mary	Luvenia	Jul. 14, 1913	Mar. 31, 1957	In loving memory	MAC030
King	Octavia	J.	Dec. 20, 1937	Sep. 16, 1993		MAC027
King	Robert		1921	1981	A rock marks the spot / Info is from church records	PGN016
King	Ruth		1955	1990		SCL4104
King	Unknown		No Date	No Date	Number 27 is inscribed	CLV457
King	Unknown		No Date	No Date	Number 26 inscribed on the lower left of the stone	CLV456
King	Unknown		No Date	No Date	Number 25 inscribed on the lower left of the stone	CLV455
King	Unknown		No Date	No Date	Number 240 inscribed on the lower left of the stone	CLV400
King	Unknown		No Date	No Date	Number 22 inscribed on lower left of stone	CLV040
King, Jr.	W.	R.	No Date	No Date	Number 250A inscribed on the lower left of the stone	CLV387
King	Whitney		Jun. 1892	Dec. 5, 1957	Info is from church records	CLVNoStone
King	William	Robert	Dec. 22, 1897	Nov. 10, 1966	Number 246 inscribed to the right of the name on the stone	CLV396
King	William		No Date	May 13, 1951	Number 17 inscribed on the lower left of the stone / info is from church records	CLV453
King	Wilmer		No Date	Aug. 2, 1938	Aged 37 / No Marker / info is from church records	CLVNoStone
Kingdon, P.S.J.	John		No Date	Jul. 8, 1761	Buried Under Sacristy (In Priests Plot)	SIC1001
Kingsley	Angelique	Sophia	No Date	Jul. 6, 1977	Infant d/o Don & Ellen Miller Kingsley	LUM067
Kinnemon	Elizabeth		No Date	Jun. 30, 1907	In the 87th year of her age	SMCA024
Kinsey	John	W.	1939	2001		CLV116
Kinsey	Viola	V.	1910	2003		CLV124
Kinsey	Willard		1899	1957		CLV125
Kintzel	Mamie	P.	1903	1979		TRI303
Kirk	Agnes	L.	May 5, 1918	Jan. 10, 1994		SCL2023

Last Name	First Name	Middle Name	Date of Birth	Date of Death	Transcription / Notes	Cemetery Code
Kirk	James	F.	Feb. 17, 1919	Jul. 16, 1983		SCL2023
Kirk	Mary	L.	Mar. 10, 1915	Jan. 20, 1986		SCL2024
Kirk	Thomas	M.	Jan. 23, 1913	Jan. 5, 1978		SCL2024
Kirkpatrick	Willey	V.	1894	1963	Beloved h/o Rebecca Perry	NJB040
Kirkstan, Jr.	Vito	Anthony	Jul. 5, 1949	Mar. 27, 2008	Age 58 s/o the lates Vito and Anthony Kirkstan Sr. and Doris Kirkstan. h/o Jennifer Hutton Kirkstan. / MD Independent Newspaper Wed. Apr 2, 2008 Page A-10 Column 2	SCLNoStone
Kiser	Marvin	L.	1904	1954		CLV377
Kiser	S.	Kate	1912	2001		CLV377
Kiser	Unknown		No Date	No Date	Number 257-F inscribed on the lower left of the stone info is from church records	CLV375
Kisner	Jill	M.	Dec. 12, 1962	Sep. 13, 1968		OFE1009
Kisner, Jr.	Lonnie	L.	Nov. 5, 1934	Sep. 13, 1968	There's a symbol in the Upper Right corner of stone with the date 1906	OFE1008A
Kite	Edna	M.	1932	1993	"Edie"	SMC4293
Kitts	Coralie	M.	Feb. 27, 1936	Jul. 4, 1962		NZN042
Kitts	Helen		Jun. 13, 1927	Jan. 19, 1990		NZN063
Kitts-Small	Nancy	A.	Oct. 18, 1938	Jul. 24, 1998	An Angel	NSP664
Klaas	Doris	M.	1922	2002		SCL1170
Klaas	Harmond	A.	1921	1992		SCL1170
Klapthor	Frank	Edward	Jul. 19, 1914	May 12, 1994	Antiquarian	SIC6038
Klapthor	Margaret	Washington, Brown	Jan. 16, 1922	Sep. 26, 1994	Historian	SIC6039
Klimkiewicz	Albert	A.	1881	1950		SMCD003
Klimkiewicz	Bernadette		May 28, 1876	Sep. 23, 1936	May she rest in peace	SMCD046
Klimkiewicz	Francis	D.	1879	1957		SMCD124
Klimkiewicz	Jane	C.	Aug. 14, 1896	Sep. 12, 1965	In loving memory of our mother	SMCD122
Klimkiewicz	Joseph	H.	Mar. 4, 1905	Jun. 29, 1905	Son of F D & Lucy Klimkiewicz	SMCD129
Klimkiewicz	Lucy		Jul. 7, 1884	Jan. 16, 1927	In memory of Lucy Klimkiewicz / Rest in peace / Top of stone is broken off	SMCD127
Klimkiewicz	Mary	Lucy	Jan. 16, 1927	Sep. 21, 1927	Infant daughter of Francis D and Lucy Klimkiewicz / Rest in peace / Top of stone is broken off	SMCD127

Last Name	First Name	Middle Name	Date of Birth	Date of Death	Transcription / Notes	Cemetery Code
Klimkiewicz	Richard	D.	May 5, 1913	May 26, 1930	Hope / son of Francis D & Lucy	SMCD125
Klimkiewicz, Jr.	James	C.	Jun. 18, 1924	Jun. 19, 1973	District of Columbia M3 US Navy World War II	SMCD067
Kline	Betty	Bernice	Aug. 19, 1931	Dec. 14, 1988	Together Forever	HER009
Kline	Edward	C.	May 14, 1930	No Date	Loving Husband & Father / In Loving Memory / If tears could build a stairway and memories a lane, I'd walk right up to heaven and bring you home again	SAC2057
Kline					Loving Wife & Mother / In Loving Memory / If years could build a stairway and memories a lane. I'd walk right up to heaven and bring you home again / Loving Husband & Father	SAC2057
Kline	Lucia	Quagliero	Feb. 19, 1930	Feb. 5, 2005		SAC2057
Kline	Robert	Louis	Nov. 19, 1933	Jul. 20, 1990		MTR3131
Klopfer, Jr.	John	E.	1955	2004		SIC9003
Klopp	Kenneth	Eugene	Dec. 23, 1927	Nov. 29, 1977	Sweetheart / Love lives on	CHR565
Kluetsch	John		No Date	Nov. 17, 1907	Aged 79 yrs and 10 mos	OSP138
Kluetsch	Mary		No Date	May 19, 1904	Aged 70 yr and 2 mos	OSP138
Knapp	Mary	E.	1842	1915		NJB368
Knepley	Robert	J.	1918	1978	SGT US Army WW II	MTR4001
Knisley	Gwendolen	Montgomery	Dec. 27, 1915	No Date		SPL4068
Knobel	Agatha	Heinz	Nov. 20, 1902	Apr. 16, 1986		SMC2165
Knobel	Joe		Mar. 19, 1899	Jul. 3, 1982		SMC2165
Knobel	Leonard	Edward	Dec. 22, 1942	Apr. 4, 1949	Brother & Twin / We love and miss you	SMCD249
Knott	Albert		Sep. 30, 1914	Feb. 27, 1980		SCL2029
Knott	Anna		1948	No Date	Thornton Funeral Home marker	SMY2077
Knott	Charity	L.	Dec. 1, 1934	Nov. 10, 1998		SAC1046
Knott	Dorothy	E.	1925	1972	Mother	SMY2085
Knott	Edith	M.	1881	1955		SCL2067
Knott	Edith	May	1906	1984		SCL2107
Knott	Ella		1880	Apr. 1, 1941	Info is from church records	CLVNoStone
Knott	Emma	E.	1862	1938		SCL2214
Knott, Sr.	Francis	X.	1903	1978		SCL2041
Knott	H.		Oct. 8, 1876	Dec. 19, 1954	Writing on stone was done by hand / Death date on stone says Dem 19, 1954	MTR3126

Last Name	First Name	Middle Name	Date of Birth	Date of Death	Transcription / Notes	Cemetery Code
Knott	Hilda	C.	Feb. 16, 1949	Mar. 19, 2001	"Sissy"	SAC5062
Knott	James	Albert	Jul. 5, 1938	Mar. 20, 1939		SCL2062
Knott	James	Vandell	Dec. 30, 1957	Dec. 8, 1996	"Vernie" / In Loving Memory	SAC5061
Knott	Joan	Risdon	Aug. 30, 1918	Nov. 16, 2005	Loving Mother and Grandmother / ALJA / Back of Stone: To those I love and those who love Me. I won't be far away, for life goes on. So if you need me, call and I will come. And if you listen with your heart, you'll hear all my love around you soft and clear	SAC3005
Knott	John	H.	No Date	Jul. 3, 1911	In loving remembrance of my dear husband / aged 87 years Gone but not forgotten	SIC3046
Knott	John	Robert	Jul. 27, 1901	May 18, 1971	District of Columbia PVT Medical Dept World War I	SCL2213
Knott	John	R.	Jan. 25, 1879	Apr. 24, 1953		MTR4032
Knott	John		1944	1986	Thornton Funeral Home marker	SMY2078
Knott	Joseph	W.	Aug. 11, 1923	Dec. 18, 1991		HGH4008
Knott	Juanita	B.	May 5, 1914	Sep. 15, 1994		SCL2031
Knott	Katharina	T.	Jan. 29, 1926	Mar. 18, 1972		CLV319
Knott	L.	Spencer	Jan. 6, 1916	Nov. 1, 1966		SMC3253
Knott	M. E.	F.	No Date	No Date	Stone is laying on the ground	CLV320
Knott	Margaret	E.	Oct. 20, 1923	May 21, 1998		HGH4008
Knott	Mary	Alice	Apr. 26, 1893	Feb. 14, 1981		MTR4031
Knott	Mary	L.	Feb. 1, 1919	Nov. 15, 1965		SCL2030
Knott	Mary	Nettie	Feb. 20, 1912	Apr. 3, 1976		SMY2062
Knott	Mary	Catherine	Apr. 15, 1916	Jul. 9, 1917	Daughter of R.H. & Edith M. Knott / Age 1 yr 2 mos & 21 ds	SCL2064
Knott	Natalie	A.	1907	1991		SJO4130
Knott	Paul	Louis	Feb. 17, 1958	May 15, 2006		SMY2015
Knott	R.	Hugh	1876	1951		SCL2067
Knott	Regina	M.	1905	1994		SCL2041
Knott	Richard	Hugh	Dec. 18, 1909		Son of R.H. & Edith M. Knott / Age 7 mo. & 10 ds	SCL2198
Knott	Richard	T.	1849	1923		SCL2214
Knott	Spriggs	A.	1962	1994	Arehart-Echol's Funeral Home marker	SAC5060
Knott	Thomas	S.	1901	1971		SJO4130

Last Name	First Name	Middle Name	Date of Birth	Date of Death	Transcription / Notes	Cemetery Code
Knott	Wade	J.	1927	1991	Pop-Pop	SMY2010
Knott	Margaret	M.	Jun. 1, 1913	Mar. 5, 1949	w/o Robert H. Knott	SJE186
Knowlen	Elford	J.	Jan. 30, 1898	Feb. 22, 1967		SCL3080
Knowlen	Florence	V.	Jun. 2, 1899	Jun. 8, 1972		SCL3080
Koch	Carson	Daniel	No Date	Oct. 8, 2006	Forever our angel / Beloved son and brother	SIC9049
Koch	Robert	B.	Dec. 5, 1913	Jan. 26, 1996	Precious Lord take my hand	LUM030
Koch	Ruth	E.	Sep. 14, 1918	May 8, 1990	Precious Lord take my hand	LUM030
Koegler	Edward	J.	May 22, 1915	May 5, 1998		SMC3024
Koegler	Maude	E.	Oct. 7, 1914	Nov. 8, 1992		SMC3024
Koehler	Frances	A.	Apr. 7, 1918	Apr. 26, 1976		CLV118
Koehler	Gerald	Thomas	Jul. 25, 1932	Aug. 16, 1993	In Loving Memory / "Tom" TSGT US Air Force / Korea / Vietnam	SAC2009
Koehler	Joye	E.	Apr. 10, 1938	No Date	In Loving Memory	SAC2009
Koehler	William	H.	Nov. 6, 1917	No Date		CLV118
Kolitas	Earl	Paul	No Date	Apr. 16, 1976	Age 49 yrs (info is from Historical Society Research located at The College of Southern MD, LaPlata, MD)	SACNostone
Koller	Emily	E.	Feb. 24, 1920	Dec. 17, 1989		SMC1002
Koller	Mary		Mar. 18, 1886	Jun. 26, 1967		SMC1010
Koller	Wenzel		Apr. 23, 1873	Jun. 27, 1966		SMC1010
Koller	Willie	R.	Dec. 31, 1921	Dec. 22, 1990		SMC1002
Kondrup	Ludvig	Fred., Cornelius	Sep. 28, 1887	Jun. 9, 1974	B: Arhus, Denmark - D: La Plata, MD	OSM140
Kondrup	Rose Mathilda	Rasmussen	Feb. 5, 1892	May 27, 1979	B: Clinton, MN - D: La Plata, MD	OSM141
Korrow	Dorothy	F.	Jun. 5, 1918	Dec. 31, 2006		SMY3093
Korrow, Sr.	Russell	F.	Jan. 21, 1919	Oct. 20, 1977		SMY3093
Kotch	Francis	Person	No Date	Feb. 27, 1998	Name is shown on church records but burial location is unknown	CHRNoStone
Kowalski	John		1883	1975		SCL3038
Kozlowski	Alanna		Jan. 10, 1953	Aug. 22, 1959		CMX2015
Kozlowski	Cecelia	H.	1926	No Date	Together forever	SMC1083
Kozlowski	Victor	V.	1923	1994	Together forever	SMC1083
Kragh	Agnes	W.	Jun. 14, 1891	Jul. 31, 1979		MTR4171

Last Name	First Name	Middle Name	Date of Birth	Date of Death	Transcription / Notes	Cemetery Code
Kragh	Alvin	Earl	Jul. 22, 1916	Jan. 4, 2005		SJO4173
Kragh	Joseph	Edward	Aug. 10, 1983	Aug. 11, 1983	Infant s/o Joseph and Patricia Kragh	SJO4193
Kragh	M.	Helen, Edelen	May 17, 1919	Jun. 24, 1993		SJO4173
Kragh	Michael	Gerard	Jun. 16, 1958	Jun. 16, 1958		SJO4173
Kragh	Nicholin	G.	Apr. 22, 1888	Feb. 8, 1976		MTR4171
Kragh	Virginia	Lee	Jul. 21, 1943	No Date		SJO4173
Krahling	Joyce	C.	Mar. 21, 1936	Mar. 26, 2004	Married May 29, 1954	SMY2126
Krahling	Thomas	J.	Dec. 29, 1933	No Date	Married May 29, 1954	SMY2126
Kramer	Lawrence	Joseph	Sep. 27, 1950	Dec. 28, 2004		OSM151
Kranke	Wm.	Scotty	1963	1990		SJE223
Krause	Joseph	F.	Feb. 15, 1908	Jan. 24, 1984		MTR2060
Krause	Tillie	D.	Aug. 25, 1912	Dec. 14, 1994		MTR2060
Krauss	Morgan	Avry	2008	2009	Raymond funeral home marker	SMCI001
Kreft	Anthony	J.	1932	1995	Married Oct 12, 1957	SMC1046
Kreft	Anthony	L.	May 4, 1904	May 5, 1976		SMC3323
Kreft	Catherine	J.	1938	No Date	Married Oct 12, 1957	SMC1046
Kreft	Erna	R.	Jul. 22, 1914	No Date		SMC3323
Kreft	John		Mar. 8, 1868	Oct. 15, 1936		SMCD042
Kreft	Katherine		Jul. 14, 1867	Dec. 16, 1928		SMCD042
Kreft	Leona		Mar. 5, 1896	Mar. 29, 1930		SMCD042
Kreft	Marie	L.	1898	1984		SMC3320
Kreft	Paul	A.	1935	1978	PFC US Army	SMC3322
Kreft	Salome	H	1905	1981		SMC3319
Kremer	Etta	M..	1918	2002	Death year is from church records	OSM101
Kremer, Sr.	Lloyd	W.	1908	1986		OSM101
Kremer	Mildred	Elizabeth	Dec. 6, 1934	Dec. 28, 2001	Mother / Thornton Funeral Home Marker shows last name as Riley	OSM100
Krex, Jr.	Peter	H.	No Date	Jan. 19, 1969	Always in our hearts	MTR3147
Kroh	Adelaide	Milstead	May 12, 1888	Jun. 1, 1948	In memory of / At rest	CMX2131
Kroh	William	J.	Dec. 4, 1877	Feb. 7, 1958	In memory of / At rest	CMX2131
Krouse	Annie	E.	Dec. 2, 1860	Feb. 1, 1931		SJE050

Last Name	First Name	Middle Name	Date of Birth	Date of Death	Transcription / Notes	Cemetery Code
Krouse	Kentzing	P.	No Date	Apr. 5, 1931		SCL2156
Krygar	Paul	W.	Aug. 30, 1928	No Date	Husband / in loving memory	CHR283
Krygar	Rosalene	A.	Apr. 22, 1941	No Date	Daughter & wife / in loving memory	CHR283
Krynicky	John	Thomas	Sep. 2, 1930	May 28, 2008	Loving Brother	SJO1085
Krynicky	Lillian	Mary	Feb. 24, 1925	Feb. 6, 2007	Loving Sister	SJO1085
Kubick	Margaret	M.	Dec. 2, 1913	Mar. 1, 2001	NONA	SCL2016
Kulesza	Henry		Jul. 18, 1932	Oct. 22, 1991	"Hank" / In loving memory	CMX1125
Kurtz	Ella	M.	1913	1978		NJB140
Kurtz	M.	Clair	1902	1966		NJB140
Kurtz	Thomas	E.	Jan. 7, 1974	Mar. 1, 1992		SCL1124
Kutchi	Elizabeth	Ann	Aug. 11, 1983	Aug. 15, 1983	Our Little Angel	SCL3052
Kuzniar	Charles	John	Dec. 13, 1915	Nov. 6, 1977		NSP587
Kuzniar	Richard	Allen	May 31, 1940	May 9, 1985		NSP588
Kyles	Thelma	Bush	1924	2005		SCL1158
Kyro	Harley	A.	1957	1961	Our Darling Son	SCL3056

www.ingramcontent.com/pod-product-compliance
Lightning Source LLC
Chambersburg PA
CBHW060308240426
43661CB00059B/2696